THE HOUSEHOLD EDITON.

THE WORKS

OF

FREDERICK SCHILLER.

Vol. I.—HISTORICAL.

HISTORY OF THE THIRTY YEARS' WAR.
HISTORY OF THE REVOLT OF THE NETHERLANDS.

TRANSLATED FROM THE GERMAN.

ILLUSTRATED.

NEW YORK:
JOHN D. WILLIAMS,
24 West Fourteenth St.

TROW'S
PRINTING AND BOOKBINDING COMPANY,
NEW YORK.

PREFACE TO THE EDITION.

THE present is the best collected edition of the important works of Schiller which is accessible to readers in the English language. Detached poems or dramas have been translated at various times since the first publication of the original works; and in several instances these versions have been incorporated into this collection.

Schiller was not less efficiently qualified by nature for an historian than for a dramatist. He was formed to excel in all departments of literature, and the admirable lucidity of style and soundness and impartiality of judgment displayed in his historical writings will not easily be surpassed, and will always recommend them as popular expositions of the periods of which they treat.

Since the publication of the first English edition many corrections and improvements have been made, with a view to rendering it as acceptable as possible to English readers; and, notwithstanding the disadvantages of a translation, the publishers feel sure that Schiller will be heartily acceptable to English readers, and that the influence of his writings will continue to increase.

THE HISTORY OF THE REVOLT OF THE NETHERLANDS was translated by Lieut. E. B. Eastwick, and originally published abroad for students' use. But this translation was too strictly literal for general readers. It has been carefully revised, and some portions have been entirely rewritten by the Rev. A. J. W. Morrison, who also has so ably translated the HISTORY OF THE THIRTY YEARS' WAR.

THE CAMP OF WALLENSTEIN was translated by Mr. James Churchill, and first appeared in "Frazer's Magazine." It is an exceedingly happy version of what has always been deemed the most untranslatable of Schiller's works.

THE PICCOLOMINI and DEATH OF WALLENSTEIN are the admirable version of S. T. Coleridge, completed by the addition of all those passages which he has omitted, and by a restoration of Schiller's own arrangement of the acts and scenes. It is said, in defence of the variations which exist between the German original and the version given by Coleridge, that he translated from a prompter's copy in manuscript, before the drama had been printed, and that Schiller himself subsequently altered it, by omitting some passages, adding others, and even engrafting several of Coleridge's adaptations.

WILHELM TELL is translated by Theodore Martin, Esq., whose well-known position as a writer, and whose special acquaintance with German literature make any recommendation superfluous.

DON CARLOS is translated by R. D. Boylan, Esq., and, in the opinion of competent judges, the version is eminently successful. Mr. Theodore Martin kindly gave some assistance, and, it is but justice to state, has enhanced the value of the work by his judicious suggestions.

The translation of MARY STUART is that by the late Joseph Mellish, who appears to have been on terms of intimate friendship with Schiller. His version was made from the prompter's copy, before the play was published, and, like Coleridge's Wallenstein, contains many passages not found in the printed edition. These are distinguished by brackets. On the other hand, Mr. Mellish omitted many passages which now form part of the printed drama, all of which are now added. The translation, as a whole, stands out from similar works of the time (1800) in almost as marked a degree as Coleridge's Wallenstein, and some passages exhibit powers of a high order; a few, however, especially in the earlier scenes, seemed capable of improvement, and these have been revised, but, in deference to the translator, with a sparing hand.

THE MAID OF ORLEANS is contributed by Miss Anna Swanwick, whose translation of Faust has since become well known. It has been carefully revised, and is now, for the first time, published complete.

THE BRIDE OF MESSINA, which has been regarded as the poetical masterpiece of Schiller, and, perhaps of all his works, presents the greatest difficulties to the translator, is rendered by A. Lodge, Esq., M.A. This version, on its first publication in England, a few years ago, was received with deserved eulogy by distinguished critics. To the present edition has been prefixed Schiller's Essay on the Use of the Chorus in Tragedy, in which the author's favorite theory of the "Ideal of Art" is enforced with great ingenuity and eloquence.

CONTENTS.

		PAGE
Book I	. . . .	5
II	. . . .	85
III	. . . .	177
IV	. . . .	271
V	. . . .	319

HISTORY

OF THE

THIRTY YEARS' WAR IN GERMANY.

BOOK I.

FROM the beginning of the religious wars in Germany to the peace of Munster scarcely anything great or remarkable occurred in the political world of Europe in which the Reformation had not an important share. All the events of this period, if they did not originate in, soon became mixed up with, the question of religion, and no state was either too great or too little, to feel, directly or indirectly, more or less of its influence.

Against the reformed doctrine and its adherents the House of Austria directed, almost exclusively, the whole of its immense political power. In France the Reformation had enkindled a civil war which, under four stormy reigns, shook the kingdom to its foundations, brought foreign armies into the heart of the country, and for half a century rendered it the scene of the most mournful disorders. It was the Reformation, too, that rendered the Spanish yoke intolerable to the Flemings, and awakened in them both the desire and the courage to throw off its fetters, while it also principally furnished them with the means of their emancipation. And as to England, all the evils with which Philip II. threatened Elizabeth were mainly intended in revenge for her having taken his Protestant subjects under her protection, and placing herself at the head of a religious party which it was his aim and endeavor to extirpate. In Germany the schisms in the church produced also a lasting political schism, which made that country for more than a century the theatre of confusion, but at the same time threw up a firm barrier against political oppression. It was, too, the Reformation principally that first drew the northern powers, Denmark and Sweden, into the political system of Europe; and while, on the one hand, the Protestant League was strengthened by their adhesion, it, on the other, was indispensable to their interests. States which hitherto scarcely concerned themselves with one another's existence, acquired through the Reformation an attractive centre of interest, and began to be united by new political sympathies. And as through its influence new relations sprang up between citizen and citizen, and between rulers and subjects, so also entire states were forced by it into new relative positions. Thus, by a strange course of events, religious disputes were the means of cementing a closer union among the nations of Europe.

Fearful, indeed, and destructive was the first movement in which this general political sympathy announced itself; a desolating war of thirty years, which, from the interior of Bohemia to the mouth of the Scheldt, and from the banks of the Po to the coasts of the Baltic, devastated whole countries, destroyed harvests, and reduced towns and villages to ashes; which opened a grave for many thousand combatants, and for half a century smothered the glimmering sparks of civilization in Germany, and threw back the improving manners of the country into their pristine barbarity and wildness. Yet out of this fearful war Europe came forth free and independent. In it she first learned to recognize herself as a community of nations; and this intercommunion of states, which originated in the thirty years' war, may alone be sufficient to reconcile the philosopher to its horrors. The hand of industry has slowly but gradually effaced the traces of its ravages, while its beneficent influence still survives; and this general sympathy among the states of Europe, which grew out of the troubles in Bohemia, is our guarantee for the continuance of that peace which was the result of the war. As the sparks of destruction found their way from the interior of Bohemia, Moravia, and Austria, to kindle Germany, France, and the half of Europe, so also will the torch of civilization make a path for itself from the latter to enlighten the former countries.

All this was effected by religion. Religion alone could have rendered possible all that was accomplished, but it was far from being the *sole* motive of the war. Had not private advantages and state interests been closely connected with it, vain and powerless would have been the arguments of theologians; and the cry of the people would never have met with princes so willing to espouse their cause, nor the new doctrines have found such numerous, brave, and persevering champions. The Reformation is undoubtedly owing in a great measure to the invincible power of truth, or of opinions which were held as such. The abuses in the old church, the absurdity of many of its dogmas, the extravagance of its requisitions, necessarily revolted the tempers of men, already half-won with the promise of a better light, and favorably disposed them towards the new doctrines. The charm of independence, the rich plunder of monastic institutions, made the Reformation attractive in the eyes of princes, and tended not a little to strengthen their inward convictions. Nothing, however, but political considerations could have driven them to espouse it. Had not Charles V., in the intoxication of success, made an attempt on the independence of the German States, a Protestant league would scarcely have rushed to arms in defence of freedom of belief; but for the ambition of the Guises the Calvinists in France would never have beheld a Condé or a Coligny at their head. Without the exaction of the tenth and the twentieth penny, the See of Rome had never lost the United Netherlands. Princes fought in self-defence or for aggrandizement, while religious enthusiasm recruited their armies and opened to them the treasures of their subjects. Of the multitude who flocked to their standards, such as were not lured by the hope of plunder imagined they were fighting for the truth, while in fact they were shedding their blood for the personal objects of their princes.

And well was it for the people that, on this occasion, their interests coincided with those of their princes. To this coincidence alone were they indebted for their deliverance from popery. Well was it also for the rulers that the subject contended too for his own cause, while he was fighting their battles. Fortunately at this date no European sovereign was so absolute as to be able, in the pursuit of his political designs, to dispense with the good-will of his subjects. Yet how difficult was it to gain and to set to work this good-will! The most impressive arguments drawn from reasons of state fall powerless on the ear of the subject, who seldom understands, and still more rarely is interested in them. In such circumstances, the only course open to a prudent prince is to connect the interests of the cabinet with some one that sits nearer to the people's heart, if such exists, or if not, to create it.

In such a position stood a greater part of those princes who embraced the cause of the Reformation. By a strange concatenation of events the divisions of the Church were associated with two circumstances, without which, in all probability, they would have had a very different conclusion. These were the increasing power of the House of Austria, which threatened the liberties of Europe, and its active zeal for the old religion. The first aroused the princes, while the second armed the people.

The abolition of a foreign jurisdiction within their own territories, the supremacy in ecclesiastical matters, the stopping of the treasure which had so long flowed to Rome, the rich plunder of religious foundations, were tempting advantages to every sovereign. Why, then, it may be asked, did they not operate with equal force upon the princes of the House of Austria? What prevented this house, particularly in its German branch, from yielding to the pressing demands of so many of its subjects, and, after the example of other princes, enriching itself at the expense of a defenceless clergy? It is difficult to credit that a belief in the infallibility of the Romish Church had any greater influence on the pious adherence of this house than the opposite conviction had on the revolt of the Protestant princes. In fact, several circumstances combined to make the Austrian princes zealous supporters of popery. Spain and Italy, from which Austria derived its principal strength, were still devoted to the See of Rome with that blind obedience which, ever since the days of the Gothic dynasty, had been the peculiar characteristic of the Spaniard. The slightest approximation in a Spanish prince to the obnoxious tenets of Luther and Calvin would have alienated forever the affections of his subjects, and a defection from the Pope would have cost him the kingdom. A Spanish prince had no alternative but orthodoxy or abdication. The same restraint was imposed upon Austria by her Italian dominions, which she was obliged to treat, if possible, with even greater indulgence; impatient as they naturally were of a foreign yoke, and possessing also ready means of shaking it off. In regard to the latter provinces, moreover, the rival pretensions of France, and the neighborhood of the Pope, were motives sufficient to prevent the Emperor from declaring in favor of a party which strove to annihilate the papal see, and also to induce him to show the most active zeal in behalf of the old religion. These general considerations, which must have been equally weighty with every Spanish monarch, were, in the particular case of Charles V., still further enforced by peculiar and personal motives. In Italy this monarch had a formidable rival in the King of France, under whose protection that country might throw itself the instant that Charles should incur the slightest suspicion of heresy. Distrust on the part of the Roman Catholics, and a rupture with the church, would have been fatal also to many of his most cherished designs. Moreover, when Charles was first called upon to make his election between the two parties, the new doctrine had not yet attained to a full and commanding influence, and there still subsisted a prospect of its reconciliation with the old. In his son and successor, Philip II., a monastic education combined with a gloomy and despotic disposition to generate an unmitigated hostility to all innovations in religion; a feeling which the thought that his most formidable political opponents were also the enemies of his faith was not calculated to weaken. As his European possessions, scattered as they were over so many countries, were on all sides exposed to the seductions of foreign opinions, the progress of the Reformation in other quarters could not well be a matter of indifference to him. His immediate interests, therefore, urged him to attach himself devotedly to the old church, in order to close up the sources of the heretical contagion. Thus circumstances naturally placed this prince at the head of the league which the Roman Catholics formed against the Reformers. The principles which had actuated the long and active reigns of Charles V. and Philip II. remained a law for their successors; and the more the breach in the church widened the firmer became the attachment of the Spaniards to Roman Catholicism.

The German line of the House of Austria was apparently more unfettered; but in reality, though free from many of these restraints, it was yet confined by others. The possession of the imperial throne — a dignity it was impossible for a Protestant to hold (for with what consistency could an apostate from the Romish Church wear the crown of a Roman Emperor?) bound the successors of Ferdinand I. to the See of Rome. Ferdinand himself was, from conscientious motives, heartily attached to it. Besides, the German princes of the House of Austria were not powerful enough to dispense with the support of Spain, which, however, they would have forfeited by the least show of leaning towards the new doctrines. The imperial dignity, also, required them to preserve the existing political system of Germany, with which the maintenance of their own authority was closely bound up, but which it was the aim of the Protestant League to destroy. If to these grounds we add the indifference of the Protestants to the Emperor's necessities and to the common dangers of the empire, their encroachments on the temporalities of the church, and their aggressive violence when they became conscious of their own power, we can easily conceive how so many concurring motives must have determined the emperors to the side of popery, and how their own interests came to be intimately interwoven with those of the Romish Church. As its fate seemed to depend altogether on the part taken by Austria, the princes of this house came to be regarded by all Europe as the pillars of popery. The hatred, therefore, which the Protestants bore against the latter was turned exclusively upon Austria; and the cause became gradually confounded with its protector.

But this irreconcilable enemy of the Reformation —

the House of Austria — by its ambitious projects and the overwhelming force which it could bring to their support, endangered, in no small degree, the freedom of Europe, and more especially of the German States. This circumstance could not fail to rouse the latter from their security, and to render them vigilant in self-defence. Their ordinary resources were quite insufficient to resist so formidable a power. Extraordinary exertions were required from their subjects; and when even these proved far from adequate, they had recourse to foreign assistance; and, by means of a common league, they endeavored to oppose a power which, singly, they were unable to withstand.

But the strong political inducements which the German princes had to resist the pretensions of the House of Austria, naturally, did not extend to their subjects. It is only immediate advantages or immediate evils that set the people in action, and for these a sound policy cannot wait. Ill then would it have fared with these princes if by good fortune another effectual motive had not offered itself, which roused the passions of the people, and kindled in them an enthusiasm which might be directed against the political danger, as having with it a common cause of alarm.

This motive was their avowed hatred of the religion which Austria protected, and their enthusiastic attachment to a doctrine which that house was endeavoring to extirpate by fire and sword. Their attachment was ardent, their hatred invincible. Religious fanaticism anticipates even the remotest dangers. Enthusiasm never calculates its sacrifices. What the most pressing danger of the state could not gain from the citizens was effected by religious zeal. For the state, or for the prince, few would have drawn the sword; but for religion the merchant, the artist, the peasant, all cheerfully flew to arms. For the state or for the prince even the smallest additional impost would have been avoided; but for religion the people readily staked at once life, fortune, and all earthly hopes. It trebled the contributions which flowed into the exchequer of the princes, and the armies which marched to the field; and, in the ardent excitement produced in all minds by the peril to which their faith was exposed, the subject felt not the pressure of those burdens and privations under which, in cooler moments, he would have sunk exhausted. The terrors of the Spanish Inquisition, and the massacre of St. Bartholomew's, procured for the Prince of Orange, the Admiral Coligny, the British Queen Elizabeth, and the Protestant princes of Germany, supplies of men and money from their subjects to a degree which at present is inconceivable.

But, with all their exertions, they would have effected little against a power which was an overmatch for any single adversary, however powerful. At this period of imperfect policy accidental circumstances alone could determine distant states to afford one another a mutual support. The differences of government, of laws, of language, of manners, and of character, which hitherto had kept whole nations and countries as it were insulated, and raised a lasting barrier between them, rendered one state insensible to the distresses of another, save where national jealousy could indulge a malicious joy at the reverses of a rival. This barrier the Reformation destroyed. An interest more intense and more immediate than national aggrandizement or patriotism, and entirely independent of private utility, began to animate whole states and individual citizens; an interest capable of uniting numerous and distant nations, even while it frequently lost its force among the subjects of the same government. With the inhabitants of Geneva, for instance, of England, of Germany, or of Holland, the French Calvinist possessed a common point of union which he had not with his own countrymen. Thus, in one important particular, he ceased to be the citizen of a single state, and to confine his views and sympathies to his own country alone. The sphere of his views became enlarged. He began to calculate his own fate from that of other nations of the same religious profession, and to make their cause his own. Now for the first time did princes venture to bring the affairs of other countries before their own councils; for the first time could they hope for a willing ear to their own necessities, and prompt assistance from others. Foreign affairs had now become a matter of domestic policy, and that aid was readily granted to the religious confederate which would have been denied to the mere neighbor, and still more to the distant stranger. The inhabitant of the Palatinate leaves his native fields to fight side by side with his religious associate of France, against the common enemy of their faith. The Huguenot draws his sword against the country which persecutes him, and sheds his blood in defence of the liberties of Holland. Swiss is arrayed against Swiss; German against German, to determine, on the banks of the Loire and the Seine, the succession of the French crown. The Dane crosses the Eider, and the Swede the Baltic, to break the chains which are forged for Germany.

It is difficult to say what would have been the fate of the Reformation, and the liberties of the empire, had not the formidable power of Austria declared against them. This, however, appears certain, that nothing so completely damped the Austrian hopes of universal monarchy as the obstinate war which they had to wage against the new religious opinions. Under no other circumstances could the weaker princes have roused their subjects to such extraordinary exertions against the ambition of Austria, or the states themselves have united so closely against the common enemy.

The power of Austria never stood higher than after the victory which Charles V. gained over the Germans at Mühlberg. With the treaty of Smalcalde the freedom of Germany lay, as it seemed, prostrate forever; but it revived under Maurice of Saxony, once its most formidable enemy. All the fruits of the victory of Mühlberg were lost again in the Congress of Passau and the Diet of Augsburg; and every scheme of civil and religious oppression terminated in the concessions of an equitable peace.

The Diet of Augsburg divided Germany into two religious and two political parties, by recognizing the independent rights and existence of both. Hitherto the Protestants had been looked on as rebels; they were henceforth to be regarded as brethren — not, indeed, through affection, but necessity. By the Interim,* the

* A system of Theology, so called, prepared by order of the Emperor Charles V. for the use of Germany, to reconcile the differences between the Roman Catholics and the Lutherans, which, however, was rejected by both parties.— ED.

Confession of Augsburg was allowed temporarily to take a sisterly place alongside of the olden religion, though only as a tolerated neighbor. To every secular state was conceded the right of establishing the religion it acknowledged as supreme and exclusive within its own territories, and of forbidding the open profession of its rival. Subjects were to be free to quit a country where their own religion was not tolerated. The doctrines of Luther for the first time received a positive sanction; and if they were trampled under foot in Bavaria and Austria they predominated in Saxony and Thuringia. But the sovereigns alone were to determine what form of religion should prevail within their territories; the feelings of subjects who had no representatives in the Diet were little attended to in the pacification. In the ecclesiastical territories, indeed, where the unreformed religion enjoyed an undisputed supremacy, the free exercise of their religion was obtained for all who had previously embraced the Protestant doctrines; but this indulgence rested only on the personal guarantee of Ferdinand, King of the Romans, by whose endeavors chiefly this peace was effected; a guarantee, which, being rejected by the Roman Catholic members of the Diet, and only inserted in the treaty under their protest, could not of course have the force of law.

If it had been opinions only that thus divided the minds of men, with what indifference would all have regarded the division! But on these opinions depended riches, dignities, and rights; and it was this which so deeply aggravated the evils of division. Of two brothers, as it were, who had hitherto enjoyed a paternal inheritance in common, one now remained, while the other was compelled to leave his father's house, and hence arose the necessity of dividing the patrimony. For this separation, which he could not have foreseen, the father had made no provision. By the beneficent donations of pious ancestors the riches of the church had been accumulating through a thousand years, and these benefactors were as much the progenitors of the departing brother as of him who remained. Was the right of inheritance then to be limited to the paternal house, or to be extended to blood? The gifts had been made to the church in communion with Rome, because at that time no other existed, — to the first born, as it were, because he was as yet the only son. Was then a right of primogeniture to be admitted in the church, as in noble families? Were the pretensions of one party to be favored by a prescription from times when the claims of the other could not have come into existence. Could the Lutherans be justly excluded from these possessions, to which the benevolence of their forefathers had contributed, merely on the ground that, at the date of their foundation, the differences between Lutheranism and Romanism were unknown? Both parties have disputed, and still dispute, with equal plausibility, on these points. Both alike have found it difficult to prove their right. Law can be applied only to conceivable cases, and perhaps spiritual foundations are not among the number of these, and still less where the conditions of the founders generally extended to a system of doctrines; for how is it conceivable that a permanent endowment should be made of opinions left open to change?

What law cannot decide is usually determined by might, and such was the case here. The one party held firmly all that could no longer be wrested from it — the other defended what it still possessed. All the bishoprics and abbeys which had been secularized *before* the peace remained with the Protestants; but, by an express clause, the unreformed Catholics provided that none should thereafter be secularized. Every impropriator of an ecclesiastical foundation, who held immediately of the Empire, whether elector, bishop, or abbot, forfeited his benefice and dignity the moment he embraced the Protestant belief; he was obliged in that event instantly to resign its emoluments, and the chapter was to proceed to a new election, exactly as if his place had been vacated by death. By this sacred anchor of the Ecclesiastical Reservation (*Reservatum Ecclesiasticum*), which makes the temporal existence of a spiritual prince entirely depend on his fidelity to the olden religion, the Roman Catholic Church in Germany is still held fast; and precarious, indeed, would be its situation were this anchor to give way.

The principle of the Ecclesiastical Reservation was strongly opposed by the Protestants; and though it was at last adopted into the treaty of peace, its insertion was qualified with the declaration, that parties had come to no final determination on the point. Could it then be more binding on the Protestants than Ferdinand's guarantee in favor of Protestant subjects of ecclesiastical states was upon the Roman Catholics? Thus were two important subjects of dispute left unsettled in the treaty of peace, and by them the war was rekindled.

Such was the position of things with regard to religious toleration and ecclesiastical property; it was the same with regard to rights and dignities. The existing German system provided only for one church, because one only was in existence when that system was framed. The church had now divided; the Diet had broken into two religious parties; was the whole system of the Empire still exclusively to follow the one? The emperors had hitherto been members of the Romish Church, because till now that religion had no rival. But was it his connection with Rome which constituted a German emperor, or was it not rather Germany which was to be represented in its head? The Protestants were now spread over the whole Empire, and how could they justly still be represented by an unbroken line of Roman Catholic emperors? In the Imperial Chamber the German States judge themselves, for they elect the judges; it was the very end of its institution that they should do so, in order that equal justice should be dispensed to all; but would this be still possible if the representatives of both professions were not equally admissible to a seat in the Chamber? That one religion only existed in Germany at the time of its establishment was accidental; that no one estate should have the means of legally oppressing another, was the essential purpose of the institution. Now this object would be entirely frustrated if one religious party were to have the exclusive power of deciding for the other. Must, then, the design be sacrificed because that which was merely accidental had changed? With great difficulty the Protestants, at last, obtained for the representatives of their religion a place in the Supreme Council,

but still there was far from being a perfect equality
of voices. To this day no Protestant prince has been
raised to the imperial throne.

Whatever may be said of the equality which the peace
of Augsburg was to have established between the two
German churches, the Roman Catholic had unquestionably
still the advantage. All that the Lutheran Church gained
by it was toleration; all that the Romish Church conceded was a sacrifice to necessity, not an offering to
justice. Very far was it from being a peace between two
equal powers, but a truce between a sovereign and
unconquered rebels. From this principle all the proceedings of the Roman Catholics against the Protestants seemed
to flow, and still continue to do so. To join the reformed
faith was still a crime, since it was to be visited with so
severe a penalty as that which the Ecclesiastical Reservation held suspended over the apostacy of the spiritual
princes. Even to the last the Romish Church preferred
to risk the loss of everything by force than voluntarily
to yield the smallest matter to justice. The loss was
accidental and might be repaired; but the abandonment
of its pretensions, the concession of a single point to the
Protestants, would shake the foundations of the church
itself. Even in the treaty of peace this principle was not
lost sight of. Whatever in this peace was yielded to the
Protestants was always under condition. It was expressly declared that affairs were to remain on the
stipulated footing only till the next general council,
which was to be called with the view of effecting a
union between the two confessions. Then only, when
this last attempt should have failed, was the religious
treaty to become valid and conclusive. However little
hope there might be of such a reconciliation, however little
perhaps the Romanists themselves were in earnest with it,
still it was something to have clogged the peace with
these stipulations.

Thus this religious treaty, which was to extinguish forever the flames of civil war, was, in fact, but a temporary
truce, extorted by force and necessity; not dictated by
justice, nor emanating from just notions either of religion
or toleration. A religious treaty of this kind the Roman

Catholics were as incapable of granting, to be candid, as in truth the Lutherans were unqualified to receive. Far from evincing a tolerant spirit towards the Roman Catholics, when it was in their power, they even oppressed the Calvinists; who indeed just as little deserved toleration, since they were unwilling to practise it. For such a peace the times were not yet ripe — the minds of men not yet sufficiently enlightened. How could one party expect from another what itself was incapable of performing? What each side saved or gained by the treaty of Augsburg it owed to the imposing attitude of strength which it maintained at the time of its negotiation. What was won by force was to be maintained also by force; if the peace was to be permanent, the two parties to it must preserve the same relative positions. The boundaries of the two churches had been marked out with the sword; with the sword they must be preserved, or woe to that party which should be first disarmed! A sad and fearful prospect for the tranquillity of Germany when peace itself bore so threatening an aspect.

A momentary lull now pervaded the empire; a transitory bond of concord appeared to unite its scattered limbs into one body, so that for a time a feeling also for the common weal returned. But the division had penetrated its inmost being, and to restore its original harmony was impossible. Carefully as the treaty of peace appeared to have defined the rights of both parties, its interpretation was nevertheless the subject of many disputes. In the heat of conflict it had produced a cessation of hostilities; it covered, not extinguished, the fire, and unsatisfied claims remained on either side. The Romanists imagined they had lost too much, the Protestants that they had gained too little; and the treaty which neither party could venture to violate was interpreted by each in its own favor.

The seizure of the ecclesiastical benefices, the motive which had so strongly tempted the majority of the Protestant princes to embrace the doctrines of Luther, was not less powerful after than before the peace; of those whose founders had not held their fiefs immediately of the empire, such as were not already in their possession would it was evident soon be so. The whole of Lower Germany was already secularized; and if it were otherwise in Upper Germany, it was owing to the vehement resistance of the Catholics, who had there the preponderance. Each party, where it was the most powerful, oppressed the adherents of the other; the ecclesiastical princes in particular, as the most defenceless members of the empire, were incessantly tormented by the ambition of their Protestant neighbors. Those who were too weak to repel force by force took refuge under the wings of justice; and the complaints of spoliation were heaped up against the Protestants in the Imperial Chamber, which was ready enough to pursue the accused with judgments, but found too little support to carry them into effect. The peace which stipulated for complete religious toleration for the dignitaries of the Empire, had provided also for the subject, by enabling him, without interruption, to leave the country in which the exercise of his religion was prohibited. But from the wrongs which the violence of a sovereign might inflict on an obnoxious subject; from the nameless oppressions by which he might harass and annoy the emigrant; from the artful snares in which subtilty combined with power might enmesh him — from these the dead letter of the treaty could afford him no protection. The Catholic subject of Protestant princes complained loudly of violations of the religious peace — the Lutherans still more loudly of the oppression they experienced under their Romanist suzerains. The rancor and animosities of theologians infused a poison into every occurrence, however inconsiderable, and inflamed the minds of the people. Happy would it have been had this theological hatred exhausted its zeal upon the common enemy, instead of venting its virus on the adherents of a kindred faith!

Unanimity amongst the Protestants might, by preserving the balance between the contending parties, have prolonged the peace; but, as if to complete the confusion, all concord was quickly broken. The doctrines which had been propagated by Zuingli in Zurich, and by Calvin in Geneva, soon spread to Germany, and divided the Protestants among themselves, with little in unison save their common hatred to popery. The Protestants of this date bore but slight resemblance to those who, fifty years before, drew up the Confession of Augsburg; and the cause of the change is to be sought in that Confession itself. It had prescribed a positive boundary to the Protestant faith, before the newly-awakened spirit of inquiry had satisfied itself as to the limits it ought to set; and the Protestants seemed unwittingly to have thrown away much of the advantage acquired by their rejection of popery. Common complaints of the Romish hierarchy and of ecclesiastical abuses, and a common disapprobation of its dogmas, formed a sufficient centre of union for the Protestants; but not content with this, they sought a rallying point in the promulgation of a new and positive creed, in which they sought to embody the distinctions, the privileges, and the essence of the church, and to this they referred the convention entered into with their opponents. It was as professors of this creed that they had acceded to the treaty; and in the benefits of this peace the advocates of the Confession were alone entitled to participate. In any case, therefore, the situation of its adherents was embarrassing. If a blind obedience were yielded to the dicta of the Confession, a lasting bound would be set to the spirit of inquiry; if, on the other hand, they dissented from the formulæ agreed upon, the point of union would be lost. Unfortunately both incidents occurred, and the evil results of both were quickly felt. One party rigorously adhered to the original symbol of faith, and the other abandoned it, only to adopt another with equal exclusiveness.

Nothing could have furnished the common enemy a more plausible defence of his cause than this dissension; no spectacle could have been more gratifying to him than the rancor with which the Protestants alternately persecuted each other. Who could condemn the Roman Catholics if they laughed at the audacity with which the Reformers had presumed to announce the only true belief?—if from Protestants they borrowed the weapons against Protestants?—if, in the midst of this clashing of opinions, they held fast to the authority of their own church, for which, in part, there spoke an honorable antiquity, and a yet more honorable plurality of voices. But this division placed the Protestants in still more serious embarrassments. As the covenants of the treaty applied only to the partisans of the Confession, their opponents, with some reason, called upon them to explain who were to be recognized as the adherents of that creed. The Lutherans could not, without offending conscience, include the Calvinists in their communion; except at the risk of converting a useful friend into a dangerous enemy, could they exclude them. This unfortunate difference opened a way for the machinations of the Jesuits to sow distrust between both parties, and to destroy the unity of their measures. Fettered by the double fear of their direct adversaries, and of their opponents among themselves, the Protestants lost forever the opportunity of placing their church on a perfect equality with the Catholic. All these difficulties would have been avoided, and the defection of the Calvinists would not have prejudiced the common cause, if the point of union had been placed simply in the abandonment of Romanism, instead of in the Confession of Augsburg.

But however divided on other points, they concurred in this — that the security which had resulted from equality of power could only be maintained by the preservation of that balance. In the meanwhile, the continual reforms of one party, and the opposing measures of the other, kept both upon the watch, while the interpretation of the religious treaty was a never-ending subject of dispute. Each party maintained that every step taken by its opponent was an infraction of the peace, while of every movement of its own it was asserted that it was essential to its maintenance. Yet all the measures of the Catholics did not, as their opponents alleged, proceed from a spirit of encroachment — many of them were the necessary precautions of self-defence. The Protestants had shown unequivocally enough what the Romanists might expect if they were unfortunate enough to become the weaker party. The greediness of the former for the property of the church, gave no reason to expect indulgence; — their bitter hatred left no hope of magnanimity or forbearance.

But the Protestants, likewise, were excusable if they, too, placed little confidence in the sincerity of the Roman Catholics. By the treacherous and inhuman treatment which their brethren in Spain, France, and the Netherlands had suffered; by the disgraceful subterfuge of the Romish princes, who held that the Pope had power to relieve them from the obligation of the most solemn oaths; and above all, by the detestable maxim, that faith was not to be kept with heretics, the Roman Church, in the eyes of all honest men, had lost its honor. No engagement, no oath, however sacred, from a Roman Catholic, could satisfy a Protestant. What security then could the religious peace afford, when, throughout Germany, the Jesuits represented it as a measure of mere temporary convenience, and in Rome itself it was solemnly repudiated.

The General Council, to which reference had been made in the treaty, had already been held in the city of Trent; but, as might have been foreseen, without accommodating the religious differences, or taking a single step to effect such accommodation, and even without being attended by the Protestants. The latter, indeed, were now solemnly excommunicated by it in the name of the church, whose representative the Council gave itself out to be. Could, then, a secular treaty, extorted moreover by force of arms, afford them adequate protection against the ban of the church; a treaty, too, based on a condition which the decision of the Council seemed entirely to abolish? There was then a show of right for violating the peace, if only the Romanists possessed the power; and henceforward the Protestants were protected by nothing but the respect for their formidable array.

Other circumstances combined to augment this distrust. Spain, on whose support the Romanists in Germany chiefly relied, was engaged in a bloody conflict with the Flemings. By it the flower of the Spanish troops were drawn to the confines of Germany. With what ease might they be introduced within the empire, if a decisive stroke should render their presence necessary? Germany was at that time a magazine of war for nearly all the powers of Europe. The religious war had crowded it with soldiers, whom the peace left destitute; its many independent princes found it easy to assemble armies, and afterwards, for the sake of gain or the interests of party, hire them out to other powers. With German troops Philip II. waged war against the Netherlands. and with German troops they defended themselves, Every such levy in Germany was a subject of alarm to the one party or the other, since it might be intended for their oppression. The arrival of an ambassador, an extraordinary legate of the Pope, a conference of princes, every unusual incident, must, it was thought, be pregnant with destruction to some party. Thus, for nearly half a century, stood Germany, her hand upon the sword; every rustle of a leaf alarmed her.

Ferdinand I., King of Hungary, and his excellent son, Maximilian II., held at this memorable epoch the reins of government. With a heart full of sincerity, with a truly heroic patience, had Ferdinand brought about the religious peace of Augsburg, and afterwards, in the Council of Trent, labored assiduously, though vainly, at the ungrateful task of reconciling the two religions. Abandoned by his nephew, Philip of Spain, and hard pressed both in Hungary and Transylvania by the victorious armies of the Turks, it was not likely that this emperor would entertain the idea of violating the religious peace, and thereby destroying his own painful work. The heavy expenses of the perpetually recurring war with Turkey could not be defrayed by the meagre contributions of his exhausted hereditary dominions. He stood, therefore, in need of the assistance of the whole empire; and the religious peace alone preserved in one body the otherwise divided empire. Financial necessities made the Protestant as needful to him as the Romanist, and imposed upon him the obligation of treating both parties with equal justice, which, amidst so many contradictory claims, was truly a colossal task. Very far, however, was the result from answering his expectations. His indulgence of the Protestants served only to bring upon his successors a war, which death saved himself the mortification of witnessing. Scarcely more fortunate was his son Maximilian, with whom perhaps the pressure of circumstances was the only obstacle, and a longer life perhaps the only want to his establishing the new religion upon the imperial throne. Necessity had taught the father forbearance towards the Protestants — necessity and justice dictated the same course to the son. The grandson had reason to repent that he neither listened to justice nor yielded to necessity.

Maximilian left six sons, of whom the eldest, the Archduke Rodolph, inherited his dominions, and ascended the imperial throne. The other brothers were put off with petty appanages. A few mesne fiefs were held by a collateral branch, which had their uncle, Charles of Styria, at its head; and even these were afterwards under his son, Ferdinand II., incorporated with the rest of the family dominions. With this exception, the whole of the imposing power of Austria was now wielded by a single but unfortunately weak hand.

Rodolph II. was not devoid of those virtues which might have gained him the esteem of mankind had the lot of a private station fallen to him. His character was mild; he loved peace and the sciences, particularly astronomy, natural history, chemistry, and the study of antiquities. To these he applied with a passionate zeal, which at the very time when the critical posture of affairs demanded all his attention, and his exhausted finances the most rigid economy, diverted his attention from state affairs, and involved him in pernicious expenses. His taste for astronomy soon lost itself in those astrological reveries to which timid and melancholy temperaments like his are but too disposed. This, together with a youth passed in Spain, opened his ears to the evil counsels of the Jesuits and the influence of the Spanish court, by which at last he was wholly governed. Ruled by tastes so little in accordance with the dignity of his station, and alarmed by ridiculous prophecies, he withdrew, after the Spanish custom, from the eyes of his subjects, to bury himself amidst his gems and antiques, or to make experiments in his laboratory, while the most fatal discords loosened all the bands of the empire, and the flames of rebellion began to burst out at the very

footsteps of his throne. All access to his person was
denied, the most urgent matters were neglected. The
prospect of the rich inheritance of Spain was closed
against him while he was trying to make up his mind to
offer his hand to the Infanta Isabella. A fearful anarchy
threatened the Empire, for, though without an heir of his
own body, he could not be persuaded to allow the election
of a King of the Romans. The Austrian States renounced
their allegiance, Hungary and Transylvania threw off his
supremacy, and Bohemia was not slow in following their
example. The descendant of the once so formidable
Charles V. was in perpetual danger, either of losing one
part of his possessions to the Turks, or another to the
Protestants, and of sinking beyond redemption under the
formidable coalition which a great monarch of Europe
had formed against him. The events which now took
place in the interior of Germany were such as usually
happened when either the throne was without an emperor
or the emperor without a sense of his imperial dignity.
Outraged or abandoned by their head, the states of the
empire were left to help themselves; and alliances
among themselves must supply the defective authority of
the emperor. Germany was divided into two leagues,
which stood in arms arrayed against each other: between
both, Rodolph, the despised opponent of the one, and the
impotent protector of the other, remained irresolute and
useless, equally unable to destroy the former or to command the latter. What had the Empire to look for from
a prince incapable even of defending his hereditary dominions against its domestic enemies? To prevent the
utter ruin of the House of Austria, his own family
combined against him; and a powerful party threw itself
into the arms of his brother. Driven from his hereditary
dominions, nothing was now left him to lose but the
imperial dignity; and he was only spared this last disgrace by a timely death.

At this critical moment, when only a supple policy,
united with a vigorous arm, could have maintained the
tranquillity of the Empire, its evil genius gave it a Rodolph for emperor. At a more peaceful period the Ger-
manic Union would have managed its own interests, and

Rodolph, like so many others of his rank, might have hidden his deficiencies in a mysterious obscurity. But the urgent demand for the qualities in which he was most deficient revealed his incapacity. The position of Germany called for an emperor who, by his known energies, could give weight to his resolves; and the hereditary dominions of Rodolph, considerable as they were, were at present in a situation to occasion the greatest embarrassment to the governors.

The Austrian princes, it is true, were Roman Catholics, and, in addition to that, the supporters of popery, but their countries were far from being so. The reformed opinions had penetrated even these, and, favored by Ferdinand's necessities and Maximilian's mildness, had met with a rapid success. The Austrian provinces exhibited in miniature what Germany did on a larger scale. The great nobles and the ritter class or knights were chiefly evangelical, and in the cities the Protestants had a decided preponderance. If they succeeded in bringing a few of their party into the country, they contrived imperceptibly to fill all places of trust and the magistracy with their own adherents, and to exclude the Catholics. Against the numerous order of the nobles and knights, and the deputies from the towns, the voice of a few prelates was powerless; and the unseemly ridicule and offensive contempt of the former soon drove them entirely from the provincial diets. Thus the whole of the Austrian Diet had imperceptibly become Protestant, and the Reformation was making rapid strides towards its public recognition. The prince was dependent on the Estates, who had it in their power to grant or refuse supplies. Accordingly, they availed themselves of the financial necessities of Ferdinand and his son to extort one religious concession after another. To the nobles and knights Maximilian at last conceded the free exercise of their religion, but only within their own territories and castles. The intemperate enthusiasm of the Protestant preachers overstepped the boundaries which prudence had prescribed. In defiance of the express prohibition, several of them ventured to preach publicly, not only in the towns, but in Vienna itself, and

the people flocked in crowds to this new doctrine, the
best seasoning of which was personality and abuse.
Thus continued food was supplied to fanaticism, and the
hatred of two churches, that were such near neighbors,
was farther envenomed by the sting of an impure zeal.

Among the hereditary dominions of the House of
Austria, Hungary and Transylvania were the most unstable and the most difficult to retain. The impossibility
of holding these two countries against the neighboring
and overwhelming power of the Turks had already driven
Ferdinand to the inglorious expedient of recognizing, by
an annual tribute, the Porte's supremacy over Transylvania, — a shameful confession of weakness, and a still more
dangerous temptation to the turbulent nobility, when they
fancied they had any reason to complain of their master.
Not without conditions had the Hungarians submitted
to the House of Austria. They asserted the elective
freedom of their crown, and boldly contended for all
those prerogatives of their order which are inseparable
from this freedom of election. The near neighborhood
of Turkey, the facility of changing masters with impunity, encouraged the magnates still more in their presumption; discontented with the Austrian government,
they threw themselves into the arms of the Turks; dissatisfied with these, they returned again to their German
sovereigns. The frequency and rapidity of these transitions from one government to another had communicated its influences also to their mode of thinking; and as
their country wavered between the Turkish and Austrian
rule, so their minds vacillated between revolt and submission. The more unfortunate each nation felt itself in
being degraded into a province of a foreign kingdom, the
stronger desire did they feel to obey a monarch chosen
from amongst themselves, and thus it was always easy for
an enterprising noble to obtain their support. The
nearest Turkish pasha was always ready to bestow the
Hungarian sceptre and crown on a rebel against Austria;
just as ready was Austria to confirm to any adventurer the possession of provinces which he had wrested
from the Porte, satisfied with preserving thereby the
shadow of authority, and with erecting at the same

time a barrier against the Turks. In this way several of these magnates, Bathori, Boschkai, Ragoczi, and Bethlen, succeeded in establishing themselves, one after another, as tributary sovereigns in Transylvania and Hungary; and they maintained their ground by no deeper policy than that of occasionally joining the enemy, in order to render themselves more formidable to their own prince.

Ferdinand, Maximilian, and Rodolph, who were all sovereigns of Hungary and Transylvania, exhausted their other territories in endeavoring to defend these from the hostile inroads of the Turks, and to put down intestine rebellion. In this quarter destructive wars were succeeded but by brief truces, which were scarcely less hurtful: far and wide the land lay waste, while the injured serf had to complain equally of his enemy and his protector. Into these countries also the Reformation had penetrated; and protected by the freedom of the States, and under the cover of the internal disorders, had made a noticeable progress. Here, too, it was incautiously attacked, and party spirit thus became yet more dangerous from religious enthusiasm. Headed by a bold rebel, Boschkai, the nobles of Hungary and Transylvania raised the standard of rebellion. The Hungarian insurgents were upon the point of making common cause with the discontented Protestants in Austria, Moravia, and Bohemia, and uniting all those countries in one fearful revolt. The downfall of popery in these lands would then have been inevitable.

Long had the Austrian archdukes, the brothers of the Emperor, beheld with silent indignation the impending ruin of their house; this last event hastened their decision. The Archduke Matthias, Maximilian's second son, Viceroy in Hungary, and Rodolph's presumptive heir, now came forward as the stay of the falling house of Hapsburg. In his youth, misled by a false ambition, this prince, disregarding the interests of his family, had listened to the overtures of the Flemish insurgents, who invited him into the Netherlands to conduct the defence of their liberties against the oppression of his own relative, Philip II. Mistaking the voice of an insulated faction for that of the entire nation, Matthias obeyed the call. But the event answered the expectations of the men of Brabant as little as his own, and from this imprudent enterprise he retired with little credit.

Far more honorable was his second appearance in the political world. Perceiving that his repeated remonstrances with the Emperor were unavailing, he assembled the archdukes, his brothers and cousins, at Presburg, and consulted with them on the growing perils of their house, when they unanimously assigned to him, as the oldest, the duty of defending that patrimony which a feeble brother was endangering. In his hands they placed all their powers and rights, and vested him with sovereign authority to act at his discretion for the common good. Matthias immediately opened a communication with the Porte and the Hungarian rebels, and through his skilful management succeeded in saving by a peace with the Turks the remainder of Hungary, and, by a treaty with the rebels, preserved the claims of Austria to the lost provinces. But Rodolph, as jealous as he had hitherto been careless of his sovereign authority, refused to ratify this treaty, which he regarded as a criminal encroachment on his sovereign rights. He accused the Archduke of keeping up a secret understanding with the enemy, and of cherishing treasonable designs on the crown of Hungary.

The activity of Matthias was, in truth, anything but disinterested; the conduct of the Emperor only accelerated the execution of his ambitious views. Secure, from motives of gratitude, of the devotion of the Hungarians, for whom he had so lately obtained the blessings of peace; assured by his agents of the favorable disposition of the nobles, and certain of the support of a large party even in Austria, he now ventured to assume a bolder attitude, and, sword in hand, to discuss his grievances with the Emperor. The Protestants in Austria and Moravia, long ripe for revolt, and now won over to the Archduke by his promises of toleration, loudly and openly espoused his cause, and their long-menaced alliance with the Hungarian rebels was actually effected. Almost at once a formidable conspiracy was planned and matured against the Emperor. Too late did he resolve to amend his past errors; in vain did he attempt to break up this fatal alliance. Already the whole empire was in arms; Hungary, Austria, and Moravia had done homage to Matthias, who was already on his march to Bohemia to seize the Emperor in his palace, and to cut at once the sinews of his power.

Bohemia was not a more peaceable possession for Austria than Hungary; with this difference only, that, in the latter, political considerations, in the former, religious dissensions, fomented disorders. In Bohemia, a century before the days of Luther, the first spark of the religious war had been kindled; a century after Luther the first flames of the thirty years, war burst out in Bohemia. The sect which owed its rise to John Huss still existed in that country;—it agreed with the Romish Church in ceremonies and doctrines, with the single exception of the administration of the Communion, in which the Hussites communicated in both kinds. This privilege had been conceded to the followers of Huss by the Council of Basle in an express treaty (the Bohemian Compact); and though it was afterwards disavowed by the popes, they nevertheless continued to profit by it under the sanction of the government. As the use of the cup formed the only important distinction of their body, they were usually designated by the name of Utraquists; and they readily adopted an appellation which reminded them of their dearly-valued privilege. But under this title lurked also the far stricter sects of the Bohemian and Moravian Brethren, who differed from the predominant church in more important particulars, and bore, in fact, a great resemblance to the German Protestants. Among them both the German and Swiss opinions on religion made rapid progress; while the name of Utraquists, under which they managed to disguise the change of their principles, shielded them from persecution.

In truth, they had nothing in common with the Utraquists but the name; essentially they were altogether Protestant. Confident in the strength of their party, and the Emperor's toleration under Maximilian, they had openly avowed their tenets. After the example of the Germans, they drew up a Confession of their own, in which Lutherans as well as Calvinists recognized their own doctrines, and they sought to transfer to the new Confession the privileges of the original Utraquists. In this they were opposed by their Roman Catholic countrymen, and forced to rest content with the Emperor's verbal assurance of protection.

As long as Maximilian lived they enjoyed complete toleration, even under the new form they had taken. Under his successor the scene changed. An imperial edict appeared which deprived the Bohemian Brethren of their religious freedom. Now these differed in nothing from the other Utraquists. The sentence, therefore, of their condemnation obviously included all the partisans of the Bohemian Confession. Accordingly, they all combined to oppose the imperial mandate in the Diet, but without being able to procure its revocation. The Emperor and the Roman Catholic Estates took their ground on the Compact and the Bohemian Constitution; in which nothing appeared in favor of a religion which had not then obtained the voice of the country. Since that time how completely had affairs changed? What then formed but an inconsiderable opinion had now become the predominant religion of the country. And what was it then but a subterfuge to limit a newly-spreading religion by the terms of obsolete treaties? The Bohemian Protestants appealed to the verbal guarantee of Maximilian, and the religious freedom of the Germans, with whom they argued they ought to be on a footing of equality. It was in vain — their appeal was dismissed.

Such was the posture of affairs in Bohemia when Matthias, already master of Hungary, Austria, and Moravia, appeared in Kolin, to raise the Bohemian Estates also against the Emperor. The embarrassment of the latter was now at its height. Abandoned by all his other subjects, he placed his last hopes on the Bohemians, who, it might be foreseen, would take advantage of his necessities to enforce their own demands. After an interval of many years, he once more appeared publicly in the Diet at Prague; and to convince the people that he was really still in existence, orders were given that all the windows should be opened in the streets through which he was to pass — proof enough how far things had gone with him. The event justified his fears. The Estates, conscious of their own power, refused to take a single step until their privileges were confirmed, and religious toleration fully assured to them. It was in vain to have recourse now to the old system of evasion. The Emperor's fate was in their hands, and he must yield to necessity. At present, however, he only granted their other demands — religious matters he reserved for consideration at the next Diet.

The Bohemians now took up arms in defence of the Emperor, and a bloody war between the two brothers was on the point of breaking out. But Rodolph, who feared nothing so much as remaining in this slavish dependence on the Estates, waited not for a warlike issue, but hastened to effect a reconciliation with his brother by more peaceable means. By a formal act of abdication he resigned to Matthias, what indeed he had no chance of wresting from him, Austria and the kingdom of Hungary, and acknowledged him as his successor to the crown of Bohemia.

Dearly enough had the Emperor extricated himself from one difficulty only to get immediately involved in another. The settlement of the religious affairs of Bohemia had been referred to the next Diet, which was held in 1609. The reformed Bohemians demanded the free exercise of their faith, as under the former emperors; a Consistory of their own; the cession of the University of Prague; and the right of electing *Defenders, or Protectors* of *Liberty*, from their own body. The answer was the same as before; for the timid Emperor was now entirely fettered by the unreformed party. However often, and in however threatening language the Estates renewed their remonstrances, the Emperor persisted in his first declaration of granting nothing beyond the old compact. The Diet broke up without coming to a decision; and the Estates, exasperated against the Emperor, arranged a general meeting at Prague, upon their own authority, to right themselves.

They appeared at Prague in great force. In defiance

of the imperial prohibition they carried on their deliberations almost under the very eyes of the Emperor. The yielding compliance which he began to show only proved how much they were feared, and increased their audacity. Yet on the main point he remained inflexible. They fulfilled their threats, and at last resolved to establish, by their own power, the free and universal exercise of their religion, and to abandon the Emperor to his necessities until he should confirm this resolution. They even went farther, and elected for themselves the DEFENDERS which the Emperor had refused them. Ten were nominated by each of the three Estates; they also determined to raise, as soon as possible, an armed force, at the head of which Count Thurn, the chief organizer of the revolt, should be placed as general defender of the liberties of Bohemia. Their determination brought the Emperor to submission, to which he was now counselled even by the Spaniards. Apprehensive lest the exasperated Estates should throw themselves into the arms of the King of Hungary, he signed the memorable Letter of Majesty for Bohemia, by which, under the successors of the Emperor, that people justified their rebellion.

The Bohemian Confession, which the States had laid before the Emperor Maximilian, was, by the Letter of Majesty, placed on a footing of equality with the olden profession. The Utraquists, for by this title the Bohemian Protestants continued to designate themselves, were put in possession of the University of Prague, and allowed a Consistory of their own entirely independent of the archiepiscopal see of that city. All the churches in the cities, villages, and market towns, which they held at the date of the letter, were secured to them; and if in addition they wished to erect others, it was permitted to the nobles, and knights, and the free cities to do so. This last clause in the Letter of Majesty gave rise to the unfortunate disputes which subsequently rekindled the flames of war in Europe.

The Letter of Majesty erected the Protestant part of Bohemia into a kind of republic. The Estates had learned to feel the power which they gained by perseverance, unity, and harmony in their measures. The

Emperor now retained little more than the shadow of his sovereign authority; while by the new dignity of the so-called defenders of liberty a dangerous stimulus was given to the spirit of revolt. The example and success of Bohemia afforded a tempting seduction to the other hereditary dominions of Austria, and all attempted by similar means to extort similar privileges. The spirit of liberty spread from one province to another; and as it was chiefly the disunion among the Austrian princes that had enabled the Protestants so materially to improve their advantages, they now hastened to effect a reconciliation between the Emperor and the King of Hungary.

But the reconciliation could not be sincere. The wrong was too great to be forgiven, and Rodolph continued to nourish at heart an unextinguishable hatred of Matthias. With grief and indignation he brooded over the thought that the Bohemian sceptre was finally to descend into the hands of his enemy; and the prospect was not more consoling, even if Matthias should die without issue. In that case, Ferdinand, Archduke of Grätz, whom he equally disliked, was the head of the family. To exclude the latter as well as Matthias from the succession to the throne of Bohemia, he fell upon the project of diverting that inheritance to Ferdinand's brother, the Archduke Leopold, Bishop of Passau, who among all his relatives had ever been the dearest and most deserving. The prejudices of the Bohemians in favor of the elective freedom of their crown, and their attachment to Leopold's person, seemed to favor this scheme, in which Rodolph consulted rather his own partiality and vindictiveness than the good of his house. But to carry out this project, a military force was requisite, and Rodolph actually assembled an army in the bishopric of Passau. The object of this force was hidden from all. An inroad, however, which, for want of pay, it made suddenly and without the Emperor's knowledge into Bohemia, and the outrages which it there committed, stirred up the whole kingdom against him. In vain he asserted his innocence to the Bohemian Estates; they would not believe his protestations; vainly did he attempt to restrain the violence of his soldiery; they disregarded his orders. Persuaded that the Emperor's object was to annul the Letter of Majesty, the Protectors of Liberty armed the whole of Protestant Bohemia, and invited Matthias into the country. After the dispersion of the force he had collected at Passau, the Emperor remained helpless at Prague, where he was kept shut up like a prisoner in his palace, and separated from all his counsellors. In the meantime Matthias entered Prague amidst universal rejoicings, where Rodolph was soon afterwards weak enough to acknowledge him King of Bohemia. So hard a fate befell this Emperor; he was compelled, during his life, to abdicate in favor of his enemy that very throne of which he had been endeavoring to deprive him after his own death. To complete his degradation he was obliged, by a personal act of renunciation, to release his subjects in Bohemia, Silesia, and Lusatia from their allegiance, and he did it with a broken heart. All, even those he thought he had most attached to his person, had abandoned him. When he had signed the instrument he threw his hat upon the ground, and gnawed the pen which had rendered so shameful a service.

While Rodolph thus lost one hereditary dominion after another the imperial dignity was not much better maintained by him. Each of the religious parties into which Germany was divided continued its efforts to advance itself at the expense of the other, or to guard against its attacks. The weaker the hand that held the sceptre, and the more the Protestants and Roman Catholics felt they were left to themselves, the more vigilant necessarily became their watchfulness, and the greater their distrust of each other. It was enough that the Emperor was ruled by Jesuits, and was guided by Spanish counsels, to excite the apprehension of the Protestants and to afford a pretext for hostility. The rash zeal of the Jesuits, which in the pulpit and by the press disputed the validity of the religious peace, increased this distrust, and caused their adversaries to see a dangerous design in the most indifferent measures of the Roman Catholics. Every step taken in the hereditary dominions of the Emperor for the repression of the reformed religion was sure to draw the attention of all the Protestants of Germany; and this powerful support which the reformed subjects of Austria met, or expected to meet with from their religious confederates in the rest of Germany, was no small cause of their confidence and of the rapid success of Matthias. It was the general belief of the Empire that they owed the long enjoyment of the religious peace merely to the difficulties in which the Emperor was placed by the internal troubles in his dominions; and consequently they were in no haste to relieve him from them.

Almost all the affairs of the Diet were neglected, either through the procrastination of the Emperor, or through the fault of the Protestant Estates, who had determined to make no provision for the common wants of the Empire till their own grievances were removed. These grievances related principally to the misgovernment of the Emperor; the violation of the religious treaty, and the presumptuous usurpations of the Aulic Council, which in the present reign had begun to extend its jurisdiction at the expense of the Imperial Chamber. Formerly, in all disputes between the Estates, which could not be settled by club law, the Emperors had in the last resort decided of themselves, if the case were trifling, and in conjunction with the princes, if it were important; or they determined them by the advice of imperial judges who followed the court. This superior jurisdiction they had, in the end of the fifteenth century, assigned to a regular and permanent tribunal, the Imperial Chamber of Spires, in which the Estates of the Empire, that they might not be oppressed by the arbitrary appointment of the Emperor, had reserved to themselves the right of electing the assessors, and of periodically reviewing its decrees. By the religious peace, these rights of the Estates (called the rights of presentation and visitation), were extended also to the Lutherans, so that Protestant judges had a voice in Protestant causes, and a seeming equality obtained for both religions in this supreme tribunal.

But the enemies of the Reformation and of the freedom of the Estates, vigilant to take advantage of every incident that favored their views, soon found means to neutralize the beneficial effects of this institution. A supreme jurisdiction over the Imperial States was gradually and skilfully usurped by a private imperial tribunal, the Aulic Council in Vienna, a court at first intended merely to advise the Emperor in the exercise of his undoubted, imperial, and personal prerogatives; a court whose members, being appointed and paid by him, had no law but the interest of their master, and no standard of equity but the advancement of the unreformed religion of which they were partisans. Before the Aulic Council were now brought several suits originating between Estates differing in religion, and which, therefore, properly belonged to the Imperial Chamber. It was not surprising if the decrees of this tribunal bore traces of their orgin; if the interests of the Roman Church and of the Emperor were preferred to justice by Roman Catholic judges, and the creatures of the Emperor. Although all the Estates of Germany seemed to have equal cause for resisting so perilous an abuse, the Protestants alone, who most sensibly felt it, and even these not all at once and in a body, came forward as the defenders of German liberty, which the establishment of so arbitrary a tribunal had outraged in its most sacred point, the adminstration of justice. In fact, Germany would have had little cause to congratulate itself upon the abolition of club law, and in the institution of the Imperial Chamber, if an arbitrary tribunal of the Emperor was allowed to interfere with the latter. The Estates of the German Empire would indeed have improved little upon the days of barbarism if the Chamber of Justice, in which they sat along with the Emperor as judges, and for which they had abandoned their original princely prerogative, should cease to be a court of the last resort. But the strangest contradictions were at this date to be found in the minds of men. The name of Emperor, a remnant of Roman despotism, was still associated with an idea of autocracy, which, though it formed a ridiculous inconsistency with the privileges of the Estates, was nevertheless argued for by jurists, diffused by the partisans of despotism, and believed by the ignorant.

To these general grievances was gradually added a

chain of singular incidents, which at length converted the anxiety of the Protestants into utter distrust. During the Spanish persecutions in the Netherlands several Protestant families had taken refuge in Aix-la-Chapelle, an imperial city, and attached to the Roman Catholic faith, where they settled and insensibly extended their adherents. Having succeeded by stratagem in introducing some of their members into the municipal council, they demanded a church and the public exercise of their worship, and the demand being unfavorably received, they succeeded by violence in enforcing it, and also in usurping the entire government of the city. To see so important a city in Protestant hands was too heavy a blow for the Emperor and the Roman Catholics. After all the Emperor's requests and commands for the restoration of the olden government had proved ineffectual, the Aulic Council proclaimed the city under the ban of the Empire, which, however, was not put in force till the following reign.

Of yet greater importance were two other attempts of the Protestants to extend their influence and their power. The Elector Gebhard, of Cologne (born Truchsess* of Waldburg), conceived for the young Countess Agnes, of Mansfield, Canoness of Gerresheim, a passion which was not unreturned. As the eyes of all Germany were directed to this intercourse, the brothers of the Countess, two zealous Calvinists, demanded satisfaction for the injured honor of their house, which, as long as the Elector remained a Roman Catholic prelate, could not be repaired by marriage. They threatened the Elector they would wash out this stain in his blood and their sister's unless he either abandoned all further connection with the Countess, or consented to re-establish her reputation at the altar. The Elector, indifferent to all the consequences of this step, listened to nothing but the voice of love. Whether it was in consequence of his previous inclination to the reformed doctrines, or that the charms of his mistress alone effected this wonder, he renounced the Roman Catholic faith, and led the beautiful Agnes to the altar.

* Grand-master of the kitchen.

This event was of the greatest importance. By the letter of the clause reserving the ecclesiastical states from the general operation of the religious peace, the Elector had, by his apostasy, forfeited all right to the temporalities of his bishopric; and if, in any case, it was important for the Catholics to enforce the clause, it was so especially in the case of electorates. On the other hand, the relinquishment of so high a dignity was a severe sacrifice, and peculiarly so in the case of a tender husband, who had wished to enhance the value of his heart and hand by the gift of a principality. Moreover, the Reservatum Ecclesiasticum was a disputed article of the treaty of Augsburg; and all the German Protestants were aware of the extreme importance of wresting this fourth[*] electorate from the opponents of their faith. The example had already been set in several of the ecclesiastical benefices of Lower Germany, and attended with success. Several canons of Cologne had also already embraced the Protestant confession, and were on the Elector's side, while in the city itself he could depend upon the support of a numerous Protestant party. All these considerations, greatly strengthened by the persuasions of his friends and relations, and the promises of several German courts, determined the Elector to retain his dominions, while he changed his religion.

But it was soon apparent that he had entered upon a contest which he could not carry through. Even the free toleration of the Protestant service within the territories of Cologne had already occasioned a violent opposition on the part of the canons and Roman Catholic *Estates* of that province. The intervention of the Emperor, and a papal ban from Rome, which anathematized the Elector as an apostate, and deprived him of all his dignities, temporal and spiritual, armed his own subjects and chapter against him. The Elector assembled a military force; the chapter did the same. To insure also the aid of a strong arm, they proceeded forthwith to a new election, and chose the Bishop of Liege, a prince of Bavaria.

A civil war now commenced, which, from the strong

[*] Saxony, Brandenburg, and the Palatinate were already Protestant.

interest which both religious parties in Germany necessarily felt in the conjuncture, was likely to terminate in a general breaking up of the religious peace. What most made the Protestants indignant was that the Pope should have presumed, by a pretended apostolic power, to deprive a prince of the empire of his imperial dignities. Even in the golden days of their spiritual domination this prerogative of the Pope had been disputed; how much more likely was it to be questioned at a period when his authority was entirely disowned by one party, while even with the other it rested on a tottering foundation. All the Protestant princes took up the affair warmly against the Emperor; and Henry IV. of France, then King of Navarre, left no means of negotiation untried to urge the German princes to the vigorous assertion of their rights. The issue would decide forever the liberties of Germany. Four Protestant against three Roman Catholic voices in the Electoral College must at once have given the preponderance to the former, and forever excluded the House of Austria from the imperial throne.

But the Elector Gebhard had embraced the Calvinist, not the Lutheran religion; and this circumstance alone was his ruin. The mutual rancor of these two churches would not permit the Lutheran Estates to regard the Elector as one of their party, and as such to lend him their effectual support. All indeed had encouraged and promised him assistance; but only one appanaged prince of the Palatine House, the Palsgrave John Casimir, a zealous Calvinist, kept his word. Despite of the imperial prohibition he hastened with his little army into the territories of Cologne; but without being able to effect anything, because the Elector, who was destitute even of the first necessaries, left him totally without help. So much the more rapid was the progress of the newly-chosen elector, whom his Bavarian relations and the Spaniards from the Netherlands supported with the utmost vigor. The troops of Gebhard, left by their master without pay, abandoned one place after another to the enemy; by whom others were compelled to surrender. In his Westphalian territories Gebhard held out for some time longer, till here, too, he was at last obliged to yield to superior force. After several vain attempts in Holland and England to obtain means for his restoration, he retired into the Chapter of Strasburg, and died dean of that cathedral; the first sacrifice to the Ecclesiastical Reservation, or rather to the want of harmony among the German Protestants.

To this dispute in Cologne was soon added another in Strasburg. Several Protestant canons of Cologne, who had been included in the same papal ban with the Elector, had taken refuge within this bishopric, where they likewise held prebends. As the Roman Catholic canons of Strasburg hesitated to allow them, as being under the ban, the enjoyment of their prebends, they took violent possession of their benefices, and the support of a powerful Protestant party among the citizens soon gave them the preponderance in the chapter. The other canons thereupon retired to Alsace-Saverne, where, under the protection of the bishop, they established themselves as the only lawful chapter, and denounced that which remained in Strasburg as illegal. The latter, in the meantime, had so strengthened themselves by the reception of several Protestant colleagues of high rank that they could venture, upon the death of the bishop, to nominate a new Protestant bishop in the person of John George of Brandenburg. The Roman Catholic canons, far from allowing this election, nominated the Bishop of Metz, a prince of Lorraine, to that dignity, who announced his promotion by immediately commencing hostilities against the territories of Strasburg.

That city now took up arms in defence of its Protestant chapter and the Prince of Brandendurg, while the other party, with the assistance of the troops of Lorraine, endeavored to possess themselves of the temporalities of the chapter. A tedious war was the consequence, which, according to the spirit of the times, was attended with barbarous devastations. In vain did the Emperor interpose with his supreme authority to terminate the dispute; the ecclesiastical property remained for a long time divided between the two parties, till at last the Protestant prince, for a moderate pecuniary equivalent, renounced his claims; and thus, in this dispute also, the Roman Church came off victorious.

An occurrence which, soon after the adjustment of this dispute, took place in Donauwerth, a free city of Suabia, was still more critical for the whole of Protestant Germany. In this once Roman Catholic city the Protestants, during the reigns of Ferdinand and his son, had, in the usual way, become so completely predominant that the Roman Catholics were obliged to content themselves with a church in the monastery of the Holy Cross, and, for fear of offending the Protestants, were even forced to suppress the greater part of their religious rites. At length a fanatical abbot of this monastery ventured to defy the popular prejudices, and to arrange a public procession, preceded by the cross and banners flying; but he was soon compelled to desist from the attempt. When, a year afterwards, encouraged by a favorable imperial proclamation, the same abbot attempted to renew this procession, the citizens proceeded to open violence. The inhabitants shut the gates against the monks on their return, trampled their colors under foot, and followed them home with clamor and abuse. An imperial citation was the consequence of this act of violence; and as the exasperated populace even threatened to assault the imperial commissaries, and all attempts at an amicable adjustment were frustrated by the fanaticism of the multitude, the city was at last formally placed under the ban of the Empire, the execution of which was entrusted to Maximilian, Duke of Bavaria. The citizens, formerly so insolent, were seized with terror at the approach of the Bavarian army; pusillanimity now possessed them, though once so full of defiance, and they laid down their arms without striking a blow. The total abolition of the Protestant religion within the walls of the city was the punishment of their rebellion; it was deprived of its privileges, and, from a free city of Suabia, converted into a municipal town of Bavaria.

Two circumstances connected with this proceeding must have strongly excited the attention of the Protestants, even if the interests of religion had been less powerful on their minds. First of all, the sentence had

been pronounced by the Aulic Council, an arbitrary and
exclusively Roman Catholic tribunal, whose jurisdiction
besides had been so warmly disputed by them; and
secondly, its execution had been entrusted to the Duke of
Bavaria, the head of another circle. These unconstitutional steps seemed to be the harbingers of further violent
measures on the Roman Catholic side, the result, probably, of secret conferences and dangerous designs, which
might perhaps end in the entire subversion of their
religious liberty.

In circumstances where the law of force prevails, and
security depends upon power alone, the weakest party is
naturally the most busy to place itself in a posture of
defence. This was now the case in Germany. If the
Roman Catholics really meditated any evil against the
Protestants in Germany, the probability was that the
blow would fall on the south rather than the north,
because, in Lower Germany, the Protestants were connected through a long unbroken tract of country, and
could therefore easily combine for their mutual support;
while those in the south, detached from each other, and
surrounded on all sides by Roman Catholic states, were
exposed to every inroad. If, moreover, as was to be
expected, the Catholics availed themselves of the divisions amongst the Protestants, and levelled their attack
against one of the religious parties, it was the Calvinists,
who as the weaker, and as being besides excluded from
the religious treaty, were apparently in the greatest
danger, and upon them would probably fall the first
attack.

Both these circumstances took place in the dominions
of the Elector Palatine, which possessed, in the Duke of
Bavaria, a formidable neighbor, and which, by reason of
their defection to Calvinism, received no protection from
the Religious Peace, and had little hope of succor from
the Lutheran states. No country in Germany had experienced so many revolutions in religion in such a short
time as the Palatinate. In the space of sixty years this
country, an unfortunate toy in the hands of its rulers, had
twice adopted the doctrines of Luther, and twice relinquished them for Calvinism. The Elector Frederick III.

first abandoned the confession of Augsburg, which his eldest son and successor, Lewis, immediately re-established. The Calvinists throughout the whole country were deprived of their churches, their preachers and even their teachers banished beyond the frontiers; while the prince, in his Lutheran zeal, persecuted them even in his will, by appointing none but strict and orthodox Lutherans as the guardians of his son, a minor. But this illegal testament was disregarded by his brother, the Count Palatine, John Casimir, who, by the regulations of the Golden Bull, assumed the guardianship and administration of the state. Calvinistic teachers were given to the Elector Frederick IV., then only nine years of age, who were ordered, if necessary, to drive the Lutheran heresy out of the soul of their pupil with blows. If such was the treatment of the sovereign, that of the subjects may be easily conceived.

It was under this Frederick that the Palatine Court exerted itself so vigorously to unite the Protestant states of Germany in joint measures against the House of Austria, and, if possible, bring about the formation of a general confederacy. Besides that this court had always been guided by the counsels of France, with whom hatred of the House of Austria was the ruling principle, a regard for his own safety urged him to secure in time the doubtful assistance of the Lutherans against a near and overwhelming enemy. Great difficulties, however, opposed this union, because the Lutherans' dislike of the Reformed was scarcely less than the common aversion of both to the Romanists. An attempt was first made to reconcile the two professions, in order to facilitate a political union; but all these attempts failed and generally ended in both parties adhering the more strongly to their respective opinions. Nothing then remained but to increase the fear and the distrust of the Evangelicals, and in this way to impress upon them the necessity of this alliance. The power of the Roman Catholics and the magnitude of the danger were exaggerated, accidental incidents were ascribed to deliberate plans, innocent actions misrepresented by invidious constructions, and the whole conduct of the professors of the olden religion was interpreted as the result of a well-weighed and systematic plan, which, in all probability, they were very far from having concerted.

The Diet of Ratisbon, to which the Protestants had looked forward with the hope of obtaining a renewal of the Religious Peace, had broken up without coming to a decision, and to the former grievances of the Protestant party was now added the late oppression of Donauwerth. With incredible speed the union, so long attempted, was now brought to bear. A conference took place at Anhausen, in Franconia, at which were present the Elector Frederick IV., from the Palatinate, the Palsgrave of Neuburg, two Margraves of Brandenburg, the Margrave of Baden, and the Duke John Frederick of Wirtemburg,—Lutherans as well as Calvinists,—who for themselves and their heirs entered into a close confederacy under the title of the Evangelical Union. The purport of this union was, that the allied princes should, in all matters relating to religion and their civil rights, support each other with arms and counsel against every aggressor, and should all stand as one man; that in case any member of the alliance should be attacked, he should be assisted by the rest with an armed force; that, if necessary, the territories, towns, and castles of the allied states should be open to his troops; and that whatever conquests were made should be divided among all the confederates, in proportion to the contingent furnished by each.

The direction of the whole confederacy in time of peace was conferred upon the Elector Palatine, but with a limited power. To meet the necessary expenses, sudsidies were demanded, and a common fund established. Differences of religion (betwixt the Lutherans and the Calvinists) were to have no effect on this alliance, which was to subsist for ten years, every member of the union engaged at the same time to procure new members to it. The Electorate of Brandenburg adopted the alliance, that of Saxony rejected it. Hesse-Cashel could not be prevailed upon to declare itself, the Dukes of Brunswick and Luneburg also hesitated. But the three cities of the Empire, Strasburg, Nuremburg, and Ulm, were no unimportant acquisition for the League, which was in great want of their money, while their example, besides, might be followed by other imperial cities.

After the formation of this alliance, the confederate states, dispirited and, singly, little feared, adopted a bolder language. Through Prince Christian of Anhalt they laid their common grievances and demands before the Emperor; among which the principal were the restoration of Donauwerth, the abolition of the Imperial Court, the reformation of the Emperor's own administration and that of his counsellors. For these remonstrances, they chose the moment when the Emperor had scarcely recovered breath from the troubles in his hereditary dominions, — when he had lost Hungary and Austria to Matthias, and had barely preserved his Bohemian throne by the concession of the Letter of Majesty, and finally, when through the succession of Juliers he was already threatened with the distant prospect of a new war. No wonder, then, that this dilatory prince was more irresolute than ever in his decision, and that the confederates took up arms before he could bethink himself.

The Roman Catholics regarded this confederacy with a jealous eye; the Union viewed them and the Emperor with the like distrust; the Emperor was equally suspicious of both; and thus, on all sides, alarm and animosity had reached their climax. And, as if to crown the whole, at this critical conjuncture, by the death of the Duke John William of Juliers, a highly disputable succession became vacant in the territories of Juliers and Cleves.

Eight competitors laid claim to this territory, the indivisibility of which had been guaranteed by solemn treaties; and the Emperor, who seemed disposed to enter upon it as a vacant fief, might be considered as the ninth. Four of these, the Elector of Brandenburg, the Count Palatine of Neuburg, the Count Palatine of Deux Ponts, and the Margrave of Bergau, an Austrian prince, claimed it as a female fief in name of four princesses, sisters of the late duke. Two others, the Elector of Saxony, of the line of Albert, and the Duke of Saxony, of the line of Ernest, laid claim to it under a prior right of reversion granted to them by the Emperor Frederick III., and confirmed to both Saxon houses by Maximilian I. The pretensions of some foreign princes were little regarded. The best right was perhaps on the side of Brandenburg and Neuberg, and between the claims of the two it was not easy to decide. Both courts, as soon as the succession was vacant, proceeded to take possession; Brandenburg beginning, and Neuberg following the example. Both commenced their dispute with the pen, and would probably have ended it with the sword: but the interference of the Emperor, by proceeding to bring the cause before his own cognizance, and, during the progress of the suit, sequestrating the disputed countries, soon brought the contending parties to an agreement, in order to avert the common danger. They agreed to govern the duchy conjointly. In vain did the Emperor prohibit the Estates from doing homage to their new masters; in vain did he send his own relation, the Archduke Leopold, Bishop of Passau and Strasburg, into the territory of Juliers, in order, by his presence, to strengthen the imperial party. The whole country, with the exception of Juliers itself, had submitted to the Protestant princes, and in that capital the imperialists were besieged.

The dispute about the succession of Juliers was an important one to the whole German Empire, and also attracted the attention of several European courts. It was not so much the question, who was or was not to possess the Duchy of Juliers;—the real question was, which of the two religious parties in Germany, the Roman Catholic or the Protestant, was to be strengthened by so important an accession—for which of the two *religions* this territory was to be lost or won. The question in short was, whether Austria was to be allowed to persevere in her usurpations, and to gratify her lust of dominion by another robbery; or whether the liberties of Germany, and the balance of power, were to be maintained against her encroachments. The disputed succession of Juliers, therefore, was matter which interested all who were favorable to liberty and hostile to Austria. The Evangelical Union, Holland, England, and particularly Henry IV. of France were drawn into the strife.

This monarch, the flower of whose life had been spent in opposing the House of Austria and Spain, and by persevering heroism alone had surmounted the obstacles which this house had thrown between him and the French throne, had been no idle spectator of the troubles in Germany. This contest of the Estates with the Emperor was the means of giving and securing peace to France. The Protestants and the Turks were the two salutary weights which kept down the Austrian power in the East and West: but it would rise again in all its terrors, if once it were allowed to remove this pressure. Henry IV. had before his eyes for half a lifetime the uninterrupted spectacle of Austrian ambition and Austrian lust of dominion, which neither adversity nor poverty of talents, though generally they check all human passions, could extinguish in a bosom wherein flowed one drop of the blood of Ferdinand of Arragon. Austrian ambition had destroyed for a century the peace of Europe, and effected the most violent changes in the heart of its most considerable states. It had deprived the fields of husbandmen, the workshops of artisans, to fill the land with enormous armies, and to cover the commercial sea with hostile fleets. It had imposed upon the princes of Europe the necessity of fettering the industry of their subjects by unheard-of imposts; and of wasting in self-defence the best strength of their states, which was thus lost to the prosperity of their inhabitants. For Europe there was no peace, for its states no welfare, for the people's happiness no security or permanence, so long as this dangerous house was permitted to disturb at pleasure the repose of the world.

Such considerations clouded the mind of Henry at the close of his glorious career. What had it not cost him to reduce to order the troubled chaos into which France had been plunged by the tumult of civil war, fomented and supported by this very Austria! Every great mind labors for eternity; and what security had Henry for the endurance of that prosperity, which he had gained for France, so long as Austria and Spain formed a single power, which did indeed lie exhausted for the present, but which required only one lucky chance to be speedily reunited, and to spring up again as formidable as ever. If he would bequeath to his successors a firmly established throne, and a durable prosperity to his subjects, this dangerous power must be forever disarmed. This was the source of that irreconcilable enmity which Henry had sworn to the House of Austria, a hatred unextinguishable, ardent, and well-founded as that of Hannibal against the people of Romulus, but ennobled by a purer origin.

The other European powers had the same inducements to action as Henry, but all of them had not that enlightened policy, nor that disinterested courage to act upon the impulse. All men, without distinction, are allured by immediate advantages; great minds alone are excited by distant good. So long as wisdom in its projects calculates upon wisdom, or relies upon its own strength, it forms none but chimerical schemes, and runs a risk of making itself the laughter of the world; but it is certain of success, and may reckon upon aid and admiration when it finds a place in its intellectual plans for barbarism, rapacity, and superstition, and can render the selfish passions of mankind the executors of its purposes.

In the first point of view, Henry's well-known project of expelling the House of Austria from all its possessions, and dividing the spoil among the European powers, deserves the title of a chimera, which men have so liberally bestowed upon it; but did it merit that appellation in the second? It had never entered into the head of that excellent monarch, in the choice of those who must be the instruments of his designs, to reckon on the sufficiency of such motives as animated himself and Sully to the enterprise. All the states whose co-operation was necessary were to be persuaded to the work by the strongest motives that can set a political power in action. From the Protestants in Germany nothing more was required than that which, on other grounds, had been long their object, — their throwing off the Austrian yoke; from the Flemings, a similar revolt from the Spaniards. To the Pope and all the Italian republics no inducement could be more powerful than the hope of driving the Spaniards forever from their peninsula; for England, nothing more desirable than a revolution which should free it from its bitterest enemy. By this division of the Austrian conquests every power gained either land or freedom, new possessions or security for the old; and, as all gained, the balance of power remained undisturbed. France might magnanimously decline a share in the spoil, because by the ruin of Austria it doubly profited, and was most powerful if it did not become more powerful. Finally, upon condition of ridding Europe of their presence, the posterity of Hapsburg were to be allowed the liberty of augmenting her territories in all the other known or yet undiscovered portions of the globe. But the dagger of Ravaillac delivered Austria from her danger, to postpone for some centuries longer the tranquillity of Europe.

With his view directed to this project, Henry felt the necessity of taking a prompt and active part in the important events of the Evangelical Union, and the disputed succession of Juliers. His emissaries were busy in all the courts of Germany, and the little which they published or allowed to escape of the great political secrets of their master was sufficient to win over minds inflamed by so ardent a hatred to Austria, and by so strong a desire of aggrandizement. The prudent policy of Henry cemented the Union still more closely, and the powerful aid which he bound himself to furnish raised the courage of the confederates into the firmest confidence. A numerous French army, led by the king in person, was to meet the troops of the Union on the banks of the Rhine, and to assist in effecting the conquest of Juliers and Cleves; then, in conjunction with the Germans, it was to march into Italy (where Savoy, Venice, and the Pope were even now ready with a powerful reinforcement), and to overthrow the Spanish dominion in that quarter. This victorious army was then to penetrate by Lombardy into the hereditary dominions of Hapsburg; and there, favored by a general insurrection of the Protestants, destroy the power of Austria in all its German territories, in Bohemia, Hungary, and Transylvania. The Brabanters and Hollanders, supported by French auxiliaries, would in the meantime shake off the Spanish tyranny in the Netherlands, and thus the mighty stream which, only a short time before, had so fearfully overflowed its banks, threatening to overwhelm in its troubled waters the liberties of Europe, would then roll silent and forgotten behind the Pyrenean mountains.

At other times the French had boasted of their rapidity of action, but upon this occasion they were outstripped by the Germans. An army of the confederates entered Alsace before Henry made his appearance there, and an Austrian army, which the Bishop of Strasburg and Passau had assembled in that quarter for an expedition against Juliers, was dispersed. Henry IV. had formed his plan as a statesman and a king, but he had intrusted its execution to plunderers. According to his design, no Roman Catholic state was to have cause to think this preparation aimed against itself, or to make the quarrel of Austria its own. Religion was in nowise to be mixed up with the matter. But how could the German princes forget their own purposes in furthering the plans of Henry? Actuated as they were by the desire of aggrandizement and by religious hatred, was it to be supposed that they would not gratify, in every passing opportunity, their ruling passions to the utmost? Like vultures, they stooped upon the territories of the ecclesiastical princes, and always chose those rich countries for their quarters, though to reach them they must make ever so wide a detour from their direct route. They levied contributions as in an enemy's country, seized upon the revenues, and exacted by violence what they could not obtain of free-will. Not to leave the Roman Catholics in doubt as to the true objects of their expedition, they announced, openly and intelligibly enough, the fate that awaited the property of the church. So little had Henry IV. and the German princes understood each other in their plan of operations, so much had the excellent king been mistaken in his instruments. It is an unfailing maxim, that, if policy enjoins an act of violence, its execution ought never to be entrusted to the violent; and that he only ought to be trusted with the violation of order by whom order is held sacred.

Both the past conduct of the Union, which was condemned even by several of the evangelical states, and the apprehension of even worse treatment, aroused the Roman Catholics to something beyond mere inactive indignation. As to the Emperor, his authority had sunk too low to afford them any security against such an enemy. It was their Union that rendered the confederates so formidable and so insolent; and another union must now be opposed to them.

The Bishop of Wurtzburg formed the plan of the Catholic Union, which was distinguished from the evangelical by the title of the League. The objects agreed upon were nearly the same as those which constituted the groundwork of the Union. Bishops formed its principal members, and at its head was placed Maximilian, Duke of Bavaria. As the only influential secular member of the confederacy, he was entrusted with far more extensive powers than the Protestants had committed to their chief. In addition to the Duke's being the sole head of the League's military power, whereby their operations acquired a speed and weight unattainable by the Union, they had also the advantage that supplies flowed in much more regularly from the rich prelates, than the latter could obtain them from the poor evangelical states. Without offering to the Emperor, as the sovereign of a Roman Catholic state, any share in their confederacy, without ever communicating its existence to him as Emperor, the League arose at once formidable and threatening; with strength sufficient to crush the Protestant Union and to maintain itself under three emperors. It contended, indeed, for Austria, in so far as it fought against the Protestant princes; but Austria herself had soon cause to tremble before it.

The arms of the Union had, in the meantime, been tolerably successful in Juliers and in Alsace; Juliers was closely blockaded, and the whole bishopric of Strasburg was in their power. But here their splendid achievements came to an end. No French army appeared upon the Rhine; for he who was to be its leader, he who was the animating soul of the whole enterprise, Henry IV., was no more! Their supplies were on the wane; the Estates refused to grant new subsidies; and the confederate free cities were offended that their money should be liberally, but their advice so sparingly called for. Especially were they displeased at being put to expense for the expedition against Juliers, which had been expressly excluded from the affairs of the Union — at the united princes appropriating to themselves large pensions out of the common treasure — and, above all, at their refusing to give any account of its expenditure.

The Union was thus verging to its fall at the moment when the League started to oppose it in the vigor of its strength. Want of supplies disabled the confederates from any longer keeping the field. And yet it was dangerous to lay down their weapons in the sight of an armed enemy. To secure themselves at least on one side they hastened to conclude a peace with their old enemy, the Archduke Leopold; and both parties agreed to withdraw their troops from Alsace, to exchange prisoners, and to bury all that had been done in oblivion. Thus ended in nothing all these promising preparations.

The same imperious tone with which the Union, in the confidence of its strength, had menaced the Roman Catholics of Germany, was now retorted by the League upon themselves and their troops. The traces of their march were pointed out to them, and plainly branded with the hard epithets they had deserved. The chapters of Wurtzburg, Bamberg, Strasburg, Mentz, Treves, Cologne, and several others, had experienced their destructive presence; to all these the damage done was to be made good, the free passage by land and by water restored (for the Protestants had even seized on the navigation of the Rhine), and everything replaced on its former footing. Above all, the parties to the Union were called on to declare expressly and unequivocally its intentions. It was now their turn to yield to superior strength. They had not calculated on so formidable an opponent; but they themselves had taught the Roman Catholics the secret of their strength. It was humiliating to their pride to sue for peace, but they might think themselves fortunate in obtaining it. The one party promised restitution, the other forgiveness. All laid down their arms. The storm of war once more rolled by, and a temporary calm succeeded. The insurrection in Bohemia then broke out, which deprived the Emperor of the last of his hereditary dominions, but in this dispute neither the Union nor the League took any share.

At length the Emperor died, in 1612, as little regretted in his coffin as noticed on the throne. Long afterwards, when the miseries of succeeding reigns had made the misfortunes of his reign forgotten, a halo spread about his memory, and so fearful a night set in upon Germany that, with tears of blood, people prayed for the return of such an emperor.

Rodolph never could be prevailed upon to choose a successor in the Empire, and all awaited with anxiety the approaching vacancy of the throne; but, beyond all hope, Matthias at once ascended it, and without opposition. The Roman Catholics gave him their voices, because they hoped the best from his vigor and activity; the Protestants gave him theirs, because they hoped everything from his weakness. It was not difficult to reconcile this contradiction. The one relied on what he had once appeared; the other judged him by what he seemed at present.

The moment of a new accession is always a day of hope; and the first Diet of a king in elective monarchies is usually his severest trial. Every old grievance is brought forward, and new ones are sought out, that they may be included in the expected reform; quite a new world is expected to commence with the new reign. The important services which, in his insurrection, their religious confederates in Austria had rendered to Matthias, were still fresh in the minds of the Protestant free cities, and, above all, the price which they had exacted for their services seemed now to serve them also as a model.

It was by the favor of the Protestant Estates in Austria and Moravia that Matthias had sought and really found the way to his brother's throne; but, hurried on by his ambitious views, he never reflected that a way was thus opened for the States to give laws to their sovereign. This discovery soon awoke him from the intoxication of success. Scarcely had he shown himself in triumph to his Austrian subjects, after his victorious expedition to Bohemia, when an humble petition awaited him which was quite sufficient to poison his whole triumph. They required, before doing homage, unlimited religious toleration in the cities and market towns, perfect equality of rights between Roman Catholics and Protestants, and a full and equal admissibility of the latter to all offices of state. In several places they of themselves assumed these privileges, and, reckoning on a change of administration, restored the Protestant religion where the late Emperor had suppressed it. Matthias, it is true, had not scrupled to make use of the grievances of the Protestants for his own ends against the Emperor; but it was far from being his intention to relieve them. By a firm and resolute tone he hoped to check at once these presumptuous demands. He spoke of his hereditary title to these territories, and would hear of no stipulations before the act of homage. A like unconditional submission had been rendered by their neighbors, the inhabitants of Styria, to the Archduke Ferdinand, who, however, had soon reason to repent of it. Warned by this example, the Austrian States persisted in their refusal; and, to avoid being compelled by force to do homage, their deputies (after urging their Roman Catholic colleagues to a similar resistance) immediately left the capital, and began to levy troops.

They took steps to renew their old alliance with Hungary, drew the Protestant princes into their interests, and set themselves seriously to work to accomplish their object by force of arms.

With the more exorbitant demands of the Hungarians Matthias had not hesitated to comply. For Hungary was an elective monarchy, and the republican constitution of the country justified to himself their demands, and to the Roman Catholic world his concessions. In Austria, on the contrary, his predecessors had exercised far higher prerogatives, which he could not relinquish at the demand of the Estates without incurring the scorn of Roman Catholic Europe, the enmity of Spain and Rome, and the contempt of his own Roman Catholic subjects. His exclusively Romish council, among which the Bishop of Vienna, Melchio Kiesel, had the chief influence, exhorted him to see all the churches extorted from him by the Protestants rather than to concede one to them as a matter of right.

But by ill luck this difficulty occurred at a time when the Emperor Rodolph was yet alive and a spectator of this scene, and who might easily have been tempted to employ against his brother the same weapons which the latter had successfully directed against him — namely, an understanding with his rebellious subjects. To avoid this blow, Matthias willingly availed himself of the offer made by Moravia, to act as mediator between him and the Estates of Austria. Representatives of both parties met in Vienna, when the Austrian deputies held language which would have excited surprise even in the English Parliament. "The Protestants," they said, "are determined to be not worse treated in their native country than the handful of Romanists. By the help of his Protestant nobles had Matthias reduced the Emperor to submission; where eighty Papists were to be found three hundred Protestant barons might be counted. The example of Rodolph should be a warning to Matthias. He should take care that he did not lose the terrestrial in attempting to make conquests for the celestial." As the Moravian States, instead of using their powers as mediators for the Emperor's advantage, finally adopted the cause of their co-religionists of Austria; as the Union in Germany came forward to afford them its most active support, and as Matthias dreaded reprisals on the part of the Emperor, he was at length compelled to make the desired declaration in favor of the Evangelical Church.

This behavior of the Austrian Estates towards their Archduke was now imitated by the Protestant Estates of the Empire towards their Emperor, and they promised themselves the same favorable results. At his first Diet at Ratisbon, in 1613, when the most pressing affairs were waiting for decision — when a general contribution was indispensable for a war against Turkey, and against Bethlem Gabor in Transylvania, who by Turkish aid had forcibly usurped the sovereignty of that land, and even threatened Hungary — they surprised him with an entirely new demand. The Roman Catholic votes were still the most numerous in the Diet; and as everything was decided by a plurality of voices, the Protestant party, however closely united, were entirely without consideration. The advantage of this majority the Roman Catholics were now called on to relinquish; henceforward no one religious party was to be permitted to dictate to the other by means of its invariable superiority. And, in truth, if the evangelical religion was really to be represented in the Diet, it was self-evident that it must not be shut out from the possibility of making use of that privilege, merely from the constitution of the Diet itself. Complaints of the judicial usurpations of the Aulic Council, and of the oppression of the Protestants, accompanied this demand, and the deputies of the Estates were instructed to take no part in any general deliberations till a favorable answer should be given on this preliminary point.

The Diet was torn asunder by this dangerous division, which threatened to destroy forever the unity of its deliberations. Sincerely as the Emperor might have wished, after the example of his father, Maximilian, to preserve a prudent balance between the two religions, the present conduct of the Protestants seemed to leave him nothing but a critical choice between the two. In his present necessities a general contribution from the Estates was indispensable to him; and yet he could not conciliate the one party without sacrificing the support of the other. Insecure as he felt his situation to be in his own hereditary dominions, he could not but tremble at the idea, however remote, of an open war with the Protestants. But the eyes of the whole Roman Catholic world, which were attentively regarding his conduct, the remonstrances of the Roman Catholic Estates, and of the Courts of Rome and Spain, as little permitted him to favor the Protestant at the expense of the Romish religion.

So critical a situation would have paralyzed a greater mind than Matthias; and his own prudence would scarcely have extricated him from his dilemma. But the interests of the Roman Catholics were closely interwoven with the imperial authority; if they suffered this to fall the ecclesiastical princes in particular would be without a bulwark against the attacks of the Protestants. Now, then, that they saw the Emperor wavering, they thought it high time to reassure his sinking courage. They imparted to him the secret of their League, and acquainted him with its whole constitution, resources, and power. Little comforting as such a revelation must have been to the Emperor, the prospect of so powerful a support gave him greater boldness to oppose the Protestants. Their demands were rejected, and the Diet broke up without coming to a decision. But Matthias was the victim of this dispute. The Protestants refused him their supplies, and made him alone suffer for the inflexibility of the Roman Catholics.

The Turks, however, appeared willing to prolong the cessation of hostilities, and Bethlem Gabor was left in peaceable possession of Transylvania. The empire was now free from foreign enemies; and even at home, in the midst of all these fearful disputes, peace still reigned. An unexpected accident had given a singular turn to the dispute as to the succession of Juliers. This duchy was still ruled conjointly by the Electoral House of Brandenburg and the Palatine of Neuberg: and a marriage between the Prince of Neuberg and a Princess of Brandenburg was to have inseparably united the interests of the two houses. But the whole scheme was upset by a box on the ear, which, in a drunken brawl, the Elector of Brandenburg unfortunately inflicted upon his intended son-in-law. From this moment the good understanding between the two houses was at an end. The Prince of Neuberg embraced popery. The hand of a princess of Bavaria rewarded his apostasy, and the strong support of Bavaria and Spain was the natural result of both. To secure to the Palatine the exclusive possession of Juliers, the Spanish troops from the Netherlands were marched into the Palatinate. To rid himself of these guests, the Elector of Brandenburg called the Flemings to his assistance, whom he sought to propitiate by embracing the Calvinist religion. Both Spanish and Dutch armies appeared, but, as it seemed, only to make conquests for themselves.

The neighboring war of the Netherlands seemed now about to be decided on German ground; and what an inexhaustible mine of combustibles lay here ready for it! The Protestants saw with consternation the Spaniards establishing themselves upon the Lower Rhine; with still greater anxiety did the Roman Catholics see the Hollanders bursting through the frontiers of the empire. It was in the west that the mine was expected to explode which had long been dug under the whole of Germany. To the west apprehension and anxiety turned; but the spark which kindled the flame came unexpectedly from the east.

The tranquillity which the *Letter of Majesty* of Rodolph II. had established in Bohemia lasted for some time under the administration of Matthias, till the nomination of a new heir to this kingdom in the person of Ferdinand of Grätz.

This prince, whom we shall afterwards become better acquainted with under the title of Ferdinand II., Emperor of Germany, had, by the violent extirpation of the Protestant religion within his hereditary dominions, announced himself as an inexorable zealot for popery, and was consequently looked upon by the Roman Catholic part of Bohemia as the future pillar of their church. The declining health of the Emperor brought on this hour rapidly; and, relying on so powerful a supporter, the Bohemian Papists began to treat the Protestants with little moderation. The Protestant vassals of Roman Catholic nobles, in particular, experienced the harshest treatment. At length several of the former were incautious enough to speak somewhat loudly of their hopes, and by threatening hints to awaken among the Protestants a suspicion of their future sovereign. But this mistrust would never have broken out into actual violence had the Roman Catholics confined themselves to general expressions, and not by attacks on individuals furnished the discontent of the people with enterprising leaders.

Henry Matthias, Count Thurn, not a native of Bohemia, but proprietor of some estates in that kingdom, had, by his zeal for the Protestant cause, and an enthusiastic attachment to his newly-adopted country, gained the entire confidence of the Utraquists, which opened him the way to the most important posts. He had fought with great glory against the Turks, and won by a flattering address the hearts of the multitude. Of a hot and impetuous disposition, which loved tumult because his talents shone in it — rash and thoughtless enough to undertake things which cold prudence and a calmer temper would not have ventured upon — unscrupulous enough, where the gratification of his passions was concerned, to sport with the fate of thousands, and at the same time politic enough to hold in leading-strings such a people as the Bohemians then were. He had already taken an active part in the troubles under Rodolph's administration; and the Letter of Majesty which the States had extorted from that Emperor was chiefly to be laid to his merit. The court had entrusted to him, as burgrave or castellan of Calstein, the custody of the Bohemian crown and of the national charter. But the nation had placed in his hands something far more important — *itself* — with the office of defender or protector of the faith. The aristocracy, by which the Emperor was ruled, imprudently deprived him of this harmless guardianship of the dead, to leave him his full influence over the living. They took him from his office of burgrave, or constable of the castle, which had rendered him dependent on the court, thereby opening his eyes to the importance of the other which remained, and wounded his vanity, which yet was the thing that made his ambition harmless. From this moment he was actuated solely by a desire of revenge; and the opportunity of gratifying it was not long wanting.

In the Royal Letter which the Bohemians had extorted from Rodolph II., as well as in the German religious treaty, one material article remained undetermined. All the privileges granted by the latter to the Protestants were conceived in favor of the Estates or governing bodies, not of the subjects; for only to those of the ecclesiastical states had a toleration, and that precarious, been conceded. The Bohemian Letter of Majesty, in the same manner, spoke only of the Estates and imperial towns, the magistrates of which had contrived to obtain equal privileges with the former. These alone were free to erect churches and schools, and openly to celebrate their Protestant worship; in all other towns, it was left entirely to the government to which they belonged to determine the religion of the inhabitants. The Estates of the Empire had availed themselves of this privilege in its fullest extent; the secular, indeed, without opposition;

while the ecclesiastical, in whose case the declaration of Ferdinand had limited this privilege, disputed, not without reason, the validity of that limitation. What was a disputed point in the religious treaty was left still more doubtful in the Letter of Majesty; in the former the construction was not doubtful, but it was a question how far obedience might be compulsory; in the latter the interpretation was left to the states. The subjects of the ecclesiastical Estates in Bohemia thought themselves entitled to the same rights which the declaration of Ferdinand secured to the subjects of German bishops; they considered themselves on an equality with the subjects of imperial towns, because they looked upon the ecclesiastical property as part of the royal demesnes. In the little town of Klostergrab, subject to the Archbishop of Prague, and in Braunau, which belonged to the abbot of that monastery, churches were founded by the Protestants, and completed, notwithstanding the opposition of their superiors and the disapprobation of the Emperor.

In the meantime the vigilance of the defenders had somewhat relaxed, and the court thought it might venture on a decisive step. By the Emperor's orders the church at Klostergrab was pulled down, that at Braunau forcibly shut up, and the most turbulent of the citizens thrown into prison. A general commotion among the Protestants was the consequence of this measure; a loud outcry was everywhere raised at this violation of the Letter of Majesty; and Count Thurn, animated by revenge, and particularly called upon by his office of defender, showed himself not a little busy inflaming the minds of the people. At his instigation deputies were summoned to Prague from every circle in the empire, to concert the necessary measures against the common danger. It was resolved to petition the Emperor to press for the liberation of the prisoners. The answer of the Emperor, already offensive to the states, from its being addressed, not to them, but to his viceroy, denounced their conduct as illegal and rebellious, justified what had been done at Klostergarb and Braunau as the result of an imperial mandate, and contained some passages that might be construed into threats.

Count Thurn did not fail to augment the unfavorable impression which this imperial edict made upon the assembled Estates. He pointed out to them the danger in which all who had signed the petition were involved, and sought by working on their resentment and fears to hurry them into violent resolutions. To have caused their immediate revolt against the Emperor would have been, as yet, too bold a measure. It was only step by step that he would lead them on to this unavoidable result. He held it, therefore, advisable first to direct their indignation against the Emperor's counsellors; and for that purpose circulated a report that the imperial proclamation had been drawn up by the government at Prague, and only signed in Vienna. Among the imperial delegates, the chief objects of the popular hatred, were the President of the Chamber, Slawata, and Baron Martinitz, who had been elected in place of Count Thurn, Burgrave of Calstein. Both had long before evinced pretty openly their hostile feelings towards the Protestants, by alone refusing to be present at the sitting at which the Letter of Majesty had been inserted in the Bohemian constitution. A threat was made at the time to make them responsible for every violation of the Letter of Majesty; and from this moment, whatever evil befell the Protestants was set down, and not without reason, to their account. Of all the Roman Catholic nobles, these two had treated their Protestant vassals with the greatest harshness. They were accused of hunting them with dogs to the mass, and of endeavoring to drive them to popery by a denial of the rites of baptism, marriage, and burial. Against two characters so unpopular the public indignation was easily excited, and they were marked out for a sacrifice to the general indignation.

On the 23d of May, 1618, the deputies appeared armed, and in great numbers, at the royal palace, and forced their way into the hall where the Commissioners Sternberg, Martinitz, Lobkowitz, and Slawata were assembled. In a threatening tone they demanded to know from each of them, whether he had taken any part, or had consented to, the imperial proclamation. Sternberg received them with composure, Martinitz and Slawata with defiance.

This decided their fate; Sternberg and Lobkowitz, less hated and more feared, were led by the arm out of the room; Martinitz and Slawata were seized, dragged to a window, and precipitated from a height of eighty feet into the castle trench. Their creature, the secretary Fabricius, was thrown after them. This singular mode of execution naturally excited the surprise of civilized nations. The Bohemians justified it as a national custom, and saw nothing remarkable in the whole affair, excepting that any one should have got up again safe and sound after such a fall. A dunghill, on which the imperial commissioners chanced to be deposited, had saved them from injury.

It was not to be expected that this summary mode of proceeding would much increase the favor of the parties with the Emperor, but this was the very position to which Count Thurn wished to bring them. If, from the fear of uncertain danger, they had permitted themselves such an act of violence, the certain expectation of punishment, and the now urgent necessity of making themselves secure, would plunge them still deeper into guilt. By this brutal act of self-redress no room was left for irresolution or repentance, and it seemed as if a single crime could be absolved only by a series of violences. As the deed itself could not be undone, nothing was left but to disarm the hand of punishment. Thirty directors were appointed to organize a regular insurrection. They seized upon all the offices of state, and all the imperial revenues, took into their own service the royal functionaries and the soldiers, and summoned the whole Bohemian nation to avenge the common cause. The Jesuits, whom the common hatred accused as the instigators of every previous oppression, were banished the kingdom, and this harsh measure the Estates found it necessary to justify in a formal manifesto. These various steps were taken for the preservation of the royal authority and the laws — the language of all rebels till fortune has decided in their favor.

The emotion which the news of the Bohemian insurrection excited at the imperial court was much less lively than such intelligence deserved. The Emperor Matthias

was no longer the resolute spirit that formerly sought out
his king and master in the very bosom of his people, and
hurled him from three thrones. The confidence and
courage which had animated him in an usurpation deserted him in a legitimate self-defense. The Bohemian
rebels had first taken up arms, and the nature of circumstances drove him to join them. But he could not hope
to confine such a war to Bohemia. In all the territories
under his dominion the Protestants were united by a
dangerous sympathy — the common danger of their
religion might suddenly combine them all into a formidable republic. What could he oppose to such an enemy,
if the Protestant portion of his subjects deserted him?
And would not both parties exhaust themselves in so
ruinous a civil war? How much was at stake if he lost;
and if he won, whom else would he destroy but his own
subjects?

Considerations such as these inclined the Emperor and
his council to concessions and pacific measures, but it was
in this very spirit of concession that, as others would have
it, lay the origin of the evil. The Archduke Ferdinand
of Grätz congratulated the Emperor upon an event which
would justify in the eyes of all Europe the severest
measures against the Bohemian Protestants. "Disobedience, lawlessness, and insurrection," he said, "went
always hand-in-hand with Protestantism. Every privilege
which had been conceded to the Estates by himself and
his predecessor had had no other effect than to raise
their demands. All the measures of the heretics were
aimed against the imperial authority. Step by step had
they advanced from defiance to defiance up to this last
aggression; in a short time they would assail all that remained to be assailed, in the person of the Emperor. In
arms alone was there any safety against such an enemy —
peace and subordination could be only established on
the ruins of their dangerous privileges; security for the
Catholic belief was to be found only in the total destruction of this sect. Uncertain, it was true, might be the
event of the war, but inevitable was the ruin if it were
pretermitted. The confiscation of the lands of the rebels
would richly indemnify them for its expenses, while the

terror of punishment would teach the other states the
wisdom of a prompt obedience in future." Were the
Bohemian Protestants to blame if they armed themselves
in time against the enforcement of such maxims? The
insurrection in Bohemia, besides, was directed only
against the successor of the Emperor, not against himself, who had done nothing to justify the alarm of the
Protestants. To exclude this prince from the Bohemian
throne, arms had before been taken up under Matthias,
though as long as this Emperor lived his subjects had
kept within the bounds of an apparent submission.

But Bohemia was in arms, and, unarmed, the Emperor
dared not even offer them peace. For this purpose Spain
supplied gold, and promised to send troops from Italy
and the Netherlands. Count Bucquoi, a native of the
Netherlands, was named generalissimo, because no native
could be trusted, and Count Dampierre, another foreigner,
commanded under him. Before the army took the field
the Emperor endeavored to bring about an amicable
arrangement by the publication of a manifesto. In this
he assured the Bohemians, "that he held sacred the
Letter of Majesty — that he had not formed any resolutions inimical to their religion or their privileges, and
that his present preparations were forced upon him by
their own. As soon as the nation laid down their arms,
he also would disband his army." But this gracious letter
failed of its effect, because the leaders of the insurrection
contrived to hide from the people the Emperor's good
intentions. Instead of this, they circulated the most
alarming reports from the pulpit, and by pamphlets, and
terrified the deluded populace with threatened horrors of
another Saint Bartholomew's that existed only in their
own imagination. All Bohemia, with the exception of
three towns, Budweiss, Krummau, and Pilsen, took part
in this insurrection. These three towns, inhabited principally by Roman Catholics, alone had the courage, in this
general revolt, to hold out for the Emperor, who promised
them assistance. But it could not escape Count Thurn
how dangerous it was to leave in hostile hands three
places of such importance, which would at all times keep
open for the imperial troops an entrance into the kingdom.

With prompt determination he appeared before Budweiss and Krummau in the hope of terrifying them into a surrender. Krummau surrendered, but all his attacks were steadfastly repulsed by Budweiss.

And now, too, the Emperor began to show more earnestness and energy. Bucquoi and Dampierre, with two armies, fell upon the Bohemian territories, which they treated as a hostile country. But the imperial generals found the march to Prague more difficult than they had expected. Every pass, every position that was the least tenable, must be opened by the sword, and resistance increased at each fresh step they took, for the outrages of their troops, chiefly consisting of Hungarians and Walloons, drove their friends to revolt and their enemies to despair. But even now that his troops had penetrated into Bohemia, the Emperor continued to offer the Estates peace, and to show himself ready for an amicable adjustment. But the new prospects which opened upon them raised the courage of the revolters. Moravia espoused their party; and from Germany appeared to them a defender equally intrepid and unexpected, in the person of Count Mansfeld.

The heads of the Evangelic Union had been silent but not inactive spectators of the movements in Bohemia. Both were contending for the same cause and against the same enemy. In the fate of the Bohemians their confederates in the faith might read their own; and the cause of this people was represented as of solemn concern to the whole German union. True to these principles, the Unionists supported the courage of the insurgents by promises of assistance; and a fortunate accident now enabled them, beyond their hopes, to fulfil them.

The instrument by which the House of Austria was humbled in Germany was Peter Ernest, Count Mansfeld, the son of a distinguished Austrian officer, Ernest von Mansfeld, who for some time had commanded with repute the Spanish army in the Netherlands. His first campaigns in Juliers and Alsace had been made in the service of this house, and under the banner of the Archduke Leopold, against the Protestant religion and the liberties of Germany. But insensibly won by the principles of this religion, he abandoned a leader whose selfishness denied him the reimbursement of the moneys expended in his cause, and he transferred his zeal and a victorious sword to the Evangelic Union. It happened just then that the Duke of Savoy, an ally of the Union, demanded assistance in a war against Spain. They assigned to him their newly-acquired servant, and Mansfeld received instructions to raise an army of four thousand men in Germany, in the cause and in the pay of the duke. The army was ready to march at the very moment when the flames of war burst out in Bohemia, and the duke, who at the time did not stand in need of its services, placed it at the disposal of the Union. Nothing could be more welcome to these troops than the prospect of aiding their confederates in Bohemia at the cost of a third party. Mansfeld received orders forthwith to march with these four thousand men into that kingdom; and a pretended Bohemian commission was given to blind the public as to the true author of this levy.

This Mansfeld now appeared in Bohemia, and, by the occupation of Pilsen, strongly fortified and favorable to the Emperor, obtained a firm footing in the country. The courage of the rebels was farther increased by succors which the Silesian States despatched to their assistance. Between these and the Imperialists several battles were fought, far indeed from decisive, but only on that account the more destructive, which served as the prelude to a more serious war. To check the vigor of his military operations, a negotiation was entered into with the Emperor, and a disposition was shown to accept the proffered mediation of Saxony. But before the event could prove how little sincerity there was in these proposals, the Emperor was removed from the scene by death.

What now had Matthias done to justify the expectations which he had excited by the overthrow of his predecessor? Was it worth while to ascend a brother's throne through guilt, and then maintain it with so little dignity, and leave it with so little renown? As long as Matthias sat on the throne he had to atone for the imprudence by which he had gained it. To enjoy the real dignity a few years sooner he had shackled the free exercise of its prerogatives. The slender portion of independence left him by the growing power of the Estates, was still farther lessened by the encroachments of his relations. Sickly and childless he saw the attention of the world turned to an ambitious heir who was impatiently anticipating his fate; and who, by his interference with the closing administration, was already opening his own.

With Matthias the reigning line of the German House of Austria was in a manner extinct; for of all the sons of Maximilian one only was now alive, the weak and childless Archduke Albert, in the Netherlands, who had already renounced his claims to the inheritance in favor of the line of Grätz. The Spanish House had also, in a secret bond, resigned its pretensions to the Austrian possessions in behalf of the Archduke Ferdinand of Styria, in whom the branch of Hapsburg was about to put forth new shoots, and the former greatness of Austria to experience a revival.

The father of Ferdinand was the Archduke Charles of Carniola, Carinthia, and Styria, the youngest brother of Emperor Maximilian II.; his mother a princess of Bavaria. Having lost his father at twelve years of age, he was entrusted by the archduchess to the guardianship of her brother William, Duke of Bavaria, under whose eyes he was instructed and educated by Jesuits at the Academy of Ingolstadt. What principles he was likely to imbibe by his intercourse with a prince, who from motives of devotion had abdicated his government, may be easily conceived. Care was taken to point out to him, on the one hand, the weak indulgence of Maximilian's house towards the adherents of the new doctrines, and the consequent troubles of their dominions; on the other, the blessings of Bavaria, and the inflexible religious zeal of its rulers; between these two examples he was left to choose for himself.

Formed in this school to be a stout champion of the faith, and a prompt instrument of the church, he left Bavaria, after a residence of five years, to assume the government of his hereditary dominions. The Estates of Carniola, Carinthia, and Styria, who, before doing homage,

demanded a guarantee for freedom of religion, were told
that religious liberty has nothing to do with their allegiance. The oath was put to them without conditions, and
unconditionally taken. Many years, however, elapsed,
ere the designs which had been planned at Ingolstadt
were ripe for execution. Before attempting to carry
them into effect, he sought in person at Loretto the favor
of the Virgin, and received the apostolic benediction in
Rome at the feet of Clement VIII.

These designs were nothing less than the expulsion of
Protestantism from a country where it had the advantage
of numbers, and had been legally recognized by a formal
act of toleration, granted by his father to the noble and
knightly estates of the land. A grant so formally ratified
could not be revoked without danger; but no difficulties
could deter the pious pupil of the Jesuits. The example
of other states, both Roman Catholic and Protestant,
which within their own territories had exercised un-
questioned a right of reformation, and the abuse which the
Estates of Styria made of their religious liberties, would
serve as a justification of this violent procedure. Under
the shelter of an absurd positive law those of equity and
prudence might, it is thought, be safely despised. In
the execution of these unrighteous designs Ferdinand
did, it must be owned, display no common courage and
perseverance. Without tumult, and we may add, without cruelty, he suppressed the Protestant service in one
town after another, and in a few years, to the astonishment of Germany, this dangerous work was brought to a
successful end.

But, while the Roman Catholics admired him as a hero,
and the champion of the church, the Protestants began
to combine against him as their most dangerous enemy.
And yet Matthias' intention to bequeath to him the succession met with little or no opposition in the elective
states of Austria. Even the Bohemians agreed to receive
him as their future king on very favorable conditions.
It was not until afterwards, when they had experienced
the pernicious influence of his councils on the administration of the Emperor, that their anxiety was first excited;
and then several projects, in his handwriting, which an

unlucky chance threw into their hands, as they plainly evinced his disposition towards them, carried their apprehension to the utmost pitch. In particular, they were alarmed by a secret family compact with Spain, by which, in default of heirs-male of his own body, Ferdinand bequeathed to that crown the kingdom of Bohemia, without first consulting the wishes of that nation, and without regard to its rights of free election. The many enemies, too, which by his reforms in Styria that prince had provoked among the Protestants, were very prejudicial to his interests in Bohemia; and some Styrian emigrants, who had taken refuge there, bringing with them into their adopted country hearts overflowing with a desire of revenge, were particularly active in exciting the flame of revolt. Thus ill-affected did Ferdinand find the Bohemians when he succeeded Matthias.

So bad an understanding between the nation and the candidate for the throne would have raised a storm even in the most peaceable succession; how much more so at the present moment, before the ardor of insurrection had cooled; when the nation had just recovered its dignity, and reasserted its rights; when they still held arms in their hands, and the consciousness of unity had awakened an enthusiastic reliance on their own strength; when by past success, by the promises of foreign assistance, and by visionary expectations of the future, their courage had been raised to an undoubting confidence. Disregarding the rights already conferred on Ferdinand, the Estates declared the throne vacant, and their right of election entirely unfettered. All hopes of their peaceful submission were at an end, and if Ferdinand wished still to wear the crown of Bohemia he must choose between purchasing it at the sacrifice of all that would make a crown desirable, or winning it sword in hand.

But with what means was it to be won? Turn his eyes where he would the fire of revolt was burning. Silesia had already joined the insurgents in Bohemia; Moravia was on the point of following its example. In Upper and Lower Austria the spirit of liberty was awake, as it had been under Rodolph, and the Estates refused to do homage. Hungary was menaced with an inroad by

Prince Bethlen Gabor, on the side of Transylvania; a secret arming among the Turks spread consternation among the provinces to the eastward; and, to complete his perplexities, the Protestants also in his hereditary dominions, stimulated by the general example, were again raising their heads. In that quarter their numbers were overwhelming; in most places they had possession of the revenues which Ferdinand would need for the maintenance of the war. The neutral began to waver, the faithful to be discouraged, the turbulent alone to be animated and confident. One half of Germany encouraged the rebels, the other inactively awaited the issue; Spanish assistance was still very remote. The moment which had brought him everything threatened also to deprive him of all.

And when he now, yielding to the stern law of necessity, made overtures to the Bohemian rebels, all his proposals for peace were insolently rejected. Count Thurn, at the head of an army, entered Moravia to bring this province, which alone continued to waver, to a decision. The appearance of their friends is the signal of revolt for the Moravian Protestants. Brunn is taken, the remainder of the country yields with free will; throughout the province government and religion are changed. Swelling as it flows, the torrent of rebellion pours down upon Austria, where a party, holding similar sentiments, receives it with a joyful concurrence. Henceforth there should be no more distinctions of religion; equality of rights should be guaranteed to all Christian churches. They hear that a foreign force has been invited into the country to oppress the Bohemians. Let them be sought out, and the enemies of liberty pursued to the ends of the earth. Not an arm is raised in defence of the Archduke, and the rebels, at length, encamp before Vienna to besiege their sovereign.

Ferdinand had sent his children from Grätz, where they were no longer safe, to the Tyrol; he himself awaited the insurgents in his capital. A handful of soldiers was all he could oppose to the enraged multitude; these few were without pay or provisions, and therefore little to be depended on. Vienna was unprepared for a long siege.

The party of the Protestants, ready at any moment to join the Bohemians, had the preponderance in the city; those in the country had already begun to levy troops against him. Already, in imagination, the Protestant populace saw the Emperor shut up in a monastery, his territories divided, and his children educated as Protestants. Confiding in secret, and surrounded by public enemies, he saw the chasm every moment widening to engulf his hopes and even himself. The Bohemian bullets were already falling upon the imperial palace, when sixteen Austrian barons forcibly entered his chamber, and inveighing against him with loud and bitter reproaches, endeavored to force him into a confederation with the Bohemians. One of them seizing him by the button of his doublet, demanded, in a tone of menace, "Ferdinand, wilt thou sign it?"

Who would not be pardoned had he wavered in this frightful situation? Yet Ferdinand still remembered the dignity of a Roman emperor. No alternative seemed left to him but an immediate flight or submission; laymen urged him to the one, priests to the other. If he abandoned the city it would fall into the enemy's hands; with Vienna, Austria was lost; with Austria, the imperial throne. Ferdinand abandoned not his capital, and as little would he hear of conditions.

The Archduke is still engaged in altercation with the deputed barons, when all at once a sound of trumpets is heard in the palace square. Terror and astonishment take possession of all present; a fearful report pervades the palace; one deputy after another disappears. Many of the nobility and the citizens hastily take refuge in the camp of Thurn. This sudden change is effected by a regiment of Dampierre's cuirassiers, who at that moment marched into the city to defend the Archduke. A body of infantry soon followed; reassured by their appearance, several of the Roman Catholic citizens, and even the students themselves, take up arms. A report which arrived just at the same time from Bohemia made his deliverance complete. The Flemish general, Bucquoi, had totally defeated Count Mansfeld at Budweiss, and was marching upon Prague. The Bohemians hastily

broke up their camp before Vienna to protect their own
capital.

And now also the passes were free which the enemy
had taken possession of in order to obstruct Ferdinand's
progress to his coronation at Frankfort. If the accession
to the imperial throne was important for the plans of the
King of Hungary, it was of still greater consequence at the
present moment, when his nomination as Emperor would
afford the most unsuspicious and decisive proof of the
dignity of his person, and of the justice of his cause,
while, at the same time, it would give him a hope of
support from the Empire. But the same cabal which
opposed him in his hereditary dominions labored also to
counteract him in his canvass for the imperial dignity.
No Austrian prince, they maintained, ought to ascend
the throne; least of all Ferdinand, the bigoted persecutor
of their religion, the slave of Spain and of the Jesuits.
To prevent this the crown had been offered, even during
the lifetime of Matthias, to the Duke of Bavaria, and, on
his refusal, to the Duke of Savoy. As some difficulty
was experienced in settling with the latter the conditions
of acceptance, it was sought, at all events, to delay the
election till some decisive blow in Austria or Bohemia
should annihilate all the hopes of Ferdinand, and incapa-
citate him from any competition for this dignity. The
members of the Union left no stone unturned to gain over
from Ferdinand the Electorate of Saxony, which was
bound to Austrian interests; they represented to this
court the dangers with which the Protestant religion, and
even the constitution of the empire, were threatened by the
principles of this prince and his Spanish alliance. By
the elevation of Ferdinand to the imperial throne,
Germany, they further asserted, would be involved in
the private quarrels of this prince, and bring upon itself
the arms of Bohemia. But in spite of all opposing
influences the day of election was fixed, Ferdinand
summoned to it as lawful King of Bohemia, and his
electoral vote, after a fruitless resistance on the part of
the Bohemian Estates, acknowledged to be good. The
votes of the three ecclesiastical electorates were for him,
Saxony was favorable to him, Brandenburg made no

opposition, and a decided majority declared him Emperor in 1619. Thus he saw the most doubtful of his crowns placed first of all on his head; but a few days after he lost that which he had reckoned among the most certain of his possessions. While he was thus elected Emperor in Frankfort, he was in Prague deprived of the Bohemian throne.

Almost all of his German hereditary dominions had in the meantime entered into a formidable league with the Bohemians, whose insolence now exceeded all bounds. In a general Diet, the latter, on the 17th of August, 1619, proclaimed the Emperor an enemy to the Bohemian religion and liberties, who by his pernicious counsels had alienated from them the affections of the late Emperor, had furnished troops to oppress them, had given their country as a prey to foreigners, and finally, in contravention of the national rights, had bequeathed the crown, by a secret compact, to Spain; they therefore declared that he had forfeited whatever title he might otherwise have had to the crown, and immediately proceeded to a new election. As this sentence was pronounced by Protestants, their choice could not well fall upon a Roman Catholic prince, though, to save appearances, some voices were raised for Bavaria and Savoy. But the violent religious animosities which divided the evangelical and the reformed parties among the Protestants impeded for some time the election even of a Protestant king; till at last the address and activity of the Calvinists carried the day from the numerical superiority of the Lutherans.

Among all the princes who were competitors for this dignity, the Elector Palatine Frederick V. had the best grounded claims on the confidence and gratitude of the Bohemians; and, among them all, there was no one in whose case the private interests of particular Estates, and the attachment of the people, seemed to be justified by so many considerations of state. Frederick V. was a free and lively spirit, of great goodness of heart and regal liberality. He was the head of the Calvinistic party in Germany, the leader of the Union, whose resources were at his disposal, a near relation of the Duke of Bavaria, and a son-in-law of the King of Great Britain, who might lend him his powerful support. All these considerations were prominently and successfully brought forward by the Calvinists, and Frederick V. was chosen king by the Assembly at Prague amidst prayers and tears of joy.

The whole proceedings of the Diet at Prague had been premeditated, and Frederick himself had taken too active a share in the matter to feel at all surprised at the offer made to him by the Bohemians. But now the immediate glitter of this throne dazzled him, and the magnitude both of his elevation and his delinquency made his weak mind to tremble. After the usual manner of pusillanimous spirits, he sought to confirm himself in his purpose by the opinions of others; but these opinions had no weight with him when they ran counter to his own cherished wishes. Saxony and Bavaria, of whom he sought advice, all his brother electors, all who compared the magnitude of the design with his capacities and resources, warned him of the danger into which he was about to rush. Even King James of England preferred to see his son-in-law deprived of this crown than that the sacred majesty of kings should be outraged by so dangerous a precedent. But of what avail was the voice of prudence against the seductive glitter of a crown? In the moment of boldest determination, when they are indignantly rejecting the consecrated branch of a race which had governed them for two centuries, a free people throws itself into his arms. Confiding in his courage, they choose him as their leader in the dangerous career of glory and liberty. To him, as to its born champion, an oppressed religion looks for shelter and support against its persecutors. Could he have the weakness to listen to his fears, and to betray the cause of religion and liberty? This religion proclaims to him its own preponderance and the weakness of its rival, — two-thirds of the power of Austria are now in arms against Austria itself, while a formidable confederacy, already formed in Transylvania, would, by a hostile attack, further distract even the weak remnant of its power. Could inducements such as these fail to awaken his ambition, or such hopes to animate and inflame his resolution?

A few moments of calm consideration would have sufficed to show the danger of the undertaking and the comparative worthlessness of the prize. But the temptation spoke to his feelings; the warning only to his reason. It was his misfortune that his nearest and most influential counsellors espoused the side of his passions. The aggrandizement of their master's power opened to the ambition and avarice of his Palatine servants an unlimited field for their gratification; this anticipated triumph of their church kindled the ardor of the Calvinistic fanatic. Could a mind so weak as that of Ferdinand resist the delusions of his counsellors, who exaggerated his resources and his strength as much as they underrated those of his enemies; or the exhortations of his preachers, who announced the effusions of their fanatical zeal as the immediate inspiration of heaven? The dreams of astrology filled his mind with visionary hopes; even love conspired, with its irresistible fascination, to complete the seduction. "Had you," demanded the Electress, "confidence enough in yourself to accept the hand of a king's daughter, and have you misgivings about taking a crown which is voluntarily offered you? I would rather eat bread at thy kingly table than feast at thy electoral board."

Frederick accepted the Bohemian crown. The coronation was celebrated with unexampled pomp at Prague, for the nation displayed all its riches in honor of its own work. Silesia and Moravia, the adjoining provinces to Bohemia, followed their example, and did homage to Frederick. The reformed faith was enthroned in all the churches of the kingdom; the rejoicings were unbounded, their attachment to their new king bordered on adoration. Denmark and Sweden, Holland and Venice, and several of the Dutch states, acknowledged him as lawful sovereign, and Frederick now prepared to maintain his new acquisition.

His principal hopes rested on Prince Bethlen Gabor of Transylvania. This formidable enemy of Austria, and of the Roman Catholic church, not content with the principality which, with the assistance of the Turks, he had wrested from his legitimate prince, Gabriel Bathori, gladly seized this opportunity of aggrandizing himself at the expense of Austria, which had hesitated to acknowledge him as sovereign of Transylvania. An attack upon Hungary and Austria was concerted with the Bohemian rebels, and both armies were to unite before the capital. Meantime, Bethlen Gabor, under the mask of friendship, disguised the true object of his warlike preparations, artfully promising the Emperor to lure the Bohemians into the toils by a pretended offer of assistance, and to deliver up to him alive the leaders of the insurrection. All at once, however, he appeared in a hostile attitude in Upper Hungary. Before him went terror, and devastation behind; all opposition yielded, and at Presburg he received the Hungarian crown. The Emperor's brother, who governed in Vienna, trembled for the capital. He hastily summoned General Bucquoi to his assistance, and the retreat of the Imperialists drew the Bohemians, a second time, before the walls of Vienna. Reinforced by twelve thousand Transylvanians, and soon after joined by the victorious army of Bethlen Gabor, they again menaced the capital with assault; all the country round Vienna was laid waste, the navigation of the Danube closed, all supplies cut off, and the horrors of famine were threatened. Ferdinand, hastily recalled to his capital by this urgent danger, saw himself a second time on the brink of ruin. But want of provisions, and the inclement weather, finally compelled the Bohemians to go into quarters, a defeat in Hungary recalled Bethlen Gabor, and thus once more had fortune rescued the Emperor.

In a few weeks the scene was changed, and by his prudence and activity Ferdinand improved his position as rapidly as Frederick, by indolence and impolicy, ruined his. The Estates of Lower Austria were regained to their allegiance by a confirmation of their privileges; and the few who still held out were declared guilty of *lèse-majesté* and high treason. During the election of Frankfort he had contrived, by personal representations, to win over to his cause the ecclesiastical electors, and also Maximilian, Duke of Bavaria, at Munich. The whole issue of the war, the fate of Frederick and the Emperor, were now dependent on the part which the Union and the

League should take in the troubles of Bohemia. It was evidently of importance to all the Protestants of Germany that the King of Bohemia should be supported, while it was equally the interests of the Roman Catholics to prevent the ruin of the Emperor. If the Protestants succeeded in Bohemia, all the Roman Catholic princes in Germany might tremble for their possessions; if they failed, the Emperor would give laws to Protestant Germany. Thus Ferdinand put the League, Frederick the Union, in motion. The ties of relationship and a personal attachment to the Emperor, his brother-in-law, with whom he had been educated at Ingolstadt, zeal for the Roman Catholic religion, which seemed to be in the most imminent peril, and the suggestions of the Jesuits, combined with the suspicious movements of the Union, moved the Duke of Bavaria, and all the princes of the League, to make the cause of Ferdinand their own.

According to the terms of a treaty with the Emperor, which assured to the Duke of Bavaria compensation for all the expenses of the war, or the losses he might sustain, Maximilian took, with full powers, the command of the troops of the League, which were ordered to march to the assistance of the Emperor against the Bohemian rebels. The leaders of the Union, instead of delaying by every means this dangerous coalition of the League with the Emperor, did everything in their power to accelerate it. Could they, they thought, but once drive the Roman Catholic League to take an open part in the Bohemian war they might reckon on similar measures from all the members and allies of the Union. Without some open step taken by the Roman Catholics against the Union no effectual confederacy of the Protestant powers was to be looked for. They seized, therefore, the present emergency of the troubles in Bohemia to demand from the Roman Catholics the abolition of their past grievances, and full security for the future exercise of their religion. They addressed this demand, which was moreover couched in threatening language, to the Duke of Bavaria, as the head of the Roman Catholics, and they insisted on an immediate and categorical answer. Maximilian might decide for or against them, still their point was gained;

his concession, if he yielded, would deprive the Roman Catholic party of its most powerful protector; his refusal would arm the whole Protestant party, and render inevitable a war in which they hoped to be the conquerors. Maximilian, firmly attached to the opposite party from so many other considerations, took the demands of the Union as a formal declaration of hostilities, and quickened his preparations. While Bavaria and the League were thus arming in the Emperor's cause negotiations for a subsidy were opened with the Spanish court. All the difficulties with which the indolent policy of that ministry met this demand were happily surmounted by the imperial ambassador at Madrid, Count Khevenhuller. In addition to a subsidy of a million of florins, which from time to time were doled out by this court an attack upon the Lower Palatinate, from the side of the Spanish Netherlands, was at the same time agreed upon.

During these attempts to draw all the Roman Catholic powers into the League, every exertion was made against the counter-league of the Protestants. To this end it was important to alarm the Elector of Saxony and the other Evangelical powers, and accordingly the Union were diligent in propagating a rumor that the preparations of the League had for their object to deprive them of the ecclesiastical foundations they had secularized. A written assurance to the contrary calmed the fears of the Duke of Saxony, whom moreover private jealousy of the Palatine, and the insinuations of his chaplain, who was in the pay of Austria, and mortification at having been passed over by the Bohemians in the election to the throne, strongly inclined to the side of Austria. The fanaticism of the Lutherans could never forgive the reformed party for having drawn, as they expressed it, so many fair provinces into the gulf of Calvinism, and rejecting the Roman Antichrist only to make way for an Helvetian one.

While Ferdinand used every effort to improve the unfavorable situation of his affairs, Frederick was daily injuring his good cause. By his close and questionable connection with the Prince of Transylvania, the open ally of the Porte, he gave offence to weak minds; and a general rumor accused him of furthering his own ambition at the expense of Christendom, and arming the Turks against Germany. His inconsiderate zeal for the Calvinistic scheme irritated the Lutherans of Bohemia, his attacks on image-worship incensed the Papists of this kingdom against him. New and oppressive imposts alienated the affections of all his subjects. The disappointed hopes of the Bohemian nobles cooled their zeal; the absence of foreign succors abated their confidence. Instead of devoting himself with untiring energies to the affairs of his kingdom, Frederick wasted his time in amusements; instead of filling his treasury by a wise economy, he squandered his revenues by a needless theatrical pomp and a misplaced munificence. With a light-minded carelessness, he did but gaze at himself in his new dignity, and in the ill-timed desire to enjoy his crown, he forgot the more pressing duty of securing it on his head.

But greatly as men erred in their opinion of him, Frederick himself had not less miscalculated his foreign resources. Most of the members of the Union considered the affairs of Bohemia as foreign to the real object of their confederacy; others, who were devoted to him, were overawed by fear of the Emperor. Saxony and Hesse Darmstadt had already been gained over by Ferdinand; Lower Austria, on which side a powerful diversion had been looked for, had made its submission to the Emperor; and Bethlen Gabor had concluded a truce with him. By its embassies the court of Vienna had induced Denmark to remain inactive, and to occupy Sweden in a war with the Poles. The republic of Holland had enough to do to defend itself against the arms of the Spaniards; Venice and Saxony remained inactive; King James of England was overreached by the artifice of Spain. One friend after another withdrew; one hope vanished after another — so rapidly in a few months was everything changed.

In the meantime the leaders of the Union assembled an army; the Emperor and the League did the same. The troops of the latter were assembled under the banners of Maximilian at Donauwerth, those of the Union at Ulm, under the Margrave of Anspach. The decisive moment seemed at length to have arrived which was to end these long dissensions by a vigorous blow, and irrevocably to settle the relation of the two churches in Germany. Anxiously on the stretch was the expectation of both parties. How great then was their astonishment when suddenly the intelligence of peace arrived, and both armies separated without striking a blow!

The intervention of France effected this peace, which was equally acceptable to both parties. The French cabinet, no longer swayed by the counsels of Henry the Great, and whose maxims of state were perhaps not applicable to the present condition of that kingdom, was now far less alarmed at the preponderance of Austria than of the increase which would accrue to the strength of the Calvinists if the Palatine house should be able to retain the throne of Bohemia. Involved at the time in a dangerous conflict with its own Calvinistic subjects, it was of the utmost importance to France that the Protestant faction in Bohemia should be suppressed before the Huguenots could copy their dangerous example. In order therefore to facilitate the Emperor's operations against the Bohemians, she offered her mediation to the Union and the League, and effected this unexpected treaty of which the main article was, "That the Union should abandon all interference in the affairs of Bohemia, and confine the aid which they might afford to Frederick V., to his Palatine territories." To this disgraceful treaty, the Union were moved by the firmness of Maximilian and the fear of being pressed at once by the troops of the League, and a new Imperial army which was on its march from the Netherlands.

The whole force of Bavaria and the League was now at the disposal of the Emperor to be employed against the Bohemians, who by the pacification of Ulm were abandoned to their fate. With a rapid movement, and before a rumor of the proceedings at Ulm could reach there, Maximilian appeared in Upper Austria, when the Estates, surprised and unprepared for an enemy, purchased the Emperor's pardon by an immediate and unconditional submission. In Lower Austria the duke formed a junction with the troops from the Low Countries, under Bucquoi, and without loss of time the united Imperial and Bavarian forces, amounting to fifty thousand men, entered Bohemia. All the Bohemian troops, which were dispersed over Lower Austria and Moravia, were driven before them; every town which attempted resistance was quickly taken by storm; others, terrified by the report of the punishment inflicted on these, voluntarily opened their gates; nothing in short interrupted the impetuous career of Maximilian. The Bohemian army, commanded by the brave Prince Christian of Anhalt, retreated to the neighborhood of Prague; where, under the walls of the city, Maximilian offered him battle.

The wretched condition in which he hoped to surprise the insurgents justified the rapidity of the duke's movements, and secured him the victory. Frederick's army did not amount to thirty thousand men. Eight thousand of these were furnished by the Prince of Anhalt; ten thousand were Hungarians, whom Bethlen Gabor had despatched to his assistance. An inroad of the Elector of Saxony upon Lusatia had cut off all succors from that country and from Silesia; the pacification of Austria put an end to all his expectations from that quarter; Bethlen Gabor, his most powerful ally, remained inactive in Transylvania; the Union had betrayed his cause to the Emperor. Nothing remained to him but his Bohemians; and they were without good-will to his cause, and without unity and courage. The Bohemian magnates were indignant that German generals should be put over their heads; Count Mansfeld remained in Pilsen, at a distance from the camp, to avoid the mortification of serving under Anhalt and Hohenlohe. The soldiers, in want of necessaries, became dispirited; and the little discipline that was observed gave occasion to bitter complaints from the peasantry. It was in vain that Frederick made his appearance in the camp, in the hope of reviving the courage of the soldiers by his presence, and of kindling the emulation of the nobles by his example.

The Bohemians had begun to entrench themselves on the White Mountain, near Prague, when they were attacked by the Imperial and Bavarian armies, on the 8th

November, 1620. In the beginning of the action some advantages were gained by the cavalry of the Prince of Anhalt; but the superior numbers of the enemy soon neutralized them. The charge of the Bavarians and Walloons was irresistible. The Hungarian cavalry was the first to retreat. The Bohemian infantry soon followed their example; and the Germans were at last carried along with them in the general flight. Ten cannons, composing the whole of Frederick's artillery, were taken by the enemy; four thousand Bohemians fell in the flight and on the field; while of the Imperialists and soldiers of the League only a few hundred were killed. In less than an hour this decisive action was over.

Frederick was seated at table in Prague while his army was thus cut to pieces. It is probable that he had not expected the attack on this day, since he had ordered an entertainment for it. A messenger summoned him from table to show him from the walls the whole frightful scene. He requested a cessation of hostilities for twenty-four hours for deliberation; but eight was all the Duke of Bavaria would allow him. Frederick availed himself of these to fly by night from the capital, with his wife and the chief officers of his army. This flight was so hurried that the Prince of Anhalt left behind him his most private papers and Frederick his crown. "I know now what I am," said this unfortunate prince to those who endeavored to comfort him; "there are virtues which misfortune only can teach us, and it is in adversity alone that princes learn to know themselves."

Prague was not irretrievably lost when Frederick's pusillanimity abandoned it. The light troops of Mansfeld were still in Pilsen, and were not engaged in the action. Bethlen Gabor might at any moment have assumed an offensive attitude, and drawn off the Emperor's army to the Hungarian frontier. The defeated Bohemians might rally. Sickness, famine, and the inclement weather might wear out the enemy; but all these hopes disappeared before the immediate alarm. Frederick dreaded the fickleness of the Bohemians, who might probably yield to the temptation to purchase, by the surrender of his person, the pardon of the Emperor.

Thurn, and those of this party who were in the same condemnation with him, found it equally inexpedient to await their destiny within the walls of Prague. They retired towards Moravia, with a view of seeking refuge in Transylvania. Frederick fled to Breslau, where, however, he only remained a short time. He removed from thence to the court of the Elector of Brandenburg, and finally took shelter in Holland.

The battle of Prague had decided the fate of Bohemia. Prague surrendered the next day to the victors; the other towns followed the example of the capital. The Estates did homage without conditions, and the same was done by those of Silesia and Moravia. The Emperor allowed three months to elapse before instituting any inquiry into the past. Reassured by this apparent clemency, many who at first had fled in terror appeared again in the capital. All at once, however, the storm burst forth; forty-eight of the most active among the insurgents were arrested on the same day and hour, and tried by an extraordinary commission, composed of native Bohemians and Austrians. Of these, twenty-seven, and of the common people an immense number, expired on the scaffold. The absenting offenders were summoned to appear to their trial, and, failing to do so, condemned to death as traitors and offenders against his Catholic Majesty, their estates confiscated, and their names affixed to the gallows. The property also of the rebels who had fallen in the field was seized. This tyranny might have been borne, as it affected individuals only, and while the ruin of one enriched another; but more intolerable was the oppression which extended to the whole kingdom without exception. All the Protestant preachers were banished from the country; the Bohemians first, and afterwards those of Germany. The *Letter of Majesty* Ferdinand tore with his own hand and burnt the seal. Seven years after the battle of Prague the toleration of the Protestant religion within the kingdom was entirely revoked. But whatever violence the Emperor allowed himself against the religious privileges of his subjects, he carefully abstained from interfering with their political constitution; and while he deprived them of the liberty of thought, he magnanimously left them the prerogative of taxing themselves.

The victory of the White Mountain put Ferdinand in possession of all his dominions. It even invested him with greater authority over them than his predecessors enjoyed, since their allegiance had been unconditionally pledged to him, and no Letter of Majesty now existed to limit his sovereignty. All his wishes were now gratified to a degree surpassing his most sanguine expectations.

It was now in his power to dismiss his allies and disband his army. If he was just, there was an end of the war — if he was both magnanimous and just, punishment was also at an end. The fate of Germany was in his hands; the happiness and misery of millions depended on the resolution he should take. Never was so great a decision resting on a single mind; never did the blindness of one man produce so much ruin.

BOOK II.

THE resolution which Ferdinand now adopted gave to the war a new direction, a new scene, and new actors. From a rebellion in Bohemia, and the chastisement of rebels, a war extended first to Germany, and afterwards to Europe. It is, therefore, necessary to take a general survey of the state of affairs both in Germany and the rest of Europe.

Unequally as the territory of Germany and the privileges of its members were divided among the Roman Catholics and the Protestants, neither party could hope to maintain itself against the encroachments of its adversary otherwise than by a prudent use of its peculiar advantages, and by a politic union among themselves. If the Roman Catholics were the more numerous party, and more favored by the constitution of the Empire, the Protestants, on the other hand, had the advantage of possessing a more compact and populous line of territories, valiant princes, a warlike nobility, numerous armies, flourishing free towns, the command of the sea, and, even at the worst, certainty of support from Roman Catholic states. If the Catholics could arm Spain and Italy in their favor, the republics of Venice, Holland, and England opened their treasures to the Protestants, while the states of the North and the formidable power of Turkey stood ready to afford them prompt assistance. Brandenburg, Saxony, and the Palatinate opposed three Protestant to three Ecclesiastical votes in the Electoral College; while to the Elector of Bohemia, as to the Archduke of Austria, the possession of the Imperial dignity was an important check if the Protestants properly availed themselves of it. The sword of the Union might keep within its sheath the sword of the League; or, if matters actually came to a war, might make the issue of it doubtful. But, unfortunately, private interests dissolved the band of union which should have held together the Protestant members of the empire. This critical conjuncture found none but second-rate actors on the political stage, and the decisive moment was neglected because the courageous were deficient in power, and the powerful in sagacity, courage, and resolution.

The Elector of Saxony was placed at the head of the German Protestants by the services of his ancestor Maurice, by the extent of his territories, and by the influence of his electoral vote. Upon the resolution he might adopt the fate of the contending parties seemed to depend; and John George was not insensible to the advantages which this important situation procured him. Equally valuable as an ally, both to the Emperor and to the Protestant Union, he cautiously avoided committing himself to either party; neither trusting himself by any irrevocable declaration entirely to the gratitude of the Emperor, nor renouncing the advantages which were to be gained from his fears. Uninfected by the contagion of religious and romantic enthusiasm which hurried sovereign after sovereign to risk both crown and life on the hazard of war, John George aspired to the more solid renown of improving and advancing the interests of his territories. His contemporaries accused him of forsaking the Protestant cause in the very midst of the storm; of preferring the aggrandizement of his house to the emancipation of his country; of exposing the whole Evangelical or Lutheran church of Germany to ruin rather than raise an arm in defence of the Reformed or Calvinists; of injuring the common cause by his suspicious friendship more seriously than the open enmity of its avowed opponents. But it would have been well if his accusers had imitated the wise policy of the Elector. If, despite of the prudent policy, the Saxons, like all others, groaned at the cruelties which marked the Emperor's progress; if all Germany was a witness how Ferdinand deceived his confederates and trifled with his engagements; if even the Elector himself at last perceived this — the more shame to the Emperor who could so basely betray such implicit confidence.

If an excessive reliance on the Emperor, and the hope of enlarging his territories, tied the hands of the Elector of Saxony, the weak George William, Elector of Brandenburg, was still more shamefully fettered by fear of Austria and of the loss of his dominions. What was made a reproach against these princes would have preserved to the Elector Palatine his fame and his kingdom. A rash confidence in his untried strength, the influence of French counsels, and the temptation of a crown had seduced that unfortunate prince into an enterprise for which he had neither adequate genius nor political capacity. The partition of his territories among discordant princes enfeebled the Palatinate, which, united, might have made a longer resistance.

This partition of territory was equally injurious to the House of Hesse, in which, between Darmstadt and Cassel, religious dissensions had occasioned a fatal division. The line of Darmstadt, adhering to the Confession of Augsburg, had placed itself under the Emperor's protection, who favored it at the expense of the Calvinists of Cassel. While his religious confederates were shedding their blood for their faith and their liberties, the Landgrave of Darmstadt was won over by the Emperor's gold. But William of Cassel, every way worthy of his ancestor, who, a century before, had defended the freedom of Germany against the formidable Charles V., espoused the cause of danger and of honor. Superior to that pusillanimity which made far more powerful princes bow before Ferdinand's might, the Landgrave William was the first to join the hero of Sweden, and set an example to the princes of Germany, which all had hesitated to begin. The boldness of his resolve was equalled by the steadfastness of his perseverance and the valor of his exploits. He placed himself with unshrinking resolution before his bleeding country, and boldly confronted the fearful enemy, whose hands were still reeking from the carnage of Magdeburg.

The Landgrave William deserves to descend to immortality with the heroic race of Ernest. Thy day of vengeance was long delayed, unfortunate John Frederick! Noble! never-to-be-forgotten prince! Slowly but brightly it broke. Thy times returned, and thy heroic spirit descended on thy grandson. An intrepid race of princes issues from the Thuringian forests to shame, by immortal deeds, the unjust sentence which robbed thee of the electoral crown — to avenge thy offended shade by heaps of bloody sacrifice. The sentence of the conqueror could deprive thee of thy territories, but not that spirit of patriotism which staked them, nor that chivalrous courage which, a century afterwards, was destined to shake the throne of his descendant. Thy vengeance and that of Germany whetted the sacred sword, and one heroic hand after the other wielded the irresistible steel. As men they achieved what as sovereigns they dared not undertake; they met in a glorious cause as the valiant soldiers of liberty. Too weak in territory to attack the enemy with their own forces, they directed foreign artillery against them, and led foreign banners to victory.

The liberties of Germany, abandoned by the more powerful states, who, however, enjoyed most of the prosperity accruing from them, were defended by a few princes for whom they were almost without value. The possession of territories and dignities deadened courage; the want of both made heroes. While Saxony, Brandenburg, and the rest drew back in terror, Anhalt, Mansfeld, the Prince of Weimar and others were shedding their blood in the field. The Dukes of Pomerania, Mecklen-

burg, Luneburg, and Wirtemberg, and the free cities of
Upper Germany, to whom the name of *Emperor* was of
course a formidable one, anxiously avoided a contest with
such an opponent, and crouched murmuring beneath his
mighty arm.

Austria and Roman Catholic Germany possessed in
Maximilian of Bavaria a champion as prudent as he was
powerful. Adhering throughout the war to one fixed
plan, never divided between his religion and his political
interests; not the slavish dependent of Austria, who was
laboring for *his* advancement, and trembled before her
powerful protector, Maximilian earned the territories and
dignities that rewarded his exertions. The other Roman
Catholic states, which were chiefly ecclesiastical, too un-
warlike to resist the multitudes whom the prosperity of
their territories allured, became the victims of the war
one after another, and were contented to persecute in the
cabinet and in the pulpit the enemy whom they could not
openly oppose in the field. All of them, slaves either to
Austria or Bavaria, sunk into insignificance by the side
of Maximilian; in his hand alone their united power
could be rendered available.

The formidable monarchy which Charles V. and his
son had unnaturally constructed of the Netherlands,
Milan, and the two Sicilies, and their distant possessions
in the East and West Indies, was under Philip III. and
Philip IV. fast verging to decay. Swollen to a sudden
greatness by unfruitful gold, this power was now sinking
under a visible decline, neglecting, as it did, agriculture,
the natural support of states. The conquests in the West
Indies had reduced Spain itself to poverty, while they
enriched the markets of Europe; the bankers of Antwerp,
Venice, and Genoa were making profit on the gold which
was still buried in the mines of Peru. For the sake of
India Spain had been depopulated, while the treasures
drawn from thence were wasted in the reconquest of
Holland, in the chimerical project of changing the succession to the crown of France, and in an unfortunate attack
upon England. But the pride of this court had survived
its greatness, as the hate of its enemies had outlived its
power. Distrust of the Protestants suggested to the

ministry of Philip III. the dangerous policy of his father; and the reliance of the Roman Catholics in Germany on Spanish assistance was as firm as their belief in the wonder-working bones of the martyrs. External splendor concealed the inward wounds at which the life-blood of this monarchy was oozing; and the belief of its strength survived, because it still maintained the lofty tone of its golden days. Slaves in their palaces, and strangers even upon their own thrones, the Spanish nominal kings still gave laws to their German relations; though it is very doubtful if the support they afforded was worth the dependence by which the emperors purchased it. The fate of Europe was decided behind the Pyrenees by ignorant monks or vindictive favorites. Yet, even in its debasement, a power must always be formidable which yields to none in extent; which, from custom, if not from the steadfastness of its views, adhered faithfully to one system of policy; which possessed well-disciplined armies and consummate generals; which, where the sword failed, did not scruple to employ the dagger; and converted even its ambassadors into incendiaries and assassins. What it had lost in three quarters of the globe it now sought to regain to the eastward, and all Europe was at its mercy, if it could succeed in its long-cherished design of uniting with the hereditary dominions of Austria all that lay between the Alps and the Adriatic.

To the great alarm of the native states this formidable power had gained a footing in Italy, where its continual encroachments made the neighboring sovereigns to tremble for their own possessions. The Pope himself was in the most dangerous situation,—hemmed in on both sides by the Spanish Viceroys of Naples on the one side, and that of Milan upon the other. Venice was confined between the Austrian Tyrol and the Spanish territories in Milan. Savoy was surrounded by the latter and France. Hence the wavering and equivocal policy which, from the time of Charles V., had been pursued by the Italian states. The double character which pertained to the Popes made them perpetually vacillate between two contradictory systems of policy. If the successors of St. Peter found in the Spanish princes their most obedient

disciples, and the most steadfast supporters of the Papal
See, yet the princes of the states of the Church had in
these monarchs their most dangerous neighbors and most
formidable opponents. If, in the one capacity, their
dearest wish was the destruction of the Protestants, and
the triumph of Austria in the other, they had reason to
bless the arms of the Protestants which disabled a dangerous enemy. The one or the other sentiment prevailed,
according as the love of temporal dominion or zeal for
spiritual supremacy predominated in the mind of the
Pope. But the policy of Rome was, on the whole, directed
to immediate dangers; and it is well known how far more
powerful is the apprehension of losing a present good
than anxiety to recover a long lost possession. And thus
it becomes intelligible how the Pope should first combine
with Austria for the destruction of heresy, and then conspire with these very heretics for the destruction of
Austria. Strangely blended are the threads of human
affairs! What would have become of the Reformation
and of the liberties of Germany if the Bishop of Rome
and the Prince of Rome had had but one interest?

France had lost with its great Henry all its importance
and all its weight in the political balance of Europe. A
turbulent minority had destroyed all the benefits of the
able administration of Henry. Incapable ministers, the
creatures of court intrigue, squandered in a few years the
treasures which Sully's economy and Henry's frugality had
amassed. Scarce able to maintain their ground against
internal factions, they were compelled to resign to other
hands the helm of European affairs. The same civil war
which armed Germany against itself excited a similar
commotion in France; and Louis XIII. attained majority
only to wage a war with his own mother and his Protestant subjects. This party, which had been kept quiet by
Henry's enlightened policy, now seized the opportunity
to take up arms, and under the command of some adventurous leaders, began to form themselves into a party
within the state, and to fix on the strong and powerful
town of Rochelle as the capital of their intended kingdom.
Too little of a statesman to suppress by a prudent toleration this civil commotion in its birth, and too little

master of the resources of his kingdom to direct them
with energy, Louis XIII. was reduced to the degradation
of purchasing the submission of the rebels by large sums
of money. Though policy might incline him in one point
of view to assist the Bohemian insurgents against Austria,
the son of Henry IV. was now compelled to be an inactive
spectator of their destruction, happy enough if the Calvinists in his own dominions did not unseasonably bethink
them of their confederates beyond the Rhine. A great
mind at the helm of state would have reduced the Protestants in France to obedience, while it employed them
to fight for the independence of their German brethren.
But Henry IV. was no more, and Richelieu had not yet
revived his system of policy.

While the glory of France was thus upon the wane, the
emancipated republic of Holland was completing the
fabric of its greatness. The enthusiastic courage had not
yet died away which, enkindled by the House of Orange,
had converted this mercantile people into a nation of
heroes, and had enabled them to maintain their independence in a bloody war against the Spanish monarchy.
Aware how much they owed their own liberty to foreign
support, these republicans were ready to assist their German brethren in a similar cause, and the more so as both
were opposed to the same enemy, and the liberty of Germany was the best warrant for that of Holland. But a
republic which had still to battle for its very existence,
which, with all its wonderful exertions, was scarce a
match for the formidable enemy within its own territories,
could not be expected to withdraw its troops from the
necessary work of self-defence to employ them with a
magnanimous policy in protecting foreign states.

England, too, though now united with Scotland, no
longer possessed, under the weak James, that influence
in the affairs of Europe which the governing mind of
Elizabeth had procured for it. Convinced that the welfare of her dominions depended on the security of the
Protestants, this politic princess had never swerved from
the principle of promoting every enterprise which had
for its object the diminution of the Austrian power.
Her successor was no less devoid of capacity to compre-

hend, than of vigor to execute, her views. While the
economical Elizabeth spared not her treasures to support
the Flemings against Spain, and Henry IV. against the
League, James abandoned his daughter, his son-in-law,
and his grandchild to the fury of their enemies. While
he exhausted his learning to establish the divine right of
kings, he allowed his own dignity to sink into the dust;
while he exerted his rhetoric to prove the absolute
authority of kings, he reminded the people of theirs; and
by a useless profusion, sacrificed the chief of his sovereign rights — that of dispensing with his parliament, and
thus depriving liberty of its organ. An innate horror at
the sight of a naked sword averted him from the most
just of wars; while his favorite Buckingham practised
on his weakness, and his own complacent vanity rendered him an easy dupe of Spanish artifice. While his
son-in-law was ruined, and the inheritance of his grandson given to others, this weak prince was imbibing, with
satisfaction, the incense which was offered to him by
Austria and Spain. To divert his attention from the
German war, he was amused with the proposal of a
Spanish marriage for his son, and the ridiculous parent
encouraged the romantic youth in the foolish project of
paying his addresses in person to the Spanish princess.
But his son lost his bride, as his son-in-law lost the crown
of Bohemia and the Palatine Electorate; and death alone
saved him from the danger of closing his pacific reign by
a war at home, which he never had courage to maintain,
even at a distance.

The domestic disturbances which his misgovernment
had gradually excited burst forth under his unfortunate
son, and forced him, after some unimportant attempts, to
renounce all further participation in the German war, in
order to stem within his own kingdom the rage of
faction.

Two illustrious monarchs, far unequal in personal
reputation, but equal in power and desire of fame, made
the North at this time to be respected. Under the long
and active reign of Christian IV., Denmark had risen
into importance. The personal qualifications of this
prince, an excellent navy, a formidable army, well-

ordered finances, and prudent alliances, had combined to give her prosperity at home and influence abroad. Gustavus Vasa had rescued Sweden from vassalage, reformed it by wise laws, and had introduced, for the first time, this newly-organized state into the field of European politics. What this great prince had merely sketched in rude outline was filled up by Gustavus Adolphus, his still greater grandson.

These two kingdoms, once unnaturally united and enfeebled by their union, had been violently separated at the time of the Reformation, and this separation was the epoch of their prosperity. Injurious as this compulsory union had proved to both kingdoms, equally necessary to each apart were neighborly friendship and harmony. On both the evangelical church leaned; both had the same seas to protect — a common interest ought to unite them against the same enemy. But the hatred which had dissolved the union of these monarchies continued long after their separation to divide the two nations. The Danish kings could not abandon their pretensions to the Swedish crown, nor the Swedes banish the remembrance of Danish oppression. The contiguous boundaries of the two kingdoms constantly furnished materials for international quarrels, while the watchful jealousy of both kings, and the unavoidable collision of their commercial interests in the North Seas, were inexhaustible sources of dispute.

Among the means of which Gustavus Vasa, the founder of the Swedish monarchy, availed himself to strengthen his new edifice, the Reformation had been one of the principal. A fundamental law of the kingdom excluded the adherents of popery from all offices of the state, and prohibited every future sovereign of Sweden from altering the religious constitution of the kingdom. But the second son and second successor of Gustavus had relapsed into popery, and his son Sigismund, also King of Poland, had been guilty of measures which menaced both the constitution and the established church. Headed by Charles, Duke of Sudermania, the third son of Gustavus, the Estates made a courageous resistance, which terminated, at last, in an open civil war between the uncle and nephew, and between the King and the people. Duke Charles, administrator of the kingdom during the absence of the king, had availed himself of Sigismund's long residence in Poland, and the just displeasure of the states, to ingratiate himself with the nation, and gradually to prepare his way to the throne. His views were not a little forwarded by Sigismund's imprudence. A general Diet ventured to abolish, in favor of the Protector, the rule of primogeniture which Gustavus had established in the succession, and placed the Duke of Sudermania on the throne, from which Sigismund, with his whole posterity, were solemnly excluded. The son of the new king (who reigned under the name of Charles IX.) was Gustavus Adolphus, whom, as the son of a usurper, the adherents of Sigismund refused to recognize. But if the obligations between monarchy and subjects are reciprocal, and states are not to be transmitted, like a lifeless heirloom, from hand to hand, a nation acting with unanimity must have the power of renouncing their allegiance to a sovereign who has violated his obligations to them, and of filling his place by a worthier object.

Gustavus Adolphus had not completed his seventeenth year when the Swedish throne became vacant by the death of his father. But the early maturity of his genius enabled the Estates to abridge in his favor the legal period of minority. With a glorious conquest over himself he commenced a reign which was to have victory for its constant attendant, a career which was to begin and end in success. The young Countess of Brahe, the daughter of a subject, had gained his early affections, and he had resolved to share with her the Swedish throne. But, constrained by time and circumstances, he made his attachment yield to the higher duties of a king, and heroism again took exclusive possession of a heart which was not destined by nature to confine itself within the limits of quiet domestic happiness.

Christian IV. of Denmark, who had ascended the throne before the birth of Gustavus, in an inroad upon Sweden, had gained some considerable advantages over the father of that hero. Gustavus Adolphus hastened to put an end to this destructive war, and by prudent sacrifices obtained a peace in order to turn his arms against the Czar of Muscovy. The questionable fame of a conqueror never tempted him to spend the blood of his subjects in unjust wars; but he never shrunk from a just one. His arms were successful against Russia, and Sweden was augmented by several important provinces on the east.

In the meantime, Sigismund of Poland retained against the son the same sentiments of hostility which the father had provoked, and left no artifice untried to shake the allegiance of his subjects, to cool the ardor of his friends, and to embitter his enemies. Neither the great qualities of his rival, nor the repeated proofs of devotion which Sweden gave to her loved monarch, could extinguish in this infatuated prince the foolish hope of regaining his lost throne. All Gustavus' overtures were haughtily rejected. Unwillingly was this really peaceful king involved in a tedious war with Poland, in which the whole of Livonia and Polish Prussia were successively conquered. Though constantly victorious, Gustavus Adolphus was always the first to hold out the hand of peace.

This contest between Sweden and Poland falls somewhere about the beginning of the Thirty Years' War in Germany, with which it is in some measure connected. It was enough that Sigismund, himself a Roman Catholic, was disputing the Swedish crown with a Protestant prince, to assure him the active support of Spain and Austria; while a double relationship to the Emperor gave him a still stronger claim to his protection. It was his reliance on this powerful assistance that chiefly encouraged the King of Poland to continue the war, which had hitherto turned out so unfavorably for him, and the courts of Madrid and Vienna failed not to encourage him by high-sounding promises. While Sigismund lost one place after another in Livonia, Courland, and Prussia, he saw his ally in Germany advancing from conquest after conquest to unlimited power. No wonder then if his aversion to peace kept pace with his losses. The vehemence with which he nourished his chimerical hopes blinded him to the artful policy of his confederates, who at his expense were keeping the Swedish hero employed, in order to overturn, without opposition, the liberties of Germany, and then to seize on the exhausted North as an easy conquest. One circumstance which had not been calculated on — the magnanimity of Gustavus — overthrew this deceitful policy. An eight years' war in Poland, so far from exhausting the power of Sweden, had only served to mature the military genius of Gustavus, to inure the Swedish army to warfare, and insensibly to perfect that system of tactics by which they were afterwards to perform such wonders in Germany.

After this necessary digression on the existing circumstances of Europe, I now resume the thread of my history.

Ferdinand had regained his dominions, but had not indemnified himself for the expenses of recovering them. A sum of forty millions of florins, which the confiscations in Bohemia and Moravia had produced, would have sufficed to reimburse both himself and his allies; but the Jesuits and his favorites soon squandered this sum, large as it was. Maximilian, Duke of Bavaria, to whose victorious arm, principally, the Emperor owed the recovery of his dominions; who, in the service of religion and the Emperor, had sacrificed his near relation, had the strongest claims on his gratitude; and, moreover, in a treaty which, before the war, the duke had concluded with the Emperor, he had expressly stipulated for the reimbursement of all expenses. Ferdinand felt the full weight of the obligation imposed upon him by this treaty and by these services, but he was not disposed to discharge it at his own cost. His purpose was to bestow a brilliant reward upon the duke, but without detriment to himself. How could this be done better than at the expense of the unfortunate prince who, by his revolt, had given the Emperor a right to punish him, and whose offences might be painted in colors strong enough to justify the most violent measures under the appearance of law. That, then, Maximilian may be rewarded, Frederick must be further persecuted and totally ruined; and to defray the expenses of the old war a new one must be commenced.

But a still stronger motive combined to enforce the first. Hitherto Ferdinand had been contending for existence alone; he had been fulfilling no other duty than that of self-defence. But now, when victory gave him freedom to act, a higher duty occurred to him, and he remembered the vow which he had made at Loretto and at Rome, to his generalissimo, the Holy Virgin, to extend her worship even at the risk of his crown and life. With this object the oppression of the Protestants was inseparably connected. More favorable circumstances for its accomplishment could not offer than those which presented themselves at the close of the Bohemian war. Neither the power, nor a pretext of right, were now wanting to enable him to place the Palatinate in the hands of the Catholics, and the importance of this change to the Catholic interests in Germany would be incalculable. Thus, in rewarding the Duke of Bavaria with the spoils of his relation, he at once gratified his meanest passions and fulfilled his most exalted duties; he crushed an enemy whom he hated, and spared his avarice a painful sacrifice, while he believed he was winning an heavenly crown.

In the Emperor's cabinet the ruin of Frederick had been resolved upon long before fortune had decided against him; but it was only after this event that they ventured to direct against him the thunders of arbitrary power. A decree of the Emperor, destitute of all the formalities required on such occasions by the laws of the Empire, pronounced the Elector, and three other princes who had borne arms for him at Silesia and Bohemia, as offenders against the imperial majesty, and disturbers of the public peace, under the ban of the empire, and deprived them of their titles and territories. The execution of this sentence against Frederick, namely, the seizure of his lands, was, in further contempt of law, committed to Spain as Sovereign of the circle of Burgundy, to the Duke of Bavaria, and the League. Had the Evangelic Union been worthy of the name it bore, and of the cause which it pretended to defend, insuperable obstacles might have prevented the execution of the sentence; but it was hopeless for a power which was far from a match even for the Spanish troops in the Lower Palatinate, to contend against the united strength of the Emperor, Bavaria, and the League. The sentence of proscription pronounced upon the Elector soon detached the free cities from the Union; and the princes quickly followed their example. Fortunate in preserving their own dominions, they abandoned the Elector, their former chief, to the Emperor's mercy, renounced the Union, and vowed never to revive it again.

But while thus ingloriously the German princes deserted the unfortunate Frederick, and while Bohemia, Silesia, and Moravia submitted to the Emperor, a single man, a soldier of fortune, whose only treasure was his sword, Ernest Count Mansfeld, dared, in the Bohemian town of Pilsen, to defy the whole power of Austria. Left without assistance after the battle of Prague by the Elector, to whose service he had devoted himself, and even uncertain whether Frederick would thank him for his perseverance, he alone for some time held out against the imperialists, till the garrison, mutinying for want of pay, sold the town to the Emperor. Undismayed by this reverse, he immediately commenced new levies in the Upper Palatinate, and enlisted the disbanded troops of the Union. A new army of twenty thousand men was soon assembled under his banners, the more formidable to the provinces which might be the object of its attack, because it must subsist by plunder. Uncertain where this swarm might light, the neighboring bishops trembled for their rich possessions, which offered a tempting prey to its ravages. But, pressed by the Duke of Bavaria, who now entered the Upper Palatinate, Mansfeld was compelled to retire. Eluding, by a successful stratagem, the Bavarian general, Tilly, who was in pursuit of him, he suddenly appeared in the Lower Palatinate, and there wreaked upon the bishoprics of the Rhine the severities he had designed for those of Franconia. While the imperial and Bavarian allies thus overran Bohemia, the Spanish general, Spinola, had penetrated with a numerous army from the Netherlands, into the Lower Palatinate, which, however, the pacification of Ulm permitted the Union to defend. But their measures were so badly concerted that one place after another fell into the hands of the Spaniards; and at last, when the Union broke up, the greater part of the country was in the possession of Spain. The Spanish general, Corduba, who commanded these troops after the recall of Spinola, hastily raised the siege of Frankenthal, when Mansfeld entered the Lower Palatinate. But instead of driving the Spaniards out of this province, he hastened across the Rhine to secure for his needy troops shelter and subsistence in Alsace. The open countries on which this swarm of maurauders threw themselves were converted into frightful deserts, and only by enormous contributions could the cities purchase an exemption from plunder. Reinforced by this expedition, Mansfeld again appeared on the Rhine to cover the Lower Palatinate.

So long as such an arm fought for him the cause of the Elector Frederick was not irretrievably lost. New prospects began to open, and misfortune raised up friends who had been silent during his prosperity. King James of England, who had looked on with indifference while his son-in-law lost the Bohemian crown, was aroused from his insensibility when the very existence of his daughter and grandson was at stake, and the victorious enemy ventured an attack upon the Electorate. Late enough, he at last opened his treasures, and hastened to afford supplies of money and troops, first to the Union, which at that time was defending the Lower Palatinate, and afterwards, when they retired, to Count Mansfeld. By his means his near relation, Christian, King of Denmark, was induced to afford his active support. At the same time, the approaching expiration of the truce between Spain and Holland deprived the Emperor of all the supplies which otherwise he might expect from the side of the Netherlands. More important still was the assistance which the Palatinate received from Transylvania and Hungary. The cessation of hostilities between Gabor and the Emperor was scarcely at an end, when this old and formidable enemy of Austria overran Hungary anew, and caused himself to be crowned king in Presburg. So rapid was his progress that, to protect Austria and Hungary, Boucquoi was obliged to evacuate

Bohemia. This brave general met his death at the siege of Neuhausel, as, shortly before, the no less valiant Dampierre had fallen before Presburg. Gabor's march into the Austrian territory was irresistible; the old Count Thurn, and several other distinguished Bohemians, had united their hatred and their strength with this irreconcilable enemy of Austria. A vigorous attack on the side of Germany, while Gabor pressed the Emperor on that of Hungary, might have retrieved the fortunes of Frederick; but, unfortunately, the Bohemians and Germans had always laid down their arms when Gabor took the field; and the latter was always exhausted at the very moment that the former began to recover their vigor.

Meanwhile Frederick had not delayed to join his protector, Mansfeld. In disguise he entered the Lower Palatinate, of which the possession was at that time disputed betwen Mansfeld and the Bavarian general, Tilly, the Upper Palatinate having been long conquered. A ray of hope shone upon him as, from the wreck of the Union, new friends came forward. A former member of the Union, George Frederick, Margrave of Baden, had for some time been engaged in assembling a military force, which soon amounted to a considerable army. Its destination was kept a secret till he suddenly took the field and joined Mansfeld. Before commencing the war, he resigned his Margravate to his son, in the hope of eluding, by this precaution, the Emperor's revenge, if his enterprise should be unsuccessful. His neighbor, the Duke of Wirtemberg, likewise began to augment his military force. The courage of the Palatine revived, and he labored assiduously to renew the Protestant Union. It was now time for Tilly to consult for his own safety, and he hastily summoned the Spanish troops, under Corduba, to his assistance. But while the enemy was uniting his strength, Mansfeld and the Margrave separated, and the latter was defeated by the Bavarian general near Wimpfen (1622).

To defend a king whom his nearest relation persecuted, and who was deserted even by his own father-in-law, there had come forward an adventurer without money, and whose very legitimacy was questioned. A sovereign had resigned possessions over which he reigned in peace to hazard the uncertain fortune of war in behalf of a stranger. And now another soldier of fortune, poor in territorial possessions, but rich in illustrious ancestry, undertook the defence of a cause which the former despaired of. Christian, Duke of Brunswick, administrator of Halberstadt, seemed to have learnt from Count Mansfeld the secret of keeping in the field an army of twenty thousand men without money. Impelled by youthful presumption, and influenced partly by the wish of establishing his reputation at the expense of the Roman Catholic priesthood, whom he cordially detested, and partly by a thirst for plunder, he assembled a considerable army in Lower Saxony, under the pretext of espousing the defence of Frederick, and of the liberties of Germany. "God's Friend, Priests' Foe," was the motto he chose for his coinage, which was struck out of church plate; and his conduct belied one-half at least of the device.

The progress of these banditti was, as usual, marked by the most frightful devastation. Enriched by the spoils of the chapters of Lower Saxony and Westphalia, they gathered strength to plunder the bishoprics upon the Upper Rhine. Driven from thence, both by friends and foes, the Administrator approached the town of Hoechst on the Maine, which he crossed after a murderous action with Tilly, who disputed with him the passage of the river. With the loss of half his army he reached the opposite bank, where he quickly collected his shattered troops, and formed a junction with Mansfeld. Pursued by Tilly, this united host threw itself again into Alsace, to repeat their former ravages. While the Elector Frederick followed, almost like a fugitive mendicant, this swarm of plunderers, which acknowledged him as its lord, and dignified itself with his name, his friends were busily endeavoring to effect a reconciliation between him and the Emperor. Ferdinand took care not to deprive them of all hope of seeing the Palatine restored to his dominion. Full of artifice and dissimulation, he pretended to be willing to enter into a negotiation, hoping thereby to cool their ardor in the field, and to prevent them from driving matters to extremity. James I., ever the dupe of Spanish cunning, contributed not a little, by his foolish intermeddling, to promote the Emperor's schemes. Ferdinand insisted that Frederick, if he would appeal to his clemency, should, first of all, lay down his arms, and James considered this demand extremely reasonable. At his instigation the Elector dismissed his only real defenders, Count Mansfeld and the Administrator, and in Holland awaited his own fate from the mercy of the Emperor.

Mansfeld and Duke Christian were now at a loss for some new name; the cause of the Elector had not set them in motion, so his dismissal could not disarm them. War was their object; it was all the same to them in whose cause or name it was waged. After some vain attempts on the part of Mansfeld to be received into the Emperor's service, both marched into Lorraine, where the excesses of their troops spread terror even to the heart of France. Here they long waited in vain for a master willing to purchase their services; till the Dutch, pressed by the Spanish General Spinola, offered to take them into pay. After a bloody fight at Fleurus with the Spaniards, who attempted to intercept them, they reached Holland, where their appearance compelled the Spanish general forthwith to raise the siege of Bergen-op-Zoom. But even Holland was soon weary of these dangerous guests, and availed herself of the first moment to get rid of their unwelcome assistance. Mansfeld allowed his troops to recruit themselves for new enterprises in the fertile province of East Friezeland. Duke Christian, passionately enamoured of the Electress Palatine, with whom he had become acquainted in Holland, and more disposed for war than ever, led back his army into Lower Saxony, bearing that princess's glove in his hat, and on his standards the motto, "All for God and Her." Neither of these adventurers had as yet run their career in this war.

All the imperial territories were now free from the enemy; the Union was dissolved; the Margrave of Baden, Duke Christian, and Mansfeld driven from the field, and the Palatinate overrun by the executive troops of the empire. Manheim and Heidelberg were in possession of Bavaria, and Frankenthal was shortly afterwards ceded to the Spaniards. The Palatine, in a distant corner of Holland, awaited the disgraceful permission to appease, by abject submission, the vengeance of the Emperor; and an Electoral Diet was at last summoned to decide his fate. That fate, however, had been long before decided at the court of the Emperor; though now, for the first time, were circumstances favorable for giving publicity to the decision. After his past measures towards the Elector, Ferdinand believed that a sincere reconciliation was not to be hoped for. The violent course he had once begun must be completed sucessfully, or recoil upon himself. What was already lost was irrecoverable; Frederick could never hope to regain his dominions; and a prince without territory and without subjects had little chance of retaining the electoral crown. Deeply as the Palatine had offended against the House of Austria, the services of the Duke of Bavaria were no less meritorious. If the House of Austria and the Roman Catholic church had much to dread from the resentment and religious rancor of the Palatine family, they had as much to hope from the gratitude and religious zeal of the Bavarian. Lastly, by the cession of the Palatine Electorate to Bavaria, the Roman Catholic religion would obtain a decisive preponderance in the Electoral College, and secure a permanent triumph in Germany.

The last circumstance was sufficient to win the support of the three Ecclesiastical Electors to this innovation; and among the Protestants the vote of Saxony was alone of any importance. But could John George be expected to dispute with the Emperor a right, without which he would expose to question his own title to the electoral dignity? To a prince whom descent, dignity, and political power placed at the head of the Protestant church in Germany, nothing, it is true, ought to be more sacred than the defence of the rights of that church against all the encroachments of the Roman Catholics. But the question here was not whether the interests of the Protestants were to be supported against the Roman Catholics, but which of two religions equally detested, the Calvinistic and the Popish, was to triumph over the other; to which of the two enemies, equally dangerous, the Palatinate was to be assigned; and in this clashing of opposite duties, it was natural that private hate and private gain should determine the event. The born protector of the liberties of Germany, and of the Protestant religion, encouraged the Emperor to dispose of the Palatinate by his imperial prerogative; and to apprehend no resistance on the part of Saxony to his measures on the mere ground of form. If the Elector was afterwards disposed to retract this consent, Ferdinand himself, by driving the Evangelical preachers from Bohemia, was the cause of this change of opinion; and, in the eyes of the Elector, the transference of the Palatine Electorate to Bavaria ceased to be illegal as soon as Ferdinand was prevailed upon to cede Lusatia to Saxony, in consideration of six millions of dollars, as the expenses of the war.

Thus, in defiance of all Protestant Germany, and in mockery of the fundamental laws of the empire, which, at his election, he had sworn to maintain, Ferdinand at Ratisbon solemnly invested the Duke of Bavaria with the Palatinate, without prejudice, as the form ran, to the rights which the relations or descendants of Frederick might afterwards establish. That unfortunate prince thus saw himself irrevocably driven from his possessions, without having been even heard before the tribunal which condemned him — a privilege which the law allows to the meanest subject, and even to the most atrocious criminal.

This violent step at last opened the eyes of the King of England; and as the negotiations for the marriage of his son with the Infanta of Spain were now broken off, James began seriously to espouse the cause of his son-in-law. A change in the French ministry had placed Cardinal Richelieu at the head of affairs, and this fallen kingdom soon began to feel that a great mind was at the helm of state. The attempts of the Spanish Viceroy in Milan to gain possession of the Valtelline, and thus to form a junction with the Austrian hereditary dominions, revived the olden dread of this power, and with it the policy of Henry the Great. The marriage of the Prince of Wales with Henrietta of France established a close union between the two crowns; and to this alliance,

Holland, Denmark, and some of the Italian states presently acceded. Its object was to expel, by force of arms, Spain from the Valtelline, and to compel Austria to reinstate Frederick; but only the first of these designs was prosecuted with vigor. James I. died, and Charles I., involved in disputes with his Parliament, could not bestow attention on the affairs of Germany. Savoy and Venice withheld their assistance; and the French minister thought it necessary to subdue the Huguenots at home before he supported the German Protestants against the Emperor. Great as were the hopes which had been formed from this alliance, they were yet equalled by the disappointment of the event.

Mansfeld, deprived of all support, remained inactive on the Lower Rhine; and Duke Christian of Brunswick, after an unsuccessful campaign, was a second time driven out of Germany. A fresh irruption of Bethlen Gabor into Moravia, frustrated by the want of support from the Germans, terminated, like all the rest, in a formal peace with the Emperor. The Union was no more; no Protestant prince was in arms; and on the frontiers of Lower Germany, the Bavarian General Tilly, at the head of a victorious army, encamped in the Protestant territory. The movements of the Duke of Brunswick had drawn him into this quarter, and even into the circle of Lower Saxony, when he made himself master of the Administrator's magazines at Lippstadt. The necessity of observing this enemy, and preventing him from new inroads, was the pretext assigned for continuing Tilly's stay in the country. But, in truth, both Mansfeld and Duke Christian had, from want of money, disbanded their armies, and Count Tilly had no enemy to dread. Why, then, still burden the country with his presence?

It is difficult, amidst the uproar of contending parties, to distinguish the voice of truth; but certainly it was matter for alarm that the League did not lay down its arms. The premature rejoicings of the Roman Catholics, too, were calculated to increase apprehension. The Emperor and the League stood armed and victorious in Germany without a power to oppose them, should they venture to attack the Protestant states and to annul the religious treaty. Had Ferdinand been in reality far from disposed to abuse his conquests, still the defenceless position of the Protestants was most likely to suggest the temptation. Obsolete conventions could not bind a prince who thought that he owed all to religion, and believed that a religious creed would sanctify any deed, however violent. Upper Germany was already overpowered. Lower Germany alone could check his despotic authority. Here the Protestants still predominated; the church had been forcibly deprived of most of its endowments; and the present appeared a favorable moment for recovering these lost possessions. A great part of the strength of the Lower German princes consisted in these Chapters, and the plea of restoring its own to the church afforded an excellent pretext for weakening these princes.

Unpardonable would have been their negligence had they remained inactive in this danger. The remembrance of the ravages which Tilly's army had committed in Lower Saxony was too recent not to arouse the Estates to measures of defence. With all haste the circle of Lower Saxony began to arm itself. Extraordinary contributions were levied, troops collected, and magazines filled. Negotiations for subsidies were set on foot with Venice, Holland, and England. They deliberated, too, what power should be placed at the head of the confederacy. The kings of the Sound and the Baltic, the natural allies of this circle, would not see with indifference the Emperor treating it as a conqueror, and establishing himself as their neighbor on the shores of the North Sea. The twofold interests of religion and policy urged them to put a stop to his progress in Lower Germany. Christian IV., of Denmark, as Duke of Holstein, was himself a prince of this circle, and by considerations equally powerful Gustavus Adolphus of Sweden was induced to join the confederacy.

These two kings vied with each other for the honor of defending Lower Saxony, and of opposing the formidable power of Austria. Each offered to raise a well-disciplined army, and to lead it in person. His victorious campaigns against Moscow and Poland gave weight to the promises of the King of Sweden. The shores of the Baltic were full of the name of Gustavus. But the fame of his rival excited the envy of the Danish monarch; and the more success he promised himself in this campaign the less disposed was he to show any favor to his envied neighbor. Both laid their conditions and plans before the English ministry, and Christian IV. finally succeeded in outbidding his rival. Gustavus Adolphus, for his own security, had demanded the cession of some places of strength in Germany, where he himself had no territories to afford, in case of need, a place of refuge for his troops. Christian IV. possessed Holstein and Jutland, through which, in the event of a defeat, he could always secure a retreat.

Eager to get the start of his competitor, the King of Denmark hastened to take the field. Appointed generalissimo of the circle of Lower Saxony, he soon had an army of sixty thousand men in motion; the administrator of Magdeburg, and the Dukes of Brunswick and Mecklenburgh entered into an alliance with him. Encouraged by the hope of assistance from England, and the possession of so large a force, he flattered himself he should be able to terminate the war in a single campaign.

At Vienna it was officially notified that the only object of these preparations was the protection of the circle, and the maintenance of the peace. But the negotiations with Holland, England, and even France, the extraordinary exertions of the circle, and the raising of so formidable an army, seemed to have something more in view than defensive operations, and to contemplate nothing less than the complete restoration of the Elector Palatine, and the humiliation of the dreaded power of Austria.

After negotiations, exhortations, commands, and threats had in vain been employed by the Emperor in order to induce the King of Denmark and the circle of Lower Saxony to lay down their arms, hostilities commenced, and Lower Germany became the theatre of war. Count Tilly, marching along the left bank of the Weser, made himself master of all the passes as far as Minden. After an unsuccessful attack on Nieuburg, he crossed the river and overran the principality of Calemberg, in which he quartered his troops. The king conducted his operations on the right bank of the river, and spread his forces over the territories of Brunswick, but having weakened his main body by too powerful detachments, he could not engage in any enterprise of importance. Aware of his opponent's superiority, he avoided a decisive action as anxiously as the general of the League sought it.

With the exception of the troops from the Spanish Netherlands, which had poured into the Lower Palatinate, the Emperor had hitherto made use only of the arms of Bavaria and the League in Germany. Maximilian conducted the war as executor of the ban of the empire, and Tilly, who commanded the army of execution, was in the Bavarian service. The Emperor owed superiority in the field to Bavaria and the League, and his fortunes were in their hands. This dependence on their good-will but ill accorded with the grand schemes which the brilliant commencement of the war had led the imperial cabinet to form.

However active the League had shown itself in the Emperior's defence, while thereby it secured its own welfare, it could not be expected that it would enter as readily into his views of conquest. Or, if they still continued to lend their armies for that purpose, is was too much to be feared that they would share with the Emperor nothing but general odium, while they appropriated to themselves all advantages. A strong army under his own orders could alone free him from this debasing dependence upon Bavaria, and restore to him his former pre-eminence in Germany. But the war had already exhausted the imperial dominions, and they were unequal to the expense of such an armament. In these circumstances nothing could be more welcome to the Emperor than the proposal with which one of his officers surprised him.

This was Count Wallenstein, an experienced officer, and the richest nobleman in Bohemia. From his earliest youth he had been in the service of the House of Austria, and several campaigns against the Turks, Venetians, Bohemians, Hungarians, and Transylvanians had established his reputation. He was present as colonel at the battle of Prague, and afterwards, as major-general, had defeated a Hungarian force in Moravia. The Emperor's gratitude was equal to his services, and a large share of the confiscated estates of the Bohemian insurgents was their reward. Possessed of immense property, excited by ambitious views, confident in his own good fortune, and still more encouraged by the existing state of circumstances, he offered, at his own expense and that of his friends, to raise and clothe an army for the Emperor, and even undertook the cost of maintaining it, if he were allowed to augment it to fifty thousand men. The project was universally ridiculed as the chimerical offspring of a visionary brain; but the offer was highly valuable, if its promises should be but partially fulfilled. Certain circles in Bohemia were assigned to him as depôts, with authority to appoint his own officers. In a few months he had twenty thousand men under arms, with which, quitting the Austrian territories, he soon afterwards appeared on the frontiers of Lower Saxony with thirty thousand. The Emperor had lent this armament nothing but his name. The reputation of the general, the prospect of rapid promotion, and the hope of plunder, attracted to his standard adventurers from all quarters of Germany; and even sovereign princes, stimulated by the desire of glory or of gain, offered to raise regiments for the service of Austria.

Now, therefore, for the first time in this war, an imperial army appeared in Germany; an event which, if it was menacing to the Protestants, was scarcely more acceptable to the Catholics. Wallenstein had orders to unite his army with the troops of the League, and in conjunction with the Bavarian general to attack the King of Denmark. But, long jealous of Tilly's fame, he showed no disposition to share with him the laurels of the campaign or in the splendors of his rival's achievements to dim the lustre of his own. His plan of operations was to support the latter, but to act entirely independently of him. As he had not resources, like Tilly, for supplying the wants of his army, he was obliged to march his troops into fertile countries which had not as yet suffered from war. Disobeying, therefore, the order to form a junction with the general of the League, he marched into the territories of Halberstadt and Magdeburg, and at Dessau made himself master of the Elbe. All the lands on either bank of this river were at his command, and from them he could either attack the King of Denmark in the rear, or, if prudent, enter the territories of that prince.

Christian IV. was fully aware of the danger of his situation between two such powerful armies. He had already been joined by the administrator of Halberstadt, who had lately returned from Holland; he now also acknowledged Mansfeld, whom previously he had refused to recognize, and supported him to the best of his ability. Mansfeld amply requited this service. He alone kept at bay the army of Wallenstein upon the Elbe, and prevented its junction with that of Tilly, and a combined attack on the King of Denmark. Notwithstanding the enemy's superiority, this intrepid general even approached the bridge of Dessau and ventured to entrench himself in the presence of the imperial lines. But attacked in the rear by the whole force of the Imperialists, he was obliged to yield to superior numbers, and to abandon his post with the loss of three thousand killed. After this defeat Mansfeld withdrew into Brandenburg, where he soon recruited and reinforced his army, and suddenly turned into Silesia, with the view of marching from thence into Hungary, and, in conjunction with Bethlen Gabor, carrying the war into the heart of Austria. As the Austrian dominions in that quarter were entirely defenceless, Wallenstein received immediate orders to leave the King of Denmark, and if possible to intercept Mansfeld's progress through Silesia.

The diversion which this movement of Mansfeld had made in the plans of Wallenstein enabled the king to detach a part of his force into Westphalia, to seize the bishoprics of Munster and Osnaburg. To check this movement, Tilly suddenly moved from the Weser; but the operations of Duke Christian, who threatened the territories of the League with an inroad in the direction of Hesse, and to remove thither the seat of war, recalled him as rapidly from Westphalia. In order to keep open his communications with these provinces, and to prevent the junction of the enemy with the Landgrave of Hesse, Tilly hastily seized all the tenable posts on the Werha and Fulda, and took up a strong position in Minden, at the foot of the Hessian Mountains, and at the confluence of these rivers with the Weser. He soon made himself master of Göttingen, the key of Brunswick and Hesse, and was meditating a similar attack upon Nordheim, when the king advanced upon him with his whole army. After throwing into this place the necessary supplies for a long siege, the latter attempted to open a new passage through Eichsfield and Thuringia into the territories of the League. He had already reached Dunderstadt when Tilly, by forced marches, came up with him. As the army of Tilly, which had been reinforced by some of Wallenstein's regiments, was superior in numbers to his own, the king, in order to avoid a battle, retreated towards Brunswick. But Tilly incessantly harassed his retreat, and after three days' skirmishing he was at length obliged to await the enemy near the village of Lutter in Barenberg. The Danes began the attack with great bravery, and thrice did their intrepid monarch lead them in person against the enemy; but at length the superior numbers and discipline of the Imperialists prevailed, and the general of the League obtained a complete victory. The Danes lost sixty standards and their whole artillery, baggage, and ammunition. Several officers of distinction and about four thousand men were killed in the field of battle, and several companies of foot in the flight, who had thrown themselves into the town-house of Lutter, laid down their arms and surrendered to the conqueror.

The king fled with his cavalry and soon collected the wreck of his army which had survived this serious defeat. Tilly pursued his victory, made himself master of the Weser and Brunswick, and forced the king to retire into Bremen. Rendered more cautious by defeat, the latter now stood upon the defensive, and determined at all events to prevent the enemy from crossing the Elbe. But while he threw garrisons into every tenable place, he reduced his own diminished army to inactivity;

and one after another his scattered troops were either defeated or dispersed. The forces of the League in command of the Weser spread themselves along the Elbe and Havel, and everywhere drove the Danes before them. Tilly, himself crossing the Elbe, penetrated with his victorious army into Brandenburg, while Wallenstein entered Holstein to remove the seat of war to the king's own dominions.

This general had just returned from Hungary, whither he had pursued Mansfeld, without being able to obstruct his march or prevent his junction with Bethlen Gabor. Constantly persecuted by fortune, but always superior to his fate, Mansfeld had made his way against countless difficulties through Silesia and Hungary to Transylvania, where, after all, he was not very welcome. Relying upon the assistance of England, and a powerful diversion in Lower Saxony, Gabor had again broken the truce with the Emperor. But in place of the expected diversion in his favor, Mansfeld had drawn upon himself the whole strength of Wallenstein, and instead of bringing, required pecuniary assistance. The want of concert in the Protestant counsels cooled Gabor's ardor; and he hastened, as usual, to avert the coming storm by a speedy peace. Firmly determined, however, to break it, with the first ray of hope, he directed Mansfeld in the meantime to apply for assistance to Venice.

Cut off from Germany, and unable to support the weak remnant of his troops in Hungary, Mansfeld sold his artillery and baggage train and disbanded his soldiers. With a few followers he proceeded through Bosnia and Dalmatia towards Venice. New schemes swelled his bosom; but his career was ended. Fate, which had so restlessly sported with him throughout, now prepared for him a peaceful grave in Dalmatia. Death overtook him in the vicinity of Zara in 1626; and a short time before him died the faithful companion of his fortunes, Christian, Duke of Brunswick — two men worthy of immortality had they but been as superior to their times as they were to their adversities.

The King of Denmark, with his whole army, was unable to cope with Tilly alone; much less, therefore, with a shattered force could he hold his ground against the two imperial generals. The Danes retired from all their posts on the Weser, the Elbe, and the Havel, and the army of Wallenstein poured like a torrent into Brandenburg, Mecklenburgh, Holstein, and Sleswick. That general, too proud to act in conjunction with another, had despatched Tilly across the Elbe to watch, as he gave out, the motions of the Dutch in that quarter, but in reality that he might terminate the war against the king, and reap for himself the fruits of Tilly's conquests. Christian had now lost all his fortresses in the German States, with the exception of Gluckstadt; his armies were defeated or dispersed; no assistance came from Germany; from England little consolation; while his confederates in Lower Saxony were at the mercy of the conqueror. The Landgrave of Hesse Cassel had been forced by Tilly, soon after the battle of Lutter, to renounce the Danish alliance. Wallenstein's formidable appearance before Berlin reduced the Elector of Brandenburg to submission, and compelled him to recognize as legitimate Maximilian's title to the Palatine Electorate. The greater part of Mecklenburgh was now overrun by imperial troops, and both dukes, as adherents of the King of Denmark, placed under the ban of the empire and driven from their dominions. The defence of the German liberties against illegal encroachments was punished as a crime deserving the loss of all dignities and territories; and yet this was but the prelude to the still more crying enormities which shortly followed.

The secret how Wallenstein had purposed to fulfil his extravagant designs was now manifest. He had learned the lesson from Count Mansfeld; but the scholar surpassed his master. On the principle that war must support war, Mansfeld and the Duke of Brunswick had subsisted their troops by contributions levied indiscriminately on friend and enemy; but this predatory life was attended with all the inconvenience and insecurity which accompany robbery. Like a fugitive banditti, they were obliged to steal through exasperated and vigilant enemies; to roam from one end of Germany to another; to watch their opportunity with anxiety, and to abandon the most fertile territories whenever they were defended by a superior army. If Mansfeld and Duke Christian had done such great things in the face of these difficulties, what might not be expected if the obstacles were removed; when the army raised was numerous enough to overawe in itself the most powerful states of the empire; when the name of the Emperor insured impunity to every outrage; and when, under the highest authority, and at the head of an overwhelming force, the same system of warfare was pursued which these two adventurers had adopted at their own risk, and with only an untrained multitude?

Wallenstein had all this in view when he made his bold offer to the Emperor, which now seemed extravagant to no one. The more his army was augmented the less cause was there to fear for its subsistence, because it could irresistibly bear down on the refractory states; the more violent its outrages the more probable was impunity. Towards hostile states it had the plea of right; towards the favorably disposed it could allege necessity. The inequality, too, with which it dealt out its oppressions prevented any dangerous union among the states, while the exhaustion of their territories deprived them of the power of vengeance. Thus the whole of Germany became a kind of magazine for the imperial army, and the Emperor was enabled to deal with the other states as absolutely as with his own hereditary dominions. Universal was the clamor for redress before the imperial throne; but there was nothing to fear from the revenge of the injured princes so long as they appealed for justice. The general discontent was directed equally against the Emperor, who had lent his name to these barbarities, and the general who exceeded his power and openly abused the authority of his master. They applied to the Emperor for protection against the outrages of his generals, but Wallenstein had no sooner felt himself absolute in the army than he threw off his obedience to his sovereign.

The exhaustion of the enemy made a speedy peace probable; yet Wallenstein continued to augment the imperial armies until they were at least one hundred thousand men strong. Numberless commissions to colonelcies and inferior commands, the regal pomp of the commander-in-chief, immoderate largesses to his favorites (for he never gave less than a thousand florins), enormous sums lavished in corrupting the court at Vienna — all this had been effected without burdening the Emperor. These immense sums were raised by the contributions levied from the lower German provinces, where no distinction was made between friend and foe; and the territories of all princes were subjected to the same system of marching and quartering, of extortion and outrage. If credit is to be given to an extravagant contemporary statement, Wallenstein, during his seven years command, had exacted not less than sixty thousand millions of dollars from one-half of Germany. The greater his extortions the greater the rewards of his soldiers, and the greater the concourse to his standard, for the world always follows fortune. His armies flourished while all the states through which they passed withered. What cared he for the detestation of the people and the complaints of princes? His army adored him, and the very enormity of his guilt enabled him to bid defiance to its consequences.

It would be unjust to Ferdinand were we to lay all these irregularities to his charge. Had he foreseen that he was abandoning the German states to the mercy of his officer, he would have been sensible how dangerous to himself so absolute a general would prove. The closer the connection became between the army and the leader from whom flowed favor and fortune, the more the ties which united both to the Emperor were relaxed. Everything, it is true, was done in the name of the latter; but Wallenstein only availed himself of the supreme majesty of the Emperor to crush the authority of other states. His object was to depress the princes of the empire, to destroy all gradation of rank between them and the Emperor, and to elevate the power of the latter above all competition. If the Emperor was absolute in Germany who then would be equal to the man entrusted with the execution of his will? The height to which Wallenstein had raised the imperial authority astonished even the Emperor himself; but as the greatness of the master was entirely the work of the servant, the creation of Wallenstein would necessarily sink again into nothing upon the withdrawal of its creative hand. Not without an object, therefore, did Wallenstein labor to poison the minds of the German princes against the Emperor. The more violent their hatred of Ferdinand, the more indispensable to the Emperor would become the man who alone could render their ill-will powerless. His design unquestionably was that his sovereign should stand in fear of no one in all Germany besides himself, the source and engine of this despotic power.

As a step towards this end, Wallenstein now demanded the cession of Mecklenburgh, to be held in pledge till the repayment of his advances for the war. Ferdinand had already created him Duke of Friedland, apparently with the view of exalting his own general over Bavaria; but an ordinary recompense would not satisfy Wallenstein's ambition. In vain was this new demand, which could be granted only at the expense of two princes of the empire, actively resisted in the Imperial Council. In vain did the Spaniards, who had long been offended by his pride, oppose his elevation. The powerful support which Wallenstein had purchased from the imperial councillors prevailed, and Ferdinand was determined, at whatever cost, to secure the devotion of so indispensable a minister. For a slight offence one of the oldest German houses was expelled from their hereditary dominions, that a creature of the Emperor might be enriched by their spoils (1628).

Wallenstein now began to assume the title of generalissimo of the Emperor by sea and land. Wismar was taken, and a firm footing gained on the Baltic. Ships were required from Poland and the Hans towns to carry the war to the other side of the Baltic; to pursue the Danes into the heart of their own country, and to compel them to a peace which might prepare the way to more important conquests. The communication between the Lower German States and the Northern powers would be broken could the Emperor place himself between them, and encompass Germany from the Adriatic to the

Sound (the intervening kingdom of Poland being already dependent on him) with an unbroken line of territory. If such was the Emperor's plan, Wallenstein had a peculiar interest in its execution. These possessions on the Baltic should, he intended, form the first foundation of a power which had long been the object of his ambition, and which should enable him to throw off his dependence on the Emperor.

To effect this object it was of extreme importance to gain possession of Stralsund, a town on the Baltic. Its excellent harbor, and the short passage from it to the Swedish and Danish coasts, peculiarly fitted it for a naval station in a war with these powers. This town, the sixth of the Hanseatic League, enjoyed great privileges under the Duke of Pomerania, and, totally independent of Denmark, had taken no share in the war. But neither its neutrality nor its privileges could protect it against the encroachments of Wallenstein when he had once cast a longing look upon it.

The request he made, that Stralsund should receive an imperial garrison, had been firmly and honorably rejected by the magistracy, who also refused his cunningly demanded permission to march his troops through the town. Wallenstein therefore now proposed to besiege it.

The independence of Stralsund, as securing the free navigation of the Baltic, was equally important to the two Northern kings. A common danger overcame at last the private jealousies which had long divided these princes. In a treaty concluded at Copenhagen in 1628 they bound themselves to assist Stralsund with their combined force, and to oppose in common every foreign power which should appear in the Baltic with hostile views. Christian IV. also threw a sufficient garrison into Stralsund, and by his personal presence animated the courage of the citizens. Some ships-of-war which Sigismund, King of Poland, had sent to the assistance of the imperial general were sunk by the Danish fleet; and as Lubeck refused him the use of its shipping, this imperial generalissimo of the sea had not even ships enough to blockade this single harbor.

Nothing could appear more adventurous than to attempt the conquest of a strongly fortified seaport without first blockading its harbor. Wallenstein, however, who as yet had never experienced a check, wished to conquer nature itself, and to perform impossibilities. Stralsund, open to the sea, continued to be supplied with provisions and reinforcements; yet Wallenstein maintained his blockade on the land side, and endeavored, by boasting menaces, to supply his want of real strength. "I will take this town," said he, "though it were fastened by a chain to the heavens." The Emperor himself, who might have cause to regret an enterprise which promised no very glorious result, joyfully availed himself of the apparent submission and acceptable propositions of the inhabitants, to order the general to retire from the town. Wallenstein despised the command, and continued to harass the besieged by incessant assaults. As the Danish garrison, already much reduced, was unequal to the fatigue of this prolonged defence, and the king was unable to detach any further troops to their support, Stralsund, with Christian's consent, threw itself under the protection of the King of Sweden. The Danish commander left the town to make way for a Swedish governor, who gloriously defended it. Here Wallenstein's good fortune forsook him; and, for the first time, his pride experienced the humiliation of relinquishing his prey, after the loss of many months and of twelve thousand men. The necessity to which he reduced the town of applying for protection to Sweden laid the foundation of a close alliance between Gustavus Adolphus and Stralsund, which greatly facilitated the entrance of the Swedes into Germany.

Hitherto invariable success had attended the arms of the Emperor and the League, and Christian IV., defeated in Germany, had sought refuge in his own island; but the Baltic checked the further progress of the conquerors. The want of ships not only stopped the pursuit of the king, but endangered their previous acquisitions. The union of the two northern monarchs was not to be dreaded, because, so long as it lasted, it effectually prevented the Emperor and his general from acquiring a footing on the Baltic, or effecting a landing in Sweden. But if they could succeed in dissolving this union, and especially in securing the friendship of the Danish king, they might hope to overpower the insulated force of Sweden. The dread of the interference of foreign powers, the insubordination of the Protestants in his own states, and still more the storm which was gradually darkening along the whole of Protestant Germany, inclined the Emperor to peace, which his general, from opposite motives, was equally desirous to effect. Far from wishing for a state of things which would reduce him from the meridian of greatness and glory to the obscurity of private life, he only wished to change the theatre of war, and by a partial peace to prolong the general confusion. The friendship of Denmark, whose neighbor he had become as Duke of Mecklenburgh, was most important for the success of his ambitious views; and he resolved, even at the sacrifice of his sovereign's interests, to secure its alliance.

By the treaty of Copenhagen, Christian IV., had expressly engaged not to conclude a separate peace with the Emperor without the consent of Sweden. Notwithstanding, Wallenstein's proposition was readily received by him. In a conference at Lubeck in 1629, from which Wallenstein, with studied contempt, excluded the Swedish ambassadors who came to intercede for Mecklenburgh, all the conquests taken by the imperialists were restored to the Danes. The conditions imposed upon the king were, that he should interfere no farther with the affairs of Germany than was called for by his character of Duke of Holstein; that he should on no pretext harass the Chapters of Lower Germany, and should leave the Dukes of Mecklenbargh to their fate. By Christian himself had these princes been involved in the war with the Emperor; he now sacrificed them to gain the favor of the usurper of their territories. Among the motives which had engaged him in a war with the Emperor, not the least was the restoration of his relation, the Elector Palatine — yet the name of that unfortunate prince was not even mentioned in the treaty; while in one of its articles the legitimacy of the Bavarian election was expressly recognized. Thus meanly and ingloriously did Christian IV. retire from the field.

Ferdinand had it now in his power, for the second time, to secure the tranquillity of Germany; and it depended solely on his will whether the treaty with Denmark should or should not be the basis of a general peace. From every quarter arose the cry of the unfortunate, petitioning for an end of their sufferings; the cruelties of his soldiers, and the rapacity of his generals, had exceeded all bounds. Germany, laid waste by the desolating bands of Mansfeld and the Duke of Brunswick, and by the still more terrible hordes of Tilly and Wallenstein, lay exhausted, bleeding, wasted, and sighing for repose. An anxious desire for peace was felt by all conditions, and by the Emperor himself, involved as he was in a war with France in Upper Italy, exhausted by his past warfare in Germany, and apprehensive of the day of reckoning which was approaching. But, unfortunately, the conditions on which alone the two religious parties were willing respectively to sheath the sword were irreconcilable. The Roman Catholics wished to terminate the war to their own advantage; the Protestants advanced equal pretensions. The Emperor, instead of uniting both parties by a prudent moderation, sided with one; and thus Germany was again plunged in the horrors of a bloody war.

From the very close of the Bohemian troubles, Ferdinand had carried on a counter reformation in his hereditary dominions, in which, however, from regard to some of the Protestant Estates, he proceeded, at first, with moderation. But the victories of his generals in Lower Germany encouraged him to throw off all reserve. Accordingly he had it intimated to all the Protestants in these dominions that they must either abandon their religion or their native country, — a bitter and dreadful alternative, which excited the most violent commotions among his Austrian subjects. In the Palatinate, immediately after the expulsion of Frederick, the Protestant religion had been suppressed, and its professors expelled from the University of Heidelberg.

All this was but the prelude to greater changes. In

the Electoral Congress held at Mühlhausen, the Roman
Catholics had demanded of the Emperor that all the
archbishoprics, bishoprics, mediate and immediate, abbacies and monasteries, which, since the Diet of Augsburg,
had been secularized by the Protestants, should be
restored to the church, in order to indemnify them for
the losses and sufferings in the war. To a Roman
Catholic prince so zealous as Ferdinand was, such a hint
was not likely to be neglected; but he still thought it
would be premature to arouse the whole Protestants of
Germany by so decisive a step. Not a single Protestant
prince but would be deprived, by this revocation of the
religious foundations, of a part of his lands; for where
these revenues had not actually been diverted to secular
purposes they had been made over to the Protestant church.
To this source many princes owed the chief part of their
revenues and importance. All, without exception, would
be irritated by this demand for restoration. The religious
treaty did not expressly deny their right to these chapters,
although it did not allow it. But a possession which had
now been held for nearly a century, the silence of four
preceding emperors, and the law of equity, which gave
them an equal right with the Roman Catholics to the
foundations of their common ancestors, might be strongly
pleaded by them as a valid title. Besides the actual loss
of power and authority, which the surrender of these
foundations would occasion, besides the inevitable confusion which would necessarily attend it, one important
disadvantage to which it would lead, was, that the
restoration of the Roman Catholic bishops would increase
the strength of that party in the Diet by so many additional votes. Such grievous sacrifices likely to fall on
the Protestants made the Emperor apprehensive of a
formidable opposition; and until the military ardor should
have cooled in Germany, he had no wish to provoke a
party formidable by its union, and which in the Elector
of Saxony had a powerful leader. He resolved, therefore,
to try the experiment at first on a small scale, in order to
ascertain how it was likely to succeed on a larger one.
Accordingly, some of the free cities in Upper Germany,
and the Duke of Wirtemberg, received orders to sur-

render to the Roman Catholics several of the confiscated chapters.

The state of affairs in Saxony enabled the Emperor to make some bolder experiments in that quarter. In the bishoprics of Magdeburg and Halberstadt the Protestant canons had not hesitated to elect bishops of their own religion. Both bishoprics, with the exception of the town of Magdeburg itself, were overrun by the troops of Wallenstein. It happened, moreover, that by the death of the Administrator, Duke Christian of Brunswick, Halberstadt was vacant, as was also the Archbishopric of Magdeburg by the deposition of Christian William, a prince of the House of Brandenburg. Ferdinand took advantage of the circumstance to restore the see of Halberstadt to a Roman Catholic bishop, and a prince of his own house. To avoid a similar coercion, the Chapter of Magdeburg hastened to elect a son of the Elector of Saxony as archbishop. But the pope, who with his arrogated authority interfered in this matter, conferred the Archbishopric of Magdeburg also on the Austrian prince. Thus, with all his pious zeal for religion, Ferdinand never lost sight of the interests of his family.

At length, when the peace of Lubeck had delivered the Emperor from all apprehensions on the side of Denmark, and the German Protestants seemed entirely powerless, the League becoming louder and more urgent in its demands, Ferdinand, in 1629, signed the Edict of Restitution (so famous by its disastrous consequences), which he had previously laid before the four Roman Catholic electors for their approbation. In the preamble, he claimed the prerogative, in right of his imperial authority, to interpret the meaning of the religious treaty, the ambiguities of which had already caused so many disputes, and to decide as supreme arbiter and judge between the contending parties. This prerogative he founded upon the practice of his ancestors, and its previous recognition even by Protestant states. Saxony had actually acknowledged this right of the Emperor; and it now became evident how deeply this court had injured the Protestant cause by its dependence on the House of Austria. But though the meaning of the religious treaty was really ambiguous, as a century of religious disputes sufficiently proved, yet for the Emperor, who must be either a Protestant or a Roman Catholic, and therefore an interested party, to assume the right of deciding between the disputants, was clearly a violation of an essential article of the pacification. He could not be judge in his own cause without reducing the liberties of the empire to an empty sound.

And now, in virtue of this usurpation, Ferdinand decided, "That every secularization of a religious foundation, mediate or immediate, by the Protestants, subsequent to the date of the treaty, was contrary to its spirit, and must be revoked as a breach of it." He further decided, "That, by the religious peace, Catholic proprietors of estates were no further bound to their Protestant subjects than to allow them full liberty to quit their territories." In obedience to this decision, all unlawful possessors of benefices — the Protestant states in short without exception — were ordered, under pain of the ban of the empire, immediately to surrender their usurped possessions to the imperial commissioners.

This sentence applied to no less than two archbishoprics and twelve bishoprics, besides innumerable abbacies. The edict came like a thunderbolt on the whole of Protestant Germany; dreadful even in its immediate consequences; but yet more so from the further calamities it seemed to threaten. The Protestants were now convinced that the suppression of their religion had been resolved on by the Emperor and the League, and that the overthrow of German liberty would soon follow. Their remonstrances were unheeded; the commissioners were named, and an army assembled to enforce obedience. The edict was first put in force in Augsburg, where the treaty was concluded; the city was again placed under the government of its bishop, and six Protestant churches in the town were closed. The Duke of Wirtemberg was, in like manner, compelled to surrender his abbacies. These severe measures, though they alarmed the Protestant states, were yet insufficient to rouse them to an active resistance. Their fear of the Emperor was too strong, and many were disposed to quiet submission. The hope of attaining their end by gentle measures induced the Roman Catholics likewise to delay for a year the execution of the edict, and this saved the Protestants; before the end of that period the success of Swedish arms had totally changed the state of affairs.

In a Diet held at Ratisbon, at which Ferdinand was present in person (in 1630), the necessity of taking some measures for the immediate restoration of a general peace to Germany, and for the removal of all grievances, was debated. The complaints of the Roman Catholics were scarcely less numerous than those of the Protestants, although Ferdinand had flattered himself that by the Edict of Restitution he had secured the members of the League, and its leader by the gift of the electoral dignity, and the cession of great part of the Palatinate. But the good understanding between the Emperor and the princes of the League had rapidly declined since the employment of Wallenstein. Accustomed to give law to Germany, and even to sway the Emperor's own destiny, the haughty Elector of Bavaria now at once saw himself supplanted by the imperial general, and with that of the League, his own importance completely undermined. Another had now stepped in to reap the fruits of his victories, and to bury his past services in oblivion. Wallenstein's imperious character, whose dearest triumph was in degrading the authority of the princes, and giving an odious latitude to that of the Emperor, tended not a little to augment the irritation of the Elector. Discontented with the Emperor, and distrustful of his intentions, he had entered into an alliance with France, which the other members of the League were suspected of favoring. A fear of the Emperor's plans of aggrandizement, and discontent with existing evils, had extinguished among them all feelings of gratitude. Wallenstein's exactions had become altogether intolerable. Brandenburg estimated its losses at twenty, Pomerania at ten, Hesse Cassel at seven millions of dollars, and the rest in proportion. The cry of redress was loud, urgent, and universal; all prejudices were hushed; Roman Catholics and Protestants were alike on this point. The terrified Emperor was assailed on all sides by petitions against Wallenstein, and his ear filled with the most fearful descriptions of his outrages. Ferdinand was not naturally cruel. If not totally innocent of the atrocities which were practised in Germany under the shelter of his name, he was ignorant of their extent; and he was not long in yielding to the representation of the princes, and reduced his standing army by eighteen thousand cavalry. While this reduction took place, the Swedes were actively preparing an expedition into Germany, and the greater part of the disbanded Imperialists enlisted under their banners.

The Emperor's concessions only encouraged the Elector of Bavaria to bolder demands. So long as the Duke of Friedland retained the supreme command his triumph over the Emperor was incomplete. The princes of the League were meditating a severe revenge on Wallenstein for that haughtiness with which he had treated them all alike. His dismissal was demanded by the whole college of electors, and even by Spain, with a degree of unanimity and urgency which astonished the Emperor. The anxiety with which Wallenstein's enemies pressed for his dismissal ought to have convinced the Emperor of the importance of his services. Wallenstein, informed of the cabals which were forming against him in Ratisbon, lost no time in opening the eyes of the Emperor to the real views of the Elector of Bavaria. He himself appeared in Ratisbon, with a pomp which threw his master into the shade, and increased the hatred of his opponents.

Long was the Emperor undecided. The sacrifice demanded was a painful one. To the Duke of Friedland alone he owed his preponderance; he felt how much he would lose in yielding him to the indignation of the princes. But at this moment, unfortunately, he was under the necessity of conciliating the Electors. His son Ferdinand had already been chosen King of Hungary, and he was endeavoring to procure his election as his successor in the empire. For this purpose the support of Maximilian was indispensable. This consideration was the weightiest, and to oblige the Elector of Bavaria he scrupled not to sacrifice his most valuable servant.

At the Diet at Ratisbon there were present ambassadors from France, empowered to adjust the differences which seemed to menace a war in Italy between the Emperor and their sovereign. Vincent, Duke of Mantua and Montferrat, dying without issue, his next relation, Charles Duke of Nevers, had taken possession of this inheritance, without doing homage to the Emperor as liege lord of the principality. Encouraged by the support of France and Venice, he refused to surrender these territories into the hands of the imperial commissioners, until his title to them should be decided. On the other hand, Ferdinand had taken up arms at the instigation of the Spaniards, to whom, as possessors of Milan, the near neighborhood of a vassal of France was peculiarly alarming, and who welcomed this prospect of making, with the assistance of the Emperor, additional conquests in Italy. In spite of all the exertions of Pope Urban VIII. to avert a war in that country, Ferdinand marched a German army across the Alps, and threw the Italian states into a general consternation. His arms had been successful throughout Germany, and exaggerated fears revived the olden apprehension of Austria's projects of universal monarchy. All the horrors of the German war now spread like a deluge over those favored countries which the Po waters; Mantua was taken by storm, and the surrounding districts given up to the ravages of a lawless soldiery. The curse of Italy was thus added to the maledictions upon the Emperor which resounded through Germany; and even in the Roman Conclave, silent prayers were offered for the success of the Protestant arms.

Alarmed by the universal hatred which this Italian campaign had drawn upon him, and wearied out by the urgent remonstrances of the Electors, who zealously supported the application of the French ambassador, the Emperor promised the investiture to the new Duke of Mantua.

This important service on the part of Bavaria of course required an equivalent from France. The adjustment of the treaty gave the envoys of Richelieu, during their residence in Ratisbon, the desired opportunity of entangling the Emperor in dangerous intrigues, of inflaming the discontented princes of the League still more strongly against him, and of turning to his disadvantage all the transactions of the Diet. For this purpose Richelieu had chosen an admirable instrument in Father Joseph, a Capuchin friar, who accompanied the ambassadors without exciting the least suspicion. One of his principal instructions was assiduously to bring about the dismissal of Wallenstein. With the general who had led it to victory the army of Austria would lose its principal strength; many armies could not compensate for the loss of this individual. It would therefore be a master-stroke of policy, at the very moment when a victorious monarch, the absolute master of his operations, was arming against the Emperor, to remove from the head of the imperial armies the only general who, by ability and military experience, was able to cope with the French king. Father Joseph, in the interests of Bavaria, undertook to overcome the irresolution of the Emperor, who was now in a manner besieged by the Spaniards and the Electoral Council. "It would be expedient," he thought, "to gratify the Electors on this occasion, and thereby facilitate his son's election to the Roman Crown. This object once gained Wallenstein could at any time resume his former station." The artful Capuchin was too sure of his man to touch upon this ground of consolation.

The voice of a monk was to Ferdinand II. the voice of God. "Nothing on earth," writes his own confessor, "was more sacred in his eyes than a priest. If it could happen, he used to say, that an angel and a Regular were to meet him at the same time and place, the Regular should receive his first, and the angel his second obeisance." Wallenstein's dismissal was determined upon.

In return for this pious concession, the Capuchin dexterously counteracted the Emperor's scheme to procure for the King of Hungary the further dignity of King of the Romans. In an express clause of the treaty just concluded, the French ministers engaged in the name of their sovereign to observe a complete neutrality between the Emperor and his enemies; while at the same time, Richelieu was actually negotiating with the King of Sweden to declare war, and pressing upon him the alliance of his master. The latter, indeed, disavowed the lie as soon as it had served its purpose, and Father Joseph, confined to a convent, must atone for the alleged offence of exceeding his instructions. Ferdinand perceived, when too late, that he had been imposed upon. "A wicked Capuchin," he was heard to say, "has disarmed me with his rosary, and thrust nothing less than six electoral crowns into his cowl."

Artifice and trickery thus triumphed over the Emperor at the moment when he was believed to be omnipotent in Germany, and actually was so in the field. With the loss of eighteen thousand men, and of a general who alone was worth whole armies, he left Ratisbon without gaining the end for which he had made such sacrifices. Before the Swedes had vanquished him in the field, Maximilian of Bavaria and Father Joseph had given him a mortal blow. At this memorable Diet at Ratisbon the war with Sweden was resolved upon, and that of Mantua terminated. Vainly had the princes present at it interceded for the Dukes of Mecklenburgh; and equally fruitless had been an application by the English ambassadors for a pension to the Palatine Frederick.

Wallenstein was at the head of an army of nearly a hundred thousand men who adored him when the sentence of his dismissal arrived. Most of the officers were his creatures: — with the common soldiers his hint was law. His ambition was boundless, his pride indomitable, his imperious spirit could not brook an injury unavenged. One moment would now precipitate him from the height of grandeur into the obscurity of a private station. To execute such a sentence upon such a delinquent seemed to require more address than it cost to obtain it from the judge. Accordingly, two of Wallenstein's most intimate friends were selected as heralds of these evil tidings, and instructed to soften them as much as possible by flattering assurances of the continuance of the Emperor's favor.

Wallenstein had ascertained the purport of their message before the imperial ambassadors arrived. He had time to collect himself, and his countenance exhibited an external calmness, while grief and rage were storming in his bosom. He had made up his mind to obey. The Emperor's decision had taken him by surprise before circumstances were ripe, or his preparations complete, for the bold measures he had contemplated. His extensive estates were scattered over Bohemia and Moravia; and by their confiscation the Emperor might at once destroy the sinews of his power. He looked, therefore, to the future for revenge; and in this hope he was encouraged by the predictions of an Italian astrologer, who led his imperious spirit like a child in leading-strings. Seni had read in the stars that his master's brilliant career was not yet ended; and that bright and glorious prospects still awaited him. It was, indeed, unnecessary to consult the stars to foretell that an enemy, Gustavus Adolphus, would ere long render indispensable the services of such a general as Wallenstein.

"The Emperor is betrayed," said Wallenstein to the messengers; "I pity but forgive him. It is plain that the grasping spirit of the Bavarian dictates to him. I grieve that, with so much weakness, he has sacrificed me, but I will obey." He dismissed the emissaries with princely presents; and in an humble letter besought the continuance of the Emperor's favor, and of the dignities he had bestowed upon him.

The murmurs of the army were universal on hearing of the dismissal of their general; and the greater part of his officers immediately quitted the imperial service. Many followed him to his estates in Bohemia and Moravia; others he attached to his interests by pensions, in order to command their services when the opportunity should offer.

But repose was the last thing that Wallenstein contemplated when he returned to private life. In his retreat he surrounded himself with a regal pomp which seemed to mock the sentence of degradation. Six gates led to the palace he inhabited in Prague, and a hundred houses were pulled down to make way for his courtyard. Similar palaces were built on his other numerous estates. Gentlemen of the noblest houses contended for the honor of serving him, and even imperial chamberlains resigned the golden key to the Emperor to fill a similar office under Wallenstein. He maintained sixty pages, who were instructed by the ablest masters. His ante-chamber was protected by fifty life-guards. His table never consisted of less than one hundred covers, and his seneschal was a person of distinction. When he travelled, his baggage and suite accompanied him in a hundred wagons, drawn by six or four horses; his court followed in sixty carriages, attended by fifty led horses. The pomp of his liveries, the splendor of his equipages, and the decorations of his apartments, were in keeping with all the rest. Six barons and as many knights were in constant attendance about his person, and ready to execute his slightest order. Twelve patrols went their rounds about his palace to prevent any disturbance. His busy genius required silence. The noise of coaches was to be kept away from his residence, and the streets leading to it were frequently blocked up with chains. His own circle was as silent as the approaches to his palace; dark, reserved and impenetrable, he was more sparing of his words than of his gifts; while the little that he spoke was harsh and imperious. He never smiled, and the coldness of his temperament was proof against sensual seductions. Ever occupied with grand schemes, he despised all those idle amusements in which so many waste their lives. The correspondence he kept up with the whole of Europe was chiefly managed by himself, and, that as little as possible might be trusted to the silence of others, most of the letters were written by his own hand. He was a man of large stature, thin, of a sallow complexion, with short red hair, and small sparkling eyes. A gloomy and forbidding seriousness sat upon his brow; and his magnificent presents alone retained the trembling crowd of his dependents.

In this stately obscurity did Wallenstein silently but not inactively await the hour of revenge. The victorious career of Gustavus Adolphus soon gave him a presentiment of its approach. Not one of his lofty schemes had been abandoned; and the Emperor's ingratitude had loosened the curb of his ambition. The dazzling splendor of his private life bespoke high-soaring projects; and, lavish as a king, he seemed already to reckon among his certain possessions those which he contemplated with hope.

After Wallenstein's dismissal, and the invasion of Gustavus Adolphus, a new generalissimo was to be appointed; and it now appeared advisable to unite both the imperial army and that of the League under one general. Maximilian of Bavaria sought this appointment, which would have enabled him to dictate to the Emperor, who, from a conviction of this, wished to procure the command for his eldest son, the King of Hungary. At last, in order to avoid offence to either of the competitors, the appointment was given to Tilly, who now exchanged the Bavarian for the Austrian service. The imperial army in Germany, after the retirement of Wallenstein, amounted to about forty thousand men; that of the League to nearly the same number, both commanded by excellent officers, trained by the experience of several campaigns, and proud of a long series of victories. With such a force little apprehension was felt at the invasion of the King of Sweden, and the less so as it commanded both Pomerania and Mecklenburgh, the only countries through which he could enter Germany.

After the unsuccessful attempt of the King of Denmark to check the Emperor's progress, Gustavus Adolphus was the only prince in Europe from whom oppressed liberty could look for protection — the only one who, while he was personally qualified to conduct such an enterprise, had both political motives to recommend and wrongs to justify it. Before the commencement of the war in Lower Saxony, important political interests induced him, as well as the King of Denmark, to offer his services and his army for the defence of Germany; but the offer of the latter had, to his own misfortune, been preferred. Since that time Wallenstein and the Emperor had adopted measures which must have been equally offensive to him as a man and as a king. Imperial troops had been despatched to the aid of the Polish king, Sigismund, to defend Prussia against the Swedes. When the king complained to Wallenstein for this act of hostility, he received for answer, "The Emperor has more soldiers than he wants for himself, he must help his friends." The Swedish ambassadors had been insolently ordered by Wallenstein to withdraw from the conference at

Lubeck; and when, unawed by this command, they were courageous enough to remain, contrary to the law of nations, he had threatened them with violence. Ferdinand had also insulted the Swedish flag, and intercepted the king's despatches to Transylvania. He also threw every obstacle in the way of a peace betwixt Poland and Sweden, supported the pretensions of Sigismund to the Swedish throne, and denied the right of Gustavus to the title of king. Deigning no regard to the repeated remonstrances of Gustavus, he rather aggravated the offence by new grievances than acceded the required satisfaction.

So many personal motives, supported by important considerations, both of policy and religion, and seconded by pressing invitations from Germany, had their full weight with a prince, who was naturally the more jealous of his royal prerogative the more it was questioned; who was flattered by the glory he hoped to gain as Protector of the Oppressed, and passionately loved war as the element of his genius. But until a truce or peace with Poland should set his hands free, a new and dangerous war was not to be thought of.

Cardinal Richelieu had the merit of effecting this truce with Poland. This great statesman, who guided the helm of Europe, while in France he repressed the rage of faction and the insolence of the nobles, pursued steadily, amidst the cares of a stormy administration, his plan of lowering the ascendancy of the House of Austria. But circumstances opposed considerable obstacles to the execution of his designs; and even the greatest minds cannot, with impunity, defy the prejudices of the age. The minister of a Roman Catholic king, and a Cardinal, he was prevented by the purple he bore from joining the enemies of that church in an open attack on a power which had the address to sanctify its ambitious encroachments under the name of religion. The external deference which Richelieu was obliged to pay to the narrow views of his contemporaries limited his exertions to secret negotiations, by which he endeavored to gain the hand of others to accomplish the enlightened projects of his own mind. After a fruitless attempt to prevent the peace between Denmark and the Emperor, he had recourse to Gustavus Adolphus, the hero of his age. No exertion was spared to bring this monarch to a favorable decision, and at the same time to facilitate the execution of it. Charnasse, an unsuspected agent of the Cardinal, proceeded to Polish Prussia, where Gustavus Adolphus was conducting the war against Sigismund, and alternately visited these princes, in order to persuade them to a truce or peace. Gustavus had been long inclined to it, and the French minister succeeded at last in opening the eyes of Sigismund to his true interests, and to the deceitful policy of the Emperor. A truce for six years was agreed on, Gustavus being allowed to retain all his conquests. This treaty gave him also what he had so long desired, the liberty of directing his arms against the Emperor. For this the French ambassador offered him the alliance of his sovereign and considerable subsidies. But Gustavus Adolphus was justly apprehensive lest the acceptance of the assistance should make him dependent upon France, and fetter him in his career of conquests, while an alliance with a Roman Catholic power might excite distrust among the Protestants.

If the war was just and necessary, the circumstances under which it was undertaken were not less promising. The name of the Emperor, it is true, was formidable, his resources inexhaustible, his power hitherto invincible. So dangerous a contest would have dismayed any other than Gustavus. He saw all the obstacles and dangers which opposed his undertaking, but he knew also the means by which, as he hoped, they might be conquered. His army, though not numerous, was well disciplined, inured to hardship by a severe climate and campaigns, and trained to victory in the war with Poland. Sweden, though poor in men and money, and overtaxed by an eight years' war, was devoted to its monarch with an enthusiasm which assured him of the ready support of his subjects. In Germany the name of the Emperor was at least as much hated as feared. The Protestant princes only awaited the arrival of a deliverer to throw off his intolerable yoke, and openly declare for the Swedes. Even the Roman Catholic states would welcome an antagonist to the Emperor, whose opposition might control his overwhelming influence. The first victory gained on German ground would be decisive. It would encourage those princes who still hesitated to declare themselves, strengthen the cause of his adherents, augment his troops, and open resources for the maintenance of the campaign. If the greater part of the German states were improverished by oppression the flourishing Hanse towns had escaped, and they could not hesitate, by a small voluntary sacrifice, to avert the general ruin. As the imperialists should be driven from the different provinces, their armies would diminish, since they were subsisting on the countries in which they were encamped. The strength, too, of the Emperor had been lessened by ill-timed detachments to Italy and the Netherlands; while Spain weakened, by the loss of the Manila galleons, and engaged in a serious war in the Netherlands, could afford him little support. Great Britian, on the other hand, gave the King of Sweden hope of considerable subsidies; and France, now at peace with itself, came forward with the most favorable offers.

But the strongest pledge for the success of his undertaking Gustavus found — in himself. Prudence demanded that he should embrace all the foreign assistance he could in order to guard his enterprise from the imputation of rashness; but all his confidence and courage were entirely derived from himself. He was indisputably the greatest general of his age, and the bravest soldier in the army which he had formed. Familiar with the tactics of Greece and Rome, he had discovered a more effective system of warfare, which was adopted as a model by the most eminent commanders of subsequent times. He reduced the unwieldy squadrons of cavalry, and rendered their movements more light and rapid; and, with the same view, he widened the intervals between his battalions. Instead of the usual array in a single line, he disposed his forces in two lines, that the second might advance in the event of the first giving way.

He made up for his want of cavalry by placing infantry among the horse; a practice which frequently decided the victory. Europe first learned from him the importance of infantry. All Germany was astonished at the strict discipline which, at the first, so creditably distinguished the Swedish army within their territories; all disorders were punished with the utmost severity, particularly impiety, theft, gambling, and duelling. The Swedish articles of war enforced frugality. In the camp, the King's tent not excepted, neither silver nor gold was to be seen. The general's eye looked as vigilantly to the morals as to the martial bravery of his soldiers; every regiment was ordered to form round its chaplain for morning and evening prayers. In all these points the lawgiver was also an example. A sincere and ardent piety exalted his courage. Equally free from the coarse infidelity which leaves the passions of the barbarian without a control, — and from the grovelling superstition of Ferdinand, who humbled himself to the dust before the Supreme Being, while he haughtily trampled on his fellow-creature — in the height of his success he was ever a man and a Christian — in the height of his devotion, a king and hero. The hardships of war he shared with the meanest soldier in his army; maintained a calm serenity amidst the hottest fury of battle; his glance was omnipresent, and he intrepidly forgot the danger while he exposed himself to the greatest peril. His natural courage, indeed, too often made him forget the duty of a general; and the life of a king ended in the death of a common soldier. But such a leader was followed to victory alike by the coward and the brave, and his eagle glance marked every heroic deed which his example had inspired. The fame of their sovereign excited in the nation an enthusiastic sense of their own importance; proud of their king, the peasant in Finland and Gothland joyfully contributed his pittance; the soldier willingly shed his blood; and the lofty energy which his single mind had imparted to the nation long survived its creator.

The necessity of the war was acknowledged, but the best plan of conducting it was a matter of much question. Even to the bold Chancellor Oxenstiern, an offensive war appeared too daring a measure; the resources of his poor and conscientious master appeared to him too

slender to compete with those of a despotic sovereign
who held all Germany at his command. But the minis-
ister's timid scruples were overruled by the hero's penetrating prudence. "If we await the enemy in Sweden,"
said Gustavus, "in the event of a defeat everything
would be lost; by a fortunate commencement in Germany everything would be gained. The sea is wide, and
we have a long line of coast in Sweden to defend. If
the enemy's fleet should escape us, or our own be defeated, it would, in either case, be impossible to prevent
the enemy's landing. Everything depends on the reten-
tion of Stralsund. So long as this harbor is open to us
we shall both command the Baltic and secure a retreat
from Germany. But to protect this port we must not
remain in Sweden, but advance at once into Pomerania.
Let us talk no more, then, of a defensive war, by which
we should sacrifice our greatest advantages. Sweden
must not be doomed to behold a hostile banner; if we
are vanquished in Germany, it will be time enough to
follow your plan."

Gustavus resolved to cross the Baltic and attack the
Emperor. His preparations were made with the utmost
expedition, and his precautionary measures were not less
prudent than the resolution itself was bold and magnanimous. Before engaging in so distant a war it was necessary to secure Sweden against its neighbors. At a personal interview with the King of Denmark at Markaroed
Gustavus assured himself of the friendship of that monarch; his frontier on the side of Moscow was well guarded;
Poland might be held in check from Germany, if it
betrayed any design of infringing the truce. Falkenberg, a Swedish ambassador, who visited the courts of
Holland and Germany, obtained the most flattering
promises from several Protestant princes, though none of
them yet ·possessed courage or self-devotion enough to
enter into a formal alliance with him. Lubeck and
Hamburg engaged to advance him money, and to accept
Swedish copper in return. Emissaries were also despatched to the Prince of Transylvania to excite that
implacable enemy of Austria to arms.

In the meantime Swedish levies were made in Germany and the Netherlands, the regiments increased to their full complement, new ones raised, transports provided, a fleet fitted out, provisions, military stores, and money collected. Thirty ships-of-war were in a short time prepared, fifteen thousand men equipped, and two hundred transports were ready to convey them across the Baltic. A greater force Gustavus Adolphus was unwilling to carry into Germany, and even the maintenance of this exceeded the revenues of his kingdom. But however small his army, it was admirable in all points of discipline, courage, and experience, and might serve as the nucleus of a more powerful armament if it once gained the German frontier and its first attempts were attended with success. Oxenstiern, at once general and chancellor, was posted with ten thousand men in Prussia to protect that province against Poland. Some regular troops, and a considerable body of militia, which served as a nursery for the main body, remained in Sweden as a defence against a sudden invasion by any treacherous neighbor.

These were the measures taken for the external defence of the kingdom. Its internal administration was provided for with equal care. The government was entrusted to the Council of State, and the finances to the Palatine John Casimir, the brother-in-law of the King, while his wife, tenderly as he was attached to her, was excluded from all share in the government, for which her limited talents incapacitated her. He set his house in order like a dying man. On the 20th May, 1630, when all his measures were arranged, and all was ready for his departure, the King appeared in the Diet at Stockholm to bid the States a solemn farewell. Taking in his arms his daughter Christina, then only four years old, who, in the cradle had been acknowledged as his successor, he presented her to the States as the future sovereign, exacted from them a renewal of the oath of allegiance to her, in case he should never more return, and then read the ordinances for the government of the kingdom during his absence or the minority of his daughter. The whole assembly was dissolved in tears, and the King himself was some time before he could attain sufficient composure to deliver his farewell address to the States.

"Not lightly or wantonly," said he, "am I about to involve myself and you in this new and dangerous war; God is my witness that *I* do not fight to gratify my own ambition. But the Emperor has wronged me most shamefully in the person of my ambassadors. He has supported my enemies, persecuted my friends and brethren, trampled my religion in the dust, and even stretched his revengeful arm against my crown. The oppressed states of Germany call loudly for aid, which, by God's help, we will give them.

"I am fully sensible of the dangers to which my life will be exposed. I have never yet shrunk from them, nor is it likely that I shall escape them all. Hitherto, Providence has wonderfully protected me, but I shall at last fall in defence of my country. I commend you to the protection of Heaven. Be just, be conscientious, act uprightly, and we shall meet again in eternity.

"To you, my Councillors of State, I address myself first. May God enlighten you and fill you with wisdom to promote the welfare of my people. You, too, my brave nobles, I commend to the divine protection. Continue to prove yourselves the worthy successors of those Gothic heroes whose bravery humbled to the dust the pride of ancient Rome. To you, ministers of religion, I recommend moderation and unity; be yourselves examples of the virtues which you preach, and abuse not your influence over the minds of my people. On you, deputies of the burgesses, and the peasantry, I entreat the blessing of heaven; may your industry be rewarded by a prosperous harvest; your stores plenteously filled, and may you be crowned abundantly with all the blessings of this life. For the prosperity of all my subjects, absent and present, I offer my warmest prayers to Heaven. I bid you all a sincere, it may be, an eternal farewell."

The embarkation of the troops took place at Elfsknaben, where the fleet lay at anchor. An immense concourse flocked thither to witness this magnificent spectacle. The hearts of the spectators were agitated by varied emotions as they alternately considered the vastness of the enterprise and the greatness of the leader. Among the superior officers who commanded in this army were Gustavus Horn, the Rhinegrave Otto Lewis, Henry Matthias, Count Thurn, Ottenburg, Baudissen, Banner, Teufel, Tott, Mutsenfahl, Falkenberg, Kniphausen, and other distinguished names. Detained by contrary winds, the fleet did not sail till June, and on the 24th of that month reached the island of Rugen, in Pomerania.

Gustavus Adolphus was the first who landed. In the presence of his suite he knelt on the shore of Germany to return thanks to the Almighty for the safe arrival of his fleet and his army. He landed his troops on the Islands of Wollin and Usedom; upon his approach the imperial garrisons abandoned their intrenchments and fled. He advanced rapidly on Stettin, to secure this important place before the appearance of the Imperialists. Bogislaus XIV., Duke of Pomerania, a feeble and superannuated prince, had been long tired out by the outrages committed by the latter within his territories; but too weak to resist he had contented himself with murmurs. The appearance of his deliverer, instead of animating his courage, increased his fear and anxiety. Severely as his country had suffered from the Imperialists, the risk of incurring the Emperor's vengeance prevented him from declaring openly for the Swedes. Gustavus Adolphus, who was encamped under the walls of the town, summoned the city to receive a Swedish garrison. Bogislaus appeared in person in the camp of Gustavus to deprecate this condition. "I come to you," said Gustavus, "not as an enemy but a friend. I wage no war against Pomerania, nor against the German empire, but against the enemies of both. In my hands this duchy shall be sacred; and it shall be restored to you at the conclusion of the campaign, by me, with more certainty than by any other. Look to the traces of the imperial force within your territories, and to mine in Usedom; and decide whether you will have the Emperor or me as your friend. What have you to expect if the Emperor should make himself master of your capital? Will he deal with you more leniently than I? Or is it your intention to stop my progress? The

case is pressing; decide at once, and do not compel me to have recourse to more violent measures."

The alternative was a painful one. On the one side, the King of Sweden was before his gates with a formidable army; on the other, he saw the inevitable vengeance of the Emperor, and the fearful example of so many German princes who were now wandering in misery, the victims of that revenge. The more immediate danger decided his resolution. The gates of Stettin were opened to the king; the Swedish troops entered; and the Austrians, who were advancing by rapid marches, anticipated. The capture of this place procured for the king a firm footing in Pomerania, the command of the Oder, and a magazine for his troops. To prevent a charge of treachery, Bogislaus was careful to excuse this step to the Emperor on the plea of necessity; but aware of Ferdinand's implacable disposition, he entered into a close alliance with his new protector. By this league with Pomerania, Gustavus secured a powerful friend in Germany, who covered his rear, and maintained his communication with Sweden.

As Ferdinand was already the aggressor in Prussia, Gustavus Adolphus thought himself absolved from the usual formalties, and commenced hostilities without any declaration of war. To the other European powers he justified his conduct in a manifesto, in which he detailed the grounds which had led him to take up arms. Meanwhile he continued his progress in Pomerania, while he saw his army daily increasing. The troops which had fought under Mansfeld, Duke Christian of Brunswick, the King of Denmark, and Wallenstein came in crowds, both officers and soldiers, to join his victorious standard.

At the Imperial court the invasion of the King of Sweden at first excited far less attention than it merited. The pride of Austria, extravagantly elated by its unheard-of successes, looked down with contempt upon a prince, who, with a handful of men, came from an obscure corner of Europe, and who owed his past successes, as they imagined, entirely to the incapacity of a weak opponent. The depreciatory representation which Wallenstein had artfully given of the Swedish power increased the Emperor's security; for what had he to fear from an enemy whom his general undertook to drive with such ease from Germany? Even the rapid progress of Gustavus Adolphus in Pomerania could not entirely dispel this prejudice, which the mockeries of the courtiers continued to feed. He was called in Vienna the Snow King, whom the cold of the north kept together, but who would infallibly melt as he advanced southward. Even the electors, assembled in Ratisbon, disregarded his representations; and, influenced by an abject complaisance to Ferdinand, refused him even the title of king. But while they mocked him in Ratisbon and Vienna, in Mecklenburgh and Pomerania one strong town after another fell into his hands.

Notwithstanding this contempt the Emperor thought it proper to offer to adjust his differences with Sweden by negotiation, and for that purpose sent plenipotentiaries to Denmark. But their instructions showed how little he was in earnest in these proposals, for he still continued to refuse to Gustavus the title of king. He hoped by this means to throw on the King of Sweden the odium of being the aggressor, and thereby to insure the support of the States of the empire. The conference at Dantzic proved, as might be expected, fruitless, and the animosity of both parties was increased to its utmost by an intemperate correspondence.

An imperial general, Torquato Conti, who commanded in Pomerania, had, in the meantime, made a vain attempt to wrest Stettin from the Swedes. The Imperialists were driven out from one place after another; Damm, Stargard, Camin, and Wolgast, soon fell in the hands of Gustavus. To revenge himself upon the Duke of Pomerania, the imperial general permitted his troops, upon his retreat, to exercise every barbarity on the unfortunate inhabitants of Pomerania, who had already suffered but too severely from his avarice. On pretence of cutting off the resources of the Swedes, the whole country was laid waste and plundered; and often, when the Imperialists were unable any longer to maintain a place, it was laid in ashes, in order to leave the enemy nothing but ruins. But these barbarities only served to place in a more favorable light the opposite conduct of the Swedes, and to win all hearts to their humane monarch. The Swedish soldier paid for all he required; no private property was injured on his march. The Swedes consequently were received with open arms both in town and country, whilst every Imperialist that fell into the hands of the Pomeranian peasantry was ruthlessly murdered. Many Pomeranians entered into the service of Sweden, and the estates of this exhausted country willingly voted the king a contribution of one hundred thousand florins.

Torquato Conti, who, with all his severity of character, was a consummate general, endeavored to render Stettin useless to the King of Sweden, as he could not deprive him of it. He intrenched himself upon the Oder, at Gratz, above Stettin, in order, by commanding that river, to cut off the water communication of the town with the rest of Germany. Nothing could induce him to attack the King of Sweden, who was his superior in numbers, while the latter was equally cautious not to storm the strong intrenchments of the Imperialists. Torquato, too deficient in troops and money to act upon the offensive against the king, hoped by this plan of operations to give time for Tilly to hasten to the defence of Pomerania, and then, in conjunction with that general, to attack the Swedes. Seizing the opportunity of the temporary absence of Gustavus, he made a sudden attempt upon Stettin, but the Swedes were not unprepared for him. A vigorous attack of the Imperialists was firmly repulsed, and Torquato was forced to retire with great loss. For this auspicious commencement of the war, however, Gustavus was, it must be owned, as much indebted to his good fortune as to his military talents. The imperial troops in Pomerania had been greatly reduced since Wallenstein's dismissal; moreover, the outrages they had committed were now severely revenged upon them; wasted and exhausted, the country no longer afforded them a subsistence. All discipline was at an end; the orders of the officers were disregarded, while their numbers daily decreased by desertion, and by a general mortality, which the piercing cold of a strange climate had produced among them.

Under these circumstances, the imperial general was anxious to allow his troops the repose of winter quarters, but he had to do with an enemy to whom the climate of Germany had no winter. Gustavus had taken the precaution of providing his soldiers with dresses of sheepskin, to enable them to keep the field even in the most inclement season. The imperial plenipotentiaries, who came to treat with him for a cessation of hostilities, received this discouraging answer: "The Swedes are soldiers in winter as well as in summer, and not disposed to oppress the unfortunate peasantry. The Imperialists may act as they think proper, but they need not expect to remain undisturbed." Torquato Conti soon after resigned a command in which neither riches nor reputation were to be gained.

In this inequality of the two armies the advantage was necessarily on the side of the Swedes. The Imperialists were incessantly harassed in their winter quarters; Greifenhagen, an important place upon the Oder, taken by storm, and the towns of Gratz and Piritz were at last abandoned by the enemy. In the whole of Pomerania Griefswald, Demmin, and Colberg alone remained in their hands, and these the king made great preparations to besiege. The enemy directed their retreat towards Brandenburg, in which much of their artillery and baggage, and many prisoners fell into the hands of the pursuers.

By seizing the passes of Riebnitz and Damgarden Gustavus had opened a passage into Mecklenburg, whose inhabitants were invited to return to their allegiance under their legitimate sovereigns, and to expel the adherents of Wallenstein. The Imperialists, however, gained the important town of Rostock by stratagem, and thus prevented the farther advance of the king, who was unwilling to divide the forces. The exiled dukes of Mecklenburgh had ineffectually employed the princes assembled at Ratisbon to intercede with the Emperor; in vain they had endeavored to soften Ferdinand, by renouncing the alliance of the king and every idea of resistance. But, driven to despair by the Emperor's inflexibility, they openly espoused the side of Sweden, and raising troops, gave the command of them to Francis Charles, Duke of Saxe-Lauenburg. That general made himself master of several strong places on the Elbe, but lost them afterwards to the Imperial General Pappenheim, who was despatched to oppose him. Soon afterwards, besieged by the latter in the town of Ratzeburg, he was compelled to surrender with all his troops. Thus ended the attempt which these unfortunate princes made to recover their territories; and it was reserved for the victorious arm of Gustavus Adolphus to render them that brilliant service.

The Imperialists had thrown themselves into Brandenburg, which now became the theatre of the most barbarous atrocities. These outrages were inflicted upon the subjects of a prince who had never injured the Emperor, and whom, moreover, he was at the very time inciting to take up arms against the King of Sweden. The sight of the disorders of their soldiers, which want of money compelled them to wink at, and of authority over their troops, excited the disgust even of the Imperial generals, and, from very shame, their commander-in-chief, Count Schaumburg, wished to resign.

Without a sufficient force to protect his territories, and left by the Emperor, in spite of the most pressing remonstrances, without assistance, the Elector of Brandenburg at last issued an edict, ordering his subjects to repel force by force, and to put to death without mercy every Imperial soldier who should henceforth be detected in plundering. To such a height had the violence of outrage and the misery of the government risen that nothing was left to the sovereign but the desperate extremity of sanctioning private vengeance by a formal law.

The Swedes had pursued the Imperialists into Brandenburg; and only the Elector's refusal to open to him the fortress of Custrin for his march obliged the King to lay aside his design of besieging Frankfort on the Oder. He therefore returned to complete the conquest of Pomerania by the capture of Demmin and Colberg. In the meantime, Field-Marshal Tilly was advancing to the defence of Brandenburg.

This general, who could boast as yet of never having suffered a defeat; the conqueror of Mansfeld, of Duke

Christian of Brunswick, of the Margrave of Baden, and the King of Denmark, was now, in the Swedish monarch, to meet an opponent worthy of his fame. Descended of a noble family in Liege, Tilly had formed his military talents in the wars of the Netherlands, which was then the great school for generals. He soon found an opportunity of distinguishing himself under Rodolph II. in Hungary, where he rapidly rose from one step to another. After the peace he entered into the service of Maximilian of Bavaria, who made him commander-in-chief with absolute powers. Here, by his excellent regulations, he was the founder of the Bavarian army; and to him, chiefly, Maximilian was indebted for his superiority in the field. Upon the termination of the Bohemian war he was appointed commander of the troops of the League; and, after Wallenstein's dismissal, generalissimo of the Imperial armies. Equally stern towards his soldiers and implacable towards his enemies, and as gloomy and impenetrable as Wallenstein, he was greatly his superior in probity and disinterestedness. A bigoted zeal for religion and a bloody spirit of persecution co-operated with the natural ferocity of his character to make him the terror of the Protestants. A strange and terrific aspect bespoke his character; of low stature, thin, with hollow cheeks, a long nose, a broad and wrinkled forehead, large whiskers and a pointed chin; he was generally attired in a Spanish doublet of green satin, with slashed sleeves, with a small high-peaked hat upon his head, surmounted by a red feather, which hung down to his back. His whole aspect recalled to recollection the Duke of Alva, the scourge of the Flemings; and his actions were far from effacing the impression. Such was the general who was now to be opposed to the hero of the north.

Tilly was far from undervaluing his antagonist. "The King of Sweden," said he, in the Diet at Ratisbon, "is an enemy both prudent and brave, inured to war, and in the flower of his age. His plans are excellent, his resources considerable, his subjects enthusiastically attached to him. His army, composed of Swedes, Germans, Livonians, Finlanders, Scots, and English, by its devoted obedience to their leader, is blended into one nation; he is a gamester in playing with whom not to have lost is to have won a great deal."

The progress of the King of Sweden in Brandenburg and Pomerania left the new generalissimo no time to lose; and his presence was now urgently called for by those who commanded in that quarter. With all expedition he collected the imperial troops which were dispersed over the empire; but it required time to obtain from the exhausted and impoverished provinces the necessary supplies. At last, about the middle of winter, he appeared at the head of twenty thousand men before Frankfort on the Oder, where he was joined by Schaumburg. Leaving to this general the defence of Frankfort, with a sufficient garrison, he hastened to Pomerania with a view of saving Demmin and relieving Colberg, which was already hard pressed by the Swedes. But even before he had left Brandenburg, Demmin, which was but poorly defended by the Duke of Savelli, had surrendered to the king, and Colberg, after a five months' siege, was starved into a capitulation. As the passes in Upper Pomerania were well guarded, and the king's camp near Schwedt defied attack, Tilly abandoned his offensive plan of operations and retreated towards the Elbe to besiege Magdeburg.

The capture of Demmin opened to the king a free passage into Mecklenburg; but a more important enterprise drew his arms into another quarter. Scarcely had Tilly commenced his retrograde movement, when suddenly breaking up his camp at Schwedt, the king marched his whole force against Frankfort on the Oder. This town, badly fortified, was defended by a garrison of eight thousand men, mostly composed of those ferocious bands who had so cruelly ravaged Pomerania and Brandenburg. It was now attacked with such impetuosity that on the third day it was taken by storm. The Swedes, assured of victory, rejected every offer of capitulation, as they were resolved to exercise the dreadful right of retaliation. For Tilly, soon after his arrival, had surrounded a Swedish detachment, and, irritated by their obstinate resistance, had cut them in pieces to a man. This cruelty was not forgotten by the Swedes. "New Brandenburg

Quarter," they replied to the Imperialists who begged their lives, and slaughtered them without mercy. Several thousands were either killed or taken, and many were drowned in the Oder; the rest fled to Silesia. All their artillery fell into the hands of the Swedes. To satisfy the rage of his troops Gustavus Adolphus was under the necessity of giving up the town for three hours to plunder.

While the king was thus advancing from one conquest to another, and by his success encouraging the Protestants to active resistance, the Emperor proceeded to enforce the Edict of Restitution, and by his exorbitant pretensions to exhaust the patience of the states. Compelled by necessity, he continued the violent course which he had begun with such arrogant confidence; the difficulties into which his arbitrary conduct had plunged him he could only extricate himself from by measures still more arbitrary. But in so complicated a body as the German empire despotism must always create the most dangerous convulsions. With astonishment the princes beheld the constitution of the empire overthrown, and the state of nature to which matters were again verging, suggested to them the idea of self-defence, the only means of protection in such a state of things. The steps openly taken by the Emperor against the Lutheran church had at last removed the veil from the eyes of John George, who had been so long the dupe of his artful policy. Ferdinand, too, had personally offended him by the exclusion of his son from the archbishopric of Magdeburg; and field-marshal Arnheim, his new favorite and minister, spared no pains to increase the resentment of his master. Arnheim had formerly been an imperial general under Wallenstein, and being still zealously attached to him, he was eager to avenge his old benefactor and himself on the Emperor by detaching Saxony from the Austrian interests. Gustavus Adolphus, supported by the Protestant states, would be invincible; a consideration which already filled the Emperor with alarm. The example of Saxony would probably influence others, and the Emperor's fate seemed now in a manner to depend upon the Elector's decision. The

artful favorite impressed upon his master this idea of his
own importance, and advised him to terrify the Emperor
by threatening an alliance with Sweden, and thus to
extort from his fears what he had sought in vain from his
gratitude. The favorite, however, was far from wishing
him actually to enter into the Swedish alliance, but, by
holding aloof from both parties, to maintain his own
importance and independence. Accordingly he laid before him a plan which only wanted a more able hand to
carry it into execution, and recommended him, by head-
ing the Protestant party, to erect a third power in Germany, and thereby maintain the balance between Sweden
and Austria.

This project was peculiarly flattering to the Saxon
Elector, to whom the idea of being dependent on Sweden,
or of longer submitting to the tyranny of the Emperor,
was equally hateful. He could not, with indifference,
see the control of German affairs wrested from him by a
foreign prince; and incapable as he was of taking a principal part, his vanity would not condescend to act a
subordinate one. He resolved, therefore, to draw every
possible advantage from the progress of Gustavus, but to
pursue, independently, his own separate plans. With
this view, he consulted with the Elector of Brandenburg,
who, from similar causes, was ready to act against the
Emperor, but, at the same time, was jealous of Sweden.
In a Diet at Torgau, having assured himself of the support of his Estates, he invited the Protestant States of
the empire to a general convention, which took place at
Leipzig on the 6th February, 1631. Brandenburg, Hesse
Cassel, with several princes, counts, estates of the empire,
and Protestant bishops were present, either personally or
by deputy, at this assembly, which the chaplain to the
court, Dr. Hoe von Hohenegg, opened with a vehement
discourse from the pulpit. The Emperor had in vain
endeavored to prevent this self-appointed convention,
whose object was evidently to provide for its own defence, and which the presence of the Swedes in the empire
rendered more than usually alarming. Emboldened by
the progress of Gustavus Adolphus the assembled princes
asserted their rights, and after a session of two months

broke up with adopting a resolution which placed the Emperor in no slight embarrassment. Its import was to demand of the Emperor, in a general address, the revocation of the Edict of Restitution, the withdrawal of his troops from their capitals and fortresses, the suspension of all existing proceedings, and the abolition of abuses; and, in the meantime, to raise an army of forty thousand men to enable them to redress their own grievances if the Emperor should still refuse satisfaction.

A further incident contributed not a little to increase the firmness of the Protestant princes. The King of Sweden had at last overcome the scruples which had deterred him from a closer alliance with France, and, on the 13th January, 1631, concluded a formal treaty with this crown. After a serious dispute respecting the treatment of the Roman Catholic princes of the empire, whom France took under her protection, and against whom Gustavus claimed the right of retaliation, and after some less important differences with regard to the title of majesty, which the pride of France was loth to concede to the King of Sweden, Richelieu yielded the second, and Gustavus Adolphus the first point, and the treaty was signed at Beerwald, in Neumark. The contracting parties mutually covenanted to defend each other with a military force, to protect their common friends, to restore to their dominions the deposed princes of the empire, and to replace everything, both on the frontier and in the interior of Germany, on the same footing on which it stood before the commencment of the war. For this end Sweden engaged to maintain an army of thirty thousand men in Germany, and France agreed to furnish the Swedes with an annual subsidy of four hundred thousand dollars. If the arms of Gustavus were successful he was to respect the Catholic religion and the constitution of the empire in all the conquered places, and to make no attempt against either. All Estates and princes, whether Protestant or Roman Catholic, either in Germany or in other countries, were to be invited to become parties to the treaty; neither France nor Sweden was to conclude a separate peace without the knowledge and consent of the other; and the treaty itself was to continue in force for five years.

Great as was the struggle to the King of Sweden to receive subsidies from France, and sacrifice his independence in the conduct of the war, this alliance with France decided his cause in Germany. Protected as he now was by the greatest power in Europe, the German states began to feel confidence in his undertaking, for the issue of which they had hitherto good reason to tremble. He became truly formidable to the Emperor. The Roman Catholic princes, too, who, though they were anxious to humble Austria, had witnessed his progress with distrust, were less alarmed now that an alliance with a Roman Catholic power insured his respect for their religion. And thus, while Gustavus Adolphus protected the Protestant religion and the liberties of Germany against the aggression of Ferdinand, France secured those liberties, and the Roman Catholic religion, against Gustavus himself, if the intoxication of success should hurry him beyond the bounds of moderation.

The King of Sweden lost no time in apprizing the members of the confederacy of Leipzig of the treaty concluded with France, and inviting them to a closer union with himself. The application was seconded by France, who spared no pains to win over the Elector of Saxony. Gustavus was willing to be content with secret support, if the princes should deem it too bold a step as yet to declare openly in his favor. Several princes gave him hopes of his proposals being accepted on the first favorable opportunity; but the Saxon Elector, full of jealousy and distrust towards the King of Sweden, and true to the selfish policy he had pursued, could not be prevailed upon to give a decisive answer.

The resolution of the confederacy of Leipzig, and the alliance betwixt France and Sweden, were news equally disagreeable to the Emperor. Against them he employed the thunder of imperial ordinances, and the want of an army saved France from the full weight of his displeasure. Remonstrances were addressed to all the members of the confederacy, strongly prohibiting them from enlisting troops. They retorted with explanations equally vehement, justified their conduct upon the principles of natural right, and continued their preparations.

Meantime, the imperial generals, deficient both in troops and money, found themselves reduced to the disagreeable alternative of losing sight either of the King of Sweden, or of the Estates of the empire, since with a divided force they were not a match for either. The movements of the Protestants called their attention to the interior of the empire, while the progress of the king in Brandenburg, by threatening the hereditary possessions of Austria, required them to turn their arms to that quarter. After the conquest of Frankfort, the king had advanced upon Landsberg on the Warta, and Tilly, after a fruitless attempt to relieve it, had again returned to Magdeburg, to prosecute with vigor the siege of that town.

The rich archbishopric, of which Magdeburg was the capital, had long been in the possession of princes of the house of Brandenburg, who introduced the Protestant religion into the province. Christian William, the last administrator, had, by his alliance with Denmark, incurred the ban of the empire, on which account the chapter, to avoid the Emperor's displeasure, had formally deposed him. In his place they had elected Prince John Augustus, the second son of the Elector of Saxony, whom the Emperor rejected, in order to confer the archbishopric on his son Leopold. The Elector of Saxony complained ineffectually to the imperial court; but Christian William of Brandenburg took more active measures. Relying on the attachment of the magistracy and inhabitants of Brandenburg, and excited by chimerical hopes, he thought himself able to surmount all the obstacles which the vote of the chapter, the competition of two powerful rivals, and the Edict of Restitution opposed to his restoration. He went to Sweden, and, by the promise of a diversion in Germany, sought to obtain assistance from Gustavus. He was dismissed by that monarch not without hopes of effectual protection, but with the advice to act with caution.

Scarcely had Christian William been informed of the landing of his protector in Pomerania than he entered

Magdeburg in disguise. Appearing suddenly in the town council, he reminded the magistrates of the ravages which both town and country had suffered from the imperial troops, of the pernicious designs of Ferdinand, and the danger of the Protestant church. He then informed them that the moment of deliverance was at hand, and that Gustavus Adolphus offered them his alliance and assistance. Magdeburg, one of the most flourishing towns in Germany, enjoyed under the government of its magistrates a republican freedom, which inspired its citizens with a brave heroism. Of this they had already given proofs, in the bold defence of their rights against Wallenstein, who, tempted by their wealth, made on them the most extravagant demands. Their territory had been given up to the fury of his troops, though Magdeburg itself had escaped his vengeance. It was not difficult, therefore, for the Administrator to gain the concurrence of men in whose minds the remembrance of these outrages was still recent. An alliance was formed between the city and the Swedish king, by which Magdeburg granted to the king a free passage through its gates and territories, with liberty of enlisting soldiers within its boundaries, and, on the other hand, obtained promises of effectual protection for its religion and its privileges.

The Administrator immediately collected troops and commenced hostilities, before Gustavus Adolphus was near enough to co-operate with him. He defeated some imperial detachments in the neighborhood, made a few conquests, and even surprised Halle. But the approach of an imperial army obliged him to retreat hastily, and not without loss, to Magdeburg. Gustavus Adolphus, though displeased with his premature measures, sent Dietrich Falkenberg, an experienced officer, to direct the Administrator's military operations, and to assist him with his counsel. Falkenberg was named by the magistrates governor of the town during the war. The Prince's army was daily augmented by recruits from the neighboring towns; and he was able for some months to maintain a petty warfare with success.

At length Count Pappenheim, having brought his expedition against the Duke of Saxe-Lauenburg to a close, approached the town. Driving the troops of the Administrator from their entrenchments, he cut off his communication with Saxony, and closely invested the place. He was soon followed by Tilly, who haughtily summoned the Elector forthwith to comply with the Edict of Restitution, to submit to the Emperor's orders, and surrender Magdeburg. The Prince's answer was spirited and resolute, and obliged Tilly at once to have recourse to arms.

In the meanwhile the siege was prolonged, by the progress of the King of Sweden, which called the Austrian general from before the place; and the jealousy of the officers who conducted the operations in his absence delayed for some months the fall of Magdeburg. On the 30th March, 1631, Tilly returned, to push the siege with vigor.

The outworks were soon carried, and Falkenberg, after withdrawing the garrisons from the points which he could no longer hold, destroyed the bridge over the Elbe. As his troops were barely sufficient to defend the extensive fortifications, the suburbs of Sudenburg and Neustadt were abandoned to the enemy, who immediately laid them in ashes. Pappenheim, now separated from Tilly, crossed the Elbe at Schonenbeck, and attacked the town from the opposite side.

The garrison, reduced by the defence of the outworks, scarcely exceeded two thousand infantry and a few hundred horse; a small number for so extensive and irregular a fortress. To supply this deficiency, the citizens were armed, a desperate expedient, which produced more evils than those it prevented. The citizens, at best but indifferent soldiers, by their disunion threw the town into confusion. The poor complained that they were exposed to every hardship and danger, while the rich, by hiring substitutes, remained at home in safety. These rumors broke out at last in an open mutiny; indifference succeeded to zeal; weariness and negligence took the place of vigilance and foresight. Dissension, combined with growing scarcity, gradually produced a feeling of despondency; many began to tremble at the desperate nature of their undertaking, and the magnitude of the power to which they were opposed. But religious zeal, an ardent love of liberty, an invincible hatred to the Austrian yoke, and the expectation of speedy relief, banished as yet the idea of a surrender; and, divided as they were in everything else, they were united in the resolve to defend themselves to the last extremity.

Their hopes of succor were apparently well founded. They knew that the confederacy of Leipzig was arming; they were aware of the near approach of Gustavus Adolphus. Both were alike interested in the preservation of Magdeburg; and a few days might bring the King of Sweden before its walls. All this was also known to Tilly, who, therefore, was anxious to make himself speedily master of the place. With this view he had despatched a trumpeter with letters to the Administrator, the commandant, and the magistrates, offering terms of capitulation; but he received for answer, that they would rather die than surrender. A spirited sally of the citizens also convinced him that their courage was as earnest as their words, while the king's arrival at Potsdam, with the incursions of the Swedes as far as Zerbst, filled him with uneasiness, but raised the hopes of the garrison. A second trumpeter was now despatched; but the more moderate tone of his demands increased the confidence of the besieged, and unfortunately their negligence also.

The besiegers had now pushed their approaches as far as the ditch, and vigorously cannonaded the fortifications from the abandoned batteries. One tower was entirely overthrown, but this did not facilitate an assault, as it fell sidewise upon the wall, and not into the ditch. Notwithstanding the continual bombardment the walls had not suffered much; and the fire balls, which were intended to set the town in flames, were deprived of their effect by the excellent precautions adopted against them. But the ammunition of the besieged was nearly expended, and the cannon of the town gradually ceased to answer the fire of the Imperialists. Before a new supply could be obtained Magdeburg would be either relieved or taken. The hopes of the besieged were on the stretch, and all eyes anxiously directed towards the quarter in which the Swedish banners were expected to appear. Gustavus Adolphus was near enough to reach

Magdeburg within three days; security grew with hope, which all things contributed to augment. On the 9th of May, the fire of the Imperialists was suddenly stopped, and the cannon withdrawn from several of the batteries. A deathlike stillness reigned in the Imperial camp. The besieged were convinced that deliverance was at hand. Both citizens and soldiers left their posts upon the ramparts early in the morning to indulge themselves, after their long toils, with the refreshment of sleep, but it was indeed a dear sleep, and a frightful awakening.

Tilly had abandoned the hope of taking the town, before the arrival of the Swedes, by the means which he had hitherto adopted; he therefore determined to raise the siege, but first to hazard a general assault. This plan, however, was attended with great difficulties, as no breach had been effected, and the works were scarcely injured. But the council of war assembled on this occasion declared for an assault, citing the example of Maestricht, which had been taken early in the morning, while the citizens and soldiers were reposing themselves. The attack was to be made simultaneously on four points; the night betwixt the 9th and 10th of May was employed in the neccessary preparations. Everything was ready and awaiting the signal, which was to be given by cannon at five o'clock in the morning. The signal, however, was not given for two hours later, during which Tilly, who was still doubtful of success, again consulted the council of war. Pappenheim was ordered to attack the works of the new town, where the attempt was favored by a sloping rampart, and a dry ditch of moderate depth. The citizens and soldiers had mostly left the walls, and the few who remained were overcome with sleep. This general, therefore, found little difficulty in mounting the wall at the head of his troops.

Falkenberg, roused by the report of musketry, hastened from the town-house, where he was employed in despatching Tilly's second trumpeter, and hurried with all the force he could hastily assemble towards the gate of the new town, which was already in the possession of the enemy. Beaten back, this intrepid general flew to another quarter, where a second party of the enemy were preparing to scale the walls. After an ineffectual resistance he fell in the commencement of the action. The roaring of musketry, the pealing of the alarm-bells, and the growing tumult apprised the awakening citizens of their danger. Hastily arming themselves, they rushed in blind confusion against the enemy. Still some hope of repulsing the besiegers remained; but the governor being killed, their efforts were without plan and co-operation, and at last their ammunition began to fail them. In the meanwhile, two other gates, hitherto unattacked, were stripped of their defenders, to meet the urgent danger within the town. The enemy quickly availed themselves of this confusion to attack these posts. The resistance was nevertheless spirited and obstinate, until four imperial regiments, at length, masters of the ramparts, fell upon the garrison in the rear, and completed their rout. Amidst the general tumult, a brave captain, named Schmidt, who still headed a few of the more resolute against the enemy, succeeded in driving them to the gates; here he fell mortally wounded, and with him expired the hopes of Magdeburg. Before noon all the works were carried, and the town was in the enemy's hands.

Two gates were now opened by the storming-party for the main body, and Tilly marched in with part of his infantry. Immediately occupying the principal streets, he drove the citizens with pointed cannon into their dwellings, there to await their destiny. They were not long held in suspense; a word from Tilly decided the fate of Magdeburg.

Even a more humane general would in vain have recommended mercy to such soldiers; but Tilly never made the attempt. Left by their general's silence masters of the lives of all the citizens, the soldiery broke into the houses to satiate their most brutal appetites. The prayers of innocence excited some compassion in the hearts of the Germans, but none in the rude breasts of Pappenheim's Walloons. Scarcely had the savage cruelty commenced when the other gates were thrown open, and the cavalry, with the fearful hordes of the Croats, poured in upon the devoted inhabitants.

Here commenced a scene of horrors for which history has no language, poetry no pencil. Neither innocent childhood, nor helpless old age; neither youth, sex, rank, nor beauty could disarm the fury of the conquerors. Wives were abused in the arms of their husbands, daughters at the feet of their parents; and the defenceless sex exposed to the double sacrifice of virtue and life. No situation, however obscure, or however sacred, escaped the rapacity of the enemy. In a single church fifty-three women were found beheaded. The Croats amused themselves with throwing children into the flames; Pappenheim's Walloons with stabbing infants at the mother's breast. Some officers of the League, horror-struck at this dreadful scene, ventured to remind Tilly that he had it in his power to stop the carnage. "Return in an hour," was his answer; "I will see what I can do; the soldier must have some reward for his dangers and toils." These horrors lasted with unabated fury, till at last the smoke and flames proved a check to the plunderers. To augment the confusion, and to divert the resistance of the inhabitants, the imperialists had, in the commencement of the assault, fired the town in several places. The wind rising rapidly, spread the flames, till the blaze became universal. Fearful, indeed, was the tumult amid clouds of smoke, heaps of dead bodies, the clash of swords, the crash of falling ruins, and streams of blood. The atmosphere glowed; and the intolerable heat forced at last even the murderers to take refuge in their camp. In less than twelve hours this strong, populous, and flourishing city, one of the finest in Germany, was reduced to ashes, with the exception of two churches and a few houses. The Administrator, Christian William, after receiving several wounds, was taken prisoner, with three of the burgomasters; most of the officers and magistrates had already met an enviable death. The avarice of the officers had saved four hundred of the richest citizens in the hope of extorting from them an exorbitant ransom. But this humanity was confined to the officers of the League, whom the ruthless barbarity of the Imperialists caused to be regarded as guardian angels.

Scarcely had the fury of the flames abated when the

Imperialists returned to renew the pillage amid the ruins and ashes of the town. Many were suffocated by the smoke; many found rich booty in the cellars, where the citizens had concealed their more valuable effects. On the 13th of May Tilly himself appeared in the town, after the streets had been cleared of ashes and dead bodies. Horrible and revolting to humanity was the scene that presented itself. The living crawling from under the dead, children wandering about with heart-rending cries, calling for their parents; and infants still sucking the breasts of their lifeless mothers. More than six thousand bodies were thrown into the Elbe to clear the streets; a much greater number had been consumed by the flames. The whole number of the slain was reckoned at not less than thirty thousand.

The entrance of the general, which took place on the 14th, put a stop to the plunder, and saved the few who had hitherto contrived to escape. About a thousand people were taken out of the cathedral, where they had remained three days and two nights without food, and in momentary fear of death. Tilly promised them quarter, and commanded bread to be distributed among them. The next day a solemn mass was performed in the cathedral, and *Te Deum* sung amidst the discharge of artillery. The imperial general rode through the streets, that he might be able as an eye-witness to inform his master that no such conquest had been made since the destruction of Troy and Jerusalem. Nor was this an exaggeration, whether we consider the greatness, importance, and prosperity of the city razed, or the fury of its ravagers.

In Germany the tidings of the dreadful fate of Magdeburg caused triumphant joy to the Roman Catholics, while it spread terror and consternation among the Protestants. Loudly and generally they complained against the King of Sweden, who, with so strong a force, and in the very neighborhood, had left an allied city to its fate. Even the most reasonable deemed his inaction inexplicable; and lest he should lose irretrievably the good-will of the people, for whose deliverance he had engaged in this war, Gustavus was under the necessity of publishing to the world a justification of his own conduct.

He had attacked, and on the 16th April, carried Landsberg, when he was apprised of the danger of Magdeburg. He resolved immediately to march to the relief of that town; and he moved with all his cavalry, and ten regiments of infantry towards the Spree. But the position which he held in Germany made it necessary that he should not move forward without securing his rear. In traversing a country where he was surrounded by suspicious friends and dangerous enemies, and where a single premature movement might cut off his communication with his own kingdom, the utmost vigilance and caution were necessary. The Elector of Brandenburg had already opened the fortress of Custrin to the flying Imperialists, and closed the gates against their pursuers. If now Gustavus should fail in his attack upon Tilly the Elector might again open his fortresses to the Imperialists, and the king, with an enemy both in front and rear, would be irrecoverably lost. In order to prevent this contingency he demanded that the Elector should allow him to hold the fortresses of Custrin and Spandau till the siege of Magdeburg should be raised.

Nothing could be more reasonable than this demand. The services which Gustavus had lately rendered the Elector, by expelling the Imperialists from Brandenburg, claimed his gratitude, while the past conduct of the Swedes in Germany entitled them to confidence. But by the surrender of his fortresses, the Elector would in some measure make the King of Sweden master of his country; besides that, by such a step, he must at once break with the Emperor, and expose his States to his future vengeance. The Elector's struggle with himself was long and violent, pusillanimity and self-interest for awhile prevailed. Unmoved by the fate of Magdeburg, cold in the cause of religion and the liberties of Germany, he saw nothing but his own danger; and this anxiety was greatly stimulated by his minister Van Schwartzenburgh, who was secretly in the pay of Austria. In the meantime the Swedish troops approached Berlin, and the king took up his residence with the Elector. When he witnessed the timorous hesitation of that prince, he could not restrain his indignation: " My road is to Magdeburg," said he;

"not for my own advantage, but for that of the Protestant religion. If no one will stand by me I shall immediately retreat, conclude a peace with the Emperor, and return to Stockholm. I am convinced that Ferdinand will readily grant me whatever conditions I may require. But if Magdeburg is once lost, and the Emperor relieved from all fear of me, then it is for you to look to yourselves and the consequences." This timely threat, and perhaps, too, the aspect of the Swedish army, which was strong enough to obtain by force what was refused to entreaty, brought at last the Elector to his senses, and Spandau was delivered into the hands of the Swedes.

The king had now two routes to Magdeburg; one westward led through an exhausted country, and filled with the enemy's troops, who might dispute with him the passage of the Elbe; the other more to the southward, by Dessau and Wittenberg, where bridges were to be found for crossing the Elbe, and where supplies could easily be drawn from Saxony. But he could not avail himself of the latter without the consent of the Elector, whom Gustavus had good reason to distrust. Before setting out on his march, therefore, he demanded from that prince a free passage and liberty for purchasing provisions for his troops. His application was refused, and no remonstrances could prevail on the Elector to abandon his system of neutrality. While the point was still in dispute the news of the dreadful fate of Magdeburg arrived.

Tilly announced its fall to the Protestant princes in the tone of a conquerer, and lost no time in making the most of the general consternation. The influence of the Emperor, which had sensibly declined during the rapid progress of Gustavus, after this decisive blow rose higher than ever; and the change was speedily visible in the imperious tone he adopted towards the Protestant states. The decrees of the Confederation of Leipzig were annulled by a proclamation, the Convention itself suppressed by an imperial decree, and all the refractory states threatened with the fate of Magdeburg. As the executor of this imperial mandate, Tilly immediately ordered troops to march against the Bishop of Bremen, who was a member of the Confederacy, and had himself enlisted soldiers.

The terrified bishop immediately gave up his forces to Tilly, and signed the revocation of the acts of the Confederation. An imperial army, which had lately returned from Italy, under the command of Count Furstenberg, acted in the same manner towards the Administrator of Wirtemberg. The duke was compelled to submit to the Edict of Restitution, and all the decrees of the Emperor, and even to pay a monthly subsidy of one hundred thousand dollars for the maintenance of the imperial troops. Similar burdens were inflicted upon Ulm and Nuremberg, and the entire circles of Franconia and Swabia. The hand of the Emperor was stretched in terror over all Germany. The sudden preponderance, more in appearance, perhaps, than in reality, which he had obtained by this blow, carried him beyond the bounds even of the moderation which he had hitherto observed, and misled him into hasty and violent measures, which at last turned the wavering resolution of the German princes in favor of Gustavus Adolphus. Injurious as the immediate consequences of the fall of Magdeburg were to the Protestant cause, its remoter effects were most advantageous. The past surprise made way for active resentment, despair inspired courage, and the German freedom rose, like a phœnix, from the ashes of Magdeburg.

Among the princes of the Leipzig Confederation the Elector of Saxony and the Landgrave of Hesse were the most powerful; and, until they were disarmed, the universal authority of the Emperor was unconfirmed. Against the Landgrave, therefore, Tilly first directed his attack, and marched straight from Magdeburg into Thuringia. During this march the territories of Saxe, Ernest, and Schwartzburg were laid waste, and Frankenhausen plundered before the very eyes of Tilly, and laid in ashes with impunity. The unfortunate peasant paid dear for his master's attachment to the interests of Sweden. Erfurt, the key of Saxony and Franconia, was threatened with a siege, but redeemed itself by a voluntary contribution of money and provisions. From thence Tilly despatched his emissaries to the Landgrave, demanding of him the immediate disbanding of his army, a renunciation of the league of Leipzig, the reception of imperial garrisons into his territories and fortresses, with the necessary contributions, and the declaration of friendship or hostility. Such was the treatment which a prince of the Empire was compelled to submit to from a servant of the Emperor. But these extravagant demands acquired a formidable weight from the power which supported them; and the dreadful fate of Magdeburg, still fresh in the memory of the Landgrave, tended still farther to enforce them. Admirable, therefore, was the intrepidity of the Landgrave's answer: "To admit foreign troops into his capital and fortresses the Landgrave is not disposed; his troops he requires for his own purposes; as for an attack, he can defend himself. If General Tilly wants money or provisions, let him go to Munich, where there is plenty of both." The irruption of two bodies of imperial troops into Hesse Cassel was the immediate result of this spirited reply, but the Landgrave gave them so warm a reception that they could effect nothing; and just as Tilly was preparing to follow with his whole army, to punish the unfortunate country for the firmness of its sovereign, the movements of the King of Sweden recalled him to another quarter.

Gustavus Adolphus had learned the fall of Magdeburg with deep regret; and the demand now made by the Elector, George William, in terms of their agreement, for the restoration of Spandau, greatly increased this feeling. The loss of Magdeburg had rather augmented than lessened the reasons which made the possession of this fortress so desirable; and the nearer became the necessity of a decisive battle between himself and Tilly, the more unwilling he felt to abandon the only place which, in the event of a defeat, could insure him a refuge. After a vain endeavor by entreaties and representations to bring over the Elector to his views, whose coldness and lukewarmness daily increased, he gave orders to his general to evacuate Spandau, but at the same time declared to the Elector that he would henceforth regard him as an enemy.

To give weight to this declaration, he appeared with his whole force before Berlin. "I will not be worse treated that the imperial generals," was his reply to the ambassadors whom the bewildered Elector despatched to his camp. "Your master has received them into his territories, furnished them with all necessary supplies, ceded to them every place which they required, and yet, by all these concessions he could not prevail upon them to treat his subjects with common humanity. All that I require of him is security, a moderate sum of money, and provisions for my troops; in return I promise to protect his country, and to keep the war at a distance from him. On these points, however, I must insist; and my brother, the Elector, must instantly determine to have me as a friend, or to see his capital plundered." This decisive tone produced a due impression; and the cannon pointed against the town put an end to the doubts of George William. In a few days, a treaty was signed, by which the Elector engaged to furnish a monthly subsidy of thirty thousand dollars, to leave Spandau in the king's hands, and to open Custrin at all times to the Swedish troops. This now open alliance of the Elector of Brandenburg with the Swedes excited no less displeasure at Vienna than did formerly the similar procedure of the Duke of Pomerania; but the changed fortune which now attended his arms obliged the Emperor to confine his resentment to words.

The king's satisfaction, on this favorable event, was increased by the agreeable intelligence that Griefswald, the only fortress which the Imperialists still held in Pomerania, had surrendered, and that the whole country was now free of the enemy. He appeared once more in this duchy, and was gratified at the sight of the general joy which he had caused to the people. A year had elapsed since Gustavus first entered Germany, and this event was now celebrated by all Pomerania as a national festival. Shortly before the Czar of Moscow had sent ambassadors to congratulate him, to renew his alliance, and even to offer him troops. He had great reason to rejoice at the friendly disposition of Russia, as it was indispensable to his interests that Sweden itself should remain undisturbed by any dangerous neighbor during the war in which he himself was engaged. Soon after his queen, Maria Eleonora, landed in Pomerania, with a reinforcement of eight thousand Swedes; and the arrival of six thousand English, under the Marquis of Hamilton, requires more particular notice, because this is all that history mentions of the English during the Thirty Year's War.

During Tilly's expedition into Thuringia, Pappenheim commanded in Magdeburg; but was unable to prevent the Swedes from crossing the Elbe at various points, routing some imperial detachments, and seizing several posts. He himself, alarmed at the approach of the King of Sweden, anxiously recalled Tilly, and prevailed upon him to return by rapid marches to Magdeburg. Tilly encamped on this side of the river at Wolmerstadt; Gustavus on the same side, near Werben, not far from the confluence of the Havel and the Elbe. His very arrival portended no good to Tilly. The Swedes routed three of his regiments which were posted in villages at some distance from the main body, carried off half their baggage, and burned the remainder. Tilly in vain advanced within cannon-shot of the king's camp, and offered him battle. Gustavus, weaker by one-half than his adversary, prudently declined it; and his position was too strong for an attack. Nothing more ensued but a distant cannonade, and a few skirmishes, in which the Swedes had invariably the advantage. In his retreat to Wolmerstadt, Tilly's army was weakened by numerous desertions. Fortune seemed to have forsaken him since the carnage of Magdeburg.

The King of Sweden, on the contrary, was followed by uninterrupted success. While he himself was encamped in Werben, the whole of Mecklenburg, with the exception of a few towns, was conquered by his General Tott and the Duke Adolphus Frederick; and he enjoyed the satisfaction of reinstating both dukes in their dominions. He proceeded in person to Gustrow, where the reinstatement was solemnly to take place, to give additional dignity to the ceremony by his presence. The two dukes, with their deliverer between them, and attended by a splendid train of princes, made a public entry into the city, which the joy of their subjects converted into an affecting solemnity. Soon after his return to Werben, the Landgrave of Hesse Cassel appeared in his camp, to conclude an offensive and defensive alliance; the first sovereign prince in Germany who voluntary and openly declared against the Emperor, though not wholly uninfluenced by strong motives. The Landgrave bound himself to act against the king's enemies as his own, to open to him his towns and territory, and to furnish his army with provisions and necessaries. The king, on the other hand, declared himself his ally and protector; and engaged to conclude no peace with the Emperor without first obtaining for the Landgrave a full redress of grievances. Both parties honorably performed their agreement. Hesse Cassel adhered to the Swedish alliance during the whole of this tedious war; and at the peace of Westphalia had no reason to regret the friendship of Sweden.

Tilly, from whom this bold step on the part of the Landgrave was not long concealed, despatched Count Fugger with several regiments against him; and at the same time endeavored to excite his subjects to rebellion by inflammatory letters. But these made as little impression as his troops, which subsequently failed him so decidedly at the battle of Breitenfeld. The Estates of Hesse could not for a moment hesitate between their oppressor and their protector.

But the imperial general was far more disturbed by the equivocal conduct of the Elector of Saxony, who, in defiance of the imperial prohibition, continued his preparations, and adhered to the confederation at Leipzig. At this conjuncture, when the proximity of the King of Sweden made a decisive battle ere long inevitable, it appeared extremely dangerous to leave Saxony in arms, and ready in a moment to declare for the enemy. Tilly had just received a reinforcement of twenty-five thousand veteran troops under Furstenberg, and, confident in his strength, he hoped either to disarm the Elector by the mere terror of his arrival, or at least to conquer him with little difficulty. Before quitting his camp at Wolmerstadt, he commanded the Elector, by a special messenger, to open his territories to the imperial troops; either to disband his own or to join them to the imperial army; and to assist, in conjunction with himself, in driving the King of Sweden out of Germany. While he reminded him that, of all the German states, Saxony had hitherto been most respected, he threatened it, in case of refusal, with the most destructive ravages.

But Tilly had chosen an unfavorable moment for so imperious a requisition. The ill-treatment of his religious and political confederates, the destruction of Magdeburg, the excesses of the Imperialists in Lusatia, all combined to incense the Elector against the Emperor. The approach, too, of Gustavus Adolphus (however slender his claims were to the protection of that prince) tended to fortify his resolution. He accordingly forbade the quartering of the imperial soldiers in his territories, and announced his firm determination to persist in his warlike preparations. However surprised he should be, he added, "To see an imperial army on its march against his territories, when that army had enough to do in watching the operations of the King of Sweden, nevertheless he did not expect, instead of the promised and well-merited rewards, to be repaid with ingratitude and the ruin of his country." To Tilly's deputies, who were entertained in a princely style, he gave a still plainer answer on the occasion. "Gentlemen," said he, "I perceive that the Saxon confectionery, which has been so long kept back, is at length to be set upon the table. But as it is usual to mix it with nuts and garnish of all kinds, take care of your teeth."

Tilly instantly broke up his camp, and, with the most frightful devastation, advanced upon Halle; from this place he renewed his demands on the Elector, in a tone still more urgent and threatening. The previous policy of this prince, both from his own inclination, and the persuasions of his corrupt ministers, had been to promote the interests of the Emperor, even at the expense of his own sacred obligations, and but very little tact had hitherto kept him inactive. All this but renders more astonishing the infatuation of the Emperor or his ministers in abandoning, at so critical a moment, the policy they had hitherto adopted, and, by extreme measures, incensing a prince so easily led. Was this the very object which Tilly had in view? Was it his purpose to convert an equivocal friend into an open enemy, and thus to relieve himself from the necessity of that indulgence in the treatment of this prince which the secret instructions of the Emperor had hitherto imposed upon him? Or was it the Emperor's wish, by driving the Elector to open hostilities, to get quit of his obligations to him, and so cleverly to break off at once the difficulty of a reckoning? In either case we must be equally surprised at the daring presumption of Tilly, who hesitated not, in presence of one formidable enemy, to provoke another; and at his negligence in permitting, without opposition, the union of the two.

The Saxon Elector, rendered desperate by the entrance of Tilly into his territories, threw himself, though not without a violent struggle, under the protection of Sweden.

Immediately after dismissing Tilly's first embassy, he had despatched his field-marshal Arnheim in all haste to the camp of Gustavus, to solicit the prompt assistance of that monarch whom he had so long neglected. The king concealed the inward satisfaction he felt at this long wished for result. "I am sorry for the Elector," said he, with dissembled coldness, to the ambassador; "had he heeded my repeated remonstrances his country would never have seen the face of an enemy, and Magdeburg would not have fallen. Now, when necessity leaves him no alternative, he has recourse to my assistance. But tell him, that I cannot, for the sake of the Elector of Saxony, ruin my own cause and that of my confederates. What pledge have I for the sincerity of a prince whose minister is in the pay of Austria, and who will abandon me as soon as the Emperor flatters him, and withdraws his troops from his frontiers? Tilly, it is true, has received a strong reinforcement; but this shall not prevent me from meeting him with confidence, as soon as I have covered my rear."

The Saxon minister could make no other reply to these reproaches than that it was best to bury the past in oblivion.

He pressed the king to name the conditions on which he would afford assistance to Saxony, and offered to guarantee their acceptance. "I require," said Gustavus, "that the Elector shall cede to me the fortress of Wittenberg, deliver to me his eldest sons as hostages, furnish my troops with three months' pay, and deliver up to me the traitors among his ministry."

"Not Wittenberg alone," said the Elector, when he received this answer, and hurried back his minister to the Swedish camp, "not Wittenberg alone, but Torgau, and all Saxony, shall be open to him; my whole family shall be his hostages, and if that is insufficient, I will place myself in his hands. Return and inform him I am ready to deliver to him any traitors he shall name, to furnish his army with the money he requires, and to venture my life and fortune in the good cause."

The king had only desired to test the sincerity of the Elector's new sentiments. Convinced of it, he now retracted these harsh demands. "The distrust," he said, "which was shown to myself when advancing to the relief of Magdeburg had naturally excited mine; the Elector's present confidence demands a return. I am satisfied, provided he grants my army one month's pay, and even for his advance I hope to indemnify him."

Immediately upon the conclusion of the treaty, the king crossed the Elbe, and next day joined the Saxons. Instead of preventing this junction, Tilly had advanced against Leipzig, which he summoned to receive an imperial garrison. In hopes of speedy relief, Hans Von der Pforta, the commandant, made preparations for his defence, and laid the suburb towards Halle in ashes. But the ill condition of the fortifications made resistance vain, and on the second day the gates were opened. Tilly had fixed his headquarters in the house of a grave-digger, the only one still standing in the suburb of Halle; here he signed the capitulation, and here, too, he arranged his attack on the King of Sweden. Tilly grew pale at the representation of the death's-head and cross-bones with which the proprietor had decorated his house; and, contrary to all expectations, Leipzig experienced moderate treatment.

Meanwhile, a council of war was held at Torgau between the King of Sweden and the Elector of Saxony, at which the Elector of Brandenburg was also present. The resolution which should now be adopted was to decide irrevocably the fate of Germany and the Protestant religion, the happiness of nations and the destiny of their princes. The anxiety of suspense which, before every decisive resolve, oppresses even the hearts of heroes, appeared now for a moment to overshadow the great mind of Gustavus Adolphus. "If we decide upon battle," said he, "the stake will be nothing less than a crown and two electorates. Fortune is changeable, and the inscrutable decrees of Heaven may, for our sins, give the victory to our enemies. My kingdom, it is true, even after the loss of my life and my army, would still have a hope left. Far removed from the scene of action, defended by a powerful fleet, a well-guarded frontier, and a warlike population, it would at least be safe from the worst consequences of a defeat. But what chances of escape are there for you, with an enemy so close at hand?" Gustavus Adolphus displayed the modest diffidence of a hero, whom an overweening belief of his own strength did not blind to the greatness of his danger; John George, the confidence of a weak man, who knows that he has a hero by his side. Impatient to rid his territories as soon as possible of the oppressive presence of two armies, he burned for a battle, in which he had no former laurels to lose. He was ready to march with his Saxons alone against Leipzig, and attack Tilly. At last Gustavus acceded to his opinion; and it was resolved that the attack should be made without delay, before the arrival of the reinforcements, which were on their way, under Altringer and Tiefenbach. The united Swedish and Saxon armies now crossed the Mulda, while the Elector returned homeward.

Early on the morning of the 7th September, 1631, the hostile armies came in sight of each other. Tilly, who, since he had neglected the opportunity of overpowering the Saxons before their union with the Swedes, was disposed to await the arrival of the reinforcements, had taken up a strong and advantageous position not far from Leipzig, where he expected he should be able to avoid the battle. But the impetuosity of Pappenheim obliged him, as soon as the enemy were in motion, to alter his plans, and to move to the left, in the direction of the hills which run from the village of Wahren towards Lindenthal. At the foot of these heights his army was drawn up in a single line, and his artillery placed upon the heights behind, from which it could sweep the whole extensive plain of Breitenfeld. The Swedish and Saxon army advanced in two columns, having to pass the Lober near Podelwitz, in Tilly's front.

To defend the passage of this rivulet, Pappenheim advanced at the head of two thousand cuirassiers, though after great reluctance on the part of Tilly, and with express orders not to commence a battle. But, in disobedience to this command, Pappenheim attacked the vanguard of the Swedes, and after a brief struggle was driven to retreat. To check the progress of the enemy, he set fire to Podelwitz, which, however, did not prevent the two columns from advancing and forming in order of battle.

On the right, the Swedes drew up in a double line, the infantry in the centre, divided into such small battalions as could be easily and rapidly manœuvred without breaking their order; the cavalry upon their wings, divided in the same manner into small squadrons, interspersed with bodies of musqueteers, so as both to give an appearance of greater numerical force, and to annoy the enemy's horse. Colonel Teufel commanded the centre, Gustavus Horn the left, while the right was led by the king in person, opposed to Count Pappenheim.

On the left, the Saxons formed at a considerable distance from the Swedes, by the advice of Gustavus, which was justified by the event. The order of battle had been arranged between the Elector and his field-marshal, and the king was content with merely signifying his approval. He was anxious apparently to separate the Swedish prowess from that of the Saxons, and fortune did not confound them.

The enemy was drawn up under the heights towards the west, in one immense line, long enough to outflank the Swedish army, the infantry being divided in large battalions, the cavalry in equally unwieldly squadrons. The artillery being on the heights behind, the range of its fire was over the heads of his men. From this position of his artillery it was evident that Tilly's purpose was to await rather than to attack the enemy; since this arrangement rendered it impossible for him to do so without exposing his men to the fire of his own cannons. Tilly himself commanded the centre, Count Furstenberg the right wing, and Pappenheim the left. The united troops of the Emperor and the League on this day did not amount to thirty-four thousand or thirty-five thousand men; the Swedes and Saxons were about the same number. But had a million been confronted with a million it could only have rendered the action more bloody, certainly not more important and decisive. For this day Gustavus had crossed the Baltic to court danger in a distant country, and expose his crown and life to the caprice of fortune. The two greatest generals of the time, both hitherto invincible, were now to be matched against each other in a contest which both had long avoided; and on this field of battle the hitherto untarnished laurels of one leader must droop forever. The two parties in Germany had beheld the approach of this day with fear and trembling; and the whole age awaited with deep anxiety its issue, and posterity was either to bless or deplore it forever.

Tilly's usual intrepidity and resolution seemed to forsake him on this eventful day. He had formed no regular plan for giving battle to the king, and he displayed as little firmness in avoiding it. Contrary to his own judgment, Pappenheim had forced him to action. Doubts which he had never before felt struggled in his bosom; gloomy forebodings clouded his ever-open brow; the shade of Magdeburg seemed to hover over him.

A cannonade of two hours commenced the battle; the wind, which was from the west, blew thick clouds of smoke and dust from the newly-ploughed and parched fields into the faces of the Swedes. This compelled the king insensibly to wheel northwards, and the rapidity with which this movement was executed left no time to the enemy to prevent it.

Tilly at last left his heights, and began the first attack upon the Swedes; but to avoid their hot fire, he filed off towards the right, and fell upon the Saxons with such

impetuosity that their line was broken, and the whole
army thrown into confusion. The Elector himself retired
to Eilenburg, though a few regiments still maintained
their ground upon the field, and by a bold stand saved
the honor of Saxony. Scarcely had the confusion began
ere the Croats commenced plundering, and messengers
were despatched to Munich and Vienna with the news of
the victory.

Pappenheim had thrown himself with the whole force
of his cavalry upon the right wing of the Swedes, but
without being able to make it waver. The king commanded here in person, and under him General Banner.
Seven times did Pappenheim renew the attack, and seven
times was he repulsed. He fled at last with great loss,
and abandoned the field to his conqueror.

In the meantime, Tilly, having routed the remainder
of the Saxons, attacked with his victorious troops the left
wing of the Swedes. To this wing the king, as soon as
he perceived that the Saxons were thrown into disorder,
had, with a ready foresight, detached a reinforcement of
three regiments to cover its flank, which the flight of the
Saxons had left exposed. Gustavus Horn, who commanded here, showed the enemy's cuirassiers a spirited
resistance, which the infantry, interspersed among the
squadrons of horse, materially assisted. The enemy were
already beginning to relax the vigor of their attack, when
Gustavus Adolphus appeared to terminate the contest.
The left wing of the Imperialists had been routed; and
the king's division, having no longer any enemy to
oppose, could now turn their arms wherever it would be
to the most advantage. Wheeling, therefore, with his
right wing and main body to the left, he attacked the
heights on which the enemy's artillery was planted.
Gaining possession of them in a short time, he turned
upon the enemy the full fire of their own cannon.

The play of artillery upon their flank, and the terrible
onslaught of the Swedes in front, threw this hitherto invincible army into confusion. A sudden retreat was the
only course left to Tilly, but even this was to be made
through the midst of the enemy. The whole army was
in disorder, with the exception of four regiments of

veteran soldiers, who never as yet had fled from the field, and were resolved not to do so now. Closing their ranks, they broke through the thickest of the victorious army, and gained a small thicket, where they opposed a new front to the Swedes, and maintained their resistance till night, when their number was reduced to six hundred men. With them fled the wreck of Tilly's army, and the battle was decided.

Amid the dead and the wounded, Gustavus Adolphus threw himself on his knees; and the first joy of his victory gushed forth in fervent prayer. He ordered his cavalry to pursue the enemy as long as the darkness of the night would permit. The pealing of the alarm-bells set the inhabitants of all the neighboring villages in motion, and utterly lost was the unhappy fugitive who fell into their hands. The king encamped with the rest of his army between the field of battle and Leipzig, as it was impossible to attack the town the same night. Seven thousand of the enemy were killed in the field, and more than five thousand either wounded or taken prisoners. Their whole artillery and camp fell into the hands of the Swedes, and more than a hundred standards and colors were taken. Of the Saxons about two thousand had fallen, while the loss of the Swedes did not exceed seven hundred. The rout of the Imperialists was so complete that Tilly, on his retreat to Halle and Halberstadt, could not rally above six hundred men, or Pappenheim more than one thousand four hundred — so rapidly was this formidable army dispersed which so lately was the terror of Italy and Germany.

Tilly himself owed his escape merely to chance. Exhausted by his wounds, he still refused to surrender to a Swedish captain of horse, who summoned him to yield; but who, when he was on the point of putting him to death, was himself stretched on the ground by a timely pistol-shot. But more grievous than danger or wounds was the pain of surviving his reputation, and of losing in a single day the fruits of a long life. All former victories were as nothing, since he had failed in gaining the one that should have crowned them all. Nothing remained of all his past exploits but the general execration which had followed them. From this period he never recovered his cheerfulness or his good fortune. Even his last consolation, the hope of revenge, was denied to him, by the express command of the Emperor not to risk a decisive battle.

The disgrace of this day is to be ascribed principally to three mistakes: his planting the cannon on the hills behind him, his afterwards abandoning these heights, and his allowing the enemy, without opposition, to form in order of battle. But how easily might those mistakes have been rectified, had it not been for the cool presence of mind and superior genius of his adversary!

Tilly fled from Halle to Halberstadt, where he scarcely allowed time for the cure of his wounds before he hurried towards the Weser to recruit his force by the imperial garrisons in Lower Saxony.

The Elector of Saxony had not failed, after the danger was over, to appear in Gustavus' camp. The king thanked him for having advised a battle; and the Elector, charmed at his friendly reception, promised him, in the first transports of joy, the Roman crown. Gustavus set out next day for Merseburg, leaving the Elector to recover Leipzig. Five thousand Imperialists, who had collected together after the defeat, and whom he met on his march, were either cut in pieces or taken prisoners, of whom again the greater part entered into his service. Merseburg quickly surrendered; Halle was soon after taken, whither the Elector of Saxony, after making himself master of Leipzig, repaired to meet the king, and to concert their future plan of operations.

The victory was gained, but only a prudent use of it could render it decisive. The imperial armies were totally routed, Saxony free from the enemy, and Tilly had retired into Brunswick. To have followed him thither would have been to renew the war in Lower Saxony, which had scarcely recovered from the ravages of the last. It was therefore determined to carry the war into the enemy's country, which, open and defenceless as far as Vienna, invited attack. On their right, they might fall upon the territories of the Roman Catholic princes, or penetrate, on the left, into the hereditary do-

minions of Austria, and make the Emperor tremble in his
palace. Both plans were resolved on; and the question
that now remained was to assign its respective parts.
Gustavus Adolphus, at the head of a victorious army, had
little resistance to apprehend in his progress from Leipzig
to Prague, Vienna, and Presburg. As to Bohemia,
Moravia, Austria, and Hungary, they had been stripped
of their defenders, while the oppressed Protestants in
these countries were ripe for a revolt. Ferdinand was
no longer secure in his capital; Vienna, on the first terror
of surprise, would at once open its gates. The loss of his
territories would deprive the enemy of the resources by
which alone the war could be maintained; and Ferdinand
would, in all probability, gladly accede, on the hardest
conditions, to a peace which would remove a formidable
enemy from the heart of his dominions. This bold plan
of operations was flattering to a conqueror, and success
perhaps might have justified it. But Gustavus Adolphus,
as prudent as he was brave, and more a statesman than a
conqueror, rejected it, because he had a higher end in
view, and would not trust the issue either to bravery or
good fortune alone.

By marching towards Bohemia, Franconia and the
Upper Rhine would be left to the Elector of Saxony.
But Tilly had already began to recruit his shattered army
from the garrisons in Lower Saxony, and was likely to be
at the head of a formidable force upon the Weser, and
to lose no time in marching against the enemy. To so
experienced a general it would not do to oppose an
Arnheim, of whose military skill the battle of Leipzig
had afforded but equivocal proof; and of what avail
would be the rapid and brilliant career of the king in
Bohemia and Austria if Tilly should recover his superiority in the Empire, animating the courage of the
Roman Catholics, and disarming, by a new series of victories, the allies and confederates of the king? What
would he gain by expelling the Emperor from his hereditary dominions if Tilly succeeded in conquering for that
Emperor the rest of Germany? Could he hope to reduce
the Emperor more than had been done, twelve years
before, by the insurrection of Bohemia, which had failed

to shake the firmness or exhaust the resources of that prince, and from which he had risen more formidable than ever?

Less brilliant, but more solid, were the advantages which he had to expect from an incursion into the territories of the League. In this quarter his appearance in arms would be decisive. At this very conjuncture the princes were assembled in a Diet at Frankfort to deliberate upon the Edict of Restitution, where Ferdinand employed all his artful policy to persuade the intimidated Protestants to accede to a speedy and disadvantageous arrangement. The advance of their protector could alone encourage them to a bold resistance and disappoint the Emperor's designs. Gustavus Adolphus hoped by his presence to unite the discontented princes, or by the terror of his arms to detach them from the Emperor's party. Here, in the centre of Germany, he could paralyze the nerves of the imperial power, which, without the aid of the League, must soon fall; here, in the neighborhood of France, he could watch the movements of a suspicious ally; and however important to his secret views it was to cultivate the friendship of the Roman Catholic electors, he saw the necessity of making himself first of all master of their fate, in order to establish, by his magnanimous forbearance, a claim to their gratitude.

He accordingly chose the route to Franconia and the Rhine, and left the conquest of Bohemia to the Elector of Saxony.

BOOK III.

The glorious battle of Leipzig effected a great change in the conduct of Gustavus Adolphus, as well as in the opinion which both friends and foes entertained of him. Successfully had he confronted the greatest general of the age, and had matched the strength of his tactics and the courage of his Swedes against the élite of the imperial army, the most experienced troops in Europe. From this moment he felt a firm confidence in his own powers; self-confidence has always been the parent of great actions. In all his subsequent operations more boldness and decision are observable; greater determination, even amidst the most unfavorable circumstances, a more lofty tone towards his adversaries, a more dignified bearing towards his allies, and even in his clemency, something of the forbearance of a conqueror. His natural courage was farther heightened by the pious ardor of his imagination. He saw in his own cause that of heaven, and in the defeat of Tilly beheld the decisive interference of Providence against his enemies, and in himself the instrument of divine vengeance. Leaving his crown and his country far behind he advanced on the wings of victory into the heart of Germany, which for centuries had seen no foreign conqueror within its bosom. The warlike spirit of its inhabitants, the vigilance of its numerous princes, the artful confederation of its states, the number of its strong castles, its many and broad rivers had long restrained the ambition of its neighbors; and frequently as its extensive frontier had been attacked, its interior had been free from invasion. The empire had hitherto enjoyed the equivocal privilege of being its own enemy, though invincible from without. Even now it was merely the disunion of its members and the intolerance of religious zeal that paved the way for the Swedish invader. The bond of union between the states, which alone had rendered the empire invincible, was now dissolved; and Gustavus derived from Germany itself the power by which he subdued it. With as much courage as prudence he availed himself of all that the favorable moment afforded; and, equally at home in the cabinet and the field, he tore asunder the web of the artful policy with as much ease as he shattered walls with the thunder of his cannon. Uninterruptedly he pursued his conquests from one end of Germany to the other without breaking the line of posts which commanded a secure retreat at any moment; and whether on the banks of the Rhine, or at the mouth of the Lech, alike maintaining his communication with his hereditary dominions.

The consternation of the Emperor and the League at Tilly's defeat at Leipzig was scarcely greater than the surprise and embarrassment of the allies of the King of Sweden at his unexpected success. It was beyond both their expectations and their wishes. Annihilated in a moment was that formidable army which, while it checked his progress and set bounds to his ambition, rendered him in some measure dependent on themselves. He now stood in the heart of Germany alone without a rival or without an adversary who was a match for him. Nothing could stop his progress or check his pretensions if the intoxication of success should tempt him to abuse his victory. If formerly they had dreaded the Emperor's irresistible power, there was no less cause now to fear everything for the Empire from the violence of a foreign conqueror, and for the Catholic Church, from the religious zeal of a Protestant king. The distrust and jealousy of some of the combined powers, which a stronger fear of the Emperor had for a time repressed, now revived; and scarcely had Gustavus Adolphus merited by his courage and success their confidence, when they began covertly to circumvent all his plans. Through a continual struggle with the arts of enemies, and the distrust of his own allies, must his victories henceforth be won; yet resolution, penetration, and prudence made their way through all impediments. But while his success excited the jealousy of his more powerful allies, France and Saxony, it gave courage to the weaker, and emboldened them openly to declare their sentiments and join his party. Those who could neither vie with Gustavus Adolphus in importance, nor suffer from his ambition, expected the more from the magnanimity of their powerful ally, who enriched them with the spoils of their enemies and protected them against the oppression of their stronger neighbors. His strength covered their weakness, and, inconsiderable in themselves, they acquired weight and influence from their union with the Swedish hero. This was the case with most of the free cities, and particularly with the weaker Protestant states. It was these that introduced the king into the heart of Germany; these covered his rear, supplied his troops with necessaries, received them into their fortresses, while they exposed their own lives in his battles. His prudent regard to their national pride, his popular deportment, some brilliant acts of justice, and his respect for the laws were so many ties by which he bound the German Protestants to his cause; while the crying atrocities of the Imperialists, the Spaniards, and the troops of Lorraine powerfully contributed to set his own conduct and that of his army in a favorable light.

If Gustavus Adolphus owed his success chiefly to his own genius, at the same time, it must be owned, he was greatly favored by fortune and by circumstances. Two great advantages gave him a decided superiority over the enemy. While he removed the scene of war into the lands of the League, drew their youth as recruits, enriched himself with booty, and used the revenues of their fugitive princes as his own, he at once took from the enemy the means of effectual resistance, and maintained an expensive war with little cost to himself. And, moreover, while his opponents, the princes of the League, divided among themselves, and governed by different and often conflicting interests, acted without unanimity, and therefore without energy; while their generals were deficient in authority, their troops in obedience, the operations of their scattered armies without concert; while the general was separated from the lawgiver and the statesman; these several functions were united in Gustavus Adolphus, the only source from which authority flowed, the sole object to which the eye of the warrior turned; the soul of his party, the inventor as well as the executor of his plans. In him, therefore, the Protestants had a centre of unity and harmony, which was altogether wanting to their opponents. No wonder, then, if, favored by such advantages, at the head of such an army, with such a genius to direct it, and guided by such political prudence, Gustavus Adolphus was irresistible.

With a sword in one hand and mercy in the other, he traversed Germany as a conqueror, a lawgiver, and a judge in as short a time almost as the tourist of pleasure. The keys of towns and fortresses were delivered to him as if to the native sovereign. No fortress was inaccessible; no river checked his victorious career. He conquered by the very terror of his name. The Swedish standards were planted along the whole stream of the Maine; the Lower Palatinate was free, the troops of Spain and Lorraine had fled across the Rhine and the Moselle. The Swedes and Hessians poured like a torrent into the territories of Mentz, of Wurtzburg, and Bamberg, and three fugitive bishops, at a distance from their sees, suffered dearly for their unfortunate attachment to the Emperor. It was now the turn for Maximilian, the leader of the League, to feel in his own dominions the miseries he had inflicted upon others. Neither the terrible fate of his allies, nor the peaceful overtures of Gustavus, who, in the midst of conquest, ever held out the hand of friendship, could conquer the obstinacy of this prince. The torrent of war now poured into Bavaria. Like the banks of the Rhine, those of the Lecke and the Donau were crowded with Swedish troops. Creeping into his fortresses, the defeated Elector abandoned to the ravages of the foe his dominions, hitherto unscathed by war, and on which the bigoted violence of the Bavarians seemed to invite retaliation. Munich itself opened its gates to the invincible monarch, and the fugitive Palatine, Frederick V., in the forsaken residence of his rival, consoled himself for a time for the loss of his dominions.

While Gustavus Adolphus was extending his conquests in the south, his generals and allies were gaining similar triumphs in the other provinces. Lower Saxony shook off the yoke of Austria, the enemy abandoned Mecklenburg, and the imperial garrisons retired from the banks of the Weser and the Elbe. In Westphalia and the Upper Rhine William, Landgrave of Hesse, rendered himself formidable; the Duke of Weimar in Thuringia, and the French in the Electorate of Treves; while to the eastward the whole kingdom of Bohemia was conquered by the Saxons. The Turks were preparing to attack Hungary, and in the heart of Austria a dangerous insurrection was threatened. In vain did the Emperor look around to the courts of Europe for support; in vain did he summon the Spaniards to his assistance, for the bravery of the Flemings afforded them ample employment beyond the Rhine;

in vain did he call upon the Roman court and the whole church to come to his rescue. The offended Pope sported, in pompous processions and idle anathemas, with the embarrassments of Ferdinand, and instead of the desired subsidy he was shown the devastation of Mantua.

On all sides of his extensive monarchy hostile arms surrounded him. With the states of the League, now overrun by the enemy, those ramparts were thrown down behind which Austria had so long defended herself, and the embers of war were now smouldering upon her unguarded frontiers. His most zealous allies were disarmed; Maximilian of Bavaria, his firmest support, was scarce able to defend himself. His armies, weakened by desertion and repeated defeat, and dispirited by continued misfortunes, had unlearnt, under beaten generals, that warlike impetuosity which as it is the consequence, so it is the guarantee of success. The danger was extreme, and extraordinary means alone could raise the imperial power from the degradation into which it was fallen.

The most urgent want was that of a general; and the only one from whom he could hope for the revival of his former splendor had been removed from his command by an envious cabal. So low had the Emperor now fallen that he was forced to make the most humiliating proposals to his injured subject and servant, and meanly to press upon the imperious Duke of Friedland the acceptance of the powers which no less meanly had been taken from him. A new spirit began from this moment to animate the expiring body of Austria; and a sudden change in the aspect of affairs bespoke the firm hand which guided them. To the absolute King of Sweden a general equally absolute was now opposed; and one victorious hero was confronted with another. Both armies were again to engage in the doubtful struggle; and the prize of victory, already almost secured in the hands of Gustavus Adolphus, was to be the object of another and a severer trial. The storm of war gathered around Nuremberg; before its walls the hostile armies encamped; gazing on each other with dread and respect, longing for, and yet shrinking from, the moment that was to close them together in the shock of battle. The eyes of Europe turned to the scene in curiosity and alarm, while Nuremberg, in dismay, expected soon to lend its name to a more decisive battle than that of Leipzig. Suddenly the clouds broke and the storm rolled away from Franconia, to burst upon the plains of Saxony. Near Lutzen fell the thunder that had menaced Nuremberg; the victory, half lost, was purchased by the death of the king. Fortune, which had never deserted him in his lifetime, favored the King of Sweden even in his death, with the rare privilege of falling in the fulness of his glory and an untarnished fame. By a timely death his protecting genius rescued him from the inevitable fate of man — that of forgetting moderation in the intoxication of success, and justice in the plenitude of power. It may be doubted whether, had he lived longer, he would still have deserved the tears which Germany shed over his grave, or maintained his title to the admiration with which posterity regards him, as the first and only *just* conqueror that the world has produced. The untimely fall of their great leader seemed to threaten the ruin of his party; but to the Power which rules the world, no loss of a single man is irreparable. As the helm of war dropped from the hand of the falling hero, it was seized by two great statesmen, Oxenstiern and Richelieu. Destiny still pursued its relentless course, and for full sixteen years longer the flames of war blazed over the ashes of the long-forgotten king and soldier.

I may now be permitted to take a cursory retrospect of Gustavus Adolphus in his victorious career, glance at the scene in which he alone was the great actor, and then, when Austria becomes reduced to extremity by the successes of the Swedes, and by a series of disasters is driven to the most humiliating and desperate expedients, to return to the history of the Emperor.

As soon as the plan of operations had been concerted at Halle between the King of Sweden and the Elector of Saxony, as soon as the alliance had been concluded with the neighboring princes of Weimar and Anhalt, and preparations made for the recovery of the bishopric of Magdeburg, the king began his march into the empire. He had here no despicable foe to contend with. Within the empire the Emperor was still powerful; throughout Franconia, Swabia, and the Palatinate imperial garrisons were posted with whom the possession of every place of importance must be disputed sword in hand. On the Rhine he was opposed by the Spaniards, who had overrun the territory of the banished Elector Palatine, seized all its strong places, and would everywhere dispute with him the passage over that river. On his rear was Tilly, who was fast recruiting his force, and would soon be joined by the auxiliaries from Lorraine. Every Papist presented an inveterate foe, while his connection with France did not leave him at liberty to act with freedom against the Roman Catholics. Gustavus had foreseen all these obstacles, but at the same time the means by which they were to be overcome. The strength of the Imperialists was broken and divided among different garrisons, while he would bring against them one by one his whole united force. If he was to be opposed by the fanaticism of the Roman Catholics, and the awe in which the lesser states regarded the Emperor's power, he might depend on the active support of the Protestants and their hatred to Austrian oppression. The ravages of the Imperialist and Spanish troops also powerfully aided him in these quarters; where the ill-treated husbandman and citizen sighed alike for a deliverer, and where the mere change of yoke seemed to promise a relief. Emissaries were despatched to gain over to the Swedish side the principal free cities, particularly Nuremburg and Frankfort. The first that lay in the king's march, and which he could not leave unoccupied in his rear, was Erfurt. Here the Protestant party among the citizens opened to him, without a blow, the gates of the town and the citadel. From the inhabitants of this, as of every important place which afterwards submitted, he exacted an oath of allegiance, while he secured its possession by a sufficient garrison. To his ally, Duke William of Weimar, he entrusted the command of an army to be raised in Thuringia. He also left his queen in Erfurt, and promised to increase its privileges. The Swedish army now crossed the Thuringian forest in two columns, by Gotha and Arnstadt, and, having delivered in its march the county of Henneberg from the Imperialists, formed a junction on the third day near Koenigshofen, on the frontiers of Franconia.

Francis, Bishop of Wurtzburg, the bitter enemy of the Protestants, and the most zealous member of the League, was the first to feel the indignation of Gustavus Adolphus. A few threats gained for the Swedes possession of his fortress of Koenigshofen, and with it the key of the whole province. At the news of this rapid conquest dismay seized all the Roman Catholic towns of the circle. The Bishops of Wurtzburg and Bamberg trembled in their castles; they already saw their sees tottering, their churches profaned, and their religion degraded. The malice of his enemies had circulated the most frightful representations of the persecuting spirit and the mode of warfare pursued by the Swedish king and his soldiers, which neither the repeated assurances of the king nor the most splendid examples of humanity and toleration ever entirely effaced. Many feared to suffer at the hands of another what in similar circumstances they were conscious of inflicting themselves. Many of the richest Roman Catholics hastened to secure by flight their property, their religion, and their persons from the sanguinary fanaticism of the Swedes. The bishop himself set the example. In the midst of the alarm which his bigoted zeal had caused he abandoned his dominions and fled to Paris to excite, if possible, the French ministry against the common enemy of religion.

The further progress of Gustavus Adolphus in the ecclesiastical territories agreed with this brilliant commencement. Schweinfurt, and soon after Wurtzburg, abandoned by their Imperial garrisons, surrendered; but Marienberg he was obliged to carry by storm. In this place, which was believed to be impregnable, the enemy had collected a large store of provisions and ammunition, all of which fell into the hands of the Swedes. The king found a valuable prize in the library of the Jesuits, which he sent to Upsal, while his soldiers found a still more agreeable one in the prelate's well-filled cellars; his treasures the bishop had in good time removed. The whole bishopric followed the example of the capital and submitted to the Swedes. The king compelled all the bishop's subjects to swear allegiance to himself, and in the absence of the lawful sovereign appointed a regency, one-half of whose members were Protestants. In every Roman Catholic town which Gustavus took he opened the churches to the Protestant people, but without retaliating on the Papists the cruelties which they had practised on the former. On such only as sword in hand refused to submit were the fearful rights of war enforced; and for the occasional acts of violence committed by a few of the more lawless soldiers, in the blind rage of their first attack, their humane leader is not justly responsible. Those who were peaceably disposed, or defenceless, were treated with mildness. It was a sacred principle with Gustavus to spare the blood of his enemies as well as that of his own troops.

On the first news of the Swedish irruption the Bishop of Wurtzburg, without regarding the treaty which he had entered into with the King of Sweden, had earnestly pressed the general of the League to hasten to the assistance of the bishopric. That defected commander had, in the meantime, collected on the Weser the shattered remnant of his army, reinforced himself from the garrisons of Lower Saxony, and effected a junction in Hesse with Altringer and Fugger, who commanded under him. Again at the head of a considerable force Tilly burned with impatience to wipe out the stain of his first defeat by a splendid victory. From his camp at Fulda, whither he had marched with his army, he earnestly requested permission from the Duke of Bavaria to give battle to Gustavus Adolphus. But, in the event of Tilly's defeat, the League had no second army to fall back upon, and Maximilian was too cautious to risk again the fate of his party on a single battle. With tears in his eyes Tilly read the commands of his superior which compelled him to inactivity. Thus his march to Franconia was delayed, and Gustavus Adolphus gained time to overrun the whole bishopric. It was in vain that Tilly, reinforced at Aschaffenburg by a body of twelve thousand men from Lorraine, marched with an overwhelming force to the relief of Wurtzburg. The town and citadel were already in the hands of the Swedes, and Maximilian of Bavaria was generally blamed (and not without cause, perhaps) for having by his scruples occasioned the loss of the bishopric. Commanded to avoid a battle, Tilly contented himself with checking the farther advance of the enemy; but he could save only a few of the towns from the impetuosity of the Swedes. Baffled in an attempt to reinforce the weak garrison of Hanau, which it was highly important for the Swedes to gain, he crossed the Maine near Seligenstadt and took the direction of the Bergestrasse, to protect the Palatinate from the conqueror.

Tilly, however, was not the sole enemy whom Gustavus Adolphus met in Franconia and drove before him. Charles, Duke of Lorraine, celebrated in the annals of the time for his unsteadiness of character, his vain projects, and his misfortunes, ventured to raise a weak arm against the Swedish hero in the hope of obtaining from the Emperor the electoral dignity. Deaf to the suggestions of a rational policy, he listened only to the dictates of heated ambition; by supporting the Emperor he exasperated France, his formidable neighbor, and in pursuit of a visionary phantom in another country left undefended his own dominions, which were instantly overrun by a French army. Austria willingly conceded to him, as well as to the other princes of the League, the honor of being ruined in her cause. Intoxicated with vain hopes this prince collected a force of seventeen thousand men which he proposed to lead in person against the Swedes. If these troops were deficient in discipline and courage they were at least attractive by the splendor of their accoutrements; and however sparing they were of their prowess against the foe, they were liberal enough with it against the defenceless citizens and peasantry whom they were summoned to defend. Against the bravery and the formidable discipline of the Swedes this splendidly attired army, however, made no long stand. On the first advance of the Swedish cavalry a panic seized them, and they were driven without difficulty from their cantonments in Wurtzburg; the defeat of a few regiments occasioned a general rout, and the scattered remnant sought a covert from the Swedish valor in the towns beyond the Rhine. Loaded with shame and ridicule the duke hurried home by Strasburg, too fortunate in escaping, by a submissive written apology, the indignation of his conqueror, who had first beaten him out of the field, and then called upon him to account for his hostilities. It is related upon this occasion that in a village on the Rhine a peasant struck the horse of the duke as he rode past, exclaiming, "Haste, sir; you must go quicker to escape the great King of Sweden."

The example of his neighbors' misfortunes had taught the Bishop of Bamberg prudence. To avert the plundering of his territories he made offers of peace, though these were intended only to delay the king's course till the arrival of assistance. Gustavus Adolphus, too honorable himself to suspect dishonesty in another, readily accepted the bishop's proposals and named the conditions on which he was willing to save his territories from hostile treatment. He was the more inclined to peace, as he had no time to lose in the conquest of Bamberg, and his other designs called him to the Rhine. The rapidity with which he followed up these plans cost him the loss of those pecuniary supplies which, by a longer residence in Franconia, he might easily have extorted from the weak and terrified bishop. This artful prelate broke off the negotiation the instant the storm of war passed away from his own territories. No sooner had Gustavus marched onwards than he threw himself under the protection of Tilly, and received the troops of the Emperor into the very towns and fortresses which shortly before he had shown himself ready to open to the Swedes. By this stratagem, however, he only delayed for a brief interval the ruin of his bishopric. A Swedish general who had been left in Franconia undertook to punish the perfidy of the bishop, and the ecclesiastical territory became the seat of war and was ravaged alike by friends and foes.

The formidable presence of the Imperialists had hitherto been a check upon the Franconian States; but their retreat, and the humane conduct of the Swedish king, emboldened the nobility and other inhabitants of this circle to declare in his favor. Nuremberg joyfully committed itself to his protection, and the Franconian nobles were won to his cause by flattering proclamations in which he condescended to apologize for his hostile appearance in their dominions. The fertility of Franconia, and the rigorous honesty of the Swedish soldiers in their dealings with the inhabitants, brought abundance to the camp of the king. The high-esteem which the nobility of the circle felt for Gustavus, the respect and admiration with which they regarded his brilliant exploits, the promises of rich booty which the service of this monarch held out, greatly facilitated the recruiting of his troops; a step which was made necessary by detaching so many garrisons from the main body. At the sound of his drums recruits flocked to his standard from all quarters.

The king had scarcely spent more time in conquering Franconia than he would have required to cross it. He now left behind him Gustavus Horn, one of his best generals, with a force of eight thousand men, to complete and retain his conquest. He himself with his main army, reinforced by the late recruits, hastened towards the Rhine in order to secure this frontier of the empire from the Spaniards, to disarm the ecclesiastical electors, and to obtain from their fertile territories new resources for the prosecution of the war. Following the course of the Maine, he subjected in the course of his march Seligenstadt, Aschaffenburg, Steinheim, the whole territory on both sides of the river. The imperial garrisons seldom awaited his approach, and never attempted resistance. In the meanwhile one of his colonels had been fortunate enough to take by suprise the town and citadel of Hanau, for whose preservation Tilly had shown such anxiety. Eager to be free of the oppressive burden of the Imperialists, the Count of Hanau gladly placed himself under the milder yoke of the King of Sweden.

Gustavus Adolphus now turned his whole attention to Frankfort, for it was his constant maxim to cover his rear by the friendship and possession of the more important towns. Frankfort was among the free cities which, even from Saxony, he had endeavored to prepare for his reception; and he now called upon it, by a summons from Offenbach, to allow him a free passage, and to admit a Swedish garrison. Willingly would this city have dispensed with the necessity of choosing between the King of Sweden and the Emperor, for, whatever party they might embrace, the inhabitants had a like reason to fear for their privileges and trade. The Emperor's vengeance would certainly fall heavily upon them if they were in a hurry to submit to the King of Sweden, and afterwards he should prove unable to protect his adherents in Germany. But still more ruinous for them would be the displeasure of an irresistible conqueror who, with a formidable army, was already before their gates, and who might punish their opposition by the ruin of their commerce and prosperity. In vain did their deputies plead the danger which menaced their fairs, their privileges, perhaps their constitution itself, if by espousing the party of the Swedes they were to incur the Emperor's displeasure. Gustavus Adolphus expressed to them his astonishment that when the liberties of Germany and the Protestant religion were at stake the citizens of Frankfort should talk of their annual fairs, and postpone for temporal interests the great cause of their country and their conscience. He had, he continued in a menacing tone, found the keys of every town and fortress from the Isle of Rugen to the Maine, and knew also where to find a key to Frankfort. The safety of Germany and the freedom of the Protestant Church were, he assured them, the sole objects of his invasion; conscious of the justice of his cause, he was determined not to allow any obstacle to impede his progress. "The inhabitants of Frankfort, he was well aware, wished to stretch out only a finger to him, but he must have the whole hand in order to have something to grasp." At the head of the army he closely followed the deputies as they carried back his answer, and in order of battle awaited near Saxenhausen the decision of the council.

If Frankfort hesitated to submit to the Swedes it was solely from fear of the Emperor; their own inclinations did not allow them a moment to doubt between the oppressor of Germany and its protector. The menacing preparations amidst which Gustavus Adolphus now compelled them to decide would lessen the guilt of their revolt in the eyes of the Emperor, and by an appearance of compulsion justify the step which they willingly took. The gates were therefore opened to the King of Sweden, who marched his army through this imperial town in magnificent procession and in admirable order. A garrison of six hundred men was left in Saxenhausen, while the king himself advanced the same evening with the rest of his army against the town of Höchst, in Mentz, which surrendered to him before night.

While Gustavus was thus extending his conquests along the Maine, fortune crowned also the efforts of his generals and allies in the North of Germany. Rostock, Wismar, and Doemitz, the only strong places in the Duchy of Mecklenburg which still sighed under the yoke of the Imperialists, were recovered by their legitimate sovereign, the Duke John Albert, under the Swedish General Achatius Tott. In vain did the Imperial general, Wolf Count von Mansfeld, endeavor to recover from the Swedes the territories of Halberstadt, of which they had taken possession immediately upon the victory of Leipzig; he was even compelled to leave Magdeburg itself in their hands. The Swedish general, Banner, who with eight thousand men remained upon the Elbe, closely blockaded that city, and had defeated several imperial regiments which had been sent to its relief. Count Mansfeld defended it in person with great resolution, but his garrison being too weak to oppose for any length of time the numerous force of the besiegers, he was already about to surrender on conditions when Pappenheim advanced to his assistance and gave employment elsewhere to the Swedish arms. Magdeburg, however, or rather the wretched huts that peeped out miserably from among the ruins of that once great town, was afterwards voluntarily abandoned by the Imperialists and immediately taken possession of by the Swedes.

Even Lower Saxony, encouraged by the progress of the king, ventured to raise its head from the disasters of the unfortunate Danish war. They held a congress at Hamburg and resolved upon raising three regiments, which they hoped would be sufficient to free them from the oppressive garrisons of the Imperialists. The Bishop of Bremen, a relation of Gustavus Adolphus, was not content even with this, but assembled troops of his own, and terrified the unfortunate monks and priests of the neighborhood, but was quickly compelled by the imperial general, Count Gronsfeld, to lay down his arms. Even George, Duke of Lunenburg, formerly a colonel in the Emperor's service, embraced the party of Gustavus, for whom he raised several regiments, and, by occupying the attention of the Imperialists in Lower Saxony, materially assisted him.

But more important service was rendered to the king by the Landgrave William of Hesse Cassel, whose victorious arms struck with terror the greater part of Westphalia and Lower Saxony, the bishopric of Fulda, and even the Electorate of Cologne. It has been already stated that immediately after the conclusion of the alliance between the Landgrave and Gustavus Adolphus at Werben, two imperial generals, Fugger and Altringer, were ordered by Tilly to march into Hesse, to punish the Landgrave for his revolt from the Emperor. But this prince had as firmly withstood the arms of his enemies as his subjects had the proclamations of Tilly inciting them to rebellion, and the battle of Leipzig presently relieved him of their presence. He availed himself of their absence with courage and resolution; in a short time, Vach, Münden, and Hoexter surrendered to him, while his rapid advance alarmed the bishoprics of Fulda, Paderborn, and the ecclesiastical territories which bordered on Hesse. The terrified states hastened by a speedy submission to set limits to his progress, and by considerable contributions to purchase exemption from plunder. After these successful enterprises, the Landgrave united his victorious army with that of Gustavus Adolphus, and concerted with him at Frankfort their future plan of operations.

In this city a number of princes and ambassadors were assembled to congratulate Gustavus on his success, and either to conciliate his favor or to appease his indignation. Among them was the fugitive King of Bohemia, Palatine

Frederick V., who had hastened from Holland to throw himself into the arms of his avenger and protector. Gustavus gave him the unprofitable honor of greeting him as a crowned head, and endeavored by a respectful sympathy to soften his sense of his misfortunes. But great as the advantages were which Frederick had promised himself from the power and good fortune of his protector, and high as were the expectations he had built on his justice and magnanimity, the chance of this unfortunate prince's reinstatement in his kingdom was as distant as ever. The inactivity and contradictory politics of the English court had abated the zeal of Gustavus Adolphus, and an irritability, which he could not always repress, made him on this occasion forget the glorious vocation of protector of the oppressed, in which on his invasion of Germany he had so loudly announced himself.

The terrors of the king's irresistible strength, and the near prospect of his vengeance, had also compelled George, Landgrave of Hesse Darmstadt, to a timely submission. His connection with the Emperor, and his indifference to the Protestant cause, were no secret to the king, but he was satisfied with laughing at so impotent an enemy. As the Landgrave knew his own strength and the political situation of Germany so little, as to offer himself as mediator between the contending parties, Gustavus used jestingly to call him the peacemaker. He was frequently heard to say, when at play he was winning from the Landgrave, "that the money afforded double satisfaction, as it was Imperial coin." To his affinity with the Elector of Saxony, whom Gustavus had cause to treat with forbearance, the Landgrave was indebted for the favorable terms he obtained from the king, who contented himself with the surrender of his fortress of Russelheim, and his promise of observing a strict neutrality during the war. The Counts of Westerwald and Wetterau also visited the King in Frankfort, to offer him their assistance against the Spaniards, and so conclude an alliance, which was afterwards of great service to him. The town of Frankfort itself had reason to rejoice at the presence of this monarch, who took their commerce under his protection, and by the most effectual measures restored the fairs, which had been greatly interrupted by the war.

The Swedish army was now reinforced by ten thousand Hessians, which the Landgrave of Casse commanded. Gustavus Adolphus had already invested Königstein; Kostheim and Flörsheim surrendered after a short siege; he was in command of the Maine; and transports were preparing with all speed at Hoechst to carry his troops across the Rhine. These preparations filled the Elector of Mentz, Anselm Casimir, with consternation; and he no longer doubted but that the storm of war would next fall upon him. As a partisan of the Emperor, and one of the most active members of the League, he could expect no better treatment than his confederates, the Bishops of Wurtzburg and Bamberg, had already experienced. The situation of his territories upon the Rhine made it necessary for the enemy to secure them, while the fertility afforded an irresistible temptation to a necessitous army. Miscalculating his own strength and that of his adversaries, the Elector flattered himself that he was able to repel force by force, and weary out the valor of the Swedes by the strength of his fortresses. He ordered the fortifications of his capital to be repaired with all diligence, provided it with every necessary for sustaining a long siege, and received into the town a garrison of two thousand Spaniards, under Don Philip de Sylva. To prevent the approach of the Swedish transports, he endeavored to close the mouth of the Maine by driving piles, and sinking large heaps of stones and vessels. He himself, however, accompanied by the Bishop of Worms, and carrying with him his most precious effects, took refuge in Cologne, and abandoned his capital and territories to the rapacity of a tyrannical garrison. But these preparations, which bespoke less of true courage than of weak and overweening confidence, did not prevent the Swedes from marching against Mentz, and making serious preparations for an attack upon the city. While one body of their troops poured into the Rheingau, routed the Spaniards who remained there, and levied contributions on the inhabitants, another laid the Roman Catholic towns in Westerwald and Wetterau under similar contributions. The main army had encamped at Cassel, opposite Mentz; and Bernhard, Duke of Weimar, made himself master of the Mäusethurm and the castle of Ehrenfels, on the other side of the Rhine. Gustavus was now actively preparing to cross the river, and to blockade the town on the land side, when the movements of Tilly in Franconia suddenly called him from the siege, and obtained for the Elector a short repose.

The danger of Nuremburg, which, during the absence of Gustavus Adolphus on the Rhine, Tilly had made a show of besieging, and, in the event of resistance, threatened with the cruel fate of Magdeburg, occasioned the king suddenly to retire from before Mentz. Lest he should expose himself a second time to the reproaches of Germany, and the disgrace of abandoning a confederate city to a ferocious enemy, he hastened to its relief by forced marches. On his arrival at Frankfort, however, he heard of its spirited resistance, and of the retreat of Tilly, and lost not a moment in prosecuting his designs against Mentz. Failing in an attempt to cross the Rhine at Cassel, under the cannon of the besieged, he directed his march towards the Bergstrasse, with a view of approaching the town from an opposite quarter. Here he quickly made himself master of all the places of importance, and at Stockstadt, between Gernsheim and Oppenheim, appeared a second time upon the banks of the Rhine. The whole of the Bergstrasse was abandoned by the Spaniards, who endeavored obstinately to defend the other bank of the river. For this purpose they had burned or sunk all the vessels in the neighborhood, and arranged a formidable force on the banks in case the king should attempt the passage at that place.

On this occasion, the king's impetuosity exposed him to great danger of falling into the hands of the enemy. In order to reconnoitre the opposite bank, he crossed the river in a small boat; he had scarcely landed when he was attacked by a party of Spanish horse, from whose hands he only saved himself by a precipitate retreat. Having at last, with the assistance of the neighboring fishermen, succeeded in procuring a few transports, he despatched two of them across the river, bearing Count Brahe and three hundred Swedes. Scarcely had this officer time to entrench himself on the opposite bank, when he was attacked by fourteen squadrons of Spanish dragoons and cuirassiers. Superior as the enemy was in number, Count Brahe, with his small force, bravely defended himself, and gained time for the king to support him with fresh troops. The Spaniards at last retired with the loss of six hundred men, some taking refuge in Oppenheim, and others in Mentz. A lion of marble on a high pillar, holding a naked sword in his paw, and a helmet on his head, was erected seventy years after the event, to point out to the traveller the spot where the immortal monarch crossed the great river of Germany.

Gustavus Adolphus now conveyed his artillery and the greater part of his troops over the river, and laid siege to Oppenheim, which, after a brave resistance, was, on the 8th December, 1631, carried by storm. Five hundred Spaniards, who had so courageously defended the place, fell indiscriminately a sacrifice to the fury of the Swedes. The crossing of the Rhine by Gustavus struck terror into the Spaniards and Lorrainers, who had thought themselves protected by the river from the vengeance of the Swedes. Rapid flight was now their only security; every place incapable of an effectual defence was immediately abandoned. After a long train of outrages on the defenceless citizens, the troops of Lorraine evacuated Worms, which, before their departure, they treated with wanton cruelty. The Spaniards hastened to shut themselves up in Frankenthal, where they hoped to defy the victorious arms of Gustavus Adolphus.

The king lost no time in prosecuting his designs against Mentz, into which the flower of the Spanish troops had thrown themselves. While he advanced on the left bank of the Rhine, the Landgrave of Hesse Cassel moved forward on the other, reducing several strong places on his march. The besieged Spaniards, though hemmed in on both sides, displayed at first a bold determination, and threw, for several days, a shower of bombs into the Swedish camp, which cost the king many of his bravest soldiers. But, notwithstanding, the Swedes continually gained ground, and had at last advanced so close to the ditch that they prepared seriously for storming the place. The courage of the besieged now began to droop. They trembled before the furious impetuosity of the Swedish soldiers, of which Marienberg, in Wurtzburg, had afforded so fearful an example. The same dreadful fate awaited Mentz if taken by storm ; and the enemy might even be easily tempted to revenge the carnage of Magdeburg on this rich and magnificent residence of a Roman Catholic prince. To save the town, rather than their own lives, the Spanish garrison capitulated on the fourth day, and obtained from the magnanimity of Gustavus a safe conduct to Luxembourg ; the greater part of them, however, following the example of many others, enlisted in the service of Sweden.

On the 13th December, 1631, the king made his entry into the conquered town, and fixed his quarters in the palace of the Elector. Eighty pieces of cannon fell into his hands, and the citizens were obliged to redeem their property from pillage by a payment of eighty thousand florins. The benefits of this redemption did not extend to the Jews and the clergy, who were obliged to make large and separate contributions for themselves. The library of the Elector was seized by the king as his share, and presented by him to his chancellor, Oxenstiern, who intended it for the Academy of Westerrah, but the vessel in which it was shipped to Sweden foundered at sea.

After the loss of Mentz misfortune still pursued the Spaniards on the Rhine. Shortly before the capture of that city, the Landgrave of Hesse Cassel had taken Falkenstein and Reifenberg, and the fortress of Koningstein surrendered to the Hessians. The Rhinegrave, Otto Louis, one of the king's generals, defeated nine Spanish squadrons who were on their march for Frankenthal, and made himself master of the most important towns upon the Rhine, from Boppart to Bacharach. After the capture of the fortress of Braunfels, which was effected by the Count of Wetterau, with the co-operation of the Swedes, the Spaniards quickly lost every place in Wetterau, while in the Palatinate they retained few places besides Frankenthal. Landau and Kronweisenberg openly declared for the Swedes ; Spires offered troops for the king's service ; Manheim was gained through the prudence of the Duke Bernard of Weimar, and the negligence of its governor, who, for this misconduct, was tried before the council of war, at Heidelberg, and beheaded.

The king had protracted the campaign into the depth of winter, and the severity of the season was perhaps one cause of the advantage his soldiers gained over those of the enemy. But the exhausted troops now stood in need of the repose of winter quarters, which, after the surrender of Mentz, Gustavus assigned to them, in its neighborhood. He himself employed the interval of inactivity in the field, which the season of the year enjoined, in arranging, with his chancellor, the affairs of his cabinet, in treating for a neutrality with some of his enemies, and adjusting some political disputes which had sprung up with a neighboring ally. He chose the city of Mentz for his winter quarters, and the settlement of these state affairs, and showed a greater partiality for this town than seemed consistent with the interests of the German princes, or the shortness of his visit to the Empire. Not content with strongly fortifying it, he erected at the opposite angle, which the Maine forms with the Rhine, a new citadal, which was named Gustavusburg from its founder, but which is better known under the title of Pfaffenraub or Pfaffenzwang.*

While Gustavus Adolphus made himself master of the Rhine, and threatened the three neighboring electorates with his victorious arms, his vigilant enemies in Paris and St. Germain's made use of every artifice to deprive him of the support of France, and, if possible, to involve him in a war with that power. By his sudden and equivocal march to the Rhine he had surprised his friends, and furnished his enemies with the means of exciting a distrust of his intentions. After the conquest of Wurtzburg, and of the greater part of Franconia, the road into Bavaria and Austria lay open to him through Bamberg and the Upper Palatinate; and the expectation was as general as it was natural, that he would not delay to attack the Emperor and the Duke of Bavaria in the

---

* Priests' plunder; alluding to the means by which the expense of its erection had been defrayed.

very centre of their power, and, by the reduction of his two principal enemies, bring the war immediately to an end. But to the surprise of both parties, Gustavus left the path which general expectation had thus marked out for him; and instead of advancing to the right, turned to the left, to make the less important and more innocent princes of the Rhine feel his power, while he gave time to his more formidable opponents to recruit their strength. Nothing but the paramount design of reinstating the unfortunate Palatine, Frederick V., in the possession of his territories, by the expulsion of the Spaniards, could seem to account for this strange step; and the belief that Gustavus was about to effect that restoration silenced for a while the suspicions of his friends and the calumnies of his enemies. But the Lower Palatinate was now almost entirely cleared of the enemy; and yet Gustavus continued to form new schemes of conquest on the Rhine, and to withhold the reconquered country from the Palatine, its rightful owner. In vain did the English ambassador remind him of what justice demanded, and what his own solemn engagement made a duty of honor; Gustavus replied to these demands with bitter complaints of the inactivity of the English court, and prepared to carry his victorious standard into Alsace, and even into Lorraine.

A distrust of the Swedish monarch was now loud and open, while the malice of his enemies busily circulated the most injurious reports as to his intentions. Richelieu, the minister of Louis XIII., had long witnessed with anxiety the king's progress towards the French frontier, and the suspicious temper of Louis rendered him but too accessible to the evil surmises which the occasion gave rise to. France was at this time involved in a civil war with her Protestant subjects, and the fear was not altogether groundless that the approach of a victorious monarch of their party might revive their drooping spirit, and encourage them to a more desperate resistance. This might be the case, even if Gustavus Adolphus was far from showing a disposition to encourage them, or to act unfaithfully towards his ally, the King of France. But the vindictive Bishop of Wurtzburg, who was anxious to avenge the loss of his dominions, the envenomed rhetoric of the Jesuits, and the active zeal of the Bavarian minister, represented this dreaded alliance between the Huguenots and the Swedes as an undoubted fact, and filled the timid mind of Louis with the most alarming fears. Not merely chimerical politicians, but many of the best informed Roman Catholics, fully believed that the king was on the point of breaking into the heart of France, to make common cause with the Huguenots, and to overturn the Catholic religion within the kingdom. Fanatical zealots already saw him, with his army, crossing the Alps and dethroning the Vicegerent of Christ in Italy. Such reports no doubt soon refute themselves; yet it cannot be denied that Gustavus, by his manœuvres on the Rhine, gave a dangerous handle to the malice of his enemies, and in some measure justified the suspicion that he directed his arms, not so much against the Emperor and the Duke of Bavaria, as against the Roman Catholic religion itself.

The general clamor of discontent which the Jesuits raised in all the Catholic courts against the alliance between France and the enemy of the church at last compelled Cardinal Richelieu to take a decisive step for the security of his religion, and at once to convince the Roman Catholic world of the zeal of France, and of the selfish policy of the ecclesiastical states of Germany. Convinced that the views of the King of Sweden, like his own, aimed solely at the humiliation of the power of Austria, he hesitated not to promise to the princes of the League, on the part of Sweden, a complete neutrality, immediately they abandoned their alliance with the Emperor and withdrew their troops. Whatever the resolution these princes should adopt Richelieu would equally attain his object. By their separation from the Austrian interest Ferdinand would be exposed to the combined attack of France and Sweden; and Gustavus Adolphus, freed from his other enemies in Germany, would be able to direct his undivided force against the hereditary dominions of Austria. In that event the fall of Austria was inevitable, and this great object of Richelieu's policy would be gained without injury to the church. If, on

the other hand, the princes of the League persisted in
their opposition, and adhered to the Austrian alliance, the
result would indeed be more doubtful, but still France
would have sufficiently proved to all Europe the sincerity
of her attachment to the Catholic cause, and performed
her duty as a member of the Roman Church. The
princes of the League would then appear the sole authors of those evils which the continuance of the war
would unavoidably bring upon the Roman Catholics of
Germany; they alone, by their wilful and obstinate adherence to the Emperor, would frustrate the measures
employed for their protection, involve the church in
danger, and themselves in ruin.

Richelieu pursued this plan with greater zeal, the more
he was embarrassed by the repeated demands of the
Elector of Bavaria for assistance from France; for this
prince, as already stated, when he first began to entertain suspicions of the Emperor, entered immediately into
a secret alliance with France, by which, in the event of
any change in the Emperor's sentiments, he hoped to
secure the possession of the Palatinate. But though the
origin of the treaty clearly showed against what enemy
it was directed, Maximilian now thought proper to make
use of it against the King of Sweden, and did not hesitate to demand from France that assistance against her
ally which she had simply promised against Austria.
Richelieu, embarrassed by this conflicting alliance with
two hostile powers, had no resource left but to endeavor
to put a speedy termination to their hostilities; and as
little inclined to sacrifice Bavaria, as he was disabled, by
his treaty with Sweden, from assisting it, he set himself,
with all diligence, to bring about a neutrality as the only
means of fulfilling his obligations to both. For this purpose the Marquis of Breze was sent, as his plenipotentiary, to the King of Sweden at Mentz, to learn his sentiments on this point, and to procure from him favorable
conditions for the allied princes. But if Louis XIII. had
powerful motives for wishing for this neutrality, Gustavus
Adolphus had as grave reasons for desiring the contrary.
Convinced by numerous proofs that the hatred of the
princes of the League to the Protestant religion was in-

vincible, their aversion to the foreign power of the Swedes inextinguishable, and their attachment to the House of Austria irrevocable, he apprehended less danger from their open hostility than from a neutrality which was so little in unison with their real inclinations; and, moreover, as he was constrained to carry on the war in Germany at the expense of the enemy, he manifestly sustained great loss if he diminished their number without increasing that of his friends. It was not surprising, therefore, if Gustavus evinced little inclination to purchase the neutrality of the League, by which he was likely to gain so little, at the expense of the advantages he had already obtained.

The conditions, accordingly, upon which he offered to adopt the neutrality towards Bavaria were severe, and suited to these views. He required of the whole League a full and entire cessation from all hostilities; the recall of their troops from the imperial army, from the conquered towns, and from all the Protestant countries; the reduction of their military force; the exclusion of the imperial armies from their territories, and from supplies either of men, provisions, or ammunition. Hard as the conditions were which the victor thus imposed upon the vanquished the French mediator flattered himself he should be able to induce the Elector of Bavaria to accept them. In order to give time for an accommodation, Gustavus had agreed to a cessation of hostilities for a fortnight. But at the very time when this monarch was receiving from the French agents repeated assurances of the favorable progress of the negotiation, an intercepted letter from the Elector to Pappenheim, the imperial general in Westphalia, revealed the perfidy of that prince, as having no other object in view by the whole negotiation than to gain time for his measures of defence. Far from intending to fetter his military operations by a truce with Sweden, the artful prince hastened his preparations, and employed the leisure which his enemy afforded him, in making the most active dispositions for resistance. The negotiation accordingly failed, and served only to increase the animosity of the Bavarians and the Swedes.

Tilly's augmented force, with which he threatened to overrun Franconia, urgently required the king's presence in that circle; but it was necessary to expel previously the Spaniards from the Rhine, and to cut off their means of invading Germany from the Netherlands. With this view, Gustavus Adolphus had made an offer of neutrality to the Elector of Treves, Philip von Zeltern, on condition that the fortress of Hermanstein should be delivered up to him, and a free passage granted to his troops through Coblentz. But unwillingly as the Elector had beheld the Spaniards within his territories, he was still less disposed to commit his estates to the suspicious protection of a heretic, and to make the Swedish conqueror master of his destinies. Too weak to maintain his independence between two such powerful competitors, he took refuge in the protection of France. With his usual prudence, Richelieu profited by the embarrassments of this prince to augment the power of France, and to gain for her an important ally on the German frontier. A numerous French army was despatched to protect the territory of Treves, and a French garrison was received into Ehrenbreitstein. But the object which had moved the Elector to this bold step was not completely gained, for the offended pride of Gustavus Adolphus was not appeased till he had obtained a free passage for his troops through Treves.

Pending these negotiations with Treves and France, the king's generals had entirely cleared the territory of Mentz of the Spanish garrisons, and Gustavus himself completed the conquest of this district by the capture of Kreutznach. To protect these conquests the Chancellor Oxenstiern was left with a division of the army upon the Middle Rhine, while the main body, under the king himself, began its march against the enemy in Franconia.

The possession of this circle had, in the meantime, been disputed with variable success, between Count Tilly and the Swedish General Horn, whom Gustavus had left there with eight thousand men; and the Bishopric of Bamberg, in particular, was at once the prize and the scene of their struggle. Called away to the Rhine by his other projects, the king had left to his general the chastisement of the bishop, whose perfidy had excited his indignation, and the activity of Horn justified the choice. In a short time he subdued the greater part of the bishopric; and the capital itself, abandoned by its imperial garrison, was carried by storm. The banished bishop urgently demanded assistance from the Elector of Bavaria, who was at length persuaded to put an end to Tilly's inactivity. Fully empowered by his master's order to restore the bishop to his possessions, this general collected his troops, who were scattered over the Upper Palatinate, and with an army of twenty thousand men advanced upon Bamberg. Firmly resolved to maintain his conquest, even against this overwhelming force, Horn awaited the enemy within the walls of Bamberg; but was obliged to yield to the vanguard of Tilly what he had thought to be able to dispute with his whole army. A panic which suddenly seized his troops, and which no presence of mind of their general could check, opened the gates to the enemy, and it was with difficulty that the troops, baggage, and artillery were saved. The reconquest of Bamberg was the fruit of this victory; but Tilly, with all his activity, was unable to overtake the Swedish general, who retired in good order behind the Maine. The king's appearance in Franconia, and his junction with Gustavus Horn at Kitzingen, put a stop to Tilly's conquests, and compelled him to provide for his own safety by a rapid retreat.

The king made a general review of his troops at Aschaffenburg. After his junction with Gustavus Horn, Banner, and Duke William of Weimar, they amounted to nearly forty thousand men. His progress through Franconia was uninterrupted; for Tilly, far too weak to encounter an enemy so superior in numbers, had retreated, by rapid marches, towards the Danube. Bohemia and Bavaria were now equally near to the king, and, uncertain whither his victorious course might be directed, Maximilian could form no immediate resolution. The choice of the king, and the fate of both provinces, now depended on the road that should be left open to Count Tilly. It was dangerous, during the approach of so formidable an enemy, to leave Bavaria undefended, in order to protect Austria; still more dangerous, by receiving Tilly into Bavaria, to draw thither the enemy also, and to render it the seat of a destructive war. The cares of the sovereign finally overcame the scruples of the statesman, and Tilly received orders, at all hazards, to cover the frontiers of Bavaria with his army.

Nuremberg received with triumphant joy the protector of the Protestant religion and German freedom, and the enthusiasm of the citizens expressed itself on his arrival in loud transports of admiration and joy. Even Gustavus could not contain his astonishment to see himself in this city, which was the very centre of Germany, where he had never expected to be able to penetrate. The noble appearance of his person completed the impression produced by his glorious exploits, and the condescension with which he received the congratulations of this free city won all hearts. He now confirmed the alliance he had concluded with it on the shores of the Baltic, and excited the citizens to zealous activity and fraternal unity against the common enemy. After a short stay in Nuremberg he followed his army to the Danube, and appeared unexpectedly before the frontier town of Donauwerth. A numerous Bavarian garrison defended the place, and their commander, Rodolph Maximilian, Duke of Saxe Lauenburg, showed at first a resolute determination to defend it till the arrival of Tilly. But the vigor with which Gustavus Adolphus prosecuted the siege soon compelled him to take measures for a speedy and secure retreat, which, amidst a tremendous fire from the Swedish artillery, he successfully executed.

The conquest of Donauwerth opened to the king the further side of the Danube, and now the small river Lech alone separated him from Bavaria. The immediate danger of his dominions aroused all Maximilian's activity, and however little he had hitherto disturbed the enemy's progress to his frontier, he now determined to dispute as resolutely the remainder of their course. On the opposite bank of the Lech, near the small town of Rain, Tilly occupied a strongly fortified camp, which, surrounded by three rivers, bade defiance to all attack. All the bridges over the Lech were destroyed; the whole course of the stream protected by strong garrisons as far as Augsburg, and that town itself, which had long betrayed its impatience to follow the example of Nuremberg and Frankfort, secured by a Bavarian garrison, and the disarming of its inhabitants. The Elector himself, with all the troops he could collect, threw himself into Tilly's camp, as if all his hopes centred on this single point, and here the good fortune of the Swedes was to suffer shipwreck forever.

Gustavus Adolphus, after subduing the whole territory of Augsburg, on his own side of the river, and opening to his troops a rich supply of necessaries from that quarter, soon appeared on the bank opposite the Bavarian intrenchments. It was now the month of March, when the river, swollen by frequent rains and the melting of the snow from the mountains of the Tyrol, flowed full and rapid between its steep banks. Its boiling current threatened the rash assailants with certain destruction, while from the opposite side the enemy's cannon showed their murderous mouths. If, in despite of the fury both of fire and water, they should accomplish this almost impossible passage, a fresh and vigorous enemy awaited the exhausted troops in an impregnable camp; and when they needed repose and refreshment they must prepare for battle. With exhausted powers they must ascend the hostile intrenchments, whose strength seemed to bid defiance to every assault. A defeat sustained upon this shore would be attended with inevitable destruction, since the same stream which impeded their advance would also cut off their retreat if fortune should abandon them.

The Swedish council of war, which the king now assembled, strongly urged upon him all these considerations, in order to deter him from this dangerous undertaking. The most intrepid were appalled, and a troop of honorable warriors, who had grown gray in the field, did not hesitate to express their alarm. But the king's resolution was fixed. "What!" said he to Gustavus Horn, who spoke for the rest, "have we crossed the Baltic, and so many great rivers of Germany, and shall we now be checked by a brook like the Lech?" Gustavus had already at great personal risk reconnoitred the whole country, and discovered that his own side of the river was higher than the other, and consequently gave a considerable advantage to the fire of the Swedish artillery over that of the enemy. With great presence of mind he determined to profit by this circumstance. At the point where the left bank of the Lech forms an angle with the right he immediately caused three batteries to be erected, from which seventy-two field-pieces maintained a cross fire upon the enemy. While this tremendous cannonade drove the Bavarians from the opposite bank, he caused to be erected a bridge over the river with all possible rapidity. A thick smoke, kept up by burning wood and wet straw, concealed for some time the progress of the work from the enemy, while the continued thunder of the cannon overpowered the noise of the axes. He kept alive by his own example the courage of his troops, and discharged more than sixty cannon with his own hand. The cannonade was returned by the Bavarians with equal vivacity for two hours, though with less effect, as the Swedish batteries swept the lower opposite bank, while their height served as a breastwork to their own troops. In vain, therefore, did the Bavarians attempt to destroy these works; the superior fire of the Swedes threw them into disorder, and the bridge was completed under their very eyes. On this dreadful day Tilly did everything in his power to encourage his troops, and no danger could drive him from the bank. At length he found the death which he sought, a cannon-ball shattered his leg; and Altringer, his brave companion-in-arms, was soon after dangerously wounded in the head. Deprived of the animating presence of their two generals the Bavarians gave way at last, and Maximilian, in spite of his own judgment, was driven to adopt a pusillanimous resolve. Overcome by the persuasions of the dying Tilly, whose wonted firmness was overpowered by the near approach of death, he gave up his impregnable position for lost; and the discovery by the Swedes of a ford by which their cavalry were on the point of passing, accelerated his inglorious retreat. The same night, before a single soldier of the enemy had crossed the Lech, he broke up his camp, and without giving time for the king to harass him in his march, retreated in good order to Neuburgh and Ingolstadt. With astonishment did Gustavus Adolphus, who completed the passage of the river on the following day, behold the hostile camp abandoned; and the Elector's flight surprised him still more when he saw the strength of the position he had quitted. "Had I been the Bavarian," said he, "though a cannon-ball had carried away my beard and chin, never would I have abandoned a position like this and laid open my territory to my enemies."

Bavaria now lay exposed to the conquerer; and, for the first time the tide of war, which had hitherto only beat against its frontier, now flowed over its long spared and fertile fields. Before, however, the king proceeded to the conquest of these provinces, he delivered the town of Augsburg from the yoke of Bavaria, exacted an oath of allegiance from the citizens, and to secure its observance left a garrison in the town. He then advanced by rapid marches against Ingolstadt, in order, by the capture of this important fortress, which the Elector covered with the greater part of his army, to secure his conquests in Bavaria and obtain a firm footing on the Danube.

Shortly after the appearance of the Swedish King before Ingoldstadt, the wounded Tilly, after experiencing the caprice of unstable fortune, terminated his career within the walls of that town. Conquered by the superior generalship of Gustavus Adolphus, he lost at the close of his days all the laurels of his earlier victories, and appeased by a series of misfortunes the demands of justice and the avenging manes of Magdeburg. In his death the Imperial army and that of the League sustained an irreparable loss; the Roman Catholic religion was deprived of its most zealous defender, and Maximilian of Bavaria of the most faithful of his servants, who sealed his fidelity by his death, and even in his dying moments fulfilled the duties of a general. His last message to the Elector was an urgent advice to take possession of Ratisbon, in order to maintain the command of the Danube, and to keep open the communication with Bohemia.

With the confidence which was the natural fruit of so many victories, Gustavus Adolphus commenced the siege of Ingolstadt, hoping to gain the town by the fury of his first assault. But the strength of its fortifications and the bravery of its garrison presented obstacles greater than any he had had to encounter since the battle of Breitenfeld, and the walls of Ingolstadt were near putting an end to his career. While reconnoitring the works a twenty-four-pounder killed his horse under him and he fell to the ground, while almost immediately afterwards another ball struck his favorite, the young Margrave of Baden, by his side. With perfect self-possession the king rose and quieted the fears of his troops by immediately mounting another horse.

The occupation of Ratisbon by the Bavarians, who, by the advice of Tilly, had surprised this town by stratagem, and placed in it a strong garrison, quickly changed the king's plan of operations. He had flattered himself with the hope of gaining this town, which favored the Protestant cause, and to find in it an ally as devoted to him as Nuremberg, Augsburg, and Frankfort. Its seizure by the Bavarians seemed to postpone for a long time the fulfilment of his favorite project of making himself master of the Danube, and cutting off his adversaries' supplies from Bohemia. He suddenly raised the siege of Ingoldstadt, before which he had wasted both his time and his troops, and penetrated into the interior of Bavaria, in order to draw the Elector into that quarter for the defence of his territories, and thus to strip the Danube of its defenders.

The whole country as far as Munich now lay open to the conqueror. Mosberg, Landshut, and the whole territory of Freysingen submitted; nothing could resist his arms. But if he met with no regular force to oppose his progress he had to contend against a still more implacable enemy in the heart of every Bavarian — religious fanaticism. Soldiers who did not believe in the Pope were, in this country, a new and unheard-of phenomenon; the blind zeal of the priests represented them to the peasantry as monsters, the children of hell, and their leader as Antichrist. No wonder, then, if they thought themselves released from all the ties of nature and humanity towards this brood of Satan, and justified in committing the most savage atrocities upon them. Woe to the Swedish soldier who fell into their hands! All the torments which inventive malice could devise were exercised upon these unhappy victims; and the sight of their mangled bodies exasperated the army to a fearful retaliation. Gustavus Adolphus, alone, sullied the lustre of his heroic character by no act of revenge; and the aversion which the Bavarians felt towards his religion, far from making him depart from the obligations of humanity towards that unfortunate people, seemed to impose upon him the stricter duty to honor his religion by a more constant clemency.

The approach of the king spread terror and consternation in the capital, which, stripped of its defenders, and abandoned by its principal inhabitants, placed all its hopes in the magnanimity of the conqueror. By an unconditional and voluntary surrender it hoped to disarm his vengeance; and sent deputies even to Freysingen to lay at his feet the keys of the city. Strongly as the king might have been tempted by the inhumanity of the Bavarians, and the hostility of their sovereign, to make a dreadful use of the rights of victory; pressed as he was by Germans to avenge the fate of Magdeburg on the capital of its destroyer, this great prince scorned this mean revenge; and the very helplessness of his enemies disarmed his severity. Contented with the more noble triumph of conducting the Palatine Frederick with the pomp of a victor into the very palace of the prince who had been the chief instrument of his ruin, and the usurper of his territories, he heightened the brilliancy of his triumphal entry by the brighter splendor of moderation and clemency.

The king found in Munich only a forsaken palace, for the Elector's treasures had been transported to Werfen. The magnificence of the building astonished him; and he asked the guide who showed the apartments who was the architect. "No other," replied he, "than the Elector himself." "I wish," said the king, "I had this architect to send to Stockholm." "That," he was answered, "the architect will take care to prevent." When the arsenal was examined, they found nothing but carrriages, stripped of their cannon. The latter had been so artfully concealed under the floor that no traces of them remained; but for the treachery of a workman, the deceit would not have been detected. "Rise up from the dead," said the king, "and come to judgment." The floor was pulled up, and one hundred and forty pieces of cannon discovered, some of extraordinary calibre, which had been principally taken in the Palatinate and Bohemia. A treasure of thirty thousand gold ducats, concealed in one of the largest, completed the pleasure which the king received from this valuable acquisition.

A far more welcome spectacle still would have been the Bavarian army itself; for his march into the heart of Bavaria had been undertaken chiefly with the view of luring them from their intrenchments. In this expectation he was disappointed. No enemy appeared; no entreaties, however urgent, on the part of his subjects, could induce the Elector to risk the remainder of his army to the chances of a battle. Shut up in Ratisbon, he awaited the reinforcements which Wallenstein was bringing from Bohemia; and endeavored, in the meantime, to amuse his enemy and keep him inactive by reviving the negotiation for a neutrality. But the king's distrust, too often and too justly excited by his previous conduct, frustrated this design; and the intentional delay of Wallenstein abandoned Bavaria to the Swedes.

Thus far had Gustavus advanced from victory to victory without meeting with an enemy able to cope with him. A part of Bavaria and Swabia, the bishoprics of Franconia, the Lower Palatinate, and the archbishopric of Mentz lay conquered in his rear. An uninterrupted career of conquest had conducted him to the threshold of Austria; and the most brilliant success had fully justified the plan of operations which he had formed after the battle of Breitenfeld. If he had not succeeded to his wish in promoting a confederacy among the Protestant States, he had at least disarmed or weakened the League, carried on the war chiefly at its expense, lessened the Emperor's resources, emboldened the weaker States, and while he laid under contribution the allies of the Emperor, forced a way through their territories into Austria itself. Where arms were unavailing, the greatest service was rendered by the friendship of the free cities, whose affections he had gained by the double ties of policy and religion; and, as long as he should maintain his superiority in the field, he might reckon on everything from their zeal. By his conquests on the Rhine, the Spaniards were cut off from the Lower Palatinate, even if the state of the war in the Netherlands left them at liberty to interfere in the affairs of Germany. The Duke of Lorraine, too, after his unfortunate campaign, had been glad to adopt a neutrality. Even the numerous garrisons he had left behind him in his progress through Germany had not diminished his army; and, fresh and vigorous as when he first began his march, he now stood in the centre of Bavaria, determined and prepared to carry the war into the heart of Austria.

While Gustavus Adolphus thus maintained his superiority within the empire, fortune, in another quarter, had been no less favorable to his ally, the Elector of Saxony. By the arrangement concerted between these princes at Halle, after the battle of Leipzig, the conquest of Bohemia was intrusted to the Elector of Saxony, while the king reserved for himself the attack upon the territories of the League. The first fruits which the Elector reaped from the battle of Breitenfeld, was the reconquest of Leipzig, which was shortly followed by the expulsion of the Austrian garrisons from the entire circle. Reinforced by the troops who deserted to him from the hostile garrisons, the Saxon General, Arnheim, marched towards Lusatia, which had been overrun by an Imperial general, Rudolph von Tiefenbach, in order to chastise the Elector for embracing the cause of the enemy. He had already commenced in this weakly defended province the usual course of devastation, taken several towns, and terrified Dresden itself by his approach, when his destructive progress was suddenly stopped by an express mandate from the Emperor to spare the possessions of the King of Saxony.

Ferdinand had perceived too late the errors of that policy, which had reduced the Elector of Saxony to extremities, and forcibly driven this powerful monarch into an alliance with Sweden. By moderation, equally ill-timed, he now wished to repair if possible the consequences of his haughtiness; and thus committed a second error in endeavoring to repair the first. To deprive his enemy of so powerful an ally, he had opened, through the intervention of Spain, a negotiation with the Elector; and in order to facilitate an accommodation, Tiefenbach was ordered immediately to retire from Saxony. But these concessions of the Emperor, far from producing the desired effect, only revealed to the Elector the embarrassment of his adversary and his own importance, and emboldened him the more to prosecute the advantages he had already obtained. How could he, moreover, without becoming chargeable with the most shameful ingratitude, abandon an ally to whom he had given the most solemn assurances of fidelity, and to whom he was indebted for the preservation of his dominions, and even of his Electoral dignity?

The Saxon army, now relieved from the necessity of marching into Lusatia, advanced towards Bohemia, where a combination of favorable circumstances seemed to insure them an easy victory. In this kingdom, the first scene of this fatal war, the flames of dissension still smouldered beneath the ashes, while the discontent of the inhabitants was fomented by daily acts of oppression and tyranny. On every side this unfortunate country showed signs of a mournful change. Whole districts had changed their proprietors, and groaned under the hated yoke of Roman Catholic masters, whom the favor of the Emperor and the Jesuits had enriched with the plunder and possessions of the exiled Protestants. Others, taking advantage themselves of the general distress, had purchased, at a low rate, the confiscated estates. The blood of the most eminent champions of liberty had been shed upon the scaffold; and such as by a timely flight avoided that fate were wandering in misery far from their native land, while the obsequious slaves of despotism enjoyed their patrimony. Still more insupportable than the oppression of these petty tyrants, was the restraint of conscience which was imposed without distinction on all the Protestants of that kingdom. No external danger, no opposition on the part of the nation, however steadfast, not even the fearful lessons of past experience could check in the Jesuits the rage of proselytism; where fair means were ineffectual, recourse was had to military force to bring the deluded wanderers within the pale of the church. The inhabitants of Joachimsthal, on the frontiers between Bohemia and Meissen, were the chief sufferers from this violence. Two imperial commissaries, accompanied by as many Jesuits, and supported by fifteen musketeers, made their appearance in this peaceful valley to preach the gospel to the heretics. Where the rhetoric of the former was ineffectual, the forcibly quartering the latter upon the houses, and threats of banishment and fines were tried. But on this occasion, the good cause prevailed, and the bold resistance of this small district compelled the Emperor disgracefully to recall his mandate of conversion. The example of the court had, however, afforded a precedent to the Roman Catholics of the empire, and seemed to justify every act of oppression which their insolence tempted them to wreak upon the Protestants. It is not surprising, then, if this persecuted party was favorable to a revolution, and saw with pleasure their deliverers on the frontiers.

The Saxon army was already on its march towards Prague, the imperial garrisons everywhere retired before them; Schloeckenau, Tetschen, Aussig, Leutmeritz, soon fell into the enemy's hands, and every Roman Catholic place was abandoned to plunder. Consternation seized all the Papists of the Empire; and conscious of the outrages which they themselves had committed on the Protestants, they did not venture to abide the vengeful arrival of a Protestant army. All the Roman Catholics who had anything to lose fled hastily from the country to the capital, which again they presently abandoned. Prague was unprepared for an attack, and was too weakly garrisoned to sustain a long siege. Too late had the Emperor resolved to despatch Field-Marshal Tiefenbach to the defence of this capital. Before the imperial orders could reach the headquarters of that general, in Silesia, the Saxons were already close to Prague, the

Protestant inhabitants of which showed little zeal, while the weakness of the garrison left no room to hope a long resistance. In this fearful state of embarrassment the Roman Catholics of Prague looked for security to Wallenstein, who now lived in that city as a private individual. But far from lending his military experience, and the weight of his name, towards its defence, he seized the favorable opportunity to satiate his thirst for revenge. If he did not actually invite the Saxons to Prague, at least his conduct facilitated its capture. Though unprepared, the town might still hold out until succors could arrive; and an imperial colonel, Count Maradas, showed serious intentions of undertaking its defence. But without command and authority, and having no support but his own zeal and courage, he did not dare to venture upon such a step without the advice of a superior. He therefore consulted the Duke of Friedland, whose approbation might supply the want of authority from the Emperor, and to whom the Bohemian generals were referred by an express edict of the court in the last extremity. He, however, artfully excused himself, on the plea of holding no official appointment, and his long retirement from the political world; while he weakened the resolution of the subalterns by the scruples which he suggested, and painted in the strongest colors. At last, to render the consternation general and complete, he quitted the capital with his whole court, however little he had to fear from its capture; and the city was lost, because, by his departure, he showed that he despaired of its safety. His example was followed by all the Roman Catholic nobility, the generals with their troops, the clergy, and all the officers of the crown. All night the people were employed in saving their persons and effects. The roads to Vienna were crowded with fugitives, who scarcely recovered from their consternation till they reached the imperial city. Maradas himself, despairing of the safety of Prague, followed the rest, and led his small detachment to Tabor, where he awaited the event.

Profound silence reigned in Prague, when the Saxons next morning appeared before it; no preparations were made for defence; not a single shot from the walls announced an intention of resistance. On the contrary, a crowd of spectators from the town, allured by curiosity, came flocking round, to behold the foreign army; and the peaceful confidence with which they advanced resembled a friendly salutation more than a hostile reception. From the concurrent reports of these people the Swedes learned that the town had been deserted by the troops, and that the government had fled to Budweiss. This unexpected and inexplicable absence of resistance excited Arnheim's distrust the more, as the speedy approach of the Silesian succors was no secret to him, and as he knew that the Saxon army was too indifferently provided with materials for undertaking a siege, and by far too weak in numbers to attempt to take the place by storm. Apprehensive of stratagem, he redoubled his vigilance; and he continued in this conviction until Wallenstein's house-steward, whom he discovered among the crowd, confirmed to him this intelligence. "The town is ours without a blow!" exclaimed he in astonishment to his officers, and immediately summoned it by a trumpeter.

The citizens of Prague, thus shamefully abandoned by their defenders, had long taken their resolution; all that they had to do was to secure their properties and liberties by an advantageous capitulation. No sooner was the treaty signed by the Saxon general, in his master's name, than the gates were opened, without farther opposition; and upon the 11th of November, 1631, the army made their triumphal entry. The Elector soon after followed in person, to receive the homage of those whom he had newly taken under his protection: for it was only in the character of protector that the three towns of Prague had surrendered to him. Their allegiance to the Austrian monarchy was not to be dissolved by the step they had taken. In proportion as the Papists' apprehensions of reprisals on the part of the Protestants had been exaggerated, so was their surprise great at the moderation of the Elector, and the discipline of his troops. Field-Marshal Arnheim plainly evinced, on this occasion, his respect for Wallenstein. Not content with sparing his estates on his march, he now placed guards over his palace, in Prague, to prevent the plunder of any of his effects. The Roman Catholics of the town were allowed the fullest liberty of conscience; and of all the churches they had wrested from the Protestants four only were now taken back from them. From this general indulgence none were excluded but the Jesuits, who were generally considered as the authors of all past grievances, and thus banished the kingdom.

John George belied not the submission and dependence with which the terror of the imperial name inspired him; nor did he indulge at Prague in a course of conduct which would assuredly have been pursued against himself in Dresden by imperial generals, such as Tilly or Wallenstein. He carefully distinguished between the enemy with whom he was at war, and the head of the Empire, to whom he owed obedience. He did not venture to touch the household furniture of the latter, while, without scruple, he appropriated and transported to Dresden the cannon of the former. He did not take up his residence in the imperial palace, but the house of Lichtenstein; too modest to use the apartments of one whom he had deprived of a kingdom. Had this trait been related of a great man and a hero it would irresistibly excite our admiration; but the character of this prince leaves us in doubt whether this moderation ought to be ascribed to a noble self-command or to the littleness of a weak mind, which even good fortune could not embolden, and liberty itself could not strip of its habituated fetters.

The surrender of Prague, which was quickly followed by that of most of the other towns, effected a great and sudden change in Bohemia. Many of the Protestant nobility, who had hitherto been wandering about in misery now returned to their native country; and Count Thurn, the famous author of the Bohemian insurrection, enjoyed the triumph of returning as a conqueror to the scene of his crime and his condemnation. Over the very bridge where the heads of his adherents, exposed to view, held out a fearful picture of the fate which had threatened himself, he now made his triumphal entry; and to remove these ghastly objects was his first care. The exiles again took possession of their properties, without thinking of recompensing for the purchase-money the present possessors, who had mostly taken to flight. Even though they had received a price for their estates, they seized on everything which had once been their own; and many had reason to rejoice at the economy of the late possessors. The lands and cattle had greatly improved in their hands; the apartments were now decorated with the most costly furniture; the cellars, which had been left empty, were richly filled; the stables supplied; the magazines stored with provisions. But distrusting the constancy of that good fortune which had so unexpectedly smiled upon them, they hastened to get quit of these insecure possessions, and to convert their immovable into transferable property.

The presence of the Saxons inspired all the Protestants of the kingdom with courage; and both in the country and the capital crowds flocked to the newly-opened Protestant churches. Many, whom fear alone had retained in their adherence to Popery, now openly professed the new doctrine; and many of the late converts to Roman Catholicism gladly renounced a compulsory persuasion to follow the earlier conviction of their conscience. All the moderation of the new regency could not restrain the manifestation of that just displeasure which this persecuted people felt against their oppressors. They made a fearful and cruel use of their newly-recovered rights; and, in many parts of the kingdom, their hatred of the religion which they had been compelled to profess could be satiated only by the blood of its adherents.

Meantime the succors which the imperial generals, Goetz and Tiefenbach, were conducting from Silesia, had entered Bohemia, where they were joined by some of Tilly's regiments, from the Upper Palatinate. In order to disperse them before they should receive any further reinforcements, Arnheim advanced with part of his army from Prague, and made a vigorous attack on their intrenchments near Limburg, on the Elbe. After a severe action, not without great loss, he drove the enemy from their fortified camp, and forced them, by his heavy fire, to recross the Elbe, and to destroy the bridge which they had built over that river. Nevertheless, the Imperialists obtained the advantage in several skirmishes, and the Croats pushed their incursions to the very gates of Prague. Brilliant and promising as the opening of the Bohemian campaign had been, the issue by no means satisfied the expectations of Gustavus Adolphus. Instead of vigorously following up their advantages, by forcing a passage to the Swedish army through the conquered country, and then, with it, attacking the imperial power in its centre, the Saxons weakened themselves in a war of skirmishes, in which they were not always successful, while they lost the time which should have been devoted to greater undertakings. But the Elector's subsequent conduct betrayed the motives which had prevented him from pushing his advantage over the Emperor, and by consistent measures promoting the plans of the King of Sweden.

The Emperor had now lost the greater part of Bohemia, and the Saxons were advancing against Austria, while the Swedish monarch was rapidly moving to the same point through Franconia, Swabia, and Bavaria. A long war had exhausted the strength of the Austrian monarchy, wasted the country, and diminished its armies. The renown of its victories was no more, as well as the confidence inspired by constant success; its troops had lost the obedience and discipline to which those of the Swedish monarch owed all their superiority in the field. The confederates of the Emperor were disarmed, or their fidelity shaken by the danger which threatened themselves. Even Maximilian of Bavaria, Austria's most powerful ally, seemed disposed to yield to the seductive proposition of neutrality; while his suspicious alliance with France had long been a subject of apprehension to the Emperor. The Bishops of Wurtzburg and Bamberg, the Elector of Mentz, and the Duke of Lorraine, were either expelled from their territories, or threatened with immediate attack; Treves had placed itself under the protection of France. The bravery of the Hollanders gave full employment to the Spanish arms in the Netherlands; while Gustavus had driven them from the Rhine. Poland was still fettered by the truce which subsisted between that country and Sweden. The Hungarian frontier was threatened by the Transylvanian Prince, Ragotsky, a successor of Bethlem Gabor, and the inheritor of his restless mind; while the Porte was making great preparation to profit by the favorable conjuncture for aggression. Most of the Protestant states, encouraged by their protector's success, were openly and actively declaring against the Emperor. All the resources which had been obtained by the violent and oppressive extortions of Tilly and Wallenstein were exhausted; all these depôts, magazines, and rallying-points were now lost to the Emperor; and the war could no longer be carried on, as before, at the cost of others. To complete his embarrassment, a dangerous insurrection broke out in the territory of the Ens, where the ill-timed religious zeal of the government had provoked the Protestants to resistance; and thus fanaticism lit its torch within the empire, while a foreign enemy was already on its frontier. After so long a continuance of good fortune, such brilliant victories and extensive conquests, such fruitless effusion of blood, the Emperor saw himself a second time on the brink of that abyss into which he was so near falling at the commencement of his reign. If Bavaria should embrace the neutrality; if Saxony should resist the tempting offers he had held out; and France resolve to attack the Spanish power at the same time in the Netherlands, in Italy, and in Catalonia, the ruin of Austria would be complete; the allied powers would divide its spoils, and the political system of Germany would undergo a total change.

The chain of these disasters began with the battle of Breitenfeld, the unfortunate issue of which plainly revealed the long-decided decline of the Austrian power, whose weakness had hitherto been concealed under the dazzling glitter of a grand name. The chief cause of the Swedes' superiority in the field was evidently to be ascribed to the unlimited power of their leader, who concentrated in himself the whole strength of his party; and, unfettered in his enterprises by any higher authority, was complete master of every favorable opportunity, could control all his means to the accomplishment of his ends, and was responsible to none but himself. But since

Wallenstein's dismissal, and Tilly's defeat, the very reverse of this course was pursued by the Emperor and the League. The generals wanted authority over their troops, and liberty of acting at their discretion; the soldiers were deficient in discipline and obedience; the scattered corps in combined operation; the states in attachment to the cause; the leaders in harmony among themselves, in quickness to resolve, and firmness to execute. What gave the Emperor's enemy so decided an advantage over him was not so much their superior power as their manner of using it. The League and the Emperor did not want means, but a mind capable of directing them with energy and effect. Even had Count Tilly not lost his old renown, distrust of Bavaria would not allow the Emperor to place the fate of Austria in the hands of one who had never concealed his attachment to the Bavarian Elector. The urgent want which Ferdinand felt was for a general possessed of sufficient experience to form and to command an army, and willing at the same time to dedicate his services, with blind devotion, to the Austrian monarchy.

This choice now occupied the attention of the Emperor's privy council, and divided the opinions of its members. In order to oppose one monarch to another, and by the presence of their sovereign to animate the courage of the troops, Ferdinand, in the ardor of the moment, had offered himself to be the leader of his army; but little trouble was required to overturn a resolution which was the offspring of despair alone, and which yielded at once to calm reflection. But the situation which his dignity, and the duties of administration, prevented the Emperor from holding, might be filled by his son, a youth of talents and bravery, and of whom the subjects of Austria had already formed great expectations. Called by his birth to the defence of a monarchy, of whose crowns he wore two already, Ferdinand III., King of Hungary and Bohemia, united, with the natural dignity of heir to the throne, the respect of the army, and the attachment of the people, whose co-operation was indispensable to him in the conduct of the war. None but the beloved heir to the crown could venture to impose new burdens on a people already severely oppressed; his personal presence with the army could alone suppress the pernicious jealousies of the several leaders, and, by the influence of his name, restore the neglected discipline of the troops to its former rigor. If so young a leader was devoid of the maturity of judgment, prudence, and military experience, which practice alone could impart, this deficiency might be supplied by a judicious choice of counsellors and assistants, who, under the cover of his name, might be vested with supreme authority.

But plausible as were the arguments with which a part of the ministry supported this plan, it was met by difficulties not less serious, arising from the distrust, perhaps even the jealousy of the Emperor, and also from the desperate state of affairs. How dangerous was it to entrust the fate of the monarchy to a youth who was himself in need of counsel and support! How hazardous to oppose to the greatest general of his age a tyro, whose fitness for so important a post had never yet been tested by experience; whose name, as yet unknown to fame, was far too powerless to inspire a dispirited army with the assurance of future victory! What a new burden on the country, to support the state a royal leader was required to maintain, and which the prejudices of the age considered as inseparable from his presence with the army! How serious a consideration for the prince himself, to commence his political career with an office which must make him the scourge of his people, and the oppressor of the territories which he was hereafter to rule.

But not only was a general to be found for the army; an army must also be found for the general. Since the compulsory resignation of Wallenstein the Emperor had defended himself more by the assistance of Bavaria and the League than by his own armies; and it was this dependence on equivocal allies which he was endeavoring to escape by the appointment of a general of his own. But what possibility was there of raising an army out of nothing, without the all-powerful aid of gold, and the inspiriting name of a victorious commander; above all, an army which, by its discipline, warlike spirit, and activity should be fit to cope with the experienced troops of the northern conqueror? In all Europe, there was but one man equal to this, and that one had been mortally affronted.

The moment had at last arrived when more than ordinary satisfaction was to be done to the wounded pride of the Duke of Friedland. Fate itself had been his avenger, and an unbroken chain of disasters, which had assailed Austria from the day of his dismissal, had wrung from the Emperor the humiliating confession that with this general he had lost his right arm. Every defeat of his troops opened afresh this wound; every town which he lost revived in the mind of the deceived monarch the memory of his own weakness and ingratitude. It would have been well for him if, in the offended general, he had only lost a leader of his troops, and a defender of his dominions; but he was destined to find in him an enemy, and the most dangerous of all, since he was least armed against the stroke of treason.

Removed from the theatre of war, and condemned to irksome inaction, while his rivals gathered laurels on the field of glory, the haughty duke had beheld these changes of fortune with affected composure, and concealed, under a glittering and theatrical pomp, the dark designs of his restless genius. Torn by burning passions within, while all without bespoke calmness and indifference, he brooded over projects of ambition and revenge, and slowly, but surely, advanced towards his end. All that he owed to the Emperor was effaced from his mind; what he himself had done for the Emperor was imprinted in burning characters on his memory. To his insatiable thirst for power the Emperor's ingratitude was welcome, as it seemed to tear in pieces the record of past favors, to absolve from him every obligation towards his former benefactor. In the disguise of a righteous retaliation, the projects dictated by his ambition now appeared to him just and pure. In proportion as the external circle of his operations was narrowed, the world of hope expanded before him, and his dreamy imagination revelled in boundless projects, which, in any mind but such as his, madness alone could have given birth to. His services had raised him to the proudest height which it was possible for a man, by his own efforts, to attain. Fortune had denied him nothing which the subject and the citizen could lawfully enjoy. Till the moment of his dismissal his demands had met with no refusal, his ambition had met with no check; but the blow which, at the Diet of Ratisbon, humbled him, showed him the difference between *original* and *deputed* power, the distance between the subject and his sovereign. Roused from the intoxication of his own greatness by this sudden reverse of fortune, he compared the authority which he had possessed with that which had deprived him of it; and his ambition marked the steps which it had yet to surmount upon the ladder of fortune. From the moment he had so bitterly experienced the weight of sovereign power, his efforts were directed to attain it for himself; the wrong which he himself had suffered made him a robber. Had he not been outraged by injustice he might have obediently moved in his orbit round the majesty of the throne, satisfied with the glory of being the brightest of its satellites. It was only when violently forced from its sphere, that his wandering star threw in disorder the system to which it belonged, and came in destructive collision with its sun.

Gustavus Adolphus had overrun the north of Germany; one place after another was lost; and at Leipzig the flower of the Austrian army had fallen. The intelligence of this defeat soon reached the ears of Wallenstein, who, in the retired obscurity of a private station in Prague, contemplated from a calm distance the tumult of war. The news, which filled the breasts of the Roman Catholics with dismay, announced to him the return of greatness and good fortune. For him was Gustavus Adolphus laboring. Scarce had the king begun to gain reputation by his exploits when Wallenstein lost not a moment to court his friendship, and to make common cause with this successful enemy of Austria. The banished Count Thurn who had long entered the service of Sweden, undertook to convey Wallenstein's congratulations to the king, and to invite him to a close alliance with the duke. Wallenstein required fifteen thousand men from the king; and with these, and the troops he himself engaged to raise, he undertook to conquer Bohemia and Moravia, to surprise Vienna, and drive his master, the Emperor, before him into Italy. Welcome as was this unexpected proposition, its extravagant promises were naturally calculated to excite suspicion. Gustavus Adolphus was too good a judge of merit to reject with coldness the offers of one who might be so important a friend. But when Wallenstein, encouraged by the favorable reception of his first message, renewed it after the battle of Breitenfeld, and pressed for a decisive answer, the prudent monarch hesitated to trust his reputation to the chimerical projects of so daring an adventurer, and to commit so large a force to the honesty of a man who felt no shame in openly avowing himself a traitor. He excused himself, therefore, on the plea of the weakness of his army, which, if diminished by so large a detachment, would certainly suffer in its march through the empire; and thus, perhaps, by excess of caution, lost an opportunity of putting an immediate end to the war. He afterwards endeavored to renew the negotiations; but the favorable moment was past, and Wallenstein's offended pride never forgave the first neglect.

But the king's hesitation, perhaps, only accelerated the breach which their characters made inevitable sooner or later. Both framed by nature to give laws, not to receive them, they could not long have co-operated in an enterprise which eminently demanded mutual submission and sacrifices. Wallenstein was *nothing* where he was not *everything;* he must either act with unlimited power or not at all. So cordially, too, did Gustavus dislike control, that he had almost renounced his advantageous alliance with France because it threatened to fetter his own independent judgment. Wallenstein was lost to a party if he could not lead; the latter was, if possible, still less disposed to obey the instructions of another. If the pretensions of a rival would be so irksome to the Duke of Friedland, in the conduct of combined operations, in the division of the spoil they would be insupportable. The proud monarch might condescend to accept the assistance of a rebellious subject against the Emperor, and to reward his valuable services with regal munificence; but he never could so far lose sight of his own dignity, and the majesty of royalty, as to bestow the recompense which the extravagant ambition of Wallenstein demanded; and requite an act of treason, however useful, with a crown. In him, therefore, even if all Europe should tacitly acquiesce, Wallenstein had reason to expect the most decided and formidable opponent to his views on the Bohemian crown; and in all Europe he was the only one who could enforce his opposition. Constituted Dictator in Germany by Wallenstein himself, he might turn his arms against him, and consider himself bound by no obligation to one who was himself a traitor. There was no room for a Wallenstein under such an ally; and it was, apparently, this conviction, and not any supposed designs upon the imperial throne, that he alluded to, when, after the death of the King of Sweden, he exclaimed, "It is well for him and me that he is gone. The German Empire does not require two such leaders."

His first scheme of revenge on the house of Austria had indeed failed; but the purpose itself remained unalterable; the choice of means alone was changed. What he had failed in effecting with the King of Sweden, he hoped to obtain with less difficulty and more advantage from the Elector of Saxony. Him he was as certain of being able to bend to his views as he had always been doubtful of Gustavus Adolphus. Having always maintained a good understanding with his old friend Arnheim, he now made use of him to bring about an alliance with Saxony, by which he hoped to render himself equally formidable to the Emperor and the King of Sweden. He had reason to expect that a scheme, which, if successful, would deprive the Swedish monarch of his influence in Germany, would be welcomed by the Elector of Saxony, who he knew was jealous of the power and offended at the lofty pretensions of Gustavus Adolphus. If he succeeded in separating Saxony from the Swedish alliance, and in establishing, conjointly with that power, a third party in the Empire, the fate of the war would be placed in his hand; and by this single step he would succeed in gratifying his revenge against the Emperor, revenging the neglect of the Swedish monarch, and on the ruin of both raising the edifice of his own greatness.

But whatever course he might follow in the prosecution of his designs he could not carry them into effect without an army entirely devoted to him. Such a force could not be secretly raised without its coming to the knowledge of the imperial court, where it would naturally excite suspicion, and thus frustrate his design in the very outset. From the army, too, the rebellious purposes for which it was destined must be concealed till the very moment of execution, since it could scarcely be expected that they would at once be prepared to listen to the voice of a traitor, and serve against their legitimate sovereign. Wallenstein, therefore, must raise it publicly, and in name of the Emperor, and be placed at its head, with unlimited authority, by the Emperor himself. But how could this be accomplished otherwise than by his being appointed to the command of the army, and entrusted with full powers to conduct the war. Yet neither his pride nor his interest permitted him to sue in person for this post, and as a suppliant to accept from the favor of the Emperor a limited power, when an unlimited authority might be extorted from his fears. In order to make himself the master of the terms on which he would resume the command of the army, his course was to wait until the post should be forced upon him. This was the advice he received from Arnheim, and this the end for which he labored with profound policy and restless activity.

Convinced that extreme necessity would alone conquer the Emperor's irresolution, and render powerless the opposition of his bitter enemies, Bavaria and Spain, he henceforth occupied himself in promoting the success of the enemy, and in increasing the embarrassments of his master. It was apparently by his instigation and advice that the Saxons, when on the route to Lusatia and Silesia, had turned their march towards Bohemia, and overrun that defenceless kingdom, where their rapid conquests was partly the result of his measures. By the fears which he affected to entertain he paralyzed every effort at resistance; and his precipitate retreat caused the delivery of the capital to the enemy. At a conference with the Saxon general, which was held at Kaunitz under the pretext of negotiating for a peace, the seal was put to the conspiracy, and the conquest of Bohemia was the first fruits of this mutual understanding. While Wallenstein was thus personally endeavoring to heighten the perplexities of Austria, and while the rapid movements of the Swedes upon the Rhine effectually promoted his designs, his friends and bribed adherents in Vienna uttered loud complaints of the public calamities, and represented the dismissal of the general as the sole cause of all these misfortunes. "Had Wallenstein commanded, matters would never have come to this," exclaimed a thousand voices; while their opinions found supporters, even in the Emperor's privy council.

Their repeated remonstrances were not needed to convince the embarrassed Emperor of his general's merits, and of his own error. His dependence on Bavaria and the League had soon become insupportable; but hitherto this dependence permitted him not to show his distrust, or irritate the Elector by the recall of Wallenstein. But now, when his necessities grew every day more pressing, and the weakness of Bavaria more apparent, he could no longer hesitate to listen to the friends of the duke, and to consider their overtures for his restoration to command. The immense riches Wallenstein possessed, the universal reputation he enjoyed, the rapidity with which six years before he had assembled an army of forty thousand men, the little expense at which he had maintained this formidable force, the actions he had performed at its head, and, lastly, the zeal and fidelity he had displayed for his master's honor, still lived in the Emperor's recollection, and made Wallenstein seem to him the ablest instrument to restore the balance between the belligerent powers, to save Austria, and preserve the Catholic religion. However sensibly the imperial pride might feel the humiliation in being forced to make so unequivocal an admission of past errors and present necessity; however painful it was to descend to humble entreaties from the height of imperial command; however doubtful the fidelity of so deeply-injured and implacable a character; however loudly and urgently the Spanish minister and the Elector of Bavaria protested against this step, the immediate pressure of necessity finally overcame every other consideration, and the friends of the duke were empowered to consult him on the subject, and to hold out the prospect of his restoration.

Informed of all that was transacted in the Emperor's cabinet to his advantage, Wallenstein possessed sufficient self-command to conceal his inward triumph and to assume the mask of indifference. The moment of vengeance was at last come, and his proud heart exulted in the prospect of repaying with interest the injuries of the Emperor. With artful eloquence he expatiated upon the happy tranquillity of a private station, which had blessed him since his retirement from a political stage. Too long, he said, had he tasted the pleasures of ease and independence to sacrifice to the vain phantom of glory the uncertain favor of princes. All his desire of power and distinction were extinct: tranquillity and repose were now the sole object of his wishes. The better to conceal his real impatience, he declined the Emperor's invitation to the court, but at the same time, to facilitate the negotiations, came to Znaim, in Moravia.

At first it was proposed to limit the authority to be entrusted to him, by the presence of a superior, in order by this expedient to silence the objections of the Elector of Bavaria. The imperial deputies, Questenberg and Werdenberg, who, as old friends of the duke, had been employed in this delicate mission, were instructed to propose that the King of Hungary should remain with the army, and learn the art of war under Wallenstein. But the very mention of his name threatened to put a period to the whole negotiation. "No! never," exclaimed Wallenstein, "will I submit to a colleague in my office. No — not even if it were God himself with whom I should have to share my command." But even when this obnoxious point was given up, Prince Eggenberg, the Emperor's minister and favorite, who had always been the steady friend and zealous champion of Wallenstein, and was therefore expressly sent to him, exhausted his eloquence in vain to overcome the pretended reluctance of the duke. "The Emperor," he admitted, "had, in Wallenstein, thrown away the most costly jewel in his crown: but unwillingly and compulsorily only had he taken this step, which he had since deeply repented of; while his esteem for the duke had remained unaltered, his favor for him undiminished. Of these sentiments he now gave the most decisive proof, by reposing unlimited confidence in his fidelity and capacity to repair the mistakes of his predecessors, and to change the whole aspect of affairs. It would be great and noble to sacrifice his just indignation to the good of his country; dignified and worthy of him to refute the evil calumny of his enemies by the double warmth of his zeal. This victory over himself," concluded the prince, " would crown his other unparalleled services to the empire, and render him the greatest man of his age."

These humiliating confessions, and flattering assurances, seemed at last to disarm the anger of the duke; but not before he had disburdened his heart of his reproaches against the Emperor, pompously dwelt upon his own services, and humbled to the utmost the monarch who solicited his assistance, did he condescend to listen to the attractive proposals of the minister. As if he yielded entirely to the force of their arguments, he condescended with a haughty reluctance to that which was the most ardent wish of his heart; and deigned to favor the ambassadors with a ray of hope. But far from putting an end to the Emperor's embarrassments, by giving at once a full and unconditional consent, he only acceded to a part of his demands, that he might exalt the value of that which still remained, and was of most importance. He accepted the command, but only for three months; merely for the purpose of raising, but not of leading an army. He wished only to show his power and ability in its organization, and to display before the eyes of the Emperor the greatness of that assistance which he still retained in his hands. Convinced that an army raised by his name alone would, if deprived of its creator, soon sink again into nothing, he intended it to serve only as a decoy to draw more important concessions from his master. And yet Ferdinand congratulated himself, even in having gained so much as he had.

Wallenstein did not long delay to fulfil those promises

which all Germany regarded as chimerical, and which Gustavus Adolphus had considered as extravagant. But the foundation for the present enterprise had been long laid, and he now only put in motion the machinery which many years had been prepared for the purpose. Scarcely had the news spread of Wallenstein's levies, when, from every quarter of the Austrian monarchy, crowds of soldiers repaired to try their fortunes under this experienced general. Many, who had before fought under his standards, had been admiring eye-witnesses of his great actions, and experienced his magnanimity, came forward from their retirement to share with him a second time both booty and glory. The greatness of the pay he promised attracted thousands, and the plentiful supplies the soldier was likely to enjoy at the cost of the peasant was to the latter an irresistible inducement to embrace the military life at once, rather than be the victim of its oppression. All the Austrian provinces were compelled to assist in the equipment. No class was exempt from taxation — no dignity or privilege from capitation. The Spanish court, as well as the King of Hungary, agreed to contribute a considerable sum. The ministers made large presents, while Wallenstein himself advanced two hundred thousand dollars from his own income to hasten the armament. The poorer officers he supported out of his own revenues; and, by his own example, by brilliant promotions, and still more brilliant promises, he induced all who were able to raise troops at their own expense. Whoever raised a corps at his own cost was to be its commander. In the appointment of officers, religion made no difference. Riches, bravery, and experience were more regarded than creed. By this uniform treatment of different religious sects, and still more by his express declaration, that his present levy had nothing to do with religion, the Protestant subjects of the empire were tranquillized, and reconciled to bear their share of the public burdens. The duke, at the same time, did not omit to treat, in his own name, with foreign states for men and money. He prevailed on the Duke of Lorraine, a second time, to espouse the cause of the Emperor. Poland was urged to supply him with

Cossacks, and Italy with warlike necessaries. Before the three months were expired the army, which was assembled in Moravia, amounted to no less than forty thousand men, chiefly drawn from the unconquered parts of Bohemia, from Moravia, Silesia, and the German provinces of the House of Austria. What to every one had appeared impracticable, Wallenstein, to the astonishment of all Europe, had in a short time effected. The charm of his name, his treasures, and his genius had assembled thousands in arms, where before Austria had only looked for hundreds. Furnished, even to superfluity, with all necessaries, commanded by experienced officers, and inflamed by enthusiasm which assured itself of victory, this newly-created army only awaited the signal of their leader to show themselves, by the bravery of their deeds, worthy of his choice.

The duke had fulfilled his promise, and the troops were ready to take the field; he then retired, and left to the Emperor to choose a commander. But it would have been as easy to raise a second army like the first as to find any other commander for it than Wallenstein. This promising army, the last hope of the Emperor, was nothing but an illusion as soon as the charm was dissolved which had called it into existence; by Wallenstein it had been raised, and without him it sank like a creation of magic into its original nothingness. Its officers were either bound to him as his debtors, or, as his creditors, closely connected with his interests, and the preservation of his power. The regiments he had entrusted to his own relations, creatures, and favorites. He, and he alone, could discharge to the troops the extravagant promises by which they had been lured into his service. His pledged word was the only security on which their bold expectations rested; a blind reliance on his omnipotence, the only tie which linked together in one common life and soul the various impulses of their zeal. There was an end of the good fortune of each individual if he retired, who alone was the voucher of its fulfilment.

However little Wallenstein was serious in his refusal, he successfully employed this means to terrify the Emperor into consenting to his extravagant conditions. The progress of the enemy every day increased the pressure of the Emperor's difficulties, while the remedy was also close at hand; a word from him might terminate the general embarrassment. Prince Eggenberg at length received orders, for the third and last time, at any cost and sacrifice, to induce his friend, Wallenstein, to accept the command.

He found him at Znaim, in Moravia, pompously surrounded by the troops, the possession of which he made the Emperor so earnestly to long for. As a suppliant did the haughty subject receive the deputy of his sovereign. "He never could trust," he said, "to a restoration to command, which he owed to the Emperor's necessities, and not to his sense of justice. He was now courted because the danger had reached its height, and safety was hoped for from his arm only; but his successful services would soon cause the servant to be forgotten, and the return of security would bring back renewed ingratitude. If he deceived the expectations formed of him, his long-earned renown would be forfeited; even if he fulfilled them, his repose and happiness must be sacrificed. Soon would envy be excited anew, and the dependent monarch would not hesitate a second time to make an offering of convenience to a servant whom he could now dispense with. Better for him at once, and voluntarily, to resign a post from which sooner or later the intrigues of his enemies would expel him. Security and content were to be found in the bosom of private life; and nothing but the wish to oblige the Emperor had induced him, reluctantly enough, to relinquish for a time his blissful repose."

Tired of this long farce, the minister at last assumed a serious tone, and threatened the obstinate duke with the Emperor's resentment if he persisted in his refusal. "Low enough had the imperial dignity," he added, "stooped already; and yet, instead of exciting his magnanimity by its condescension, had only flattered his pride and increased his obstinacy. If this sacrifice had been made in vain, he would not answer but that the suppliant might be converted into the sovereign, and that the monarch might not avenge his injured dignity on his rebellious subject. However greatly Ferdinand may have erred, the Emperor at least had a claim to obedience; the man might be mistaken, but the monarch could not confess his error. If the Duke of Friedland had suffered by an unjust decree, he might yet be recompensed for all his losses; the wound which it had itself inflicted the hand of Majesty might heal. If he asked security for his person and his dignities, the Emperor's equity would refuse him no reasonable demand. Majesty contemned, admitted not of any atonement; disobedience to its commands cancelled the most brilliant services. The Emperor required his services, and as Emperor he demanded them. Whatever price Wallenstein might set upon them, the Emperor would readily agree to; but he demanded obedience, or the weight of his indignation should crush the refractory servant."

Wallenstein, whose extensive possessions within the Austrian monarchy were momentarily exposed to the power of the Emperor, was keenly sensible that this was no idle threat; yet it was not fear that at last overcame his affected reluctance. This imperious tone of itself was to his mind a plain proof of the weakness and despair which dictated it, while the Emperor's readiness to yield all his demands convinced him that he had attained the summit of his wishes. He now made a show of yielding to the persuasions of Eggenberg; and left him in order to write down the conditions on which he accepted the command.

Not without apprehension did the minister receive the writing in which the proudest of subjects had prescribed laws to the proudest of sovereigns. But however little confidence he had in the moderation of his friend, the extravagant contents of his writing surpassed even his worst expectations. Wallenstein required the uncontrolled command over all the German armies of Austria and Spain, with unlimited powers to reward and punish. Neither the King of Hungary, nor the Emperor himself, were to appear in the army, still less to exercise any act of authority over it. No commission in the army, no pension or letter of grace, was to be granted by the Emperor without Wallenstein's approval. All the conquests and

confiscations that should take place were to be placed
entirely at Wallenstein's disposal, to the exclusion of
every other tribunal. For his ordinary pay, an imperial
hereditary estate was to be assigned him, with another of
the conquered estates within the empire for his extraordinary expenses. Every Austrian province was to be
opened to him if he required it in case of retreat. He
farther demanded the assurance of the possession of the
Duchy of Mecklenburg, in the event of a future peace;
and a formal and timely intimation, if it should be
deemed necessary a second time to deprive him of the
command.

In vain the minister entreated him to moderate his
demands, which, if granted, would deprive the Emperor
of all authority over his own troops, and make him
absolutely dependent on his general. The value placed on
his services had been too plainly manifested to prevent
him dictating the price at which they were to be purchased. If the pressure of circumstances compelled the
Emperor to grant these demands, it was more than a
mere feeling of haughtiness and desire of revenge which
induced the duke to make them. His plans of rebellion were formed to their success, every one of the
conditions for which Wallenstein stipulated in this treaty
with the court was indispensable. Those plans required
that the Emperor should be deprived of all authority in
Germany, and be placed at the mercy of his general; and
this object would be attained the moment Ferdinand
subscribed the required conditions. The use which Wallenstein intended to make of his army (widely different
indeed from that for which it was entrusted to him),
brooked not of a divided power, and still less of an
authority superior to his own. To be the sole master of
the will of his troops, he must also be the sole master of
their destinies; insensibly to supplant his sovereign, and
to transfer permanently to his own person the rights of
sovereignty, which were only lent to him for a time by a
higher authority, he must cautiously keep the latter out
of the view of the army. Hence his obstinate refusal to
allow any prince of the house of Austria to be present
with the army. The liberty of free disposal of all the

conquered and confiscated estates in the empire would also afford him fearful means of purchasing dependents and instruments of his plans, and of acting the dictator in Germany more absolutely than ever any emperor did in time of peace. By the right to use any of the Austrian provinces as a place of refuge, in case of need, he had full power to hold the Emperor a prisoner by means of his own forces, and within his own dominions; to exhaust the strength and resources of these countries, and to undermine the power of Austria in its very foundation.

Whatever might be the issue he had equally secured his own advantage by the conditions he had extorted from the Emperor. If circumstances proved favorable to his daring project, this treaty with the Emperor facilitated its execution; if, on the contrary, the course of things ran counter to it, it would at least afford him a brilliant compensation for the failure of his plans. But how could he consider an agreement valid which was extorted from his sovereign and based upon treason? How could he hope to blind the Emperor by a written agreement, in the face of a law which condemned to death every one who should have the presumption to impose conditions upon him? But this criminal was the most indispensable man in the empire, and Ferdinand, well practised in dissimulation, granted him for the present all he required.

At last then the imperial army had found a commander-in-chief worthy of the name. Every other authority in the army, even that of the Emperor himself, ceased from the moment Wallenstein assumed the commander's baton, and every act was invalid which did not proceed from him. From the banks of the Danube to those of the Weser and the Oder, was felt the life-giving dawning of this new star; a new spirit seemed to inspire the troops of the Emperor, a new epoch of the war began. The Papists form fresh hopes, the Protestant beholds with anxiety the changed course of affairs.

The greater the price at which the services of the new general had been purchased, the greater justly were the expectations from those which the court of the Emperor entertained. But the duke was in no hurry to fulfil these expectations. Already in the vicinity of Bohemia, and at the head of a formidable force, he had but to show himself there in order to overpower the exhausted force of the Saxons, and brilliantly to commence his new career by the reconquest of that kingdom. But, contented with harassing the enemy with indecisive skirmishes of his Croats, he abandoned the best part of that kingdom to be plundered, and moved calmly forward in pursuit of his own selfish plans. His design was, not to conquer the Saxons, but to unite with them. Exclusively occupied with this important object, he remained inactive in the hope of conquering more surely by means of negotiation. He left no expedient untried to detach this prince from the Swedish alliance; and Ferdinand himself, ever inclined to an accommodation with this prince, approved of this proceeding. But the great debt which Saxony owed to Sweden was as yet too freshly remembered to allow of such an act of perfidy; and even had the Elector been disposed to yield to the temptation, the equivocal character of Wallenstein, and the bad character of Austrian policy, precluded any reliance in the integrity of its promises. Notorious already as a treacherous statesman, he met not with faith upon the very occasion when perhaps he intended to act honestly; and, moreover, was denied, by circumstances, the opportunity of proving the sincerity of his intentions by the disclosure of his real motives.

He therefore unwillingly resolved to extort by force of arms what he could not obtain by negotiation. Suddenly assembling his troops, he appeared before Prague ere the Saxons had time to advance to its relief. After a short resistance the treachery of some Capuchins opens the gates to one of his regiments; and the garrison, who had taken refuge in the citadel, soon laid down their arms upon disgraceful conditions. Master of the capital, he hoped to carry on more successfully his negotiations at the Saxon court; but even while he was renewing his proposals to Arnheim, he did not hesitate to give them weight by striking a decisive blow. He hastened to seize the narrow passes between Aussig and Pirna, with a view of cutting off the retreat of the Saxons into their own country; but the rapidity of Arnheim's operations fortunately extricated them from the danger. After the retreat of this general, Egra and Leutmeritz, the last strongholds of the Saxons, surrendered to the conqueror, and the whole kingdom was restored to its legitimate sovereign in less time than it had been lost.

Wallenstein, less occupied with the interests of his master than with the furtherance of his own plans, now purposed to carry the war into Saxony, and by ravaging his territories compel the Elector to enter into a private treaty with the Emperor, or rather with himself. But, however little accustomed he was to make his will bend to circumstances, he now perceived the necessity of postponing his favorite scheme for a time to a more pressing emergency. While he was driving the Saxons from Bohemia, Gustavus Adolphus had been gaining the victories, already detailed, on the Rhine and Danube, and carried the war through Franconia and Swabia to the frontiers of Bavaria. Maximilian, defeated on the Lech, and deprived by death of Count Tilly, his best support, urgently solicited the Emperor to send with all speed the Duke of Friedland to his assistance, from Bohemia, and by the defence of Bavaria to avert the danger from Austria itself. He also made the same request of Wallenstein, and entreated him, till he could himself come with the main force, to despatch in the meantime a few regiments to his aid. Ferdinand seconded the request with all his influence, and one messenger after another was sent to Wallenstein urging him to move towards the Danube.

It now appeared how completely the Emperor had sacrificed his authority in surrendering to another the supreme command of his troops. Indifferent to Maximilian's entreaties, and deaf to the Emperor's repeated commands, Wallenstein remained inactive in Bohemia and abandoned the Elector to his fate. The remembrance of the evil service which Maximilian had rendered him with the Emperor at the Diet at Ratisbon was deeply engraved on the implacable mind of the duke, and the Elector's late attempts to prevent his reinstatement were no secret to him. The moment of avenging this affront had now arrived, and Maximilian was doomed to pay dearly for his folly in provoking the most revengeful of men. Wallenstein maintained that Bohemia ought not to be left exposed, and that Austria could not be better protected than by allowing the Swedish army to waste its strength before the Bavarian fortress. Thus, by the arm of the Swedes, he chastised his enemy; and, while one place after another fell into their hands, he allowed the Elector vainly to await his arrival in Ratisbon. It was only when the complete subjugation of Bohemia left him without excuse, and the conquests of Gustavus Adolphus in Bavaria threatened Austria itself, that he yielded to the pressing entreaties of the Elector and the Emperor, and determined to effect the long-expected union with the former; an event, which, according to the general anticipation of the Roman Catholics, would decide the fate of the campaign.

Gustavus Adolphus, too weak in numbers to cope even with Wallenstein's force alone, naturally dreaded the junction of such powerful armies; and the little energy he used to prevent it was the occasion of great surprise. Apparently he reckoned too much on the hatred which alienated the leaders, and seemed to render their effectual co-operation improbable. When the event contradicted his views it was too late to repair his error. On the first certain intelligence he received of their designs he hastened to the Upper Palatinate for the purpose of intercepting the Elector, but the latter had already arrived there, and the junction had been effected at Egra.

This frontier town had been chosen by Wallenstein for the scene of his triumph over his proud rival. Not content with having seen him, as it were, a suppliant at his feet, he imposed upon him the hard condition of leaving his territories in his rear exposed to the enemy, and declaring by this long march to meet him, the necessity and distress to which he was reduced. Even to this humiliation the haughty prince patiently submitted. It had cost him a severe struggle to ask for protection of the man who, if his own wishes had been consulted, would never have had the power of granting it; but having once made up his mind to it, he was ready to bear all the annoyances which were inseparable from that resolve, and sufficiently master of himself to put up with petty grievances when an important end was in view.

But whatever pains it had cost to effect this junction, it was equally difficult to settle the conditions on which it was to be maintained. The united army must be placed under the command of one individual, if any object was to be gained by the union, and each general was equally averse to yield to the superior authority of the other. If Maximilian rested his claim on his electoral dignity, the nobleness of his descent, and his influence in the empire, Wallenstein's military renown and the unlimited command conferred on him by the Emperor, gave an equally strong title to it. If it was deeply humiliating to the pride of the former to serve under an imperial subject, the idea of imposing laws on so imperious a spirit flattered in the same degree the haughtiness of Wallenstein. An obstinate dispute ensued, which, however, terminated in a mutual compromise to Wallenstein's advantage. To him was assigned the unlimited command of both armies, particularly in battle, while the Elector was deprived of all power of altering the order of battle, or even the route of the army. He retained only the bare right of punishing and rewarding his own troops, and the free use of these when not acting in conjunction with the Imperialists.

After these preliminaries were settled the two generals at last ventured upon an interview; but not until they had mutually promised to bury the past in oblivion, and all the outward formalities of a reconciliation had been settled. According to agreement, they publicly embraced in the sight of their troops, and made mutual professions of friendship, while in reality the hearts of both were overflowing with malice. Maximilian, well versed in dissimulation, had sufficient command over himself not to betray in a single feature his real feelings; but a malicious triumph sparkled in the eyes of Wallenstein, and the constraint which was visible in all his movements betrayed the violence of the emotion which overpowered his proud soul.

The combined Imperial and Bavarian armies amounted

to nearly sixty thousand men, chiefly veterans. Before this force the King of Sweden was not in a condition to keep the field. As his attempt to prevent their junction had failed, he commenced a rapid retreat into Franconia, and awaited there for some decisive movement on the part of the enemy in order to form his own plans. The position of the combined armies between the frontiers of Saxony and Bavaria left it for some time doubtful whether they would remove the war into the former or endeavor to drive the Swedes from the Danube and deliver Bavaria. Saxony had been stripped of troops by Arnheim, who was pursuing his conquests in Silesia, not without a secret design, it was generally supposed, of favoring the entrance of the Duke of Friedland into that electorate, and of thus driving the irresolute John George into peace with the Emperor. Gustavus Adolphus himself, fully persuaded that Wallenstein's views were directed against Saxony, hastily despatched a strong reinforcement to the assistance of his confederate, with the intention, as soon as circumstances would allow, of following with the main body. But the movements of Wallenstein's army soon led him to suspect that he himself was the object of attack; and the duke's march through the Upper Palatinate placed the matter beyond a doubt. The question now was, how to provide for his own security, and the prize was no longer his supremacy, but his very existence. His fertile genius must now supply the means, not of conquest, but of preservation. The approach of the enemy had surprised him before he had time to concentrate his troops, which were scattered all over Germany, or to summon his allies to his aid. Too weak to meet the enemy in the field, he had no choice left but either to throw himself into Nuremberg, and run the risk of being shut up in its walls, or to sacrifice that city and await a reinforcement under the cannon of Donauwerth. Indifferent to danger or difficulty, while he obeyed the call of humanity or honor, he chose the first without hesitation, firmly resolved to bury himself with his whole army under the ruins of Nuremberg rather than to purchase his own safety by the sacrifice of his confederates.

Measures were immediately taken to surround the city

and suburbs with redoubts, and to form an intrenched camp. Several thousand workmen immediately commenced this extensive work, and an heroic determination to hazard life and property in the common cause animated the inhabitants of Nuremberg. A trench eight feet deep and twelve broad surrounded the whole fortification; the lines were defended by redoubts and batteries, the gates by half-moons. The river Pegnitz, which flows through Nuremberg, divided the whole camp into two semicircles, whose communication was secured by several bridges. About three hundred pieces of cannon defended the town-walls and the intrenchments. The peasantry from the neighboring villages, and the inhabitants of Nuremberg, assisted the Swedish soldiers so zealously that on the seventh day the army was able to enter the camp, and in a fortnight this great work was completed.

While these operations were carried on without the walls, the magistrates of Nuremberg were busily occupied in filling the magazines with provisions and ammunition for a long siege. Measures were taken, at the same time, to secure the health of the inhabitants, which was likely to be endangered by the conflux of so many people; cleanliness was enforced by the strictest regulations. In order, if necessary, to support the king, the youth of the city were embodied and trained to arms, the militia of the town considerably reinforced, and a new regiment raised, consisting of four-and-twenty names, according to the letters of the alphabet. Gustavus had, in the meantime, called to his assistance his allies, Duke William of Weimar and the Landgrave of Hesse Cassel; and ordered his generals on the Rhine, in Thuringia and Lower Saxony, to commence their march immediately, and join him with their troops in Nuremberg. His army, which was encamped within the lines, did not amount to more than sixteen thousand men, scarcely a third of the enemy.

The Imperialists had, in the meantime, by slow marches, advanced to Neumark, where Wallenstein made a general review. At the sight of this formidable force he could not refrain from indulging in a childish boast: "In four days," said he, "it will be shown whether I or the King of Sweden is to be master of the world." Yet, notwithstanding his superiority, he did nothing to fulfil his promise; and even let slip the opportunity of crushing his enemy, when the latter had the hardihood to leave his lines to meet him. "Battles enough have been fought," was his answer to those who advised him to attack the king, "it is now time to try another method." Wallenstein's well-founded reputation required not any of those rash enterprises on which younger soldiers rush in hope of gaining a name. Satisfied that the enemy's despair would dearly sell a victory, while a defeat would irretrievably ruin the Emperor's affairs, he resolved to wear out the ardor of his opponent by a tedious blockade, and by thus depriving him of every opportunity of availing himself of his impetuous bravery, take from him the very advantage which had hitherto rendered him invincible. Without making any attack, therefore, he erected a strong fortified camp on the other side of the Pegnitz, and opposite Nuremberg; and, by this well-chosen position, cut off from the city and the camp of Gustavus all supplies from Franconia, Swabia, and Thuringia. Thus he held in siege at once the city and the king, and flattered himself with the hope of slowly, but surely, wearing out by famine and pestilence the courage of his opponent whom he had no wish to encounter in the field.

Little aware, however, of the resources and strength of his adversary, Wallenstein had not taken sufficient precautions to avert from himself the fate he was designing for others. From the whole of the neighboring country, the peasantry had fled with their property; and what little provision remained must be obstinately contested with the Swedes. The king spared the magazines within the town, as long as it was possible to provision his army from without; and these forays produced constant skirmishes between the Croats and the Swedish cavalry, of which the surrounding country exhibited the most melancholy traces. The necessaries of life must be obtained sword in hand; and the foraging parties could not venture out without a numerous escort. And when this supply failed, the town opened its magazines to the king, but Wallenstein had to support his troops from a distance. A large convoy from Bavaria was on its way to him with an escort of a thousand men. Gustavus Adolphus having received intelligence of its approach, immediately sent out a regiment of cavalry to intercept it; and the darkness of the night favored the enterprise. The whole convoy, with the town in which it was, fell into the hands of the Swedes; the imperial escort was cut to pieces; about twelve hundred cattle carried off; and a thousand wagons loaded with bread, which could not be brought away, were set on fire. Seven regiments, which Wallenstein had sent forward to Altdorp to cover the entrance of the long and anxiously expected convoy, were attacked by the king, who had, in like manner, advanced to cover the retreat of his cavalry, and routed after an obstinate action, being driven back into the imperial camp with the loss of four hundred men. So many checks and difficulties, and so firm and unexpected a resistance on the part of the king, made the Duke of Friedland repent that he had declined to hazard a battle. The strength of the Swedish camp rendered an attack impracticable; and the armed youth of Nuremberg served the king as a nursery from which he could supply his loss of troops. The want of provisions, which began to be felt in the imperial camp as strongly as in the Swedish, rendered it uncertain which party would be first compelled to give way.

Fifteen days had the two armies now remained in view of each other, equally defended by inaccessible intrenchments, without attempting anything more than slight attacks and unimportant skirmishes. On both sides infectious diseases, the natural consequence of bad food and a crowded population, had occasioned a greater loss than the sword. And this evil daily increased. But at length the long-expected succors arrived in the Swedish camp; and by this strong reinforcement the king was now enabled to obey the dictates of his native courage, and to break the chains which had hitherto fettered him.

In obedience to his requisitions, the Duke of Weimar had hastily drawn together a corps from the garrisons in Lower Saxony and Thuringia, which, at Schweinfurt, in

Franconia, was joined by four Saxon regiments, and at Kitzingen by the corps of the Rhine, which the Landgrave of Hesse and the Palatine of Birkenfeld despatched to the relief of the king. The chancellor, Oxenstiern, undertook to lead this force to its destination. After being joined at Windsheim by the Duke of Weimar himself, and the Swedish general, Banner, he advanced by rapid marches to Bruck and Eltersdorf, where he passed the Rednitz, and reached the Swedish camp in safety. This reinforcement amounted to nearly fifty thousand men, and was attended by a train of sixty pieces of cannon, and four thousand baggage wagons. Gustavus now saw himself at the head of an army of nearly seventy thousand strong, without reckoning the militia of Nuremberg, which in case of necessity, could bring into the field about thirty thousand fighting men; a formidable force, opposed to another not less formidable. The war seemed at length compressed to the point of a single battle, which was to decide its fearful issue. With divided sympathies, Europe looked with anxiety to this scene, where the whole strength of the two contending parties was fearfully drawn, as it were, to a focus.

If, before the arrival of the Swedish succors, a want of provisions had been felt, the evil was now fearfully increased to a dreadful height in both camps, for Wallenstein had also received reinforcements from Bavaria. Besides the one hundred and twenty thousand men confronted to each other, and more than fifty thousand horses in the two armies, and besides the inhabitants of Nuremberg, whose number far exceeded the Swedish army, there were in the camp of Wallenstein about fifteen thousand women, with as many drivers, and nearly the same number in that of the Swedes. The custom of the time permitted the soldier to carry his family with him to the field. A number of prostitutes followed the Imperialists; while, with the view of preventing such excesses, Gustavus' care for the morals of his soldiers promoted marriages. For the rising generation who had this camp for their home and country, regular military schools were established, which educated a race of excellent warriors, by which means the army might in a manner recruit itself in the course of a long campaign. No wonder, then, if these wandering nations exhausted every territory in which they encamped, and by their immense consumption raised the necessaries of life to an exorbitant price. All the mills of Nuremberg were insufficient to grind the corn required for each day; and fifteen thousand pounds of bread, which were daily delivered by the town into the Swedish camp, excited without allaying the hunger of the soldiers. The laudable exertions of the magistrates of Nuremberg could not prevent the greater part of the horses from dying for want of forage, while the increasing mortality in the camp consigned more than a hundred men daily to the grave.

To put an end to these distresses, Gustavus Adolphus, relying on his numerical superiority, left his lines on the twenty-fifth day, forming before the enemy in order of battle, while he cannonaded the duke's camp from three batteries erected on the side of the Rednitz. But the duke remained immovable in his intrenchments and contented himself with answering this challenge by a distant fire of cannon and musketry. His plan was to wear out the king by his inactivity, and by the force of famine to overcome his resolute determination; and neither the remonstrances of Maximilian, and the impatience of his army, nor the ridicule of his opponent, could shake his purpose. Gustavus, deceived in his hope of forcing a battle, and compelled by his increasing necessities, now attempted impossibilities, and resolved to storm a position which art and nature had combined to render impregnable.

Entrusting his own camp to the militia of Nuremberg on the fifty-eighth day of his encampment (the festival of St. Bartholomew), he advanced in full order of battle, and passing the Rednitz at Furth, easily drove the enemy's outposts before him. The main army of the Imperialists was posted on the steep heights between the Biber and the Rednitz, called the Old Fortress and Altenberg; while the camp itself, commanded by these eminences, spread out immeasurably along the plain. On these heights the whole of the artillery was placed. Deep trenches surrounded inaccessible redoubts, while thick barricades, with pointed palisades, defended the approaches to the heights, from the summits of which Wallenstein calmly and securely discharged the lightnings of his artillery from amid the dark thunder-clouds of smoke. A destructive fire of musketry was maintained behind the breastworks, and a hundred pieces of cannon threatened the desperate assailant with certain destruction. Against this dangerous post Gustavus now directed his attack; five hundred musketeers, supported by a few infantry (for a greater number could not act in the narrow space), enjoyed the unenvied privilege of first throwing themselves into the open jaws of death. The assault was furious, the resistance obstinate. Exposed to the whole fire of the enemy's artillery, and infuriate by the prospect of inevitable death, these determined warriors rushed forward to storm the heights; which, in an instant, converted into a flaming volcano, discharged on them a shower of shot. At the same moment, the heavy cavalry rushed forward into the openings which the artillery had made in the close ranks of the assailants, and divided them; till the intrepid band, conquered by the strength of nature and of man, took to flight, leaving a hundred dead upon the field. To Germans had Gustavus yielded this post of honor. Exasperated at their retreat, he now led on his Finlanders to the attack, thinking, by their northern courage, to shame the cowardice of the Germans. But they, also, after a similar hot reception, yielded to the superiority of the enemy; and a third regiment succeeded them to experience the same fate. This was replaced by a fourth, a fifth, and a sixth; so that, during a ten hour's action every regiment was brought to the attack to retire with bloody loss from the contest. A thousand mangled bodies covered the field; yet Gustavus undauntedly maintained the attack, and Wallenstein held his position unshaken.

In the meantime a sharp contest had taken place between the imperial cavalry and the left wing of the Swedes, which was posted in a thicket on the Rednitz, with varying success, but with equal intrepidity and loss

on both sides. The Duke of Friedland and Prince
Bernard of Weimar had each a horse shot under them;
the king himself had the sole of his boot carried off by a
cannon ball. The combat was maintained with undiminished obstinacy, till the approach of night separated
the combatants. But the Swedes had advanced too far
to retreat without hazard. While the king was seeking
an officer to convey to the regiments the order to retreat,
he met Colonel Hepburn, a brave Scotchman, whose
native courage alone had drawn him from the camp to
share in the dangers of the day. Offended with the king
for having not long before preferred a younger officer
for some post of danger, he had rashly vowed never
again to draw his sword for the king. To him Gustavus
now addressed himself, praising his courage, and requesting him to order the regiments to retreat. "Sire,"
replied the brave soldier, " it is the only service I cannot
refuse to your Majesty; for it is a hazardous one,"—and
immediately hastened to carry the command. One of
the heights above the old fortress had, in the heat of the
action, been carried by the Duke of Weimar. It commanded the hills and the whole camp. But the heavy
rain which fell during the night rendered it impossible
to draw up the cannon; and this post, which had been
gained with so much bloodshed, was also voluntarily abandoned Diffident of fortune, which forsook him on this decisive day, the king did not venture the following morning
to renew the attack with his exhausted troops; and vanquished for the first time, even because he was not victor,
he led back his troops over the Rednitz. Two thousand
dead which he left behind him on the field testified to
the extent of his loss; and the Duke of Friedland remained unconquered within his lines.

For fourteen days after this action the two armies still
continued in front of each other, each in the hope that
the other would be the first to give way. Every day
reduced their provisions, and as scarcity became greater,
the excesses of the soldiers, rendered furious, exercised
the wildest outrages on the peasantry. The increasing
distress broke up all discipline and order in the Swedish
camp; and the German regiments, in particular, distin-

guished themselves for the ravages they practised indiscriminately on friend and foe. The weak hand of a single individual could not check excesses encouraged by the silence, if not the actual example, of the inferior officers. These shameful breaches of discipline, on the maintenance of which he had hitherto justly prided himself, severely pained the king; and the vehemence with which he reproached the German officers for their negligence bespoke the liveliness of his emotion. "It is you yourselves, Germans," said he, "that rob your native country and ruin your own confederates in the faith. As God is my judge, I abhor you, I loathe you; my heart sinks within me whenever I look upon you. Ye break my orders; ye are the cause that the world curses me, that the tears of poverty follow me, that complaints ring in my ear — 'The king, our friend, does us more harm than even our worst enemies.' On your account I have stripped my own kingdom of its treasures, and spent upon you more than forty tons of gold;* while from your German empire I have not received the least aid. I gave you a share of all that God had given to me; and had ye regarded my orders I would have gladly shared with you all my future acquisitions. Your want of discipline convinces me of your evil intentions, whatever cause I might otherwise have to applaud your bravery."

Nuremberg had exerted itself, almost beyond its power, to subsist for eleven weeks the vast crowd which was compressed within its boundaries; but its means were at length exhausted, and the king's more numerous party was obliged to determine on a retreat. By the casualties of war and sickness Nuremberg had lost more than ten thousand of its inhabitants, and Gustavus Adolphus nearly twenty thousand of his soldiers. The fields around the city were trampled down, the villages lay in ashes, the plundered peasantry lay faint and dying on the highways; foul odors infected the air, and bad food, the exhalations from so dense a population, and so many putrifying carcasses, together with the heat of the dog-days, produced a desolating pestilence which raged among men and beasts, and long after the retreat of both

* A ton of gold in Sweden amounts to one hundred thousand rix dollars.

armies continued to load the country with misery and distress. Affected by the general distress, and despairing of conquering the steady determination of the Duke of Friedland, the king broke up his camp on the 8th September, leaving in Nuremberg a sufficient garrison. He advanced in full order of battle before the enemy, who remained motionless, and did not attempt in the least to harass his retreat. His route lay by the Aisch and Windsheim towards Neustadt, where he halted five days to refresh his troops, and also to be near to Nuremberg in case the enemy should make an attempt upon the town. But Wallenstein, as exhausted as himself, had only awaited the retreat of the Swedes to commence his own. Five days afterwards he broke up his camp at Zirndorf, and set it on fire. A hundred columns of smoke, rising from all the burning villages in the neighborhood, announced his retreat, and showed the city the fate it had escaped. His march, which was directed on Forchheim, was marked by the most frightful ravages; but he was too far advanced to be overtaken by the king. The latter now divided his army, which the exhausted country was unable to support, and leaving one division to protect Franconia, with the other he prosecuted in person his conquests in Bavaria.

In the meantime the imperial Bavarian army had marched into the Bishopric of Bamberg, where the Duke of Friedland a second time mustered his troops. He found this force, which so lately had amounted to sixty thousand men, diminished by the sword, desertion, and disease to about twenty-four thousand, and of these a fourth were Bavarians. Thus had the encampments before Nuremberg weakened both parties more than two great battles would have done, apparently without advancing the termination of the war, or satisfying, by any decisive result, the expectations of Europe. The king's conquests in Bavaria, were, it is true, checked for a time by this diversion before Nuremberg, and Austria itself secured against the danger of immediate invasion; but by the retreat of the king from that city, he was again left at full liberty to make Bavaria the seat of war. Indifferent towards the fate of that country, and weary of the restraint which his union with the Elector imposed upon him, the Duke of Friedland eagerly seized the opportunity of separating from this burdensome associate, and prosecuting, with renewed earnestness, his favorite plans. Still adhering to his purpose of detaching Saxony from its Swedish alliance, he selected that country for his winter quarters, hoping by his destructive presence to force the Elector the more readily into his views.

No conjuncture could be more favorable for his designs. The Saxons had invaded Silesia, where, reinforced by troops from Brandenburg and Sweden, they had gained several advantages over the Emperor's troops. Silesia would be saved by a diversion against the Elector in his own territories, and the attempt was the more easy as Saxony, left undefended during the war in Silesia, lay open on every side to attack. The pretext of rescuing from the enemy an hereditary dominion of Austria would silence the remonstrances of the Elector of Bavaria, and, under the mask of a patriotic zeal for the Emperor's interests, Maximilian might be sacrificed without much difficulty. By giving up the rich country of Bavaria to the Swedes he hoped to be left unmolested by them in his enterprise against Saxony, while the increasing coldness between Gustavus and the Saxon Court gave him little reason to apprehend any extraordinary zeal for the deliverance of John George. Thus a second time abandoned by his artful protector, the Elector separated from Wallenstein at Bamberg, to protect his defenceless territory with the small remains of his troops, while the imperial army, under Wallenstein, directed its march through Beyreuth and Coburg towards the Thuringian Forest.

An imperial general, Holk, had previously been sent into Vogtland with six thousand men to waste this defenceless province with fire and sword; he was soon followed by Gallus, another of the duke's generals, and an equally faithful instrument of his inhuman orders. Finally, Pappenheim, too, was recalled from Lower Saxony, to reinforce the diminished army of the duke, and to complete the miseries of the devoted country. Ruined churches, villages in ashes, harvests wilfully destroyed, families plundered, and murdered peasants marked the progress of these barbarians, under whose scourge the whole of Thuringia, Vogtland, and Meissen lay defenceless. Yet this was but the prelude to greater sufferings, with which Wallenstein himself, at the head of the main army, threatened Saxony. After having left behind him fearful monuments of his fury, in his march through Franconia and Thuringia, he arrived with his whole army in the Circle of Leipzig, and compelled the city, after a short resistance, to surrender. His design was to push on to Dresden, and by the conquest of the whole country, to prescribe laws to the Elector. He had already approached the Mulda, threatening to overpower the Saxon army which had advanced as far as Torgau to meet him, when the King of Sweden's arrival at Erfurt gave an unexpected check to his operations. Placed between the Saxon and Swedish armies, which were likely to be farther reinforced by the troops of George, Duke of Lunenburg, from Lower Saxony, he hastily retired upon Merseberg, to form a junction there with Count Pappenheim, and to repel the further advance of the Swedes.

Gustavus Adolphus had witnessed with great uneasiness the arts employed by Spain and Austria to detach his allies from him. The more important his alliance with Saxony the more anxiety the inconstant temper of John George caused him. Between himself and the Elector a sincere friendship could never subsist. A prince proud of his political importance, and accustomed to consider himself as the head of his party, could not see without annoyance the interference of a foreign power in the affairs of the Empire; and nothing but the extreme danger of his dominions could overcome the aversion with which he had long witnessed the progress of this unwelcome intruder. The increasing influence of the king in Germany, his authority with the Protestant states, the unambiguous proofs which he gave of his ambitious views, which were of a character calculated to excite the jealousies of all the states of the Empire, awakened in the Elector's breast a thousand anxieties, which the imperial emissaries did not fail skilfully to keep alive and cherish. Every arbitrary step on the part of the king, every demand, however reasonable, which he addressed to the princes of the Empire, was followed by bitter complaints from the Elector, which seemed to announce an approaching rupture. Even the generals of the two powers, whenever they were called upon to act in common, manifested the same jealousy as divided their leaders. John George's natural aversion to war, and a lingering attachment to Austria, favored the efforts of Arnheim; who, maintaining a constant correspondence with Wallenstein, labored incessantly to effect a private treaty between his master and the Emperor; and if his representations were long disregarded, still the event proved that they were not altogether without effect.

Gustavus Adolphus, naturally apprehensive of the consequences which the defection of so powerful an ally would produce on his future prospects in Germany, spared no pains to avert so pernicious an event; and his remonstrances had hitherto had some effect upon the Elector. But the formidable power with which the Emperor seconded his seductive proposals, and the miseries which, in the case of hesitation, he threatened to accumulate upon Saxony, might at length overcome the resolution of the Elector should he be left exposed to the vengeance of his enemies; while an indifference to the fate of so powerful a confederate would irreparably destroy the confidence of the other allies in their protector. This consideration induced the king a second time to yield to the pressing entreaties of the Elector, and to sacrifice his own brilliant prospects to the safety of this ally. He had already resolved upon a second attack on Ingoldstadt; and the weakness of the Elector of Bavaria gave him hopes of soon forcing this exhausted enemy to accede to a neutrality. An insurrection of the peasantry in Upper Austria opened to him a passage into that country, and the capital might be in his possession before Wallenstein could have time to advance to its defence. All these views he now gave up for the sake of an ally who, neither by his services nor his fidelity, was worthy of the sacrifice; who, on the pressing occasions of common good, had steadily adhered to his own selfish projects; and who was important, not for the services he was expected to render, but merely for the injuries he had it in his power to inflict. Is it possible, then, to refrain from indignation, when we know that in this expedition, undertaken for the benefit of such an ally, the great king was destined to terminate his career?

Rapidly assembling his troops in Franconia, he followed the route of Wallenstein through Thuringia. Duke Bernard of Weimar, who had been despatched to act against Pappenheim, joined the king at Armstadt, who now saw himself at the head of twenty thousand veterans. At Erfurt he took leave of his queen, who was not to behold him, save in his coffin, at Weissenfels. Their anxious adieus seemed to forbode an eternal separation.

He reached Naumburg on the 1st November, 1632, before the corps, which the Duke of Friedland had despatched for that purpose, could make itself master of that place. The inhabitants of the surrounding country flocked in crowds to look upon the hero, the avenger, the great king, who, a year before, had first appeared in that quarter like a guardian angel. Shouts of joy everywhere attended his progress; the people knelt before him and struggled for the honor of touching the sheath of his sword or the hem of his garment. The modest hero disliked this innocent tribute which a sincerely grateful and admiring multitude paid him. "Is it not," said he, "as if this people would make a God of me? Our affairs prosper, indeed; but I fear the vengeance of Heaven will punish me for this presumption, and soon enough reveal to this deluded multitude my human weakness and mortality!" How amiable does Gustavus appear before us at this moment, when about to leave us forever! Even in the plenitude of success he honors an avenging Nemesis, declines that homage which is due only to the Immortal, and strengthens his title to our tears the nearer the moment approaches that is to call them forth!

In the meantime the Duke of Friedland had determined to advance to meet the king as far as Weissenfels, and, even at the hazard of a battle, to secure his winter-quarters in Saxony. His inactivity before Nuremberg had occasioned a suspicion that he was unwilling to measure his powers with those of the Hero of the North, and his hard-earned reputation would be at stake if a second time he should decline a battle. His present superiority in numbers, though much less than what it was at the beginning of the siege of Nuremberg, was still enough to give him hopes of victory if he could compel the king to give battle before his junction with the Saxons. But his present reliance was not so much in his numerical superiority as in the predictions of his astrologer, Seni, who had read in the stars that the good fortune of the Swedish monarch would decline in the month of November. Besides, between Naumburg and Weissenfels there was also a range of narrow defiles, formed by a long mountainous ridge and the river Saal, which ran at their foot, along which the Swedes could not advance without difficulty, and which might with the assistance of a few troops be rendered almost impassable. If attacked there the king would have no choice but either to penetrate with great danger through the defiles, or commence a laborious retreat through Thuringia, and to expose the greater part of his army to a march through a desert country deficient in every necessary for their support. But the rapidity with which Gustavus Adolphus had taken possession of Naumburg disappointed this plan, and it was now Wallenstein himself who awaited the attack.

But in this expectation he was disappointed; for the king, instead of advancing to meet him at Weissenfels, made preparations for intrenching himself near Naumburg, with the intention of awaiting there the reinforcements which the Duke of Lunenburg was bringing up. Undecided whether to advance against the king through the narrow passes between Weissenfels and Naumburg, or to remain inactive in his camp, he called a council of war in order to have the opinion of his most experienced generals. None of these thought it prudent to attack the king in his advantageous position. On the other hand, the preparations which the latter made to fortify his camp plainly showed that it was not his intention soon to abandon it. But the approach of winter rendered it impossible to prolong the campaign, and by a continued encampment to exhaust the strength of the army, already so much in need of repose. All voices were in favor of immediately terminating the campaign; and the more so as the important city of Cologne upon the Rhine was threatened by the Dutch, while the progress of the enemy in Westphalia and the Lower Rhine called for effective reinforcements in that quarter. Wallenstein yielded to the weight of these arguments, and almost convinced that at this season he had no reason to apprehend an attack from the king, he put his troops into winter quarters, but so that, if necessary, they might be rapidly assembled. Count Pappenheim was despatched, with great part of the army, to the assistance of Cologne, with orders to take possession on his march of the fortress of Moritzburg, in the territory of Halle. Different corps took up their winter quarters in the neighboring towns, to watch on all sides the motions of the enemy. Count Colloredo guarded the castle of Weissenfels, and Wallenstein himself encamped with the remainder not far from Merseburg, between Flotzgaben and the Saal, from whence he purposed to march to Leipzig, and to cut off the communication between the Saxons and the Swedish army.

Scarcely had Gustavus Adolphus been informed of Pappenheim's departure when, suddenly breaking up his camp at Naumburg, he hastened with his whole force to attack the enemy, now weakened to one-half. He advanced by rapid marches towards Weissenfels, from whence the news of his arrival quickly reached the enemy, and greatly astonished the Duke of Friedland. But a speedy resolution was now necessary; and the measures of Wallenstein were soon taken. Though he had little more than twelve thousand men to oppose to the twenty thousand of the enemy, he might hope to maintain his ground until the return of Pappenheim, who could not have advanced farther than Halle, five miles distant. Messengers were hastily despatched to recall him, while Wallenstein moved forward into the wide plain between the Canal and Lutzen, where he awaited the king in full order of battle, and by this position cut off his communication with Leipzig and the Saxon auxiliaries.

Three cannon shots, fired by Count Colloredo from the Castle of Weissenfels, announced the king's approach;

and at this concerted signal the light troops of the Duke of Friedland, under the command of the Croatian General Isolani, moved forward to possess themselves of the villages lying upon the Rippach. Their weak resistance did not impede the advance of the enemy, who crossed the Rippach, near the village of that name, and formed in line below Lutzen, opposite the Imperialists. The high road which goes from Weissenfels to Leipzig is intersected between Lutzen and Markranstadt by the canal which extends from Zeitz to Merseburg, and unites the Elster with the Saal. On this canal rested the left wing of the Imperialists and the right of the King of Sweden; but so that the cavalry of both extended themselves along the opposite side. To the northward, behind Lutzen, was Wallenstein's right wing, and to the south of that town was posted the left wing of the Swedes; both armies fronted the high road, which ran between them and divided their order of battle; but the evening before the battle Wallenstein, to the great disadvantage of his opponent, had possessed himself of this highway, deepened the trenches which ran along its sides, and planted them with musketeers so as to make the crossing of it both difficult and dangerous. Behind these, again, was erected a battery of seven large pieces of cannon, to support the fire from the trenches; and at the windmills, close behind Lutzen, fourteen smaller field-pieces were ranged on an eminence, from which they could sweep the greater part of the plain. The infantry, divided into no more than five unwieldy brigades, was drawn up at the distance of three hundred paces from the road, and the cavalry covered the flanks. All the baggage was sent to Leipzig, that it might not impede the movements of the army; and the ammunition-wagons alone remained, which were placed in rear of the line. To conceal the weakness of the Imperialists all the camp-followers and sutlers were mounted, and posted on the left wing, but only until Pappenheim's troops arrived. These arrangements were made during the darkness of the night; and when the morning dawned all was ready for the reception of the enemy.

On the evening of the same day Gustavus Adolphus

appeared on the opposite plain, and formed his troops in the order of attack. His disposition was the same as that which had been so successful the year before at Leipzig. Small squadrons of horse were interspersed among the divisions of the infantry, and troops of musketeers placed here and there among the cavalry. The army was arranged in two lines, the canal on the right and in its rear, the high road in front, and the town on the left. In the centre the infantry was formed, under the command of Count Brahe; the cavalry on the wings; the artillery in front. To the German hero, Bernard, Duke of Weimar, was entrusted the command of the German cavalry of the left wing; while on the right the king led on the Swedes in person, in order to excite the emulation of the two nations to a noble competition. The second line was formed in the same manner; and behind these was placed the reserve, commanded by Henderson, a Scotchman.

In this position they awaited the eventful dawn of morning to begin a contest, which long delay, rather than the probability of decisive consequences, and the picked body, rather than the number of combatants, was to render so terrible and remarkable. The strained expectation of Europe, so disappointed before Nuremberg, was now to be gratified on the plains of Lutzen. During the whole course of the war two such generals, so equally matched in renown and ability, had not before been pitted against each other. Never as yet had daring been cooled by so awful a hazard, or hope animated by so glorious a prize. Europe was next day to learn who was her greatest general — to-morrow, the leader, who had hitherto been invincible, must acknowledge a victor. This morning was to place it beyond a doubt whether the victories of Gustavus at Leipzig and on the Lech were owing to his own military genius or to the incompetency of his opponent; whether the services of Wallenstein were to vindicate the Emperor's choice, and justify the high price at which they had been purchased. The victory was as yet doubtful, but certain were the labor and the bloodshed by which it must be earned. Every private in both armies felt a jealous share in their leader's reputation, and under every corslet beat the same emotions that inflamed the bosoms of the generals. Each army knew the enemy to which it was to be opposed; and the anxiety which each in vain attempted to repress was a convincing proof of their opponent's strength.

At last the fatal morning dawned; but an impenetrable fog, which spread over the plain, delayed the attack till noon. Kneeling in front of his lines the king offered up his devotions; and the whole army at the same moment dropping on their knees burst into a moving hymn, accompanied by the military music. The king then mounted his horse, and clad only in a leathern doublet and surtout (for a wound he had formerly received prevented his wearing armor), he rode along the ranks to animate the courage of his troops with a joyful confidence, which, however, the forboding presentment of his own bosom contradicted. "God with us!" was the warcry of the Swedes; "Jesus Maria!" that of the Imperialists. About eleven the fog began to disperse and the enemy became visible. At the same moment Lutzen was seen in flames, having been set on fire by command of the duke to prevent his being outflanked on that side. The charge was now sounded; the cavalry rushed upon the enemy, and the infantry advanced against the trenches.

Received by a tremendous fire of musketry and heavy artillery, these intrepid battalions maintained the attack with undaunted courage till the enemy's musketeers abandoned their posts, the trenches were passed, the battery carried and turned against the enemy. They pressed forward with irresistible impetuosity; the first of the five imperial brigades was immediately routed, the second soon after, and the third put to flight. But here the genius of Wallenstein opposed itself to their progress. With the rapidity of lightning he was on the spot to rally his discomfited troops; and his powerful word was itself sufficient to stop the flight of the fugitives. Supported by three regiments of cavalry the vanquished brigades, forming anew, faced the enemy and pressed vigorously into the broken ranks of the Swedes. A murderous conflict ensued. The nearness of the enemy left no room for firearms, the fury of the attack no time for loading; man was matched to man, the useless musket exchanged for the sword and pike, and science gave way to desperation. Overpowered by numbers the wearied Swedes at last retire beyond the trenches, and the captured battery is again lost by the retreat. A thousand mangled bodies already strewed the plain, and as yet not a single step of ground had been won.

In the meantime the king's right wing, led by himself, had fallen upon the enemy's left. The first impetuous shock of the heavy Finland cuirassiers dispersed the lightly-mounted Poles and Croats who were posted here, and their disorderly flight spread terror and confusion among the rest of the cavalry. At this moment notice was brought to the king that his infantry were retreating over the trenches, and also that his left wing, exposed to a severe fire from the enemy's cannon posted at the windmills, was beginning to give way. With rapid decision he committed to General Horn the pursuit of the enemy's left, while he flew, at the head of the regiment of Steinbock, to repair the disorder of his right wing. His noble charger bore him with the velocity of lightning across the trenches, but the squadrons that followed could not come on with the same speed, and only a few horsemen, among whom was Francis Albert, Duke of Saxe Lauenburg, were able to keep up with the king. He rode directly to the place where his infantry were most closely pressed, and while he was reconnoitring the enemy's line for an exposed point of attack the shortness of his sight unfortunately led him too close to their ranks. An imperial Gefreyter,* remarking that every one respectfully made way for him as he rode along, immediately ordered a musketeer to take aim at him. "Fire at him yonder," said he, "that must be a man of consequence." The soldier fired, and the king's left arm was shattered. At that moment his squadrons came hurrying up, and a confused cry of "the king bleeds! the king is shot!" spread terror and consternation through all the ranks. "It is nothing — follow me," cried the king, collecting his whole

---

* Gefreyter, a person exempt from watching duty, nearly corresponding to the corporal.

strength; but overcome by pain, and nearly fainting, he requested the Duke of Lauenburg, in French, to lead him unobserved out of the tumult. While the duke proceeded towards the right wing with the king, making a long circuit to keep this discouraging sight from the disordered infantry, his majesty received a second shot through the back, which deprived him of his remaining strength. "Brother," said he, with a dying voice, "I have enough! look only to your own life." At the same moment he fell from his horse pierced by several more shots, and abandoned by all his attendants he breathed his last amidst the plundering hands of the Croats. His charger, flying without its rider, and covered with blood, soon made known to the Swedish cavalry the fall of their king. They rushed madly forward to rescue his sacred remains from the hands of the enemy. A murderous conflict ensued over the body till his mangled remains were buried beneath a heap of slain.

The mournful tidings soon ran through the Swedish army; but instead of destroying the courage of these brave troops, it but excited it into a new, a wild, and consuming flame. Life had lessened in value now that the most sacred life of all was gone; death had no terrors for the lowly since the anointed head was not spared. With the fury of lions the Upland, Småland, Finland, East and West Gothland regiments rushed a second time upon the left wing of the enemy, which, already making but feeble resistance to General Horn, was now entirely beaten from the field. Bernard, Duke of Saxe-Weimar, gave to the bereaved Swedes a noble leader in his own person; and the spirit of Gustavus led his victorious squadrons anew. The left wing quickly formed again and vigorously pressed the right of the Imperialists. The artillery at the windmills, which had maintained so murderous a fire upon the Swedes, was captured and turned against the enemy. The centre also of the Swedish infantry, commanded by the duke and Knyphausen, advanced a second time against the trenches, which they successfully passed, and retook the battery of seven cannons. The attack was now renewed with redoubled fury upon the heavy battalions of the enemy's centre; their resistance became gradually less, and chance conspired with Swedish valor to complete the defeat. The imperial powder-wagons took fire, and, with a tremendous explosion, grenades and bombs filled the air. The enemy, now in confusion, thought they were attacked in the rear, while the Swedish brigades pressed them in front. Their courage began to fail them. Their left wing was already beaten, their right wavering, and their artillery in the enemy's hands. The battle seemed to be almost decided; another moment would decide the fate of the day, when Pappenheim appeared on the field with his cuirassiers and dragoons; all the advantages already gained were lost, and the battle was to be fought anew.

The order which recalled that general to Lutzen had reached him in Halle, while his troops were still plundering the town. It was impossible to collect the scattered infantry with that rapidity which the urgency of the order and Pappenheim's impatience required. Without waiting for it, therefore, he ordered eight regiments of cavalry to mount, and at their head he galloped at full speed for Lutzen to share in the battle. He arrived in time to witness the flight of the imperial right wing, which Gustavus Horn was driving from the field, and to be at first involved in their rout. But with rapid presence of mind he rallied the flying troops and led them once more against the enemy. Carried away by his wild bravery, and impatient to encounter the king, who he supposed was at the head of this wing, he burst furiously upon the Swedish ranks, which, exhausted by victory and inferior in numbers, were, after a noble resistance, overpowered by this fresh body of enemies. Pappenheim's unexpected appearance revived the drooping courage of the Imperialists, and the Duke of Friedland quickly availed himself of the favorable moment to reform his line. The closely serried battalion of the Swedes were, after a tremendous conflict, again driven across the trenches, and the battery, which had been twice lost, again rescued from their hands. The whole yellow regiment, the finest of all that distingushed themselves in this dreadful day, lay dead on the field, covering the ground almost in the same excellent order which, when alive, they maintained with such unyielding courage. The same fate befel another regiment of Blues which Count Piccolomini attacked with the imperial cavalry, and cut down after a desperate contest. Seven times did this intrepid general renew the attack; seven horses were shot under him, and he himself was pierced with six musket balls; yet he would not leave the field until he was carried along in the general rout of the whole army. Wallenstein himself was seen riding through his ranks with cool intrepidity, amidst a shower of balls, assisting the distressed, encouraging the valiant with praise, and the wavering by his fearful glance. Around and close by him his men were falling thick, and his own mantle was perforated by several shots. But avenging destiny this day protected that breast for which another weapon was reserved; on the same field where the noble Gustavus expired Wallenstein was not allowed to terminate his guilty career.

Less fortunate was Pappenheim, the Telamon of the army, the bravest soldier of Austria and the church. An ardent desire to encounter the king in person carried this daring leader into the thickest of the fight, where he thought his noble opponent was most surely to be met. Gustavus had also expressed a wish to meet his brave antagonist, but these hostile wishes remained ungratified; death first brought together these two great heroes. Two musket-balls pierced the breast of Pappenheim; and his men forcibly carried him from the field. While they were conveying him to the rear a murmur reached him that he whom he had sought lay dead upon the plain. When the truth of the report was confirmed to him, his look became brighter, his dying eye sparkled with a last gleam of joy. "Tell the Duke of Friedland," said he, "that I lie without hope of life, but that I die happy, since I know that the implacable enemy of my religion has fallen on the some day."

With Pappenheim the good fortune of the Imperialists departed. The cavalry of the left wing, already beaten, and only rallied by his exertions, no sooner missed their victorious leader than they gave up everything for lost, and abandoned the field of battle in spiritless despair.

The right wing fell into the same confusion, with the exception of a few regiments, which the bravery of their colonels, Gotz, Terzky, Colloredo, and Piccolomini, compelled to keep their ground. The Swedish infantry, with prompt determination, profited by the enemy's confusion. To fill up the gaps which death had made in the front line they formed both lines into one, and with it made the final and decisive charge. A third time they crossed the trenches, and a third time they captured the battery. The sun was setting when the two lines closed. The strife grew hotter as it drew to an end; the last efforts of strength were mutually exerted, and skill and courage did their utmost to repair in these precious moments the fortune of the day. It was in vain; despair endows every one with superhuman strength; no one can conquer, no one will give way. The art of war seemed to exhaust its powers on one side only to unfold some new and untried masterpiece of skill on the other. Night and darkness at last put an end to the fight before the fury of the combatants was exhausted; and the contest only ceased when no one could any longer find an antagonist. Both armies separated as if by tacit agreement; the trumpets sounded and each party, claiming the victory, quitted the field.

The artillery on both sides, as the horses could not be found, remained all night upon the field, at once the reward and the evidence of victory to him who should hold it. Wallenstein, in his haste to leave Leipzig and Saxony, forgot to remove his part. Not long after the battle was ended Pappenheim's infantry, who had been unable to follow the rapid movements of their general, and who amounted to six regiments, marched on the field, but the work was done. A few hours earlier so considerable a reinforcement would perhaps have decided the day in favor of the Imperialists; and, even now, by remaining on the field, they might have saved the duke's artillery, and made a prize of that of the Swedes. But they had received no orders to act; and uncertain as to the issue of the battle, they retired to Leipzig, where they hoped to join the main body.

The Duke of Friedland had retreated thither, and was

followed on the morrow by the scattered remains of his army, without artillery, without colors, and almost without arms. The Duke of Weimar, it appears, after the toils of this bloody day, allowed the Swedish army some repose, between Lutzen and Weissenfels, near enough to the field of battle to oppose any attempt the enemy might make to recover it. Of the two armies more than nine thousand men lay dead; a still greater number were wounded, and among the Imperialists scarcely a man escaped from the field uninjured. The entire plain from Lutzen to the Canal was strewed with the wounded, the dying, and the dead. Many of the principal nobility had fallen on both sides. Even the Abbot of Fulda, who had mingled in the combat as a spectator, paid for his curiosity and his ill-timed zeal with his life. History says nothing of prisoners; a further proof of the animosity of the combatants, who neither gave nor took quarter.

Pappenheim died the next day of his wounds at Leipzig; an irreparable loss to the imperial army, which this brave warrior had so often led on to victory. The battle of Prague, where, together with Wallenstein, he was present as colonel, was the beginning of his heroic career. Dangerously wounded, with a few troops he made an impetuous attack on a regiment of the enemy, and lay for several hours mixed with the dead upon the field beneath the weight of his horse, till he was discovered by some of his own men in plundering. With a small force he defeated, in three different engagements, the rebels in Upper Austria, though forty thousand strong. At the battle of Leipzig he for a long time delayed the defeat of Tilly by his bravery, and led the arms of the Emperor on the Elbe and the Weser to victory. The wild, impetuous fire of his temperament, which no danger, however apparent, could cool, or impossibilities check, made him the most powerful arm of the imperial force, but unfitted him for acting at its head. The battle of Leipzig, if Tilly may be believed, was lost through his rash ardor. At the destruction of Magdeburg his hands were deeply steeped in blood; war rendered savage and ferocious his disposition, which had been cultivated by youthful studies and various travels. On his forehead

two red streaks, like swords, were perceptible, with which
nature had marked him at his very birth. Even in his
later years these became visible as often as his blood was
stirred by passion; and superstition easily persuaded
itself that the future destiny of the man was thus impressed upon the forehead of the child. As a faithful
servant of the House of Austria he had the strongest
claims on the gratitude of both its lines, but he did not
survive to enjoy the most brilliant proof of their regard.
A messenger was already on his way from Madrid, bearing to him the order of the Golden Fleece, when death
overtook him at Leipzig.

Though Te Deum, in all Spanish and Austrian lands,
was sung in honor of a victory, Wallenstein himself, by
the haste with which he quitted Leipzig, and soon after
all Saxony, and by renouncing his original design of
fixing there his winter quarters, openly confessed his
defeat. It is true he made one more feeble attempt to
dispute, even in his flight, the honor of victory, by sending out his Croats next morning to the field; but the
sight of the Swedish army drawn up in order of battle
immediately dispersed these flying bands, and Duke Bernard, by keeping possession of the field, and soon after by
the capture of Leipzig, maintained indisputably his claim
to the title of victor.

But it was a dear conquest, a dearer triumph! It was
not till the fury of the conquest was over that the full
weight of the loss sustained was felt, and the shout of
triumph died away into a silent gloom of despair. He
who had led them to the charge returned not with them;
there he lay upon the field which he had won, mingled
with the dead bodies of the common crowd. After a
long and almost fruitless search, the corpse of the king
was discovered, not far from the great stone, which, for a
hundred years before had stood between Lutzen and the
Canal, and which, from the memorable disaster of that
day, still bears the name of the Stone of the Swede.
Covered with blood and wounds so as scarcely to be
recognized, trampled beneath the horses' hoofs, stripped
by the rude hands of plunderers of his ornaments and
clothes, his body was drawn from beneath a heap of dead,

conveyed to Weissenfels, and there delivered up to the
lamentations of his soldiers and the last embraces of his
queen. The first tribute had been paid to revenge, and
blood had atoned for the blood of the monarch; but now
affection assumes its rights, and tears of grief must flow
for the man. The universal sorrow absorbs all individual
woes. The generals, still stupefied by the unexpected
blow, stood speechless and motionless around his bier,
and no one trusted himself enough to contemplate the full
extent of their loss.

The Emperor, we are told by Khevenhuller, showed
symptoms of deep and apparently sincere feeling at the
sight of the king's doublet stained with blood, which had
been stripped from him during the battle, and carried to
Vienna. "Willingly," said he, "would I have granted
to the unfortunate prince a longer life, and a safe return
to his kingdom, had Germany been at peace." But when
a trait, which is nothing more than a proof of a yet
lingering humanity, and which a mere regard to appearances and even self-love would have extorted from the
most insensible, and the absence of which could exist only
in the most inhuman heart, has, by a Roman Catholic
writer of modern times and acknowledged merit, been
made the subject of the highest eulogium, and, compared
with the magnanimous tears of Alexander for the fall of
Darius, our distrust is excited of the other virtues of the
writer's hero, and what is still worse, of his own ideas of
moral dignity. But even such praise, whatever its amount,
is much for one whose memory his biographer has to clear
from the suspicion of being privy to the assassination of a
king.

It was scarcely to be expected that the strong leaning
of mankind to the marvellous would leave to the common
course of nature the glory of ending the career of Gustavus Adolphus. The death of so formidable a rival was
too important an event for the Emperor not to excite in
his bitter opponent a ready suspicion that what was so
much to his interests was also the result of his instigation. For the execution, however, of this dark deed the
Emperor would require the aid of a foreign arm, and this
it was generally believed he had found in Francis Albert,

Duke of Saxe Lauenburg. The rank of the latter permitted him a free access to the king's person, while it at the same time seemed to place him above the suspicion of so foul a deed. This prince however was in fact not incapable of this atrocity, and he had moreover sufficient motives for its commission.

Francis Albert, the youngest of four sons of Francis II., Duke of Lauenburg, and related by the mother's side to the race of Vasa, had in his early years found a most friendly reception at the Swedish court. Some offence which he had committed against Gustavus Adolphus in the queen's chamber was, it is said, repaid by this fiery youth with a box on the ear; which, though immediately repented of, and amply apologized for, laid the foundation of an irreconcilable hate in the vindictive heart of the duke. Francis Albert subsequently entered the imperial service, where he rose to the command of a regiment, and formed a close intimacy with Wallenstein, and condescended to be the instrument of a secret negotiation with the Saxon court which did little honor to his rank. Without any sufficient cause being assigned, he suddenly quitted the Austrian service, and appeared in the king's camp at Nuremberg to offer his services as a volunteer. By his show of zeal for the Protestant cause, and prepossessing and flattering deportment, he gained the heart of the king, who, warned in vain by Oxenstiern, continued to lavish his favor and friendship on this suspicious newcomer. The battle of Lutzen soon followed, in which Francis Albert, like an evil genius, kept close to the king's side and did not leave him till he fell. He owed, it was thought, his own safety amidst the fire of the enemy to a green sash which he wore, the color of the Imperialists. He was at any rate the first to convey to his friend Wallenstein the intelligence of the king's death. After the battle he exchanged the Swedish service for the Saxon; and, after the murder of Wallenstein, being charged with being an accomplice of that general, he only escaped the sword of justice by abjuring his faith. His last appearance in life was as commander of an imperial army in Silesia, where he died of the wounds he had received before Schweidnitz. It requires some effort to believe in the innocence of a man who had run through a career like this of the act charged against him; but however great may be the moral and physical possibility of his committing such a crime, it must still be allowed that there are no certain grounds for imputing it to him. Gustavus Adolphus it is well known exposed himself to danger, like the meanest soldier in his army, and where thousands fell he too might naturally meet his death. How it reached him remains indeed buried in mystery; but here, more than anywhere, does the maxim apply, that where the ordinary course of things is fully sufficient to account for the fact the honor of human nature ought not to be stained by any suspicion of moral atrocity.

But by whatever hand he fell his extraordinary destiny must appear a great interposition of Providence. History, too often confined to the ungrateful task of analyzing the uniform play of human passions, is occasionally rewarded by the appearance of events which strike, like a hand from heaven, into the nicely adjusted machinery of human plans, and carry the contemplative mind to a higher order of things. Of this kind is the sudden retirement of Gustavus Adolphus from the scene; stopping for a time the whole movement of the political machine, and disappointing all the calculations of human prudence. Yesterday the very soul, the great and animating principle of his own creation; to-day struck unpitiably to the ground in the very midst of his eagle flight; untimely torn from a whole world of great designs, and from the ripening harvest of his expectations, he left his bereaved party disconsolate; and the proud edifice of his past greatness sunk into ruins. The Protestant party had identified its hopes with its invincible leader, and scarcely can it now separate them from him; with him they now fear all good fortune is buried. But it was no longer the benefactor of Germany who fell at Lutzen; the beneficent part of his career Gustavus Adolphus had already terminated; and now the greatest service which he could render to the liberties of Germany was—to die. The all-engrossing power of an individual was at an end, but many came forward to essay their strength; the equivocal assistance of an over-powerful protector gave place to a more noble self-exertion on the part of the Estates; and those who were formerly the mere instruments of his aggrandizement, now began to work for themselves. They now looked to their own exertions for the emancipation which could not be received without danger from the hand of the mighty; and the Swedish power, now incapable of sinking into the oppressor, was henceforth restricted to the more modest part of an ally.

The ambition of the Swedish monarch aspired unquestionably to establish a power within Germany, and to attain a firm footing in the centre of the empire, which was inconsistent with the liberties of the Estates. His aim was the imperial crown; and this dignity, supported by his power, and maintained by his energy and activity, would in his hands be liable to more abuse than had ever been feared from the House of Austria. Born in a foreign country, educated in the maxims of arbitrary power, and by principles and enthusiasm a determined enemy to Popery, he was ill-qualified to maintain inviolate the constitution of the German States or to respect their liberties. The coercive homage which Augsburg, with many other cities, was forced to pay to the Swedish crown bespoke the conqueror rather than the protector of the empire; and this town, prouder of the title of a royal city than of the higher dignity of the freedom of the empire, flattered itself with the anticipation of becoming the capital of his future kingdom. His ill-disguised attempts upon the Electorate of Mentz, which he first intended to bestow upon the Elector of Brandenburg as the dower of his daughter Christina, and afterwards destined for his chancellor and friend, Oxenstiern, evinced plainly what liberties he was disposed to take with the constitution of the empire. His allies, the Protestant princes, had claims on his gratitude which could be satisfied only at the expense of their Roman Catholic neighbors, and particularly of the immediate Ecclesiastical Chapters; and it seems probable a plan was early formed for dividing the conquered provinces (after the precedent of the barbarian hordes who overran the German empire), as a common spoil, among the German and Swedish confederates. In his treatment of the Elector

Palatine he entirely belied the magnanimity of the hero, and forgot the sacred character of a protector. The Palatinate was in his hands, and the obligations both of justice and honor demanded its full and immediate restoration to the legitimate sovereign. But by a subtlety unworthy of a great mind, and disgraceful to the honorable title of protector of the oppressed, he eluded that obligation. He treated the Palatinate as a conquest wrested from the enemy, and thought that this circumstance gave him a right to deal with it as he pleased. He surrendered it to the Elector as a favor, not as a debt; and that, too, as a Swedish fief, fettered by conditions which diminished half its value, and degraded this unfortunate prince into an humble vassal of Sweden. One of these conditions obliged the Elector, after the conclusion of the war, to furnish, along with the other princes, his contribution towards the maintenance of the Swedish army, a condition which plainly indicates the fate which, in the event of the ultimate success of the king, awaited Germany. His sudden disappearance secured the liberties of Germany, and saved his reputation, while it probably spared him the mortification of seeing his own allies in arms against him, and all the fruits of his victories torn from him by a disadvantageous peace. Saxony was already disposed to abandon him, Denmark viewed his success with alarm and jealousy; and even France, the firmest and most potent of his allies, terrified at the rapid growth of his power and the imperious tone which he assumed, looked around at the very moment he passed the Lech for foreign alliances, in order to check the progress of the Goths and restore to Europe the balance of power.

BOOK IV.

THE weak bond of union by which Gustavus Adolphus contrived to hold together the Protestant members of the empire was dissolved by his death; the allies were now again at liberty, and their alliance to last must be formed anew. By the former event, if unremedied, they would lose all the advantages they had gained at the cost of so much bloodshed, and expose themselves to the inevitable danger of becoming, one after the other, the prey of an enemy whom, by their union alone, they had been able to oppose and to master. Neither Sweden nor any of the states of the empire was singly a match with the Emperor and the League; and, by seeking a peace under the present state of things, they would necessarily be obliged to receive laws from the enemy. Union was, therefore, equally indispensable, either for concluding a peace or continuing the war. But a peace sought under the present circumstances could not fail to be disadvantageous to the allied powers. With the death of Gustavus Adolphus the enemy had formed new hopes; and however gloomy might be the situation of his affairs after the battle of Lutzen, still the death of his dreaded rival was an event too disastrous to the allies, and too favorable for the Emperor, not to justify him in entertaining the most brilliant expectations, and not to encourage him to the prosecution of the war. Its inevitable consequence, for the moment at least, must be want of union among the allies, and what might not the Emperor and the League gain from such a division of their enemies? He was not likely to sacrifice such prospects as the present turn of affairs held out to him for any peace not highly beneficial to himself; and such a peace the allies would not be disposed to accept. They naturally determined, therefore, to continue the war, and for this purpose the maintenance of the existing union was acknowledged to be indispensable.

But how was this union to be renewed; and whence were to be derived the necessary means for continuing the war? It was not the power of Sweden, but the talents and personal influence of its late king, which had given him so overwhelming an influence in Germany, so great a command over the minds of men; and even he had innumerable difficulties to overcome before he could establish among the states even a weak and wavering alliance. With his death vanished all which his personal qualities alone had rendered practicable; and the mutual obligation of the states seemed to cease with the hopes on which it had been founded. Several impatiently threw off the yoke which had always been irksome; others hastened to seize the helm which they had unwillingly seen in the hands of Gustavus, but which, during his lifetime, they did not dare to dispute with him. Some were tempted by the seductive promises of the Emperor to abandon the alliance; others, oppressed by the heavy burdens of a fourteen years' war, longed for the repose of peace upon any conditions, however ruinous. The generals of the army, partly German princes, acknowledged no common head, and no one would stoop to receive orders from another. Unanimity vanished alike from the cabinet and the field, and their common weal was threatened with ruin by the spirit of disunion.

Gustavus had left no male heir to the crown of Sweden; his daughter, Christina, then six years old, was the natural heir. The unavoidable weakness of a regency suited ill with the energy and resolution which Sweden would be called upon to display in this trying conjuncture. The wide-reaching mind of Gustavus Adolphus had raised this unimportant and hitherto unknown kingdom to a rank among the powers of Europe which it could not retain without the fortune and genius of its author, and from which it could not recede without a humiliating confession of weakness. Though the German war had been conducted chiefly on the resources of Germany, yet even the small contribution of men and money which Sweden furnished had sufficed to exhaust the finances of that poor kingdom, and the peasantry groaned beneath the imposts necessarily laid upon them. The plunder gained in Germany enriched only a few individuals among the nobles and the soldiers, while Sweden itself remained poor as before. For a time, it is true, the national glory reconciled the subject to these burdens, and the sums exacted seemed but as a loan placed at interest in the fortunate hand of Gustavus Adolphus, to be richly repaid by the grateful monarch at the conclusion of a glorious peace. But with the king's death this hope vanished, and the deluded people now loudly demanded relief from their burdens.

But the spirit of Gustavus Adolphus still lived in the men to whom he had confided the administration of the kingdom. However dreadful to them and unexpected was the intelligence of his death, it did not deprive them of their manly courage; and the spirit of ancient Rome, under the invasion of Brennus and Hannibal, animated this noble assembly. The greater the price at which these hard-gained advantages had been purchased the less readily could they reconcile themselves to renounce them; not unrevenged was a king to be sacrified. Called on to choose between a doubtful and exhausting war and a profitable but disgraceful peace, the Swedish council of state boldly espoused the side of danger and honor; and with agreeable surprise men beheld this venerable senate acting with all the energy and enthusiasm of youth. Surrounded with watchful enemies, both within and without, and threatened on every side with danger, they armed themselves against them all, with equal prudence and heroism, and labored to extend their kingdom, even at the moment when they had to struggle for its existence.

The decease of the king, and the minority of his daughter Christina, renewed the claims of Poland to the Swedish throne; and King Ladislaus, the son of Sigismund, spared no intrigues to gain a party in Sweden. On this ground the regency lost no time in proclaiming the young queen and arranging the administration of the regency. All the officers of the kingdom were summoned to do homage to their new princess; all correspondence with Poland prohibited, and the edicts of previous monarchs against the heirs of Sigismund confirmed by a solemn act of the nation. The alliance with the Czar of Muscovy was carefully renewed in order, by the arms of this prince, to keep the hostile Poles in check. The death of Gustavus Adolphus had put an end to the jealousy of Denmark, and removed the grounds of alarm which had stood in the way of a good understanding between the two states. The representations by which the enemy sought to stir up Christian IV. against Sweden were no longer listened to; and the strong wish the Danish monarch entertained for the marriage of his son Ulrick with the young princess, combined, with the dictates of a sounder policy, to incline him to a neutrality. At the same time England, Holland, and France came forward with the gratifying assurances to the regency of continued friendship and support, and encouraged them, with one voice, to prosecute with activity the war which hitherto had been conducted with so much glory. Whatever reason France might have to congratulate itself on the death of the Swedish conqueror, it was as fully sensible of the expediency of maintaining the alliance with Sweden. Without exposing itself to great danger it could not allow the power of Sweden to sink in Germany. Want of resources of its own would either drive Sweden to conclude a hasty and disadvantageous peace with Austria, and then all the past efforts to lower the ascendancy of this dangerous power would be thrown away; or necessity and despair would drive the armies to extort from the Roman Catholic states the means of support, and France would then be regarded as the betrayer of those very states who had placed themselves under her powerful protection. The death of Gustavus, far from breaking up the alliance between France and Sweden, had only rendered it more necessary for both and more profitable for France. Now, for the first time, since he was dead who had stretched his protecting arm over Germany, and guarded its frontiers against the encroaching designs of France, could the latter safely pursue its designs upon Alsace, and thus be enabled to sell its aid to the German Protestants at a dearer rate.

Strengthened by these alliances, secured in its interior, and defended from without by strong frontier garrisons and fleets, the regency did not delay an instant to continue a war by which Sweden had little of its own to lose, while, if success attended its arms, one or more of the German provinces might be won, either as a conquest or indemnification of its expenses. Secure amidst its seas, Sweden, even if driven out of Germany, would scarcely be exposed to greater peril than if it voluntarily retired from the contest, while the former measure was as honorable as the latter was disgraceful. The more boldness the regency displayed the more confidence would they inspire among their confederates, the more respect among their enemies, and the more favorable conditions might they anticipate in the event of peace. If they found themselves too weak to execute the wide-ranging projects of Gustavus they at least owed it to this lofty model to do their utmost and to yield to no difficulty short of absolute necessity. Alas, that motives of self-interest had too great a share in this noble determination to demand our unqualified admiration! For those who had nothing themselves to suffer from the calamities of war, but were rather to be enriched by it, it was an easy matter to resolve upon its continuation; for the German empire was, in the end, to defray the expenses; and the provinces on which they reckoned would be cheaply purchased with the few troops they sacrificed to them, and with the generals who were placed at the head of armies, composed for the most part of Germans, and with the honorable superintendence of all the operations, both military and political.

But this superintendence was irreconcilable with the distance of the Swedish regency from the scene of action, and with the slowness which necessarily accompanies all the movements of a council.

To one comprehensive mind must be entrusted the management of Swedish interests in Germany, and with full powers to determine at discretion all questions of war and peace, the necessary alliances, or the acquisitions made. With dictatorial power, and with the whole influence of the crown which he was to represent, must this important magistrate be invested, in order to maintain its dignity, to enforce united and combined operations, to give effect to his orders, and to supply the place of the monarch whom he succeeded. Such a man was found in the Chancellor Oxenstiern, the first minister, and, what is more, the friend of the deceased king, who, acquainted with all the secrets of his master, versed in the politics of Germany, and in the relations of all the states of Europe, was unquestionably the fittest instrument to carry out the plans of Gustavus Adolphus in their full extent.

Oxenstiern was on his way to Upper Germany in order to assemble the four Upper Circles when the news of the king's death reached him at Hanau. This was a heavy blow, both to the friend and the statesman. Sweden, indeed, had lost but a king, Germany a protector; but Oxenstiern, the author of his fortunes, the friend of his soul, and the object of his admiration. Though the greatest sufferer in the general loss, he was the first who by his energy rose from the blow, and the only one qualified to repair it. His penetrating glance foresaw all the obstacles which would oppose the execution of his plans, the discouragements of the estates, the intrigues of hostile courts, the breaking up of the confederacy, the jealousy of the leaders, and the dislike of princes of the empire to submit to foreign authority. But even this deep insight into the existing state of things, which revealed the whole extent of the evil, showed him also the means by which it might be overcome. It was essential to revive the drooping courage of the weaker states, to meet the secret machinations of the enemy, to allay the jealousy of the more powerful allies, to rouse the friendly powers, and France in particular, to active assistance; but, above all, to repair the ruined edifice of the German alliance, and to reunite the scattered strength of the party by a close and permanent bond of union. The dismay which the loss of their leader occasioned the German Protestants might as readily dispose them to a closer alliance with Sweden as to a hasty peace with the Emperor; and it depended entirely upon the course pursued which of these alternatives they would adopt. Everything might be lost by the slightest sign of despondency; nothing but the confidence which Sweden showed in herself could kindle among the Germans a noble feeling of self-confidence. All the attempts of Austria to detach these princes from the Swedish alliance would be unavailing the moment their eyes became opened to their true interests, and they were instigated to a public and formal breach with the Emperor.

Before these measures could be taken, and the necessary points settled between the regency and their minister, a precious opportunity of action would, it is true, be lost to the Swedish army, of which the enemy would be sure to take the utmost advantage. It was, in short, in the power of the Emperor totally to ruin the Swedish interest in Germany, and to this he was actually invited by the prudent councils of the Duke of Friedland. Wallenstein advised him to proclaim an universal amnesty and to meet the Protestant states with favorable conditions. In the first consternation produced by the fall of Gustavus Adolphus such a declaration would have had the most powerful effects, and probably would have brought the wavering states back to their allegiance. But blinded by this unexpected turn of fortune, and infatuated by the Spanish counsels, he anticipated a more brilliant issue from war; and instead of listening to these propositions of an accommodation he hastened to augment his forces. Spain, enriched by the grant of the tenth of the ecclesiastical possessions, which the Pope confirmed, sent him considerable supplies, negotiated for him at the Saxon court, and hastily levied troops for him in Italy to be employed in Germany. The Elector of Bavaria also considerably increased his military force; and the restless disposition of the Duke of Lorraine did not permit him to remain inactive in this favorable change of fortune. But while the enemy were thus busy to profit by the disaster of Sweden Oxenstiern was diligent to avert its most fatal consequences.

Less apprehensive of open enemies than of the jealousy of the friendly powers, he left Upper Germany, which he had secured by conquests and alliances, and set out in person to prevent a total defection of the Lower German states, or, what would have been almost equally ruinous to Sweden, a private alliance among themselves. Offended at the boldness with which the chancellor assumed the direction of affairs, and inwardly exasperated at the thought of being dictated to by a Swedish nobleman, the Elector of Saxony again meditated a dangerous separation from Sweden; and the only question in his mind was whether he should make full terms with the Emperor or place himself at the head of the Protestants and form a third party in Germany. Similar ideas were cherished by Duke Ulric of Brunswick, who, indeed, showed them openly enough by forbidding the Swedes from recruiting within his dominions, and inviting the Lower Saxon states to Luneburg for the purpose of forming a confederacy among themselves. The Elector of Brandenburg, jealous of the influence which Saxony was likely to attain in Lower Germany, alone manifested any zeal for the interests of the Swedish throne, which, in thought, he already destined for his son. At the court of Saxony Oxenstiern was no doubt honorably received; but, notwithstanding the personal efforts of the Elector of Brandenburg, empty promises of continued friendship were all which he could obtain. With the Duke of Brunswick he was more successful, for with him he ventured to assume a bolder tone. Sweden was at the time in possession of the see of Magdeburg, the bishop of which had the power of assembling the Lower Saxon circle. The chancellor now asserted the rights of the crown, and by this spirited proceeding put a stop for the present to this dangerous assembly designed by the duke. The main object, however, of his present journey and of his future endeavors, a general confederacy of the Protestants, miscarried entirely, and he was obliged to content himself with some unsteady alliances in the Saxon circles, and with the weaker assistance of Upper Germany.

As the Bavarians were too powerful on the Danube the assembly of the four Upper Circles, which should have been held at Ulm, was removed to Heilbronn, where deputies of more than twelve cities of the empire, with a brilliant crowd of doctors, counts, and princes, attended. The ambassadors of foreign powers, likewise, France, England, and Holland, attended this congress, at which Oxenstiern appeared in person with all the splendor of the crown whose representative he was. He himself opened the proceedings and conducted the deliberations. After receiving from all the assembled estates assurances of unshaken fidelity, perseverance, and unity, he required of them solemnly and formally to declare the Emperor and the League as enemies. But desirable as it was for Sweden to exasperate the ill-feeling between the Emperor and the estates into a formal rupture, the latter, on the other hand, were equally indisposed to shut out the possibility of reconciliation by so decided a step, and to place themselves entirely in the hands of the Swedes. They maintained that any formal declaration of war was useless and superfluous, where the act would speak for itself, and their firmness on this point silenced at last the chancellor. Warmer disputes arose on the third and principal article of the treaty, concerning the means of prosecuting the war, and the quota which the several states ought to furnish for the support of the army. Oxenstiern's maxim, to throw as much as possible of the common burden on the states, did not suit very well with their determination to give as little as possible. The Swedish chancellor now experienced what had been felt by thirty emperors before him to their cost, that of all difficult undertakings the most difficult was to extort money from the Germans. Instead of granting the necessary sums for the new armies to be raised, they eloquently dwelt upon the calamities occasioned by the former, and demanded relief from the old burdens when they were required to submit to new. The irritation which the chancellor's demand for money raised among the states gave rise to a thousand complaints; and the outrages committed by the troops in their marches and quarters were dwelt upon with a startling minuteness and truth.

In the service of two absolute monarchs Oxenstiern had but little opportunity to become accustomed to the formalities and cautious proceedings of republican deliberations, or to bear opposition with patience. Ready to act the instant the necessity of action was apparent, and inflexible in his resolution when he had once taken it, he was at a loss to comprehend the inconsistency of most men, who, while they desire the end, are yet averse to the means. Prompt and impetuous by nature, he was so on this occasion from principle; for everything depended on concealing the weakness of Sweden under a firm and confident speech, and by assuming the tone of a lawgiver, really to become so. It was nothing wonderful, therefore, if, amidst these interminable discussions with German doctors and deputies, he was entirely out of his sphere, and if the deliberateness which distinguishes the character of the Germans in their public deliberations had driven him almost to despair. Without respecting a custom, to which even the most powerful of the emperors had been obliged to conform, he rejected all written deliberations, which suited so well with the national slowness of resolve. He could not conceive how ten days could be spent in debating a measure which with himself was decided upon its bare suggestion. Harshly, however, as he treated the states he found them ready enough to assent to his fourth motion, which concerned himself. When he pointed out the necessity of giving a director to the new confederation that honor was unanimously assigned to Sweden, and he himself was humbly requested to give to the common cause the benefit of his enlightened experience, and to take upon himself the burden of the supreme command. But in order to prevent his abusing the great powers thus conferred upon him it was proposed, not without French influence, to appoint a number of overseers, in fact, under the name of assistants, to control the expenditure of the common treasure and to consult with him as to the levies, marches, and quarterings of the troops. Oxenstiern long and strenuously resisted this limitation of his authority, which could not fail to trammel him in the execution of every enterprise requiring promptitude or secrecy, and at last succeeded, with difficulty, in obtaining so far a modification of it that his management in affairs of war was to be uncontrolled. The chancellor finally approached the delicate point of the indemnification which Sweden was to expect at the conclusion of the war from the gratitude of the allies, and flattered himself with the hope that Pomerania, the main object of Sweden, would be assigned to her, and that he would obtain from the provinces assurances of effectual cooperation in its acquisition. But he could obtain nothing more than a vague assurance that in a general peace the interests of all parties would be attended to. That on this point the caution of the estates was not owing to any regard for the constitution of the empire became manifest from the liberality they evinced towards the chancellor at the expense of the most sacred laws of the empire. They were ready to grant him the archbishopric of Mentz (which he already held as a conquest), and only with difficulty did the French ambassador succeed in preventing a step which was as impolitic as it was disgraceful. Though, on the whole, the result of the congress had fallen far short of Oxenstiern's expectations, he had at least gained for himself and his crown his main object, namely, the direction of the whole confederacy; he had also succeeded in strengthening the bond of union between the four upper circles, and obtained from the states a yearly contribution of two millions and a half of dollars for the maintenance of the army.

These concessions on the part of the States demanded some return from Sweden. A few weeks after the death of Gustavus Adolphus sorrow ended the days of the unfortunate Elector Palatine. For eight months he had swelled the pomp of his protector's court and expended on it the small remainder of his patrimony. He was at last approaching the goal of his wishes, and the prospect of a brighter future was opening when death deprived him of his protector. But what he regarded as the greatest calamity was highly favorable to his heirs. Gustavus might venture to delay the restoration of his dominions or to load the gift with hard conditions; but Oxenstiern, to whom the friendship of England, Holland, and Brandenburg, and the good opinion of the Reformed States were indispensable, felt the necessity of immediately fulfilling the obligations of justice. At this assembly at Heilbronn, therefore, he engaged to surrender to Frederick's heirs the whole Palatinate, both the part already conquered, and that which remained to be conquered, with the exception of Manheim, which the Swedes were to hold until they should be indemnified for their expenses. The chancellor did not confine his liberality to the family of the Palatine alone; the other allied princes received proofs, though at a later period, of the gratitude of Sweden, which, however, she dispensed at little cost to herself.

Impartiality, the most sacred obligation of the historian, here compels us to an admission not much to the honor of the champions of German liberty. However the Protestant princes might boast of the justice of their cause, and the sincerity of their conviction, still the motives from which they acted were selfish enough; and the desire of stripping others of their possessions had at least as great a share in the commencement of hostilities as the fear of being deprived of their own. Gustavus soon found that he might reckon much more on these selfish motives than on their patriotic zeal, and did not fail to avail himself of them. Each of his confederates received from him the promise of some possession, either already wrested or to be afterwards taken from the enemy; and death alone prevented him from fulfilling these engagements. What prudence had suggested to the king necessity now prescribed to his successor. If it was his object to continue the war he must be ready to divide the spoil among the allies, and promise them advantages from the confusion which it was his object to continue. Thus he promised to the Landgrave of Hesse the abbacies of Paderborn, Corvey, Munster, and Fulda; to Duke Bernard of Weimar the Franconian bishoprics; to the Duke of Wirtemberg the Ecclesiastical domains, and the Austrian countries lying within his territories, all under the title of fiefs of Sweden. This spectacle, so strange and so dishonorable to the German character, surprised the chancellor, who found it difficult to repress his contempt, and on one occasion exclaimed, "Let it be writ in our records for an everlasting memorial that a German prince made such a request of a Swedish nobleman, and that the Swedish nobleman granted it to the German upon German ground!"

After these successful measures he was in a condition to take the field and prosecute the war with fresh vigor. Soon after the victory at Lutzen the troops of Saxony and Lunenburg united with the Swedish main body; and the Imperialists were in a short time totally driven from Saxony. The united army again divided; the Saxons marched towards Lusatia and Silesia, to act in conjunction with Count Thurn against the Austrians in that quarter; a part of the Swedish army was led by the Duke of Weimar into Franconia, and the other by George, Duke of Brunswick, into Westphalia and Lower Saxony.

The conquests on the Lech and the Danube during Gustavus' expedition into Saxony had been maintained by the Palatine of Birkenfeld and the Swedish General Banner against the Bavarians; but, unable to hold their ground against the victorious progress of the latter, supported as they were by the bravery and military experience of the Imperial General Altringer, they were under the necessity of summoning the Swedish General Horn to their assistance from Alsace. This experienced general having captured the towns of Benfeld, Schlettstadt, Colmar, and Hagenau, committed the defence of them to the Rhinegrave Otto Louis, and hastily crossed the Rhine to form a junction with Banner's army. But although the combined force amounted to more than sixteen thousand they could not prevent the enemy from obtaining a strong position on the Swabian frontier, taking Kempten, and being joined by seven regiments from Bohemia. In order to retain the command of the important banks of the Lech and the Danube they were under the necessity of recalling the Rhinegrave Otto Louis from Alsace, where he had, after the departure of Horn, found it difficult to defend himself against the exasperated peasantry. With his army he was now summoned to strengthen the army on the Danube, and as even this reinforcement was insufficient, Duke Bernard of Weimar was earnestly pressed to turn his arms into this quarter.

Duke Bernard, soon after the opening of the campaign of 1633, had made himself master of the town and territory of Bamberg, and was now threatening Wurtzburg. But on receiving the summons of General Horn without delay he began his march towards the Danube, defeated on his way a Bavarian army under John de Werth, and joined the Swedes near Donauwerth. This numerous force, commanded by excellent generals, now threatened Bavaria with a fearful inroad. The Bishopric of Eichstadt was completely overrun, and Ingoldstadt was on the point of being delivered up by treachery to the Swedes. Altringer, fettered in his movements by the express order of the Duke of Friedland, and left without assistance from Bohemia, was unable to check the progress of the enemy. The most favorable circumstances combined to further the progress of the Swedish arms in this quarter, when the operations of the army were at once stopped by a mutiny among the officers.

All the previous successes in Germany were owing altogether to arms; the greatness of Gustavus himself was the work of the army, the fruit of their discipline, their bravery, and their persevering courage under numberless dangers and privations. However wisely his plans were laid in the cabinet it was to the army ultimately that he was indebted for their execution; and the expanding designs of the general did but continually impose new burdens on the soldiers. All the decisive advantages of the war had been violently gained by a barbarous sacrifice of the soldiers' lives in winter campaigns, forced marches, stormings, and pitched battles, for it was Gustavus' maxim never to decline a battle so long as it cost him nothing but men. The soldiers could not long be kept ignorant of their own importance, and they justly demanded a share in the spoil which had been won by their own blood. Yet, frequently they hardly received their pay, and the rapacity of individual generals or the wants of the state generally swallowed up the greater part of the sums raised by contributions or levied upon the conquered provinces. For all the privations he endured the soldier had no other recompense than the doubtful chance either of plunder or promotion, in both of which he was often disappointed. During the lifetime of Gustavus Adolphus the combined influence of fear and hope had suppressed any open complaint, but after his death the murmurs were loud and universal, and the soldiery seized the most dangerous moment to impress their superiors with a sense of their importance. Two officers, Pfuhl and Mitschefal, notorious as restless characters even during the king's life, set the example in the camp on the Danube, which in a few days was imitated by almost all the officers of the army. They solemnly bound themselves to obey no orders till these arrears, now outstanding for months, and even years, should be paid up, and a gratuity, either in money or lands, made to each man according to his services. "Immense sums," they said, "were daily raised by contributions and all dissipated by a few. They were called out to serve amidst frost and snow and no reward requited their incessant labors. The soldiers' excesses at Heilbronn had been blamed, but no one ever talked of their services. The world rung with the tidings of conquests and victories, but it was by their hands that they had been fought and won."

The number of the malcontents daily increased, and they even attempted by letters (which were fortunately intercepted) to seduce the armies on the Rhine and in Saxony. Neither the representations of Bernard of Weimar nor the stern reproaches of his harsher associate in command could suppress the mutiny, while the vehemence of Horn seemed only to increase the insolence of the insurgents. The conditions they insisted on were that certain towns should be assigned to each regiment for the payment of arrears. Four weeks were allowed to the Swedish chancellor to comply with these demands; and in case of refusal they announced that they would pay themselves, and never more draw a sword for Sweden.

These pressing demands made at the very time when the military chest was exhausted, and credit at a low ebb, greatly embarassed the chancellor. The remedy he saw must be found quickly before the contagion should spread to the other troops, and he should be deserted by all his armies at once. Among all the Swedish generals there was only one of sufficient authority and influence with the soldiers to put an end to this dispute. The Duke of Weimar was the favorite of the army, and his prudent moderation had won the good-will of the soldiers, while his military experience had excited their admiration. He now undertook the task of appeasing the discontented troops; but, aware of his importance, he embraced the opportunity to make advantageous stipulations for himself, and to make the embarassment of the chancellor subservient to his own views.

Gustavus Adolphus had flattered him with the promise of the Duchy of Franconia, to be formed out of the Bishoprics of Wurtzburg and Bamberg, and he now insisted on the performance of this pledge. He at the same time demanded the chief command as generalissimo of Sweden. The abuse which the Duke of Weimar thus made of his influence so irritated Oxenstiern that, in the first moment of his displeasure, he gave him his dismissal from the Swedish service. But he soon thought better of it, and determined, instead of sacrificing so important a leader, to attach him to the Swedish interests at any cost. He therefore granted to him the Franconian bishoprics as a fief of the Swedish crown, reserving, however, the two fortresses of Wurtzburg and Konigshofen, which were to be garrisoned by the Swedes; and also engaged in name of the Swedish crown to secure these territories to the duke. His demand of the supreme authority was evaded on some specious pretext. The duke did not delay to display his gratitude for this valuable grant, and by his influence and activity soon restored tranquillity to the army. Large sums of money, and still more extensive estates, were divided among the officers, amounting in value to about five millions of dollars, and to which they had no other right but that of conquest. In the meantime, however, the opportunity for a great undertaking had been lost, and the united generals divided their forces to oppose the enemy in other quarters.

Gustavus Horn, after a short inroad into the Upper Palatinate and the capture of Neumark, directed his march towards the Swabian frontier, where the Imperialists, strongly reinforced, threatened Wurtemberg. At his approach the enemy retired to the Lake of Constance, but only to show the Swedes the road into a district hitherto unvisited by war. A post on the entrance to Switzerland would be highly serviceable to the Swedes, and the town of Kostnitz seemed peculiarly well-fitted to be a point of communication between him and the confederated cantons. Accordingly Gustavus Horn immediately commenced the siege of it; but destitute of artillery, for which he was obliged to send to Wirtemberg, he could not press the attack with sufficient vigor to prevent the enemy from throwing supplies into the town, which the lake afforded them convenient opportunity of doing. He therefore, after an ineffectual attempt, quitted the place and its neighborhood and hastened to meet a more threatening danger upon the Danube.

At the Emperor's instigation the Cardinal Infante, the

brother of Philip IV. of Spain, and the Viceroy of Milan, had raised an army of fourteen thousand men, intended to act upon the Rhine independently of Wallenstein, and to protect Alsace. This force now appeared in Bavaria, under the command of the Duke of Feria, a Spaniard; and that they might be directly employed against the Swedes Altringer was ordered to join them with his corps. Upon the first intelligence of their approach Horn had summoned to his assistance the Palsgrave of Birkenfeld from the Rhine; and, being joined by him at Stockach, boldly advanced to meet the enemy's army of thirty thousand men.

The latter had taken the route across the Danube into Swabia, where Gustavus Horn came so close upon them that the two armies were only separated from each other by half a German mile. But instead of accepting the offer of battle the Imperialists moved by the Forest towns towards Briesgau and Alsace, where they arrived in time to relieve Breysack and to arrest the victorious progress of the Rhinegrave, Otto Louis. The latter had shortly before taken the Forest towns, and, supported by the Palatine of Birkenfeld, who had liberated the Lower Palatinate and beaten the Duke of Lorraine out of the field, had once more given the superiority to the Swedish arms in that quarter. He was now forced to retire before the superior numbers of the enemy; but Horn and Birkenfeld quickly advanced to his support, and the Imperialists after a brief triumph were again expelled from Alsace. The severity of the autumn in which this hapless retreat had to be conducted proved fatal to most of the Italians; and their leader, the Duke of Feria, died of grief at the failure of his enterprise.

In the meantime Duke Bernard of Weimar had taken up his position on the Danube, with eighteen regiments of infantry and one hundred and forty squadrons of horse, to cover Franconia and to watch the movements of the Imperial-Bavarian army upon that river. No sooner had Altringer departed to join the Italians under Feria than Bernard, profiting by his absence, hastened across the Danube, and with the rapidity of lightning appeared before Ratisbon. The possession of this town would insure the success of the Swedish designs upon Bavaria and Austria; it would establish them firmly on the Danube, and provide a safe refuge in case of defeat, while it alone could give permanence to their conquests in that quarter. To defend Ratisbon was the urgent advice which the dying Tilly left to the Elector; and Gustavus Adolphus had lamented it as an irreparable loss that the Bavarians had anticipated him in taking possession of this place. Indescribable, therefore, was the consternation of Maximilian when Duke Bernard suddenly appeared before the town and prepared in earnest to besiege it.

The garrison consisted of not more than fifteen companies, mostly newly-raised soldiers; although that number was more than sufficient to weary out an enemy of far superior force if supported by well-disposed and warlike inhabitants. But this was not the greatest danger which the Bavarian garrison had to contend against. The Protestant inhabitants of Ratisbon, equally jealous of their civil and religious freedom, had unwillingly submitted to the yoke of Bavaria, and had long looked with impatience for the appearance of a deliverer. Bernard's arrival before the walls filled them with lively joy, and there was much reason to fear that they would support the attempts of the besiegers without by exciting a tumult within. In this perplexity the Elector addressed the most pressing entreaties to the Emperor and the Duke of Friedland to assist him, were it only with five thousand men. Seven messengers in succession were despatched by Ferdinand to Wallenstein, who promised immediate succors, and even announced to the Elector the near advance of twelve thousand men under Gallas, but at the same time forbade that general, under pain of death, to march. Meanwhile the Bavarian commandant of Ratisbon, in the hope of speedy assistance, made the best preparations for defence, armed the Roman Catholic peasants, disarmed and carefully watched the Protestant citizens lest they should attempt any hostile design against the garrison. But as no relief arrived, and the enemy's artillery incessantly battered the walls, he consulted his own safety and that of the garrison by an honorable capitulation, and abandoned the Bavarian officials and ecclesiastics to the conqueror's mercy.

The possession of Ratisbon enlarged the projects of the duke, and Bavaria itself now appeared too narrow a field for his bold designs. He determined to penetrate to the frontiers of Austria, to arm the Protestant peasantry against the Emperor, and restore to them their religious liberty. He had already taken Straubingen, while another Swedish army was advancing successfully along the northern bank of the Danube. At the head of his Swedes, bidding defiance to the severity of the weather, he reached the mouth of the Iser, which he passed in the presence of the Bavarian General Werth, who was encamped on that river. Passau and Lintz trembled for their fate; the terrified Emperor redoubled his entreaties and commands to Wallenstein to hasten with all speed to the relief of the hard-pressed Bavarians. But here the victorious Bernard of his own accord checked his career of conquest. Having in front of him the river Inn, guarded by a number of strong fortresses, and behind him two hostile armies, a disaffected country, and the river Iser, while his rear was covered by no tenable position, and no intrenchment could be made in the frozen ground; and threatened by the whole force of Wallenstein, who had at last resolved to march to the Danube, by a timely retreat he escaped the danger of being cut off from Ratisbon and surrounded by the enemy. He hastened across the Iser to the Danube to defend the conquests he had made in the Upper Palatinate against Wallenstein, and fully resolved not to decline a battle, if necessary, with that general. But Wallenstein, who was not disposed for any great exploits on the Danube, did not wait for his approach, and before the Bavarians could congratulate themselves on his arrival he suddenly withdrew again into Bohemia. The duke thus ended his victorious campaign, and allowed his troops their well-earned repose in winter quarters upon an enemy's country.

While in Swabia the war was thus successfully conducted by Gustavus Horn, and on the Upper and Lower Rhine by the Palatine of Birkenfeld, General Baudissen, and the Rhinegrave, Otto Louis, and by Duke Bernard on the Danube, the reputation of the Swedish arms was as gloriously sustained in Lower Saxony and Westphalia by the Duke of Lunenburg and the Landgrave of Hesse Cassel. The fortress of Hamel was taken by Duke George, after a brave defence, and a brilliant victory obtained over the imperial General Gronsfeld by the united Swedish and Hessian armies near Oldendorf. Count Wasaburg, a natural son of Gustavus Adolphus, showed himself in this battle worthy of his descent. Sixteen pieces of cannon, the whole baggage of the Imperialists, together with seventy-four colors, fell into the hands of the Swedes; three thousand of the enemy perished on the field, and nearly the same number were taken prisoners. The town of Osnaburg surrendered to the Swedish Colonel Knyphausen, and Paderborn to the Landgrave of Hesse; while, on the other hand, Bückeburg, a very important place for the Swedes, fell into the hands of the Imperialists. The Swedish banners were victorious in almost every quarter of Germany; and the year after the death of Gustavus left no trace of the loss which had been sustained in the person of that great leader.

In a review of the important events which signalized the campaign of 1633 the inactivity of a man of whom the highest expectations had been formed justly excites astonishment. Among all the generals who distinguished themselves in this campaign none could be compared with Wallenstein in experience, talents, and reputation; and yet after the battle of Lutzen we lose sight of him entirely. The fall of his great rival had left the whole theatre of glory open to him; all Europe was now attentively awaiting those exploits which should efface the remembrance of his defeat and still prove to the world his military superiority. Nevertheless, he continued inactive in Bohemia, while the Emperor's losses in Bavaria, Lower Saxony, and the Rhine pressingly called for his presence — a conduct equally unintelligible to friend and foe — the terror, and at the same time the last hope of the Emperor. After the defeat of Lutzen he had hastened into Bohemia, where he instituted the strictest inquiry into the conduct of his officers in that battle. Those whom the council of war declared guilty of misconduct were put to death without mercy, those who had behaved with bravery rewarded with princely munificence, and the memory of the dead honored by splendid monuments. During the winter he oppressed the imperial provinces by enormous contributions, and exhausted the Austrian territories by his winter quarters, which he purposely avoided taking up in an enemy's country. And in the spring of 1633, instead of being the first to open the campaign with this well-chosen and well-appointed army, and to make a worthy display of his great abilities, he was the last who appeared in the field; and even then it was an hereditary province of Austria which he selected as the seat of war.

Of all the Austrian provinces Silesia was most exposed to danger. Three different armies, a Swedish under Count Thurn, a Saxon under Arnheim and the Duke of Lauenburg, and one of Brandenburg under Borgsdorf, had at the same time carried the war into this country; they had already taken possession of the most important places, and even Breslau had embraced the cause of the allies. But this crowd of commanders and armies was the very means of saving this province to the Emperor; for the jealousy of the generals, and the mutual hatred of the Saxons and the Swedes, never allowed them to act with unanimity. Arnheim and Thurn contended for the chief command; the troops of Brandenburg and Saxony combined against the Swedes, whom they looked upon as troublesome strangers who ought to be got rid of as soon as possible. The Saxons, on the contrary, lived on a very intimate footing with the Imperialists, and the officers of both these hostile armies often visited and entertained each other. The Imperialists were allowed to remove their property without hinderance, and many did not affect to conceal that they had received large sums from Vienna. Among such equivocal allies the Swedes saw themselves sold and betrayed; and any great enterprise was out of the question while so bad an understanding prevailed between the troops. General Arnheim, too, was absent the greater part of the time; and when he at last returned Wallenstein was fast approaching the frontiers with a formidable force.

His army amounted to forty thousand men, while to oppose him the allies had only twenty-four thousand. They nevertheless resolved to give him battle, and marched to Munsterberg, where he had formed an intrenched camp. But Wallenstein remained inactive for eight days; he then left his intrenchments and marched slowly and with composure to the enemy's camp. But even after quitting his position, and when the enemy, emboldened by his past delay, manfully prepared to receive him, he declined the opportunity of fighting. The caution with which he avoided a battle was imputed to fear; but the well-established reputation of Wallenstein enabled him to despise this suspicion. The vanity of the allies allowed them not to see that he purposely saved them a defeat because a victory at that time would not have served his own ends. To convince them of his superior power, and that his inactivity proceeded not from any fear of them, he put to death the commander of a castle that fell into his hands because he had refused at once to surrender an untenable place.

For nine days did the two armies remain within musket-shot of each other, when Count Terzky, from the camp of the Imperialists, appeared with a trumpeter in that of the allies inviting General Arnheim to a conference. The purport was that Wallenstein, notwithstanding his superiority, was willing to agree to a cessation of arms for six weeks. "He was come," he said, "to conclude a lasting peace with the Swedes, and with the princes of the empire, to pay the soldiers, and to satisfy every one. All this was in his power; and if the Austrian court hesitated to confirm his agreement he would unite with the allies, and (as he privately whispered to Arnheim) hunt the Emperor to the devil." At the second conference he expressed himself still more plainly to Count Thurn. "All the privileges of the Bohemians," he engaged, "should be confirmed anew, the exiles recalled and restored to their estates, and he himself would be the first to resign his share of them. The Jesuits, as the authors of all past grievances, should be banished, the Swedish crown indemnified by stated payments, and all the superfluous troops on both sides employed against the Turks." The last article explained the whole mystery. "If," he continued, "*he* should obtain the crown of Bohemia all the exiles would have reason to applaud his generosity; perfect toleration of religions should be established within the kingdom, the Palatine family be reinstated in its rights, and he would accept the Margraviate of Moravia as a compensation for Mecklenburg. The allied armies would then, under his command, advance upon Vienna, and, sword in hand, compel the Emperor to ratify the treaty."

Thus was the veil at last removed from the schemes over which he had brooded for years in mysterious silence. Every circumstance now convinced him that not a moment was to be lost in its execution. Nothing but a blind confidence in the good fortune and military genius of the Duke of Friedland had induced the Emperor, in the face of the remonstrances of Bavaria and Spain, and at the expense of his own reputation, to confer upon this imperious leader such an unlimited command. But this belief in Wallenstein's being invincible had been much weakened by the inaction, and almost entirely overthrown by the defeat at Lutzen. His enemies at the imperial court now renewed their intrigues; and the Emperor's disappointment at the failure of his hopes procured for their remonstrances a favorable reception. Wallenstein's whole conduct was now reviewed with the most malicious criticism; his ambitious haughtiness, his disobedience to the Emperor's orders, were recalled to the recollection of that jealous prince, as well as the complaints of the Austrian subjects against his boundless oppression; his fidelity was questioned, and alarming hints thrown out as to his secret views. These insinuations, which the conduct of the duke seemed but too well to justify, failed not to make a deep impression on Ferdinand; but the step had been taken, and the great power with which Wallenstein had been invested could not be taken from him without danger. Insensibly to diminish that power was the only course that now remained, and to effect this it must in the first place be divided; but, above all, the Emperor's present dependence on the goodwill of his general put an end to. But even this right had been resigned in his engagement with Wallenstein, and the Emperor's own handwriting secured him against every attempt to unite another general with him in the command or to exercise any immediate act of authority over the troops. As this disadvantageous contract could neither be kept nor broken recourse was had to artifice. Wallenstein was Imperial Generalissimo in Germany, but his command extended no further, and he could not presume to exercise any authority over a foreign army. A Spanish army was accordingly raised in Milan and marched into Germany under a Spanish general. Wallenstein now ceased to be indispensable because he was no longer supreme, and in case of necessity the Emperor was now provided with the means of support even against him.

The duke quickly and deeply felt whence this blow came and whither it was aimed. In vain did he protest against this violation of the compact to the Cardinal Infante; the Italian army continued its march and he was forced to detach General Altringer to join it with a reinforcement. He took care, indeed, so closely to fetter the latter as to prevent the Italian army from acquiring any great reputation in Alsace and Swabia; but this bold step of the court awakened him from his security, and warned him of the approach of danger. That he might not a second time be deprived of his command and lose the fruit of all his labors he must accelerate the accomplishment of his long-meditated designs. He secured the attachment of his troops by removing the doubtful officers and by his liberality to the rest. He had sacrificed to the welfare of the army every other order in the state, every consideration of justice and humanity, and therefore he reckoned upon their gratitude. At the very moment when he meditated an unparalleled act of ingratitude against the author of his own good fortune he founded all his hopes upon the gratitude which was due to himself.

The leaders of the Silesian armies had no authority from their principals to consent on their own discretion to such important proposals as those of Wallenstein, and they did not even feel themselves warranted in granting for more than a fortnight the cessation of hostilities which he demanded. Before the duke disclosed his designs to Sweden and Saxony he had deemed it advisable to secure the sanction of France to his bold undertaking. For this purpose a secret negotiation had been carried on with the greatest possible caution and distrust by Count Kinsky with Feuquieres, the French ambassador at Dresden, and had terminated according to his wishes. Feuquieres received orders from his court to promise every assistance on the part of France, and to offer the duke a considerable pecuniary aid in case of need.

But it was this excessive caution to secure himself on all sides that led to his ruin. The French ambassador with astonishment discovered that a plan which, more than any other, required secrecy, had been communicated to the Swedes and the Saxons. And yet it was generally known that the Saxon ministry was in the interests of the Emperor, and on, the other hand, the conditions offered to the Swedes fell too far short of their expectations to be likely to be accepted. Feuquieres therefore could not believe that the duke could be serious in calculating upon the aid of the latter and the silence of the former. He communicated accordingly his doubts and anxieties to the Swedish chancellor, who equally distrusted the views of Wallenstein and disliked his plans. Although it was no secret to Oxenstiern that the duke had formerly entered into a similar negotiation with Gustavus Adolphus he could not credit the possibility of inducing a whole army to revolt, and of his extravagant promises. So daring a design, and such imprudent conduct, seemed not to be consistent with the duke's reserved and suspicious temper, and he was the more inclined to consider the whole as the result of dissimulation and treachery because he had less reason to doubt his prudence than his honesty.

Oxenstiern's doubts at last affected Arnheim himself, who, in full confidence in Wallenstein's sincerity, had repaired to the chancellor at Gelnhausen to persuade him to lend some of his best regiments to the duke to aid him in the execution of the plan. They began to suspect that the whole proposal was only a snare to disarm the allies, and to betray the flower of their troops into the hands of the Emperor. Wallenstein's well-known character did not contradict the suspicion, and the inconsistencies in which he afterwards involved himself entirely destroyed all confidence in his sincerity. While he was endeavoring to draw the Swedes into this alliance, and requiring the help of their best troops, he declared to Arnheim that they must begin with expelling the Swedes from the empire; and while the Saxon officers, relying upon the security of the truce, repaired in great numbers to his camp he made an unsuccessful attempt to seize them. He was the first to break the truce, which some months afterwards he renewed, though not without great difficulty. All confidence in his sincerity was lost; his whole conduct was regarded as a tissue of deceit and low cunning, devised to weaken the allies and repair his own strength. This indeed he actually did effect, as his own army daily augmented, while that of the allies was reduced nearly one-half by desertion and bad provisions. But he did not make that use of his superiority which Vienna expected. When all men were looking for a decisive blow to be struck he suddenly renewed the negotiations; and when the truce lulled the allies into security he as suddenly recommenced hostilities. All these contradictions arose out of the double and irreconcilable designs to ruin at once the Emperor and the Swedes, and to conclude a separate peace with the Saxons.

Impatient at the ill-success of his negotiations he at last determined to display his strength; the more so as the pressing distress within the empire, and the growing dissatisfaction of the imperial court, admitted not of his making any longer delay. Before the last cessation of hostilities General Holk from Bohemia had attacked the circle of Meissen, laid waste everything on his route with fire and sword, driven the Elector into his fortresses, and taken the town of Leipzig. But the truce in Silesia put a period to his ravages, and the consequences of his excesses brought him to the grave at Adorf. As soon as hostilities were recommenced Wallenstein made a movement as if he designed to penetrate through Lusatia into Saxony, and circulated the report that Piccolomini had already invaded that country. Arnheim immediately broke up his camp in Silesia to follow him, and hastened to the assistance of the Electorate. By this means the Swedes were left exposed, who were encamped in small force under Count Thurn at Steinau, on the Oder, and this was exactly what Wallenstein desired. He allowed the Saxon general to advance sixteen miles towards Meissan, and then, suddenly turning towards the Oder, surprised the Swedish army in the most complete security. Their cavalry were first beaten by General Schafgotsch, who was sent against them, and the infantry completely surrounded at Steinau by the duke's army, which followed. Wallenstein gave Count Thurn half an hour to deliberate whether he would defend himself with two thousand five hundred men against more than twenty thousand, or surrender at discretion. But there was no room for deliberation. The army surrendered, and the most complete victory was obtained without bloodshed. Colors, baggage, and artillery all fell into the hands of the victors, the officers were taken into custody, the privates drafted into the army of Wallenstein. And now at last, after a banishment of fourteen years, after numberless changes of fortune, the author of the Bohemian insurrection, and the remote origin of this destructive war, the notorious Count Thurn, was in the power of his enemies. With bloodthirsty impatience the arrival of this great criminal was looked for in Vienna, where they already anticipated the malicious triumph of sacrificing so distinguished a victim to public justice. But to deprive the Jesuits of this pleasure was still a sweeter triumph to Wallenstein, and Thurn was set at liberty. Fortunately for him he knew more than it was prudent to have divulged in Vienna, and his enemies were also those of Wallenstein. A defeat might have been forgiven in Vienna, but this disappointment of their hopes they could not pardon. "What should I have done with this madman?" he writes with a malicious sneer to the minister who called him to account for this unseasonable magnanimity. "Would to Heaven the enemy had no generals but such as he. At the head of the Swedish army he will render us much better service than in prison."

The victory of Steinau was followed by the capture of Liegnitz, Grossglogau, and even of Frankfort on the Oder. Schafgotsch, who remained in Silesia to complete the subjugation of that province, blockaded Breig, and threatened Breslau, though in vain, as that free town was jealous of its privileges and devoted to the Swedes. Colonels Illo and Goetz were ordered by Wallenstein to the Warta, to push forward into Pomerania, and to the coasts of the Baltic, and actually obtained possession of Landsberg, the key of Pomerania. While thus the Elector of Brandenburg and the Duke of Pomerania were made to tremble for their dominions, Wallenstein himself with the remainder of his army burst suddenly into Lusatia, where he took Goerlitz by storm, and forced Bautzen to surrender. But his object was merely to alarm the Elector of Saxony, not to follow up the advantages already obtained; and therefore, even with the sword in his hand, he continued his negotiations for peace with Brandenburg and Saxony, but with no better success than before, as the inconsistencies of his conduct had destroyed all confidence in his sincerity. He was therefore on the point of turning his whole force in earnest against the unfortunate Saxons, and effecting his object by force of arms, when circumstances compelled him to leave these territories. The conquests of Duke Bernard upon the Danube, which threatened Austria itself with immediate danger, urgently demanded his presence in Bavaria; and the expulsion of the Saxons and Swedes from Silesia deprived him of every pretext for longer resisting the imperial orders and leaving the Elector of Bavaria without assistance. With his main body, therefore, he immediately set out for the Upper Palatinate, and his retreat freed Upper Saxony forever of this formidable enemy.

So long as was possible he had delayed to move to the rescue of Bavaria, and on every pretext evaded the commands of the Emperor. He had, indeed, after reiterated remonstrances, despatched from Bohemia a reinforcement of some regiments to Count Altringer, who was defending the Lech and the Danube against Horn and Bernard, but under the express condition of his acting merely on the defensive. He referred the Emperor and the Elector, whenever they applied to him for aid, to Altringer, who, as he publicly gave out, had received unlimited powers; secretly, however, he tied up his hands by the strictest injunctions, and even threatened him with death if he exceeded his orders. When Duke Bernard had appeared before Ratisbon, and the Emperor as well as the Elector repeated still more urgently their demand for succor, he pretended he was about to despatch General Gallas with a considerable army to the Danube; but this movement also was delayed, and Ratisbon, Straubing, and Cham, as well as the Bishopric of Eichstädt, fell into the hands of the Swedes. When at last he could no longer neglect the orders of the court he marched slowly toward the Bavarian frontier, where he invested the town of Cham, which had been taken by the Swedes. But no sooner did he learn that on the Swedish side a diversion was contemplated by an inroad of the Saxons into Bohemia than he availed himself of the report as a pretext for immediately retreating into that kingdom. Every consideration, he urged, must be postponed to the defence and preservation of the hereditary dominions of the Emperor; and on this plea he remained firmly fixed in Bohemia, which he guarded as if it had been his own property. And when the Emperor laid upon him his commands to move towards the Danube, and prevent the Duke of Weimar from establishing himself in so dangerous a position on the frontiers of Austria, Wallenstein thought proper to conclude the campaign a second time, and quartered his troops for the winter in this exhausted kingdom.

Such continued insolence and unexampled contempt of the imperial orders, as well as obvious neglect of the common cause, joined to his equivocal behavior towards the enemy, tended at last to convince the Emperor of the truth of those unfavorable reports with regard to the duke which were current through Germany. The latter had for a long time succeeded in glozing over his criminal correspondence with the enemy, and persuading the Emperor, still prepossessed in his favor, that the sole object of his secret conferences was to obtain peace for

Germany. But, impenetrable as he himself believed his proceedings to be, in the course of his conduct enough transpired to justify the insinuations with which his rivals incessantly loaded the ear of the Emperor. In order to satisfy himself of the truth or falsehood of these rumors Ferdinand had already, at different times, sent spies into Wallenstein's camp; but as the duke took the precaution never to commit anything in writing they returned with nothing but conjectures. But when at last those ministers who had formerly been his champions at the court, in consequence of their estates not being exempted by Wallenstein from the general exactions, joined his enemies; when the Elector of Bavaria threatened, in case of Wallenstein being any longer retained in the supreme command, to unite with the Swedes; when the Spanish ambassador insisted on his dismissal, and threatened in case of refusal to withdraw the subsidies furnished by his crown, the Emperor found himself a second time compelled to deprive him of the command.

The Emperor's authoritative and direct interference with the army soon convinced the duke that the compact with himself was regarded as at an end, and that his dismissal was inevitable. One of his inferior generals in Austria, whom he had forbidden under pain of death to obey the orders of the court, received the positive commands of the Emperor to join the Elector of Bavaria; and Wallenstein himself was imperiously ordered to send some regiments to reinforce the army of the Cardinal Infante, who was on his march from Italy. All these measures convinced him that the plan was finally arranged to disarm him by degrees, and at once, when he was weak and defenceless, to complete his ruin.

In self-defence must he now hasten to carry into execution the plans which he had originally formed only with the view of aggrandizement. He had delayed too long, either because the favorable configuration of the stars had not yet presented itself, or, as he used to say, to check the impatience of his friends, because *the time was not yet come.* The time even now was not come; but the pressure of circumstances no longer allowed him to await the favor of the stars. The first step was to assure himself of the sentiments of his principal officers, and then to try the attachment of the army, which he had so long confidently reckoned on. Three of them, Colonels Kinsky, Terzky, and Illo, had long been in his secrets, and the two first were further united to his interests by the ties of relationship. The same wild ambition, the same bitter hatred of the government, and the hope of enormous rewards, bound them in the closest manner to Wallenstein, who, to increase the number of his adherents, could stoop to the lowest means. He had once advised Colonel Illo to solicit in Vienna the title of count, and had promised to back his application with his powerful mediation. But he secretly wrote to the ministry, advising them to refuse his request, as to grant it would give rise to similar demands from others whose services and claims were equal to his. On Illo's return to the camp Wallenstein immediately demanded to know the success of his mission; and when informed by Illo of its failure, he broke out into the bitterest complaints against the court. "Thus," said he, "are our faithful services rewarded. My recommendation is disregarded, and your merit denied so trifling a reward! Who would any longer devote his services to so ungrateful a master? No, for my part, I am henceforth the determined foe of Austria." Illo agreed with him, and a close alliance was cemented between them.

But what was known to these three confidants of the duke was long an impenetrable secret to the rest; and the confidence with which Wallenstein spoke of the devotion of his officers was founded merely on the favors he had lavished on them, and on their known dissatisfaction with the court. But this vague presumption must be converted into certainty before he could venture to lay aside the mask or take any open step against the Emperor. Count Piccolomini, who had distinguished himself by his unparalleled bravery at Lutzen, was the first whose fidelity he put to the proof. He had he thought gained the attachment of this general by large presents, and preferred him to all others because born under the same constellations with himself. He disclosed to him that in consequence of the Emperor's ingratitude, and the

near approach of his own danger, he had irrevocably
determined entirely to abandon the party of Austria, to
join the enemy with the best part of his army, and to
make war upon the House of Austria on all sides of its
dominions till he had wholly extirpated it. In the
execution of this plan he principally reckoned on the
services of Piccolomini, and had beforehand promised
him the greatest rewards. When the latter, to conceal
his amazement at this extraordinary communication,
spoke of the dangers and obstacles which would oppose
so hazardous an enterprise, Wallenstein ridiculed his
fears. "In such enterprises," he maintained, "nothing
was difficult but the commencement. The stars were
propitious to him, the opportunity the best that could be
wished for, and something must always be trusted to
fortune. His resolution was taken, and if it could not be
otherwise he would encounter the hazard at the head of
a thousand horse." Piccolomini was careful not to excite
Wallenstein's suspicions by longer opposition, and yielded
apparently to the force of his reasoning. Such was the
infatuation of the duke that, notwithstanding the warnings of Count Terzky, he never doubted the sincerity of
this man, who lost not a moment in communicating to
the court at Vienna this important conversation.

Preparatory to taking the last decisive step he, in
January, 1634, called a meeting of all the commanders of
the army at Pilsen, whither he had marched after his
retreat from Bavaria. The Emperor's recent orders to
spare his hereditary dominions from winter quarterings,
to recover Ratisbon in the middle of winter, and to
reduce the army by a detachment of six thousand horse
to the Cardinal Infante, were matters sufficiently grave to
be laid before a council of war; and this plausible pretext
served to conceal from the curious the real object of the
meeting. Sweden and Saxony received invitations to be
present in order to treat with the Duke of Friedland for
a peace; to the leaders of more distant armies written
communications were made. Of the commanders thus
summoned twenty appeared; but three most influential,
Gallas, Colloredo and Altringer were absent. The duke
reiterated his summons to them, and in the meantime, in

expectation of their speedy arrival, proceeded to execute his designs.

It was no light task that he had to perform; a nobleman, proud, brave, and jealous of his honor was to declare himself capable of the basest treachery, in the very presence of those who had been accustomed to regard him as the representative of majesty, the judge of their actions, and the supporter of their laws, and to show himself suddenly as a traitor, a cheat, and a rebel. It was no easy task either to shake to its foundations a legitimate sovereignty, strengthened by time and consecrated by laws and religion; to dissolve all the charms of the senses and the imagination, those formidable guardians of an established throne, and to attempt forcibly to uproot those invincible feelings of duty which plead so loudly and so powerfully in the breast of the subject in favor of his sovereign. But, blinded by the splendor of a crown, Wallenstein observed not the precipice that yawned beneath his feet; and in full reliance on his own strength, the common case with energetic and daring minds, he stopped not to consider the magnitude and the number of the difficulties that opposed him. Wallenstein saw nothing but an army, partly indifferent and partly exasperated against the court, accustomed with a blind submission to do homage to his great name, to bow to him as their legislator and judge, and with trembling reverence to follow his orders as the decrees of fate. In the extravagant flatteries which were paid to his omnipotence, in the bold abuse of the court government in which a lawless soldiery indulged, and which the wild license of the camp excused, he thought he read the sentiments of the army; and the boldness with which they were ready to censure the monarch's measures, passed with him for a readiness to renounce their allegiance to a sovereign so little respected. But that which he had regarded as the lightest matter proved the most formidable obstacle with which he had to contend; the soldiers' feelings of allegiance were the rock on which his hopes were wrecked. Deceived by the profound respect in which he was held by these lawless bands, he ascribed the whole to his own personal greatness, without distinguishing how much he owed to himself and how much to tne dignity with which he was invested. All trembled before him while he exercised a legitimate authority, while obedience to him was a duty, and while his consequence was supported by the majesty of the sovereign. Greatness in and of itself may excite terror and admiration; but legitimate greatness alone can inspire reverence and submission; and of this decisive advantage he deprived himself the instant he avowed himself a traitor.

Field-Marshal Illo undertook to learn the sentiments of the officers and to prepare them for the step which was expected of them. He began by laying before them the new orders of the court to the general and the army; and by the obnoxious turn he skilfully gave to them he found it easy to excite the indignation of the assembly. After this well-chosen introduction he expatiated with much eloquence upon the merits of the army and the general and the ingratitude with which the Emperor was accustomed to requite them. Spanish influence, he maintained, governed the court; the ministry were in the pay of Spain; the Duke of Friedland alone had hitherto opposed this tyranny, and had thus drawn down upon himself the deadly enmity of the Spaniards. To remove him from the command or to make away with him entirely, he continued, had long been the end of their desires; and until they could succeed in one or the other they endeavored to abridge his power in the field. The command was to be placed in the hands of the King of Hungary for no other reason than the better to promote the Spanish power in Germany; because this prince, as the ready instrument of foreign counsels, might be led at pleasure. It was merely with the view of weakening the army that the six thousand troops were required for the Cardinal Infante; it was solely for the purpose of harassing it by a winter campaign that they were now called on in this inhospitable season to undertake the recovery of Ratisbon. The means of subsistence were everywhere rendered difficult, while the Jesuits and the ministry enriched themselves with the sweat of the provinces and squandered the money intended for the pay of the troops. The general abandoned by the court acknowledges his inability to keep his engagements to the army. For all the services which for two-and-twenty years he had rendered the House of Austria; for all the difficulties with which he had struggled; for all the treasures of his own which he had expended in the imperial service, a second disgraceful dismissal awaited him. But he was resolved the matter should not come to this; he was determined voluntarily to resign the command before it should be wrested from his hands; and this, continued the orator, is what through me he now makes known to his officers. It was now for them to say whether it would be advisable to lose such a general. Let each consider who was to refund him the sums he had expended in the Emperor's service, and where he was now to reap the reward of their bravery when he who was their evidence was removed from the scene."

A universal cry that they would not allow their general to be taken from them interrupted the speaker. Four of the principal officers were deputed to lay before him the wish of the assembly, and earnestly to request that he would not leave the army. The duke made a show of resistance and only yielded after the second deputation. This concession on his side seemed to demand a return on theirs; as he engaged not to quit the service without the knowledge and consent of the generals, he required of them, on the other hand, a written promise to truly and firmly adhere to him, neither to separate nor to allow themselves to be separated from him, and to shed their last drop of blood in his defence. Whoever should break this covenant was to be regarded as a perfidious traitor, and treated by the rest as a common enemy. The express condition, which was added,." *As long as Wallenstein shall employ the army in the Emperor's service,*" seemed to exclude all misconception, and none of the assembled generals hesitated at once to accede to a demand apparently so innocent and so reasonable.

This document was publicly read before an entertainment which Field-Marshal Illo had expressly prepared for the purpose; it was to be signed after they rose from table. The host did his utmost to stupify his guests by strong potations; and it was not until he saw them affected with the wine that he had produced the paper for signature. Most of them wrote their names without knowing what they were subscribing; a few only, more curious or more distrustful, read the paper over again, and discovered with astonishment that the clause " as long as Wallenstein shall employ the army for the Emperor's service" was omitted. Illo had, in fact, artfully contrived to substitute for the first another copy in which these words were wanting. The trick was manifest and many refused now to sign. Piccolomini, who had seen through the whole cheat, and had been present at this scene merely with the view of giving information of the whole to the court, forgot himself so far in his cups as to drink the Emperor's health. But Count Terzky now rose and declared that all were perjured villains who should recede from their engagement. His menaces, the idea of the inevitable danger to which they who resisted any longer would be exposed, the example of the rest, and Illo's rhetoric, at last overcame their scruples, and the paper was signed by all without exception.

Wallenstein had now effected his purpose; but the unexpected resistance he had met with from the commanders roused him at last from the fond illusions in which he had hitherto indulged. Besides, most of the names were scrawled so illegibly that some deceit was evidently intended. But instead of being recalled to his discretion by this warning he gave vent to his injured pride in undignified complaints and reproaches. He assembled the generals the next day, and undertook personally to confirm the whole tenor of the agreement which Illo had submitted to them the day before. After pouring out the bitterest reproaches and abuse against the court, he reminded them of their opposition to the proposition of the previous day, and declared that this circumstance had induced him to retract his own promise. The generals withdrew in silence and confusion; but after a short consultation in the ante-chamber they returned to apologize for their late conduct and offered to sign the paper anew.

Nothing now remained but to obtain a similar assurance from the absent generals, or, on their refusal, to seize their persons. Wallenstein renewed his invitation to them, and earnestly urged them to hasten their arrival. But a rumor of the doings at Pilsen reached them on their journey and suddenly stopped their further progress. Altringer, on pretence of sickness, remained in the strong fortress of Frauenberg. Gallas made his appearance, but merely with the design of better qualifying himself as an eye-witness, to keep the Emperor informed of all Wallenstein's proceedings. The intelligence which he and Piccolomini gave at once converted the suspicions of the court into an alarming certainty. Similar disclosures, which were at the same time made from other quarters, left no room for further doubt; and the sudden change of the commanders in Austria and Silesia appeared to be the prelude to some important enterprise. The danger was pressing and the remedy must be speedy, but the court was unwilling to proceed at once to the execution of the sentence till the regular forms of justice were complied with. Secret instructions were therefore issued to the principal officers, on whose fidelity reliance could be placed, to seize the persons of the Duke of Friedland and of his two associates, Illo and Terzky, and keep them in close confinement till they should have an opportunity of being heard and of answering for their conduct; but if this could not be accomplished quietly the public danger required that they should be taken dead or alive. At the same time General Gallas received a patent commission, by which these orders of the Emperor were made known to the colonels and officers, and the army was released from its obedience to the traitor, and placed under Lieutenant-General Gallas till a new generalissimo could be appointed. In order to bring back the seduced and deluded to their duty, and not to drive the guilty to despair, a general amnesty was proclaimed in regard to all offences against the imperial majesty committed at Pilsen.

General Gallas was not pleased with the honor which was done him. He was at Pilsen under the eye of the person whose fate he was to dispose of; in the power of an enemy who had a hundred eyes to watch his motions. If Wallenstein once discovered the secret of his commission nothing could save him from the effects of his vengeance and despair. But if it was thus dangerous to be the secret depositary of such a commission how much more so to execute it? The sentiments of the generals were uncertain; and it was at least doubtful whether, after the step they had taken, they would be ready to trust the Emperor's promises, and at once to abandon the brilliant expectations they had built upon Wallenstein's enterprise. It was also hazardous to attempt to lay hands on the person of a man who till now had been considered inviolable; who from long exercise of supreme power, and from habitual obedience, had become the object of deepest respect; who was invested with every attribute of outward majesty and inward greatness; whose very aspect inspired terror, and who by a nod disposed of life and death! To seize such a man, like a common criminal, in the midst of the guards by whom he was surrounded, and in a city apparently devoted to him; to convert the object of this deep and habitual veneration into a subject of compassion or of contempt was a commission calculated to make even the boldest hesitate. So deeply was fear and veneration for their general engraven in the breasts of the soldiers that even the atrocious crime of high treason could not wholly eradicate these sentiments.

Gallas perceived the impossibility of executing his commission under the eyes of the duke; and his most anxious wish was before venturing on any steps to have an interview with Altringer. As the long absence of the latter had already begun to excite the duke's suspicions Gallas offered to repair in person to Frauenberg, and to prevail on Altringer, his relation, to return with him. Wallenstein was so pleased with this proof of his zeal that he even lent him his own equipage for the journey. Rejoicing at the success of his stratagem, he left Pilsen without delay, leaving to Count Piccolomini the task of watching Wallenstein's further movements. He did not fail as he went along to make use of the imperial patent, and the sentiments of the troops proved more favorable than he had expected. Instead of taking back his friend to Pilsen he despatched him to Vienna, to warn the Emperor against the intended attack, while he himself repaired to Upper Austria, of which the safety was threatened by the near approach of Duke Bernard. In Bohemia the towns of Budweiss and Tabor were again garrisoned for the Emperor, and every precaution taken to oppose with energy the designs of the traitor.

As Gallas did not appear disposed to return, Piccolomini determined to put Wallenstein's credulity once more to the test. He begged to be sent to bring back Gallas, and Wallenstein suffered himself a second time to be overreached. This inconceivable blindness can only be accounted for as the result of his pride, which never retracted the opinion it had once formed of any person, and would not acknowledge even to itself the possibility of being deceived. He conveyed Count Piccolomini in his own carriage to Lintz, where the latter immediately followed the example of Gallas, and even went a step farther. He had promised the duke to return. He did so, but it was at the head of an army, intending to surprise the duke in Pilsen. Another army under General Suys hastened to Prague to secure that capital in its allegiance and to defend it against the rebels. Gallas at the same time announced himself to the different imperial armies as the commander-in-chief, from whom they were henceforth to receive orders. Placards were circulated through all the imperial camps denouncing the duke and his four confidants, and absolving the soldiers from all obedience to him.

The example which had been set at Lintz was universally followed; imprecations were showered on the traitor, and he was forsaken by all the armies. At last, when even Piccolomini returned no more, the mist fell from Wallenstein's eyes, and in consternation he awoke from his dream. Yet his faith in the truth of astrology and in the fidelity of the army was unshaken. Immediately after the intelligence of Piccolomini's defection he issued orders that in future no commands were to be obeyed which did not proceed directly from himself, or from Terzky, or Illo. He prepared in all haste to advance upon Prague, where he intended to throw off the mask and to openly declare against the Emperor. All the troops were to assemble before that city, and from thence to pour down with rapidity upon Austria. Duke Bernard, who had joined the conspiracy, was to support the operations of the duke with the Swedish troops, and to effect a diversion upon the Danube.

Terzky was already upon his march towards Prague; and nothing but the want of horses prevented the duke from following him with the regiments who still adhered faithfully to him. But when with the most anxious expectation he awaited intelligence from Prague he suddenly received information of the loss of that town, the defection of his generals, the desertion of his troops, the discovery of his whole plot, and the rapid advance of Piccolomini, who was sworn to his destruction. Suddenly and fearfully had all his projects been ruined — all his hopes annihilated. He stood alone, abandoned by all to whom he had been a benefactor, betrayed by all on whom he had depended. But it is under such circumstances that great minds reveal themselves. Though deceived in all his expectations he refused to abandon one of his designs; he despaired of nothing so long as life remained. The time was now come when he absolutely required that assistance which he had so often solicited from the Swedes and the Saxons, and when all doubts of the sincerity of his purposes must be dispelled. And now, when Oxenstiern and Arnheim were convinced of the sincirity of his intentions, and were aware of his necessities, they no longer hesitated to embrace the favorable opportunity and to offer him their protection. On the part of Saxony, the Duke Francis Albert of Saxe Lauenberg was to join him with four thousand men, and Duke Bernard and the Palatine Christian of Birkenfeld with six thousand from Sweden, all chosen troops.

Wallenstein left Pilsen with Terzky's regiment and the few who either were or pretended to be faithful to him, and hastened to Egra, on the frontiers of the kingdom, in order to be near the Upper Palatinate and to facilitate his junction with Duke Bernard. He was not yet informed of the decree by which he was proclaimed a public enemy and traitor; this thunder-stroke awaited him at Egra. He still reckoned on the army which General Schafgotsch was preparing for him in Silesia, and

flattered himself with the hope that many even of those
who had forsaken him would return with the first dawning of success. Even during his flight to Egra (so little
humility had he learned from melancholy experience) he
was still occupied with the colossal scheme of dethroning the Emperor. It was under these circumstances that
one of his suite asked leave to offer him his advice.
"Under the Emperor," said he, "your highness is certain
of being a great and respected noble; with the enemy
you are at best but a precarious king. It is unwise to
risk a certainty for uncertainty. The enemy will avail
themselves of your personal influence while the opportunity lasts; but you will ever be regarded with suspicion, and they will always be fearful lest you should
treat them as you have done the Emperor. Return,
then, to your alligiance, while there is yet time." "And
how is that to be done?" said Wallenstein, interrupting
him. "You have forty thousand men-at-arms," rejoined
he (meaning ducats, which were stamped with the
figure of an armed man), "take them with you and go
straight to the imperial court; then declare that the
steps you have hitherto taken were merely designed to
test the fidelity of the Emperor's servants, and of distinguishing the loyal from the doubtful; and since most
have shown a disposition to revolt, say you are come to
warn his imperial majesty against those dangerous men.
Thus you will make those appear as traitors who are
laboring to represent you as a false villain. At the imperial court a man is sure to be welcome with forty
thousand ducats, and Friedland will be again as he was
at first." "The advice is good," said Wallenstein, after
a pause, "but let the devil trust to it."

While the duke in his retirement in Egra was energetically pushing his negotiations with the enemy, consulting the stars, and indulging in new hopes, the dagger
which was to put an end to his existence was unsheathed
almost under his very eyes. The imperial decree which
proclaimed him an outlaw had not failed of its effect;
and an avenging Nemesis ordained that the ungrateful
should fall beneath the blow of ingratitude. Among
his officers Wallenstein had particularly distinguished

one Leslie,* an Irishman, and had made his fortune. This was the man who now felt himself called on to execute the sentence against him and to earn the price of blood. No sooner had he reached Egra in the suite of the duke than he disclosed to the commandant of the town, Colonel Butler, and to Lieutenant-Colonel Gordon, two Protestant Scotchmen, the treasonable designs of the duke, which the latter had imprudently enough communicated to him during the journey. In these two individuals he had found men capable of a determined resolution. They were now called upon to chose between treason and duty, between their legitimate sovereign and a fugitive abandoned rebel; and though the latter was their common benefactor the choice could not remain for a moment doubtful. They were solemnly pledged to the allegiance of the Emperor, and this duty required them to take the most rapid measures against the public enemy. The opportunity was favorable; his evil genius seemed to have delivered him into the hands of vengeance. But not to encroach on the province of justice they resolved to deliver up their victim alive; and they parted with the bold resolve to take their general prisoner. This dark plot was buried in the deepest silence, and Wallenstein, far from suspecting his impending ruin, flattered himself that in the garrison of Egra he possessed his bravest and most faithful champions.

At this time he became acquainted with the imperial proclamations containing his sentence and which had been published in all the camps. He now became aware of the full extent of the danger which encompassed him, the utter impossibility of retracing his steps, his fearfully forlorn condition, and the absolute necessity of at once trusting himself to the faith and honor of the Emperor's enemies. To Leslie he poured forth all the anguish of his wounded spirit, and the vehemence of his agitation extracted from him his last remaining secret. He disclosed to this officer his intention to deliver up Egra and Ellenbogen, the passes of the kingdom to the Palatine of

---

* Schiller is mistaken as to this point. Leslie was a Scotchman and Buttler an Irishman and a papist. He died a general in the Emperor's service, and founded at Prague a convent of Irish Franciscans which still exists.

Birkenfeld, and at the same time informed him of the near approach of Duke Bernard, of whose arrival he hoped to receive tidings that very night. These disclosures, which Leslie immediately communicated to the conspirators, made them change their original plan. The urgency of the danger admitted not of half measures. Egra might in a moment be in the enemy's hands, and a sudden revolution set their prisoner at liberty. To anticipate this mischance they resolved to assassinate him and his associates the following night.

In order to execute this design with less noise it was arranged that the fearful deed should be perpetrated at an entertainment which Colonel Buttler should give in the castle of Egra. All the guests except Wallenstein made their appearance, who, being in too great anxiety of mind to enjoy company, excused himself. With regard to him, therefore, their plan must be again changed; but they resolved to execute their design against the others. The three colonels, Illo, Terzky, and William Kinsky, came in with careless confidence, and with them Captain Neumann, an officer of ability, whose advice Terzky sought in every intricate affair. Previous to their arrival trusty soldiers of the garrison, to whom the plot had been communicated, were admitted into the castle, all the avenues leading from it guarded, and six of Buttler's dragoons concealed in an appartment close to the banqueting-room, who, on a concerted signal, were to rush in and kill the traitors. Without suspecting the danger that hung over them, the guests gayly abandoned themselves to the pleasures of the table, and Wallenstein's health was drunk in full bumpers, not as a servant of the Emperor but as a sovereign prince. The wine opened their hearts, and Illo, with exultation, boasted that in three days an army would arrive such as Wallenstein had never before been at the head of. "Yes," cried Neumann, "and then he hopes to bathe his hands in Austrian blood." During this conversation the desert was brought in, and Leslie gave the concerted signal to raise the drawbridges, while he himself received the keys of the gates. In an instant the hall was filled with armed men, who, with the unexpected greeting of "Long live Ferdinand!"

placed themselves behind the chairs of the marked guests. Surprised, and with a presentiment of their fate, they sprang from the table. Kinsky and Terzky were killed upon the spot and before they could put themselves upon their guard. Neumann during the confusion in the hall escaped into the court, where, however, he was instantly recognized and cut down. Illo alone had the presence of mind to defend himself. He placed his back against a window, from whence he poured the bitterest reproaches upon Gordon, and challenged him to fight him fairly and honorably. After a gallant resistance, in which he slew two of his assailants, he fell to the ground overpowered by numbers and pierced with ten wounds. The deed was no sooner accomplished than Leslie hastened into the town to prevent a tumult. The sentinels at the castle gate seeing him running and out of breath, and believing he belonged to the rebels, fired their muskets after him, but without effect. The firing, however, aroused the town guard, and all Leslie's presence of mind was requisite to allay the tumult. He hastily detailed to them all the circumstances of Wallenstein's conspiracy, the measures which had been already taken to counteract it, the fate of the four rebels, as well as that which awaited their chief. Finding the troops well-disposed he exacted from them a new oath of fidelity to the Emperor, and to live and die for the good cause. A hundred of Buttler's dragoons were sent from the castle into the town to patrol the streets, to overawe the partisans of the duke, and to prevent tumult. All the gates of Egra were at the same time seized, and every avenue to Wallenstein's residence, which adjoined the market-place, guarded by a numerous and trusty body of troops sufficient to prevent either his escape or his receiving any assistance from without.

But before they proceeded finally to execute the deed a long conference was held among the conspirators in the castle whether they should kill him or content themselves with making him prisoner. Besprinkled as they were with the blood, and deliberating almost over the very corpses of his murdered associates, even these furious men yet shuddered at the horror of taking away so illustrious a life. They saw him before their mind's eye their leader in battle in the days of his good fortune, surrounded by his victorious army, clothed with all the pomp of military greatness; and long-accustomed awe again seized their minds. But this transitory emotion was soon effaced by the thought of the immediate danger. They remembered the hints which Neumann and Illo had thrown out at table, the near approach of a formidable army of Swedes and Saxons, and they clearly saw that the death of the traitor was their only chance of safety. They adhered, therefore, to their first resolution, and Captain Deveroux, an Irishman, who had already been retained for the murderous purpose, received decisive orders to act.

While these three officers were thus deciding upon his fate in the castle of Egra, Wallenstein was occupied in reading the stars with Seni. "The danger is not yet over, said the astrologer, with prophetic spirit, "*It is*," replied the duke, who would give the law even to heaven. "But," he continued with equally prophetic spirit, "that thou friend Seni thyself shall soon be thrown into prison, that also is written in the stars." The astrologer had taken his leave and Wallenstein had retired to bed, when Captain Deveroux appeared before his residence with six halberdiers, and was immediately admitted by the guard, who were accustomed to see him visit the general at all hours. A page who met him upon the stairs and attempted to raise an alarm was run through the body with a pike. In the ante-chamber the assassins met a servant who had just come out of the sleeping-room of his master and had taken with him the key. Putting his finger upon his mouth the terrified domestic made a sign to them to make no noise, as the duke was asleep. "Friend," cried Deveroux, "it is time to awake him;" and with these wards he rushed against the door, which was also bolted from within, and burst it open.

Wallenstein had been roused from his first sleep by the report of a musket which had accidentally gone off, and had sprung to the window to call the guard. At the same moment he heard from the adjoining building the shrieks of the Countesses Terzky and Kinsky, who had just

learned the violent fate of their husbands. Ere he had
time to reflect on these terrible events Deveroux, with
the other murderers, was in his chamber. The duke was
in his shirt, as he had leaped out of bed, and leaning on a
table near the window. "Art thou the villain," cried Deveroux to him, "who intends to deliver up the Emperor's
troops to the enemy, and to tear the crown from the head
of his majesty? Now thou must die!" He paused for
a few moments as if expecting an answer; but scorn and
astonishment kept Wallenstein silent. Throwing his arms
wide open he received in his breast the deadly blow of
the halberts, and, without uttering a groan, fell weltering
in his blood.

The next day an express arrived from the Duke of
Lauenburg announcing his approach. The messenger was
secured, and another in Wallenstein's livery despatched to
the duke to decoy him into Egra. The stratagem succeeded, and Francis Albert fell into the hands of the
enemy. Duke Bernard of Weimar, who was on his march
towards Egra, was nearly sharing the same fate. Fortunately he heard of Wallenstein's death in time to save
himself by a retreat. Ferdinand shed a tear over the fate
of his general, and ordered three thousand masses to be
said for his soul at Vienna; but at the same time he did
not forget to reward his assassins with gold chains, chamberlains' keys, dignities, and estates.

Thus did Wallenstein, at the age of fifty, terminate his
active and extraordinary life. To ambition he owed both
his greatness and his ruin; with all his failings he possessed great and admirable qualities, and had he kept
himself within due bounds he would have lived and died
without an equal. The virtues of the ruler and of the
hero, prudence, justice, firmness, and courage, are strik-
ingly prominent features in his character; but he wanted
the gentler virtues of the man which adorn the hero and
make the ruler beloved. Terror was the talisman with
which he worked; extreme in his punishments as in his
rewards, he knew how to keep alive the zeal of his followers, while no general of ancient or modern times could
boast of being obeyed with equal alacrity. Submission
to his will was more prized by him than bravery; for if

the soldiers work by the latter it is on the former that the general depends. He continually kept up the obedience of his troops by capricious orders, and profusely rewarded the readiness to obey even in trifles, because he looked rather to the act itself than its object. He once issued a decree, with the penalty of death on disobedience that none but red sashes should be worn in the army. A captain of horse no sooner heard the order than pulling off his gold-embroidered sash he trampled it under foot; Wallenstein, on being informed of the circumstance, promoted him on the spot to the rank of colonel. His comprehensive glance was always directed to the whole, and in all his apparent caprice he steadily kept in view some general scope or bearing. The robberies committed by the soldiers in a friendly country had led to the severest orders against marauders; and all who should be caught thieving were threatened with the halter. Wallenstein himself having met a straggler in the open country upon the field commanded him to be seized without trial as a transgressor of the law, and in his usual voice of thunder exclaimed, "Hang the fellow," against which no opposition ever availed. The soldier pleaded and proved his innocence, but the irrevocable sentence had gone forth. "Hang, then, innocent," cried the inexorable Wallenstein, "the guilty will have then more reason to tremble." Preparations were already making to execute the sentence when the soldier, who gave himself up for lost, formed the desperate resolution of not dying without revenge. He fell furiously upon his judge, but was overpowered by numbers and disarmed before he could fulfil his design. "Now let him go," said the duke, "it will excite sufficient terror."

His munificence was supported by an immense income, which was estimated at three millions of florins yearly, without reckoning the enormous sums which he raised under the name of contributions. His liberality and clearness of understanding raised him above the religious prejudices of his age; and the Jesuits never forgave him for having seen through their system and for regarding the Pope as nothing more than a bishop of Rome.

But as no one ever yet came to a fortunate end who quarrelled with the Church, Wallenstein also must augment the number of its victims. Through the intrigues of monks he lost at Ratisbon the command of the army, and at Egra his life; by the same arts, perhaps, he lost, what was of more consequence, his honorable name and good repute with posterity. For in justice it must be admitted that the pens which have traced the history of this extraordinary man are not untinged with partiality, and that the treachery of the duke, and his designs upon the throne of Bohemia, rest not so much upon proven facts as upon probable conjecture. No documents have yet been brought to light which disclose with historical certainty the secret motives of his conduct; and among all his public and well-attested actions there is, perhaps, not one which could not have had an innocent end. Many of his most obnoxious measures proved nothing but the earnest wish he entertained for peace; most of the others are explained and justified by the well-founded distrust he entertained of the Emperor and the excusable wish of maintaining his own importance. It is true that his conduct towards the Elector of Bavaria looks too like an unworthy revenge and the dictates of an implacable spirit; but still none of his actions, perhaps, warrant us in holding his treason to be proved. If necessity and despair at last forced him to deserve the sentence which had been pronounced against him while innocent, still this, if true, will not justify that sentence. Thus Wallenstein fell, not because he was a rebel, but he became a rebel because he fell. Unfortunate in life that he made a victorious party his enemy, and still more unfortunate in death that the same party survived him and wrote his history.

BOOK V.

WALLENSTEIN's death rendered necessary the appointment of a new generalissimo; and the Emperor yielded at last to the advice of the Spaniards to raise his son Ferdinand, King of Hungary, to that dignity. Under him Count Gallas commanded, who performed the functions of commander-in-chief, while the prince brought to this post nothing but his name and dignity. A considerable force was soon assembled under Ferdinand; the Duke of Lorraine brought up a considerable body of auxiliaries in person, and the Cardinal Infante joined him from Italy with ten thousand men. In order to drive the enemy from the Danube the new general undertook the enterprise in which his predecessor had failed, the siege of Ratisbon. In vain did Duke Bernard of Weimar penetrate into the interior of Bavaria with a view to draw the enemy from the town; Ferdinand continued to press the siege with vigor, and the city, after a most obstinate resistance, was obliged to open its gates to him. Donauwerth soon shared the same fate, and Nordlingen in Swabia was now invested. The loss of so many of the imperial cities was severely felt by the Swedish party; as the friendship of these towns had so largely contributed to the success of their arms, indifference to their fate would have been inexcusable. It would have been an indelible disgrace had they deserted their confederates in their need, and abandoned them to the revenge of an implacable conqueror. Moved by these considerations the Swedish army, under the command of Horn and Bernard of Weimar, advanced upon Nordlingen, determined to relieve it even at the expense of a battle.

The undertaking was a dangerous one, for in numbers the enemy was greatly superior to that of the Swedes. There was also a further reason for avoiding a battle at present; the enemy's force was likely soon to divide, the Italian troops being destined for the Netherlands. In the meantime such a position might be taken up as to cover Nordlingen and cut off their supplies. All these grounds were strongly urged by Gustavus Horn in the Swedish council of war; but his remonstrances were disregarded by men who, intoxicated by a long career of success, mistook the suggestions of prudence for the voice of timidity. Overborne by the superior influence of Duke Bernard, Gustavus Horn was compelled to risk a contest whose unfavorable issue a dark foreboding seemed

already to announce. The fate of the battle depended upon the possession of a height which commanded the imperial camp. An attempt to occupy it during the night failed, as the tedious transport of the artillery through woods and hollow ways delayed the arrival of the troops. When the Swedes arrived about midnight they found the heights in possession of the enemy, strongly intrenched. They waited, therefore, for daybreak to carry them by storm. Their impetuous courage surmounted every obstacle; the intrenchments, which were in the form of a crescent, were successfully scaled by each of the two brigades appointed to the service; but as they entered at the same moment from opposite sides they met and threw each other into confusion. At this unfortunate moment a barrel of powder blew up and created the greatest disorder among the Swedes. The imperial cavalry charged upon their broken ranks and the flight became universal. No persuasion on the part of their general could induce the fugitives to renew the assault.

He resolved, therefore, in order to carry this important post, to lead fresh troops to the attack. But in the interim some Spanish regiments had marched in, and every attempt to gain it was repulsed by their heroic intrepidity. One of the duke's own regiments advanced seven times, and was as often driven back. The disadvantage of not occupying this post in time was quickly and sensibly felt. The fire of the enemy's artillery from the heights caused such slaughter in the adjacent wing of the Swedes that Horn, who commanded there, was forced to give orders to retire. Instead of being able to cover the retreat of his colleague, and to check the pursuit of the enemy, Duke Bernard, overpowered by numbers, was himself driven into the plain, where his routed cavalry spread confusion among Horn's brigade and rendered the defeat complete. Almost the entire infantry were killed or taken prisoners. More than twelve thousand men remained dead upon the field of battle; eighty field-pieces, about four thousand wagons, and three hundred standards and colors fell into the hands of the Imperialists. Horn himself, with three other generals, were taken prisoners. Duke Bernard with difficulty saved a feeble remnant of his army, which joined him at Frankfort.

The defeat at Nordlingen cost the Swedish Chancellor the second sleepless night* he had passed in Germany. The consequences of this disaster were terrible. The Swedes had lost by it at once their superiority in the field, and with it the confidence of their confederates, which they had gained solely by their previous military success. A dangerous division threatened the Protestant Confederation with ruin. Consternation and terror seized upon the whole party, while the Papists arose with exulting triumph from the deep humiliation into which they had sunk. Swabia and the adjacent circles first felt the consequences of the defeat of Nordlingen; and Wirtemberg in particular was overrun by the conquering army. All the members of the League of Heilbronn trembled at the prospect of the Emperor's revenge; those who could fled to Strasburg, while the helpless free cities awaited their fate with alarm. A little more of moderation towards the conquered would have quickly reduced all the weaker states under the Emperor's authority; but the severity which was practised, even against those who voluntarily surrendered, drove the rest to despair, and roused them to a vigorous resistance.

In this perplexity all looked to Oxenstiern for counsel and assistance; Oxenstiern applied for both to the German States. Troops were wanted, money likewise to raise new levies and to pay to the old the arrears which the men were clamorously demanding. Oxenstiern addressed himself to the Elector of Saxony; but he shamefully abandoned the Swedish cause to negotiate for a separate peace with the Emperor at Pirna. He solicited aid from the Lower Saxon States; but they, long wearied of the Swedish pretensions and demands for money, now thought only of themselves; and George, Duke of Lunenburg, in place of flying to the assistance of Upper Germany, laid siege to Minden, with the intention of keeping possession of it for himself. Abandoned by his German allies, the chancellor exerted himself to obtain the

* The first was occasioned by the death of Gustavus Adolphus.

assistance of foreign powers. England, Holland, and Venice were applied to for troops and money; and, driven to the last extremity, the chancellor reluctantly resolved to take the disagreeable step which he had so long avoided, and to throw himself under the protection of France.

The moment had at last arrived which Richelieu had long waited for with impatience. Nothing, he was aware, but the impossibility of saving themselves by any other means could induce the Protestant States in Germany to support the pretensions of France upon Alsace. This extreme necessity had now arrived; the assistance of that power was indispensable, and she was resolved to be well paid for the active part which she was about to take in the German war. Full of lustre and dignity it now came upon the political stage. Oxenstiern, who felt little reluctance in bestowing the rights and possessions of the empire, had already ceded the fortress of Philipsburg, and the other long-coveted places. The Protestants of Upper Germany now, in their own names, sent a special embassy to Richelieu, requesting him to take Alsace, the fortress of Breyssach, which was still to be recovered from the enemy, and all the places upon the Upper Rhine, which were the keys of Germany, under the protection of France. What was implied by French protection had been seen in the conduct of France towards the Bishoprics of Metz, Toul, and Verdun, which it had held for centuries against the rightful owners. Treves was already in the possession of French garrisons; Lorraine was in a manner conquered, as it might at any time be overrun by an army, and could not alone and with its own strength withstand its formidable neighbor. France now entertained the hope of adding Alsace to its large and numerous possessions, and, — since a treaty was soon to be concluded with the Dutch for the partition of the Spanish Netherlands — the prospect of making the Rhine its natural boundary towards Germany. Thus shamefully were the rights of Germany sacrificed by the German States to this treacherous and grasping power, which, under the mask of a disinterested friendship, aimed only at its own aggrandizement; and while it boldly claimed the honorable title of a protectress, was solely occupied with promoting its own schemes and advancing its own interests amid the general confusion.

In return for these important cessions France engaged to effect a diversion in favor of the Swedes by commencing hostilities against the Spaniards; and if this should lead to an open breach with the Emperor, to maintain an army upon the German side of the Rhine, which was to act in conjunction with the Swedes and Germans against Austria. For a war with Spain the Spaniards themselves soon afforded the desired pretext. Making an inroad from the Netherlands upon the city of Treves, they cut in pieces the French garrison; and, in open violation of the law of nations, made prisoner the Elector, who had placed himself under the protection of France, and carried him into Flanders. When the Cardinal Infante, as Viceroy of the Spanish Netherlands, refused satisfaction for these injuries, and delayed to restore the prince to liberty, Richelieu, after the old custom, formally proclaimed war at Brussels by a herald, and the war was at once opened by three different armies in Milan, in the Valteline, and in Flanders. The French minister was less anxious to commence hostilities with the Emperor, which promised fewer advantages and threatened greater difficulties. A fourth army, however, was detached across the Rhine into Germany, under the command of Cardinal Lavalette, which was to act in conjunction with Duke Bernard against the Emperor without a previous declaration of war.

A heavier blow for the Swedes than even the defeat of Nordlingen was the reconciliation of the Elector of Saxony with the Emperor. After many fruitless attempts, both to bring about and to prevent it, it was at last effected in 1634, at Pirna, and the following year reduced into a formal treaty of peace at Prague. The Elector of Saxony had always viewed with jealousy the pretensions of the Swedes in Germany; and his aversion to this foreign power, which now gave laws within the Empire, had grown with every fresh requisition that Oxenstiern was obliged to make upon the German States. This ill-feeling was kept alive by the Spanish court, who labored earnestly to effect a peace between Saxony and the Emperor. Wearied with the calamities of a long and destructive contest which had selected Saxony above all others for its theatre; grieved by the miseries which both friend and foe inflicted upon his subjects, and seduced by the tempting propositions of the House of Austria, the Elector at last abandoned the common cause; and caring little for the fate of his confederates, or the liberties of Germany, thought only of securing his own advantages, even at the expense of the whole body.

In fact the misery of Germany had risen to such a height that all clamorously vociferated for peace; and even the most disadvantageous pacification would have been hailed as a blessing from heaven. The plains which formerly had been thronged with a happy and industrious population, where nature had lavished her choicest gifts, and plenty and prosperity had reigned, were now a wild and desolate wilderness. The fields, abandoned by the industrious husbandman, lay waste and uncultivated; and no sooner had the young crops given the promise of a smiling harvest than a single march destroyed the labors of a year and blasted the last hope of an afflicted peasantry. Burnt castles, wasted fields, villages in ashes, were to be seen extending far and wide on all sides, while the ruined peasantry had no resource left but to swell the horde of incendiaries, and fearfully to retaliate upon their fellows, who had hitherto been spared the miseries which they themselves had suffered. The only safeguard against oppression was to become an oppressor. The towns groaned under the licentiousness of undisciplined and plundering garrisons, who seized and wasted the property of the citizens, and under the license of their position committed the most remorseless devastation and cruelty. If the march of an army converted whole provinces into deserts, if others were impoverished by winter quarters or exhausted by contributions, these still were but passing evils, and the industry of a year might efface the miseries of a few months. But there was no relief for those who had a garrison within their walls or in the neighborhood; even the change of fortune could not improve their unfortunate fate, since the victor trod in the steps of the vanquished, and friends were not more merciful than enemies. The neglected farms, the destruction of the crops, and the numerous armies which overran the exhausted country, were inevitably followed by scarcity and the high price of provisions, which in the later years was still further increased by a general failure in the crops. The crowding together of men in camps and quarters — want upon one side and excesses on the other, occasioned contagious distempers, which were more fatal than even the sword. In this long and general confusion all the bonds of social life were broken up; — respect for the rights of their fellow-men, the fear of the laws, purity of morals, honor, and religion were laid aside where might ruled supreme with iron sceptre. Under the shelter of anarchy and impunity every vice flourished, and men became as wild as the country. No station was too dignified for outrage, no property too holy for rapine and avarice. In a word, the soldier reigned supreme; and that most brutal of despots often made his own officer feel his power. The leader of an army was a far more important person within any country where he appeared than its lawful governor, who was frequently obliged to fly before him into his own castles for safety. Germany swarmed with these petty tyrants, and the country suffered equally from its enemies and its protectors. These wounds rankled the deeper when the unhappy victims recollected that Germany was sacrificed to the ambition of foreign powers, who for their own ends prolonged the miseries of war. Germany bled under the scourge to extend the conquests and influence of Sweden; and the torch of discord was kept alive within the Empire that the services of Richelieu might be rendered indispensable in France.

But in truth it was not merely interested voices which opposed a peace; and if both Sweden and the German States were anxious from corrupt motives to prolong the conflict they were seconded in their views by sound policy. After the defeat of Nordlingen an equitable peace was not to be expected from the Emperor; and this being the case, was it not too great a sacrifice, after seventeen years of war with all its miseries, to abandon the contest, not only without advantage, but even with loss? What would avail so much bloodshed if all was to remain as it had been; if their rights and pretensions were neither larger nor safer; if all that had been won with so much difficulty was to be surrendered for a peace at any cost? Would it not be better to endure for two or three years more the burdens they had borne so long, and to reap at last some recompense for twenty years of suffering? Neither was it doubtful that peace might at last be obtained on favorable terms, if only the Swedes and the German Protestants should continue united in the cabinet and in the field, and pursued their common interests with a reciprocal sympathy and zeal. Their divisions alone had rendered the enemy formidable, and protracted the acquisition of a lasting and general peace. And this great evil the Elector of Saxony had brought upon the Protestant cause by concluding a separate treaty with Austria.

He, indeed, had commenced his negotiations with the Emperor even before the battle of Nordlingen; and the unfortunate issue of that battle only accelerated their conclusion. By it all his confidence in the Swedes was lost; and it was even doubted whether they would ever recover from the blow. The jealousies among their generals, the insubordination of the army, and the exhaustion of the Swedish kingdom, shut out any reasonable prospect of effective assistance on their part. The Elector hastened, therefore, to profit by the Emperor's magnanimity, who, even after the battle of Nordlingen, did not recall the conditions previously offered. While Oxenstiern, who had assembled the estates in Frankfort, made further demands upon them and him, the Emperor, on the contrary, made concessions; and therefore it required no long consideration to decide between them.

In the meantime, however, he was anxious to escape the charge of sacrificing the common cause and attending only to his own interests. All the German States, and even the Swedes, were publicly invited to become parties to this peace, although Saxony and the Emperor were the only powers who deliberated upon it, and who assumed the right to give law to Germany. By this self-appointed tribunal the grievances of the Protestants were discussed, their rights and privileges decided, and even the fate of religions determined without the presence of those who were most deeply interested in it. Between them a general peace was resolved on, and it was to be enforced by an imperial army of execution as a formal decree of the Empire. Whoever opposed it was to be treated as a public enemy; and thus, contrary to their rights, the states were to be compelled to acknowledge a law in the passing of which they had no share. Thus, even in form, the pacification at Prague was an arbitrary measure; nor was it less so in its contents. The Edict of Restitution had been the chief cause of dispute between the Elector and the Emperor; and therefore it was first considered in their deliberations. Without formally annulling it, it was determined by the treaty of Prague that all the ecclesiastical domains holding immediately of the Empire, and, among the mediate ones, those which had been seized by the Protestants subsequently to the treaty at Passau, should for forty years remain in the same position as they had been in before the Edict of Restitution, but without any formal decision of the Diet to that effect. Before the expiration of this term a commission, composed of equal numbers of both religions, should proceed to settle the matter peaceably and according to law; and if this commission should be unable to come to a decision each party should remain in possession of the rights which it had exercised before the Edict of Restitution. This arrangement, therefore, far from removing the grounds of dissension, only suspended the dispute for a time; and this article of the treaty of Prague only covered the embers of a future war.

The Archbishopric of Magdeburg remained in possession of Prince Augustus of Saxony, and Halberstadt in that of the Archduke Leopold William. Four estates were taken from the territory of Magdeburg and given to Saxony, for which the Administrator of Magdeburg, Christian William of Brandenburg, was otherwise to be indemnified. The Dukes of Mecklenburg, upon acceding to this treaty, were to be acknowledged as rightful possessors of their territories, in which the magnanimity of

Gustavus Adolphus had long ago reinstated them. Donauwerth recovered its liberties. The important claims of the heirs of the Palatine, however important it might be for the Protestant cause not to lose this electorate vote in the Diet, were passed over in consequence of the animosity subsisting between the Lutherans and the Calvinists. All the conquests which, in the course of the war, had been made by the German States, or by the League and the Emperor, were to be mutually restored; all which had been appropriated by the foreign powers of France and Sweden was to be forcibly wrested from them by the united powers. The troops of the contracting parties were to be formed into one imperial army, which, supported and paid by the Empire, was, by force of arms, to carry into execution the covenants of the treaty.

As the peace of Prague was intended to serve as a general law of the Empire, those points which did not immediately affect the latter formed the subject of a separate treaty. By it Lusatia was ceded to the Elector of Saxony as a fief of Bohemia, and special articles guaranteed the freedom of religion of this country and of Silesia.

All the Protestant states were invited to accede to the treaty of Prague, and on that condition were to benefit by the amnesty. The Princes of Wurtemberg and Baden, whose territories the Emperor was already in possession of, and which he was not disposed to restore unconditionally; and such vassals of Austria as had borne arms against their sovereign; and those states which, under the direction of Oxenstiern, composed the council of the Upper German Circle, were excluded from the treaty,— not so much with the view of continuing the war against them as of compelling them to purchase peace at a dearer rate. Their territories were to be retained in pledge till everything should be restored to its former footing. Such was the treaty of Prague. Equal justice, however, towards all might perhaps have restored confidence between the head of the Empire and its members — between the Protestants and the Roman Catholics — between the Reformed and the Lutheran party; and the Swedes, abandoned by all their allies, would in all probability have been driven from Germany with disgrace. But this inequality strengthened in those who were more severely treated the spirit of mistrust and opposition, and made it an easier task for the Swedes to keep alive the flames of war and to maintain a party in Germany.

The peace of Prague, as might have been expected, was received with very various feelings throughout Germany. The attempt to conciliate both parties had rendered it obnoxious to both. The Protestants complained of the restraints imposed upon them; the Roman Catholics thought that these hated sectaries had been favored at the expense of the true church. In the opinion of the latter the church had been deprived of its inalienable rights by the concession to the Protestants of forty years' undisturbed possession of the ecclesiastical benefices; while the former murmured that the interests of the Protestant church had been betrayed because toleration had not been granted to their coreligionists in the Austrian dominions. But no one was so bitterly reproached as the Elector of Saxony, who was publicly denounced as a deserter, a traitor to religion and the liberties of the Empire, and a confederate of the Emperor.

In the meantime he consoled himself with the triumph of seeing most of the Protestant states compelled by necessity to embrace this peace. The Elector of Brandenburg, Duke William of Weimar, the Princes of Anhalt, the Dukes of Mecklenburg, the Dukes of Brunswick-Lunenburg, the Hanse towns, and most of the imperial cities acceded to it. The Landgrave William of Hesse long wavered, or affected to do so, in order to gain time and to regulate his measures by the course of events. He had conquered several fertile provinces of Westphalia, and derived from them principally the means of continuing the war: these, by the terms of the treaty, he was bound to restore. Bernard, Duke of Weimar, whose states as yet existed only on paper, as a belligerent power was not affected by the treaty, but as a general was so materially; and in either view he must equally be disposed to reject it. His whole riches consisted in his bravery, his possessions in his sword. War alone gave him greatness and importance, and war alone could realize the projects which his ambition suggested.

But of all who declaimed against the treaty of Prague none were so loud in their clamors as the Swedes, and none had so much reason for their opposition. Invited to Germany by the Germans themselves, the champions of the Protestant church and the freedom of the states which they had defended with so much bloodshed and with the sacred life of their king, they now saw themselves suddenly and shamefully abandoned, disappointed in all their hopes, without reward and without gratitude driven from the empire for which they had toiled and bled, and exposed to the ridicule of the enemy by the very princes who owed everything to them. No satisfaction, no indemnification for the expenses which they had incurred, no equivalent for the conquests which they were to leave behind them, was provided by the treaty of Prague. They were to be dismissed poorer than they came, or if they resisted to be expelled by the very powers who had invited them. The Elector of Saxony at last spoke of a pecuniary indemnification, and mentioned the small sum of two million five hundred thousand florins; but the Swedes had already expended considerably more, and this disgraceful equivalent in money was both contrary to their true interests and injurious to their pride. "The Electors of Bavaria and Saxony," replied Oxenstiern, "have been paid for their services, which, as vassals, they were bound to render the Emperor, with the possession of important provinces; and shall we who have sacrificed our king for Germany be dismissed with the miserable sum of two million five hundred thousand florins?" The disappointment of their expectations was the more severe because the Swedes had calculated upon being recompensed with the Duchy of Pomerania, the present possessor of which was old and without heirs. But the succession of this territory was confirmed by the treaty of Prague to the Elector of Brandenburg; and all the neighboring powers declared against allowing the Swedes to obtain a footing within the empire.

Never in the whole course of the war had the prospects

of the Swedes looked more gloomy than in the year 1635, immediately after the conclusion of the treaty of Prague. Many of their allies, particularly among the free cities, abandoned them to benefit by the peace; others were compelled to accede to it by the victorious arms of the Emperor. Augsburg, subdued by famine, surrendered under the severest conditions; Wurtzburg and Coburg were lost to the Austrians. The League of Heilbronn was formally dissolved. Nearly the whole of Upper Germany, the chief seat of the Swedish power, was reduced under the Emperor. Saxony on the strength of the treaty of Prague demanded the evacuation of Thuringia, Halberstadt, and Magdeburg. Philipsburg, the military depôt of France, was surprised by the Austrians with all the stores it contained; and this severe loss checked the activity of France. To complete the embarrassments of Sweden the truce with Poland was drawing to a close. To support a war at the same time with Poland and in Germany was far beyond the power of Sweden; and all that remained was to choose between them. Pride and ambition declared in favor of continuing the German war at whatever sacrifice on the side of Poland. An army however was necessary to command the respect of Poland and to give weight to Sweden in any negotiations for a truce or a peace.

The mind of Oxenstiern, firm and inexhaustible in expedients, set itself manfully to meet these calamities which all combined to overwhelm Sweden; and his shrewd understanding taught him how to turn even misfortunes to his advantage. The defection of so many German cities of the empire deprived him, it is true, of a great part of his former allies, but at the same time it freed him from the necessity of paying any regard to their interests. The more the number of his enemies increased the more provinces and magazines were opened to his troops. The gross ingratitude of the states and the haughty contempt with which the Emperor behaved (who did not even condescend to treat directly with him about a peace), excited in him the courage of despair and a noble determination to maintain the struggle to the last. The continuance of war, however unfortunate it might prove, could not render the situation of Sweden worse than it now was; and if Germany was to be evacuated it was at least better and nobler to do so sword in hand, and to yield to force rather than to fear.

In the extremity in which the Swedes were now placed by the desertion of their allies they addressed themselves to France, who met them with the greatest encouragement. The interest of the two crowns were closely united, and France would have injured herself by allowing the Swedish power in Germany to decline. The helpless situation of the Swedes was rather an additional motive with France to cement more closely their alliance, and to take a more active part in the German war. Since the alliance with Sweden at Beerwald, in 1632, France had maintained the war against the Emperor by the arms of Gustavus Adolphus, without any open or formal breach, by furnishing subsidies and increasing the number of his enemies. But alarmed at the unexpected rapidity and success of the Swedish arms, France, in anxiety to restore the balance of power which was disturbed by the preponderance of the Swedes, seemed for a time to have lost sight of her original designs. She endeavored to protect the Roman Catholic princes of the empire against the Swedish conqueror by the treaties of neutrality, and when this plan failed she even meditated herself to declare war against him. But no sooner had the death of Gustavus Adolphus, and the desperate situation of the Swedish affairs, dispelled this apprehension, than she returned with fresh zeal to her first design, and readily afforded in this misfortune the aid which in the hour of success she had refused. Freed from the checks which the ambition and vigilance of Gustavus Adolphus placed upon her plans of aggrandizement, France availed herself of the favorable opportunity afforded by the defeat of Nordlingen to obtain the entire direction of the war, and to prescribe laws to those who sued for her powerful protection. The moment seemed to smile upon her boldest plans, and those which had formerly seemed chimerical now appeared to be justified by circumstances. She now turned her whole attention to the war in Germany; and as soon as she had secured her own private ends by a treaty with the Germans she suddenly entered the political arena as an active and a commanding power. While the other belligerent states had been exhausting themselves in a tedious contest, France had been reserving her strength and maintained the contest by money alone; but now, when the state of things called for more active measures, she seized the sword and astonished Europe by the boldness and magnitude of her undertakings. At the same moment she fitted out two fleets and sent six different armies into the field, while she subsidized a foreign crown and several of the German princes. Animated by this powerful cooperation, the Swedes and Germans awoke from the consternation, and hoped, sword in hand, to obtain a more honorable peace than that of Prague. Abandoned by their confederates, who had been reconciled to the Emperor, they formed a still closer alliance with France, which increased her support with their growing necessities, at the same time taking a more active although secret share in the German war, until at last she threw off the mask altogether, and in her own name made an unequivocal declaration of war against the Emperor.

To leave Sweden at full liberty to act against Austria, France commenced her operations by liberating it from all fear of a Polish war. By means of the Count d'Avaux, its minister, an agreement was concluded between the two powers at Stummsdorf in Prussia, by which the truce was prolonged for twenty-six years, though not without a great sacrifice on the part of the Swedes, who ceded by a single stroke of the pen almost the whole of Polish Prussia, the dear-bought conquest of Gustavus Adolphus. The treaty of Beerwald was, with certain modifications, which circumstances rendered necessary, renewed at different times at Compiegne, and afterwards at Wismar and Hamburg. France had already come to a rupture with Spain in May, 1635, and the vigorous attack which it made upon that power deprived the Emperor of his most valuable auxiliaries from the Netherlands. By supporting the Landgrave William of Cassel and Duke Bernard of Weimar the Swedes were enabled to act with more vigor upon the Elbe and the Danube, and a diversion upon the Rhine compelled the Emperor to divide his force.

At length the Elector, having formed a junction with the Imperial General Hatzfeld, advanced against Magdeburg, which Banner in vain hastened to relieve. The united army of the Imperialists and the Saxons now spread itself over Brandenburg, wrested several places from the Swedes, and almost drove them to the Baltic. But, contrary to all expectation, Banner, who had been given up as lost, attacked the allies on the 24th of September, 1636, at Wittstock, where a bloody battle took place. The onset was terrific, and the whole force of the enemy was directed against the right wing of the Swedes, which was led by Banner in person. The contest was long maintained with equal animosity and obstinacy on both sides. There was not a squadron among the Swedes which did not return ten times to the charge, to be as often repulsed, when at last Banner was obliged to retire before the superior numbers of the enemy. His left wing sustained the combat until night, and the second line of the Swedes, which had not as yet been engaged, was prepared to renew it the next morning. But the Elector did not wait for a second attack. His army was exhausted by the efforts of the preceding day; and as the drivers had fled with the horses his artillery was unserviceable. He accordingly retreated in the night with Count Hatzfeld and relinquished the ground to the Swedes. About five thousand of the allies fell upon the field, exclusive of those who were killed in the pursuit, or who fell into the hands of the exasperated peasantry. One hundred and fifty standards and colors, twenty-three pieces of cannon, the whole baggage and silver plate of the Elector were captured, and more than two thousand men taken prisoners. This brilliant victory, achieved over an enemy far superior in numbers, and in a very advantageous position, restored the Swedes at once to their former reputation; their enemies were discouraged and their friends inspired with new hopes. Banner instantly followed up this decisive success, and, hastily crossing the Elbe, drove the Imperialists before him through Thuringia and Hesse into Westphalia. He then returned and took up his winter quarters in Saxony.

But, without the material aid furnished by the diversion upon the Rhine, and the activity there of Duke Bernard and the French, these important successes would have been unattainable. Duke Bernard, after the defeat of Nordlingen, reorganized his broken army at Wetterau, but, abandoned by the confederates of the League of Heilbronn, which had been dissolved by the peace of Prague, and receiving but little support from the Swedes, he found himself unable to maintain an army or to perform any enterprise of importance. The defeat at Nordlingen had terminated all his hopes on the Duchy of Franconia, while the weakness of the Swedes destroyed the chance of retrieving his fortunes through their assistance. Tired, too, of the constraint imposed upon him by the imperious chancellor, he turned his attention to France, who could easily supply him with money, the only aid which he required; and France readily acceded to his proposals. Richelieu desired nothing so much as to diminish the influence of the Swedes in the German war, and to obtain the direction of it for himself. To secure this end nothing appeared more effectual than to detach from the Swedes their bravest general, to win him to the interests of France, and to secure for the execution of its projects the services of his arm. From a prince like Bernard, who could not maintain himself without foreign support, France had nothing to fear, since no success, however brilliant, could render him independent of that crown. Bernard himself came into France, and in October, 1635, concluded a treaty at St. Germaine en Laye, not as a Swedish general, but in his own name, by which it was stipulated that he should receive for himself a yearly pension of one million five hundred thousand livres, and four millions for the support of his army, which he was to command under orders of the French king. To inflame his zeal, and to accelerate the conquest of Alsace, France did not hesitate, by a secret article, to promise him that province for his services; a promise which Richelieu had little intention of performing, and which the duke also estimated at its real worth. But Bernard confided in his good fortune and in his arms, and met artifice with dissimulation. If he could once succeed in wresting Alsace from the enemy he did not despair of being able, in case of need, to maintain it also against a friend. He now raised an army at the expense of France, which he commanded nominally under the orders of that power, but in reality without any limitation whatever, and without having wholly abandoned his engagements with Sweden. He began his operations upon the Rhine, where another French army, under Cardinal Lavalette, had already, in 1635, commenced hostilities against the Emperor.

Against this force the main body of the Imperialists, after the great victory of Nordlingen and the reduction of Swabia and Franconia, had advanced under the command of Gallas, had driven them as far as Metz, cleared the Rhine, and took from the Swedes the towns of Mentz and Frankenthal, of which they were in possession. But frustrated by the vigorous resistance of the French in his main object, of taking up his winter quarters in France, he led back his exhausted troops into Alsace and Swabia. At the opening of the next campaign he passed the Rhine at Breysach and prepared to carry the war into the interior of France. He actually entered Burgundy, while the Spaniards from the Netherlands made progress in Picardy; and John De Werth, a formidable general of the League and a celebrated partisan, pushed his march into Champagne and spread consternation even to the gates of Paris. But an insignificant fortress in Franche Comté completely checked the Imperialists, and they were obliged a second time to abandon their enterprise.

The activity of Duke Bernard had hitherto been impeded by his dependence on a French general more suited to the priestly robe than to the baton of command; and although in conjunction with him he conquered Alsace Saverne he found himself unable in the years 1636 and 1637 to maintain his position upon the Rhine. The ill-success of the French arms in the Netherlands had checked the activity of operations in Alsace and Breisgau, but in 1638 the war in that quarter took a more brilliant turn. Relieved from his former restraint, and with unlimited command of his troops, Duke Bernard in the beginning of February left his winter quarters in the

Bishopric of Basle and unexpectedly appeared upon the Rhine, where at this rude season of the year an attack was little anticipated. The forest towns of Laufenburg, Waldshut, and Seckingen were surprised and Rhinefeldt besieged. The Duke of Savelli, the imperial general who commanded in that quarter, hastened by forced marches to the relief of this important place, succeeded in raising the siege, and compelled the Duke of Weimar, with great loss, to retire. But, contrary to all human expectation, he appeared on the third day after (21st February, 1638) before the Imperialists in order of battle, and defeated them in a bloody engagement, in which the four imperial generals, Savelli, John De Werth, Enkeford, and Sperreuter, with two thousand men, were taken prisoners. Two of these, De Werth and Enkeford, were afterwards sent by Richelieu's orders into France in order to flatter the vanity of the French by the sight of such distinguished prisoners, and by the pomp of military trophies to withdraw the attention of the populace from the public distress. The captured standards and colors were, with the same view, carried in solemn procession to the church of Notre Dame, thrice exhibited before the altar, and committed to sacred custody.

The war was now prosecuted with increasing activity. By the treaty of Prague the Emperor had lessened the number of his adversaries within the Empire; though at the same time the zeal and activity of his foreign enemies had been augmented by it. In Germany his influence was almost unlimited, for, with the exception of a few states, he had rendered himself absolute master of the German body and its resources, and was again enabled to act in the character of emperor and sovereign. The first fruit of his power was the elevation of his son, Ferdinand III., to the dignity of King of the Romans, to which he was elected by a decided majority of votes notwithstanding the opposition of Treves and of the heirs of the Elector Palatine. But, on the other hand, he had exasperated the Swedes to desperation, had armed the power of France against him, and drawn its troops into the heart of the kingdom. France and Sweden, with their German allies, formed from this moment one firm and compactly-united power; the Emperor, with the German states which adhered to him, were equally firm and united. The Swedes, who no longer fought for Germany but for their own lives, showed no more indulgence; relieved from the necessity of consulting their German allies, or accounting to them for the plans which they adopted, they acted with more precipitation, rapidity, and boldness. Battles, though less decisive, became more obstinate and bloody; greater achievements, both in bravery and military skill, were performed; but they were but insulated efforts; and being neither dictated by any consistent plan nor improved by any commanding spirit, had comparatively little influence upon the course of the war.

Saxony had bound herself by the treaty of Prague to expel the Swedes from Germany. From this moment the banners of the Saxons and Imperialists were united; the former confederates were converted into implacable enemies. The Archbishopric of Magdeburg, which by the treaty was ceded to the Prince of Saxony, was still held by the Swedes, and every attempt to acquire it by negotiations had proved ineffectual. Hostilities commenced by the Elector of Saxony recalling all his subjects from the army of Banner, which was encamped upon the Elbe. The officers, long irritated by the accumulation of their arrears, obeyed the summons and evacuated one quarter after another. As the Saxons at the same time made a movement towards Mecklenburg to take Dömitz, and to drive the Swedes from Pomerania and the Baltic, Banner suddenly marched thither, relieved Dömitz and totally defeated the Saxon General Baudissin, with seven thousand men, of whom one thousand were slain, and about the same number taken prisoners. Reinforced by the troops and artillery which had hitherto been employed in Polish Prussia, but which the treaty of Stummsdorf rendered unnecessary, this brave and impetuous general made the following year (1636) a sudden inroad into the Electorate of Saxony, where he gratified his inveterate hatred of the Saxons by the most destructive ravages. Irritated by the memory of old grievances which, during their common campaigns, he and the Swedes had suffered from the haughtiness of the Saxons, and now exasperated to the utmost by the late defection of the Elector, they wreaked upon the unfortunate inhabitants all their rancor. Against Austria and Bavaria the Swedish soldier had fought from a sense, as it were, of duty; but against the Saxons they contended with all the energy of private animosity and personal revenge, detesting them as deserters and traitors; for the hatred of former friends is of all the most fierce and irreconcilable. The powerful diversion made by the Duke of Weimar and the Landgrave of Hesse upon the Rhine and in Westphalia prevented the Emperor from affording the necessary assistance to Saxony, and left the whole Electorate exposed to the destructive ravages of Banner's army.

The taking of Rhinefeldt, Röteln, and Fribourg was the immediate consequence of the duke's victory. His army now increased by considerable recruits, and his projects expanded in proportion as fortune favored him. The fortress of Breysach upon the Rhine was looked upon as holding the command of that river and as the key of Alsace. No place in this quarter was of more importance to the Emperor, and upon none had more care been bestowed. To protect Breysach was the principal destination of the Italian army under the Duke of Feria; the strength of its works and its natural defences bade defiance to assault, while the imperial generals who commanded in that quarter had orders to retain it at any cost. But the duke, trusting to his good fortune, resolved to attempt the siege. Its strength rendered it impregnable; it could, therefore, only be starved into a surrender; and this was facilitated by the carelessness of the commandant, who, expecting no attack, had been selling off his stores. As under these circumstances the town could not long hold out it must be immediately relieved or victualled. Accordingly the imperial General Goetz rapidly advanced at the head of twelve thousand men, accompanied by three thousand wagons loaded with provisions, which he intended to throw into the place. But he was attacked with such vigor by Duke Bernard at Witteweyer that he lost his whole force, except three thousand men, together with the entire transport. A similar fate at Ochsenfeld, near Thann, overtook the

Duke of Lorraine, who, with five or six thousand men, advanced to relieve the fortress. After a third attempt of General Goetz for the relief of Breysach had proved ineffectual the fortress, reduced to the greatest extremity by famine, surrendered, after a blockade of four months, on the 17th December, 1638, to its equally persevering and humane conqueror.

The capture of Breysach opened a boundless field to the ambition of the Duke of Weimar, and the romance of his hopes was fast approaching to reality. Far from intending to surrender his conquests in France he destined Breysach for himself, and revealed this intention by exacting allegiance from the vanquished in his own name, and not in that of any other power. Intoxicated by his past success, and excited by the boldest hopes, he believed that he should be able to maintain his conquests even against France herself. At a time when everything depended upon bravery, when even personal strength was of importance, when troops and generals were of more importance than territories, it was natural for a hero like Bernard to place confidence in his own powers, and, at the head of an excellent army, who under his command had proved invincible, to believe himself capable of accomplishing the boldest and largest designs. In order to secure himself one friend among the crowd of enemies whom he was about to provoke, he turned his eyes upon the Landgravine Amelia of Hesse, the widow of the lately desceased Landgrave William, a princess whose talents were equal to her courage, and who, along with her hand, would bestow valuable conquests, an extensive principality, and a well-disciplined army. By the union of the conquests of Hesse with his own upon the Rhine, and the junction of their forces, a power of some importance, and perhaps a third party, might be formed in Germany, which might decide the fate of the war. But a premature death put a period to these extensive schemes.

"Courage, Father Joseph, Breysach is ours!" whispered Richelieu in the ear of the Capuchin who had long held himself in readiness to be despatched into that quarter, so delighted was he with this joyful intelligence.

Already in imagination he held Alsace, Breisgau, and all the frontiers in Austria in that quarter without regard to his promise to Duke Bernard. But the firm determination which the latter had unequivocally shown to keep Breysach for himself greatly embarrassed the cardinal, and no efforts were spared to retain the victorious Bernard in the interests of France. He was invited to court to witness the honors by which his triumph was to be commemorated; but he perceived and shunned the seductive snare. The cardinal even went so far as to offer him the hand of his niece in marriage; but the proud German prince declined the offer, and refused to sully the blood of Saxony by a misalliance. He was now considered as a dangerous enemy and treated as such. His subsidies were withdrawn; and the governor of Breysach and his principal officers were bribed, at least upon the event of the duke's death, to take possession of his conquests and to secure his troops. These intrigues were no secret to the duke, and the precautions he took in the conquered places clearly bespoke the distrust of France. But this misunderstanding with the French court had the most prejudicial influence upon his future operations. The preparations he was obliged to make in order to secure his conquests against an attack on the side of France compelled him to divide his military strength, while the stoppage of his subsidies delayed his appearance in the field. It had been his intention to cross the Rhine, to support the Swedes, and to act against the Emperor and Bavaria on the banks of the Danube. He had already communicated his plan of operations to Banner, who was about to carry the war into the Austrian territories, and had promised to relieve him so, when a sudden death cut short his heroic career, in the thirty sixth year of his age, at Neuburg upon the Rhine (in July, 1639).

He died of a pestilential disorder, which, in the course of two days, had carried off nearly four hundred men in his camp. The black spots which appeared upon his body, his own dying expressions, and the advantages which France was likely to reap from his sudden decease, gave rise to a suspicion that he had been removed by poison — a suspicion sufficiently refuted by the symptoms of his disorder. In him the allies lost their greatest general after Gustavus Adolphus, France a formidable competitor for Alsace, and the Emperor his most dangerous enemy. Trained to the duties of a soldier and a general in the school of Gustavus Adolphus, he successfully imitated his eminent model, and wanted only a longer life to equal if not to surpass it. With the bravery of the soldier he united the calm and cool penetration of the general, the persevering fortitude of the man with the daring resolution of youth; with the wild ardor of the warrior, the sober dignity of the prince, the moderation of the sage, and the conscientious of the man of honor. Discouraged by no misfortune, he quickly rose again in full vigor from the severest defeats; no obstacles could check his enterprise, no disappointments conquer his indomitable perseverance. His genius, perhaps, soared after unattainable objects; but the prudence of such men is to be measured by a different standard from that of ordinary people. Capable of accomplishing more, he might venture to form more daring plans. Bernard affords, in modern history, a spendid example of those days of chivalry, when personal greatness had its full weight and influence, when individual bravery could conquer provinces, and the heroic exploits of a German knight raised him even to the imperial throne.

The best part of the duke's possessions were his army, which, together with Alsace, he bequeathed to his brother William. But to this army, both France and Sweden thought that they had well-grounded claims; the latter, because it had been raised in the name of that crown and had done homage to it; the former because it had been supported by its subsidies. The Electoral Prince of the Palatinate also negotiated for its services, and attempted, first by his agents, and latterly in his own person, to win it over to his interests, with the view of employing it in the reconquest of his territories. Even the Emperor endeavored to secure it, a circumstance the less surprising, when we reflect that at this time the justice of the cause was comparatively unimportant, and the extent of the recompense the main object to which the soldier looked;

and when bravery, like every other commodity, was disposed of to the highest bidder. But France, richer and more determined, outbade all competitors; it bought over General Erlach, the commander of Breysach, and the other officers, who soon placed that fortress, with the whole army, in their hands.

The young Palatine, Prince Charles Louis, who had already made an unsuccessful campaign against the Emperor, saw his hopes again deceived. Although intending to do France so ill a service as to compete with her for Bernard's army he had the imprudence to travel through that kingdom. The cardinal, who dreaded the justice of the Palatine's cause, was glad to seize any opportunity to frustrate his views. He accordingly caused him to be seized at Moulin, in violation of the law of nations, and did not set him at liberty until he learned that the army of the Duke of Weimar had been secured. France was now in possession of a numerous and well-disciplined army in Germany, and from this moment began to make open war upon the Emperor.

But it was no longer against Ferdinand II. that its hostilities were to be conducted, for that prince had died in February, 1637, in the fifty-ninth year of his age. The war which his ambition had kindled, however, survived him. During a reign of eighteen years he had never once laid aside the sword, nor tasted the blessings of peace as long as his hand swayed the imperial sceptre. Endowed with the qualities of a good sovereign, adorned with many of those virtues which insure the happiness of a people, and by nature gentle and humane, we see him from erroneous ideas of the monarch's duty become at once the instrument and the victim of the evil passions of others, his benevolent intentions frustrated, and the friend of justice converted into the oppressor of mankind, the enemy of peace, and the scourge of his people. Amiable in domestic life, and respectable as a sovereign, but in his policy ill-advised, while he gained the love of his Roman Catholic subjects, he incurred the execration of the Protestants. History exhibits many and greater despots than Ferdinand II., yet he alone has had the unfortunate celebrity of kindling a thirty years' war; but to produce its lamentable consequences his ambition must have been seconded by a kindred spirit of the age, a congenial state of previous circumstances, and existing seeds of discord. At a less turbulent period the spark would have found no fuel, and the peacefulness of the age would have choked the voice of individual ambition; but now the flash fell upon a pile of accumulated combustibles, and Europe was in flames.

His son, Ferdinand III., who a few months before his father's death had been raised to the dignity of King of the Romans, inherited his throne, his principles, and the war which he had caused. But Ferdinand III. had been a closer witness of the sufferings of the people and the devastation of the country, and felt more keenly and ardently the necessity of peace. Less influenced by the Jesuits and the Spaniards, and more moderate towards the religious views of others, he was more likely than his father to listen to the voice of reason. He did so, and ultimately restored to Europe the blessing of peace, but not till after a contest of eleven years waged with sword and pen; not till after he had experienced the impossibility of resistance, and necessity had laid upon him its stern laws.

Fortune favored him at the commencement of his reign, and his arms were victorious against the Swedes. The latter, under the command of the victorious Banner, had after their success at Wittstock taken up their winter quarters in Saxony, and the campaign of 1637 opened with the siege of Leipzig. The vigorous resistance of the garrison and the approach of the Electoral and Imperial armies saved the town, and Banner, to prevent his communication with the Elbe being cut off, was compelled to retreat into Torgau. But the superior number of the Imperialists drove him even from that quarter; and surrounded by the enemy, hemmed in by rivers, and suffering from famine, he had no course open to him but to attempt a highly dangerous retreat into Pomerania, of which the boldness and successful issue border upon romance. The whole army crossed the Oder at a ford near Furstenberg; and, the soldiers, wading up to the neck in water, dragged the artillery across, when the horses refused to draw. Banner had expected to be joined by General Wrangel on the farther side of the Oder in Pomerania; and, in conjunction with him, to be able to make head against the enemy. But Wrangel did not appear, and in his stead he found an imperial army posted at Landsberg with a view to cut off the retreat of the Swedes. Banner now saw that he had fallen into a dangerous snare from which escape appeared impossible. In his rear lay an exhausted country, the Imperialists, and the Oder on his left; the Oder, too, guarded by the Imperial General Bucheim, offered no retreat; in front Landsberg, Custrin, the Warta, and a hostile army; and on the right Poland, in which, notwithstanding the truce, little confidence could be placed. In these circumstances his position seemed hopeless, and the Imperialists were already triumphing in the certainty of his fall. Banner, with just indignation, accused the French as the authors of this misfortune. They had neglected to make, according to their promise, a diversion upon the Rhine, and by their inaction allowed the Emperor to combine his whole force upon the Swedes. "When the day comes," cried the incensed general to the French commissioner, who followed the camp, "that the Swedes and Germans join their arms against France we shall cross the Rhine with less ceremony." But reproaches were now useless; what the emergency demanded was energy and resolution. In the hope of drawing the enemy by stratagem from the Oder, Banner pretended to march towards Poland, and despatched the greater part of his baggage in this direction, with his own wife and those of the other officers. The Imperialists immediately broke up their camp and hurried towards the Polish frontier to block up the route; Bucheim left his station, and the Oder was stripped of its defenders. On a sudden, and under cloud of night, Banner turned towards that river, and crossed it about a mile above Custrin, with his troops, baggage, and artillery, without bridges or vessels, as he had done before at Furstenberg. He reached Pomerania without loss, and prepared to share with Wrangel the defence of that province.

But the Imperialists, under the command of Gallas, entered that duchy at Ribses, and overran it by their superior strength. Usedom and Wolgast were taken by storm, Demmin capitulated, and the Swedes were driven far into Lower Pomerania. It was, too, more important for them at this moment than ever to maintain a footing in that country, for Bogislaus XIV. had died that year, and Sweden must prepare to establish its title to Pomerania. To prevent the Elector of Brandenburg from making good the title to that duchy, which the treaty of Prague had given him, Sweden exerted her utmost energies, and supported its generals to the extent of her ability, both with troops and money. In other quarters of the kingdom the affairs of the Swedes began to wear a more favorable aspect, and to recover from the humiliation into which they had been thrown by the inaction of France and the desertion of their allies. For, after their hasty retreat into Pomerania, they had lost one place after another in Upper Saxony; the Princes of Mecklenburg, closely pressed by the troops of the Emperor, began to lean to the side of Austria, and even George, Duke of Lunenburg, declared against them. Ehrenbreitstein was starved into a surrender by the Bavarian General de Werth, and the Austrians possessed themselves of all the works which had been thrown up on the Rhine. France had been the sufferer in the contest with Spain; and the event had by no means justified the pompous expectations which had accompanied the opening of the campaign. Every place which the Swedes had held in the interior of Germany was lost; and only the principal towns in Pomerania still remained in their hands. But a single campaign raised them from this state of humiliation; and the vigorous diversion, which the victorious Bernard had effected upon the Rhine, gave quite a new turn to affairs.

The misunderstandings between France and Sweden were now at last adjusted, and the old treaty between these powers confirmed at Hamburg, with fresh advantages for Sweden. In Hesse the politic Landgravine Amelia had, with the approbation of the Estates, assumed the government after the death of her husband, and resolutely maintained her rights against the Emperor and the House of Darmstadt. Already zealously attached to the Swedish Protestant party on religious grounds, she only awaited a favorable opportunity openly to declare herself. By artful delays and by prolonging the negotiations with the Emperor she had succeeded in keeping him inactive, till she had concluded a secret compact with France, and the victories of Duke Bernard had given a favorable turn to the affairs of the Protestants. She now at once threw off the mask, and renewed her former alliance with the Swedish crown. The Electoral Prince of the Palatinate was also stimulated by the success of Bernard to try his fortune against the common enemy. Raising troops in Holland with English money, he formed a magazine at Meppen and joined the Swedes in Westphalia. His magazine was, however, quickly lost; his army defeated near Flotha by Count Hatzfeld; but his attempt served to occupy for some time the attention of the enemy, and thereby facilitated the operations of the Swedes in other quarters. Other friends began to appear as fortune declared in their favor; and the circumstance that the states of Lower Saxony embraced a neutrality was of itself no inconsiderable advantage.

Under these advantages, and reinforced by fourteen thousand fresh troops from Sweden and Livonia, Banner opened with the most favorable prospects the campaign of 1638. The Imperialists who were in possession of Upper Pomerania and Mecklenburg either abandoned their positions or deserted in crowds to the Swedes to avoid the horrors of famine, the most formidable enemy in this exhausted country. The whole country betwixt the Elbe and the Oder was so desolated by the past marchings and quarterings of the troops that, in order to support his army on its march into Saxony and Bohemia, Banner was obliged to take a circuitous route from Lower Pomerania into Lower Saxony, and then into the Electorate of Saxony through the territory of Halberstadt. The impatience of the Lower Saxon states to get rid of such troublesome guests procured him so plentiful a supply of provisions that he was provided with bread in Magdeburg itself, where famine had even overcome the natural antipathy of men to human flesh. His approach spread consternation among the Saxons; but his views were directed not against this exhausted country, but against the hereditary dominions of the Emperor. The victories of Bernard encouraged him, while the prosperity of the Austrian provinces excited his hopes of booty. After defeating the Imperial General Salis at Elsterberg, totally routing the Saxon army at Chemnitz, and taking Pirna, he penetrated with irresistible impetuosity into Bohemia, crossed the Elbe, threatened Prague, took Brandeis and Leutmeritz, defeated General Hofkirchen with ten regiments, and spread terror and devastation through that defenceless kingdom. Booty was his sole object, and whatever he could not carry off he destroyed. In order to remove more of the corn the ears were cut from the stalks, and the latter burnt. Above a thousand castles, hamlets, and villages were laid in ashes; sometimes more than a hundred were seen burning in one night. From Bohemia he crossed into Silesia, and it was his intention to carry his ravages even into Moravia and Austria. But to prevent this Count Hatzfeld was summoned from Westphalia, and Piccolomini from the Netherlands, to hasten with all speed to this quarter. The Archduke Leopold, brother to the Emperor, assumed the command in order to repair the errors of his predecessor, Gallas, and to raise the army from the low ebb to which it had fallen.

The result justified the change, and the campaign of 1640 appeared to take a most unfortunate turn for the Swedes. They were successively driven out of all their posts in Bohemia, and, anxious only to secure their plunder, they precipitately crossed the heights of Meissen. But being followed into Saxony by the pursuing enemy, and defeated at Plauen, they were obliged to take refuge in Thuringia. Made masters of the field in a single summer, they were as rapidly dispossessed, but only to acquire it a second time, and to hurry from one extreme to another. The army of Banner, weakened and on the brink of destruction in its camp at Erfurt, suddenly recovered itself. The Duke of Lunenburg abandoned the treaty of Prague, and joined Banner with the very troops which the year before had fought against him.

Hesse Cassel sent reinforcements, and the Duke of Longueville came to his support with the army of the late Duke Bernard. Once more numerically superior to the Imperialists Banner offered them battle near Saalfeld, but their leader, Piccolomini, prudently declined an engagement, having chosen too strong a position to be forced. When the Bavarians at length separated from the Imperialists and marched towards Franconia Banner attempted an attack upon this divided corps, but the attempt was frustrated by the skill of the Bavarian General Von Mercy and the near approach of the main body of the Imperialists. Both armies now moved into the exhausted territory of Hesse, where they formed intrenched camps near each other, till at last famine and the severity of the winter compelled them both to retire. Piccolomini chose the fertile banks of the Weser for his winter quarters, but being outflanked by Banner he was obliged to give way to the Swedes and to impose on the Franconian sees the burden of maintaining his army.

At this period a diet was held in Ratisbon, where the complaints of the states were to be heard, measures taken for securing the repose of the Empire, and the question of peace or war finally settled. The presence of the Emperor, the majority of the Roman Catholic voices in the Electoral College, the great number of bishops, and the withdrawal of several of the Protestant votes, gave the Emperor a complete command of the deliberations of the assembly, and rendered this diet anything but a fair representative of the opinions of the German Empire. The Protestants with reason considered it as a mere combination of Austria and its creatures against their party, and it seemed to them a laudable effort to interrupt its deliberations and to dissolve the Diet itself.

Banner undertook this bold enterprise. His military reputation had suffered by his last retreat from Bohemia, and it stood in need of some great exploit to restore its former lustre. Without communicating his designs to any one, in the depth of the winter of 1641, as soon as the roads and rivers were frozen, he broke up from his quarters in Lunenburg. Accompanied by Marshal Guebriant, who commanded the armies of France and Weimar, he took the route towards the Danube, through Thuringia and Vogtland, and appeared before Ratisbon ere the Diet could be apprised of his approach. The consternation of the assembly was indescribable, and in the first alarm the deputies prepared for flight. The Emperor alone declared that he would not leave the town, and encouraged the rest by his example. Unfortunately for the Swedes a thaw came on, which broke up the ice upon the Danube so that it was no longer passable on foot, while no boats could cross it on account of the quantities of ice which were swept down by the current. In order to perform something and to humble the pride of the Emperor, Banner discourteously fired five hundred cannon-shots into the town, which however did little mischief. Baffled in his designs, he resolved to penetrate farther into Bavaria and the defenceless province of Moravia, where a rich booty and comfortable quarters awaited his troops. Guebriant, however, began to fear that the purpose of the Swedes was to draw the army of Bernard away from the Rhine and to cut off its communication with France till it should be either entirely won over or incapacitated from acting independently. He therefore separated from Banner to return to the Maine, and the latter was exposed to the whole force of the Imperialists, which had been secretly drawn together between Ratisbon and Ingoldstadt, and was on its march against him. It was now time to think of a rapid retreat, which having to be effected in the face of an army superior in cavalry, and betwixt woods and rivers through a country entirely hostile, appeared almost impracticable. He hastily retired towards the Forest, intending to penetrate through Bohemia into Saxony, but he was obliged to sacrifice three regiments at Neuburg. These with a truly Spartan courage defended themselves for four days behind an old wall, and gained time for Banner to escape. He retreated by Egra to Annaberg; Piccolomini took a shorter route in pursuit by Schlakenwald, and Banner succeeded only by a single half hour in clearing the Pass of Prisnitz and saving his whole army from the Imperialists. At Zwickau he was again joined by Guebriant, and both generals directed their march towards Halberstadt after in vain attempting to defend the Saal and to prevent the passage of the Imperialists.

Banner at length terminated his career at Halberstadt, in May, 1641, a victim to vexation and disappointment. He sustained with great renown though with varying success the reputation of the Swedish arms in Germany, and by a train of victories showed himself worthy of his great master in the art of war. He was fertile in expedients, which he planned with secrecy and executed with boldness, cautious in the midst of dangers, greater in adversity than in prosperity, and never more formidable than when upon the brink of destruction. But the virtues of the hero were united with all the failings and vices which a military life creates, or at least fosters. As imperious in private life as he was at the head of his army, rude as his profession, and proud as a conqueror, he oppressed the German princes no less by his haughtiness than their country by his contributions. He consoled himself for the toils of war in voluptuousness and the pleasures of the table, in which he indulged to excess, and was thus brought to an early grave. But though as much addicted to pleasure as Alexander or Mahomet II., he hurried from the arms of luxury into the hardest fatigues, and placed himself in all his vigor at the head of his army at the very moment his soldiers were murmuring at his luxurious excesses. Nearly eighty thousand men fell in the numerous battles which he fought, and about six hundred hostile standards and colors, which he sent to Stockholm, were the trophies of his victories. The want of this great general was soon severely felt by the Swedes, who feared with justice that the loss would not readily be replaced. The spirit of rebellion and insubordination, which had been overawed by the imperious demeanor of this dreaded commander, awoke upon his death. The officers, with an alarming unanimity, demanded payment of their arrears, and none of the four generals who shared the command possessed influence enough to satisfy these demands or to silence the malcontents. All discipline was at an end; increasing want and the imperial citations were daily diminishing the number of the army; the troops of France and Weimar showed little zeal; those of Lunenburg forsook the Swedish colors; the Princes also of the House of Brunswick, after the death of Duke George, had formed a separate treaty with the Emperor, and at last even those of Hesse quitted them to seek better quarters in Westphalia. The enemy profited by these calamitous divisions, and although defeated with loss in two pitched battles, succeeded in making considerable progress in Lower Saxony.

At length appeared the new Swedish generalissimo with fresh troops and money. This was Bernard Torstensohn, a pupil of Gustavus Adolphus, and his most successful imitator, who had been his page during the Polish war. Though a martyr to the gout and confined to a litter, he surpassed all his opponents in activity; and his enterprises had wings while his body was held by the most frightful of fetters. Under him the scene of war was changed and new maxims adopted which necessity dictated and the issue justified. All the countries in which the contest had hitherto raged were exhausted, while the House of Austria, safe in its more distant tertories, felt not the miseries of the war under which the rest of Germany groaned. Torstensohn first furnished them with this bitter experience, glutted his Swedes on the fertile fields of Austria, and carried the torch of war to the very footsteps of the imperial throne.

In Silesia the enemy had gained considerable advantage over the Swedish General Stalhantsch, and driven him as far as Neumark. Torstenohn, who had joined the main body of the Swedes in Lunenburg, summoned him to unite with his force, and in the year 1642 hastily marched into Silesia through Brandenburg, which, under its great Elector, had begun to maintain an armed neutrality. Glogau was carried, sword in hand, without a breach or formal approaches, the Duke Francis Albert of Lauenburg defeated and killed at Schweidnitz, and Schweidnitz itself with almost all the towns on that side of the Oder taken. He now penetrated with irresistible violence into the interior of Moravia, where no enemy of

Austria had hitherto appeared, took Olmutz and threw Vienna itself into consternation.

But in the meantime Piccolomini and the Archduke Leopold had collected a superior force which speedily drove the Swedish conquerors from Moravia, and, after a fruitless attempt upon Brieg, from Silesia. Reinforced by Wrangel, the Swedes again attempted to make head against the enemy, and relieved Grossglogau, but could neither bring the Imperialists to an engagement nor carry into effect their own views upon Bohemia. Overrunning Lusatia they took Zittau in presence of the enemy, and after a short stay in that country directed their march toward the Elbe, which they passed at Torgau. Torstensohn now threatened Leipzig with a siege, and hoped to raise a large supply of provisions and contributions from that prosperous town, which for ten years had been unvisited with the scourge of war.

The Imperialists under Leopold and Piccolomini immediately hastened by Dresden to its relief, and Torstensohn to avoid being inclosed between this army and the town boldly advanced to meet them in order of battle. By a strange coincidence the two armies met upon the very spot which eleven years before Gustavus Adolphus had rendered remarkable by a decisive victory; and the heroism of their predecessors now kindled in the Swedes a noble emulation on this consecrated ground. The Swedish Generals Stahlhantsch and Wellenberg led their divisions with such impetuosity upon the left wing of the Imperialists, before it was completely formed, that the whole cavalry that covered it were dispersed and rendered unserviceable. But the left of the Swedes was threatened with a similar fate when the victorious right advanced to its assistance, took the enemy in flank and rear and divided the Austrian line. The infantry on both sides stood firm as a wall, and when their ammunition was exhausted maintained the combat with the butt ends of their muskets, till at last the Imperialists, completely surrounded, after a contest of three hours, were compelled to abandon the field. The generals on both sides had more than once to rally their flying troops; and the Archduke Leopold with his regiment was the first in the attack and last in fight. But this bloody victory cost the Swedes more than three thousand men and two of their best generals, Schlangen and Lilienhoeck. More than five thousand of the Imperialists were left upon the field, and nearly as many taken prisoners. Their whole artillery, consisting of forty-six field-pieces, the silver plate and portfolio of the archduke, with the whole baggage of the army, fell into the hands of the victors. Torstensohn, too greatly disabled by his victory to pursue the enemy, moved upon Leipzig. The defeated army retreated into Bohemia, where its shattered regiments reassembled. The Archduke Leopold could not recover from the vexation caused by this defeat, and the regiment of cavalry which by its premature flight had occasioned the disaster experienced the effects of his indignation. At Raconitz, in Bohemia, in presence of the whole army, he publicly declared it infamous, deprived it of its horses, arms, and ensigns, ordered its standards to be torn, condemned to death several of the officers, and decimated the privates.

The surrender of Leipzig, three weeks after the battle, was its brilliant result. The city was obliged to clothe the Swedish troops anew, and to purchase an exemption from plunder by a contribution of three hundred thousand rix-dollars, to which all the foreign merchants who had warehouses in the city were to furnish their quota. In the middle of the winter Torstensohn advanced against Freyberg, and for several weeks defied the inclemency of the season, hoping by his perseverance to weary out the obstinacy of the besieged. But he found that he was merely sacrificing the lives of his soldiers; and at last the approach of the imperial general, Piccolomini, compelled him with his weakened army to retire. He considered it, however, as equivalent to a victory to have disturbed the repose of the enemy in their winter quarters, who, by the severity of the weather, sustained a loss of three thousand horses. He now made a movement towards the Oder, as if with the view of reinforcing himself with the garrisons of Pomerania and Silesia; but with the rapidity of lightning he again appeared upon the Bohemian frontier, penetrated through that kingdom and relieved

Olmutz in Moravia, which was hard pressed by the Imperialists. His camp at Dobitschau, two miles from Olmutz, commanded the whole of Moravia, on which he levied heavy contributions, and carried his ravages almost to the gates of Vienna. In vain did the Emperor attempt to arm the Hungarian nobility in defence of this province; they appealed to their privileges and refused to serve beyond the limits of their own country. Thus the time that should have been spent in active resistance was lost in fruitless negotiation, and the entire province was abandoned to the ravages of the Swedes.

While Torstensohn by his marches and his victories astonished friend and foe the armies of the allies had not been inactive in other parts of the empire. The troops of Hesse, under Count Eberstein, and those of Weimar, under Mareschal de Guebriant, had fallen into the Electorate of Cologne, in order to take up their winter quarters there. To get rid of these troublesome guests the Elector called to his assistance the imperial General Hatzfeld and assembled his own troops under General Lamboy. The latter was attacked by the allies in January, 1642, and in a decisive action near Kempen defeated with a loss of about two thousand men killed and about twice as many prisoners. This important victory opened to them the whole Electorate and neighboring territories so that the allies were not only enabled to maintain their winter quarters there, but drew from the country large supplies of men and horses.

Guebriant left the Hessians to defend their conquests on the Lower Rhine against Hatzfeld, and advanced towards Thuringia, as if to second the operations of Torstensohn in Saxony. But instead of joining the Swedes he soon hurried back to the Rhine and the Maine, from which he seemed to think he had removed farther than was expedient. But being anticipated in the Margravate of Baden by the Bavarians under Mercy and John De Werth he was obliged to wander about for several weeks exposed without shelter to the inclemency of the winter and generally encamping upon the snow till he found a miserable refuge in Bavaria. He at last took the field, and in the next summer by keeping the Bavarian army employed in Swabia prevented it from relieving Thionville, which was besieged by Condé. But the superiority of the enemy soon drove him back to Alsace, where he awaited a reinforcement.

The death of Cardinal Richelieu took place in November, 1642, and the subsequent change in the throne and in the ministry, occasioned by the death of Louis XIII., had for some time withdrawn the attention of France from the German war, and was the cause of the inaction of its troops in the field. But Mazarin, the inheritor not only of Richelieu's power, but also of his principles and his projects, followed out with renewed zeal the plans of his predecessor, though the French subject was destined to pay dearly enough for the political greatness of his country. The main strength of its armies, which Richelieu had employed against the Spaniards, was by Mazarin directed against the Emperor; and the anxiety with which he carried on the war in Germany proved the sincerity of his opinion, that the German army was the right arm of his king and a wall of safety around France. Immediately upon the surrender of Thionville he sent a considerable reinforcement to Field-Marshal Guebriant in Alsace; and to encourage the troops to bear the fatigues of the German war, the celebrated victor of Rocroi, the Duke of Enghien, afterwads Prince of Condé, was placed at their head. Guebriant now felt himself strong enough to appear again in Germany with repute. He hastened across the Rhine with the view of procuring better winter quarters in Swabia, and actually made himself master of Rothweil, where a Bavarian magazine fell into his hands. But the place was too dearly purchased for its worth, and was again lost even more speedily than it had been taken. Guebriant received a wound in the arm, which the surgeon's unskilfulness rendered mortal, and the extent of his loss was felt on the very day of his death.

The French army, sensibly weakened by an expedition undertaken at so severe a season of the year, had after the taking of Rowtheil withdrawn into the neighborhood of Duttlingen, where it lay in complete security without expectation of a hostile attack. In the meantime the enemy collected a considerable force with a view to prevent the French from establishing themselves beyond the Rhine and so near to Bavaria, and to protect that quarter from their ravages. The Imperialists under Hatzfeld had formed a junction with the Bavarians under Mercy; and the Duke of Lorraine, who, during the whole course of the war, was generally found everywhere except in his own duchy, joined their united forces. It was resolved to force the quarters of the French in Duttlingen and the neighboring villages by surprise; a favorite mode of proceeding in this war, and which being commonly accompanied by confusion occasioned more bloodshed than a regular battle. On the present occasion there was the more to justify it, as the French soldiers, unaccustomed to such enterprises, conceived themselves protected by the security of the winter against any surprise. John de Werth, a master in this species of warfare, which he had often put in practice against Gustavus Horn, conducted the enterprise and succeeded contrary to all expectation.

The attack was made on a side where it was least looked for, on account of the woods and narrow passes; and a heavy snow-storm which fell upon the same day (the 24th November, 1643), concealed the approach of the vanguard till it halted before Duttlingen. The whole of the artillery without the place, as well as the neighboring Castle of Honberg, were taken without resistance, Duttlingen itself was gradually surrounded by the enemy, and all connection with the other quarters in the adjacent villages silently and suddenly cut off. The French were vanquished without firing a cannon. The cavalry owed their escape to the swiftness of their horses and the few minutes in advance which they had gained upon their pursuers. The infantry were cut to pieces or voluntarily laid down their arms. About two thousand men were killed, and seven thousand, with twenty-five staff-officers and ninety captains, taken prisoners. This was perhaps the only battle in the whole course of the war which produced nearly the same effect upon the party which gained and that which lost; — both these parties were Germans; the French disgraced themselves. The memory of this unfortunate day, which was renewed one hundred years after at Rosbach, was indeed erased by the subsequent heroism of a Turenne and Condé; but the Germans may be pardoned if they indemnified themselves for the miseries which the policy of France had heaped upon them by these severe reflections upon her intrepidity.

Meantime this defeat of the French was calculated to prove highly disastrous to Sweden, as the whole power of the Emperor might now act against them, while the number of their enemies was increased by a formidable accession. Torstensohn had, in September, 1643, suddenly left Moravia and moved into Silesia. The cause of this step was a secret, and the frequent changes which took place in the direction of his march contributed to increase this perplexity. From Silesia after numberless circuits he advanced towards the Elbe, while the Imperialists followed him into Lusatia. Throwing a bridge across the Elbe at Torgau, he gave out that he intended to penetrate through Meissen into the Upper Palatinate in Bavaria; at Barby he also made a movement as if to pass that river, but continued to move down the Elbe as far as Havelburg, where he astonished his troops by informing them that he was leading them against the Danes in Holstein.

The partiality which Christian IV. had displayed against the Swedes in his office of mediator, the jealousy which led him to do all in his power to hinder the progress of their arms, the restraints which he laid upon their navigation of the Sound, and the burdens which he imposed upon their commerce, had long roused the indignation of Sweden; and at last when these grievances increased daily had determined the Regency to measures of retaliation. Dangerous as it seemed to involve the nation in a new war, when even amidst its conquests it was almost exhausted by the old, the desire of revenge, and the deep-rooted hatred which subsisted between Danes and Swedes, prevailed over all other considerations; and even the embarassment in which hostilities with Germany had plunged it only served as an additional motive to try its fortune against Denmark.

Matters were in fact arrived at last to that extremity, that the war was prosecuted merely for the purpose of furnishing food and employment to the troops; that good winter quarters formed the chief subject of contention; and that success in this point was more valued than a decisive victory. But now the provinces of Germany were almost all exhausted and laid waste. They were wholly destitute of provisions, horses, and men, which in Holstein were to be found in profusion. If by this movement Torstensohn should succeed merely in recruiting his army, providing subsistence for his horses and soldiers, and remounting his cavalry, all the danger and difficulty would be well repaid. Besides it was highly important on the eve of negotiations for peace to diminish the injurious influence which Denmark might exercise upon these deliberations to delay the treaty itself, which threatened to be prejudicial to the Swedish interests, by sowing confusion among the parties interested, and with a view to the amount of indemnification to increase the number of her conquests in order to be the more sure of securing those which alone she was anxious to retain. Moreover the present state of Denmark justified even greater hopes, if only the attempts were executed with rapidity and silence. The secret was in fact so well kept in Stockholm that the Danish minister had not the slightest suspicion of it; and neither France nor Holland were let into the scheme. Actual hostilities commenced with the declaration of war; and Torstensohn was in Holstein before even an attack was expected. The Swedish troops meeting with no resistance, quickly overran this duchy and made themselves masters of all its strong places except Rensburg and Gluckstadt. Another army penetrated into Schonen, which made as little opposition; and nothing but the severity of the season prevented the enemy from passing the Lesser Baltic and carrying the war into Funen and Zealand. The Danish fleet was unsuccessful at Femeru; and Christian himself, who was on board, lost his right eye by a splinter. Cut off from all communication with the distant force of the Emperor, his ally, this king was on the point of seeing his whole kindom overrun by the Swedes; and all things threatened the speedy fulfilment of the old prophecy of the famous Tycho Brahe, that in the year 1644 Christian IV. should wander in the greatest misery from his dominions.

But the Emperor could not look on with indifference while Denmark was sacrificed to Sweden, and the latter strengthened by so great an acquisition. Notwithstanding great difficulties lay in the way of so long a march through desolated provinces, he did not hesitate to despatch an army into Holstein under Count Gallas, who, after Piccolomini's retirement, had resumed the supreme command of the troops. Gallas accordingly appeared in the duchy, took Keil, and hoped by forming a junction with the Danes to be able to shut up the Swedish army in Jutland. Meantime the Hessians and the Swedish General Koenigsmark were kept in check by Hatzfeld and the Archbishop of Bremen, the son of Christian IV.; and afterwards the Swedes drawn into Saxony by an attack upon Meissen. But Torstensohn, with his augmented army, penetrated to the unoccupied pass betwixt Schleswig and Stapelholm, met Gallas, and drove him along the whole course of the Elbe as far as Bernburg, where the Imperialists took up an intrenched position. Torstensohn passed the Saal, and by posting himself in the rear of the enemy, cut off their communication with Saxony and Bohemia. Scarcity and famine began now to destroy them in great numbers, and forced them to retreat to Magdeburg, where, however, they were not much better off. The cavalry which endeavored to escape into Silesia was overtaken and routed by Torstensohn, near Juterbock; the rest of the army, after a vain attempt to fight its way through the Swedish lines, was almost wholly destroyed near Magdeburg. From this expedition Gallas brought back only a few thousand men of all his formidable force, and the reputation of being a consummate master in the art of ruining an army. The King of Denmark after this unsuccessful effort to relieve him sued for peace, which he obtained at Bremsebor in the year 1645 under very unfavorable conditions.

Torstensohn rapidly followed up his victory; and while Axel Lilienstern, one of the generals who commanded under him, overawed Saxony, and Koenigsmark subdued the whole of Bremen, he himself penetrated into Bohemia with sixteen thousand men and eighty pieces of artillery, and endeavored a second time to remove the seat of war into the hereditary dominions of Austria. Ferdinand, upon this intelligence, hastened in person to Prague, in order to animate the courage of the people by his presence; and as a skilful general was much required, and so little unanimity prevailed among the numerous leaders, he hoped in the immediate neighborhood of the war to be able to give more energy and activity. In obedience to his orders Hatzfeld assembled the whole Austrian and Bavarian force, and, contrary to his own inclination and advice, formed the Emperor's last army and the last bulwark of his states in order of battle to meet the enemy, who were approaching, at Jankowitz, on the 24th of February, 1645. Ferdinand depended upon his cavalry, which outnumbered that of the enemy by three thousand, and upon the promise of the Virgin Mary, who had appeared to him in a dream, and given him the strongest assurances of a complete victory.

The superiority of the Imperialists did not intimidate Torstensohn, who was not accustomed to number his antagonists. On the very first onset the left wing, which Goetz, the general of the League, had entangled in a disadvantageous position among marshes and thickets, was totally routed; the general, with the greater part of his men, killed, and almost the whole ammunition of the army taken. This unfortunate commencement decided the fate of the day. The Swedes constantly advancing successively carried all the most commanding heights. After a bloody engagement of eight hours, a desperate attack on the part of the imperial cavalry, and a vigorous resistance by the Swedish infantry, the latter remained in possession of the field. Two thousand Austrians were killed upon the spot, and Hatzfeld himself, with three thousand men, taken prisoners. Thus on the same day did the Emperor lose his best general and his last army.

This decisive victory at Jankowitz at once exposed all the Austrian territory to the enemy. Ferdinand hastily fled to Vienna, to provide for its defence and to save his

family and his treasures. In a very short time the victorious Swedes poured like an inundation upon Moravia and Austria. After they had subdued nearly the whole of Moravia, invested Brunn, and taken all the strongholds as far as the Danube, and carried the intrenchments at the Wolf's bridge, near Vienna, they at last appeared in sight of that capital, while the care which they had taken to fortify their conquests showed that their visit was not likely to be a short one. After a long and destructive circuit through every province of Germany the stream of war had at last rolled backwards to its source, and the roar of the Swedish artillery now reminded the terrified inhabitants of those balls which, twenty-seven years before, the Bohemian rebels had fired into Vienna. The same theatre of war brought again similar actors on the scene. Torstensohn invited Ragotsky, the successor of Bethlen Gabor, to his assistance, as the Bohemian rebels had solicited that of his predecessor; Upper Hungary was already inundated by his troops, and his union with the Swedes was daily apprehended. The Elector of Saxony, driven to despair by the Swedes taking up their quarters within his territories, and abandoned by the Emperor, who, after the defeat at Jankowitz, was unable to defend himself, at length adopted the last and only expedient which remained, and concluded a truce with Sweden, which was renewed from year to year till the general peace. The Emperor thus lost a friend, while a new enemy was appearing at his very gates, his armies dispersed, and his allies in other quarters of Germany defeated. The French army had effaced the disgrace of their defeat at Duttlingen by a brilliant campaign, and had kept the whole force of Bavaria employed upon the Rhine and in Swabia. Reinforced with fresh troops from France, which the great Turenne, already distinguished by his victories in Italy, brought to the assistance of the Duke of Enghien, they appeared on the 3d of August, 1644, before Fribourg, which Mercy had lately taken and now covered with his whole army strongly intrenched. But against the steady firmness of the Bavarians all the impetuous valor of the French was exerted in vain, and after a fruitless sacrifice of six thousand men, the Duke of Enghien was compelled to retreat. Mazarin shed tears over this great loss, which Condé, who had no feeling for anything but glory, disregarded. "A single night in Paris," said he, "gives birth to more men than this action has destroyed." The Bavarians, however, were so disabled by this murderous battle that, far from being in a condition to relieve Austria from the menaced dangers, they were too weak even to defend the banks of the Rhine. Spires, Worms, and Manheim capitulated; the strong fortress of Philipsburg was forced to surrender by famine; and by a timely submission Mentz hastened to disarm the conquerors.

Austria and Moravia, however, were now freed from Torstensohn, by a similar means of deliverance as in the beginning of the war had saved them from the Bohemians. Ragotzky, at the head of twenty-five thousand men, had advanced into the neighborhood of the Swedish quarters upon the Danube. But these wild, undisciplined hordes, instead of seconding the operations of Torstensohn by any vigorous enterprise, only ravaged the country, and increased the distress which, even before their arrival, had begun to be felt in the Swedish camp. To extort tribute from the Emperor, and money and plunder from his subjects, was the sole object that had allured Ragotzky, or his predecessor, Bethlen Gabor, into the field; and both departed as soon as they had gained their end. To get rid of him, Ferdinand granted the barbarian whatever he asked, and, by a small sacrifice, freed his states of this formidable enemy.

In the meantime the main body of the Swedes had been greatly weakened by a tedious encampment before Brunn. Torstensohn, who commanded in person, for four entire months employed in vain all his knowledge of military tactics; the obstinacy of the resistance was equal to that of the assault; while despair roused the courage of Souches, the commandant, a Swedish deserter, who had no hope of pardon. The ravages caused by pestilence, arising from famine, want of cleanliness, and the use of unripe fruit, during their tedious and unhealthy encampment, with the sudden retreat of the Prince of Transylvania, at last compelled the Swedish leader to raise the siege. As all the passes upon the Danube were occupied, and his army greatly weakened by famine and sickness, he at last relinquished his intended plan of operations against Austria and Moravia, and contented himself with securing a key to these provinces by leaving behind him Swedish garrisons in the conquered fortresses. He then directed his march into Bohemia, whither he was followed by the Imperialists under the Archduke Leopold. Such of the lost places as had not been retaken by the latter were recovered after his departure by the Austrian General Bucheim; so that in the course of the following year the Austrian frontier was again cleared of the enemy, and Vienna escaped with mere alarm. In Bohemia and Silesia, too, the Swedes maintained themselves only with a very variable fortune; they traversed both countries without being able to hold their ground in either. But if the designs of Torstensohn were not crowned with all the success which they were promised at the commencement, they were, nevertheless, productive of the most important consequences to the Swedish party. Denmark had been compelled to a peace, Saxony to a truce. The Emperor, in the deliberations for a peace, offered greater concessions; France became more manageable; and Sweden itself bolder and more confident in its bearing towards these two crowns. Having thus nobly performed his duty, the author of these advantages retired, adorned with laurels, into the tranquillity of private life, and endeavored to restore his shattered health.

By the retreat of Torstensohn the Emperor was relieved from all fears of an irruption on the side of Bohemia. But a new danger soon threatened the Austrian frontier from Swabia and Bavaria. Turenne, who had separated from Condé and taken the direction of Swabia, had, in the year 1645, been totally defeated by Mercy near Mergentheim; and the victorious Bavarians, under their brave leader, poured into Hesse. But the Duke of Enghien hastened with considerable succors from Alsace, Koenigsmark from Moravia, and the Hessians from the Rhine, to recruit the defeated army, and the Bavarians were in turn compelled to retire to the extreme limits of Swabia. Here they posted themselves at the village of Allersheim, near Nordlingen, in order to cover the Bavarian frontier. But no obstacle could check the impetuosity of the Duke of Enghien. In person he led on his troops against the enemy's intrenchments, and a battle took place which the heroic resistance of the Bavarians rendered most obstinate and bloody; till at last the death of the great Mercy, the skill of Turenne, and the iron firmness of the Hessians decided the day in favor of the allies. But even this second barbarous sacrifice of life had little effect either on the course of the war or on the negotiations for peace. The French army, exhausted by this bloody engagement, was still further weakened by the departure of the Hessians, and the Bavarians being reinforced by the Archduke Leopold, Turenne was again obliged hastily to recross the Rhine.

The retreat of the French enabled the enemy to turn his whole force upon the Swedes in Bohemia. Gustavus Wrangel, no unworthy successor of Banner and Torstensohn had, in 1646, been appointed commander-in-chief of the Swedish army, which, besides Koenigsmark's flying corps and the numerous garrisons dispersed throughout the empire, amounted to about eight thousand horse and fifteen thousand foot. The archduke, after reinforcing his army, which already amounted to twenty-four thousand men, with twelve Bavarian regiments of cavalry and eighteen regiments of infantry, moved against Wrangel in the hope of being able to overwhelm him by his superior force before Koenigsmark could join him, or the French effect a diversion in his favor. Wrangel, however, did not await him, but hastened through Upper Saxony to the Weser, where he took Hoester and Paderborn. From thence he marched into Hesse in order to join Turenne, and at his camp at Wetzlar was joined by the flying corps of Koenigsmark. But Turenne, fettered by the instructions of Mazarin, who had seen with jealousy the warlike prowess and increasing power of the Swedes, excused himself on the plea of a pressing necessity to defend the frontier of France on the side of the Netherlands in consequence of the Flemings having failed to make the promised diversion. But as Wrangel continued to press his just demand, and a longer opposition might have

excited distrust on the part of the Swedes, or induce them
to conclude a private treaty with Austria, Turenne at last
obtained the wished-for permission to join the Swedish
army.

The junction took place at Giessen, and they now felt
themselves strong enough to meet the enemy. The latter
had followed the Swedes into Hesse in order to intercept their commissariat and to prevent their union with
Turenne. In both designs they had been unsuccessful;
and the Imperialists now saw themselves cut off from the
Maine and exposed to great scarcity and want from
the loss of their magazines. Wrangel took advantage of
their weakness to execute a plan by which he hoped to
give a new turn to the war. He, too, had adopted the
maxim of his predecessor, to carry the war into the
Austrian States. But discouraged by the ill-success of
Torstensohn's enterprise, he hoped to gain his end with
more certainty by another way. He determined to follow the course of the Danube, and to break into the
Austrian territories through the midst of Bavaria. A
similar design had been formerly conceived by Gustavus
Adolphus, which he had been prevented carrying into
effect by the approach of Wallenstein's army and the
danger of Saxony. Duke Bernard moving in his footsteps, and more fortunate than Gustavus, had spread his
victorious banners between the Iser and the Inn; but the
near approach of the enemy, vastly superior in force,
obliged him to halt in his victorious career, and lead back
his troops. Wrangel now hoped to accomplish the object
in which his predecessors had failed, the more so as the
Imperial and Bavarian army was far in his rear upon the
Lahn, and could only reach Bavaria by a long march
through Franconia and the Upper Palatinate. He moved
hastily upon the Danube, defeated a Bavarian corps near
Donauwerth, and passed that river, as well as the Lech,
unopposed. But by wasting his time in the unsuccessful
siege of Augsburg, he gave opportunity to the Imperialists
not only to relieve that city, but also to repulse him as
far as Lauingen. No sooner, however, had they turned
towards Swabia with a view to remove the war from
Bavaria, than, seizing the opportunity, he repassed the

Lech, and guarded the passage of it against the Imperialists themselves. Bavaria now lay open and defenceless before him; the French and Swedes quickly overran it; and the soldiery indemnified themselves for all dangers by frightful outrages, robberies, and extortions. The arrival of the imperial troops, who at last succeeded in passing the Lech at Thierhaupten, only increased the misery of this country, which friend and foe indiscriminately plundered.

And now for the first time during the whole course of this war the courage of Maximilian, which for eight-and-twenty years had stood unshaken amidst fearful dangers, began to waver. Ferdinand II., his school-companion at Ingoldstadt, and the friend of his youth, was no more, and with the death of his friend and benefactor the strong tie was dissolved which had linked the Elector to the House of Austria. To the father, habit, inclination, and gratitude had attached him; the son was a stranger to his heart, and political interests alone could preserve his fidelity to the latter prince.

Accordingly the motives which the artifices of France now put in operation in order to detach him from the Austrian alliance, and to induce him to lay down his arms, were drawn entirely from political considerations. It was not without a selfish object that Mazarin had so far overcome his jealousy of the growing power of the Swedes as to allow the French to accompany them into Bavaria. His intention was to expose Bavaria to all the horrors of war, in the hope that the persevering fortitude of Maximilian might be subdued by necessity and despair, and the Emperor deprived of his first and last ally. Brandenburg had under its great sovereign embraced the neutrality; Saxony had been forced to accede to it; the war with France prevented the Spaniards from taking any part in that of Germany; the peace with Sweden had removed Denmark from the theatre of war; and Poland had been disarmed by a long truce. If they could succeed in detaching the Elector of Bavaria also from the Austrian alliance the Emperor would be without a friend in Germany and left to the mercy of the allied powers.

Ferdinand III. saw his danger and left no means untried to avert it. But the Elector of Bavaria was unfortunately led to believe that the Spaniards alone were disinclined to peace, and that nothing but Spanish influence had induced the Emperor so long to resist a cessation of hostilities. Maximilian detested the Spaniards, and could never forgive their having opposed his application for the Palatine Electorate. Could it then be supposed that, in order to gratify this hated power, he would see his people sacrificed, his country laid waste, and himself ruined, when, by a cessation of hostilities, he could at once emancipate himself from all these distresses, procure for his people the repose of which they stood so much in need, and perhaps accelerate the arrival of a general peace? All doubts disappeared; and, convinced of the necessity of this step, he thought he should sufficiently discharge his obligations to the Emperor if he invited him also to share in the benefit of the truce.

The deputies of the three crowns, and of Bavaria, met at Ulm to adjust the conditions. But it was soon evident from the instructions of the Austrian ambassadors that it was not the intention of the Emperor to second the conclusion of a truce, but if possible to prevent it. It was obviously necessary to make the terms acceptable to the Swedes, who had the advantage, and had more to hope than to fear from the continuance of the war. They were the conquerors; and yet the Emperor presumed to dictate to them. In the first transports of their indignation the Swedish ambassadors were on the point of leaving the congress, and the French were obliged to have recourse to threats in order to detain them.

The good intentions of the Elector of Bavaria to include the Emperor in the benefit of the truce having been thus rendered unavailing, he felt himself justified in providing for his own safety. However hard were the conditions on which the truce was to be purchased, he did not hesitate to accept it on any terms. He agreed to the Swedes extending their quarters in Swabia and Franconia, and to his own being restricted to Bavaria and the Palatinate. The conquests which he had made in Swabia were ceded to the allies, who, on their part, restored to him what they had taken from Bavaria. Cologne and Hesse Cassel were also included in the truce. After the conclusion of this treaty, upon the 14th March, 1647, the French and Swedes left Bavaria, and in order not to interfere with each other, took up different quarters, the former in Wurtemburg, the latter in Upper Swabia, in the neighborhood of the Lake of Constance. On the extreme north of this lake, and on the most southern frontier of Swabia, the Austrian town of Bregentz, by its steep and narrow passes, seemed to defy attack; and in this persuasion the whole peasantry of the surrounding villages had, with their property, taken refuge in this natural fortress. The rich booty which the store of provisions it contained gave reason to expect, and the advantage of possessing a pass into the Tyrol, Switzerland, and Italy, induced the Swedish general to venture an attack upon this supposed impregnable post and town, in which he succeeded. Meantime, Turenne, according to agreement, marched into Wurtemburg, where he forced the Landgrave of Darmstadt and the Elector of Mentz to imitate the example of Bavaria, and to embrace the neutrality.

And now at last France seemed to have attained the great object of its policy, that of depriving the Emperor of the support of the League and of his Protestant allies, and of dictating to him, sword in hand, the conditions of peace. Of all his once formidable power an army not exceeding twelve thousand was all that remained to him; and this force he was driven to the necessity of entrusting to the command of a Calvinist, the Hessian deserter, Melander, as the casualties of war had stripped him of his best generals. But as this war had been remarkable for the sudden changes of fortune it displayed, and as every calculation of state policy had been frequently baffled by some unforeseen event, in this case also the issue disappointed expectation; and after a brief crisis the fallen power of Austria rose again to a formidable strength. The jealousy which France entertained of Sweden prevented it from permitting the total ruin of the Emperor, or allowing the Swedes to obtain such a preponderance in Germany as might have been destructive to France herself. Accordingly the French minister declined to take advantage of the distresses of Austria; and the army of Turenne, separating from that of Wrangel, retired to the frontier of the Netherlands. Wrangel, indeed, after moving from Swabia into Franconia, taking Schweinfurt, and incorporating the imperial garrison of that place with his own army, attempted to make his way into Bohemia, and laid siege to Egra, the key of that kingdom. To relieve this fortress the Emperor put his last army into motion, and placed himself at his head. But obliged to take a long circuit, in order to spare the lands of Von Schlick, the president of the council of war, he protracted his march; and on his arrival Egra was already taken. Both armies were now in sight of each other, and a decisive battle was momentarily expected, as both were suffering from want, and the two camps were only separated from each other by the space of the intrenchments. But the Imperialists, although superior in numbers, contented themselves with keeping close to the enemy, and harassing them by skirmishes, by fatiguing marches and famine, until the negotiations which had been opened with Bavaria were brought to a bearing.

The neutrality of Bavaria was a wound under which the imperial court writhed impatiently, and after in vain attempting to prevent it, Austria now determined, if possible, to turn it to advantage. Several officers of the Bavarian army had been offended by this step of their master, which at once reduced them to inaction, and imposed a burdensome restraint on their restless dispositions. Even the brave John de Werth was at the head of the malcontents, and, encouraged by the Emperor, he formed a plot to seduce the whole army from their allegiance to the Elector and lead it over to the Emperor. Ferdinand did not blush to patronize this act of treachery against his father's most trusty ally. He formally issued a proclamation to the Bavarian troops, in which he recalled them to himself, reminded them that they were the troops of the Empire, which the Elector had merely commanded in name of the Emperor. Fortunately for

Maximilian he detected the conspiracy time enough to anticipate and prevent it by the most rapid and effective measures.

This disgraceful conduct of the Emperor might have justified a reprisal, but Maximilian was too old a statesman to listen to the voice of passion where policy alone ought to be heard. He had not derived from the truce the advantages he expected. Far from tending to accelerate a general peace, it had a pernicious influence upon the negotiations at Münster and Osnaburg, and had made the allies bolder in their demands. The French and Swedes had indeed removed from Bavaria; but by the loss of his quarters in the Swabian circle he found himself compelled either to exhaust his own territories by the subsistence of his troops, or at once to disband them and throw aside the shield and spear at the very moment when the sword alone seemed to be the arbiter of right. Before embracing either of these certain evils he determined to try a third step, the unfavorable issue of which was, at least, not so uncertain, viz., to renounce the truce and resume the war.

This resolution, and the assistance which he immediately dispatched to the Emperor in Bohemia, threatened materially to injure the Swedes, and Wrangel was compelled in haste to evacuate that kingdom. He retired through Thuringia into Westphalia and Lunenburg, in the hope of forming a junction with the French army under Turenne, while the Imperial and Bavarian army followed him to the Weser, under Melander and Gronsfeld. His ruin was inevitable if the enemy should overtake him before his junction with Turenne; but the same consideration which had just saved the Emperor now proved the salvation of the Swedes. Even amidst all the fury of the conquest cold calculations of prudence guided the course of the war, and the vigilance of the different courts increased as the prospect of peace approached. The Elector of Bavaria could not allow the Emperor to obtain so decisive a preponderance as by the sudden alteration of affairs might delay the chances of a general peace. Every change of fortune was important now, when a pacification was so ardently desired by all, and when the disturbance of the balance of power among the contracting parties might at once annihilate the work of years, destroy the fruit of long and tedious negotiations, and indefinitely protract the repose of Europe. If France sought to restrain the Swedish crown within due bounds, and measured out her assistance according to her successes and defeats, the Elector of Bavaria silently undertook the same task with the Emperor, his ally, and determined by prudently dealing out his aid to hold the fate of Austria in his own hands. And now that the power of the Emperor threatened once more to attain a dangerous superiority, Maximilian at once ceased to pursue the Swedes. He was also afraid of reprisals from France, who had threatened to direct Turenne's whole force against him if he allowed his troops to cross the Weser.

Melander, prevented by the Bavarians from further pursuing Wrangel, crossed by Jena and Erfurt into Hesse, and now appeared as a dangerous enemy in the country which he had formerly defended. If it was the desire of revenge upon his former sovereign which led him to choose Hesse for the scene of his ravage, he certainly had his full gratification. Under this scourge the miseries of that unfortunate state reached their height. But he had soon reason to regret that in the choice of his quarters he had listened to the dictates of revenge rather than of prudence. In this exhausted country his army was oppressed by want, while Wrangel was recruiting his strength and remounting his cavalry in Lunenburg. Too weak to maintain his wretched quarters against the Swedish general, when he opened the campaign in the winter of 1648, and marched against Hesse, he was obliged to retire with disgrace, and take refuge on the banks of the Danube.

France had once more disappointed the expectations of Sweden; and the army of Turenne, disregarding the remonstrances of Wrangel, had remained upon the Rhine. The Swedish leader revenged himself by drawing into his service the cavalry of Weimar, which had abandoned the standard of France, though by this step he further increased the jealousy of that power. Turenne received permission to join the Swedes; and the last campaign of this eventful war was now opened by the united armies. Driving Melander before them along the Danube, they threw supplies into Egra, which was besieged by the Imperialists, and defeated the Imperial and Bavarian armies on the Danube, which ventured to oppose them at Susmarshausen, where Melander was mortally wounded. After this overthrow, the Bavarian general, Gronsfeld, placed himself on the farther side of the Lech, in order to guard Bavaria from the enemy.

But Gronsfeld was not more fortunate than Tilly, who in this same position had sacrificed his life for Bavaria. Wrangel and Turenne chose the same spot for passing the river which was so gloriously marked by the victory of Gustavus Adolphus, and accomplished it by the same means, too, which had favored their predecessor. Bavaria was now a second time overrun, and the breach of the truce punished by the severest treatment of its inhabitants. Maximilian sought shelter in Salzburg, while the Swedes crossed the Iser, and forced their way as far as the Inn. A violent and continued rain, which in a few days swelled this inconsiderable stream into a broad river, saved Austria once more from the threatened danger. The enemy ten times attempted to form a bridge of boats over the Inn, and as often it was destroyed by the current. Never, during the whole course of the war, had the Imperialists been in so great consternation as at present, when the enemy were in the centre of Bavaria, and when they had no longer a general left who could be matched against a Turenne, a Wrangel, and a Koenigsmark. At last the brave Piccolomini arrived from the Netherlands to assume the command of the feeble wreck of the Imperialists. By their own ravages in Bohemia the allies had rendered their subsistence in that country impracticable, and were at last driven by scarcity to retreat into the Upper Palatinate, where the news of the peace put a period to their activity.

Koenigsmark, with his flying corps, advanced towards Bohemia, where Ernest Odowalsky, a disbanded captain, who, after being disabled in the imperial service, had been dismissed without a pension, laid before him a plan for surprising the lesser side of the city of Prague. Koenigsmark successfully accomplished the bold enterprise, and acquired the reputation of closing the thirty years' war by the last brilliant achievement. This decisive stroke, which vanquished the Emperor's irresolution, cost the Swedes only the loss of a single man. But the old town, the larger half of Prague, which is divided into two parts by the Moldau, by its vigorous resistance wearied out the efforts of the Palatine, Charles Gustavus, the successor of Christina on the throne, who had arrived from Sweden with fresh troops, and had assembled the whole Swedish force in Bohemia and Silesia before its walls. The approach of winter at last drove the besiegers into their quarters, and in the meantime, the intelligence arrived that a peace had been signed at Münster, on the 24th October.

The colossal labor of concluding this solemn, and ever-memorable and sacred treaty, which is known by the name of the peace of Westphalia; the endless obstacles which were to be surmounted; the contending interests which it was necessary to reconcile; the concatenation of circumstances which must have co-operated to bring to a favorable termination this tedious, but precious and permanent work of policy; the difficulties which beset the very opening of the negotiations, and maintaining them, when opened, during the ever-fluctuating vicissitudes of the war; finally, arranging the conditions of peace, and, still more, the carrying them into effect;— what were the conditions of this peace; what each contending power gained or lost, by the toils and sufferings of a thirty years' war; what modification it wrought upon the general system of European policy;— these are matters which must be relinquished to another pen. The history of the peace of Westphalia constitutes a whole, as important as the history of the war itself. A mere abridgment of it would reduce to a mere skeleton one of the most interesting and characteristic monuments of human policy and passions, and deprive it of every feature calculated to fix the attention of the public, for which I write, and of which I now respectfully take my leave.

WORKS OF FREDERICK SCHILLER.

THE HISTORY

OF THE

REVOLT OF THE NETHERLANDS.

CONTENTS.

	PAGE
AUTHOR'S PREFACE	5
INTRODUCTION	8
BOOK I.—EARLIER HISTORY OF THE NETHERLANDS UP TO THE SIXTEENTH CENTURY	22
BOOK II.—CARDINAL GRANVELLA	31
BOOK III.—CONSPIRACY OF THE NOBLES	142
BOOK IV.—THE ICONOCLASTS	187
TRIAL AND EXECUTION OF COUNTS EGMONT AND HORN	279
SIEGE OF ANTWERP BY THE PRINCE OF PARMA, IN THE YEARS 1584 AND 1585	287

HISTORY

OF THE

REVOLT OF THE UNITED NETHERLANDS.

THE AUTHOR'S PREFACE.

MANY years ago, when I read the History of the Belgian Revolution in Watson's excellent work, I was seized with an enthusiasm which political events but rarely excite. On further reflection I felt that this enthusiastic feeling had arisen less from the book itself than from the ardent workings of my own imagination, which had imparted to the recorded materials the particular form that so fascinated me. These imaginations, therefore, I felt a wish to fix, to multiply, and to strengthen; these exalted sentiments I was anxious to extend by communicating them to others. This was my principal motive for commencing the present history, my only vocation to write it. The execution of this design carried me farther than in the beginning I had expected. A closer acquaintance with my materials enabled me to discover defects previously unnoticed, long waste tracts to be filled up, apparent contradictions to be reconciled, and isolated facts to be brought into connection with the rest of the subject. Not so much with the view of enriching my history with new facts as of seeking a key to old ones, I betook myself to the original sources, and thus what was originally intended to be only a general outline expanded under my hands into an elaborate history. The first part, which concludes with the Duchess of Parma's departure from the Netherlands, must be looked upon only as the introduction to the history of the Revolution itself, which did not come to an open outbreak till the government of her successor. I have bestowed the more care and attention upon this introductory period the more the generality of writers who had previously treated of it seemed to me deficient in these very qualities. Moreover, it is in my opinion the more important as being the root and source of all the subsequent events. If, then, the first volume should appear to any as barren in important incident, dwelling prolixly on trifles, or, rather, should seem at first sight profuse of reflections, and in general tediously minute, it must be remembered that it was precisely out of small beginnings that the Revolution was gradually developed; and that all the great results which follow sprang out of a countless number of trifling and little circumstances.

A nation like the one before us invariably takes its first steps with doubts and uncertainty, to move afterwards only the more rapidly for its previous hesitation. I proposed, therefore, to follow the same method in describing this rebellion. The longer the reader delays on the introduction the more familiar he becomes with the actors in this history, and the scene in which they took a part, so much the more rapidly and unerringly shall I be able to lead him through the subsequent periods, where the accumulation of materials will forbid a slowness of step or minuteness of attention.

As for the authorities of our history there is not so much cause to complain of their paucity as of their extreme abundance, since it is indispensable to read them all to obtain that clear view of the whole subject to which the perusal of a part, however large, is always prejudicial. From the unequal, partial, and often contradictory narratives of the same occurrences it is often extremely difficult to seize the truth, which in all is alike partly concealed and to be found complete in none. In this first volume, besides de Thou, Strada, Reyd, Grotius, Meteren, Burgundius, Meursius, Bentivoglio, and some moderns, the Memoirs of Counsellor Hopper, the life and correspondence of his friend Viglius, the records of the trials of the Counts of Hoorne and Egmont, the defence of the Prince of Orange, and some few others have been my guides. I must here acknowledge my obligations to a work compiled with much industry and critical acumen,

and written with singular truthfulness and impartiality.
I allude to the general history of the United Netherlands
which was published in Holland during the present century.
Besides many original documents which I could
not otherwise have had access to, it has abstracted all
that is valuable in the excellent works of Bos, Hooft,
Brandt, Le Clerc, which either were impossible for me to
procure or were not available to my use, as being written
in Dutch, which I do not understand. An otherwise
ordinary writer, Richard Dinoth, has also been of service
to me by the many extracts he gives from the pamphlets
of the day, which have been long lost. I have in vain
endeavored to procure the correspondence of Cardinal
Granvella, which also would no doubt have thrown much
light upon the history of these times. The lately published
work on the Spanish Inquisition by my excellent
countryman, Professor Spittler of Göttingen, reached me
too late for its sagacious and important contents to be
available for my purpose.

The more I am convinced of the importance of the
French history, the more I lament that it was not in my
power to study, as I could have wished, its copious annals
in the original sources and contemporary documents, and
to reproduce it abstracted of the form in which it was
transmitted to me by the more intelligent of my predecessors,
and thereby emancipate myself from the influence
which every talented author exercises more or less upon
his readers. But to effect this the work of a few years
must have become the labor of a life. My aim in making
this attempt will be more than attained if it should convince
a portion of the reading public of the possibility of
writing a history with historic truth without making
a trial of patience to the reader; and if it should extort
from another portion the confession that history can
borrow from a cognate art without thereby, of necessity,
becoming a romance.

WEIMAR, Michaelmas Fair, 1788.

INTRODUCTION.

OF those important political events which make the sixteenth century to take rank among the brightest of the world's epochs, the foundation of the freedom of the Netherlands appears to me one of the most remarkable. If the glittering exploits of ambition and the pernicious lust of power claim our admiration, how much more so should an event in which oppressed humanity struggled for its noblest rights, where with the good cause unwonted powers were united, and the resources of resolute despair triumphed in unequal contest over the terrible arts of tyranny.

Great and encouraging is the reflection that there is a resource left us against the arrogant usurpations of despotic power; that its best-contrived plans against the liberty of mankind may be frustrated; that resolute opposition can weaken even the outstretched arm of tyranny; and that heroic perseverance can eventually exhaust its fearful resources. Never did this truth affect me so sensibly as in tracing the history of that memorable rebellion which forever severed the United Netherlands from the Spanish Crown. Therefore I thought it not unworth the while to attempt to exhibit to the world this grand memorial of social union, in the hope that it may awaken in the breast of my reader a spirit-stirring consciousness of his own powers, and give a new and irrefragable example of what in a good cause men may both dare and venture, and what by union they may accomplish. It is not the extraordinary or heroic features of this event that induce me to describe it. The annals of the world record perhaps many similar enterprises, which may have been even bolder in the conception and more brilliant in the execution. Some states have fallen after a nobler struggle; others have risen with more exalted strides. Nor are we here to look for eminent heroes, colossal talents, or those marvellous exploits which the history of past times presents in such rich abundance. Those times are gone; such men are no more. In the soft lap of refinement we have suffered the energetic powers to become enervate which those ages called into action and rendered indispensable. With admiring awe we wonder at these gigantic images of the past as a feeble old man gazes on the athletic sports of youth.

Not so, however, in the history before us. The people here presented to our notice were the most peaceful in our quarter of the globe, and less capable than their neighbors of that heroic spirit which stamps a lofty character even on the most insignificant actions. The pressure of circumstances with its peculiar influence surprised them and forced a transitory greatness upon them, which they never could have possessed and perhaps will never possess again. It is, indeed, exactly this want of heroic grandeur which renders this event peculiarly instructive; and while others aim at showing the superiority of genius over chance, I shall here paint a scene where necessity creates genius and accident makes heroes.

If in any case it be allowable to recognize the intervention of Providence in human affairs it is certainly so in the present history, its course appears so contradictory to reason and experience. Philip II., the most powerful sovereign of his line—whose dreaded supremacy menaced the independence of Europe—whose treasures surpassed the collective wealth of all the monarchs of Christendom besides—whose ambitious projects were backed by numerous and well-disciplined armies—whose troops, hardened by long and bloody wars, and confident in past victories and in the irresistible prowess of this nation, were eager for any enterprise that promised glory and spoil, and ready to second with prompt obedience the daring genius of their leaders—this dreaded potentate here appears before us obstinately pursuing one favorite project, devoting to it the untiring efforts of a long reign, and bringing all these terrible resources to bear upon it; but forced, in the evening of his reign, to abandon it— here we see the mighty Philip II. engaging in combat with a few weak and powerless adversaries, and retiring from it at last with disgrace.

And with what adversaries? Here, a peaceful tribe of fishermen and shepherds, in an almost-forgotten corner of Europe, which with difficulty they had rescued from the ocean; the sea their profession, and at once their wealth and their plague; poverty with freedom their highest blessing, their glory, their virtue. There, a harmless, moral, commercial people, revelling in the abundant fruits of thriving industry, and jealous of the maintenance of laws which had proved their benefactors. In the happy leisure of affluence they forsake the narrow circle of immediate wants and learn to thirst after higher and nobler gratifications. The new views of truth, whose benignant dawn now broke over Europe, cast a fertilizing beam on this favored clime, and the free burgher admitted with joy the light which oppressed and miserable slaves shut out. A spirit of independence, which is the ordinary companion of prosperity and freedom, lured this people on to examine the authority of antiquated opinions and to break an ignominious chain. But the stern rod of despotism was held suspended over them; arbitrary power threatened to tear away the foundation of their happiness; the guardian of their laws became their tyrant. Simple in their statecraft no less than in their manners, they dared to appeal to ancient treaties and to remind the lord of both Indies of the rights of nature. A name decides the whole issue of things. In Madrid that was called rebellion which in Brussels was simply styled a lawful remonstrance. The complaints of Brabant required a prudent mediator; Philip II. sent an executioner. The signal for war was given. An unparalleled tyranny assailed both property and life. The despairing citizens, to whom the choice of deaths was all that was left, chose the nobler one on the battle-field. A wealthy and luxurious nation loves peace, but becomes warlike as soon as it becomes poor. Then it ceases to tremble for a life which is deprived of everything that had made it desirable. In an instant the contagion of rebellion seizes at once the most distant provinces; trade and commerce are at a standstill, the ships disappear from the harbors, the artisan abandons his workshop, the rustic his uncultivated fields. Thousands fled to distant lands, a thousand victims fell on the bloody field, and fresh thousands pressed on. Divine, indeed, must that doctrine be for which men could die so joyfully. All that was wanting was the last finishing hand, the enlightened, enterprising spirit, to seize on this great political crisis and to mould the offspring of chance into the ripe creation of wisdom. William the Silent, like a second Brutus, devoted himself to the great cause of liberty. Superior to all selfishness, he resigned honorable offices which entailed on him objectionable duties, and, magnanimously divesting himself of all his princely dignities, he descended to a state of voluntary poverty, and became but a citizen of the world. The cause of justice was staked upon the hazardous game of battle; but the newly-raised levies of mercenaries and peaceful husbandmen were unable to withstand the terrible onset of an experienced force. Twice did the brave William lead his dispirited troops against the tyrant. Twice was he abandoned by them, but not by his courage.

Philip II. sent as many reinforcements as the dreadful importunity of his viceroy demanded. Fugitives, whom their country rejected, sought a new home on the ocean, and turned to the ships of their enemy to satisfy the cravings both of vengeance and of want. Naval heroes were now formed out of corsairs, and a marine collected out of piratical vessels; out of morasses arose a republic. Seven provinces threw off the yoke at the same time, to form a new, youthful state, powerful by its waters and its union and despair. A solemn decree of the whole nation deposed the tyrant, and the Spanish name was erased from all its laws.

For such acts no forgiveness remained; the republic became formidable only because it was impossible for her to retrace her steps. But factions distracted her within; without, her terrible element, the sea itself, leaguing with her oppressors, threatened her very infancy with a premature grave. She felt herself succumb to the superior force of the enemy, and cast herself a suppliant before the most powerful thrones of Europe, begging them to accept a dominion which she herself could no longer protect. At last, but with difficulty — so despised at first was this state that even the rapacity of foreign monarchs spurned her opening bloom — a stranger deigned to accept their importunate offer of a dangerous crown. New hopes began to revive her sinking courage; but in this new father of his country destiny gave her a traitor, and in the critical emergency, when the foe was in full force before her very gates, Charles of Anjou invaded the liberties which he had been called to protect. In the midst of the tempest, too, the assassin's hand tore the steersman from the helm, and with William of Orange the career of the infant republic was seemingly at an end, and all her guardian angels fled. But the ship continued to scud along before the storm, and the swelling canvas carried her safe without the pilot's help.

Philip II. missed the fruits of a deed which cost him his royal honor, and perhaps, also, his self-respect. Liberty struggled on still with despotism in obstinate and dubious contest; sanguinary battles were fought; a brilliant array of heroes succeeded each other on the field of glory, and Flanders and Brabant were the schools which educated generals for the coming century. A long, devastating war laid waste the open country; victor and vanquished alike waded through blood; while the rising republic of the waters gave a welcome to fugitive industry, and out of the ruins of despotism erected the noble edifice of its own greatness. For forty years lasted the war whose happy termination was not to bless the dying eye of Philip; which destroyed one paradise in Europe to form a new one out of its shattered fragments; which destroyed the choicest flower of military youth, and while it enriched more than a quarter of the globe impoverished the possessor of the golden Peru. This monarch, who could expend nine hundred tons of gold without oppressing his subjects, and by tyrannical measures extorted far more, heaped, moreover, on his exhausted people a debt of one hundred and forty millions of ducats. An implacable hatred of liberty swallowed up all these treasures, and consumed on the fruitless task the labor of a royal life. But the Reformation throve amidst the devastations of the sword, and over the blood of her citizens the banner of the new republic floated victorious.

This improbable turn of affairs seems to border on a miracle; many circumstances, however, combined to break the power of Philip, and to favor the progress of the infant state. Had the whole weight of his power fallen on the United Provinces there had been no hope for their religion or their liberty. His own ambition, by tempting him to divide his strength, came to the aid of their weakness. The expensive policy of maintaining traitors in every cabinet of Europe; the support of the League in France; the revolt of the Moors in Granada; the conquest of Portugal, and the magnificent fabric of the Escurial, drained at last his apparently inexhaustible treasury, and prevented his acting in the field with spirit and energy. The German and Italian troops, whom the hope of gain alone allured to his banner, mutinied when he could no longer pay them, and faithlessly abandoned their leaders in the decisive moment of action. These terrible instruments of oppression now turned their dangerous power against their employer, and wreaked their vindictive rage on the provinces which remained faithful to him. The unfortunate armament against England, on which, like a desperate gamester, he had staked the whole strength of his kingdom, completed his ruin; with the armada sank the wealth of the two Indies, and the flower of Spanish chivalry.

But in the very same proportion that the Spanish power declined the republic rose in fresh vigor. The ravages which the fanaticism of the new religion, the tyranny of the Inquisition, the furious rapacity of the soldiery, and the miseries of a long war unbroken by any interval of peace, made in the provinces of Brabant, Flanders, and Hainault, at once the arsenals and the magazines of this expensive contest, naturally rendered it every year more difficult to support and recruit the royal armies. The Catholic Netherlands had already lost a million of citizens, and the trodden fields maintained their husbandmen no longer. Spain itself had but few more men to spare. That country, surprised by a sudden affluence which brought idleness with it, had lost much of its population, and could not long support the continual drafts of men which were required both for the New World and the Netherlands. Of these conscripts few ever saw their country again; and these few having left it as youths returned to it infirm and old. Gold, which had become more common, made soldiers proportionately dearer; the growing charm of effeminacy enhanced the price of the opposite virtues. Wholly different was the posture of affairs with the rebels. The thousands whom the cruelty of the viceroy expelled from the southern Netherlands, the Huguenots whom the wars of persecution drove from France, as well as every one whom constraint of conscience exiled from the other parts of Europe, all alike flocked to unite themselves with the Belgian insurgents. The whole Christian world was their recruiting ground. The fanaticism both of the persecutor and the persecuted worked in their behalf. The enthusiasm of a doctrine newly embraced, revenge, want, and hopeless misery drew to their standard adventurers from every part of Europe. All whom the new doctrine had won, all who had suffered, or had still cause of fear from despotism, linked their own fortunes with those of the new republic. Every injury inflicted by a tyrant gave a right of citizenship in Holland. Men pressed towards a country where liberty raised her spirit-stirring banner, where respect and security were insured to a fugitive religion, and even revenge on the oppressor. If we consider the conflux in the present day of people to Holland, seeking by their entrance upon her territory to be reinvested in their rights as men, what must it have been at a time when the rest of Europe groaned under a heavy bondage, when Amsterdam was nearly the only free port for all opinions? Many hundred families sought a refuge for their wealth in a land which the ocean and domestic concord powerfully combined to protect. The republican army maintained its full complement without the plough being stripped of hands to work it. Amid the clash of arms trade and industry flourished, and the peaceful citizen enjoyed in anticipation the fruits of liberty which foreign blood was to purchase for them. At the very time when the republic of Holland was struggling for existence she extended her dominions beyond the ocean, and was quietly occupied in erecting her East Indian Empire.

Moreover, Spain maintained this expensive war with dead, unfructifying gold, that never returned into the hand which gave it away, while it raised to her the price

of every necessary. The treasuries of the republic were
industry and commerce. Time lessened the one whilst
it multiplied the other, and exactly in the same proportion that the resources of the Spanish government became
exhausted by the long continuance of the war the republic began to reap a richer harvest. Its field was sown
sparingly with the choice seed which bore fruit, though
late, yet a hundredfold; but the tree from which Philip
gathered fruit was a fallen trunk which never again
became verdant.

Philip's adverse destiny decreed that all the treasures
which he lavished for the oppression of the Provinces
should contribute to enrich them. The continual outlay
of Spanish gold had diffused riches and luxury throughout Europe; but the increasing wants of Europe were
supplied chiefly by the Netherlanders, who were masters
of the commerce of the known world, and who by their
dealings fixed the price of all merchandise. Even during
the war Philip could not prohibit his own subjects from
trading with the republic; nay, he could not even desire
it. He himself furnished the rebels with the means of
defraying the expenses of their own defence; for the very
war which was to ruin them increased the sale of their
goods. The enormous sums expended on his fleets and
armies flowed for the most part into the exchequer of the
republic, which was more or less connected with the
commercial places of Flanders and Brabant. Whatever
Philip attempted against the rebels operated indirectly
to their advantage.

The sluggish progress of this war did the king as much
injury as it benefited the rebels. His army was composed
for the most part of the remains of those victorious troops
which had gathered their laurels under Charles V. Old
and long services entitled them to repose; many of them,
whom the war had enriched, impatiently longed for their
homes, where they might end in ease a life of hardship.
Their former zeal, their heroic spirit, and their discipline
relaxed in the same proportion as they thought they had
fully satisfied their honor and their duty, and as they
began to reap at last the reward of so many battles. Besides, the troops which had been accustomed by their

irresistible impetuosity to vanquish all opponents were necessarily wearied out by a war which was carried on not so much against men as against the elements; which exercised their patience more than it gratified their love of glory; and where there was less of danger than of difficulty and want to contend with. Neither personal courage nor long military experience was of avail in a country whose peculiar features gave the most dastardly the advantage. Lastly, a single discomfiture on foreign ground did them more injury than any victories gained over an enemy at home could profit them. With the rebels the case was exactly the reverse. In so protracted a war, in which no decisive battle took place, the weaker party must naturally learn at last the art of defence from the stronger; slight defeats accustomed him to danger; slight victories animated his confidence.

At the beginning of the war the republican army scarcely dared to show itself in the field; the long continuance of the struggle practised and hardened it. As the royal armies grew wearied of victory, the confidence of the rebels rose with their improved discipline and experience. At last, at the end of half a century, master and pupil separated, unsubdued, and equal in the fight.

Again, throughout the war the rebels acted with more concord and unanimity than the royalists. Before the former had lost their first leader the government of the Netherlands had passed through as many as five hands. The Duchess of Parma's indecision soon imparted itself to the cabinet of Madrid, which in a short time tried in succession almost every system of policy. Duke Alva's inflexible sternness, the mildness of his successor Requescens, Don John of Austria's insidious cunning, and the active and imperious mind of the Prince of Parma gave as many opposite directions to the war, while the plan of rebellion remained the same in a single head, who, as he saw it clearly, pursued it with vigor. The king's greatest misfortune was that right principles of action generally missed the right moment of application. In the commencement of the troubles, when the advantage was as yet clearly on the king's side, when prompt resolution and manly firmness might have crushed the rebellion in the cradle, the reigns of government were allowed to hang loose in the hands of a woman. After the outbreak had come to an open revolt, and when the strength of the factious and the power of the king stood more equally balanced, and when a skilful flexible prudence could alone have averted the impending civil war, the government devolved on a man who was eminently deficient in this necessary qualification. So watchful an observer as William the Silent failed not to improve every advantage which the faulty policy of his adversary presented, and with quiet silent industry he slowly but surely pushed on the great enterprise to its accomplishment.

But why did not Philip II. himself appear in the Netherlands? Why did he prefer to employ every other means, however improbable, rather than make trial of the only remedy which could insure success? To curb the overgrown power and insolence of the nobility there was no expedient more natural than the presence of their master. Before royalty itself all secondary dignities must necessarily have sunk in the shade, all other splendor be dimmed. Instead of the truth being left to flow slowly and obscurely through impure channels to the distant throne, so that procrastinated measures of redress gave time to ripen ebullitions of the moment into acts of deliberation, his own penetrating glance would at once have been able to separate truth from error; and cold policy alone, not to speak of his humanity, would have saved the land a million citizens. The nearer to their source the more weighty would his edicts have been; the thicker they fell on their objects the weaker and the more dispirited would have become the efforts of the rebels. It costs infinitely more to do an evil to an enemy in his presence than in his absence. At first the rebellion appeared to tremble at its own name, and long sheltered itself under the ingenious pretext of defending the cause of its sovereign against the arbitrary assumptions of his own viceroy. Philip's appearance in Brussels would have put an end at once to this juggling. In that case, the rebels would have been compelled to act up to their pretence, or to cast aside the mask, and so, by appearing in their true shape, condemn themselves. And what a relief for the Netherlands if the king's presence had only spared them those evils which were inflicted upon them without his knowledge, and contrary to his will. What gain, too, even if it had only enabled him to watch over the expenditure of the vast sums which, illegally raised on the plea of meeting the exigencies of the war, disappeared in the plundering hands of his deputies.

What the latter were compelled to extort by the unnatural expedient of terror, the nation would have been disposed to grant to the sovereign majesty. That which made his ministers detested would have rendered the monarch feared; for the abuse of hereditary power is less painfully oppressive than the abuse of delegated authority. His presence would have saved his exchequer thousands had he been nothing more than an economical despot; and even had he been less, the awe of his person would have preserved a territory which was lost through hatred and contempt for his instruments.

In the same manner, as the oppression of the people of the Netherlands excited the sympathy of all who valued their own rights, it might have been expected that their disobedience and defection would have been a call to all princes to maintain their own prerogatives in the case of their neighbors. But jealousy of Spain got the better of political sympathies, and the first powers of Europe arranged themselves more or less openly on the side of freedom.

Although bound to the house of Spain by the ties of relationship, the Emperor Maximilian II. gave it just cause for its charge against him of secretly favoring the rebels. By the offer of his mediation he implicitly acknowledged the partial justice of their complaints, and thereby encouraged them to a resolute perseverance in their demands. Under an emperor sincerely devoted to the interests of the Spanish house, William of Orange could scarcely have drawn so many troops and so much money from Germany. France, without openly and formally breaking the peace, placed a prince of the blood at the head of the Netherlandish rebels; and it was with French gold and French troops that the operations of the latter were chiefly conducted. Elizabeth of England, too, did but exercise a just retaliation and revenge in protecting the rebels against their legitimate sovereign; and although her meagre and sparing aid availed no farther than to ward off utter-ruin from the republic, still even this was infinitely valuable at a moment when nothing but hope could have supported their exhausted courage. With both these powers Philip at the time was at peace, but both betrayed him. Between the weak and the strong honesty often ceases to appear a virtue; the delicate ties which bind equals are seldom observed towards him whom all men fear. Philip had banished truth from political intercourse; he himself had dissolved all morality between kings, and had made artifice the divinity of cabinets. Without once enjoying the advantages of his preponderating greatness, he had, throughout life, to contend with the jealousy which it awakened in others. Europe made him atone for the possible abuses of a power of which in fact he never had the full possession.

If against the disparity between the two combatants, which, at first sight, is so astounding, we weigh all the incidental circumstances which were adverse to Spain, but favorable to the Netherlands, that which is supernatural in this event will disappear, while that which is extraordinary will still remain — and a just standard will be furnished by which to estimate the real merit of these republicans in working out their freedom. It must not, however, be thought that so accurate a calculation of the opposing forces could have preceded the undertaking itself, or that, on entering this unknown sea, they already knew the shore on which they would ultimately be landed. The work did not present itself to the mind of its originator in the exact form which it assumed when completed, any more than the mind of Luther foresaw the eternal separation of creeds when he began to oppose the sale of indulgences. What a difference between the modest procession of those suitors in Brussels, who prayed for a more humane treatment as a favor, and the dreaded majesty of a free state, which treated with kings as equals, and in less than a century disposed of the throne of its former tyrant. The unseen hand of fate gave to the discharged arrow a higher flight, and quite a different direction from that which it first received from the bowstring. In the womb of happy Brabant that liberty had its birth which, torn from its mother in its earliest infancy, was to gladden the so despised Holland. But the enterprise must not be less thought of because its issue differed from the first design. Man works up, smooths, and fashions the rough stone which the times bring to him; the moment and the instant may belong to him, but accident develops the history of the world. If the passions which co-operated actively in bringing about this event were only not unworthy of the great work to which they were unconsciously subservient — if only the powers which aided in its accomplishment were intrinsically noble, if only the single actions out of whose concatenation it wonderfully arose were beautiful and great, then is the event grand, interesting, and fruitful for us, and we are at liberty to wonder at the bold offspring of chance, or rather offer up our admiration to a higher intelligence.

The history of the world, like the laws of nature, is consistent with itself, and simple as the soul of man. Like conditions produce like phenomena. On the same soil where now the Netherlanders were to resist their Spanish tyrants, their forefathers, the Batavi and Belgæ, fifteen centuries before, combated against their Roman oppressors. Like the former, submitting reluctantly to a haughty master, and misgoverned by rapacious satraps, they broke off their chain with like resolution, and tried their fortune in a similar unequal combat. The same pride of conquest, the same national grandeur, marked the Spaniard of the sixteenth century and the Roman of the first; the same valor and discipline distinguished the armies of both, their battle array inspired the same terror. There as here we see stratagem in combat with superior force, and firmness, strengthened by unanimity, wearing out a mighty power weakened by division; then as now private hatred armed a whole nation; a single man, born for his times, revealed to his fellow-slaves the dangerous secret of their power, and brought their mute grief to a bloody announcement. "Confess, Batavians," cries Claudius Civilis to his countrymen in the sacred grove, "we are no longer treated, as formerly, by these Romans as allies, but rather as slaves. We are handed over to their prefects and centurions, who, when satiated with our plunder and with our blood, make way for others, who, under different names, renew the same outrages. If even at last Rome deigns to send us a legate, he oppresses us with an ostentatious and costly retinue, and with still more intolerable pride. The levies are again at hand which tear forever children from their parents, brothers from brothers. Now, Batavians, is our time. Never did Rome lie so prostrate as now. Let not their names of legions terrify you. There is nothing in their camps but old men and plunder. Our infantry and horsemen are strong; Germany is allied to us by blood, and Gaul is ready to throw off its yoke. Let Syria serve them, and Asia and the East, who are used to bow before kings; many still live who were born among us before tribute was paid to the Romans. The gods are ever with the brave." Solemn religious rites hallowed this conspiracy, like the League of the Gueux; like that, it craftily wrapped itself in the veil of submissiveness, in the majesty of a great name. The cohorts of Civilis swear allegiance on the Rhine to Vespasian in Syria, as the League did to Philip II. The same arena furnished the same plan of defence, the same refuge to despair. Both confided their wavering fortunes to a friendly element; in the same distress Civilis preserves his island, as fifteen centuries after him William of Orange did the town of Leyden — through an artificial inundation. The valor of the Batavi disclosed the impotency of the world's ruler, as the noble courage of their descendants revealed to the whole of Europe the decay of Spanish greatness. The same fecundity of genius in the generals of both times gave to the war a similarly obstinate continuance, and nearly as doubtful an issue; one difference, nevertheless, distinguishes them: the Romans and Batavians fought humanely, for they did not fight for religion.

BOOK I.

EARLIER HISTORY OF THE NETHERLANDS UP TO THE SIXTEENTH CENTURY.

BEFORE we consider the immediate history of this great revolution, it will be advisable to go a few steps back into the ancient records of the country, and to trace the origin of that constitution which we find it possessed of at the time of this remarkable change.

The first appearance of this people in the history of the world is the moment of its fall; their conquerors first gave them a political existence. The extensive region which is bounded by Germany on the east, on the south by France, on the north and northwest by the North Sea, and which we comprehend under the general name of the Netherlands, was, at the time when the Romans invaded Gaul, divided amongst three principal nations, all originally of German descent, German institutions, and German spirit. The Rhine formed its boundaries. On the left of the river dwelt the Belgæ, on its right the Frisii, and the Batavi on the island which its two arms then formed with the ocean. All these several nations were sooner or later reduced into subjection by the Romans, but the conquerors themselves give us the most glorious testimony to their valor. The Belgæ, writes Cæsar, were the only people amongst the Gauls who repulsed the invasion of the Teutones and Cimbri. The Batavi, Tacitus tells us, surpassed all the tribes on the Rhine in bravery. This fierce nation paid its tribute in soldiers, and was reserved by its conquerors, like arrow and sword, only for battle. The Romans themselves acknowledged the Batavian horsemen to be their best cavalry. Like the Swiss at this day, they formed for a long time the body-guard of the Roman Emperor; their wild courage terrified the Dacians, as they saw them, in full armor, swimming across the Danube. The Batavi accompanied Agricola in his expedition against Britain, and helped him to conquer that island. The Frieses were, of all, the last subdued, and the first to regain their liberty. The morasses among which they dwelt attracted the conquerors later, and enhanced the price of conquest. The Roman Drusus, who made war in these regions, had a canal cut from the Rhine into the Flevo, the present Zuyder Zee, through which the Roman fleet penetrated into the North Sea, and from thence, entering the mouths of the Ems and the Weser, found an easy passage into the interior of Germany.

Through four centuries we find Batavian troops in the Roman armies, but after the time of Honorius their name disappears from history. Presently we discover their island overrun by the Franks, who again lost themselves in the adjoining country of Belgium. The Frieses threw off the yoke of their distant and powerless rulers, and again appeared as a free, and even a conquering people, who governed themselves by their own customs and a remnant of Roman laws, and extended their limits beyond the left bank of the Rhine. Of all the provinces of the Netherlands, Friesland especially had suffered the least from the irruptions of strange tribes and foreign customs, and for centuries retained traces of its original institutions, of its national spirit and manners, which have not, even at the present day, entirely disappeared.

The epoch of the immigration of nations destroyed the original form of most of these tribes; other mixed races arose in their place, with other constitutions. In the general irruption the towns and encampments of the Romans disappeared, and with them the memorials of their wise government, which they had employed the natives to execute. The neglected dikes once more yielded to the violence of the streams and to the encroachments of the ocean. Those wonders of labor, and creations of human skill, the canals, dried up, the rivers changed their course, the continent and the sea confounded their olden limits, and the nature of the soil changed with its inhabitants. So, too, the connection of the two eras seems effaced, and with a new race a new history commences.

The monarchy of the Franks, which arose out of the ruins of Roman Gaul, had, in the sixth and seventh centuries, seized all the provinces of the Netherlands, and planted there the Christian faith. After an obstinate war Charles Martel subdued to the French crown Friesland, the last of all the free provinces, and by his victories paved a way for the gospel. Charlemagne united all these countries, and formed of them one division of the mighty empire which he had constructed out of Germany, France, and Lombardy. As under his descendants this vast dominion was again torn into fragments, so the Netherlands became at times German, at others French, or then again Lotheringian Provinces; and at last we find them under both the names of Friesland and Lower Lotheringia.

With the Franks the feudal system, the offspring of the North, also came into these lands, and here, too, as in all other countries, it degenerated. The more powerful vassals gradually made themselves independent of the crown, and the royal governors usurped the countries they were appointed to govern. But the rebellious vassals could not maintain their usurpations without the aid of their own dependants, whose assistance they were compelled to purchase by new concessions. At the same time the church became powerful through pious usurpations and donations, and its abbey lands and episcopal sees acquired an independent existence. Thus were the Netherlands in the tenth, eleventh, twelfth, and thirteenth centuries split up into several small sovereignties, whose possessors did homage at one time to the German Emperor, at another to the kings of France. By purchase, marriages, legacies, and also by conquest, several of these provinces were often united under one suzerain, and thus in the fifteenth century we see the house of Burgundy in possession of the chief part of the Netherlands. With more or less right Philip the Good, Duke of Burgundy, had united as many as eleven provinces under his authority, and to these his son, Charles the Bold, added two others, acquired by force of arms. Thus imperceptibly a new state arose in Europe, which wanted nothing but the name to be the most flourishing kingdom in this quarter of the globe. These extensive possessions made the Dukes of Burgundy formidable neighbors to France, and tempted the restless spirit of Charles the Bold to devise a scheme of conquest,

embracing the whole line of country from the Zuyder
Zee and the mouth of the Rhine down to Alsace. The
almost inexhaustible resources of this prince justify in
some measure this bold project. A formidable army
threatened to carry it into execution. Already Switzerland trembled for her liberty; but deceitful fortune
abandoned him in three terrible battles, and the infatuated hero was lost in the melée of the living and the
dead.*

The sole heiress of Charles the Bold, Maria, at once
the richest princess and the unhappy Helen of that time,
whose wooing brought misery on her inheritance, was
now the centre of attraction to the whole known world.
Among her suitors appeared two great princes, King
Louis XI. of France, for his son, the young Dauphin, and
Maximilian of Austria, son of the Emperor Frederic III.
The successful suitor was to become the most powerful
prince in Europe; and now, for the first time, this quarter
of the globe began to fear for its balance of power.
Louis, the more powerful of the two, was ready to back
his suit by force of arms; but the people of the Netherlands, who disposed of the hand of their princess, passed
by this dreaded neighbor, and decided in favor of Maximilian, whose more remote territories and more limited
power seemed less to threaten the liberty of their country.
A deceitful, unfortunate policy, which, through a strange
dispensation of heaven, only accelerated the melancholy
fate which it was intended to prevent.

To Philip the Fair, the son of Maria and Maximilian, a
Spanish bride brought as her portion that extensive kingdom which Ferdinand and Isabella had recently founded;
and Charles of Austria, his son, was born lord of the
kingdoms of Spain, of the two Sicilies, of the New World,

---

* A page who had seen him fall a few days after the battle conducted the victors to the spot, and saved his remains from an ignominious oblivion. His body was dragged from out of a pool, in which it was fast frozen, naked, and so disfigured with wounds that with great difficulty he was recognized, by the well-known deficiency of some of his teeth, and by remarkably long finger-nails. But that, notwithstanding the marks, there were still incredulous people who doubted his death, and looked for his reappearance, is proved by the missive in which Louis XI. called upon the Burgundian States to return to their allegiance to the Crown of France. "If," the passage runs, "Duke Charles should still be living, you shall be released from your oath to me." Comines, t. iii., Preuves des Mémoires, 495, 497.

and of the Netherlands. In the latter country the commonalty emancipated themselves much earlier than in other feudal states, and quickly attained to an independent political existence. The favorable situation of the country on the North Sea and on great navigable rivers early awakened the spirit of commerce, which rapidly peopled the towns, encouraged industry and the arts, attracted foreigners, and diffused prosperity and affluence among them. However contemptuously the warlike policy of those times looked down upon every peaceful and useful occupation, the rulers of the country could not fail altogether to perceive the essential advantages they derived from such pursuits. The increasing population of their territories, the different imposts which they extorted from natives and foreigners under the various titles of tolls, customs, highway rates, escort money, bridge tolls, market fees, escheats, and so forth, were too valuable considerations to allow them to remain indifferent to the sources from which they were derived. Their own rapacity made them promoters of trade, and, as often happens, barbarism itself rudely nursed it, until at last a healthier policy assumed its place. In the course of time they invited the Lombard merchants to settle among them, and accorded to the towns some valuable privileges and an independent jurisdiction, by which the latter acquired uncommon extraordinary credit and influence. The numerous wars which the counts and dukes carried on with one another, or with their neighbors, made them in some measure dependent on the good-will of the towns, who by their wealth obtained weight and consideration, and for the subsidies which they afforded failed not to extort important privileges in return. These privileges of the commonalties increased as the crusades with their expensive equipment augmented the necessities of the nobles; as a new road to Europe was opened for the productions of the East, and as wide-spreading luxury created new wants to their princes. Thus as early as the eleventh and twelfth centuries we find in these lands a mixed form of government, in which the prerogative of the sovereign is greatly limited by the privileges of the estates; that is to say, of the nobility, the clergy, and the municipalities.

These, under the name of States, assembled as often as the wants of the province required it. Without their consent no new laws were valid, no war could be carried on, and no taxes levied, no change made in the coinage, and no foreigner admitted to any office of government. All the provinces enjoyed these privileges in common; others were peculiar to the various districts. The supreme government was hereditary, but the son did not enter on the rights of his father before he had solemnly sworn to maintain the existing constitution.

Necessity is the first lawgiver; all the wants which had to be met by this constitution were originally of a commercial nature. Thus the whole constitution was founded on commerce, and the laws of the nation were adapted to its pursuits. The last clause, which excluded foreigners from all offices of trust, was a natural consequence of the preceding articles. So complicated and artificial a relation between the sovereign and his people, which in many provinces was further modified according to the peculiar wants of each, and frequently of some single city, required for its maintenance the liveliest zeal for the liberties of the country, combined with an intimate acquaintance with them. From a foreigner neither could well be expected. This law, besides, was enforced reciprocally in each particular province; so that in Brabant no Fleming, in Zealand no Hollander, could hold office; and it continued in force even after all these provinces were united under one government.

Above all others, Brabant enjoyed the highest degree of freedom. Its privileges were esteemed so valuable that many mothers from the adjacent provinces removed thither about the time of their accouchment, in order to entitle their children to participate, by birth, in all the immunities of that favored country; just as, says Strada, one improves the plants of a rude climate by removing them to the soil of a milder.

After the House of Burgundy had united several provinces under its dominion, the separate provincial assemblies which, up to that time, had been independent tribunals, were made subject to a supreme court at Malines, which incorporated the various judicatures into one body, and decided in the last resort all civil and criminal appeals. The separate independence of the provinces was thus abolished, and the supreme power vested in the senate at Malines.

After the death of Charles the Bold the states did not neglect to avail themselves of the embarassment of their duchess, who, threatened by France, was consequently in their power. Holland and Zealand compelled her to sign a great charter, which secured to them the most important sovereign rights. The people of Ghent carried their insolence to such a pitch that they arbitrarily dragged the favorites of Maria, who had the misfortune to displease them, before their own tribunals, and beheaded them before the eyes of that princess. During the short government of the Duchess Maria, from her father's death to her marriage, the commons obtained powers which few free states enjoyed. After her death her husband, Maximilian, illegally assumed the government as guardian of his son. Offended by this invasion of their rights, the estates refused to acknowledge his authority, and could only be brought to receive him as a viceroy for a stated period, and under conditions ratified by oath.

Maximilian, after he became Roman Emperor, fancied that he might safely venture to violate the constitution. He imposed extraordinary taxes on the provinces, gave official appointments to Burgundians and Germans, and introduced foreign troops into the provinces. But the jealousy of these republicans kept pace with the power of their regent. As he entered Bruges with a large retinue of foreigners, the people flew to arms, made themselves masters of his person, and placed him in confinement in the castle. In spite of the intercession of the Imperial and Roman courts, he did not again obtain his freedom until security had been given to the people on all the disputed points.

The security of life and property arising from mild laws, and an equal administration of justice, had encouraged activity and industry. In continual contest with the ocean and rapid rivers, which poured their violence on the neighboring lowlands, and whose force it was requisite to break by embankments and canals, this people had early learned to observe the natural objects around them; by industry and perseverance to defy an element of superior power; and like the Egyptian, instructed by his Nile, to exercise their inventive genius and acuteness in self-defence. The natural fertility of their soil, which favored agriculture and the breeding of cattle, tended at the same time to increase the population. Their happy position on the sea and the great navigable rivers of Germany and France, many of which debouched on their coasts; the numerous artificial canals which intersected the land in all directions, imparted life to navigation; and the facility of internal communication between the provinces, soon created and fostered a commercial spirit among these people.

The neighboring coasts, Denmark and Britain, were the first visited by their vessels. The English wool which they brought back employed thousands of industrious hands in Bruges, Ghent, and Antwerp; and as early as the middle of the twelfth century cloths of Flanders were extensively worn in France and Germany. In the eleventh century we find ships of Friesland in the Belt, and even in the Levant. This enterprising people ventured, without a compass, to steer under the North Pole round to the most northerly point of Russia. From the Wendish towns the Netherlands received a share in the Levant trade, which, at that time, still passed from the Black Sea through the Russian territories to the Baltic. When, in the thirteenth century, this trade began to decline, the Crusades having opened a new road through the Mediterranean for Indian merchandise, and after the Italian towns had usurped this lucrative branch of commerce, and the great Hanseatic League had been formed in Germany, the Netherlands became the most important emporium between the north and south. As yet the use of the compass was not general, and the merchantmen sailed slowly and laboriously along the coasts. The ports on the Baltic were, during the winter months, for the most part frozen and inaccessible. Ships, therefore, which could not well accomplish within the year the long voyage from the Mediterranean to the Belt, gladly availed themselves of harbors which lay half-way between the two.

With an immense continent behind them with which navigable streams kept up their communication, and towards the west and north open to the ocean by commodious harbors, this country appeared to be expressly formed for a place of resort for different nations, and for a centre of commerce. The principal towns of the Netherlands were established marts. Portuguese, Spaniards, Italians, French, Britons, Germans, Danes, and Swedes thronged to them with the produce of every country in the world. Competition insured cheapness; industry was stimulated as it found a ready market for its productions. With the necessary exchange of money arose the commerce in bills, which opened a new and fruitful source of wealth. The princes of the country, acquainted at last with their true interest, encouraged the merchant by important immunities, and neglected not to protect their commerce by advantageous treaties with foreign powers. When, in the fifteenth century, several provinces were united under one rule, they discontinued their private wars, which had proved so injurious, and their separate interests were now more intimately connected by a common government. Their commerce and affluence prospered in the lap of a long peace, which the formidable power of their princes extorted from the neighboring monarchs. The Burgundian flag was feared in every sea, the dignity of their sovereign gave support to their undertakings, and the enterprise of a private individual became the affair of a powerful state. Such vigorous protection soon placed them in a position even to renounce the Hanseatic League, and to pursue this daring enemy through every sea. The Hanseatic merchants, against whom the coasts of Spain were closed, were compelled at last, however reluctantly, to visit the Flemish fairs, and purchase their Spanish goods in the markets of the Netherlands.

Bruges, in Flanders, was, in the fourteenth and fifteenth centuries, the central point of the whole commerce of Europe, and the great market of all nations. In the year 1468 a hundred and fifty merchant vessels were counted entering the harbor of Sluys at one time. Besides the rich factories of the Hanseatic League, there were here fifteen trading companies, with their counting-houses, and many factories and merchants' families from every European country. Here was established the market of all northern products for the south, and of all southern and Levantine products for the north. These passed through the Sound, and up the Rhine, in Hanseatic vessels to Upper Germany, or were transported by land-carriage to Brunswick and Luneburg.

As in the common course of human affairs, so here also a licentious luxury followed prosperity. The seductive example of Philip the Good could not but accelerate its approach. The court of the Burgundian dukes was the most voluptuous and magnificent in Europe, Italy itself not excepted. The costly dress of the higher classes, which afterwards served as patterns to the Spaniards, and eventually, with other Burgundian customs, passed over to the court of Austria, soon descended to the lower orders, and the meanest citizen nursed his person in velvet and silk.*

Comines, an author who travelled through the Netherlands about the middle of the fifteenth century, tells us that pride had already attended their prosperity. The pomp and vanity of dress was carried by both sexes to extravagance. The luxury of the table had never reached so great a height among any other people. The immoral assemblage of both sexes at bathing-places, and such other places of reunion for pleasure and enjoyment, had banished all shame — and we are not here speaking of the usual luxuriousness of the higher ranks; the females of the common class abandoned themselves to such extravagances without limit or measure.

But how much more cheering to the philanthropist is

* Philip the Good was too profuse a prince to amass treasures; nevertheless Charles the Bold found accumulated among his effects, a greater store of table services, jewels, carpets, and linen than three rich princedoms of that time together possessed, and over and above all a treasure of three hundred thousand dollars in ready money. The riches of this prince, and of the Burgundian people, lay exposed on the battle-fields of Granson, Murten, and Nancy. Here a Swiss soldier drew from the finger of Charles the Bold that celebrated diamond which was long esteemed the largest in Europe, which even now sparkles in the crown of France as the second in size, but which the unwitting finder sold for a florin. The Swiss exchanged the silver they found for tin, and the gold for copper, and tore into pieces the costly tents of cloth of gold. The value of the spoil of silver, gold, and jewels which was taken has been estimated at three millions. Charles and his army had advanced to the combat, not like foes who purpose battle, but like conquerors who adorn themselves after victory.

this extravagance than the miserable frugality of want, and the barbarous virtues of ignorance, which at that time oppressed nearly the whole of Europe! The Burgundian era shines pleasingly forth from those dark ages, like a lovely spring day amid the showers of February. But this flourishing condition tempted the Flemish towns at last to their ruin; Ghent and Bruges, giddy with liberty and success, declared war against Philip the Good, the ruler of eleven provinces, which ended as unfortunately as it was presumptuously commenced. Ghent alone lost many thousand men in an engagement near Havre, and was compelled to appease the wrath of the victor by a contribution of four hundred thousand gold florins. All the municipal functionaries, and two thousand of the principal citizens, went, stripped to their shirts, barefooted, and with heads uncovered, a mile out of the town to meet the duke, and on their knees supplicated for pardon. On this occasion they were deprived of several valuable privileges, an irreparable loss for their future commerce. In the year 1482 they engaged in a war, with no better success, against Maximilian of Austria, with a view to deprive him of the guardianship of his son, which, in contravention of his charter, he had unjustly assumed. In 1487 the town of Bruges placed the archduke himself in confinement, and put some of his most eminent ministers to death. To avenge his son the Emperor Frederic III. entered their territory with an army, and, blockading for ten years the harbor of Sluys, put a stop to their entire trade. On this occasion Amsterdam and Antwerp, whose jealousy had long been roused by the flourishing condition of the Flemish towns, lent him the most important assistance. The Italians began to bring their own silk-stuffs to Antwerp for sale, and the Flemish cloth-workers likewise, who had settled in England, sent their goods thither; and thus the town of Bruges lost two important branches of trade. The Hanseatic League had long been offended at their overweening pride; and it now left them and removed its factory to Antwerp. In the year 1516 all the foreign merchants left the town except only a few Spaniards; but its prosperity faded as slowly as it had bloomed.

Antwerp received, in the sixteenth century, the trade which the luxuriousness of the Flemish towns had banished; and under the government of Charles V. Antwerp was the most stirring and splendid city in the Christian world. A stream like the Scheldt, whose broad mouth, in the immediate vicinity, shared with the North Sea the ebb and flow of the tide, and could carry vessels of the largest tonnage under the walls of Antwerp, made it the natural resort for all vessels which visited that coast. Its free fairs attracted men of business from all countries.* The industry of the nation had, in the beginning of this century, reached its greatest height. The culture of grain, flax, the breeding of cattle, the chase, and fisheries, enriched the peasant; arts, manufactures, and trade gave wealth to the burghers. Flemish and Brabantine manufactures were long to be seen in Arabia, Persia, and India. Their ships covered the ocean, and in the Black Sea contended with the Genoese for supremacy. It was the distinctive characteristic of the seaman of the Netherlands that he made sail at all seasons of the year, and never laid up for the winter.

When the new route by the Cape of Good Hope was discovered, and the East India trade of Portugal undermined that of the Levant, the Netherlands did not feel the blow which was inflicted on the Italian republics. The Portuguese established their mart in Brabant, and the spices of Calicut were displayed for sale in the markets of Antwerp. Hither poured the West Indian merchandise, with which the indolent pride of Spain repaid the industry of the Netherlands. The East Indian market attracted the most celebrated commercial houses from Florence, Lucca, and Genoa; and the Fuggers and Welsers from Augsburg. Here the Hanse towns brought the wares of the north, and here the English company had a factory. Here art and nature seemed to expose to view all their riches; it was a splendid exhibition of the works of the Creator and of the creature.

Their renown soon diffused itself through the world. Even a company of Turkish merchants, towards the end

* Two such fairs lasted forty days, and all the goods sold there were duty free.

of this century, solicited permission to settle here, and to supply the products of the East by way of Greece. With the trade in goods they held also the exchange of money. Their bills passed current in the farthest parts of the globe. Antwerp, it is asserted, then transacted more extensive and more important business in a single month than Venice, at its most flourishing period, in two whole years.

In the year 1491 the Hanseatic League held its solemn meetings in this town, which had formerly assembled in Lubeck alone. In 1531 the exchange was erected, at that time the most splendid in all Europe, and which fulfilled its proud inscription. The town now reckoned one hundred thousand inhabitants. The tide of human beings, which incessantly poured into it, exceeds all belief. Between two hundred and two hundred and fifty ships were often seen loading at one time in its harbor; no day passed on which the boats entering inwards and outwards did not amount to more than five hundred; on market days the number amounted to eight or nine hundred. Daily more than two hundred carriages drove through its gates; above two thousand loaded wagons arrived every week from Germany, France, and Lorraine, without reckoning the farmers' carts and corn-vans, which were seldom less than ten thousand in number. Thirty thousand hands were employed by the English company alone. The market dues, tolls, and excise brought millions to the government annually. We can form some idea of the resources of the nation from the fact that the extraordinary taxes which they were obliged to pay to Charles V. towards his numerous wars were computed at forty millions of gold ducats.

For this affluence the Netherlands were as much indebted to their liberty as to the natural advantages of their country. Uncertain laws and the despotic sway of a rapacious prince would quickly have blighted all the blessings which propitious nature had so abundantly lavished on them. The inviolable sanctity of the laws can alone secure to the citizen the fruits of his industry, and inspire him with that happy confidence which is the soul of all activity.

The genius of this people, developed by the spirit of commerce, and by the intercourse with so many nations, shone in useful inventions; in the lap of abundance and liberty all the noble arts were carefully cultivated and carried to perfection. From Italy, to which Cosmo de Medici had lately restored its golden age, painting, architecture, and the arts of carving and of engraving on copper, were transplanted into the Netherlands, where, in a new soil, they flourished with fresh vigor. The Flemish school, a daughter of the Italian, soon vied with its mother for the prize; and, in common with it, gave laws to the whole of Europe in the fine arts. The manufactures and arts, on which the Netherlanders principally founded their prosperity, and still partly base it, require no particular enumeration. The weaving of tapestry, oil painting, the art of painting on glass, even pocket-watches and sun-dials were, as Guicciardini asserts, originally invented in the Netherlands. To them we are indebted for the improvement of the compass, the points of which are still known by Flemish names. About the year 1430 the invention of typography is ascribed to Laurence Koster, of Haarlem; and whether or not he is entitled to this honorable distinction, certain it is that the Dutch were among the first to engraft this useful art among them; and fate ordained that a century later it should reward its country with liberty. The people of the Netherlands united with the most fertile genius for inventions a happy talent for improving the discoveries of others; there are probably few mechanical arts and manufactures which they did not either produce or at least carry to a higher degree of perfection.

THE NETHERLANDS UNDER CHARLES V.

Up to this time these provinces had formed the most enviable state in Europe. Not one of the Burgundian dukes had ventured to indulge a thought of overturning the constitution; it had remained sacred even to the daring spirit of Charles the Bold, while he was preparing fetters for foreign liberty. All these princes grew up with no higher hope than to be the heads of a republic, and none of their territories afforded them experience of a higher authority. Besides, these princes possessed nothing but what the Netherlands gave them; no armies but those which the nation sent into the field; no riches but what the estates granted to them. Now all was changed. The Netherlands had fallen to a master who had at his command other instruments and other resources, who could arm against them a foreign power.*

Charles V. was an absolute monarch in his Spanish dominions; in the Netherlands he was no more than the first citizen. In the southern portion of his empire he might have learned contempt for the rights of individuals; here he was taught to respect them. The more he there

---

* The unnatural union of two such different nations as the Belgians and Spaniards could not possibly be prosperous. I cannot here refrain from quoting the comparison which Grotius, in energetic language, has drawn between the two. "With the neighboring nations," says he, " the people of the Netherlands could easily maintain a good understanding, for they were of a similar origin with themselves, and had grown up in the same manner. But the people of Spain and of the Netherlands differed in almost every respect from one another, and therefore, when they were brought together, clashed the more violently. Both had for many centuries been distinguished in war, only the latter had, in luxurious repose, become disused to arms, while the former had been inured to war in the Italian and African campaigns; the desire of gain made the Belgians more inclined to peace, but not less sensitive of offence. No people were more free from the lust of conquest, but none defended its own more zealously. Hence the numerous towns, closely pressed together in a confined tract of country; densely crowded with a foreign and native population; fortified near the sea and the great rivers. Hence for eight centuries after the northern immigration foreign arms could not prevail against them. Spain, on the contrary, often changed its masters; and when at last it fell into the hands of the Goths, its character and its manners had suffered more or less from each new conqueror. The people thus formed at last out of these several admixtures is described as patient in labor, imperturbable in danger, equally eager for riches and honor, proud of itself even to contempt of others, devout and grateful to strangers for any act of kindness, but also revengeful, and of such ungovernable passions in victory as so regard neither conscience nor honor in the case of an enemy. All this is foreign to the character of the Belgian, who is astute but not insidious, who, placed midway between France and Germany, combines in moderation the faults and good qualities of both. He is not easily to be imposed upon, nor is he to be insulted with impunity. In veneration for the Deity, too, he does not yield to the Spaniard; the arms of the Northmen could not make him apostatize from Christianity when he had once professed it. No opinion which the church condemns had, up to this time, empoisoned the purity of his faith. Nay, his pious extravagance went so far that it became requisite to curb by laws the rapacity of his clergy. In both people loyalty to their rulers is equally innate, with this difference, that the Belgian places the law above kings. Of all the Spaniards the Castilians require to be governed with the most caution; but the liberties which they arrogate for themselves they do not willingly accord to others. Hence the difficult task to their common ruler, so to distribute his attention and care between the two nations that neither the preference shown to the Castilian should offend the Belgian, nor the equal treatment of the Belgian affront the haughty spirit of the Castilian." — Grotii Annal. Belg. L. I. 4. 5. seq.

tasted the pleasures of unlimited power, and the higher he raised his opinion of his own greatness, the more reluctant he must have felt to descend elsewhere to the ordinary level of humanity, and to tolerate any check upon his arbitrary authority. It requires, indeed, no ordinary degree of virtue to abstain from warring against the power which imposes a curb on our most cherished wishes.

The superior power of Charles awakened at the same time in the Netherlands that distrust which always accompanies inferiority. Never were they so alive to their constitutional rights, never so jealous of the royal prerogative, or more observant in their proceedings. Under his reign we see the most violent outbreaks of republican spirit, and the pretensions of the people carried to an excess which nothing but the increasing encroachments of the royal power could in the least justify. A sovereign will always regard the freedom of the citizen as an alienated fief, which he is bound to recover. To the citizen the authority of a sovereign is a torrent, which, by its inundation, threatens to sweep away his rights. The Belgians sought to protect themselves against the ocean by embankments, and against their princes by constitutional enactments. The whole history of the world is a perpetually recurring struggle between liberty and the lust of power and possession; as the history of nature is nothing but the contest of the elements and organic bodies for space. The Netherlands soon found to their cost that they had become but a province of a great monarchy. So long as their former masters had no higher aim than to promote their prosperity, their condition resembled the tranquil happiness of a secluded family, whose head is its ruler. Charles V. introduced them upon the arena of the political world. They now formed a member of that gigantic body which the ambition of an individual employed as his instrument. They ceased to have their own good for their aim; the centre of their existence was transported to the soul of their ruler. As his whole government was but one tissue of plans and manœuvres to advance his power, so it was, above all things, necessary that he should be completely master of the various limbs of his mighty empire in order to move them effectually and suddenly. It was impossible, therefore, for him to embarrass himself with the tiresome mechanism of their interior political organization, or to extend to their peculiar privileges the conscientious respect which their republican jealousy demanded. It was expedient for him to facilitate the exercise of their powers by concentration and unity. The tribunal at Malines had been under his predecessor an independent court of judicature; he subjected its decrees to the revision of a royal council, which he established in Brussels, and which was the mere organ of his will. He introduced foreigners into the most vital functions of their constitution, and confided to them the most important offices. These men, whose only support was the royal favor, would be but bad guardians of privileges which, moreover, were little known to them. The ever-increasing expenses of his warlike government compelled him as steadily to augment his resources. In disregard of their most sacred privileges he imposed new and strange taxes on the provinces. To preserve their olden consideration the estates were forced to grant what he had been so modest as not to extort; the whole history of the government of this monarch in the Netherlands is almost one continued list of imposts demanded, refused, and finally accorded. Contrary to the constitution, he introduced foreign troops into their territories, directed the recruiting of his armies in the provinces, and involved them in wars, which could not advance even if they did not injure their interest, and to which they had not given their consent. He punished the offences of a free state as a monarch; and the terrible chastisement of Ghent announced to the other provinces the great change which their constitution had already undergone.

The welfare of the country was so far secured as was necessary to the political schemes of its master; the intelligent policy of Charles would certainly not violate the salutary regiment of the body whose energies he found himself necessitated to exert. Fortunately, the opposite pursuits of selfish ambition, and of disinterested philanthropy, often bring about the same end; and the well-being of a state, which a Marcus Aurelius might propose to himself as a rational object of pursuit, is occasionally promoted by an Augustus or a Louis.

Charles V. was perfectly aware that commerce was the strength of the nation, and that the foundation of their commerce was liberty. He spared its liberty because he needed its strength. Of greater political wisdom, though not more just than his son, he adapted his principles to the exigencies of time and place, and recalled an ordinance in Antwerp and in Madrid which he would under other circumstances have enforced with all the terrors of his power. That which makes the reign of Charles V. particularly remarkable in regard to the Netherlands is the great religious revolution which occurred under it; and which, as the principal cause of the subsequent rebellion, demands a somewhat circumstantial notice. This it was that first brought arbitrary power into the innermost sanctuary of the constitution; taught it to give a dreadful specimen of its might; and, in a measure, legalized it, while it placed republican spirit on a dangerous eminence. And as the latter sank into anarchy and rebellion monarchical power rose to the height of despotism.

Nothing is more natural than the transition from civil liberty to religious freedom. Individuals, as well as communities, who, favored by a happy political constitution, have become acquainted with the rights of man, and accustomed to examine, if not also to create, the law which is to govern them; whose minds have been enlightened by activity, and feelings expanded by the enjoyments of life; whose natural courage has been exalted by internal security and prosperity; such men will not easily surrender themselves to the blind domination of a dull arbitrary creed, and will be the first to emancipate themselves from its yoke. Another circumstance, however, must have greatly tended to diffuse the new religion in these countries. Italy, it might be objected, the seat of the greatest intellectual culture, formerly the scene of the most violent political factions, where a burning climate kindles the blood with the wildest passions — Italy, among all the European countries, remained the freest from this change. But to a romantic people, whom a warm and lovely sky, a luxurious, ever young and ever smiling nature, and the multifarious witcheries of art, rendered keenly susceptible of sensuous enjoyment, that form of religion must naturally have been better adapted, which by its splendid pomp captivates the senses, by its mysterious enigmas opens an unbounded range to the fancy; and which, through the most picturesque forms, labors to insinuate important doctrines into the soul. On the contrary, to a people whom the ordinary employments of civil life have drawn down to an unpoetical reality, who live more in plain notions than in images, and who cultivate their common sense at the expense of their imagination — to such a people that creed will best recommend itself which dreads not investigation, which lays less stress on mysticism than on morals, and which is rather to be understood then to be dwelt upon in meditation. In few words, the Roman Catholic religion will, on the whole, be found more adapted to a nation of artists, the Protestant more fitted to a nation of merchants.

On this supposition the new doctrines which Luther diffused in Germany, and Calvin in Switzerland, must have found a congenial soil in the Netherlands. The first seeds of it were sown in the Netherlands by the Protestant merchants, who assembled at Amsterdam and Antwerp. The German and Swiss troops, which Charles introduced into these countries, and the crowd of French, German, and English fugitives who, under the protection of the liberties of Flanders, sought to escape the sword of persecution which threatened them at home, promoted their diffusion. A great portion of the Belgian nobility studied at that time at Geneva, as the University of Louvain was not yet in repute, and that of Douai not yet founded. The new tenets publicly taught there were transplanted by the students to their various countries. In an isolated people these first germs might easily have been crushed; but in the market-towns of Holland and Brabant, the resort of so many different nations, their first growth would escape the notice of government, and be accelerated under the veil of obscurity. A difference in opinion might easily spring up and gain ground amongst those who already were divided in national character, in manners, customs, and laws. Moreover, in a country where industry was the most lauded virtue, mendicity the most abhorred vice, a slothful body of men, like that of the monks, must have been an object of long and deep aversion. Hence, the new religion, which opposed these orders, derived an immense advantage from having the popular opinion on its side. Occasional pamphlets, full of bitterness and satire, to which the newly-discovered art of printing secured a rapid circulation, and several bands of strolling orators, called Rederiker, who at that time made the circuit of the provinces, ridiculing in theatrical representations or songs the abuses of their times, contributed not a little to diminish respect for the Romish Church, and to prepare the people for the reception of the new dogmas.

The first conquests of this doctrine were astonishingly rapid. The number of those who in a short time avowed themselves its adherents, especially in the northern provinces, was prodigious; but among these the foreigners far outnumbered the natives. Charles V., who, in this hostile array of religious tenets, had taken the side which a despot could not fail to take, opposed to the increasing torrent of innovation the most effectual remedies. Unhappily for the reformed religion political justice was on the side of its persecutor. The dam which, for so many centuries, had repelled human understanding from truth was too suddenly torn away for the outbreaking torrent not to overflow its appointed channel. The reviving spirit of liberty and of inquiry, which ought to have remained within the limits of religious questions, began also to examine into the rights of kings. While in the commencement iron fetters were justly broken off, a desire was eventually shown to rend asunder the most legitimate and most indispensable of ties. Even the Holy Scriptures, which were now circulated everywhere, while they imparted light and nurture to the sincere inquirer after truth, were the source also whence an eccentric fanaticism contrived to extort the virulent poison. The good cause had been compelled to choose the evil road of rebellion, and the result was what in such cases it ever will be so long as men remain men. The bad cause, too, which had nothing in common with the good but the employment of illegal means, emboldened by this slight point of connection, appeared in the same company, and was mistaken for it. Luther had written against the invocation of saints; every audacious varlet who broke into the churches and cloisters, and plundered the altars, called himself Lutheran. Faction, rapine, fanaticism, licentiousness robed themselves in his colors; the most enormous offenders, when brought before the judges, avowed themselves his followers. The Reformation had drawn down the Roman prelate to a level with fallible humanity; an insane band, stimulated by hunger and want, sought to annihilate all distinction of ranks. It was natural that a doctrine, which to the state showed itself only in its most unfavorable aspect, should not have been able to reconcile a monarch who had already so many reasons to extirpate it; and it is no wonder, therefore, that he employed against it the arms it had itself forced upon him.

Charles must already have looked upon himself as absolute in the Netherlands since he did not think it necessary to extend to these countries the religious liberty which he had accorded to Germany. While, compelled by the effectual resistance of the German princes, he assured to the former country a free exercise of the new religion, in the latter he published the most cruel edicts for its repression. By these the reading of the Evangelists and Apostles; all open or secret meetings to which religion gave its name in ever so slight a degree; all conversations on the subject, at home or at the table, were forbidden under severe penalties. In every province special courts of judicature were established to watch over the execution of the edicts. Whoever held these erroneous opinions was to forfeit his office without regard to his rank. Whoever should be convicted of diffusing heretical doctrines, or even of simply attending the secret meetings of the Reformers, was to be condemned to death, and if a male, to be executed by the sword, if a female, buried alive. Backsliding heretics were to be committed to the flames. Not even the recantation of the offender could annul these appalling sentences. Whoever abjured his errors gained nothing by his apostacy but at farthest a milder kind of death.

The fiefs of the condemned were also confiscated, contrary to the privileges of the nation, which permitted the heir to redeem them for a trifling fine; and in defiance of an express and valuable privilege of the citizens of Holland, by which they were not to be tried out of their province, culprits were conveyed beyond the limits of the native judicature, and condemned by foreign tribunals. Thus did religion guide the hand of despotism to attack with its sacred weapon, and without danger or opposition, the liberties which were inviolable to the secular arm.

Charles V., emboldened by the fortunate progress of his arms in Germany, thought that he might now venture on everything, and seriously meditated the introduction of the Spanish Inquisition in the Netherlands. But the terror of its very name alone reduced commerce in Antwerp to a standstill. The principal foreign merchants prepared to quit the city. All buying and selling ceased, the value of houses fell, the employment of artisans stopped. Money disappeared from the hands of the citizen. The ruin of that flourishing commercial city was inevitable had not Charles V. listened to the representations of the Duchess of Parma, and abandoned this perilous resolve. The tribunal, therefore, was ordered not to interfere with the foreign merchants, and the title of Inquisitor was changed unto the milder appellation of Spiritual Judge. But in the other provinces that tribunal proceeded to rage with the inhuman despotism which has ever been peculiar to it. It has been computed that during the reign of Charles V. fifty thousand persons perished by the hand of the executioner for religion alone.

When we glance at the violent proceedings of this monarch we are quite at a loss to comprehend what it was that kept the rebellion within bounds during his reign, which broke out with so much violence under his successor. A closer investigation will clear up this seeming anomaly. Charles's dreaded supremacy in Europe had raised the commerce of the Netherlands to a height which it had never before attained. The majesty of his name opened all harbors, cleared all seas for their vessels, and obtained for them the most favorable commercial treaties with foreign powers. Through him, in particular, they destroyed the dominion of the Hanse towns in the Baltic. Through him, also, the New World, Spain, Italy, Germany, which now shared with them a common ruler, were, in a measure, to be considered as provinces of their own country, and opened new channels for their commerce. He had, moreover, united the remaining six provinces with the hereditary states of Burgundy, and thus given to them an extent and political importance which placed them by the side of the first kingdoms of Europe.*

By all this he flattered the national pride of this people. Moreover, by the incorporation of Gueldres, Utrecht, Friesland, and Gröningen with these provinces, he put an end to the private wars which had so long disturbed their commerce; an unbroken internal peace now allowed them to enjoy the full fruits of their industry. Charles was therefore a benefactor of this people. At the same time, the splendor of his victories dazzled their eyes; the glory of their sovereign, which was reflected upon them also, had bribed their republican vigilance; while the awe-inspiring halo of invincibility which encircled the conqueror of Germany, France, Italy, and Africa terrified the factious. And then, who knows not on how much may venture the man, be he a private individual or a prince, who has succeeded in enchaining the admiration of his fellow-creatures! His repeated personal visits to these lands, which he, according to his own confession, visited as often as ten different times, kept the disaffected

---

* He had, too, at one time the intention of raising it to a kingdom; but the essential points of difference between the provinces, which extended from constitution and manners to measures and weights, soon made him abandon this design. More important was the service which he designed them in the Burgundian treaty, which settled its relation to the German empire. According to this treaty the seventeen provinces were to contribute to the common wants of the German empire twice as much as an electoral prince; in case of a Turkish war three times as much; in return for which, however, they were to enjoy the powerful protection of this empire, and not to be injured in any of their various privileges. The revolution, which under Charles' son altered the political constitution of the provinces, again annulled this compact, which, on account of the trifling advantage that it conferred, deserves no further notice.

within bounds; the constant exercise of severe and prompt justice maintained the awe of the royal power. Finally, Charles was born in the Netherlands, and loved the nation in whose lap he had grown up. Their manners pleased him, the simplicity of their character and social intercourse formed for him a pleasing recreation from the severe Spanish gravity. He spoke their language, and followed their customs in his private life. The burdensome ceremonies which form the unnatural barriers between king and people were banished from Brussels. No jealous foreigner debarred natives from access to their prince; their way to him was through their own countrymen, to whom he entrusted his person. He spoke much and courteously with them; his deportment was engaging, his discourse obliging. These simple artifices won for him their love, and while his armies trod down their cornfields, while his rapacious imposts diminished their property, while his governors oppressed, his executioners slaughtered, he secured their hearts by a friendly demeanor.

Gladly would Charles have seen this affection of the nation for himself descend upon his son. On this account he sent for him in his youth from Spain, and showed him in Brussels to his future subjects. On the solemn day of his abdication he recommended to him these lands as the richest jewel in his crown, and earnestly exhorted him to respect their laws and privileges.

Philip II. was in all the direct opposite of his father. As ambitious as Charles, but with less knowledge of men and of the rights of man, he had formed to himself a notion of royal authority which regarded men as simply the servile instruments of despotic will, and was outraged by every symptom of liberty. Born in Spain, and educated under the iron discipline of the monks, he demanded of others the same gloomy formality and reserve as marked his own character. The cheerful merriment of his Flemish subjects was as uncongenial to his disposition and temper as their privileges were offensive to his imperious will. He spoke no other language but the Spanish, endured none but Spaniards about his person, and obstinately adhered to all their customs. In vain did the loyal ingenuity of the Flemish towns through which he passed vie with each other in solemnizing his arrival with costly festivities.* Philip's eye remained dark; all the profusion of magnificence, all the loud and hearty effusions of the sincerest joy could not win from him one approving smile.

Charles entirely missed his aim by presenting his son to the Flemings. They might eventually have endured his yoke with less impatience if he had never set his foot in their land. But his look forewarned them what they had to expect; his entry into Brussels lost him all hearts. The Emperor's gracious affability with his people only served to throw a darker shade on the haughty gravity of his son. They read in his countenance the destructive purpose against their liberties which, even then, he already revolved in his breast. Forewarned to find in him a tyrant they were forearmed to resist him.

The throne of the Netherlands was the first which Charles V. abdicated. Before a solemn convention in Brussels he absolved the States-General of their oath, and transferred their allegiance to King Philip, his son. "If my death," addressing the latter, as he concluded, "had placed you in possession of these countries, even in that case so valuable a bequest would have given me great claims on your gratitude. But now that of my free will I transfer them to you, now that I die in order to hasten your enjoyment of them, I only require of you to pay to the people the increased obligation which the voluntary surrender of my dignity lays upon you. Other princes esteem it a peculiar felicity to bequeath to their children the crown which death is already ravishing from them. This happiness I am anxious to enjoy during my life. I wish to be a spectator of your reign. Few will follow my example, as few have preceded me in it. But this my deed will be praised if your future life should justify my expectations, if you continue to be guided by that wisdom which you have hitherto evinced, if you remain inviolably attached to the pure faith which is the main pillar of your throne. One thing more I have to

---

* The town of Antwerp alone expended on an occasion of this kind two hundred and sixty thousand gold florins.

add: may Heaven grant you also a son, to whom you may transmit your power by choice, and not by necessity."

After the Emperor had concluded his address Philip kneeled down before him, kissed his hand, and received his paternal blessing. His eyes for the last time were moistened with a tear. All present wept. It was an hour never to be forgotten.

This affecting farce was soon followed by another. Philip received the homage of the assembled states. He took the oath administered in the following words: "I, Philip, by the grace of God, Prince of Spain, of the two Sicilies, etc., do vow and swear that I will be a good and just lord in these countries, counties, and duchies, etc.; that I will well and truly hold, and cause to be held, the privileges and liberties of all the nobles, towns, commons, and subjects which have been conferred upon them by my predecessors, and also the customs, usages and rights which they now have and enjoy, jointly and severally, and, moreover, that I will do all that by law and right pertains to a good and just prince and lord, so help me God and all His Saints."

The alarm which the arbitrary government of the Emperor had inspired, and the distrust of his son, are already visible in the formula of this oath, which was drawn up in far more guarded and explicit terms than that which had been administered to Charles V. himself and all the Dukes in Burgundy. Philip, for instance, was compelled to swear to the maintenance of their customs and usages, what before his time had never been required. In the oath which the states took to him no other obedience was promised than such as should be consistent with the privileges of the country. His officers then were only to reckon on submission and support so long as they legally discharged the duties entrusted to them. Lastly, in this oath of allegiance, Philip is simply styled the natural, the hereditary prince, and not, as the Emperor had desired, sovereign or lord; proof enough how little confidence was placed in the justice and liberality of the new sovereign.

PHILIP II., RULER OF THE NETHERLANDS.

Philip II. received the lordship of the Netherlands in the brightest period of their prosperity. He was the first of their princes who united them all under his authority. They now consisted of seventeen provinces; the duchies of Brabant, Limburg, Luxembourg, and Gueldres, the seven counties of Artois, Hainault, Flanders, Namur, Zütphen, Holland, and Zealand, the margravate of Antwerp, and the five lordships of Friesland, Mechlin (Malines), Utrecht, Overyssel, and Gröningen, which, collectively, formed a great and powerful state able to contend with monarchies. Higher than it then stood their commerce could not rise. The sources of their wealth were above the earth's surface, but they were more valuable and inexhaustible and richer than all the mines in America. These seventeen provinces which, taken together, scarcely comprised the fifth part of Italy, and do not extend beyond three hundred Flemish miles, yielded an annual revenue to their lord, not much inferior to that which Britain formerly paid to its kings before the latter had annexed so many of the ecclesiastical domains to their crown. Three hundred and fifty cities, alive with industry and pleasure, many of them fortified by their natural position and secure without bulwarks or walls; six thousand three hundred market towns of a larger size; smaller villages, farms, and castles innumerable, imparted to this territory the aspect of one unbroken flourishing landscape. The nation had now reached the meridian of its splendor; industry and abundance had exalted the genius of the citizen, enlightened his ideas, ennobled his affections; every flower of the intellect had opened with the flourishing condition of the country. A happy temperament under a severe climate cooled the ardor of their blood, and moderated the rage of their passions; equanimity, moderation, and enduring patience, the gifts of a northern clime; integrity, justice, and faith, the necessary virtues of their profession; and the delightful fruits of liberty, truth, benevolence, and a patriotic pride were blended in their character, with a slight admixture of human frailties. No people on earth was more easily governed by a prudent prince, and none with more difficulty by a charlatan or a tyrant. Nowhere was the popular voice so infallible a test of good government as here. True statesmanship could be tried in no nobler school, and a sickly artificial policy had none worse to fear.

A state constituted like this could act and endure with gigantic energy whenever pressing emergencies called forth its powers and a skilful and provident administration elicited its resources. Charles V. bequeathed to his successor an authority in these provinces little inferior to that of a limited monarchy. The prerogative of the crown had gained a visible ascendancy over the republican spirit, and that complicated machine could now be set in motion, almost as certainly and rapidly as the most absolutely governed nation. The numerous nobility, formerly so powerful, cheerfully accompanied their sovereign in his wars, or, on the civil changes of the state, courted the approving smile of royalty. The crafty policy of the crown had created a new and imaginary good, of which it was the exclusive dispenser. New passions and new ideas of happiness supplanted at last the rude simplicity of republican virtue. Pride gave place to vanity, true liberty to titles of honor, a needy independence to a luxurious servitude. To oppress or to plunder their native land as the absolute satraps of an absolute lord was a more powerful allurement for the avarice and ambition of the great, than in the general assembly of the state to share with the monarch a hundredth part of the supreme power. A large portion, moreover, of the nobility were deeply sunk in poverty and debt. Charles V. had crippled all the most dangerous vassals of the crown by expensive embassies to foreign courts, under the specious pretext of honorary distinctions. Thus, William of Orange was despatched to Germany with the imperial crown, and Count Egmont to conclude the marriage contract between Philip and Queen Mary. Both also afterwards accompanied the Duke of Alva to France to negotiate the peace between the two crowns, and the new alliance of their sovereign with Madame Elizabeth. The expenses of these journeys amounted to three hundred thousand florins, towards which the king did not contribute a single penny. When the Prince of Orange was appointed generalissimo in the place of the Duke of Savoy he was obliged to defray all the necessary expenses of his office. When foreign ambassadors or princes came to Brussels it was made incumbent on the nobles to maintain the honor of their king, who himself always dined alone, and never kept open table. Spanish policy had devised a still more ingenious contrivance gradually to impoverish the richest families of the land. Every year one of the Castilian nobles made his appearance in Brussels, where he displayed a lavish magnificence. In Brussels it was accounted an indelible disgrace to be distanced by a stranger in such munificence. All vied to surpass him, and exhausted their fortunes in this costly emulation, while the Spaniard made a timely retreat to his native country, and by the frugality of four years repaired the extravagance of one year. It was the foible of the Netherlandish nobility to contest with every stranger the credit of superior wealth, and of this weakness the government studiously availed itself. Certainly these arts did not in the sequel produce the exact result that had been calculated on; for these pecuniary burdens only made the nobility the more disposed for innovation, since he who has lost all can only be a gainer in the general ruin.

The Roman Church had ever been a main support of the royal power, and it was only natural that it should be so. Its golden time was the bondage of the human intellect, and, like royalty, it had gained by the ignorance and weakness of men. Civil oppression made religion more necessary and more dear; submission to tyrannical power prepares the mind for a blind, convenient faith, and the hierarchy repaid with usury the services of despotism. In the provinces the bishops and prelates were zealous supporters of royalty, and ever ready to sacrifice the welfare of the citizen to the temporal advancement of the church and the political interests of the sovereign.

Numerous and brave garrisons also held the cities in awe, which were at the same time divided by religious squabbles and factions, and consequently deprived of their strongest support — union among themselves. How little, therefore, did it require to insure this preponderance of Philip's power, and how fatal must have been the folly by which it was lost.

But Philip's authority in these provinces, however great, did not surpass the influence which the Spanish monarchy at that time enjoyed throughout Europe. No state ventured to enter the arena of contest with it. France, its most dangerous neighbor, weakened by a destructive war, and still more by internal factions, which boldly raised their heads during the feeble government of a child, was advancing rapidly to that unhappy condition which, for nearly half a century, made it a theatre of the most enormous crimes and the most fearful calamities. In England Elizabeth could with difficulty protect her still tottering throne against the furious storms of faction, and her new church establishment against the insidious arts of the Romanists. That country still awaited her mighty call before it could emerge from a humble obscurity, and had not yet been awakened by the faulty policy of her rival to that vigor and energy with which it finally overthrew him. The imperial family of Germany was united with that of Spain by the double ties of blood and political interest; and the victorious progress of Soliman drew its attention more to the east than to the west of Europe. Gratitude and fear secured to Philip the Italian princes, and his creatures ruled the Conclave. The monarchies of the North still lay in barbarous darkness and obscurity, or only just began to acquire form and strength, and were as yet unrecognized in the political system of Europe. The most skilful generals, numerous armies accustomed to victory, a formidable marine, and the golden tribute from the West Indies, which now first began to come in regularly and certainly — what terrible instruments were these in the firm and steady hand of a talented prince! Under such auspicious stars did King Philip commence his reign.

Before we see him act we must first look hastily into the deep recesses of his soul, and we shall there find a key to his political life. Joy and benevolence were wholly wanting in the composition of his character. His temperament, and the gloomy years of his early childhood, denied him the former; the latter could not be imparted to him by men who had renounced the sweetest and most powerful of the social ties. Two ideas, his own self and what was above that self, engrossed his narrow and contracted mind. Egotism and religion were the contents and the title-page of the history of his whole life. He was a king and a Christian, and was bad in both characters; he never was a man among men, because he never condescended but only ascended. His belief was dark and cruel; for his divinity was a being of terror, from whom he had nothing to hope but everything to fear. To the ordinary man the divinity appears as a comforter, as a Saviour; before his mind it was set up as an image of fear, a painful, humiliating check to his human omnipotence. His veneration for this being was so much the more profound and deeply rooted the less it extended to other objects. He trembled servilely before God because God was the only being before whom he had to tremble. Charles V. was zealous for religion because religion promoted his objects. Philip was so because he had real faith in it. The former let loose the fire and the sword upon thousands for the sake of a dogma, while he himself, in the person of the pope, his captive, derided the very doctrine for which he had sacrificed so much human blood. It was only with repugnance and scruples of conscience that Philip resolved on the most just war against the pope, and resigned all the fruits of his victory as a penitent malefactor surrenders his booty. The Emperor was cruel from calculation, his son from impulse. The first possessed a strong and enlightened spirit, and was, perhaps, so much the worse as a man; the second was narrow-minded and weak, but the more upright.

Both, however, as it appears to me, might have been better men than they actually were, and still, on the whole, have acted on the very same principles. What we lay to the charge of personal character of an individual is very often the infirmity, the necessary imperfection of universal human nature. A monarchy so great and so powerful was too great a trial for human pride, and too mighty a charge for human power. To combine universal happiness with the highest liberty of the individual is the sole prerogative of infinite intelligence, which diffuses itself omnipresently over all. But what resource has man when placed in the position of omnipotence? Man can only aid his circumscribed powers by classification; like the naturalist, he establishes certain marks and rules by which to facilitate his own feeble survey of the whole, to which all individualities must conform. All this is accomplished for him by religion. She finds hope and fear planted in every human breast; by making herself mistress of these emotions, and directing their affections to a single object, she virtually transforms millions of independent beings into one uniform abstract. The endless diversity of the human will no longer embarrasses its ruler—now there exists one universal good, one universal evil, which he can bring forward or withdraw at pleasure, and which works in unison with himself even when absent. Now a boundary is established before which liberty must halt; a venerable, hallowed line, towards which all the various conflicting inclinations of the will must finally converge. The common aim of despotism and of priestcraft is uniformity, and uniformity is a necessary expedient of human poverty and imperfection. Philip became a greater despot than his father because his mind was more contracted, or, in other words, he was forced to adhere the more scrupulously to general rules the less capable he was of descending to special and individual exceptions. What conclusion could we draw from these principles but that Philip II. could not possibly have any higher object of his solicitude than uniformity, both in religion and in laws, because without these he could not reign?

And yet he would have shown more mildness and forbearance in his government if he had entered upon it earlier. In the judgment which is usually formed of this prince one circumstance does not appear to be sufficiently considered in the history of his mind and heart, which, however, in all fairness, ought to be duly weighed. Philip counted nearly thirty years when he ascended the Spanish throne, and the early maturity of his understanding had anticipated the period of his majority. A mind like his, conscious of its powers, and only too early acquainted with his high expectations, could not brook the yoke of childish subjection in which he stood; the superior genius of the father, and the absolute authority of the autocrat, must have weighed heavily on the self-satisfied pride of such a son. The share which the former allowed him in the government of the empire was just important enough to disengage his mind from petty passions and to confirm the austere gravity of his character, but also meagre enough to kindle a fiercer longing for unlimited power. When he actually became possessed of uncontrolled authority it had lost the charm of novelty. The sweet intoxication of a young monarch in the sudden and early possession of supreme power; that joyous tumult of emotions which opens the soul to every softer sentiment, and to which humanity has owed so many of the most valuable and the most prized of its institutions; this pleasing moment had for him long passed by, or had never existed. His character was already hardened when fortune put him to this severe test, and his settled principles withstood the collision of occasonal emotion. He had had time, during fifteen years, to prepare himself for the change; and instead of youthful dallying with the external symbols of his new station, or of losing the morning of his government in the intoxication of an idle vanity, he remained composed and serious enough to enter at once on the full possession of his power so as to revenge himself through the most extensive employment of it for its having been so long withheld from him.

THE TRIBUNAL OF THE INQUISITION.

Philip II. no sooner saw himself, through the peace of Chateau-Cambray, in undisturbed enjoyment of his immense territory than he turned his whole attention to the great work of purifying religion, and verified the fears of his Netherlandish subjects. The ordinances which his father had caused to be promulgated against heretics were renewed in all their rigor, and terrible tribunals, to whom nothing but the name of inquisition was wanting, were appointed to watch over their execution. But his plan appeared to him scarcely more than half-fulfilled so long as he could not transplant into these countries the Spanish Inquisition in its perfect form — a design in which the Emperor had already suffered shipwreck.

The Spanish Inquisition is an institution of a new and peculiar kind, which finds no prototype in the whole course of time, and admits of comparison with no ecclesiastical or civil tribunal. Inquisition had existed from the time when reason meddled with what is holy, and from the very commencement of scepticism and innovation; but it was in the middle of the thirteenth century, after some examples of apostasy had alarmed the hierarchy, that Innocent III. first erected for it a peculiar tribunal, and separated, in an unnatural manner, ecclesiastical superintendence and instruction from its judicial and retributive office. In order to be the more sure that no human sensibilities or natural tenderness should thwart the stern severity of its statutes, he took it out of the hands of the bishops and secular clergy, who, by the ties of civil life, were still too much attached to humanity for his purpose, and consigned it to those of the monks, a half-denaturalized race of beings who had abjured the sacred feelings of nature, and were the servile tools of the Roman See. The Inquisition was received in Germany, Italy, Spain, Portugal, and France; a Franciscan monk sat as judge in the terrible court, which passed sentence on the Templars. A few states succeeded either in totally excluding or else in subjecting it to civil authority. The Netherlands had remained free from it until the government of Charles V.; their bishops exercised the spiritual censorship, and in extraordinary cases reference was made to foreign courts of inquisition; by the French provinces to that of Paris, by the Germans to that of Cologne.

But the Inquisition which we are here speaking of came from the west of Europe, and was of a different origin and form. The last Moorish throne in Granada had fallen in the fifteenth century, and the false faith of the Saracens had finally succumbed before the fortunes of Christianity. But the gospel was still new, and but imperfectly established in this youngest of Christian kingdoms, and in the confused mixture of heterogeneous laws and manners the religions had become mixed. It is true the sword of persecution had driven many thousand families to Africa, but a far larger portion, detained by the love of climate and home, purchased remission from this dreadful necessity by a show of conversion, and continued at Christian altars to serve Mohammed and Moses. So long as prayers were offered towards Mecca, Granada was not subdued; so long as the new Christian, in the retirement of his house, became again a Jew or a Moslem, he was as little secured to the throne as to the Romish See. It was no longer deemed sufficient to compel a perverse people to adopt the exterior forms of a new faith, or to wed it to the victorious church by the weak bands of ceremonials; the object now was to extirpate the roots of an old religion, and to subdue an obstinate bias which, by the slow operation of centuries, had been implanted in their manners, their language, and their laws, and by the enduring influence of a paternal soil and sky was still maintained in its full extent and vigor.

If the church wished to triumph completely over the opposing worship, and to secure her new conquest beyond all chance of relapse, it was indispensable that she should undermine the foundation itself on which the old religion was built. It was necessary to break to pieces the entire form of moral character to which it was so closely and intimately attached. It was requisite to loosen its secret roots from the hold they had taken in the innermost depths of the soul; to extinguish all traces of it, both in domestic life and in the civil world; to cause all recollection of it to perish; and, if possible, to destroy the very susceptibility for its impressions. Country and family, conscience and honor, the sacred feelings of society and of nature, are ever the first and immediate ties to which religion attaches itself; from these it derives while it imparts strength. This connection was now to be dissolved; the old religion was violently to be dissevered from the holy feelings of nature, even at the expense of the sanctity itself of these emotions. Thus arose that Inquisition which, to distinguish it from the more humane tribunals of the same name, we usually call the Spanish. Its founder was Cardinal Ximenes, a Dominican monk.

Torquemada was the first who ascended its bloody throne, who established its statutes, and forever cursed his order with this bequest. Sworn to the degradation of the understanding and the murder of intellect, the instruments it employed were terror and infamy. Every evil passion was in its pay; its snare was set in every joy of life. Solitude itself was not safe from it; the fear of its omnipresence fettered the freedom of the soul in its inmost and deepest recesses. It prostrated all the instincts of human nature before it yielded all the ties which otherwise man held most sacred. A heretic forfeited all claims upon his race; the most trivial infidelity to his mother church divested him of the rights of his nature. A modest doubt in the infallibility of the pope met with the punishment of parricide and the infamy of sodomy; its sentences resembled the frightful corruption of the plague, which turns the most healthy body into rapid putrefaction. Even the inanimate things belonging to a heretic were accursed. No destiny could snatch the victim of the Inquisition from its sentence. Its decrees were carried in force on corpses and on pictures, and the grave itself was no asylum from its tremendous arm. The presumptuous arrogance of its decrees could only be surpassed by the inhumanity which executed them. By coupling the ludicrous with the terrible, and by amusing the eye with the strangeness of its processions, it weakened compassion by the gratification of another feeling; it drowned sympathy in derision and contempt. The delinquent was conducted with solemn pomp to the place of execution, a blood-red flag was displayed before him, the universal clang of all the bells accompanied the procession. First came the priests, in the robes of the Mass and singing a sacred hymn; next followed the condemned sinner, clothed in a yellow vest, covered with figures of black devils. On his head he wore a paper cap, surmounted by a human figure, around which played lambent flames of fire, and ghastly demons flitted. The image of the crucified Saviour was carried before, but turned away from the eternally condemned sinner, for whom salvation was no longer available. His mortal body belonged to the material fire, his immortal soul to the flames of hell. A gag closed his mouth, and prevented him from alleviating his pain by lamentations, from awakening compassion by his affecting tale, and from divulging the secrets of the holy tribunal. He was followed by the clergy in festive robes, by the magistrates, and the nobility; the fathers who had been his judges closed the awful procession. It seemed like a solemn funeral procession, but on looking for the corpse on its way to the grave, behold! it was a living body whose groans are now to afford such shuddering entertainment to the people. The executions were generally held on the high festivals, for which a number of such unfortunate sufferers were reserved in the prisons of the holy house, in order to enhance the rejoicing by the multitude of the victims, and on these occasions the king himself was usually present. He sat with uncovered head, on a lower chair than that of the Grand Inquisitor, to whom, on such occasions, he yielded precedence; who, then, would not tremble before a tribunal at which majesty must humble itself?

The great revolution in the church accomplished by Luther and Calvin renewed the causes to which this tribunal owed its first origin; and that which, at its commencement, was invented to clear the petty kingdom of Granada from the feeble remnant of Saracens and Jews was now required for the whole of Christendom. All the Inquisitions in Portugal, Italy, Germany, and France adopted the form of the Spanish; it followed Europeans to the Indies, and established in Goa a fearful tribunal, whose inhuman proceedings make us shudder even at the bare recital. Wherever it planted its foot devastation followed; but in no part of the world did it rage so violently as in Spain. The victims are forgotten whom it immolated; the human race renews itself, and the lands, too, flourish again which it has devastated and depopulated by its fury; but centuries will elapse before its traces disappear from the Spanish character. A generous and enlightened nation has been stopped by it on its road to perfection; it has banished genius from a region where it was indigenous, and a stillness like that which hangs over the grave has been left in the mind of a people who, beyond most others of our world, were framed for happiness and enjoyment.

The first Inquisitor in Brabant was appointed by Charles V. in the year 1522. Some priests were associated with him as coadjutors; but he himself was a layman. After the death of Adrian VI., his successor, Clement VII., appointed three Inquisitors for all the Netherlands; and Paul III. again reduced them to two, which number continued until the commencement of the troubles. In the year 1530, with the aid and approbation of the states, the edicts against heretics were promulgated, which formed the foundation of all that followed, and in which, also, express mention is made of the Inquisition. In the year 1550, in consequence of the rapid increase of sects, Charles V. was under the necessity of reviving and enforcing these edicts, and it was on this occasion that the town of Antwerp opposed the establishment of the Inquisition, and obtained an exemption from its jurisdiction. But the spirit of the Inquisition in the Netherlands, in accordance with the genius of the country, was more humane than in Spain, and as yet had never been administered by a foreigner, much less by a Dominican. The edicts which were known to everybody served it as the rule of its decisions. On this very account it was less obnoxious; because, however severe its sentence, it did not appear a tool of arbitrary power, and it did not, like the Spanish Inquisition, veil itself in secrecy.

Philip, however, was desirous of introducing the latter tribunal into the Netherlands, since it appeared to him the instrument best adapted to destroy the spirit of this people, and to prepare them for a despotic government. He began, therefore, by increasing the rigor of the religious ordinances of his father; by gradually extending the power of the inquisitors; by making the proceedings more arbitrary, and more independent of the civil jurisdiction. The tribunal soon wanted little more than the name and the Dominicans to resemble in every point the Spanish Inquisition. Bare suspicion was enough to snatch a citizen from the bosom of public tranquillity, and from his domestic circle; and the weakest evidence was a sufficient justification for the use of the rack. Whoever fell into its abyss returned no more to the world. All the benefits of the laws ceased for him; the maternal care of justice no longer noticed him; beyond the pale of his former world malice and stupidity judged him according to laws which were never intended for man. The delinquent never knew his accuser, and very seldom his crime, — a flagitious, devilish artifice which constrained the unhappy victim to guess at his error, and in the delirium of the rack, or in the weariness of a long living interment, to acknowledge transgressions which, perhaps, had never been committed, or at least had never come to the knowledge of his judges. The goods of the condemned were confiscated, and the informer encouraged by letters of grace and rewards. No privilege, no civil jurisdiction was valid against the holy power; the secular arm lost forever all whom that power had once touched. Its only share in the judicial duties of the latter was to execute its sentences with humble submissiveness. The consequences of such an institution were, of necessity, unnatural and horrible; the whole temporal happiness, the life itself, of an innocent man was at the mercy of any worthless fellow. Every secret enemy, every envious person, had now the perilous temptation of an unseen and unfailing revenge. The security of property, the sincerity of intercourse were gone; all the ties of interest were dissolved; all of blood and of affection were irreparably broken. An infectious distrust envenomed social life; the dreaded presence of a spy terrified the eye from seeing, and choked the voice in the midst of utterance. No one believed in the existence of an honest man, or passed for one himself. Good name, the ties of country, brotherhood, even oaths, and all that man holds sacred, were fallen in estimation. Such was the destiny to which a great and flourishing commercial town was subjected, where one hundred thousand industrious men had been brought together by the single tie of mutual confidence, — every one indispensable to his neighbor, yet every one distrusted and distrustful, — all attracted by the spirit of gain, and repelled from each other by fear, — all the props of society torn away, where social union was the basis of all life and all existence.

OTHER ENCROACHMENTS ON THE CONSTITUTION OF THE NETHERLANDS.

No wonder if so unnatural a tribunal, which had proved intolerable even to the more submissive spirit of the Spaniard, drove a free state to rebellion. But the terror which it inspired was increased by the Spanish troops, which, even after the restoration of peace, were kept in the country, and, in violation of the constitution, garrisoned border towns. Charles V. had been forgiven for this introduction of foreign troops so long as the necessity of it was evident, and his good intentions were less distrusted. But now men saw in these troops only the alarming preparations of oppression and the instruments of a detested hierarchy. Moreover, a considerable body of cavalry, composed of natives, and fully adequate for the protection of the country, made these foreigners superfluous. The licentiousness and rapacity, too, of the Spaniards, whose pay was long in arrear, and who indemnified themselves at the expense of the citizens, completed the exasperation of the people, and drove the lower orders to despair. Subsequently, when the general murmur induced the government to move them from the frontiers and transport them into the islands of Zealand, where ships were prepared for their deportation, their excesses were carried to such a pitch that the inhabitants left off working at the embankments, and preferred to abandon their native country to the fury of the sea rather than to submit any longer to the wanton brutality of these lawless bands.

Philip, indeed, would have wished to retain these Spaniards in the country, in order by their presence to give weight to his edicts, and to support the innovations which he had resolved to make in the constitution of the Netherlands. He regarded them as a guarantee for the submission of the nation and as a chain by which he held it captive. Accordingly, he left no expedient untried to evade the persevering importunity of the states, who demanded the withdrawal of these troops; and for this end he exhausted all the resources of chicanery and persuasion. At one time he pretended to dread a sudden invasion by France, although, torn by furious factions, that country could scarce support itself against a domestic enemy; at another time they were, he said, to receive his son, Don Carlos, on the frontiers; whom, however, he never intended should leave Castile. Their maintenance should not be a burden to the nation; he himself would disburse all their expenses from his private purse. In order to detain them with the more appearance of reason he purposely kept back from them their arrears of pay; for otherwise he would assuredly have preferred them to the troops of the country, whose demands he fully satisfied. To lull the fears of the nation, and to appease the general discontent, he offered the chief command of these troops to the two favorites of the people, the Prince of Orange and Count Egmont. Both, however, declined his offer, with the noble-minded declaration that they could never make up their minds to serve contrary to the laws of the country. The more desire the king showed to have his Spaniards in the country the more obstinately the states insisted on their removal. In the following Diet at Ghent he was compelled, in the very midst of his courtiers, to listen to republican truth. "Why are foreign hands needed for our defence?" demanded the Syndic of Ghent. "Is it that the rest of the world should consider us too stupid, or too cowardly, to protect ourselves? Why have we made peace if the burdens of war are still to oppress us? In war necessity enforced endurance; in peace our patience is exhausted by its burdens. Or shall we be able to keep in order these licentious bands which thine own presence could not restrain? Here, Cambray and Antwerp cry for redress; there, Thionville and Marienburg lie waste; and, surely, thou hast not bestowed upon us peace that our cities should become deserts, as they necessarily must if thou freest them not from these destroyers? Perhaps thou art anxious to guard against surprise from our neighbors? This precaution is wise; but the report of their preparations will long outrun their hostilities. Why incur a heavy expense to engage foreigners who will not care for a country which they must leave to-morrow? Hast thou not still at thy command the same brave Netherlanders to whom thy father entrusted the republic in far more troubled times? Why shouldest thou now doubt their loyalty, which, to thy ancestors, they have preserved for so many centuries inviolate? Will not they be sufficient to sustain the war long enough to give time to thy confederates to join their banners, or to thyself to send succor from the neighboring country? This language was too new to the king, and its truth too obvious for him to be able at once to reply to it. "I, also, am a foreigner," he at length exclaimed, "and they would like, I suppose, to expel me from the country!" At the same time he descended from the throne, and left the assembly; but the speaker was pardoned for his boldness. Two days afterwards he sent a message to the states that if he had been apprised earlier that these troops were a burden to them he would have immediately made preparation to remove them with himself to Spain. Now it was too late, for they would not depart unpaid; but he pledged them his most sacred promise that they should not be oppressed with this burden more than four months. Nevertheless, the troops remained in this country eighteen months instead of four; and would not, perhaps, even then have left it so soon if the exigencies of the state had not made their presence indispensable in another part of the world.

The illegal appointment of foreigners to the most important offices of the country afforded further occasion of complaint against the government. Of all the privileges of the provinces none was so obnoxious to the Spaniards as that which excluded strangers from office, and none they had so zealously sought to abrogate. Italy, the two Indies, and all the provinces of this vast Empire, were indeed open to their rapacity and ambition; but from the richest of them all an inexorable fundamental law excluded them. They artfully persuaded their sovereign that his power in these countries would never be firmly established so long as he could not employ foreigners as his instruments. The Bishop of Arras, a Burgundian by birth, had already been illegally forced upon the Flemings; and now the Count of Feria, a Castilian, was to receive a seat and voice in the council of state. But this attempt met with a bolder resistance than the king's flatterers had led him to expect, and his despotic omnipotence was this time wrecked by the politic measures of William of Orange and the firmness of the states.

WILLIAM OF ORANGE AND COUNT EGMONT.

By such measures, did Philip usher in his government of the Netherlands, and such were the grievances of the nation when he was preparing to leave them. He had long been impatient to quit a country where he was a stranger, where there was so much that opposed his secret wishes, and where his despotic mind found such undaunted monitors to remind him of the laws of freedom. The peace with France at last rendered a longer stay unnecessary; the armaments of Soliman required his presence in the south, and the Spaniards also began to miss their long-absent king. The choice of a supreme Stadtholder for the Netherlands was the principal matter which still detained him. Emanuel Philibert, Duke of Savoy, had filled this place since the resignation of Mary, Queen of Hungary, which, however, so long as the king himself was present, conferred more honor than real influence. His absence would make it the most important office in the monarchy, and the most splendid aim for the ambition of a subject. It had now become vacant through the departure of the duke, whom the peace of Chateau-Cambray had restored to his dominions. The almost unlimited power with which the supreme Statholder would be entrusted, the capacity and experience which so extensive and delicate an appointment required, but, especially, the daring designs which the government had in contemplation against the freedom of the country, the execution of which would devolve on him, necessarily embarrassed the choice. The law, which excluded all foreigners from office, made an exception in the case of the supreme Stadtholder. As he could not be at the same time a native of all the provinces, it was allowable for him not to belong to any one of them; for the jealousy of the man of Brabant would concede no greater right to a Fleming, whose home was half a mile from his frontier, than to a Sicilian, who lived in another soil and under a different sky. But here the interests of the crown itself seemed to favor the appointment of a native. A Brabanter, for instance, who enjoyed the full confidence of his countrymen if he were a traitor would have half accomplished his treason before a foreign governor could have overcome the mistrust with which his most insignificant measures would be watched. If the government should succeed in carrying through its designs in one province, the opposition of the rest would then be a temerity, which it would be justified in punishing in the severest manner. In the common whole which the provinces now formed their individual constitutions were, in a measure, destroyed; the obedience of one would be a law for all, and the privilege, which one knew not how to preserve, was lost for the rest.

Among the Flemish nobles who could lay claim to the Chief Stadtholdership, the expectations and wishes of the nation were divided between Count Egmont and the Prince of Orange, who were alike qualified for this high dignity by illustrious birth and personal merits, and by an equal share in the affections of the people. Their high rank placed them both near to the throne, and if the choice of the monarch was to rest on the worthiest it must necessarily fall upon one of these two. As, in the course of our history, we shall often have occasion to mention both names, the reader cannot be too early made acquainted with their characters.

William I., Prince of Orange, was descended from the princely German house of Nassau, which had already flourished eight centuries, had long disputed the preeminence with Austria, and had given one Emperor to Germany. Besides several extensive domains in the Netherlands, which made him a citizen of this republic and a vassal of the Spanish monarchy, he possessed also in France the independent princedom of Orange. William was born in the year 1533, at Dillenburg, in the country of Nassau, of a Countess Stolberg. His father, the Count of Nassau, of the same name, had embraced the Protestant religion, and caused his son also to be educated in it; but Charles V., who early formed an attachment for the boy, took him when quite young to his court, and had him brought up in the Romish church. This monarch, who already in the child discovered the future greatness of the man, kept him nine years about his person, thought him worthy of his personal instruction in the affairs of government, and honored him with a confidence beyond his years. He alone was permitted to remain in the Emperor's presence when he gave audience to foreign ambassadors — a proof that, even as a boy, he had already begun to merit the surname of the Silent. The Emperor was not ashamed even to confess openly, on one occasion, that this young man had often made suggestions which would have escaped his own sagacity. What expectations might not be formed of the intellect of a man who was disciplined in such a school.

William was twenty-three years old when Charles abdicated the government, and had already received from the latter two public marks of the highest esteem. The Emperor had entrusted to him, in preference to all the nobles of his court, the honorable office of conveying to his brother Ferdinand the imperial crown. When the Duke of Savoy, who commanded the imperial army in the Netherlands, was called away to Italy by the exigency of his domestic affairs, the Emperor appointed him commander-in-chief against the united representations of his military council, who declared it altogether hazardous to oppose so young a tyro in arms to the experienced generals of France. Absent, and unrecommended by any, he was preferred by the monarch to the laurel-crowned band of his heroes, and the result gave him no cause to repent of his choice.

The marked favor which the prince had enjoyed with the father was in itself a sufficient ground for his exclusion from the confidence of the son. Philip, it appears, had laid it down for himself as a rule to avenge the wrongs of the Spanish nobility for the preference which Charles V. had on all important occasions shown to his Flemish nobles. Still stronger, however, were the secret motives which alienated him from the prince. William of Orange was one of those lean and pale men who, according to Cæsar's words, "sleep not at night, and think too much," and before whom the most fearless spirits quail. The calm tranquillity of a never-varying countenance concealed a busy, ardent soul, which never ruffled even the veil behind which it worked, and was alike inaccessible to artifice and love; a versatile, formidable, indefatigable mind, soft, and ductile enough to be instantaneously moulded into all forms; guarded enough to lose itself in none; and strong enough to endure every vicissitude of fortune. A greater master in reading and in winning men's hearts never existed than William. Not that, after the fashion of courts, his lips avowed a servility to which his proud heart gave the lie; but because he was neither too sparing nor too lavish of the marks of his esteem, and through a skilful economy of the favors which mostly bind men, he increased his real stock in them. The fruits of his meditation were as perfect as they were slowly formed; his resolves were as steadily and indomitably accomplished as they were long in maturing. No obstacles could defeat the plan which he had once adopted as the best; no accidents frustrated it, for they all had been foreseen before they actually occurred. High as his feelings were raised above terror and joy, they were, nevertheless, subject in the same degree to fear; but his fear was earlier than the danger, and he was calm in tumult because he had trembled in repose. William lavished his gold with a profuse hand, but he was a niggard of his movements. The hours of repast were the sole hours of relaxation, but these were exclusively devoted to his heart, his family, and his friends; this the modest deduction he allowed himself from the cares of his country. Here his brow was cleared with wine, seasoned by temperance and a cheerful disposition; and no serious cares were permitted to enter this recess of enjoyment. His household was magnificent; the splendor of a numerous retinue, the number and respectability of those who surrounded his person, made his habitation resemble the court of a sovereign prince. A sumptuous hospitality, that master-spell of demagogues, was the goddess of his palace. Foreign princes and ambassadors found here a fitting reception and entertainment, which surpassed all that luxurious Belgium could elsewhere offer. A humble submissiveness to the government bought off the blame and suspicion which this munificence might have thrown on his intentions. But this liberality secured for him the affections of the people, whom nothing gratified so much as to see the riches of their country displayed before admiring foreigners, and the high pinnacle of fortune on which he stood enhanced the value of the courtesy to which he condescended. No one, probably, was better fitted by nature for the leader of a conspiracy than William the Silent. A comprehensive and intuitive glance into the past, the present, and the future; the talent for improving every favorable opportunity; a commanding influence over the minds of men, vast schemes which only when viewed from a distance show form and symmetry; and bold calculations which were wound up in the long chain of futurity; all these faculties he possessed, and kept, moreover, under the control of that free and enlightened virtue which moves with firm step even on the very edge of the abyss.

A man like this might at other times have remained unfathomed by his whole generation; but not so by the distrustful spirit of the age in which he lived. Philip II. saw quickly and deeply into a character which, among good ones, most resembled his own. If he had not seen through him so clearly his distrust of a man, in whom were united nearly all the qualities which he prized highest and could best appreciate, would be quite inexplicable. But William had another and still more important point of contact with Philip II. He had learned his policy from the same master, and had become, it was to be feared, a more apt scholar. Not by making Machiavelli's '*Prince*' his study, but by having enjoyed the living instruction of a monarch who reduced the book to practice, had he become versed in the perilous arts by which thrones rise and fall. In him Philip had to deal with an antagonist who was armed against his policy, and who in a good cause could also command the resources of a bad one. And it was exactly this last circumstance which accounts for his having hated this man so implacably above all others of his day, and his having had so supernatural a dread of him.

The suspicion which already attached to the prince was increased by the doubts which were entertained of his religious bias. So long as the Emperor, his benefactor, lived, William believed in the pope; but it was feared, with good ground, that the predilection for the reformed religion, which had been imparted into his young heart, had never entirely left it. Whatever church he may at certain periods of his life have preferred each might console itself with the reflection that none other possessed him more entirely. In later years he went over to Calvinism with almost as little scruple as in his early childhood he deserted the Lutheran profession for the Romish. He defended the rights of the Protestants rather than their opinions against Spanish oppression; not their faith, but their wrongs, had made him their brother.

These general grounds for suspicion appeared to be justified by a discovery of his real intentions which accident had made. William had remained in France as hostage for the peace of Chateau-Cambray, in concluding which he had borne a part; and here, through the imprudence of Henry II., who imagined he spoke with a confidant of the King of Spain, he became acquainted with a secret plot which the French and Spanish courts had formed against Protestants of both kingdoms. The prince hastened to communicate this important discovery to his friends in Brussels, whom it so nearly concerned, and the letters which he exchanged on the subject fell, unfortunately, into the hands of the King of Spain. Philip was less surprised at this decisive disclosure of William's sentiments than incensed at the disappointment of his scheme; and the Spanish nobles, who had never forgiven the prince that moment, when in the last act of his life the greatest of Emperors leaned upon his shoulders, did not neglect this favorable opportunity of finally ruining, in the good opinion of their king, the betrayer of a state secret.

Of a lineage no less noble than that of William was Lamoral, Count Egmont and Prince of Gavre, a descendant of the Dukes of Gueldres, whose martial courage had wearied out the arms of Austria. His family was highly distinguished in the annals of the country; one of his ancestors, had, under Maximilian, already filled the office of Stadtholder over Holland. Egmont's marriage with the Duchess Sabina of Bavaria reflected additional lustre on the splendor of his birth, and made him powerful through the greatness of this alliance. Charles V. had, in the year 1516, conferred on him at Utrecht the order of the Golden Fleece; the wars of this Emperor were the school of his military genius, and the battle of St. Quentin and Gravelines made him the hero of his age. Every blessing of peace, for which a commercial people feel most grateful, brought to mind the remembrance of the victory by which it was accelerated, and Flemish pride, like a fond mother, exulted over the illustrious son of their country, who had filled all Europe with admiration. Nine children who grew up under the eyes of their fellow-citizens, multiplied and drew closer the ties between him and his fatherland, and the people's grateful affection for the father was kept alive by the sight of those who were dearest to him. Every appearance of Egmont in public was a triumphal procession; every eye which was fastened upon him recounted his history; his deeds lived in the plaudits of his companions-in-arms; at the games of chivalry mothers pointed him out to their children. Affability, a noble and courteous demeanor, the amiable virtues of chivalry, adorned and graced his merits. His liberal soul shone forth on his open brow; his frank-heartedness managed his secrets no better than his benevolence did his estate, and a thought was no sooner his than it was the property of all. His religion was gentle and humane, but not very enlightened, because it derived its light from the heart and not from his understanding. Egmont possessed more of conscience than of fixed principles; his head had not given him a code of its own, but had merely learnt it by rote; the mere name of any action, therefore, was often with him sufficient for its condemnation. In his judgment men were wholly bad or wholly good, and had not something bad or something good; in this system of morals there was no middle term between vice and virtue; and consequently a single good trait often decided his opinion of men. Egmont united all the eminent qualities which form the hero; he was a better soldier than the Prince of Orange, but far inferior to him as a statesman; the latter saw the world as it really was; Egmont viewed it in the magic mirror of an imagination that embellished all that it reflected. Men, whom fortune has surprised with a reward for which they can find no adequate ground in their actions, are, for the most part, very apt to forget the necessary connection between cause and effect, and to insert in the natural consequences of things a higher miraculous power to which, as Cæsar to his fortune, they at last insanely trust. Such a character was Egmont. Intoxicated with the idea of his own merits, which the love and gratitude of his fellow-citizens had exaggerated, he staggered on in this sweet reverie as in a delightful world of dreams. He feared not, because he trusted to the deceitful pledge which destiny had given him of her favor, in the general love of the people; and he believed in its justice because he himself was prosperous. Even the most terrible experience of Spanish perfidy could not afterwards eradicate this confidence from his soul, and on the scaffold itself his latest feeling was hope. A tender fear for his family kept his patriotic courage fettered by lower duties. Because he trembled for property and life he could not venture much for the republic. William of Orange broke with the throne because its arbitrary power was offensive to his pride; Egmont was vain, and therefore valued the favors of the monarch. The former was a citizen of the world; Egmont had never been more than a Fleming.

Philip II. still stood indebted to the hero of St. Quentin, and the supreme stadtholdership of the Netherlands appeared the only appropriate reward for such great services. Birth and high station, the voice of the nation and personal abilities, spoke as loudly for Egmont as for Orange; and if the latter was to be passed by it seemed that the former alone could supplant him.

Two such competitors, so equal in merit, might have embarrassed Philip in his choice if he had ever seriously thought of selecting either of them for the appointment.

But the pre-eminent qualities by which they supported their claim to this office were the very cause of their rejection; and it was precisely the ardent desire of the nation for their election to it that irrevocably annulled their title to the appointment. Philip's purpose would not be answered by a stadtholder in the Netherlands who could command the good-will and the energies of the people. Egmont's descent from the Duke of Gueldres made him an hereditary foe of the house of Spain, and it seemed impolitic to place the supreme power in the hands of a man to whom the idea might occur of revenging on the son of the oppressor the oppression of his ancestor. The slight put on their favorites could give no just offence either to the nation or to themselves, for it might be pretended that the king passed over both because he would not show a preference to either.

The disappointment of his hopes of gaining the regency did not deprive the Prince of Orange of all expectation of establishing more firmly his influence in the Netherlands. Among the other candidates for this office was also Christina, Duchess of Lorraine, and aunt of the king, who, as mediatrix of the peace of Chateau-Cambray, had rendered important service to the crown. William aimed at the hand of her daughter, and he hoped to promote his suit by actively interposing his good offices for the mother; but he did not reflect that through this very intercession he ruined her cause. The Duchess Christina was rejected, not so much for the reason alleged, namely, the dependence of her territories on France made her an object of suspicion to the Spanish court, as because she was acceptable to the people of the Netherlands and the Prince of Orange.

MARGARET OF PARMA REGENT OF THE NETHERLANDS.

While the general expectation was on the stretch as to whom the future destines of the provinces would be committed, there appeared on the frontiers of the country the Duchess Margaret of Parma, having been summoned by the king from Italy to assume the government.

Margaret was a natural daughter of Charles V. and of a noble Flemish lady named Vangeest, and born in 1522.

Out of regard for the honor of her mother's house she was at first educated in obscurity; but her mother, who possessed more vanity than honor, was not very anxious to preserve the secret of her origin, and a princely education betrayed the daughter of the Emperor. While yet a child she was entrusted to the Regent Margaret, her great-aunt, to be brought up at Brussels under her eye. This guardian she lost in her eighth year, and the care of her education devolved on Queen Mary of Hungary, the successor of Margaret in the regency. Her father had already affianced her, while yet in her fourth year, to a Prince of Ferrara; but this alliance being subsequently dissolved, she was betrothed to Alexander de Medicis, the new Duke of Florence, which marriage was, after the victorious return of the Emperor from Africa, actually consummated in Naples. In the first year of this unfortunate union, a violent death removed from her a husband who could not love her, and for the third time her hand was disposed of to serve the policy of her father. Octavius Farnese, a prince of thirteen years of age and nephew of Paul III., obtained, with her person, the Duchies of Parma and Piacenza as her portion. Thus, by a strange destiny, Margaret at the age of maturity was contracted to a boy, as in the years of infancy she had been sold to a man. Her disposition, which was anything but feminine, made this last alliance still more unnatural, for her taste and inclinations were masculine, and the whole tenor of her life belied her sex. After the example of her instructress, the Queen of Hungary, and her great-aunt, the Duchess Mary of Burgundy, who met her death in this favorite sport, she was passionately fond of hunting, and had acquired in this pursuit such bodily vigor that few men were better able to undergo its hardships and fatigues.

Her gait itself was so devoid of grace that one was far more tempted to take her for a disguised man than for a masculine woman; and Nature, whom she had derided by thus transgressing the limits of her sex, revenged itself finally upon her by a disease peculiar to men — the gout.

These unusual qualities were crowned by a monkish superstition which was infused into her mind by Ignatius

Loyola, her confessor and teacher. Among the charitable works and penances with which she mortified her vanity, one of the most remarkable was that, during Passion-Week she yearly washed, with her own hands, the feet of a number of poor men (who were most strictly forbidden to cleanse themselves beforehand), waited on them at table like a servant, and sent them away with rich presents.

Nothing more is requisite than this last feature in her character to account for the preference which the king gave her over all her rivals; but his choice was at the same time justified by excellent reasons of state. Margaret was born and also educated in the Netherlands. She had spent her early youth among the people, and had acquired much of their national manners. Two regents (Duchess Margaret and Queen Mary of Hungary), under whose eyes she had grown up, had gradually initiated her into the maxims by which this peculiar people might be most easily governed; and they would also serve her as models. She did not want either in talents; and possessed, moreover, a particular turn for business, which she had acquired from her instructors, and had afterwards carried to greater perfection in the Italian school. The Netherlands had been for a number of years accustomed to female government; and Philip hoped, perhaps, that the sharp iron of tyranny which he was about to use against them would cut more gently if wielded by the hands of a woman. Some regard for his father, who at the time was still living, and was much attached to Margaret, may have in a measure, as it is asserted, influenced this choice; as it is also probable that the king wished to oblige the Duke of Parma, through this mark of attention to his wife, and thus to compensate for denying a request which he was just then compelled to refuse him. As the territories of the duchess were surrounded by Philip's Italian states, and at all times exposed to his arms, he could, with the less danger, entrust the supreme power into her hands. For his full security her son, Alexander Farnese, was to remain at his court as a pledge for her loyalty. All these reasons were alone sufficiently weighty to turn the king's decision in her favor; but they became irresistible when supported by the Bishop of Arras and

the Duke of Alva. The latter, as it appears, because he hated or envied all the other competitors; the former, because even then, in all probability, he anticipated from the wavering disposition of this princess abundant gratification for his ambition.

Philip received the new regent on the frontiers with a splendid cortège, and conducted her with magnificent pomp to Ghent, where the States General had been convoked. As he did not intend to return soon to the Netherlands, he desired, before he left them, to gratify the nation for once by holding a solemn Diet, and thus giving a solemn sanction and the force of law to his previous regulations. For the last time he showed himself to his Netherlandish people, whose destinies were from henceforth to be dispensed from a mysterious distance. To enhance the splendor of this solemn day, Philip invested eleven knights with the Order of the Golden Fleece, his sister being seated on a chair near himself, while he showed her to the nation as their future ruler. All the grievances of the people, touching the edicts, the Inquisition, the detention of the Spanish troops, the taxes, and the illegal introduction of foreigners into the offices and administration of the country were brought forward in this Diet, and were hotly discussed by both parties; some of them were skilfully evaded, or apparently removed, others arbitrarily repelled. As the king was unacquainted with the language of the country, he addressed the nation through the mouth of the Bishop of Arras, recounted to them with vain-glorious ostentation all the benefits of his government, assured them of his favor for the future, and once more recommended to the estates in the most earnest manner the preservation of the Catholic faith and the extirpation of heresy. The Spanish troops, he promised, should in a few months evacuate the Netherlands, if only they would allow him time to recover from the numerous burdens of the last war, in order that he might be enabled to collect the means for paying the arrears of these troops; the fundamental laws of the nation should remain inviolate, the imposts should not be grievously burdensome, and the Inquisition should administer its duties with justice and moderation. In the choice of a supreme Stadtholder, he added, he had especially consulted the wishes of the nation, and had decided for a native of the country, who had been brought up in their manners and customs, and was attached to them by a love to her native land. He exhorted them, therefore, to show their gratitude by honoring his choice, and obeying his sister, the duchess, as himself. Should, he concluded, unexpected obstacles oppose his return, he would send in his place his son, Prince Charles, who should reside in Brussels.

A few members of this assembly, more courageous than the rest, once more ventured on a final effort for liberty of conscience. Every people, they argued, ought to be treated according to their natural character, as every individual must in accordance to his bodily constitution. Thus, for example, the south may be considered happy under a certain degree of constraint which would press intolerably on the north. Never, they added, would the Flemings consent to a yoke under which, perhaps, the Spaniards bowed with patience, and rather than submit to it would they undergo any extremity if it was sought to force such a yoke upon them. This remonstrance was supported by some of the king's counsellors, who strongly urged the policy of mitigating the rigor of religious edicts. But Philip remained inexorable. Better not reign at all, was his answer, than reign over heretics!

According to an arrangement already made by Charles V., three councils or chambers were added to the regent, to assist her in the administration of state affairs. As long as Philip was himself present in the Netherlands these courts had lost much of their power, and the functions of the first of them, the state council, were almost entirely suspended. Now that he quitted the reins of government, they recovered their former importance. In the state council, which was to deliberate upon war and peace, and security against external foes, sat the Bishop of Arras, the Prince of Orange, Count Egmont, the President of the Privy Council, Viglius Van Zuichem Van Aytta, and the Count of Barlaimont, President of the Chamber of Finance. All knights of the Golden

Fleece, all privy counsellors and counsellors of finance, as also the members of the great senate at Malines, which had been subjected by Charles V. to the Privy Council in Brussels, had a seat and vote in the Council of State, if expressly invited by the regent. The management of the royal revenues and crown lands was vested in the Chamber of Finance, and the Privy Council was occupied with the administration of justice, and the civil regulation of the country, and issued all letters of grace and pardon. The governments of the provinces which had fallen vacant were either filled up afresh or the former governors were confirmed. Count Egmont received Flanders and Artois; the Prince of Orange, Holland, Zealand, Utrecht, and West Friesland; the Count of Aremberg, East Friesland, Overyssel, and Gröningen; the Count of Mansfeld, Luxemburg; Barlaimont, Namur; the Marquis of Bergen, Hainault, Chateau-Cambray, and Valenciennes; the Baron of Montigny, Tournay and its dependencies. Other provinces were given to some who have less claim to our attention. Philip of Montmorency, Count of Hoorn, who had been succeeded by the Count of Megen in the government of Gueldres and Zütphen, was confirmed as admiral of the Belgian navy. Every governor of a province was at the same time a knight of the Golden Fleece and member of the Council of State. Each had, in the province over which he presided, the command of the military force which protected it, the superintendence of the civil administration and the judicature; the governor of Flanders alone excepted, who was not allowed to interfere with the administration of justice. Brabant alone was placed under the immediate jurisdiction of the regent, who, according to custom, chose Brussels for her constant residence. The induction of the Prince of Orange into his governments was, properly speaking, an infraction of the constitution, since he was a foreigner; but several estates which he either himself possessed in the provinces, or managed as guardian of his son, his long residence in the country, and above all the unlimited confidence the nation reposed in him, gave him substantial claims in default of a real title of citizenship.

The military force of the Low Countries consisted, in its full complement, of three thousand horse. At present it did not much exceed two thousand, and was divided into fourteen squadrons, over which, besides the governors of the provinces, the Duke of Arschot, the Counts of Hoogstraten, Bossu, Roeux, and Brederode held the chief command. This cavalry, which was scattered through all the seventeen provinces, was only to be called out on sudden emergencies. Insufficient as it was for any great undertaking, it was, nevertheless, fully adequate for the maintenance of internal order. Its courage had been approved in former wars, and the fame of its valor was diffused through the whole of Europe. In addition to this cavalry it was also proposed to levy a body of infantry, but hitherto the states had refused their consent to it. Of foreign troops there were still some German regiments in the service, which were waiting for their pay. The four thousand Spaniards, respecting whom so many complaints had been made, were under two Spanish generals, Mendoza and Romero, and were in garrison in the frontier towns.

Among the Belgian nobles whom the king especially distinguished in these new appointments, the names of Count Egmont and William of Orange stand conspicuous. However inveterate his hatred was of both, and particularly of the latter, Philip nevertheless gave them these public marks of his favor, because his scheme of vengeance was not yet fully ripe, and the people were enthusiastic in their devotion to them. The estates of both were declared exempt from taxes, the most lucrative governments were entrusted to them, and by offering them the command of the Spaniards whom he left behind in the country the king flattered them with a confidence which he was very far from really reposing in them. But at the very time when he obliged the prince with these public marks of his esteem he privately inflicted the most cruel injury on him. Apprehensive lest an alliance with the powerful house of Lorraine might encourage this suspected vassal to bolder measures, he thwarted the negotiation for a marriage between him and a princess of that family, and crushed his hopes on the very eve of

their accomplishment, — an injury which the prince never
forgave. Nay, his hatred to the prince on one occasion
even got completely the better of his natural dissimulation, and seduced him into a step in which we entirely
lose sight of Philip II. When he was about to embark
at Flushing, and the nobles of the country attended him·
to the shore, he so far forgot himself as roughly to accost
the prince, and openly to accuse him of being the author
of the Flemish troubles. The prince answered temperately that what had happened had been done by the
provinces of their own suggestion and on legitimate
grounds. No, said Philip, seizing his hand, and shaking
it violently, not the provinces, but You! You! You!
The prince stood mute with astonishment, and without
waiting for the king's embarkation, wished him a safe
journey, and went back to the town.

Thus the enmity which William had long harbored in
his breast against the oppressor of a free people was now
rendered irreconcilable by private hatred; and this
double incentive accelerated the great enterprise which
tore from the Spanish crown seven of its brightest
jewels.

Philip had greatly deviated from his true character in
taking so gracious a leave of the Netherlands. The legal
form of a diet, his promise to remove the Spaniards from
the frontiers, the consideration of the popular wishes,
which had led him to fill the most important offices of the
country with the favorites of the people, and, finally, the
sacrifice which he made to the constitution in withdrawing the Count of Feria from the council of state, were
marks of condescension of which his magnanimity was
never again guilty. But in fact he never stood in greater
need of the good-will of the states, that with their aid he
might, if possible, clear off the great burden of debt
which was still attached to the Netherlands from the
former war. He hoped, therefore, by propitiating them
through smaller sacrifices to win approval of more important usurpations. He marked his departure with
grace, for he knew in what hands he left them. The
frightful scenes of death which he intended for this
unhappy people were not to stain the splendor of majesty

which, like the Godhead, marks its course only with
beneficence; that terrible distinction was reserved for
his representatives. The establishment of the council of
state was, however, intended rather to flatter the vanity
of the Belgian nobility than to impart to them any real
influence. The historian Strada (who drew his information with regard to the regent from her own papers) has
preserved a few articles of the secret instructions which
the Spanish ministry gave her. Amongst other things it
is there stated if she observed that the councils were
divided by factions, or, what would be far worse, prepared by private conferences before the session, and in
league with one another, then she was to prorogue all
the chambers and dispose arbitrarily of the disputed
articles in a more select council or committee. In this
select committee, which was called the Consulta, sat the
Archbishop of Arras, the President Viglius, and the Count
of Barlaimont. She was to act in the same manner if
emergent cases required a prompt decision. Had this
arrangement not been the work of an arbitrary despotism
it would perhaps have been justified by sound policy, and
republican liberty itself might have tolerated it. In great
assemblies where many private interests and passions
co-operate, where a numerous audience presents so great
a temptation to the vanity of the orator, and parties often
assail one another with unmannerly warmth, a decree can
seldom be passed with that sobriety and mature deliberation which, if the members are properly selected, a smaller
body readily admits of. In a numerous body of men,
too, there is, we must suppose, a greater number of limited
than of enlightened intellects, who through their equal right
of vote frequently turn the majority on the side of ignorance. A second maxim which the regent was especially
to observe, was to select the very members of council
who had voted against any decree to carry it into execution. By this means not only would the people be kept
in ignorance of the originators of such a law, but the
private quarrels also of the members would be restrained,
and a greater freedom insured in voting in compliance
with the wishes of the court.

In spite of all these precautions Philip would never have

been able to leave the Netherlands with a quiet mind so long as he knew that the chief power in the council of state, and the obedience of the provinces, were in the hands of the suspected nobles. In order, therefore, to appease his fears from this quarter, and also at the same time to assure himself of the fidelity of the regent, he subjected her, and through her all the affairs of the judicature, to the higher control of the Bishop of Arras. In this single individual he possessed an adequate counterpoise to the most dreaded cabal. To him, as to an infallible oracle of majesty, the duchess was referred, and in him there watched a stern supervisor of her administration. Among all his contemporaries Granvella was the only one whom Philip II. appears to have excepted from his universal distrust; as long as he knew that this man was in Brussels he could sleep calmly in Segovia. He left the Netherlands in September, 1559, was saved from a storm which sank his fleet, and landed at Laredo in Biscay, and in his gloomy joy thanked the Deity who had preserved him by a detestable vow. In the hands of a priest and of a woman was placed the dangerous helm of the Netherlands; and the dastardly tyrant escaped in his oratory at Madrid the supplications, the complaints, and the curses of the people.

BOOK II.

CARDINAL GRANVELLA.

ANTHONY PERENOT, Bishop of Arras, subsequently Archbishop of Malines, and Metropolitan of all the Netherlands, who, under the name of Cardinal Granvella, has been immortalized by the hatred of his contemporaries, was born in the year 1516, at Besançon in Burgundy. His father, Nicolaus Perenot, the son of a blacksmith, had risen by his own merits to be the private secretary of Margaret, Duchess of Savoy, at that time regent of the Netherlands. In this post he was noticed for his habits of business by Charles V., who took him into his own service and employed him in several important negotiations. For twenty years he was a member of the Emperor's cabinet, and filled the offices of privy counsellor and keeper of the king's seal, and shared in all the state secrets of that monarch. He acquired a large fortune. His honors, his influence, and his political knowledge were inherited by his son, Anthony Perenot, who in his early years gave proofs of the great capacity which subsequently opened to him so distinguished a career. Anthony had cultivated at several colleges the talents with which nature had so lavishly endowed him, and in some respects had an advantage over his father. He soon showed that his own abilities were sufficient to maintain the advantageous position which the merits of another had procured him. He was twenty-four years old when the Emperor sent him as his plenipotentiary to the ecclesiastical council of Trent, where he delivered the first specimen of that eloquence which in the sequel gave him so complete an ascendancy over two kings. Charles employed him in several difficult embassies, the duties of which he fulfilled to the satisfaction of his sovereign, and when finally that Emperor resigned the sceptre to his son he made that costly present complete by giving him a minister who could help him to wield it.

Granvella opened his new career at once with the greatest masterpiece of political genius, in passing so easily from the favor of such a father into equal consideration with such a son. And he soon proved himself deserving of it. At the secret negotiations of which the Duchess of Lorraine had, in 1558, been the medium between the French and Spanish ministers at Peronne, he planned, conjointly with the Cardinal of Lorraine, that conspiracy against the Protestants which was afterwards matured, but also betrayed, at Chateau-Cambray, where Perenot likewise assisted in effecting the so-called peace.

A deeply penetrating, comprehensive intellect, an unusual facility in conducting great and intricate affairs, and the most extensive learning, were wonderfully united in this man with persevering industry and never-wearying patience, while his enterprising genius was associated with thoughtful mechanical regularity. Day and night the state found him vigilant and collected; the most important and the most insignificant things were alike weighed by him with scrupulous attention. Not unfrequently he employed five secretaries at one time, dictating to them in different languages, of which he is said to have spoken seven. What his penetrating mind had slowly matured acquired in his lips both force and grace, and truth, set forth by his persuasive eloquence, irresistibly carried away all hearers. He was tempted by none of the passions which make slaves of most men. His integrity was incorruptible. With shrewd penetration he saw through the disposition of his master, and could read in his features his whole train of thought, and, as it were, the approaching form in the shadow which outran it. With an artifice rich in resources he came to the aid of Philip's more inactive mind, formed into perfect thought his master's crude ideas while they yet hung on his lips, and liberally allowed him the glory of the invention. Granvella understood the difficult and useful art of depreciating his own talents; of making his own genius the seeming slave of another; thus he ruled while he concealed his sway. In this manner only could Philip II. be governed. Content with a silent but real power, Granvella did not grasp insatiably at new and outward marks of it, which with lesser minds are ever the most coveted objects; but every new distinction seemed to sit upon him as easily as the oldest. No wonder if such extraordinary endowments had alone gained him the favor of his master; but a large and valuable treasure of political secrets and experiences, which the active life of Charles V. had accumulated, and had deposited in the mind of this man, made him indispensable to his successor. Self-sufficient as the latter was, and accustomed to confide in his own understanding, his timid and crouching policy was fain to lean on a superior mind, and to aid its own irresolution not only by precedent but also by the influence and example of another. No political matter which concerned the royal interest, even when Philip himself was in the Netherlands, was decided without the intervention of Granvella; and when the king embarked for Spain he made the new regent the same valuable present of the minister which he himself had received from the Emperor, his father.

Common as it is for despotic princes to bestow unlimited confidence on the creatures whom they have raised from the dust, and of whose greatness they themselves are, in a measure, the creators, the present is no ordinary instance; pre-eminent must have been the qualities which could so far conquer the selfish reserve of such a character as Philip's as to gain his confidence, nay, even to win him into familiarity. The slightest ebullition of the most allowable self-respect, which might have tempted him to assert, however slightly, his claim to any idea which the king had once ennobled as his own, would have cost him his whole influence. He might gratify without restraint the lowest passions of voluptuousness, of rapacity, and of revenge, but the only one in which he really took delight, the sweet consciousness of his own superiority and power, he was constrained carefully to conceal from the suspicious glance of the despot. He voluntarily disclaimed all the eminent qualities, which were already his own, in order, as it were, to receive them a second time from the generosity of the king. His happiness seemed to flow from no other source, no other person could have a claim upon his gratitude. The purple, which was sent to him from Rome, was not assumed until the royal permission reached him from Spain; by laying it down on the steps of the throne he appeared, in a measure, to receive it first from the hands of majesty. Less politic, Alva erected a trophy in Antwerp, and inscribed his own name under the victory, which he had won as the servant of the crown — but Alva carried with him to the grave the displeasure of his master. He had invaded with audacious hand the royal prerogative by drawing immediately at the fountain of immortality.

Three times Granvella changed his master, and three times he succeeded in rising to the highest favor. With the same facility with which he had guided the settled pride of an autocrat, and the sly egotism of a despot, he knew how to manage the delicate vanity of a woman. His business between himself and the regent, even when they were in the same house, was, for the most part, transacted by the medium of notes, a custom which draws its date from the times of Augustus and Tiberius. When the regent was in any perplexity these notes were interchanged from hour to hour. He probably adopted this expedient in the hope of eluding the watchful jealousy of the nobility, and concealing from them, in part at least, his influence over the regent. Perhaps, too, he also believed that by this means his advice would become more permanent; and, in case of need, this written testimoney would be at hand to shield him from blame. But the vigilance of the nobles made this caution vain, and it was soon known in all the provinces that nothing was determined upon without the minister's advice.

Granvella possessed all the qualities requisite for a perfect statesman in a monarchy governed by despotic principles, but was absolutely unqualified for republics which are governed by kings. Educated between the throne and the confessional, he knew of no other relation between man and man than that of rule and subjection; and the innate consciousness of his own superiority gave him a contempt for others. His policy wanted pliability, the only virtue which was here indispensable to its success. He was naturally overbearing and insolent, and the royal authority only gave arms to the natural impetuosity of his disposition and the imperiousness of his order. He veiled his own ambition beneath the interests of the crown, and made the breach between the nation and the king incurable, because it would render him indispensable to the latter. He revenged on the nobility the lowliness of his own origin; and, after the fashion of all those who have risen by their own merits, he valued the advantages of birth below those by which he had raised himself to distinction. The Protestants saw in him their most implacable foe; to his charge were laid all the burdens which oppressed the country, and they pressed the more heavily because they came from him. Nay, he was even accused of having brought back to severity the milder sentiments to which the urgent remonstrances of the provinces had at last disposed the monarch. The Netherlands execrated him as the most terrible enemy of their liberties, and the originator of all the misery which subsequently came upon them.

1559. Philip had evidently left the provinces too soon. The new measures of the government were still strange to the people, and could receive sanction and authority from his presence alone; the new machines which he had brought into play required to be kept in motion by a dreaded and powerful hand, and to have their first movements watched and regulated. He now exposed his minister to all the angry passions of the people, who no longer felt restrained by the fetters of the royal presence; and he delegated to the weak arm of a subject the execution of projects in which majesty itself, with all its powerful supports, might have failed.

The land, indeed, flourished; and a general prosperity appeared to testify to the blessings of the peace which had so lately been bestowed upon it. An external repose deceived the eye, for within raged all the elements of discord. If the foundations of religion totter in a country they totter not alone; the audacity which begins with things sacred ends with things profane. The successful attack upon the hierarchy had awakened a spirit of boldness, and a desire to assail authority in general, and to test laws as well as dogmas — duties as well as opinions. The fanatical boldness with which men had learned to discuss and decide upon the affairs of eternity might change its subject matter; the contempt for life and property which religious enthusiasm had taught could metamorphose timid citizens into foolhardy rebels. A female government of nearly forty years had given the nation room to assert their liberty; continual wars, of which the Netherlands had been the theatre, had introduced a license with them, and the right of the stronger had usurped the place of law and order. The provinces were filled with foreign adventurers and fugitives; generally men bound by no ties of country, family, or property, who had brought with them from their unhappy homes the seeds of insubordination and rebellion. The repeated spectacles of torture and of death had rudely burst the tenderer threads of moral feeling, and had given an unnatural harshness to the national character.

Still the rebellion would have crouched timorously and silently on the ground if it had not found a support in the nobility. Charles V. had spoiled the Flemish nobles of the Netherlands by making them the participators of his glory, by fostering their national pride, by the marked preference he showed for them over the Castilian nobles, and by opening an arena to their ambition in every part of his empire. In the late war with France they had really deserved this preference from Philip; the advantages which the king reaped from the peace of Chateau-Cambray were for the most part the fruits of their valor, and they now sensibly missed the gratitude on which they had so confidently reckoned. Moreover, the separation of the German empire from the Spanish monarchy, and the less warlike spirit of the new government, had greatly narrowed their sphere of action, and, except in their own country, little remained for them to gain. And Philip now appointed his Spaniards where Charles V. had employed the Flemings. All the passions which the preceding government had raised and kept employed still survived in peace; and in default of a legitimate object these unruly feelings found, unfortunately, ample scope in the grievances of their country. Accordingly, the claims and wrongs which had been long supplanted by new passions were now drawn from oblivion. By his late appointments the king had satisfied no party; for those even who obtained offices were not much more content than those who were entirely passed over, because they had calculated on something better than they got. William of Orange had received four governments (not to reckon some smaller dependencies which, taken together, were equivalent to a fifth), but William had nourished hopes of Flanders and Brabant. He and Count Egmont forgot what had really fallen to their share, and only remembered that they had lost the regency. The majority of the nobles were either plunged into debt by their own extravagance, or had willingly enough been drawn into it by the government. Now that they were excluded from the prospect of lucrative appointments, they at once saw themselves exposed to poverty, which pained them the more sensibly when they contrasted the splendor of the affluent citizens with their own necessities. In the extremities to which they were reduced many would have readily assisted in the commission even of crimes; how then could they resist the seductive offers of the Calvinists, who liberally repaid them for their intercession and protection? Lastly, many whose estates were past redemption placed their last hope in a general devastation, and stood prepared at the first favorable moment to cast the torch of discord into the republic.

This threatening aspect of the public mind was rendered still more alarming by the unfortunate vicinity of France. What Philip dreaded for the provinces was there already accomplished. The fate of that kingdom prefigured to him the destiny of his Netherlands, and the spirit of rebellion found there a seductive example. A similar state of things had under Francis I. and Henry II. scattered the seeds of innovation in that kingdom; a similar fury of persecution and a like spirit of faction had encouraged its growth. Now Huguenots and Catholics were struggling in a dubious contest; furious parties disorganized the whole monarchy, and were violently hurrying this once-powerful state to the brink of destruction. Here, as there, private interest, ambition, and party feeling might veil themselves under the names of religion and patriotism, and the passions of a few citizens drive the entire nation to take up arms. The frontiers of both countries merged in Walloon Flanders; the rebellion might, like an agitated sea, cast its waves as far as this: would a country be closed against it whose language, manners, and character wavered between those of France and Belgium? As yet the government had taken no census of its Protestant subjects in these countries, but the new sect, it was aware, was a vast, compact republic, which extended its roots through all the monarchies of Christendom, and the slighest disturbance in any of its most distant members vibrated to its centre. It was, as it were, a chain of threatening volcanoes, which, united by subterraneous passages, ignite at the same moment with alarming sympathy. The Netherlands were, necessarily, open to all nations, because they derived their support from all. Was it possible for Philip to close a commercial state as easily as he could Spain? If he wished to purify these provinces from heresy it was necessary for him to commence by extirpating it in France.

It was in this state that Granvella found the Netherlands at the beginning of his administration (1560).

To restore to these countries the uniformity of papistry, to break the co-ordinate power of the nobility and the states, and to exalt the royal authority on the ruins of republican freedom, was the great object of Spanish policy and the express commission of the new minister. But obstacles stood in the way of its accomplishment; to conquer these demanded the invention of new resources, the application of new machinery. The Inquisition, indeed, and the religious edicts appeared sufficient to check the contagion of heresy; but the latter required superintendence, and the former able instruments for its now extended jurisdiction. The church constitution continued the same as it had been in earlier times, when the provinces were less populous, when the church still enjoyed universal repose, and could be more easily overlooked and controlled. A succession of several centuries, which changed the whole interior form of the provinces, had left the form of the hierarchy unaltered, which, moreover, was protected from the arbitrary will of its ruler by the particular privileges of the provinces. All the seventeen provinces were parcelled out under four bishops, who had their seats at Arras, Tournay, Cambray, and Utrecht, and were subject to the primates of Rheims and Cologne. Philip the Good, Duke of Burgundy, had, indeed, meditated an increase in the number of bishops to meet the wants of the increasing population; but, unfortunately, in the excitement of a life of pleasure had abandoned the project. Ambition and lust of conquest withdrew the mind of Charles the Bold from the internal concerns of his kingdom, and Maximilian had already too many subjects of dispute with the states to venture to add to their number by proposing this change. A stormy reign prevented Charles V. from the execution of this extensive plan, which Philip II. now undertook as a bequest from all these princes. The moment had now arrived when the urgent necessities of the church would excuse the innovation, and the leisure of peace favored its accomplishment. With the prodigious crowd of people from all the countries of Europe who were crowded together in the towns of the Netherlands, a multitude of religious opinions had also grown up; and it was impossible that religion could any longer be effectually superintended by so few eyes as were formerly sufficient. While the number of bishops was so small their districts must, of necessity, have been proportionally extensive, and four men could not be adequate to maintain the purity of the faith through so wide a district.

The jurisdiction which the Archbishops of Cologne and Rheims exercised over the Netherlands had long been a stumbling-block to the government, which could not look on this territory as really its own property so long as such an important branch of power was still wielded by foreign hands. To snatch this prerogative from the alien archbishops; by new and active agents to give fresh life and vigor to the superintendence of the faith, and at the same time to strengthen the number of the partisans of government at the diet, no more effectual means could be devised than to increase the number of bishops. Resolved upon doing this Philip II. ascended the throne; but he soon found that a change in the hierarchy would inevitably meet with warm opposition from the provinces, without whose consent, nevertheless, it would be vain to attempt it. Philip foresaw that the nobility would never approve of a measure which would so strongly augment the royal party, and take from the aristocracy the preponderance of power in the diet. The revenues, too, for the maintenance of these new bishops must be diverted from the abbots and monks, and these formed a considerable part of the states of the realm. He had, besides, to fear the opposition of the Protestants, who would not fail to act secretly in the diet against him. On these accounts the whole affair was discussed at Rome with the greatest possible secrecy. Instructed by, and as the agent of, Granvella, Francis Sonnoi, a priest of Louvain, came before Paul IV. to inform him how extensive the provinces were, how thriving and populous, how luxurious in their prosperity. But, he continued, in the immoderate enjoyment of liberty the true faith is neglected, and heretics prosper. To obviate this evil the Romish See must have recourse to extraordinary measures. It was not difficult to prevail on the Romish pontiff to make a change which would enlarge the sphere of his own jurisdiction.

Paul IV. appointed a tribunal of seven cardinals to deliberate upon this important matter; but death called him away, and he left to his successor, Pius IV., the duty of carrying their advice into execution. The welcome tidings of the pope's determination reached the king in Zealand when he was just on the point of setting sail for Spain, and the minister was secretly charged with the dangerous reform. The new constitution of the hierarchy was published in 1560; in addition to the then existing four bishoprics thirteen new ones were established, according to the number of seventeen provinces, and four of them were raised into archbishoprics. Six of thesee piscopal sees, viz., in Antwerp, Herzogenbusch, Ghent, Bruges, Ypres, and Ruremonde, were placed under the Archbishopric of Malines; five others, Haarlem, Middelburg, Leuwarden, Deventer, and Gröningen, under the Archbishopric of Utrecht; and the remaining four, Arras, Tournay, St. Omer, and Namur, which lie nearest to France, and have language, character, and manners in common with that country, under the Archbishopric of Cambray. Malines, situated in the middle of Brabant and in the centre of all the seventeen provinces, was made the primacy of all the rest, and was, with several rich abbeys, the reward of Granvella. The revenues of the new bishoprics were provided by an appropriation of the treasures of the cloisters and abbeys which had accumulated from pious benefactions during centuries. Some of the abbots were raised to the episcopal throne, and with the possession of their cloisters and prelacies retained also the vote at the diet which was attached to them. At the same time to every bishopric nine prebends were attached, and bestowed on the most learned juris-consult-.

ists and theologians, who were to support the Inquisition and the bishop in his spiritual office. Of these, the two who were most deserving by knowledge, experience, and unblemished life were to be constituted actual inquisitors, and to have the first voice in the Synods. To the Archbishop of Malines, as metropolitan of all the seventeen provinces, the full authority was given to appoint, or at discretion depose, archbishops and bishops; and the Romish See was only to give its ratification to his acts.

At any other period the nation would have received with gratitude and approved of such a measure of church reform since it was fully called for by circumstances, was conducive to the interests of religion, and absolutely indispensable for the moral reformation of the monkhood. Now the temper of the times saw in it nothing but a hateful change. Universal was the indignation with which it was received. A cry was raised that the constitution was trampled under foot, the rights of the nation violated, and that the Inquisition was already at the door, and would soon open here, as in Spain, its bloody tribunal. The people beheld with dismay these new servants of arbitrary power and of persecution. The nobility saw in it nothing but a strengthening of the royal authority by the addition of fourteen votes in the states' assembly, and a withdrawal of the firmest prop of their freedom, the balance of the royal and the civil power. The old bishops complained of the diminution of their incomes and the circumscription of their sees; the abbots and monks had not only lost power and income, but had received in exchange rigid censors of their morals. Noble and simple, laity and clergy, united against the common foe, and while all singly struggled for some petty private interest, the cry appeared to come from the formidable voice of patriotism.

Among all the provinces Brabant was loudest in its opposition. The inviolability of its church constitution was one of the important privileges which it had reserved in the remarkable charter of the "Joyful Entry,"— statutes which the sovereign could not violate without releasing the nation from its allegiance to him. In vain did the university of Louvain assert that in disturbed times of the church a privilege lost its power which had been granted in the period of its tranquillity. The introduction of the new bishoprics into the constitution was thought to shake the whole fabric of liberty. The prelacies, which were now transferred to the bishops, must henceforth serve another rule than the advantage of the province of whose states they had been members. The once free patriotic citizens were to be instruments of the Romish See and obedient tools of the archbishop, who again, as first prelate of Brabant, had the immediate control over them. The freedom of voting was gone, because the bishops, as servile spies of the crown, made every one fearful. "Who," it was asked, "will after this venture to raise his voice in parliament before such observers, or in their presence dare to protect the rights of the nation against the rapacious hands of the government? They will trace out the resources of the provinces, and betray to the crown the secrets of our freedom and our property. They will obstruct the way to all offices of honor; we shall soon see the courtiers of the king succeed the present men; the children of foreigners will, for the future, fill the parliament, and the private interest of their patron will guide their venal votes." "What an act of oppression," rejoined the monks, "to pervert to other objects the pious designs of our holy institutions, to contemn the inviolable wishes of the dead, and to take that which a devout charity had deposited in our chests for the relief of the unfortunate and make it subservient to the luxury of the bishops, thus inflating their arrogant pomp with the plunder of the poor?" Not only the abbots and monks, who really did suffer by this act of appropriation, but every family which could flatter itself with the slightest hope of enjoying, at some time or other, even in the most remote posterity, the benefit of this monastic foundation, felt this disappointment of their distant expectations as much as if they had suffered an actual injury, and the wrongs of a few abbot-prelates became the concern of a whole nation.

Historians have not omitted to record the covert proceedings of William of Orange during this general commotion, who labored to conduct to one end these various and conflicting passions. At his instigation the people of Brabant petitioned the regent for an advocate and protector, since they alone, of all his Flemish subjects, had the misfortune to unite, in one and the same person, their counsel and their ruler. Had the demand been granted, their choice could fall on no other than the Prince of Orange. But Granvella, with his usual presence of mind, broke through the snare. "The man who receives this office," he declared in the state council, "will, I hope, see that he divides Brabant with the king!" The long delay of the papal bull, which was kept back by a misunderstanding between the Romish and Spanish courts, gave the disaffected an opportunity to combine for a common object. In perfect secrecy the states of Brabant despatched an extraordinary messenger to Pius IV. to urge their wishes in Rome itself. The ambassador was provided with important letters of recommendation from the Prince of Orange, and carried with him considerable sums to pave his way to the father of the church. At the same time a public letter was forwarded from the city of Antwerp to the King of Spain containing the most urgent representations, and supplicating him to spare that flourishing commercial town from the threatened innovation. They knew, it was stated, that the intentions of the monarch were the best, and that the institution of the new bishops was likely to be highly conducive to the maintenance of true religion; but the foreigners could not be convinced of this, and on them depended the prosperity of their town. Among them the most groundless rumors would be as perilous as the most true. The first embassy was discovered in time, and its object disappointed by the prudence of the regent; by the second the town of Antwerp gained so far its point that it was to remain without a bishop, at least until the personal arrival of the king, which was talked of.

The example and success of Antwerp gave the signal of opposition to all the other towns for which a new bishop was intended. It is a remarkable proof of the hatred to the Inquisition and the unanimity of the Flemish towns at this date that they preferred to renounce all the advantages which the residence of a bishop would necessarily bring to their local trade rather than by their consent promote that abhorred tribunal, and thus act in opposition to the interests of the whole nation. Deventer, Ruremond, and Leuwarden placed themselves in determined opposition, and (1561) successfully carried their point; in the other towns the bishops were, in spite of all remonstrances, forcibly inducted. Utrecht, Haarlem, St. Omer, and Middelburg were among the first which opened their gates to them; the remaining towns followed their example; but in Malines and Herzogenbusch the bishops were received with very little respect. When Granvella made his solemn entry into the former town not a single nobleman showed himself, and his triumph was wanting in everything that could make it real, because those remained away over whom it was meant to be celebrated.

In the meantime, too, the period had elapsed within which the Spanish troops were to have left the country, and as yet there was no appearance of their being withdrawn. People perceived with terror the real cause of the delay, and suspicion lent it a fatal connection with the Inquisition. The detention of these troops, as it rendered the nation more vigilant and distrustful, made it more difficult for the minister to proceed with the other innovations, and yet he would fain not deprive himself of this powerful and apparently indispensable aid in a country where all hated him, and in the execution of a commission to which all were opposed. At last, however, the regent saw herself compelled by the universal murmurs of discontent, to urge most earnestly upon the king the necessity of the withdrawal of the troops. "The provinces," she writes to Madrid, "have unanimously declared that they would never again be induced to grant the extraordinary taxes required by the government as long as word was not kept with them in this matter. The danger of a revolt was far more imminent than that of an attack by the French Protestants, and if a rebellion was to take place in the Netherlands these forces would be too weak to repress it, and there was not sufficient money in the treasury to enlist new." By delaying his answer the king still sought at least to gain time, and the reiterated representations of the regent would still have remained ineffectual, if, fortunately for the provinces, a loss which he had lately suffered from the Turks had not compelled him to employ these troops in the Mediterranean. He, therefore, at last consented to their departure: they were embarked in 1561 in Zealand, and the exulting shouts of all the provinces accompanied their departure.

Meanwhile Granvella ruled in the council of state almost uncontrolled. All offices, secular and spiritual, were given away through him; his opinion prevailed against the unanimous voice of the whole assembly. The regent herself was governed by him. He had contrived to manage so that her appointment was made out for two years only, and by this expedient he kept her always in his power. It seldom happened that any important affair was submitted to the other members, and if it really did occur it was only such as had been long before decided, to which it was only necessary for formality's sake to gain their sanction. Whenever a royal letter was read Viglius received instructions to omit all such passages as were underlined by the minister. It often happened that this correspondence with Spain laid open the weakness of the government, or the anxiety felt by the regent, with which it was not expedient to inform the members, whose loyalty was distrusted. If again it occurred that the opposition gained a majority over the minister, and insisted with determination on an article which he could not well put off any longer, he sent it to the ministry at Madrid for their decision, by which he at least gained time, and in any case was certain to find support. With the exception of the Count of Barlaimont, the President Viglius, and a few others, all the other counsellors were but superfluous figures in the senate, and the minister's behavior to them marked the small value which he placed upon their friendship and adherence. No wonder that men whose pride had been so greatly indulged by the flattering attentions of sovereign princes, and to whom, as to the idols of their country, their fellow-citizens paid the most reverential submission, should be highly indignant at this arrogance of a plebeian. Many of them had been personally insulted by Granvella.

The Prince of Orange was well aware that it was he who
had prevented his marriage with the Princess of Lorraine,
and that he had also endeavored to break off the negotiations for another alliance with the Princess of Savoy.
He had deprived Count Horn of the government of
Gueldres and Zütphen, and had kept for himself an abbey
which Count Egmont had in vain exerted himself to
obtain for a relation. Confident of his superior power, he
did not even think it worth while to conceal from the
nobility his contempt for them, and which, as a rule,
marked his whole administration; William of Orange
was the only one with whom he deemed it advisable to
dissemble. Although he really believed himself to be
raised far above all the laws of fear and decorum, still
in this point, however, his confident arrogance misled
him, and he erred no less against policy than he sinned
against propriety. In the existing posture of affairs the
government could hardly have adopted a worse measure
than that of throwing disrespect on the nobility. It had
it in its power to flatter the prejudices and feelings of the
aristocracy, and thus artfully and imperceptibly win them
over to its plans, and through them subvert the edifice
of national liberty. Now it admonished them, most in-
opportunely, of their duties, their dignity, and their
power; calling upon them even to be patriots, and to
devote to the cause of true greatness an ambition which
hitherto it had inconsiderately repelled. To carry into
effect the ordinances it required the active co-operation
of the lieutenant-governors; no wonder, however, that
the latter showed but little zeal to afford this assistance.
On the contrary, it is highly probable that they silently
labored to augment the difficulties of the minister, and to
subvert his measures, and through his ill-success to
diminish the king's confidence in him, and expose his
administration to contempt. The rapid progress which
in spite of those horrible edicts the Reformation made
during Granvella's administration in the Netherlands, is
evidently to be ascribed to the lukewarmness of the
nobility in opposing it. If the minister had been sure
of the nobles he might have despised the fury of the mob,
which would have impotently dashed itself against the

dreaded barriers of the throne. The sufferings of the citizens lingered long in tears and sighs, until the arts and the example of the nobility called forth a louder expression of them.

Meanwhile the inquisitions into religion were carried on with renewed vigor by the crowd of new laborers (1561, 1562), and the edicts against heretics were enforced with fearful obedience. But the critical moment when this detestable remedy might have been applied was allowed to pass by; the nation had become too strong and vigorous for such rough treatment. The new religion could now be extirpated only by the death of all its professors. The present executions were but so many alluring exhibitions of its excellence, so many scenes of its triumphs and radiant virtue. The heroic greatness with which the victims died made converts to the opinions for which they perished. One martyr gained ten new proselytes. Not in towns only, or villages, but on the very highways, in the boats and public carriages disputes were held touching the dignity of the pope, the saints, purgatory, and indulgences, and sermons were preached and men converted. From the country and from the towns the common people rushed in crowds to rescue the prisoners of the Holy Tribunal from the hands of its satellites, and the municipal officers who ventured to support it with the civil forces were pelted with stones. Multitudes accompanied the Protestant preachers whom the Inquisition pursued, bore them on their shoulders to and from church, and at the risk of their lives concealed them from their persecutors. The first province which was seized with the fanatical spirit of rebellion was, as had been expected, Walloon Flanders. A French Calvinist, by name Lannoi, set himself up in Tournay as a worker of miracles, where he hired a few women to simulate diseases, and to pretend to be cured by him. He preached in the woods near the town, drew the people in great numbers after him, and scattered in their minds the seeds of rebellion. Similar teachers appeared in Lille and Valenciennes, but in the latter place the municipal functionaries succeeded in seizing the persons of these incendiaries; while, however, they delayed to execute them their followers increased so rapidly that they became sufficiently strong to break open the prisons and forcibly deprive justice of its victims. Troops at last were brought into the town and order restored. But this trifling occurrence had for a moment withdrawn the veil which had hitherto concealed the strength of the Protestant party, and allowed the minister to compute their prodigious numbers. In Tournay alone five thousand at one time had been seen attending the sermons, and not many less in Valenciennes. What might not be expected from the northern provinces, where liberty was greater, and the seat of government more remote, and where the vicinity of Germany and Denmark multiplied the sources of contagion? One slight provocation had sufficed to draw from its concealment so formidable a multitude. How much greater was, perhaps, the number of those who in their hearts acknowledged the new sect, and only waited for a favorable opportunity to publish their adhesion to it. This discovery greatly alarmed the regent. The scanty obedience paid to the edicts, the wants of the exhausted treasury, which compelled her to impose new taxes, and the suspicious movements of the Huguenots on the French frontiers still further increased her anxiety. At the same time she received a command from Madrid to send off two thousand Flemish cavalry to the army of the Queen Mother in France, who, in the distresses of the civil war, had recourse to Philip II. for assistance. Every affair of faith, in whatever land it might be, was made by Philip his own business. He felt it as keenly as any catastrophe which could befall his own house, and in such cases always stood ready to sacrifice his means to foreign necessities. If it were interested motives that here swayed him they were at least kingly and grand, and the bold support of his principles wins our admiration as much as their cruelty withholds our esteem.

The regent laid before the council of state the royal will on the subject of these troops, but with a very warm opposition on the part of the nobility. Count Egmont and the Prince of Orange declared that the time was ill-chosen for stripping the Netherlands of troops, when the aspect of affairs rendered rather the enlistment of new

levies advisable. The movements of the troops in France
momentarily threatened a surprise, and the commotions
within the provinces demanded, more than ever, the utmost vigilance on the part of the government. Hitherto,
they said, the German Protestants had looked idly on
during the struggles of their brethren in the faith; but
will they continue to do so, especially when we are lending our aid to strengthen their enemy? By thus acting
shall we not rouse their vengeance against us, and call
their arms into the northern Netherlands? Nearly
the whole council of state joined in this opinion; their
representations were energetic and not to be gainsaid.
The regent herself, as well as the minister, could not but
feel their truth, and their own interests appeared to forbid obedience to the royal mandate. Would it not be
impolitic to withdraw from the Inquisition its sole prop
by removing the larger portion of the army, and in a
rebellious country to leave themselves without defence,
dependent on the arbitrary will of an arrogant aristocracy? While the regent, divided between the royal
commands, the urgent importunity of her council, and
her own fears, could not venture to come to a decision,
William of Orange rose and proposed the assembling of
the States General. But nothing could have inflicted a
more fatal blow on the supremacy of the crown than by
yielding to this advice to put the nation in mind of its
power and its rights. No measure could be more hazardous at the present moment. The danger which was thus
gathering over the minister did not escape him; a sign
from him warned the regent to break off the consultation
and adjourn the council. "The government," he writes
to Madrid, "can do nothing more injurious to itself than
to consent to the assembling of the states. Such a step
is at all times perilous, because it tempts the nation to
test and restrict the rights of the crown; but it is many
times more objectionable at the present moment, when
the spirit of rebellion is already widely spread amongst
us; when the abbots, exasperated at the loss of their
income, will neglect nothing to impair the dignity of the
bishops; when the whole nobility and all the deputies
from the towns are led by the arts of the Prince of

Orange, and the disaffected can securely reckon on the assistance of the nation." This representation, which at least was not wanting in sound sense, did not fail in having the desired effect on the king's mind. The assembling of the states was rejected once and forever, the penal statutes against the heretics were renewed in all their rigor, and the regent was directed to hasten the despatch of the required auxiliaries.

But to this the council of state would not consent. All that she obtained was, instead of the troops, a supply of money for the Queen Mother, which at this crisis was still more welcome to her. In place, however, of assembling the states, and in order to beguile the nation with, at least, the semblance of republican freedom, the regent summoned the governors of the provinces and the knights of the Golden Fleece to a special congress at Brussels, to consult on the present dangers and necessities of the state. When the President, Viglius, had laid before them the matters on which they were summoned to deliberate, three days were given to them for consideration. During this time the Prince of Orange assembled them in his palace, where he represented to them the necessity of coming to some unanimous resolution before the next sitting, and of agreeing on the measures which ought to be followed in the present dangerous state of affairs.

The majority assented to the propriety of this course; only Barlaimont, with a few of the dependents of the cardinal, had the courage to plead for the interests of the crown and of the minister. "It did not behoove them," he said, "to interfere in the concerns of the government, and this previous agreement of votes was an illegal and culpable assumption, in the guilt of which he would not participate;"— a declaration which broke up the meeting without any conclusion being come to. The regent, apprised of it by the Count Barlaimont, artfully contrived to keep the knights so well employed during their stay in the town that they could find no time for coming to any further secret understanding; in this session, however, it was arranged, with their concurrence, that Florence of Montmorency, Lord of Montigny, should make a journey to Spain, in order to acquaint the king with the present posture of affairs. But the regent sent before him another messenger to Madrid, who previously informed the king of all that had been debated between the Prince of Orange and the knights at the secret conference.

The Flemish ambassador was flattered in Madrid with empty protestations of the king's favor and paternal sentiments towards the Netherlands, while the regent was commanded to thwart, to the utmost of her power, the secret combinations of the nobility, and, if possible, to sow discord among their most eminent members. Jealousy, private interest, and religious differences had long divided many of the nobles; their share in the common neglect and contempt with which they were treated, and a general hatred of the minister had again united them. So long as Count Egmont and the Prince of Orange were suitors for the regency it could not fail but that at times their competing claims should have brought them into collision. Both had met each other on the road to glory and before the throne; both again met in the republic, where they strove for the same prize, the favor of their fellow-citizens. Such opposite characters soon became estranged, but the powerful sympathy of necessity as quickly reconciled them. Each was now indispensable to the other, and the emergency united these two men together with a bond which their hearts would never have furnished. But it was on this very uncongeniality of disposition that the regent based her plans; if she could fortunately succeed in separating them she would at the same time divide the whole Flemish nobility into two parties. Through the presents and small attentions by which she exclusively honored these two she also sought to excite against them the envy and distrust of the rest, and by appearing to give Count Egmont a preference over the Prince of Orange she hoped to make the latter suspicious of Egmont's good faith. It happened that at this very time she was obliged to send an extraordinary ambassador to Frankfort, to be present at the election of a Roman emperor. She chose for this office the Duke of Arschot, the avowed enemy of the prince, in order in some degree to show in his case how splendid was the reward which hatred against the latter might look for.

The Orange faction, however, instead of suffering any diminution, had gained an important accession in Count Horn, who, as admiral of the Flemish marine, had convoyed the king to Biscay, and now again took his seat in the council of state. Horn's restless and republican spirit readily met the daring schemes of Orange and Egmont, and a dangerous Triumvirate was soon formed by these three friends, which shook the royal power in the Netherlands, but which terminated very differently for each of its members.

(1562.) Meanwhile Montigny had returned from his embassy, and brought back to the council of state the most gracious assurance of the monarch. But the Prince of Orange had, through his own secret channels of intelligence, received more credible information from Madrid, which entirely contradicted this report. By these means he learnt all the ill services which Granvella had done him and his friends with the king, and the odious appellations which were there applied to the Flemish nobility. There was no help for them so long as the minister retained the helm of government, and to procure his dismissal was the scheme, however rash and adventurous it appeared, which wholly occupied the mind of the prince. It was agreed between him and Counts Horn and Egmont to despatch a joint letter to the king, and, in the name of the whole nobility, formally to accuse the minister, and press energetically for his removal. The Duke of Arschot, to whom this proposition was communicated by Count Egmont, refused to concur in it, haughtily declaring that he was not disposed to receive laws from Egmont and Orange; that he had no cause of complaint against Granvella, and that he thought it very presumptuous to prescribe to the king what ministers he ought to employ. Orange received a similar answer from the Count of Aremberg. Either the seeds of distrust which the regent had scattered amongst the nobility had already taken root, or the fear of the minister's power outweighed the abhorrence of his measures; at any rate, the whole nobility shrunk back timidly and irresolutely from the proposal. This disappointment did not, however, discourage them. The letter was written and subscribed by all three (1563).

In it Granvella was represented as the prime cause of all the disorders in the Netherlands. So long as the highest power should be entrusted to him it would, they declared, be impossible for them to serve the nation and king effectually; on the other hand, all would revert to its former tranquillity, all opposition be discontinued, and the government regain the affections of the people as soon as his majesty should be pleased to remove this man from the helm of the state. In that case, they added, neither exertion nor zeal would be wanting on their part to maintain in these countries the dignity of the king and the purity of the faith, which was no less sacred to them than to the cardinal, Granvella.

Secretly as this letter was prepared still the duchess was informed of it in sufficient time to anticipate it by another despatch, and to counteract the effect which it might have had on the king's mind. Some months passed ere an answer came from Madrid. It was mild, but vague. "The king," such was its import, "was not used to condemn his ministers unheard on the mere accusations of their enemies. Common justice alone required that the accusers of the cardinal should descend from general imputations to special proofs, and if they were not inclined to do this in writing, one of them might come to Spain, where he should be treated with all respect. Besides this letter, which was equally directed to all three, Count Egmont further received an autograph letter from the king, wherein his majesty expressed a wish to learn from him in particular what in the common letter had been only generally touched upon. The regent, also, was specially instructed how she was to answer the three collectively, and the count singly. The king knew his man. He felt it was easy to manage Count Egmont alone; for this reason he sought to entice him to Madrid, where he would be removed from the commanding guidance of a higher intellect. In distinguishing him above his two friends by so flattering a mark of his confidence, he made a difference in the relation in which they severally stood to the throne; how could they, then, unite with equal zeal for the same object when the inducements were no longer the same? This time, indeed, the vigilance of Orange frustrated the scheme; but the sequel of the history will show that the seed which was now scattered was not altogether lost.

(1563.) The king's answer gave no satisfaction to the three confederates; they boldly determined to venture a second attempt. "It had," they wrote, "surprised them not a little, that his majesty had thought their representations so unworthy of attention. It was not as accusers of the minister, but as counsellors of his majesty, whose duty it was to inform their master of the condition of his states, that they had despatched that letter to him. They sought not the ruin of the minister, indeed it would gratify them to see him contented and happy in any other part of the world than here in the Netherlands. They were, however, fully persuaded of this, that his continued presence there was absolutely incompatible with the general tranquillity. The present dangerous condition of their native country would allow none of them to leave it, much less to take so long a journey as to Spain on Granvella's account. If, therefore, his majesty did not please to comply with their written request, they hoped to be excused for the future from attendance in the senate, where they were only exposed to the mortification of meeting the minister, and where they could be of no service either to the king or the state, but only appeared contemptible in their own sight. In conclusion, they begged his majesty would not take ill the plain simplicity of their languge, since persons of their character set more value on acting well than on speaking finely." To the same purport was a separate letter from Count Egmont, in which he returned thanks for the royal autograph. This second address was followed by an answer to the effect that "their representations should be taken into consideration, meanwhile they were requested to attend the council of state as heretofore."

It was evident that the monarch was far from intending to grant their request; they, therefore, from this time forth absented themselves from the state council, and even left Brussels. Not having succeeded in removing the minister by lawful means they sought to accomplish this end by a new mode from which more might be expected. On every occasion they and their adherents openly showed the contempt which they felt for him, and contrived to throw ridicule on everything he undertook. By this contemptuous treatment they hoped to harass the haughty spirit of the priest, and to obtain through his mortified self-love what they had failed in by other means. In this, indeed, they did not succeed; but the expedient on which they had fallen led in the end to the ruin of the minister.

The popular voice was raised more loudly against him so soon as it was perceived that he had forfeited the good opinion of the nobles, and that men whose sentiments they had been used blindly to echo preceded them in detestation of him. The contemptuous manner in which the nobility now treated him devoted him in a measure to the general scorn and emboldened calumny which never spares even what is holiest and purest, to lay its sacrilegious hand on his honor. The new constitution of the church, which was the great grievance of the nation, had been the basis of his fortunes. This was a crime that could not be forgiven. Every fresh execution — and with such spectacles the activity of the inquisitors was only too liberal — kept alive and furnished dreadful exercise to the bitter animosity against him, and at last custom and usage inscribed his name on every act of oppression. A stranger in a land into which he had been introduced against its will; alone among millions of enemies; uncertain of all his tools; supported only by the weak arm of distant royalty; maintaining his intercourse with the nation, which he had to gain, only by means of faithless instruments, all of whom made it their highest object to falsify his actions and misrepresent his motives; lastly, with a woman for his coadjutor who could not share with him the burden of the general execration — thus he stood exposed to the wantonness, the ingratitude, the faction, the envy, and all the evil passions of a licentious, insubordinate people. It is worthy of remark that the hatred which he had incurred far outran the demerits which could be laid to his charge; that it was difficult, nay impossible, for his accusers to substantiate by proof the general condemnation which fell upon him from all sides. Before and after him fanaticism dragged its victims to the altar; before and after him civil blood flowed, the rights of men were made a mock of, and men themselves rendered wretched. Under Charles V. tyranny ought to have pained more acutely through its novelty; under the Duke of Alva it was carried to far more unnatural lengths, insomuch that Granvella's administration, in comparison with that of his successor, was even merciful; and yet we do not find that his contemporaries ever evinced the same degree of personal exasperation and spite against the latter in which they indulged against his predecessor. To cloak the meanness of his birth in the splendor of high dignities, and by an exalted station to place him if possible above the malice of his enemies, the regent had made interest at Rome to procure for him the cardinal's hat; but this very honor, which connected him more closely with the papal court, made him so much the more an alien in the provinces. The purple was a new crime in Brussels, and an obnoxious, detested garb, which in a measure publicly held forth to view the principles on which his future conduct would be governed. Neither his honorable rank, which alone often consecrates the most infamous caitiff, nor his talents, which commanded esteem, nor even his terrible omnipotence, which daily revealed itself in so many bloody manifestations, could screen him from derision. Terror and scorn, the fearful and the ludicrous, were in his instance unnaturally blended.* Odious rumors branded his honor; murderous attempts on the lives of Egmont and Orange were ascribed to him; the most incredible things found cre-

---

* The nobility, at the suggestion of Count Egmont, caused their servants to wear a common livery, on which was embroidered a fool's cap. All Brussels interpreted it for the cardinal's hat, and every appearance of such a servant renewed their laughter; this badge of a fool's cap, which was offensive to the court, was subsequently changed into a bundle of arrows — an accidental jest which took a very serious end, and probably was the origin of the arms of the republic. Vit. Vigl. T. II. 35 Thuan. 489. The respect for the cardinal sunk at last so low that a caricature was publicly placed in his own hand, in which he was represented seated on a heap of eggs, out of which bishops were crawling. Over him hovered a devil with the inscription — "This is my son, hear ye him!"

dence; the most monstrous, if they referred to him or were said to emanate from him, surprised no longer. The nation had already become uncivilized to that degree where the most contradictory sentiments prevail side by side, and the finer boundary lines of decorum and moral feeling are erased. This belief in extraordinary crimes is almost invariably their immediate precursor.

But with this gloomy prospect the strange destiny of this man opens at the same time a grander view, which impresses the unprejudiced observer with pleasure and admiration. Here he beholds a nation dazzled by no splendor, and restrained by no fear, firmly, inexorably, and unpremeditatedly unanimous in punishing the crime which had been committed against its dignity by the violent introduction of a stranger into the heart of its political constitution. We see him ever aloof and ever isolated, like a foreign hostile body hovering over a surface which repels its contact. The strong hand itself of the monarch, who was his friend and protector, could not support him against the antipathies of the nation which had once resolved to withhold from him all its sympathy. The voice of national hatred was all powerful, and was ready to forego even private interest, its certain gains; his alms even were shunned, like the fruit of an accursed tree. Like pestilential vapor, the infamy of universal reprobation hung over him. In his case gratitude believed itself absolved from its duties; his adherents shunned him; his friends were dumb in his behalf. So terribly did the people avenge the insulted majesty of their nobles and their nation on the greatest monarch of the earth.

History has repeated this memorable example only once, in Cardinal Mazarin; but the instance differed according to the spirit of the two periods and nations. The highest power could not protect either from derision; but if France found vent for its indignation in laughing at its pantaloon, the Netherlands hurried from scorn to rebellion. The former, after a long bondage under the vigorous administration of Richelieu, saw itself placed suddenly in unwonted liberty; the latter had passed from ancient hereditary freedom into strange and unusual servitude; it was as natural that the Fronde should end again in subjection as that the Belgian troubles should issue in republican independence. The revolt of the Parisians was the offspring of poverty; unbridled, but not bold, arrogant, but without energy, base and plebeian, like the source from which it sprang. The murmur of the Netherlands was the proud and powerful voice of wealth. Licentiousness and hunger inspired the former; revenge, life, property, and religion were the animating motives of the latter. Rapacity was Mazarin's spring of action; Granvella's lust of power. The former was humane and mild; the latter harsh, imperious, cruel. The French minister sought in the favor of his queen an asylum from the hatred of the magnates and the fury of the people; the Netherlandish minister provoked the hatred of a whole nation in order to please one man. Against Mazarin were only a few factions and the mob they could arm; an entire and united nation against Granvella. Under the former parliament attempted to obtain, by stealth, a power which did not belong to them; under the latter it struggled for a lawful authority which he insidiously had endeavored to wrest from them. The former had to contend with the princes of the blood and the peers of the realm, as the latter had with the native nobility and the states, but instead of endeavoring, like the former, to overthrow the common enemy, in the hope of stepping themselves into his place, the latter wished to destroy the place itself, and to divide a power which no single man ought to possess entire.

While these feelings were spreading among the people the influence of the minister at the court of the regent began to totter. The repeated complaints against the extent of his power must at last have made her sensible how little faith was placed in her own; perhaps, too, she began to fear that the universal abhorrence which attached to him would soon include herself also, or that his longer stay would inevitably provoke the menaced revolt. Long intercourse with him, his instruction and example, had qualified her to govern without him. His dignity began to be more oppressive to her as he became less necessary, and his faults, to which her friendship had hitherto lent a veil, became visible as it was withdrawn. She was now as much disposed to search out and enumerate these faults as she formerly had been to conceal them. In this unfavorable state of her feelings towards the cardinal the urgent and accumulated representations of the nobles began at last to find access to her mind, and the more easily, as they contrived to mix up her own fears with their own. "It was matter of great astonishment," said Count Egmont to her, "that to gratify a man who was not even a Fleming, and of whom, therefore, it must be well known that his happiness could not be dependent on the prosperity of this country, the king could be content to see all his Netherlandish subjects suffer, and this to please a foreigner, who if his birth made him a subject of the Emperor, the purple had made a creature of the court of Rome." "To the king alone," added the count, "was Granvella indebted for his being still among the living; for the future, however, he would leave that care of him to the regent, and he hereby gave her warning." As the majority of the nobles, disgusted with the contemptuous treatment which they met with in the council of state, gradually withdrew from it, the arbitrary proceedings of the minister lost the last semblance of republican deliberation which had hitherto softened the odious aspect, and the empty desolation of the council chamber made his domineering rule appear in all its obnoxiousness. The regent now felt that she had a master over her, and from that moment the banishment of the minister was decided upon.

With this object she despatched her private secretary, Thomas Armenteros, to Spain, to acquaint the king with the circumstances in which the cardinal was placed, to apprise him of the intimations she had received of the intentions of the nobles, and in this manner to cause the resolution for his recall to appear to emanate from the king himself. What she did not like to trust to a letter Armenteros was ordered ingeniously to interweave in the oral communication which the king would probably require from him. Armenteros fulfilled his commission with all the ability of a consummate courtier; but an audience of four hours could not overthrow the work of many years, nor destroy in Philip's mind his opinion of his minister, which was there unalterably established. Long did the monarch hold counsel with his policy and his interest, until Granvella himself came to the aid of his wavering resolution and voluntarily solicited a dismissal, which, he feared, could not much longer be deferred. What the detestation of all the Netherlands could not effect the contemptuous treatment of the nobility accomplished; he was at last weary of a power which was no longer feared, and exposed him less to envy than to infamy.

Perhaps as some have believed he trembled for his life, which was certainly in more than imaginary danger; perhaps he wished to receive his dismissal from the king under the shape of a boon rather than of a sentence, and after the example of the Romans meet with dignity a fate which he could no longer avoid. Philip too, it would appear, preferred generously to accord to the nation a request rather than to yield at a later period to a demand, and hoped at least to merit their thanks by voluntarily conceding now what necessity would ere long extort. His fears prevailed over his obstinacy, and prudence overcame pride.

Granvella doubted not for a moment what the decision of the king would be. A few days after the return of Armenteros he saw humility and flattery disappear from the few faces which had till then servilely smiled upon him; the last small crowd of base flatterers and eye-servants vanished from around his person; his threshold was forsaken; he perceived that the fructifying warmth of royal favor had left him.

Detraction, which had assailed him during his whole administration, did not spare him even in the moment of resignation. People did not scruple to assert that a short time before he laid down his office he had expressed a wish to be reconciled to the Prince of Orange and Count Egmont, and even offered, if their forgiveness could be hoped for on no other terms, to ask pardon of them on his knees. It was base and contemptible to sully the memory of a great and extraordinary man with such a charge, but it is still more so to hand it down uncontradicted to posterity. Granvella submitted to the royal command with a dignified composure. Already had he written, a few months previously, to the Duke of Alva in Spain, to prepare him a place of refuge in Madrid, in case of his having to quit the Netherlands. The latter long bethought himself whether it was advisable to bring thither so dangerous a rival for the favor of his king, or to deny so important a friend such a valuable means of indulging his old hatred of the Flemish nobles. Revenge prevailed over fear, and he strenuously supported Granvella's request with the monarch. But his intercession was fruitless. Armenteros had persuaded the king that the minister's residence in Madrid would only revive, with increased violence, all the complaints of the Belgian nation, to which his ministry had been sacrificed; for then, he said, he would be suspected of poisoning the very source of that power, whose outlets only he had hitherto been charged with corrupting. He therefore sent him to Burgundy, his native place, for which a decent pretext fortunately presented itself. The cardinal gave to his departure from Brussels the appearance of an unimportant journey, from which he would return in a few days. At the same time, however, all the state counsellors, who, under his administration, had voluntarily excluded themselves from its sittings, received a command from the court to resume their seats in the senate at Brussels. Although the latter circumstance made his return not very credible, nevertheless the remotest possibility of it sobered the triumph which celebrated his departure. The regent herself appears to have been undecided what to think about the report; for, in a fresh letter to the king, she repeated all the representations and arguments which ought to restrain him from restoring this minister. Granvella himself, in his correspondence with Barlaimont and Viglius, endeavored to keep alive this rumor, and at least to alarm with fears, however unsubstantial, the enemies whom he could no longer punish by his presence. Indeed, the dread of the influence of this extraordinary man was so exceedingly great that, to appease it, he was at last driven even from his home and his country.

After the death of Pius IV., Granvella went to Rome, to be present at the election of a new pope, and at the same time to discharge some commissions of his master, whose confidence in him remained unshaken. Soon after, Philip made him viceroy of Naples, where he succumbed to the seductions of the climate, and the spirit which no vicissitudes could bend voluptuousness overcame. He was sixty-two years old when the king allowed him to revisit Spain, where he continued with unlimited powers to administer the affairs of Italy. A gloomy old age, and the self-satisfied pride of a sexagenarian administration made him a harsh and rigid judge of the opinions of others, a slave of custom, and a tedious panegyrist of past times. But the policy of the closing century had ceased to be the policy of the opening one. A new and younger ministry were soon weary of so imperious a superintendent, and Philip himself began to shun the aged counsellor, who found nothing worthy of praise but the deeds of his father. Nevertheless, when the conquest of Portugal called Philip to Lisbon, he confided to the cardinal the care of his Spanish territories. Finally, on an Italian tour, in the town of Mantua, in the seventy-third year of his life, Granvella terminated his long existence in the full enjoyment of his glory, and after possessing for forty years the uninterrupted confidence of his king.

THE COUNCIL OF STATE.

(1564.) Immediately upon the departure of the minister, all the happy results which were promised from his withdrawal were fulfilled. The disaffected nobles resumed their seats in the council, and again devoted themselves to the affairs of the state with redoubled zeal, in order to give no room for regret for him whom they had driven away, and to prove, by the fortunate administration of the state, that his services were not indispensable. The crowd round the duchess was great. All vied with one another in readiness, in submission, and zeal in her service; the hours of night were not allowed to stop the transaction of pressing business of state; the greatest unanimity existed between the three councils, the best understanding between the court and the states. From the obliging temper of the Flemish nobility everything was to be had, as soon as their pride and self-will was flattered by confidence and obliging treatment. The regent took advantage of the first joy of the nation to beguile them into a vote of certain taxes, which, under the preceding administration, she could not have hoped to extort. In this, the great credit of the nobility effectually supported her, and she soon learned from this nation the secret, which had been so often verified in the German diet — that much must be demanded in order to get a little.

With pleasure did the regent see herself emancipated from her long thraldom; the emulous industry of the nobility lightened for her the burden of business, and their insinuating humility allowed her to feel the full sweetness of power.

(1564). Granvella had been overthrown, but his party still remained. His policy lived in his creatures, whom he left behind him in the privy council and in the chamber of finance. Hatred still smouldered amongst the factious long after the leader was banished, and the names of the Orange and Royalist parties, of the Patriots and Cardinalists still continued to divide the senate and to keep up the flames of discord. Viglius Van Zuichem Van Aytta, president of the privy council, state counsellor and keeper of the seal, was now looked upon as the most important person in the senate, and the most powerful prop of the crown and the tiara. This highly meritorious old man, whom we have to thank for some valuable contributions towards the history of the rebellion of the Low Countries, and whose confidential correspondence with his friends has generally been the guide of our narrative, was one of the greatest lawyers of his time, as well as a theologian and priest, and had already, under the Emperor, filled the most important offices. Familiar intercourse with the learned men who adorned the age, and at the head of whom stood Erasmus of Rotterdam, combined with frequent travels in the imperial service, had extended the sphere of his information and experience, and in many points raised him in his principles and opinions above his contemporaries. The fame of his erudition filled the whole century in which he lived, and has handed his name down to posterity. When, in the year 1548, the connection of the Netherlands with the German empire was to be settled at the Diet of Augsburg, Charles V. sent hither this statesman to manage the interests of the provinces; and his ability principally succeeded in turning the negotiations to the advantage of the Netherlands. After the death of the Emperor, Viglius was one of the many eminent ministers bequeathed to Philip by his father, and one of the few in whom he honored his memory. The fortune of the minister, Granvella, with whom he was united by the ties of an early acquaintance, raised him likewise to greatness; but he did not share the fall of his patron, because he had not participated in his lust of power; nor, consequently, the hatred which attached to him. A residence of twenty years in the provinces, where the most important affairs were entrusted to him, approved loyalty to his king, and zealous attachment to the Roman Catholic tenets, made him one of the most distinguished instruments of royalty in the Netherlands.

Viglius was a man of learning, but no thinker; an experienced statesman, but without an enlightened mind; of an intellect not sufficiently powerful to break, like his friend Erasmus, the fetters of error, yet not sufficiently bad to employ it, like his predecessor, Granvella, in the service of his own passions. Too weak and timid to follow boldly the guidance of his reason, he preferred trusting to the more convenient path of conscience; a thing was just so soon as it became his duty; he belonged to those honest men who are indispensable to bad ones; fraud reckoned on his honesty. Half a century later he would have received his immortality from the freedom which he now helped to subvert. In the privy council at Brussels he was the servant of tyranny; in the parliament in London, or in the senate at Amsterdam, he would have died, perhaps, like Thomas More or Olden Barneveldt.

In the Count Barlaimont, the president of the council of finance, the opposition had a no less formidable antagonist than in Viglius. Historians have transmitted but little information regarding the services and the opinions of this man. In the first part of his career the dazzling greatness of Cardinal Granvella seems to have cast a shade over him; after the latter had disappeared from the stage the superiority of the opposite party kept him down, but still the little that we do find respecting him throws a favorable light over his character. More than once the Prince of Orange exerted himself to detach him from the interests of the cardinal, and to join him to his own party — sufficient proof that he placed a value on the prize. All his efforts failed, which shows that he had to do with no vacillating character. More than once we see him alone, of all the members of the council, stepping forward to oppose the dominant faction, and protecting against universal opposition the interests of the crown, which were in momentary peril of being sacrificed. When the Prince of Orange had assembled the knights of the Golden Fleece in his own palace, with a view to induce them to come to a preparatory resolution for the abolition of the Inquisition, Barlaimont was the first to denounce the illegality of this proceeding and to inform the regent of it. Some time after the prince asked him if the regent knew of that assembly, and Barlaimont hesitated not a moment to avow to him the truth. All the steps which have been ascribed to him bespeak a man whom neither influence nor fear could tempt,— who, with a firm courage and indomitable constancy, remained faithful to the party which he had once chosen, but who, it must at the same time be confessed, entertained too proud and too despotic notions to have selected any other.

Amongst the adherents of the royal party at Brussels, we have, further, the names of the Duke of Arschot, the Counts of Mansfeld, Megen, and Aremberg — all three native Netherlanders; and therefore, as it appeared, bound equally with the whole Netherlandish nobility to oppose the hierarchy and the royal power in their native country. So much the more surprised must we feel at their contrary behavior, and which is indeed the more remarkable, since we find them on terms of friendship with the most eminent members of the faction, and anything but insensible to the common grievances of their country.

But they had not self-confidence or heroism enough to venture on an unequal contest with so superior an antagonist. With a cowardly prudence they made their just discontent submit to the stern law of necessity, and imposed a hard sacrifice on their pride because their pampered vanity was capable of nothing better. Too thrifty and too discreet to wish to extort from the justice or the fear of their sovereign the certain good which they already possessed from his voluntary generosity, or to resign a real happiness in order to preserve the shadow of another, they rather employed the propitious moment to drive a traffic with their constancy, which, from the general defection of the nobility, had now risen in value. Caring little for true glory, they allowed their ambition to decide which party they should take; for the ambition of base minds prefers to bow beneath the hard yoke of compulsion rather than submit to the gentle sway of a superior intellect. Small would have been the value of the favor conferred had they bestowed themselves on the Prince of Orange; but their connection with royalty made them so much the more formidable as opponents. There their names would have been lost among his numerous adherents and in the splendor of their rival. On the almost deserted side of the court their insignificant merit acquired lustre.

The families of Nassau and Croi (to the latter belonged the Duke of Arschot) had for several reigns been competitors for influence and honor, and their rivalry had kept up an old feud between their families, which religious differences finally made irreconcilable. The house of Croi from time immemorial had been renowned for its devout and strict observance of papistic rites and ceremonies; the Counts of Nassau had gone over to the new sect — sufficient reasons why Philip of Croi, Duke of Arschot, should prefer a party which placed him the most decidedly in opposition to the Prince of Orange. The court did not fail to take advantage of this private feud, and to oppose so important an enemy to the increasing influence of the house of Nassau in the republic. The Counts Mansfeld and Megen had till lately been the confidential friends of Count Egmont. In common with him they had raised their voice against the minister, had joined him in resisting the Inquisition and the edicts, and had hitherto held with him as far as honor and duty would permit. But at these limits the three friends now separated. Egmont's unsuspecting virtue incessantly hurried him forwards on the road to ruin; Mansfeld and Megen, admonished of the danger, began in good time to think of a safe retreat. There still exist letters which were interchanged between the Counts Egmont and Mansfeld, and which, although written at a later period, give us a true picture of their former friendship. "If," replied Count Mansfeld to his friend, who in an amicable manner had reproved him for his defection to the king, "if formerly I was of opinion that the general good made the abolition of the Inquisition, the mitigation of the edicts, and the removal of the Cardinal Granvella necessary, the king has now acquiesced in this wish and removed the cause of complaint. We have already done too much against the majesty of the sovereign and the authority of the church; it is high time for us to turn, if we would wish to meet the king, when he comes, with open brow and without anxiety. As regards my own person, I do not dread his vengeance; with confident courage I would at his first summons present myself in Spain, and boldly abide my sentence from his justice and goodness. I do not say this as if I doubted whether Count Egmont can assert the same, but he will act prudently in looking more to his own safety, and in removing suspicion from his actions. If I hear," he says, in conclusion, "that he has allowed my admonitions to have their due weight, our friendship continues; if not, I feel myself in that case strong enough to sacrifice all human ties to my duty and to honor."

The enlarged power of the nobility exposed the republic to almost a greater evil than that which it had just escaped by the removal of the minister. Impoverished by long habits of luxury, which at the same time had relaxed their morals, and to which they were now too much addicted to be able to renounce them, they yielded to the perilous opportunity of indulging their ruling inclination, and of again repairing the expiring lustre of their fortunes. Extravagance brought on the thirst for gain, and this introduced bribery. Secular and ecclesiastical offices were publicly put up to sale; posts of honor, privileges, and patents were sold to the highest bidder; even justice was made a trade. Whom the privy council had condemned was acquitted by the council of state, and what the former refused to grant was to be purchased from the latter. The council of state, indeed, subsequently retorted the charge on the two other councils, but it forgot that it was its own example that corrupted them. The shrewdness of rapacity opened new sources of gain. Life, liberty, and religion were insured for a certain sum, like landed estates; for gold, murderers and malefactors were free, and the nation was plundered by a lottery. The servants and creatures of the state, counsellors and governors of provinces, were, without regard to rank or merit, pushed into the most important posts; whoever had a petition to present at court had to make his way through the governors of provinces and their inferior servants. No artifice of seduction was spared to implicate in these excesses the private secretary of the duchess, Thomas Armenteros, a man up to this time of irreproachable character. By pretended professions of attachment and friendship a successful attempt was made to gain his confidence, and by luxurious entertainments to undermine his principles; the seductive example infected his morals, and new wants overcame his hitherto incorruptible integrity. He was now blind to abuses in which he was an accomplice, and drew a veil over the crimes of others in order at the same time to cloak his own. With his knowledge the royal exchequer was robbed, and the objects of the government were defeated through a corrupt administration of its revenues. Meanwhile the regent wandered on in a fond dream of power and activity, which the flattery of the nobles artfully knew how to foster. The ambition of the factious played with the foibles of a woman, and with empty signs and an humble show of submission purchased real power from her. She soon belonged entirely to the faction, and had imperceptibly changed her principles. Diametrically opposing all her former proceedings, even in direct violation of her duty, she now brought before the council of state, which was swayed by the faction, not only questions which belonged to the other councils, but also the suggestions which Viglius had made to her in private, in the same way as formerly, under Granvella's administration, she had improperly neglected to consult it at all. Nearly all business and all influence were now diverted to the governors of provinces. All petitions were directed to them, by them all lucrative appointments were bestowed. Their usurpations were indeed carried so far that law proceedings were withdrawn from the municipal authorities of the towns and brought before their own tribunals. The respectability of the provincial courts decreased as theirs extended, and with the respectability of the municipal functionaries the administration of justice and civil order declined. The smaller courts soon followed the example of the government of the country. The spirit which ruled the council of state at Brussels soon diffused itself through the provinces. Bribery, indulgences, robbery, venality of justice, were universal in the courts of judicature of the country; morals degenerated, and the new sects availed themselves of this all-pervading licentiousness to propagate their opinions. The religious indifference or toleration of the nobles, who, either themselves inclined to the side of the innovators, or, at least, detested the Inquisition as an instrument of despotism, had mitigated the rigor of the religious edicts, and through the letters of indemnity, which were bestowed on many Protestants, the holy office was deprived of its best victims. In no way could the nobility more agreeably announce to the nation its present share in the government of the country than by sacrificing to it the hated tribunal of the Inquisition — and to this inclination impelled them still more than the dictates of policy. The nation passed in a moment from the most oppressive constraint of intolerance into a state of freedom, to which, however, it had already become too unaccustomed to support it with moderation. The inquisitors, deprived of the support of the municipal authorities, found themselves an object of derision rather than of fear. In Bruges the town council caused even some of their own servants to be placed in confinement, and kept on bread and water, for attempting to lay hands upon a supposed heretic. About this very time the mob in Antwerp, having made a futile attempt to rescue a person charged with heresy from the holy office, there was placarded in the public market-place an inscription, written in blood, to the effect that a number of persons had bound themselves by oath to avenge the death of that innocent person.

From the corruption which pervaded the whole council of state, the privy council, and the chamber of finance, in which Viglius and Barlaimont were presidents, had as yet, for the most part, kept themselves pure.

As the faction could not succeed in insinuating their adherents into those two councils the only course open to them was, if possible, to render both inefficient, and to transfer their business to the council of state. To carry out this design the Prince of Orange sought to secure the co-operation of the other state counsellors. "They were called, indeed, senators," he frequently declared to his adherents, "but others possessed the power. If gold was wanted to pay the troops, or when the question was how the spreading heresy was to be repressed, or the people kept in order, then they were consulted; although in fact they were the guardians neither of the treasury nor of the laws, but only the organs through which the other two councils operated on the state. And yet alone they were equal to the whole administration of the country, which had been uselessly portioned out amongst three separate chambers. If they would among themselves only agree to reunite to the council of state these two important branches of government, which had been dissevered from it, one soul might animate the whole body." A plan was preliminarily and secretly agreed on, in accordance with which twelve new Knights of the Fleece were to be added to the council of state, the administration of justice restored to the tribunal at Malines, to which it originally belonged, the granting of letters of grace, patents, and so forth, assigned to the president, Viglius, while the management of the finances should be committed to it. All the difficulties, indeed, which the distrust of the court and its jealousy of the increasing power of the nobility would oppose to this innovation were foreseen and provided against. In order to constrain the regent's assent, some of the principal officers of the army were put forward as a cloak, who were to annoy the court at Brussels with boisterous demands for their arrears of pay, and in case of refusal to threaten a rebellion. It was also contrived to have the regent assailed with numerous petitions and memorials complaining of the delays of justice, and exaggerating the danger which was to be apprehended from the daily growth of heresy. Nothing was omitted to darken the picture of the disorganized state of society, of the abuse of justice, and of the deficiency in the finances, which was made so alarming that she awoke with terror from the delusion of prosperity in which she had hitherto cradled herself. She called the three councils together to consult them on the means by which these disorders were to be remedied. The majority was in favor of sending an extraordinary ambassador to Spain, who by a circumstantial and vivid delineation should make the king acquainted with the true position of affairs, and if possible prevail on him to adopt efficient measures of reform. This proposition was opposed by Viglius, who, however, had not the slighest suspicion of the secret designs of the faction. "The evil complained of," he said, "is undoubtedly great, and one which can no longer be neglected with impunity, but it is not irremediable by ourselves. The administration of justice is certainly crippled, but the blame of this lies with the nobles themselves; by their contemptuous treatment they have thrown discredit on the municipal authorities, who, moreover, are very inadequately supported by the governors of provinces. If heresy is on the increase it is because the secular arm has deserted the spiritual judges, and because the lower orders, following the example of the nobles, have thrown off all respect for those in authority. The provinces are undoubtedly oppressed by a heavy debt, but it has not been accumulated, as alleged, by any malversation of the revenues, but by the expenses of former wars and the king's present exigences; still wise and prudent measures of finance might in a short time remove the burden. If the council of state would not be so profuse of its indulgences, its charters of immunity, and its exemptions; if it would commence the reformation of morals with itself, show greater respect to the laws, and do what lies in its power to restore to the municipal functionaries their former consideration; in short, if the councils and the governors of provinces would only fulfil their own duties the present grounds of complaint would soon be removed. Why, then, send an ambassador to Spain, when as yet nothing has occurred to justify so extraordinary an expedient? If, however, the council thinks otherwise, he would not oppose the general voice; only he must make it a condition of his concurrence that the principal instruction of the envoy should be to entreat the king to make them a speedy visit."

There was but one voice as to the choice of an envoy. Of all the Flemish nobles Count Egmont was the only one whose appointment would give equal satisfaction to both parties. His hatred of the Inquisition, his patriotic and liberal sentiments, and the unblemished integrity of his character, gave to the republic sufficient surety for his conduct, while for the reasons already mentioned he could not fail to be welcome to the king. Moreover, Egmont's personal figure and demeanor were calculated on his first appearance to make that favorable impression which goes so far towards winning the hearts of princes; and his engaging carriage would come to the aid of his eloquence, and enforce his petition with those persuasive arts which are indispensable to the success of even the most trifling suits to royalty. Egmont himself, too, wished for the embassy, as it would afford him the opportunity of adjusting, personally, matters with his sovereign.

About this time the Council, or rather synod, of Trent closed its sittings, and published its decrees to the whole of Christendom. But these canons, far from accomplishing the object for which the synod was originally convened, and satisfying the expectation of religious parties, had rather widened the breach between them, and made the schism irremediable and eternal.

The labors of the synod instead of purifying the

Romish Church from its corruptions had only reduced the latter to greater definiteness and precision, and invested them with the sanction of authority. All the subtilties of its teaching, all the arts and usurpations of the Roman See, which had hitherto rested more on arbitrary usage, were now passed into laws and raised into a system. The uses and abuses which during the barbarous times of ignorance and superstition had crept into Christianity were now declared essential parts of its worship, and anathemas were denounced upon all who should dare to contradict the dogmas or neglect the observances of the Romish communion. All were anathematized who should either presume to doubt the miraculous power of relics, and refuse to honor the bones of martyrs, or should be so bold as to doubt the availing efficacy of the intercession of saints. The power of granting indulgences, the first source of the defection from the See of Rome, was now propounded in an irrefragable article of faith; and the principle of monasticism sanctioned by an express decree of the synod, which allowed males to take the vows at sixteen and females at twelve. And while all the opinions of the Protestants were, without exception, condemned, no indulgence was shown to their errors or weaknesses, nor a single step taken to win them back by mildness to the bosom of the mother church. Amongst the Protestants the wearisome records of the subtle deliberations of the synod, and the absurdity of its decisions, increased, if possible, the hearty contempt which they had long entertained for popery, and laid open to their controversialists new and hitherto unnoticed points of attack. It was an ill-judged step to bring the mysteries of the church too close to the glaring torch of reason, and to fight with syllogisms for the tenets of a blind belief.

Moreover, the decrees of the Council of Trent were not satisfactory even to all the powers in communion with Rome. France rejected them entirely, both because she did not wish to displease the Huguenots, and also because she was offended by the supremacy which the pope arrogated to himself over the council; some of the Roman Catholic princes of Germany likewise declared against it. Little, however, as Philip II. was pleased with many of

its articles, which trenched too closely upon his own
rights, for no monarch was ever more jealous of his prerogative; highly as the pope's assumption of control over
the council, and its arbitrary, precipitate dissolution had
offended him; just as was his indignation at the slight
which the pope had put upon his ambassador; he nevertheless acknowedged the decrees of the synod, even in
its present form, because it favored his darling object —
the extirpation of heresy. Political considerations were
all postponed to this one religious object, and he commanded the publication and enforcement of its canons
throughout his dominions.

The spirit of revolt, which was diffused through the
Belgian provinces, scarcely required this new stimulus.
There the minds of men were in a ferment, and the character of the Romish Church had sunk almost to the lowest
point of contempt in the general opinion. Under such
circumstances the imperious and frequently injudicious
decrees of the council could not fail of being highly
offensive; but Philip II. could not belie his religious
character so far as to allow a different religion to a portion of his subjects, even though they might live on a
different soil and under different laws from the rest.
The regent was strictly enjoined to exact in the Netherlands the same obedience to the decrees of Trent which
was yielded to them in Spain and Italy.

They met, however, with the warmest opposition in the
council of state at Brussels. "The nation," William of
Orange declared, "neither would nor could acknowledge
them, since they were, for the most part, opposed to the
fundamental principles of their constitution; and, for
similar reasons, they had even been rejected by several
Roman Catholic princes." The whole council nearly was
on the side of Orange; a decided majority were for
entreating the king either to recall the decrees entirely or
at least to publish them under certain limitations. This
proposition was resisted by Viglius, who insisted on a
strict and literal obedience to the royal commands. "The
church," he said, "had in all ages maintained the purity
of its doctrines and the strictness of its discipline by
means of such general councils. No more efficacious

remedy could be opposed to the errors of opinion which had so long distracted their country than these very decrees, the rejection of which is now urged by the council of state. Even if they are occasionally at variance with the constitutional rights of the citizens this is an evil which can easily be met by a judicious and temperate application of them. For the rest it redounds to the honor of our sovereign, the King of Spain, that he alone, of all the princes of his time, refuses to yield his better judgment to necessity, and will not, for any fear of consequences, reject measures which the welfare of the church demands, and which the happiness of his subjects makes a duty."

But the decrees also contained several matters which affected the rights of the crown itself. Occasion was therefore taken of this fact to propose that these sections at least should be omitted from the proclamation. By this means the king might, it was argued, be relieved from these obnoxious and degrading articles by a happy expedient; the national liberties of the Netherlands might be advanced as the pretext for the omission, and the name of the republic lent to cover this encroachment on the authority of the synod. But the king had caused the decrees to be received and enforced in his other dominions unconditionally; and it was not to be expected that he would give the other Roman Catholic powers such an example of opposition, and himself undermine the edifice whose foundation he had been so assiduous in laying.

COUNT EGMONT IN SPAIN.

Count Egmont was despatched to Spain to make a forcible representation to the king on the subject of these decrees; to persuade him, if possible, to adopt a milder policy towards his Protestant subjects, and to propose to him the incorporation of the three councils, was the commission he received from the malcontents. By the regent he was charged to apprise the monarch of the refractory spirit of the people; to convince him of the impossibility of enforcing these edicts of religion in their full severity; and lastly to acquaint him with the bad state of the military defences and the exhausted condition of the exchequer.

The count's public instructions were drawn up by the President Viglius. They contained heavy complaints of the decay of justice, the growth of heresy, and the exhaustion of the treasury. He was also to press urgently a personal visit from the king to the Netherlands. The rest was left to the eloquence of the envoy, who received a hint from the regent not to let so fair an opportunity escape of establishing himself in the favor of his sovereign.

The terms in which the count's instructions and the representations which he was to make to the king were drawn up appeared to the Prince of Orange far too vague and general. "The president's statement," he said, "of our grievances comes very far short of the truth. How can the king apply the suitable remedies if we conceal from him the full extent of the evil? Let us not represent the numbers of the heretics inferior to what it is in reality. Let us candidly acknowledge that they swarm in every province and in every hamlet, however small. Neither let us disguise from him the truth that they despise the penal statutes and entertain but little reverence for the government. What good can come of this concealment? Let us rather openly avow to the king that the republic cannot long continue in its present condition. The privy council indeed will perhaps pronounce differently, for to them the existing disorders are welcome. For what else is the source of the abuse of justice and the universal corruption of the courts of law but its insatiable rapacity? How otherwise can the pomp and scandalous luxury of its members, whom we have seen rise from the dust, be supported if not by bribery? Do not the people daily complain that no other key but gold can open an access to them; and do not even their quarrels prove how little they are swayed by a care for the common weal? Are they likely to consult the public good who are the slaves of their private passions? Do they think forsooth that we, the governors of the provinces are, with our soldiers, to stand ready at the beck and call of an infamous lictor? Let them set bounds to their indulgences and free pardons which they so lavishly bestow on the very persons to whom we think it just and expedient to deny them. No one can remit the punishment of a crime without sinning against the society and contributing to the increase of the general evil. To my mind, and I have no hesitation to avow it, the distribution amongst so many councils of the state secrets and the affairs of government has always appeared highly objectionable. The council of state is sufficient for all the duties of the administration; several patriots have already felt this in silence, and I now openly declare it. It is my decided conviction that the only sufficient remedy for all the evils complained of is to merge the other two chambers in the council of state. This is the point which we must endeavor to obtain from the king, or the present embassy, like all others, will be entirely useless and ineffectual." The prince now laid before the assembled senate the plan which we have already described. Viglius, against whom this new proposition was individually and mainly directed, and whose eyes were now suddenly opened, was overcome by the violence of his vexation. The agitation of his feelings was too much for his feeble body, and he was found, on the following morning, paralyzed by apoplexy, and in danger of his life.

His place was supplied by Jaachim Hopper, a member of the privy council at Brussels, a man of old-fashioned morals and unblemished integrity, the president's most trusted and worthiest friend.* To meet the wishes of the Orange party he made some additions to the instructions of the ambassador, relating chiefly to the abolition of the Inquisition and the incorporation of the three councils, not so much with the consent of the regent as in the absence of her prohibition. Upon Count Egmont taking leave of the president, who had recovered from his attack, the latter requested him to procure in Spain permission to resign his appointment. His day, he declared, was past; like the example of his friend and predecessor, Granvella, he wished to retire into the quiet

* Vita Vigl. § 89. The person from whose memoirs I have already drawn so many illustrations of the times of this epoch. His subsequent journey to Spain gave rise to the correspondence between him and the president, which is one of the most valuable documents for our history.

of private life, and to anticipate the uncertainty of fortune. His genius warned him of impending storm, by which he could have no desire to be overtaken.

Count Egmont embarked on his journey to Spain in January, 1565, and was received there with a kindness and respect which none of his rank had ever before experienced. The nobles of Castile, taught by the king's example to conquer their feelings, or rather, true to his policy, seemed to have laid aside their ancient grudge against the Flemish nobility, and vied with one another in winning his heart by their affability. All his private matters were immediately settled to his wishes by the king, nay, even his expectations exceeded; and during the whole period of his stay he had ample cause to boast of the hospitality of the monarch. The latter assured him in the strongest terms of his love for his Belgian subjects, and held out hopes of his acceding eventually to the general wish, and remitting somewhat of the severity of the religious edicts. At the same time, however, he appointed in Madrid a commission of theologians to whom he propounded the question, "Is it *necessary* to grant to the provinces the religious toleration they demand?" As the majority of them were of opinion that the peculiar constitution of the Netherlands, and the fear of a rebellion might well excuse a degree of forbearance in their case, the question was repeated more pointedly. "He did not seek to know," he said, "if he might do so, but if he must." When the latter question was answered in the negative, he rose from his seat, and kneeling down before a crucifix prayed in these words: "Almighty Majesty, suffer me not at any time to fall so low as to consent to reign over those who reject thee!" In perfect accordance with the spirit of this prayer were the measures which he resolved to adopt in the Netherlands. On the article of religion this monarch had taken his resolution once forever; urgent necessity might, perhaps, have constrained him temporarily to suspend the execution of the penal statutes, but never, formally, to repeal them entirely, or even to modify them. In vain did Egmont represent to him that the public execution of the heretics daily augmented the number of their followers, while the

courage and even joy with which they met their death filled
the spectators with the deepest admiration, and awakened
in them high opinions of a doctrine which could make
such heroes of its disciples. This representation was not
indeed lost upon the king, but it had a very different
effect from what it was intended to produce. In order
to prevent these seductive scenes, without, however, compromising the severity of the edicts, he fell upon an
expedient, and ordered that in future the executions
should take place in private. The answer of the king on
the subject of the embassy was given to the count in
writing, and addressed to the regent. The king, when
he granted him an audience to take leave, did not omit
to call him to account for his behavior to Granvella, and
alluded particularly to the livery invented in derision of
the cardinal. Egmont protested that the whole affair
had originated in a convivial joke, and nothing was
further from their meaning than to derogate in the least
from the respect that was due to royalty. "If he knew,"
he said, "that any individual among them had entertained
such disloyal thoughts he himself would challenge him to
answer for it with his life."

At his departure the monarch made him a present of
fifty thousand florins, and engaged, moreover, to furnish
a portion for his daughter on her marriage. He also
consigned to his care the young Farnese of Parma, whom,
to gratify the regent, his mother, he was sending to
Brussels. The king's pretended mildness, and his professions of regard for the Belgian nation, deceived the open-
hearted Fleming. Happy in the idea of being the bearer
of so much felicity to his native country, when in fact it
was more remote than ever, he quitted Madrid satisfied
beyond measure to think of the joy with which the provinces would welcome the message of their good king; but
the opening of the royal answer in the council of state at
Brussels disappointed all these pleasing hopes. "Although in regard to the religious edicts," this was its
tenor, "his resolve was firm and immovable, and he
would rather lose a thousand lives than consent to alter
a single letter of it, still, moved by the representations of
Count Egmont, he was, on the other hand, equally deter-

mined not to leave any gentle means untried to guard the people against the delusions of heresy, and so to avert from them that punishment which must otherwise infallibly overtake them. As he had now learned from the count that the principal source of the existing errors in the faith was in the moral depravity of the clergy, the bad instruction and the neglected education of the young, he hereby empowered the regent to appoint a special commission of three bishops, and a convenient number of learned theologians, whose business it should be to consult about the necessary reforms, in order that the people might no longer be led astray through scandal, nor plunge into error through ignorance. As, moreover, he had been informed that the public executions of the heretics did but afford them an opportunity of boastfully displaying a foolhardy courage, and of deluding the common herd by an affectation of the glory of martyrdom, the commission was to devise means for putting in force the final sentence of the Inquisition with greater privacy, and thereby depriving condemned heretics of the honor of their obduracy." In order, however, to provide against the commission going beyond its prescribed limits Philip expressly required that the Bishop of Ypres, a man whom he could rely on as a determined zealot for the Romish faith, should be one of the body. Their deliberations were to be conducted, if possible, in secrecy, while the object publicly assigned to them should be the introduction of the Tridentine decrees. For this his motive seems to have been twofold; on the one hand, not to alarm the court of Rome by the assembling of a private council; nor, on the other, to afford any encouragement to the spirit of rebellion in the provinces. At its sessions the duchess was to preside, assisted by some of the more loyally disposed of her counsellors, and regularly transmit to Philip a written account of its transactions. To meet her most pressing wants he sent her a small supply in money. He also gave her hopes of a visit from himself; first, however, it was necessary that the war with the Turks, who were then expected in hostile force before Malta, should be terminated. As to the proposed augmentation of the council of state, and its union with the privy council and chamber of finance, it was passed over in perfect silence. The Duke of Arschot, however, who is already known to us as a zealous royalist, obtained a voice and seat in the latter. Viglius, indeed, was allowed to retire from the presidency of the privy council, but he was obliged, nevertheless, to continue to discharge its duties for four more years, because his successor, Carl Tyssenaque, of the council for Netherlandish affairs in Madrid, could not sooner be spared.

SEVERER RELIGIOUS EDICTS — UNIVERSAL OPPOSITION OF THE NATION.

Scarcely was Egmont returned when severer edicts against heretics, which, as it were, pursued him from Spain, contradicted the joyful tidings which he had brought of a happy change in the sentiments of the monarch. They were at the same time accompanied with a transcript of the decrees of Trent, as they were acknowledged in Spain, and were now to be proclaimed in the Netherlands also; with it came likewise the death warrants of some Anabaptists and other kinds of heretics. "The count has been beguiled," William the Silent was now heard to say, "and deluded by Spanish cunning. Self-love and vanity have blinded his penetration; for his own advantage he has forgotten the general welfare." The treachery of the Spanish ministry was now exposed, and this dishonest proceeding roused the indignation of the noblest in the land. But no one felt it more acutely than Count Egmont, who now perceived himself to have been the tool of Spanish duplicity, and to have become unwittingly the betrayer of his own country. "These specious favors then," he exclaimed, loudly and bitterly, "were nothing but an artifice to expose me to the ridicule of my fellow-citizens, and to destroy my good name. If this is the fashion after which the king purposes to keep the promises which he made to me in Spain, let who will take Flanders; for my part, I will prove by my retirement from public business that I have no share in this breach of faith." In fact, the Spanish ministry could not have adopted a surer method of breaking the credit of so important a man than by exhibiting him to his fellow-citizens, who adored him, as one whom they had succeeded in deluding.

Meanwhile the commission had been appointed, and had unanimously come to the following decision : " Whether for the moral reformation of the clergy, or for the religious instruction of the people, or for the education of youth, such abundant provision had already been made in the decrees of Trent that nothing now was requisite but to put these decrees in force as speedily as possible. The imperial edicts against the heretics already ought on no account to be recalled or modified ; the courts of justice, however, might be secretly instructed to punish with death none but obstinate heretics or preachers, to make a difference between the different sects, and to show consideration to the age, rank, sex, or disposition of the accused. If it were really the case that public executions did but inflame fanaticism, then, perhaps, the unheroic, less observed, but still equally severe punishment of the galleys, would be well-adapted to bring down all high notions of martyrdom. As to the delinquencies which might have arisen out of mere levity, curiosity, and thoughtlessness it would perhaps be sufficient to punish them by fines, exile, or even corporal chastisement."

During these deliberations, which, moreover, it was requisite to submit to the king at Madrid, and to wait for the notification of his approval of them, the time passed away unprofitably, the proceedings against the sectaries being either suspended, or at least conducted very supinely. Since the recall of Granvella the disunion which prevailed in the higher councils, and from thence had extended to the provincial courts of justice, combined with the mild feelings generally of the nobles on the subject of religion, had raised the courage of the sects, and allowed free scope to the proselytizing mania of their apostles. The inquisitors, too, had fallen into contempt in consequence of the secular arm withdrawing its support, and in many places even openly taking their victims under its protection. The Roman Catholic part of the nation had formed great expectations from the decrees of the synod of Trent, as well as from Egmont's embassy to Spain ; but in the latter case their hopes had scarcely been justified by the joyous tidings which the count had brought back, and, in the integrity of his heart, left nothing undone to make known as widely as possible. The more disused the nation had become to severity in matters pertaining to religion the more acutely was it likely to feel the sudden adoption of even still more rigorous measures. In this position of affairs the royal rescript arrived from Spain in answer to the proposition of the bishops and the last despatches of the regent. "Whatever interpretation (such was its tenor) Count Egmont may have given to the king's verbal communications, it had never in the remotest manner entered his mind to think of altering in the slightest degree the penal statutes which the Emperor, his father, had five-and-thirty years ago published in the provinces. These edicts he therefore commanded should henceforth be carried rigidly into effect, the Inquisition should receive the most active support from the secular arm, and the decrees of the council of Trent be irrevocably and unconditionally acknowledged in all the provinces of his Netherlands. He acquiesced fully in the opinion of the bishops and canonists as to the sufficiency of the Tridentine decrees as guides in all points of reformation of the clergy or instruction of the people; but he could not concur with them as to the mitigation of punishment which they proposed in consideration either of the age, sex, or character of individuals, since he was of opinion that his edicts were in no degree wanting in moderation. To nothing but want of zeal and disloyalty on the part of judges could he ascribe the progress which heresy had already made in the country. In future, therefore, whoever among them should be thus wanting in zeal must be removed from his office and make room for a more honest judge. The Inquisition ought to pursue its appointed path firmly, fearlessly, and dispassionately, without regard to or consideration of human feelings, and was to look neither before nor behind. He would always be ready to approve of all its measures however extreme if it only avoided public scandal."

This letter of the king, to which the Orange party have ascribed all the subsequent troubles of the Netherlands, caused the most violent excitement amongst the state counsellors, and the expressions which in society they either accidentally or intentionally let fall from them with regard to it spread terror and alarm amongst the people. The dread of the Spanish Inquisition returned with new force, and with it came fresh apprehensions of the subversion of their liberties. Already the people fancied they could hear prisons building, chains and fetters forging, and see piles of fagots collecting. Society was occupied with this one theme of conversation, and fear kept no longer within bounds. Placards were affixed to houses of the nobles in which they were called upon, as formerly Rome called on her Brutus, to come forward and save expiring freedom. Biting pasquinades were published against the new bishops — tormentors as they were called; the clergy were ridiculed in comedies, and abuse spared the throne as little as the Romish see.

Terrified by the rumors which were afloat, the regent called together all the counsellors of state to consult them on the course she ought to adopt in this perilous crisis. Opinion varied and disputes were violent. Undecided between fear and duty they hesitated to come to a conclusion, until at last the aged senator, Viglius, rose and surprised the whole assembly by his opinion. "It would," he said, "be the height of folly in us to think of promulgating the royal edict at the present moment; the king must be informed of the reception which, in all probability, it will now meet. In the meantime the inquisitors must be enjoined to use their power with moderation, and to abstain from severity." But if these words of the aged president surprised the whole assembly, still greater was the astonishment when the Prince of Orange stood up and opposed his advice. "The royal will," he said, "is too clearly and too precisely stated; it is the result of too long and too mature deliberation for us to venture to delay its execution without bringing on ourselves the reproach of the most culpable obstinacy." "That I take on myself," interrupted Viglius; "I oppose myself to his displeasure. If by this delay we purchase for him the peace of the Netherlands our opposition will eventually secure for us the lasting gratitude of the king." The regent already began to incline to the advice of Viglius, when the prince vehemently interposing, "What," he demanded, "what have the many representations which we have already made effected? of what avail was the embassy we so lately despatched? Nothing! And what then do we wait for more? Shall we, his state counsellors, bring upon ourselves the whole weight of his displeasure by determining, at our own peril, to render him a service for which he will never thank us?" Undecided and uncertain the whole assembly remained silent; but no one had courage enough to assent to or reply to him. But the prince had appealed to the fears of the regent, and these left her no choice. The consequences of her unfortunate obedience to the king's command will soon appear. But, on the other hand, if by a wise disobedience she had avoided these fatal consequences, is it clear that the result would not have been the same? However she had adopted the most fatal of the two counsels: happen what would the royal ordinance was to be promulgated. This time, therefore, faction prevailed, and the advice of the only true friend of the government, who, to serve his monarch, was ready to incur his displeasure, was disregarded. With this session terminated the peace of the regent: from this day the Netherlands dated all the trouble which uninterruptedly visited their country. As the counsellors separated the Prince of Orange said to one who stood nearest to him, "Now will soon be acted a great tragedy."*

* The conduct of the Prince of Orange in this meeting of the council has been appealed to by historians of the Spanish party as a proof of his dishonesty, and they have availed themselves over and over again to blacken his character. "He," say they, "who had, invariably up to this period, both by word and deed, opposed the measures of the court so long as he had any ground to fear that the king's measures could be successfully carried out, supported them now for the first time when he was convinced that a scrupulous obedience to the royal orders would inevitably prejudice him. In order to convince the king of his folly in disregarding his warnings; in order to be able to boast, 'this I foresaw,' and 'I foretold that,' he was willing to risk the welfare of his nation, for which alone he had hitherto professed to struggle. The whole tenor of his previous conduct proved that he held the enforcement of the edicts to be an evil; nevertheless, he at once becomes false to his own convictions and follows an opposite course; although, so far as the nation was concerned, the same grounds existed as had dictated his former measures; and he changed his conduct simply that the result might be different to the king." "It is clear, therefore," continue his adversaries, "that the welfare of the nation had less weight with him than his animosity to his sovereign. In order to gratify his hatred to the latter he does not

An edict, therefore, was issued to all the governors of provinces, commanding them rigorously to enforce the mandates of the Emperor against heretics, as well as those which had been passed under the present government, the decrees of the council of Trent, and those of the episcopal commission, which had lately sat to give all the aid of the civil force to the Inquisition, and also to enjoin a similar line of conduct on the officers of government under them. More effectually to secure their object, every governor was to select from his own council an efficient officer who should frequently make the circuit of the province and institute strict inquiries into the obedience shown by the inferior officers to these commands, and then transmit quarterly to the capital an exact report of their visitation. A copy of the Tridentine decrees, according to the Spanish original, was also sent to the archbishops and bishops, with an intimation that in case of their needing the assistance of the secular power, the governors of their diocese, with their troops, were placed at their disposal. Against these decrees no privilege was to avail; however, the king willed and commanded that the particular territorial rights of the provinces and towns should in no case be infringed.

These commands, which were publicly read in every town by a herald, produced an effect on the people which in the fullest manner verified the fears of the President Viglius and the hopes of the Prince of Orange.

hesitate to sacrifice the former." But is it then true that by calling for the promulgation of these edicts he sacrificed the nation? or, to speak more correctly, did he carry the edicts into effect by insisting on their promulgation? Can it not, on the contrary, be shown with far more probability that this was really the only way effectually to frustrate them? The nation was in a ferment, and the indignant people would (there was reason to expect, and as Viglius himself seems to have apprehended) show so decided a spirit of opposition as must compel the king to yield. "Now," says Orange, "my country feels all the impulse necessary for it to contend successfully with tyranny! If I neglect the present moment the tyrant will, by secret negotiation and intrigue, find means to obtain by stealth what by open force he could not. The same object will be steadily pursued, only with greater caution and forbearance; but extremity alone can combine the people to unity of purpose, and move them to bold measures." It is clear, therefore, that with regard to the king the prince did but change his language only; but that as far as the people was concerned his conduct was perfectly consistent. And what duties did he owe the king apart from those he owed the republic? Was he to oppose an arbitary act in the very moment when it was about to entail a just retribution on its author? Would he have done his duty to his country if he had deterred its oppressor from a precipitate step which alone could save it from its otherwise unavoidable misery?

Nearly all the governors of provinces refused compliance with them, and threatened to throw up their appointments if the attempt should be made to compel their obedience. "The ordinance," they wrote back, "was based on a statement of the numbers of the sectaries, which was altogether false.* Justice was appalled at the prodigious crowd of victims which daily accumulated under its hands; to destroy by the flames fifty thousand or sixty thousand persons from their districts was no commission for them." The inferior clergy too, in particular, were loud in their outcries against the decrees of Trent, which cruelly assailed their ignorance and corruption, and which moreover threatened them with a reform they so much detested. Sacrificing, therefore, the highest interests of their church to their own private advantage, they bitterly reviled the decrees and the whole council, and with liberal hand scattered the seeds of revolt in the minds of the people. The same outcry was now revived which the monks had formerly raised against the new bishops. The Archbishop of Cambray succeeded at last, but not without great opposition, in causing the decrees to be proclaimed. It cost more labor to effect this in Malines and Utrect, where the archbishops were at strife with their clergy, who, as they were accused, preferred to involve the whole church in ruin rather than submit to a reformation of morals.

Of all the provinces Brabant raised its voice the loudest. The states of this province appealed to their great privilege, which protected their members from being brought before a foreign court of justice. They spoke loudly of the oath by which the king had bound himself to observe all their statutes, and of the conditions under which they alone had sworn allegiance to him. Louvain, Antwerp, Brussels, and Herzogenbusch solemnly pro-

* The number of the heretics was very unequally computed by the two parties, according as the interests and passions of either made its increase or diminution desirable, and the same party often contradicted itself when its interest changed. If the question related to new measures of oppression, to the introduction of the inquisitional tribunals, etc., the numbers of the Protestants were countless and interminable. If, on the other hand, the question was of lenity towards them, of ordinances to their advantage, they were now reduced to such an insignificant number that it would not repay the trouble of making an innovation for this small body of ill-minded people.

tested against the decrees, and transmitted their protests in distinct memorials to the regent. The latter, always hesitating and wavering, too timid to obey the king, and far more afraid to disobey him, again summoned her council, again listened to the arguments for and against the question, and at last again gave her assent to the opinion which of all others was the most perilous for her to adopt. A new reference to the king in Spain was proposed; the next moment it was asserted that so urgen a crisis did not admit of so dilatory a remedy; it was necessary for the regent to act on her own responsibility, and either defy the threatening aspect of despair, or to yield to it by modifying or retracting the royal ordinance. She finally caused the annals of Brabant to be examined in order to discover if possible a precedent for the present case in the instructions of the first inquisitor whom Charles V. had appointed to the province. These instructions indeed did not exactly correspond with those now given; but had not the king declared that he introduced no innovation? This was precedent enough, and it was declared that the new edicts must also be interpreted in accordance with the old and existing statutes of the province. This explanation gave indeed no satisfaction to the states of Brabant, who had loudly demanded the entire abolition of the inquisition, but it was an encouragement to the other provinces to make similar protests and an equally bold opposition. Without giving the duchess time to decide upon their remonstrances they, on their own authority, ceased to obey the inquisition, and withdrew their aid from it. The inquisitors, who had so recently been expressly urged to a more rigid execution of their duties now saw themselves suddenly deserted by the secular arm, and robbed of all authority, while in answer to their application for assistance the court could give them only empty promises. The regent by thus endeavoring to satisfy all parties had displeased all.

During these negotiations between the court, the councils, and the states a universal spirit of revolt pervaded the whole nation. Men began to investigate the rights of the subject, and to scrutinize the prerogative of kings. "The Netherlanders were not so stupid," many were heard to say with very little attempt at secrecy, "as not to know right well what was due from the subject to the sovereign, and from the king to the subject; and that perhaps means would yet be found to repel force with force, although at present there might be no appearance of it." In Antwerp a placard was set up in several places calling upon the town council to accuse the King of Spain before the supreme court at Spires of having broken his oath and violated the liberties of the country, for, Brabant being a portion of the Burgundian circle, was included in the religious peace of Passau and Augsburg. About this time too the Calvinists published their confession of faith, and in a preamble addressed to the king, declared that they, although a hundred thousand strong, kept themselves nevertheless quiet, and like the rest of his subjects, contributed to all the taxes of the country; from which it was evident, they added, that of themselves they entertained no ideas of insurrection. Bold and incendiary writings were publicly disseminated, which depicted the Spanish tyranny in the most odious colors, and reminded the nation of its privileges, and occasionally also of its powers.*

The warlike preparations of Philip against the Porte, as well as those which, for no intelligible reason, Eric, Duke of Brunswick, about this time made in the vicinity, contributed to strengthen the general suspicion that the Inquisition was to be forcibly imposed on the Netherlands. Many of the most eminent merchants already spoke of quitting their houses and business to seek in some other part of the world the liberty of which they were here deprived; others looked about for a leader, and let fall hints of forcible resistance and of foreign aid.

That in this distressing position of affairs the regent might be left entirely without an adviser and without support, she was now deserted by the only person who

---

* The regent mentioned to the king a number (three thousand) of these writings. Strada 117. It is remarkable how important a part printing, and publicity in general, played in the rebellion of the Netherlands. Through this organ one restless spirit spoke to millions. Besides the lampoons, which for the most part were composed with all the low scurrility and brutality which was the distinguishing character of most of the Protestant polemical writings of the time, works were occasionally published which defended religious liberty in the fullest sense of the word,

was at the present moment indispensable to her, and who had contributed to plunge her into this embarrassment. "Without kindling a civil war," wrote to her William of Orange, "it was absolutely impossible to comply now with the orders of the king. If, however, obedience was to be insisted upon, he must beg that his place might be supplied by another who would better answer the expectations of his majesty, and have more power than he had over the minds of the nation. The zeal which on every other occasion he had shown in the service of the crown, would, he hoped, secure his present proceeding from misconstruction; for, as the case now stood, he had no alternative between disobeying the king and injuring his country and himself." From this time forth William of Orange retired from the council of state to his town of Breda, where in observant but scarcely inactive repose he watched the course of affairs. Count Horn followed his example. Egmont, ever vacillating between the republic and the throne, ever wearying himself in the vain attempt to unite the good citizen with the obedient subject — Egmont, who was less able than the rest to dispense with the favor of the monarch, and to whom, therefore, it was less an object of indifference, could not bring himself to abandon the bright prospects which were now opening for him at the court of the regent. The Prince of Orange had, by his superior intellect, gained an influence over the regent which great minds cannot fail to command from inferior spirits. His retirement had opened a void in her confidence which Count Egmont was now to fill by virtue of that sympathy which so naturally subsists between timidity, weakness, and good-nature. As she was as much afraid of exasperating the people by an exclusive confidence in the adherents to the crown, as she was fearful of displeasing the king by too close an understanding with the declared leaders of the faction, a better object for her confidence could now hardly be presented than this very Count Egmont, of whom it could not be said that he belonged to either of the two conflicting parties.

BOOK III.

CONSPIRACY OF THE NOBLES.

1565. Up to this point the general peace had it appears been the sincere wish of the Prince of Orange, the Counts Egmont and Horn, and their friends. They had pursued the true interests of their sovereign as much as the general weal; at least their exertions and their actions had been as little at variance with the former as with the latter. Nothing had as yet occurred to make their motives suspected, or to manifest in them a rebellious spirit. What they had done they had done in discharge of their bounden duty as members of a free state, as the representatives of the nation, as advisers of the king, as men of integrity and honor. The only weapons they had used to oppose the encroachments of the court had been remonstrances, modest complaints, petitions. They had never allowed themselves to be so far carried away by a just zeal for their good cause as to transgress the limits of prudence and moderation which on many occasions are so easily overstepped by party spirit. But all the nobles of the republic did not now listen to the voice of that prudence; all did not abide within the bounds of moderation.

While in the council of state the great question was discussed whether the nation was to be miserable or not, while its sworn deputies summoned to their assistance all the arguments of reason and of equity, and while the middle-classes and the people contented themselves with empty complaints, menaces, and curses, that part of the nation which of all seemed least called upon, and on whose support least reliance had been placed, began to take more active measures. We have already described a class of the nobility whose services and wants Philip at his accession had not considered it necessary to remember. Of these by far the greater number had asked for promotion from a much more urgent reason than a love of the mere honor. Many of them were deeply sunk in debt, from which by their own resources they could not hope to emancipate themselves. When then, in filling up appointments, Philip passed them over he wounded them in a point far more sensitive than their pride. In these suitors he had by his neglect raised up so many idle spies and merciless judges of his actions, so many collectors and propagators of malicious rumor. As their pride did not quit them with their prosperity, so now, driven by necessity, they trafficked with the sole capital which they could not alienate — their nobility and the political influence of their names; and brought into circulation a coin which only in such a period could have found currency — their protection. With a self-pride to which they gave the more scope as it was all they could now call their own, they looked upon themselves as a strong intermediate power between the sovereign and the citizen, and believed themselves called upon to hasten to the rescue of the oppressed state, which looked imploringly to them for succor. This idea was ludicrous only so far as their self-conceit was concerned in it; the advantages which they contrived to draw from it were substantial enough. The Protestant merchants, who held in their hands the chief part of the wealth of the Netherlands, and who believed they could not at any price purchase too dearly the undisturbed exercise of their religion, did not fail to make use of this class of people who stood idle in the market and ready to be hired. These very men whom at any other time the merchants, in the pride of riches, would most probably have looked down upon, now appeared likely to do them good service through their numbers, their courage, their credit with the populace, their enmity to the government, nay, through their beggarly pride itself and their despair. On these grounds they zealously endeavored to form a close union with them, and diligently fostered the disposition for rebellion, while they also used every means to keep alive their high opinions of themselves, and, what was most important, lured their poverty by well-applied pecuniary assistance and glittering promises. Few of them were so utterly insignificant as not to possess some influence, if not personally, yet at least by their relationship with higher and more powerful nobles; and if united they would be able to raise a formidable voice against the crown. Many of them had either already joined the new sect or were secretly inclined to it; and even those who were zealous Roman Catholics had political or private grounds enough to set them against the decrees of Trent and the Inquisition. All, in fine, felt the call of vanity sufficiently powerful not to allow the only moment to escape them in which they might possibly make some figure in the republic.

But much as might be expected from the co-operation of these men in a body it would have been futile and ridiculous to build any hopes on any one of them singly; and the great difficulty was to effect a union among them. Even to bring them together some unusual occurrence was necessary, and fortunately such an incident presented itself. The nuptials of Baron Montigny, one of the Belgian nobles, as also those of the Prince Alexander of Parma, which took place about this time in Brussels, assembled in that town a great number of the Belgian nobles. On this occasion relations met relations; new friendships were formed and old renewed; and while the distress of the country was the topic of conversation wine and mirth unlocked lips and hearts, hints were dropped of union among themselves, and of an alliance with foreign powers. These accidental meetings soon led to concealed ones, and public discussions gave rise to secret consultations. Two German barons, moreover, a Count of Holle and a Count of Schwarzenberg, who at this time were on a visit to the Netherlands, omitted nothing to awaken expectations of assistance from their neighbors. Count Louis of Nassau, too, had also a short time before visited several German courts to ascertain their sentiments.* It has even been asserted that secret emissaries of the Admiral Coligny were seen at this time in Brabant, but this, however, may be reasonably doubted.

If ever a political crisis was favorable to an attempt at revolution it was the present. A woman at the helm of

---

* It was not without cause that the Prince of Orange suddenly disappeared from Brussels in order to be present at the election of a king of Rome in Frankfort. An assembly of so many German princes must have greatly favored a negotiation.

government; the governors of provinces disaffected themselves and disposed to wink at insubordination in others; most of the state counsellors quite inefficient; no army to fall back upon; the few troops there were long since discontented on account of the outstanding arrears of pay, and already too often deceived by false promises to be enticed by new; commanded, moreover, by officers who despised the Inquisition from their hearts, and would have blushed to draw a sword in its behalf; and, lastly, no money in the treasury to enlist new troops or to hire foreigners. The court at Brussels, as well as the three councils, not only divided by internal dissensions, but in the highest degree venal and corrupt; the regent without full powers to act on the spot, and the king at a distance; his adherents in the provinces few, uncertain, and dispirited; the faction numerous and powerful; two-thirds of the people irritated against popery and desirous of a change — such was the unfortunate weakness of the government, and the more unfortunate still that this weakness was so well known to its enemies!

In order to unite so many minds in the prosecution of a common object a leader was still wanting, and a few influential names to give political weight to their enterprise. The two were supplied by Count Louis of Nassau and Henry Count Brederode, both members of the most illustrious houses of the Belgian nobility, who voluntarily placed themselves at the head of the undertaking. Louis of Nassau, brother of the Prince of Orange, united many splendid qualities which made him worthy of appearing on so noble and important a stage. In Geneva, where he studied, he had imbibed at once a hatred to the hierarchy and a love to the new religion, and on his return to his native country had not failed to enlist proselytes to his opinions. The republican bias which his mind had received in that school kindled in him a bitter hatred of the Spanish name, which animated his whole conduct and only left him with his latest breath. Popery and Spanish rule were in his mind identical — as indeed they were in reality — and the abhorrence which he entertained for the one helped to strengthen his dislike for the other. Closely as the brothers agreed in their inclinations and aversions the ways by which each sought to gratify them were widely dissimilar. Youth and an ardent temperament did not allow the younger brother to follow the tortuous course through which the elder wound himself to his object. A cold, calm circumspection carried the latter slowly but surely to his aim, and with a pliable subtilty he made all things subserve his purpose; with a foolhardy impetuosity which overthrew all obstacles, the other at times compelled success, but oftener accelerated disaster. For this reason William was a general and Louis never more than an adventurer; a sure and powerful arm if only it were directed by a wise head. Louis' pledge once given was good forever; his alliances survived every vicissitude, for they were mostly formed in the pressing moment of necessity, and misfortune binds more firmly than thoughtless joy. He loved his brother as dearly as he did his cause, and for the latter he died.

Henry of Brederode, Baron of Viane and Burgrave of Utrecht, was descended from the old Dutch counts who formerly ruled that province as sovereign princes. So ancient a title endeared him to the people, among whom the memory of their former lords still survived, and was the more treasured the less they felt they had gained by the change. This hereditary splendor increased the self-conceit of a man upon whose tongue the glory of his ancestors continually hung, and who dwelt the more on former greatness, even amidst its ruins, the more unpromising the aspect of his own condition became. Excluded from the honors and employments to which, in his opinion, his own merits and his noble ancestry fully entitled him (a squadron of light cavalry being all which was entrusted to him), he hated the government, and did not scruple boldly to canvass and to rail at its measures. By these means he won the hearts of the people. He also favored in secret the evangelical belief; less, however, as a conviction of his better reason than as an opposition to the government. With more loquacity than eloquence, and more audacity than courage, he was brave rather from not believing in danger than from being superior to it. Louis of Nassau burned for the cause which he defended; Brederode for the glory of being its defender; the former was satisfied in acting for his party, the latter discontented if he did not stand at its head. No one was more fit to lead off the dance in a rebellion, but it could hardly have a worse ballet-master. Contemptible as his threatened designs really were, the illusion of the multitude might have imparted to them weight and terror if it had occurred to them to set up a pretender in his person. His claim to the possessions of his ancestors was an empty name; but even a name was now sufficient for the general disaffection to rally round. A pamphlet which was at the time disseminated amongst the people openly called him the heir of Holland; and his engraved portrait, which was publicly exhibited, bore the boastful inscription: —

> Sum Brederodus ego, Batavæ non infima gentis
> Gloria, virtutem non unica pagina claudit.

(1565.) Besides these two, there were others also from among the most illustrious of the Flemish nobles: the young Count Charles of Mansfeld, a son of that nobleman whom we have found among the most zealous royalists; the Count Kinlemburg; two Counts of Bergen and of Battenburg; John of Marnix, Baron of Toulouse; Philip of Marnix, Baron of St. Aldegonde; with several others who joined the league, which, about the middle of November, in the year 1565, was formed at the house of Von Hammes, king at arms of the Golden Fleece. Here it was that six men decided the destiny of their country (as formerly a few confederates consummated the liberty of Switzerland), kindled the torch of a forty years' war, and laid the basis of a freedom which they themselves were never to enjoy. The objects of the league were set forth in the following declaration, to which Philip of Marnix was the first to subscribe his name: "Whereas certain ill-disposed persons, under the mask of a pious zeal, but in reality under the impulse of avarice and ambition, have by their evil counsels persuaded our most gracious sovereign the king to introduce into these countries the abominable tribunal of the Inquisition, a tribunal diametrically opposed to all laws, human and divine, and in cruelty far surpassing the barbarous institutions of heathenism; which raises the inquisitors above every other power, and debases man to a perpetual bondage, and by its snares exposes the honest citizen to a constant fear of death, inasmuch as any one (priest, it may be, or a faithless friend, a Spaniard or a reprobate), has it in his power at any moment to cause whom he will to be dragged before that tribunal, to be placed in confinement, condemned, and executed without the accused ever being allowed to face his accuser, or to adduce proof of his innocence; we, therefore, the undersigned, have bound ourselves to watch over the safety of our families, our estates, and our own persons. To this we hereby pledge ourselves, and to this end bind ourselves as a sacred fraternity, and vow with a solemn oath to oppose to the best of our power the introduction of this tribunal into these countries, whether it be attempted openly or secretly, and under whatever name it may be disguised. We at the same time declare that we are far from intending anything unlawful against the king our sovereign; rather is it our unalterable purpose to support and defend the royal prerogative, and to maintain peace, and, as far as lies in our power, to put down all rebellion. In accordance with this purpose we have sworn, and now again swear, to hold sacred the government, and to respect it both in word and deed, which witness Almighty God!

"Further, we vow and swear to protect and defend one another, in all times and places, against all attacks whatsoever touching the articles which are set forth in this covenant. We hereby bind ourselves that no accusation of any of our followers, in whatever name it may be clothed, whether rebellion, sedition, or otherwise, shall avail to annul our oath towards the accused, or absolve us from our obligation towards him. No act which is directed against the Inquisition can deserve the name of a rebellion. Whoever, therefore, shall be placed in arrest on any such charge, we here pledge ourselves to assist him to the utmost of our ability, and to endeavor by every allowable means to effect his liberation. In this, however, as in all matters, but especially in the conduct of all measures against the tribunal of the Inquisition, we submit ourselves to the general regulations of the league, or to the decision of those whom we may unanimously appoint our counsellors and leaders.

"In witness hereof, and in confirmation of this our common league and covenant, we call upon the holy name of the living God, maker of heaven and earth, and of all that are therein, who searches the hearts, the consciences, and the thoughts, and knows the purity of ours. We implore the aid of the Holy Spirit, that success and honor may crown our undertaking, to the glory of His name, and to the peace and blessing of our country!"

This covenant was immediately translated into several languages, and quickly disseminated through the provinces. To swell the league as speedily as possible each of the confederates assembled all his friends, relations, adherents, and retainers. Great banquets were held, which lasted whole days — irresistible temptations for a sensual, luxurious people, in whom the deepest wretchedness could not stifle the propensity for voluptuous living. Whoever repaired to these banquets — and every one was welcome — was plied with officious assurances of friendship, and, when heated with wine, carried away by the example of numbers, and overcome by the fire of a wild eloquence. The hands of many were guided while they subscribed their signatures; the hesitating were derided, the pusillanimous threatened, the scruples of loyalty clamored down; some even were quite ignorant what they were signing, and were ashamed afterwards to inquire. To many whom mere levity brought to the entertainment the general enthusiasm left no choice, while the splendor of the confederacy allured the mean, and its numbers encouraged the timorous. The abetters of the league had not scrupled at the artifice of counterfeiting the signature and seals of the Prince of Orange, Counts Egmont, Horn, Megen, and others, a trick which won them hundreds of adherents. This was done especially with a view of influencing the officers of the army, in order to be safe in this quarter, if matters should come at last to violence. The device succeeded with many, especially with subalterns, and Count Brederode even drew his sword upon an ensign who wished time for consideration. Men of all classes and conditions signed it. Religion made no difference. Roman Catholic priests even were associates of the league. The motives were not the same with all, but the pretext was similar. The Roman Catholics desired simply the abolition of the Inquisition, and a mitigation of the edicts; the Protestants aimed at unlimited freedom of conscience. A few daring spirits only entertained so bold a project as the overthrow of the present government, while the needy and indigent based the vilest hopes on a general anarchy. A farewell entertainment, which about this time was given to the Counts Schwarzenberg and Holle in Breda, and another shortly afterwards in Hogstraten, drew many of the principal nobility to these two places, and of these several had already signed the covenant. The Prince of Orange, Counts Egmont, Horn, and Megen were present at the latter banquet, but without any concert or design, and without having themselves any share in the league, although one of Egmont's own secretaries and some of the servants of the other three noblemen had openly joined it. At this entertainment three hundred persons gave in their adhesion to the covenant, and the question was mooted whether the whole body should present themselves before the regent armed or unarmed, with a declaration or with a petition? Horn and Orange (Egmont would not countenance the business in any way) were called in as arbiters upon this point, and they decided in favor of the more moderate and submissive procedure. By taking this office upon them they exposed themselves to the charge of having in no very covert manner lent their sanction to the enterprise of the confederates. In compliance, therefore, with their advice, it was determined to present their address unarmed, and in the form of a petition, and a day was appointed on which they should assemble in Brussels.

The first intimation the regent received of this conspiracy of the nobles was given by the Count of Megen soon after his return to the capital. "There was," he said, "an enterprise on foot; no less than three hundred of the nobles were implicated in it; it referred to religion; the members of it had bound themselves together by an oath; they reckoned much on foreign aid; she would soon know more about it." Though urgently pressed, he would give her no further information. "A nobleman," he said, "had confided it to him under the seal of secrecy, and he had pledged his word of honor to him." What really withheld him from giving her any further explanation was, in all probability, not so much any delicacy about his honor, as his hatred of the Inquisition, which he would not willingly do anything to advance. Soon after him, Count Egmont delivered to the regent a copy of the covenant, and also gave her the names of the conspirators, with some few exceptions. Nearly about the same time the Prince of Orange wrote to her: "There was, as he had heard, an army enlisted, four hundred officers were already named, and twenty thousand men would presently appear in arms." Thus the rumor was intentionally exaggerated, and the danger was multiplied in every mouth.

The regent, petrified with alarm at the first announcement of these tidings, and guided solely by her fears, hastily called together all the members of the council of state who happened to be then in Brussels, and at the same time sent a pressing summons to the Prince of Orange and Count Horn, inviting them to resume their seats in the senate. Before the latter could arrive she consulted with Egmont, Megen, and Barlaimont what course was to be adopted in the present dangerous posture of affairs. The question debated was whether it would be better to have recourse to arms or to yield to the emergency and grant the demands of the confederates; or whether they should be put off with promises, and an appearance of compliance, in order to gain time for procuring instructions from Spain, and obtaining money and troops? For the first plan the requisite supplies were wanting, and, what was equally requisite, confidence in the army, of which there seemed reason to doubt whether it had not been already gained by the conspirators. The second expedient would it was quite clear never be sanctioned by the king; besides it would serve rather to raise than depress the courage of the confederates; while, on the other hand, a compliance with their reasonable demands and a ready unconditional pardon of the past would in all probability stifle the rebellion in the cradle. The last opinion was supported by Megen and Egmont but opposed by Barlaimont. "Rumor," said the latter, "had exaggerated the matter; it is impossible that so formidable an armament could have been prepared so secretly and so rapidly. It was but a band of a few outcasts and desperadoes, instigated by two or three enthusiasts, nothing more. All will be quiet after a few heads have been struck off." The regent determined to await the opinion of the council of state, which was shortly to assemble; in the meanwhile, however, she was not inactive. The fortifications in the most important places were inspected and the necessary repairs speedily executed; her ambassadors at foreign courts received orders to redouble their vigilance; expresses were sent off to Spain. At the same time she caused the report to be revived of the near advent of the king, and in her external deportment put on a show of that imperturbable firmness which awaits attack without intending easily to yield to it. At the end of March (four whole months consequently from the framing of the covenant), the whole state council assembled in Brussels. There were present the Prince of Orange, the Duke of Arschot, Counts Egmont, Bergen, Megen, Aremberg, Horn, Hogstraten, Barlaimont, and others; the Barons Montigny and Hachicourt, all the knights of the Golden Fleece, with the President Viglius, State Counsellor Bruxelles, and the other assessors of the privy council. Several letters were produced which gave a clearer insight into the nature and objects of the conspiracy. The extremity to which the regent was reduced gave the disaffected a power which on the present occasion they did not neglect to use. Venting their long suppressed indignation, they indulged in bitter complaints against the court and against the government. "But lately," said the Prince of Orange, "the king sent forty thousand gold florins to the Queen of Scotland to support her in her undertakings against England, and he allows his Netherlands to be burdened with debt. Not to mention the unseasonableness of this subsidy and its fruitless expenditure, why should he bring upon us the resentment of a queen, who is both so important to us as a friend and as an enemy so much to be dreaded?" The prince did not even refrain on the present occasion from glancing at the concealed hatred which the king was suspected of cherishing against the family of Nassau and against him in particular. "It is well known," he said, "that he has plotted with the hereditary enemies of my house to take away my life, and that he waits with impatience only for a suitable opportunity." His example opened the lips of Count Horn also, and of many others besides, who with passionate vehemence descanted on their own merits and the ingratitude of the king. With difficulty did the regent succeed in silencing the tumult and in recalling attention to the proper subject of the debate. The question was whether the confederates, of whom it was now known that they intended to appear at court with a petition, should be admitted or not? The Duke of Arschot, Counts Aremberg, Megen, and Barlaimont gave their negative to the proposition. "What need of five hundred persons," said the latter, "to deliver a small memorial? This paradox of humility and defiance implies no good. Let them send to us one respectable man from among their number without pomp, without assumption, and so submit their application to us. Otherwise, shut the gates upon them, or if some insist on their admission let them be closely watched, and let the first act of insolence which any one of them shall be guilty of be punished with death." In this advice concurred Count Mansfeld, whose own son was among the conspirators; he had even threatened to disinherit his son if he did not quickly abandon the league.

Counts Megen, also, and Aremberg hesitated to receive the petition; the Prince of Orange, however, Counts Egmont, Horn, Hogstraten, and others voted emphatically for it. "The confederates," they declared, "were known to them as men of integrity and honor; a great part of them were connected with themselves by friendship and relationship, and they dared vouch for their behavior. Every subject was allowed to petition; a right which was enjoyed by the meanest individual in the state could not without injustice be denied to so respectable a body of men." It was therefore resolved by a majority of votes to admit the confederates on the condition that they should appear unarmed and conduct themselves temperately. The squabbles of the members of council had occupied the greater part of the sitting, so that it was necessary to adjourn the discussion to the following day. In order that the principal matter in debate might not again be lost sight of in useless complaints the regent at once hastened to the point: "Brederode, we are informed," she said, " is coming to us, with an address in the name of the league, demanding the abolition of the Inquisition and a mitigation of the edicts. The advice of my senate is to guide me in my answer to him; but before you give your opinions on this point permit me to premise a few words. I am told that there are many even amongst yourselves who load the religious edicts of the Emperor, my father, with open reproaches, and describe them to the people as inhuman and barbarous. Now I ask you, lords and gentlemen, knights of the Fleece, counsellors of his majesty and of the state, whether you did not yourselves vote for these edicts, whether the states of the realm have not recognized them as lawful? Why is that now blamed, which was formerly declared right? Is it because they have now become even more necessary than they then were? Since when is the Inquisition a new thing in the Netherlands? Is it not full sixteen years ago since the Emperor established it? And wherein is it more cruel than the edicts? If it be allowed that the latter were the work of wisdom, if the universal consent of the states has sanctioned them — why this opposition to the former, which is nevertheless far more humane than the edicts, if they are to be observed to the letter? Speak now freely; I am not desirous of fettering your decision; but it is your business to see that it is not misled by passion and prejudice." The council of state was again, as it always had been, divided between two opinions; but the few who spoke for the Inquisition and the literal execution of the edicts were outvoted by the opposite party with the Prince of Orange at its head. "Would to heaven," he began, "that my representations had been then thought worthy of attention, when as yet the grounds of apprehension were remote; things would in that case never have been carried so far as to make recourse to extreme measures indispensable, nor would men have been plunged deeper in error by the very means which were intended to beguile them from their delusion. We are all unanimous on the one main point. We all wish to see the Catholic religion safe; if this end can be secured without the aid of the Inquisition, it is well, and we offer our wealth and our blood to its service; but on this very point it is that our opinions are divided.

"There are two kinds of inquisition: the see of Rome lays claim to one, the other has, from time immemorial, been exercised by the bishops. The force of prejudice and of custom has made the latter light and supportable to us. It will find little opposition in the Netherlands, and the augmented numbers of the bishops will make it effective. To what purpose then insist on the former, the mere name of which is revolting to all the feelings of our minds? When so many nations exist without it why should it be imposed on us? Before Luther appeared it was never heard of; but the troubles with Luther happened at a time when there was an inadequate number of spiritual overseers, and when the few bishops were, moreover, indolent, and the licentiousness of the clergy excluded them from the office of judges. Now all is changed; we now count as many bishops as there are provinces. Why should not the policy of the government adjust itself to the altered circumstances of the times? We want leniency, not severity. The repugnance of the people is manifest — this we must seek to appease if we would not have it burst out into rebellion. With the death of Pius IV. the full powers of the inquisitors have expired; the new pope has as yet sent no ratification of their authority, without which no one formerly ventured to exercise his office. Now, therefore, is the time when it can be suspended without infringing the rights of any party.

"What I have stated with regard to the Inquisition holds equally good in respect to the edicts also. The exigency of the times called them forth, but are not those times passed? So long an experience of them ought at last to have taught us that against hersey no means are less successful than the fagot and sword. What incredible progress has not the new religion made during only the last few years in the provinces; and if we investigate the cause of this increase we shall find it principally in the glorious constancy of those who have fallen sacrifices to the truth of their opinions. Carried away by sympathy and admiration, men begin to weigh in silence whether what is maintained with such invincible courage may not really be the truth. In France and in England the same severities may have been inflicted on the Protestants, but have they been attended with any better success there than here? The very earliest Christians boasted that the blood of the martyrs was the seed of the church. The Emperor Julian, the most terrible enemy that Christianity ever experienced, was fully persuaded of this. Convinced that persecution did but kindle enthusiasm he betook himself to ridicule and derision, and found these weapons far more effective than force. In the Greek empire different teachers of heresy have arisen at different times. Arius under Constantine, Aetius under Constantius, Nestorius under Theodosius. But even against these arch-heretics and their disciples such cruel measures were never resorted to as are thought necessary against our unfortunate country — and yet where are all those sects now which once a whole world, I had almost said, could not contain? This is the natural course of heresy. If it is treated with contempt it crumbles into insignificance. It is as iron, which, if it lies idle, corrodes, and only becomes sharp by use. Let no notice be paid to it, and it loses its most powerful attraction, the magic of what is new and what is forbidden. Why will we not content ourselves with the measures which have been approved of by the wisdom of such great rulers? Example is ever the safest guide.

"But what need to go to pagan antiquity for guidance and example when we have near at hand the glorious precedent of Charles V., the greatest of kings, who taught at last by experience, abandoned the bloody path of persecution, and for many years before his abdication adopted milder measures. And Philip himself, our most gracious sovereign, seemed at first strongly inclined to leniency until the counsels of Granvella and of others like him changed these views; but with what right or wisdom they may settle between themselves. To me, however, it has always appeared indispensable that legislation to be wise and successful must adjust itself to the manners and maxims of the times. In conclusion, I would beg to remind you of the close understanding which subsists between the Huguenots and the Flemish Protestants. Let us beware of exasperating them any further. Let us not act the part of French Catholics towards them, lest they should play the Huguenots against us, and, like the latter, plunge their country into the horrors of a civil war." *

It was, perhaps, not so much the irresistible truth of his arguments, which, moreover, were supported by a decisive majority in the senate, as rather the ruinous state of the military resources, and the exhaustion of the treasury, that prevented the adoption of the opposite opinion which recommended an appeal to the force of arms that the Prince of Orange had chiefly to thank for the attention which now at last was paid to his representations. In order to avert at first the violence of the storm, and to gain time, which was so necessary to place the government in a better sate of preparation, it was agreed that a portion of the demands should be accorded to the confederates. It was also resolved to mitigate the penal statutes of the Emperor, as he himself would certainly mitigate them, were he again to appear among them at that day — and as, indeed, he had once shown under circumstances very similar to the present that he did not think it derogatory to his high dignity to do. The Inquisition was not to be introduced in any place where it did not already exist, and where it had been it should adopt a milder system, or even be entirely sus-

---

* No one need wonder, says Burgundias (a vehement stickler for the Roman Catholic religion and the Spanish party), that the speech of this prince evinced so much acquaintance with philosophy; he had acquired it in his intercourse with Balduin. 180. Barry, 174-178. Hopper, 72. Strada, 123, 124.

pended, especially since the inquisitors had not yet been confirmed in their office by the pope. The latter reason was put prominently forward, in order to deprive the Protestants of the gratification of ascribing the concessions to any fear of their own power, or to the justice of their demands. The privy council was commissioned to draw out this decree of the senate without delay. Thus prepared the confederates were awaited.

THE GUEUX.

The members of the senate had not yet dispersed, when all Brussels resounded with the report that the confederates were approaching the town. They consisted of no more than two hundred horse, but rumor greatly exaggerated their numbers. Filled with consternation, the regent consulted with her ministers whether it was best to close the gates on the approaching party or to seek safety in flight? Both suggestions were rejected as dishonorable; and the peaceable entry of the nobles soon allayed all fears of violence. The first morning after their arrival they assembled at Kuilemberg house, where Brederode administered to them a second oath, binding them before all other duties to stand by one another, and even with arms if necessary. At this meeting a letter from Spain was produced, in which it was stated that a certain Protestant, whom they all knew and valued, had been burned alive in that country by a slow fire. After these and similar preliminaries he called on them one after another by name to take the new oath and renew the old one in their own names and in those of the absent. The next day, the 5th of April, 1556, was fixed for the presentation of the petition. Their numbers now amounted to between three and four hundred. Amongst them were many retainers of the high nobility, as also several servants of the king himself and of the duchess.

With the Counts of Nassau and Brederode at their head, and formed in ranks of four by four, they advanced in procession to the palace; all Brussels attended the unwonted spectacle in silent astonishment. Here were to be seen a body of men advancing with too much boldness and confidence to look like supplicants, and led by two men who were not wont to be petitioners; and, on the other hand, with so much order and stillness as do not usually accompany rebellion. The regent received the procession surrounded by all her counsellors and the Knights of the Fleece. "These noble Netherlanders," thus Brederode respectfully addressed her, "who here present themselves before your highness, wish in their own name, and of many others besides who are shortly to arrive, to present to you a petition of whose importance as well as of their own humility this solemn procession must convince you. I, as speaker of this body, entreat you to receive our petition, which contains nothing but what is in unison with the laws of our country and the honor of the king."

"If this petition," replied Margaret, "really contains nothing which is at variance either with the good of the country, or with the authority of the king, there is no doubt that it will be favorably considered." "They had learnt," continued the spokesman, "with indignation and regret that suspicious objects had been imputed to their association, and that interested parties had endeavored to prejudice her highness against him; they therefore craved that she would name the authors of so grave an accusation, and compel them to bring their charges publicly, and in due form, in order that he who should be found guilty might suffer the punishment of his demerits." "Undoubtedly," replied the regent, "she had received unfavorable rumors of their designs and alliance. She could not be blamed, if in consequence she had thought it requisite to call the attention of the governors of the provinces to the matter; but, as to giving up the names of her informants to betray state secrets," she added, with an appearance of displeasure, "that could not in justice be required of her." She then appointed the next day for answering their petition; and in the meantime she proceeded to consult the members of her council upon it.

"Never" (so ran the petition which, according to some, was drawn up by the celebrated Balduin), "never had they failed in their loyalty to their king, and nothing now could be farther from their hearts; but they would rather run the risk of incurring the displeasure of their sovereign than allow him to remain longer in ignorance of the evils with which their native country was menaced, by the forcible introduction of the Inquisition and the continued enforcement of the edicts. They had long remained consoling themselves with the expectation that a general assembly of the states would be summoned to remedy these grievances; but now that even this hope was extinguished, they held it to be their duty to give timely warning to the regent. They, therefore, entreated her highness to send to Madrid an envoy, well disposed, and fully acquainted with the state and temper of the times, who should endeavor to persuade the king to comply with the demands of the whole nation, and abolish the Inquisition, to revoke the edicts, and in their stead cause new and more humane ones to be drawn up at a general assembly of the states. But, in the meanwhile, until they could learn the king's decision, they prayed that the edicts and the operations of the Inquisition be suspended." "If," they concluded, "no attention should be paid to their humble request, they took God, the king, the regent, and all her counsellors to witness that they had done their part, and were not responsible for any unfortunate result that might happen."

The following day the confederates, marching in the same order of procession, but in still greater numbers (Counts Bergen and Kuilemberg having, in the interim, joined them with their adherents), appeared before the regent in order to receive her answer. It was written on the margin of the petition, and was to the effect, "that entirely to suspend the Inquisition and the edicts, even temporarily, was beyond her powers; but in compliance with the wishes of the confederates she was ready to despatch one of the nobles to the king in Spain, and also to support their petition with all her influence. In the meantime, she would recommend the inquisitors to administer their office with moderation; but in return she should expect on the part of the league that they should abstain from all acts of violence, and undertake nothing to the prejudice of the Catholic faith." Little as these vague and general promises satisfied the confederates, they were, nevertheless, as much as they could have reasonably expected to gain at first. The granting or refusing of the petition had nothing to do with the primary object of the league. Enough for them at present that it was once recognized, enough that it was now, as it were, an established body, which by its power and threats might, if necessary, overawe the government. The confederates, therefore, acted quite consistently with their designs, in contenting themselves with this answer, and referring the rest to the good pleasure of the king. As, indeed, the whole pantomime of petitioning had only been invented to cover the more daring plan of the league, until it should have strength enough to show itself in its true light, they felt that much more depended on their being able to continue this mask, and on the favorable reception of their petition, than on its speedily being granted. In a new memorial, which they delivered three days after, they pressed for an express testimonial from the regent that they had done no more than their duty, and been guided simply by their zeal for the service of the king. When the duchess evaded a declaration, they even sent a person to repeat this request in a private interview. "Time alone and their future behavior," she replied to this person, "would enable her to judge of their designs."

The league had its origin in banquets, and a banquet gave it form and perfection. On the very day that the second petition was presented Brederode entertained the confederates in Kuilemberg house. About three hundred guests assembled; intoxication gave them courage, and their audacity rose with their numbers. During the conversation one of their number happened to remark that he had overheard the Count of Barlaimont whisper in French to the regent, who was seen to turn pale on the delivery of the petitions, that "she need not be afraid of a band of beggars (gueux);" (in fact, the majority of them had by their bad management of their incomes only too well deserved this appellation.) Now, as the very name for their fraternity was the very thing which had most perplexed them, an expression was eagerly caught up, which, while it cloaked the presumption of their enterprise in humility, was at the same time appropriate to them as petitioners. Immediately they drank to one another under this name, and the cry "long live the Gueux!" was accompanied with a general shout of applause. After the cloth had been removed Brederode appeared with a wallet over his shoulder similar to that which the vagrant pilgrims and mendicant monks of the time used to carry, and after returning thanks to all for their accession to the league, and boldly assuring them that he was ready to venture life and limb for every individual present, he drank to the health of the whole company out of a wooden beaker. The cup went round and every one uttered the same vow as he set it to his lips. Then one after the other they received the beggar's purse, and each hung it on a nail which he had appropriated to himself. The shouts and uproar attending this buffoonery attracted the Prince of Orange and Counts Egmont and Horn, who by chance were passing the spot at the very moment, and on entering the house were boisterously pressed by Brederode, as host, to remain and drink a glass with them.*

The entrance of three such influential personages renewed the mirth of the guests, and their festivities soon passed the bounds of moderation. Many were intoxicated; guests and attendants mingled together without distinction; the serious and the ludicrous, drunken fancies and affairs of state were blended one with another in a burlesque medley; and the discussions on the general distress of the country ended in the wild uproar of a bacchanalian revel. But it did not stop here; what they had resolved on in the moment of intoxication they attempted when sober to carry into execution. It was necessary to manifest to the people in some striking

* "But," Egmont asserted in his written defence, "we drank only one single small glass, and thereupon they cried "long live the king and the Gueux!' This was the first time that I heard that appellation, and it certainly did not please me. But the times were so bad that one was often compelled to share in much that was against one's inclination, and I knew not but I was doing an innocent thing." Procés criminels des Comtes d'Egmont, etc., 7. 1. Egmont's defence, Hopper, 94. Strada, 127-130. Burgund., 185, 187.

shape the existence of their protectors, and likewise to fan the zeal of the faction by a visible emblem; for this end nothing could be better than to adopt publicly this name of Gueux, and to borrow from it the tokens of the association. In a few days the town of Brussels swarmed with ash-gray garments such as were usually worn by mendicant friars and penitents. Every confederate put his whole family and domestics in this dress. Some carried wooden bowls thinly overlaid with plates of silver, cups of the same kind, and wooden knives; in short the whole paraphernalia of the beggar tribe, which they either fixed around their hats or suspended from their girdles. Round the neck they wore a golden or silver coin, afterwards called the Geusen penny, of which one side bore the effigy of the king, with the inscription, "True to the king;" on the other side were seen two hands folded together holding a wallet, with the words "as far as the beggar's scrip." Hence the origin of the name "Gueux," which was subsequently borne in the Netherlands by all who seceded from popery and took up arms against the king.

Before the confederates separated and dispersed among the provinces they presented themselves once more before the duchess, in order to remind her of the necessity of leniency towards the heretics until the arrival of the king's answer from Spain, if she did not wish to drive the people to extremities. "If, however," they added, "a contrary behavior should give rise to any evils they at least must be regarded as having done their duty."

To this the regent replied, "she hoped to be able to adopt such measures as would render it impossible for disorders to ensue; but if, nevertheless, they did occur, she could ascribe them to no one but the confederates. She therefore earnestly admonished them on their part to fulfil their engagements, but especially to receive no new members into the league, to hold no more private assemblies, and generally not to attempt any novel and unconstitutional measures." And in order to tranquillize their minds she commanded her private secretary, Berti, to show them the letters to the inquisitors and secular judges, wherein they were enjoined to observe modera tion towards all those who had not aggravated their heretical offences by any civil crime. Before their departure from Brussels they named four presidents from among their number who were to take care of the affairs of the league, and also particular administrators for each province. A few were left behind in Brussels to keep a watchful eye on all the movements of the court. Brederode, Kuilemberg, and Bergen at last quitted the town, attended by five hundred and fifty horsemen, saluted it once more beyond the walls with a discharge of musketry, and then the three leaders parted, Brederode taking the road to Antwerp, and the two others to Guelders. The regent had sent off an express to Antwerp to warn the magistrate of that town against him. On his arrival more than a thousand persons thronged to the hotel where he had taken up his abode. Showing himself at a window, with a full wineglass in his hand, he thus addressed them: "Citizens of Antwerp! I am here at the hazard of my life and my property to relieve you from the oppressive burden of the Inquisition. If you are ready to share this enterprise with me, and to acknowledge me as your leader, accept the health which I here drink to you, and hold up your hands in testimony of your approbation." Hereupon he drank to their health, and all hands were raised amidst clamorous shouts of exultation. After this heroic deed he quitted Antwerp.

Immediately after the delivery of the "petition of the nobles," the regent had caused a new form of the edicts to be drawn up in the privy council, which should keep the mean between the commands of the king and the demands of the confederates. But the next question that arose was to determine whether it would be advisable immediately to promulgate this mitigated form, or moderation, as it was commonly called, or to submit it first to the king for his ratification. The privy council who maintained that it would be presumptuous to take a step so important and so contrary to the declared sentiments of the monarch without having first obtained his sanction, opposed the vote of the Prince of Orange who supported the former proposition. Besides, they urged, there was cause to fear that it would not even content the nation.

A "moderation" devised with the assent of the states was what they particularly insisted on. In order, therefore, to gain the consent of the states, or rather to obtain it from them by stealth, the regent artfully propounded the question to the provinces singly, and first of all to those which possessed the least freedom, such as Artois, Namur, and Luxemburg. Thus she not only prevented one province encouraging another in opposition, but also gained this advantage by it, that the freer provinces, such as Flanders and Brabant, which were prudently reserved to the last, allowed themselves to be carried away by the example of the others. By a very illegal procedure the representatives of the towns were taken by surprise, and their consent exacted before they could confer with their constituents, while complete silence was imposed upon them with regard to the whole transaction. By these means the regent obtained the unconditional consent of some of the provinces to the "moderation," and, with a few slight changes, that of other provinces. Luxemburg and Namur subscribed it without scruple. The states of Artois simply added the condition that false informers should be subjected to a retributive penalty; those of Hainault demanded that instead of confiscation of the estates, which directly militated against their privileges, another discretionary punishment should be introduced. Flanders called for the entire abolition of the Inquisition, and desired that the accused might be secured in right of appeal to their own province. The states of Brabant were outwitted by the intrigues of the court. Zealand, Holland, Utrecht, Guelders, and Friesland as being provinces which enjoyed the most important privileges, and which, moreover, watched over them with the greatest jealousy, were never asked for their opinion. The provincial courts of judicature had also been required to make a report on the projected amendment of the law, but we may well suppose that it was unfavorable, as it never reached Spain. From the principal cause of this "moderation," which, however, really deserved its name, we may form a judgment of the general character of the edicts themselves. "Sectarian writers," it ran, "the heads and teachers of sects, as also those who conceal heretical meetings, or cause any other public scandal, shall be punished with the gallows, and their estates, where the law of the province permit it, confiscated; but if they abjure their errors, their punishment shall be commuted into decapitation with the sword, and their effects shall be preserved to their families." A cruel snare for parental affection! Less grievous heretics, it was further enacted, shall, if penitent, be pardoned; and if impenitent shall be compelled to leave the country, without, however, forfeiting their estates, unless by continuing to lead others astray they deprive themselves of the benefit of this provision. The Anabaptists, however, were expressly excluded from benefiting by this clause; these, if they did not clear themselves by the most thorough repentance, were to forfeit their possessions; and if, on the other hand, they relapsed after penitence, that is, were backsliding heretics, they were to be put to death without mercy. The greater regard for life and property which is observable in this ordinance as compared with the edicts, and which we might be tempted to ascribe to a change of intention in the Spanish ministry, was nothing more than a compulsory step extorted by the determined opposition of the nobles. So little, too, were the people in the Netherlands satisfied by this "moderation," which fundamentally did not remove a single abuse, that instead of "moderation" (mitigation), they indignantly called it "moorderation," that is, murdering.

After the consent of the states had in this manner been extorted from them, the "moderation" was submitted to the council of the state, and, after receiving their signatures, forwarded to the king in Spain in order to receive from his ratification the force of law.

The embassy to Madrid, which had been agreed upon with the confederates, was at the outset entrusted to the Marquis of Bergen,* who, however, from a distrust of the present disposition of the king, which was only too well grounded, and from reluctance to engage alone in so delicate a business, begged for a coadjutor. He obtained

* This Marquis of Bergen is to be distinguished from Count William of Bergen, who was among the first who subscribed the covenant. Vigl. ad Hopper, Letter VII.

one in the Baron of Montigny, who had previously been employed in a similar duty, and had discharged it with high credit. As, however, circumstances had since altered so much that he had just anxiety as to his present reception in Madrid for his greater safety, he stipulated with the duchess that she should write to the monarch previously; and that he, with his companion, should, in the meanwhile, travel slowly enough to give time for the king's answer reaching him *en route*. His good genius wished, as it appeared, to save him from the terrible fate which awaited him in Madrid, for his departure was delayed by an unexpected obstacle, the Marquis of Bergen being disabled from setting out immediately through a wound which he received from the blow of a tennis-ball. At last, however, yielding to the pressing importunities of the regent, who was anxious to expedite the business, he set out alone, not, as he hoped, to carry the cause of his nation, but to die for it.

In the meantime the posture of affairs had changed so greatly in the Netherlands, the step which the nobles had recently taken had so nearly brought on a complete rupture with the government, that it seemed impossible for the Prince of Orange and his friends to maintain any longer the intermediate and delicate position which they had hitherto held between the country and the court, or to reconcile the contradictory duties to which it gave rise. Great must have been the restraint which, with their mode of thinking, they had to put on themselves not to take part in this contest; much, too, must their natural love of liberty, their patriotism, and their principles of toleration have suffered from the constraint which their official station imposed upon them. On the other hand, Philip's distrust, the little regard which now for a long time had been paid to their advice, and the marked slights which the duchess publicly put upon them, had greatly contributed to cool their zeal for the service, and to render irksome the longer continuance of a part which they played with so much repugnance and with so little thanks. This feeling was strengthened by several intimations they received from Spain which placed beyond doubt the great displeasure of the king at the petition of the nobles, and his little satisfaction with their own behavior on that occasion, while they were also led to expect that he was about to enter upon measures, to which, as favorable to the liberties of their country, and for the most part friends or blood relations of the confederates, they could never lend their countenance or support. On the name which should be applied in Spain to the confederacy of the nobles it principally depended what course they should follow for the future. If the petition should be called rebellion no alternative would be left them but either to come prematurely to a dangerous explanation with the court, or to aid it in treating as enemies those with whom they had both a fellow-feeling and a common interest. This perilous alternative could only be avoided by withdrawing entirely from public affairs; this plan they had once before practically adopted, and under present circumstances it was something more than a simple expedient. The whole nation had their eyes upon them. An unlimited confidence in their integrity, and the universal veneration for their persons, which closely bordered on idolatry, would ennoble the cause which they might make their own and ruin that which they should abandon. Their share in the administration of the state, though it were nothing more than nominal, kept the opposite party in check; while they attended the senate violent measures were avoided because their continued presence still favored some expectations of succeeding by gentle means. The withholding of their approbation, even if it did not proceed from their hearts, dispirited the faction, which, on the contrary, would exert its full strength so soon as it could reckon even distantly on obtaining so weighty a sanction. The very measures of the government which, if they came through their hands, were certain of a favorable reception and issue, would without them prove suspected and futile; even the royal concessions, if they were not obtained by the mediation of these friends of the people, would fail of the chief part of their efficacy. Besides, their retirement from public affairs would deprive the regent of the benefit of their advice at a time when counsel was most indispensable to her; it would, moreover, leave the preponderance with a party which, blindly dependent on the court, and ignorant of the peculiarities of republican character, would neglect nothing to aggravate the evil, and to drive to extremity the already exasperated mind of the public.

All these motives (and it is open to every one, according to his good or bad opinion of the prince, to say which was the most influential) tended alike to move him to desert the regent, and to divest himself of all share in public affairs. An opportunity for putting this resolve into execution soon presented itself. The prince had voted for the immediate promulgation of the newly-revised edicts; but the regent, following the suggestion of her privy council, had determined to transmit them first to the king. "I now see clearly," he broke out with well-acted vehemence, "that all the advice which I give is distrusted. The king requires no servants whose loyalty he is determined to doubt; and far be it from me to thrust my services upon a sovereign who is unwilling to receive them. Better, therefore, for him and me that I withdraw from public affairs." Count Horn expressed himself nearly to the same effect. Egmont requested permission to visit the baths of Aix-la-Chapelle, the use of which had been prescribed to him by his physician, although (as it is stated in his accusation) he appeared health itself. The regent, terrified at the consequences which must inevitably follow this step, spoke sharply to the prince. "If neither my representations, nor the general welfare can prevail upon you, so far as to induce you to relinquish this intention, let me advise you to be more careful, at least, of your own reputation. Louis of Nassau is your brother; he and Count Brederode, the heads of the confederacy, have publicly been your guests. The petition is in substance identical with your own representations in the council of state. If you now suddenly desert the cause of your king will it not be universally said that you favor the conspiracy?" We do not find it anywhere stated whether the prince really withdrew at this time from the council of state; at all events, if he did, he must soon have altered his mind, for shortly after he appears again in public transactions. Egmont

allowed himself to be overcome by the remonstrances of
the regent; Horn alone actually withdrew himself to one
of his estates,* with the resolution of never more serving
either emperor or king. Meanwhile the Gueux had dispersed themselves through the provinces, and spread
everywhere the most favorable reports of their success.
According to their assertions, religious freedom was
finally assured; and in order to confirm their statements
they helped themselves, where the truth failed, with
falsehood. For example, they produced a forged letter
of the Knights of the Fleece, in which the latter were made
solemnly to declare that for the future no one need fear
imprisonment, or banishment, or death on account of
religion, unless he also committed a political crime; and
even in that case the confederates alone were to be his
judges; and this regulation was to be in force until the
king, with the consent and advice of the states of the
realm, should otherwise dispose. Earnestly as the knights
applied themselves upon the first information of the
fraud to rescue the nation from their delusion, still it
had already in this short interval done good service
to the faction. If there are truths whose effect is limited
to a single instant, then inventions which last so long can
easily assume their place. Besides, the report, however
false, was calculated both to awaken distrust between the
regent and the knights, and to support the courage of the
Protestants by fresh hopes, while it also furnished those
who were meditating innovation an appearance of right,
which, however unsubstantial they themselves knew it to
be, served as a colorable pretext for their proceedings.
Quickly as this delusion was dispelled, still, in the short
space of time that it obtained belief, it had occasioned so
many extravagances, had introduced so much irregularity
and license, that a return to the former state of things
became impossible, and continuance in the course already
commenced was rendered necessary as well by habit as
by despair. On the very first news of this happy result
the fugitive Protestants had returned to their homes,
which they had so unwillingly abandoned; those who had
been in concealment came forth from their hiding-places;

* Where he remained three months inactive.

those who had hitherto paid homage to the new religion
in their hearts alone, emboldened by these pretended acts
of toleration, now gave in their adhesion to it publicly
and decidedly. The name of the "Gueux" was extolled
in all the provinces; they were called the pillars of religion and liberty; their party increased daily, and many
of the merchants began to wear their insignia. The
latter made an alteration in the "Gueux" penny, by
introducing two travellers' staffs, laid crosswise, to intimate that they stood prepared and ready at any instant
to forsake house and hearth for the sake of religion.
The Gueux league, in short, had now given to things an
entirely different form. The murmurs of the people,
hitherto impotent and despised, as being the cries of
individuals, had, now that they were concentrated, become formidable; and had gained power, direction, and
firmness through union. Every one who was rebelliously
disposed now looked on himself as the member of a
venerable and powerful body, and believed that by carrying his own complaints to the general stock of discontent
he secured the free expression of them. To be called an
important acquisition to the league flattered the vain; to
be lost, unnoticed, and irresponsible in the crowd was
an inducement to the timid. The face which the confederacy showed to the nation was very unlike that
which it had turned to the court. But had its objects
been the purest, had it really been as well disposed
towards the throne as it wished to appear, still the multitude would have regarded only what was illegal in its
proceedings, and upon them its better intentions would
have been entirely lost.

PUBLIC PREACHING.

No moment could be more favorable to the Huguenots
and the German Protestants than the present to seek
a market for their dangerous commodity in the Netherlands. Accordingly, every considerable town now
swarmed with suspicious arrivals, masked spies, and the
apostles of every description of heresy. Of the religious
parties, which had sprung up by secession from the ruling

church, three chiefly had made considerable progress in the provinces. Friesland and the adjoining districts were overrun by the Anabaptists, who, however, as the most indigent, without organization and government, destitute of military resources, and moreover at strife amongst themselves, awakened the least apprehension. Of far more importance were the Calvanists, who prevailed in the southern provinces, and above all in Flanders, who were powerfully supported by their neighbors the Huguenots, the republic of Geneva, the Swiss Cantons, and part of Germany, and whose opinions, with the exception of a slight difference, were also held by the throne in England. They were also the most numerous party, especially among the merchants and common citizens. The Huguenots, expelled from France, had been the chief disseminators of the tenets of this party. The Lutherans were inferior both in numbers and wealth, but derived weight from having many adherents among the nobility. They occupied, for the most part, the eastern portion of the Netherlands, which borders on Germany, and were also to be found in some of the northern territories. Some of the most powerful princes of Germany were their allies; and the religious freedom of that empire, of which by the Burgundian treaty the Netherlands formed an integral part, was claimed by them with some appearance of right. These three religious denominations met together in Antwerp, where the crowded population concealed them, and the mingling of all nations favored liberty. They had nothing in common, except an equally inextinguishable hatred of popery, of the Inquisition in particular, and of the Spanish government, whose instrument it was; while, on the other hand, they watched each other with a jealousy which kept their zeal in exercise, and perverted the glowing ardor of fanaticism from waxing dull.

The regent, in expectation that the projected "moderation" would be sanctioned by the king, had, in the meantime, to gratify the Gueux, recommended the governors and municipal officers of the provinces to be as moderate as possible in their proceedings against heretics; instructions which were eagerly followed, and interpreted in the widest sense by the majority, who had hitherto administered the painful duty of punishment with extreme repugnance. Most of the chief magistrates were in their hearts averse to the Inquisition and the Spanish tyranny, and many were even secretly attached to one or other of the religious parties; even the others were unwilling to inflict punishment on their countrymen to gratify their sworn enemies, the Spaniards. All, therefore, purposely misunderstood the regent, and allowed the Inquisition and the edicts to fall almost entirely into disuse. This forbearance of the government, combined with the brilliant representations of the Gueux, lured from their obscurity the Protestants, who, however, had now grown too powerful to be any longer concealed. Hitherto they had contented themselves with secret assemblies by night; now they thought themselves numerous and formidable enough to venture to these meetings openly and publicly. This license commenced somewhere between Oudenarde and Ghent, and soon spread through the rest of Flanders. A certain Hermann Stricker, born at Overyssel, formerly a monk, a daring enthusiast of able mind, imposing figure, and ready tongue, was the first who collected the people for a sermon in the open air. The novelty of the thing gathered together a crowd of about seven thousand persons. A magistrate of the neighborhood, more courageous than wise, rushed amongst the crowd with his drawn sword, and attempted to seize the preacher, but was so roughly handled by the multitude, who for want of other weapons took up stones and felled him to the ground, that he was glad to beg for his life.*

This success of the first attempt inspired courage for a second. In the vicinity of Aalst they assembled again in still greater numbers; but on this occasion they provided themselves with rapiers, firearms, and halberds, placed sentries at all the approaches, which they also barricaded with carts and carriages. All passers-by were

---

* The unheard-of foolhardiness of a single man rushing into the midst of a fanatical crowd of seven thousand people to seize before their eyes one whom they adored, proves, more than all that can be said on the subject, the insolent contempt with which the Roman Catholics of the time looked down upon the so-called heretics as an inferior race of beings.

obliged, whether willing or otherwise, to take part in the religious service, and to enforce this object lookout parties were posted at certain distances round the place of meeting. At the entrance booksellers stationed themselves, offering for sale Protestant catechisms, religious tracts, and pasquinades on the bishops. The preacher, Hermann Stricker, held forth from a pulpit which was hastily constructed for the occasion out of carts and trunks of trees. A canvas awning drawn over it protected him from the sun and the rain; the preacher's position was in the quarter of the wind that the people might not lose any part of his sermon, which consisted principally of revilings against popery. Here the sacraments were administered after the Calvinistic fashion, and water was procured from the nearest river to baptize infants without further ceremony, after the practice, it was pretended, of the earliest times of Christianity. Couples were also united in wedlock, and the marriage ties dissolved between others. To be present at this meeting half the population of Ghent had left its gates; their example was soon followed in other parts, and ere long spread over the whole of East Flanders. In like manner Peter Dathen, another renegade monk, from Poperingen, stirred up West Flanders; as many as fifteen thousand persons at a time attended his preaching from the villages and hamlets; their number made them bold, and they broke into the prisons, where some Anabaptists were reserved for martyrdom. In Tournay the Protestants were excited to a similar pitch of daring by Ambrosius Ville, a French Calvinist. They demanded the release of the prisoners of their sect, and repeatedly threatened if their demands were not complied with to deliver up the town to the French. It was entirely destitute of a garrison, for the commandant, from fear of treason, had withdrawn it into the castle, and the soldiers, moreover, refused to act against their fellow-citizens. The sectarians carried their audacity to such great lengths as to require one of the churches within the town to be assigned to them; and when this was refused they entered into a league with Valenciennes and Antwerp to obtain a legal recognition of their worship, after the example of

the other towns, by open force. These three towns maintained a close connection with each other, and the Protestant party was equally powerful in all. While, however, no one would venture singly to commence the disturbance, they agreed simultaneously to make a beginning with public preaching. Brederode's appearance in Antwerp at last gave them courage. Six thousand persons, men and women, poured forth from the town on an appointed day, on which the same thing happened in Tournay and Valenciennes. The place of meeting was closed in with a line of vehicles, firmly fastened together, and behind them armed men were secretly posted, with a view to protect the service from any surprise. Of the preachers, most of whom were men of the very lowest class — some were Germans, some were Huguenots — and spoke in the Walloon dialect; some even of the citizens felt themselves called upon to take a part in this sacred work, now that no fears of the officers of justice alarmed them. Many were drawn to the spot by mere curiosity to hear what kind of new and unheard-of doctrines these foreign teachers, whose arrival had caused so much talk, would set forth. Others were attracted by the melody of the psalms, which were sung in a French version, after the custom in Geneva. A great number came to hear these sermons as so many amusing comedies: such was the buffoonery with which the pope, the fathers of the ecclesiastical council of Trent, purgatory, and other dogmas of the ruling church were abused in them. And, in fact, the more extravagant was this abuse and ridicule the more it tickled the ears of the lower orders; and a universal clapping of hands, as in a theatre, rewarded the speaker who had surpassed others in the wildness of his jokes and denunciations. But the ridicule which was thus cast upon the ruling church was, nevertheless, not entirely lost on the minds of the hearers, as neither were the few grains of truth or reason which occasionally slipped in among it; and many a one, who had sought from these sermons anything but conviction, unconsciously carried away a little also of it.

These assemblies were several times repeated, and each day augmented the boldness of the sectarians; till at last they even ventured, after concluding the service, to conduct their preachers home in triumph, with an escort of armed horsemen, and ostentatiously to brave the law. The town council sent express after express to the duchess, entreating her to visit them in person, and if possible to reside for a short time in Antwerp, as the only expedient to curb the arrogance of the populace; and assuring her that the most eminent merchants, afraid of being plundered, were already preparing to quit it. Fear of staking the royal dignity on so hazardous a stroke of policy forbade her compliance; but she despatched in her stead Count Megen, in order to treat with the magistrate for the introduction of a garrison. The rebellious mob, who quickly got an inkling of the object of his visit, gathered around him with tumultuous cries, shouting, "He was known to them as a sworn enemy of the Gueux; that it was notorious he was bringing upon them prisons and the Inquisition, and that he should leave the town instantly." Nor was the tumult quieted till Megen was beyond the gates. The Calvinists now handed in to the magistrate a memorial, in which they showed that their great numbers made it impossible for them henceforward to assemble in secrecy, and requested a separate place of worship to be allowed them inside the town. The town council renewed its entreaties to the duchess to assist, by her personal presence, their perplexities, or at least to send to them the Prince of Orange, as the only person for whom the people still had any respect, and, moreover, as specially bound to the town of Antwerp by his hereditary title of its burgrave. In order to escape the greater evil she was compelled to consent to the second demand, however much against her inclination to entrust Antwerp to the prince. After allowing himself to be long and fruitlessly entreated, for he had all at once resolved to take no further share in public affairs, he yielded at last to the earnest persuasions of the regent and the boisterous wishes of the people. Brederode, with a numerous retinue, came half a mile out of the town to meet him, and both parties saluted each other with a discharge of pistols. Antwerp appeared to have poured out all her inhabitants to welcome her deliverer. The high road swarmed with multitudes; the roofs were taken off the houses in order that they might accommodate more spectators; behind fences, from churchyard walls, even out of graves started up men. The attachment of the people to the prince showed itself in childish effusions. "Long live the Gueux!" was the shout with which young and old received him. "Behold," cried others, "the man who shall give us liberty." "He brings us," cried the Lutherans, "the Confession of Augsburg!" "We don't want the Gueux now!" exclaimed others; "we have no more need of the troublesome journey to Brussels. He alone is everything to us!" Those who knew not what to say vented their extravagant joy in psalms, which they vociferously chanted as they moved along. He, however, maintained his gravity, beckoned for silence, and at last, when no one would listen to him, exclaimed with indignation, half real and half affected, "By God, they ought to consider what they did, or they would one day repent what they had now done." The shouting increased even as he rode into the town. The first conference of the prince with the heads of the different religious sects, whom he sent for and separately interrogated, presently convinced him that the chief source of the evil was the mutual distrust of the several parties, and the suspicions which the citizens entertained of the designs of the government, and that therefore it must be his first business to restore confidence among them all. First of all he attempted, both by persuasion and artifice, to induce the Calvinists, as the most numerous body, to lay down their weapons, and in this he at last, with much labor, succeeded. When, however, some wagons were soon afterwards seen laden with ammunition in Malines, and the high bailiff of Brabant showed himself frequently in the neighborhood of Antwerp with an armed force, the Calvinists, fearing hostile interruption of their religious worship, besought the prince to allot them a place within the walls for their sermons, which should be secure from a surprise. He succeeded once more in pacifying them, and his presence fortunately prevented an outbreak on the Assumption of the Virgin, which, as usual, had drawn a crowd to the town, and from whose sentiments there was but too much reason for alarm. The image of the Virgin was, with the usual pomp, carried round the town without interruption; a few words of abuse, and a suppressed murmur about idolatry, was all that the disapproving multitudes indulged in against the procession.

1566. While the regent received from one province after another the most melancholy accounts of the excesses of the Protestants, and while she trembled for Antwerp, which she was compelled to leave in the dangerous hands of the Prince of Orange, a new terror assailed her from another quarter. Upon the first authentic tidings of the public preaching she immediately called upon the league to fulfil its promises and to assist her in restoring order. Count Brederode used this pretext to summon a general meeting of the whole league, for which he could not have selected a more dangerous moment than the present. So ostentatious a display of the strength of the league, whose existence and protection had alone encouraged the Protestant mob to go the length it had already gone, would now raise the confidence of the sectarians, while in the same degree it depressed the courage of the regent. The convention took place in the town of Liege St. Truyen, into which Brederode and Louis of Nassau had thrown themselves at the head of two thousand confederates. As the long delay of the royal answer from Madrid seemed to presage no good from that quarter, they considered it advisable in any case to extort from the regent a letter of indemnity for their persons.

Those among them who were conscious of a disloyal sympathy with the Protestant mob looked on its licentiousness as a favorable circumstance for the league; the apparent success of those to whose degrading fellowship they had deigned to stoop led them to alter their tone; their former laudable zeal began to degenerate into insolence and defiance. Many thought that they ought to avail themselves of the general confusion and the perplexity of the duchess to assume a bolder tone and heap demand upon demand. The Roman Catholic members of the league, among whom many were in their hearts still strongly inclined to the royal cause, and who had been drawn into a connection with the league by occasion and example, rather than from feeling and conviction, now heard to their astonishment propositions for establishing universal freedom of religion, and were not a little shocked to discover in how perilous an enterprise they had hastily implicated themselves. On this discovery the young Count Mansfeld withdrew immediately from it, and internal dissensions already began to undermine the work of precipitation and haste, and imperceptibly to loosen the joints of the league.

Count Egmont and William of Orange were empowered by the regent to treat with the confederates. Twelve of the latter, among whom were Louis of Nassau, Brederode, and Kuilemberg, conferred with them in Duffle, a village near Malines. "Wherefore this new step?" demanded the regent by the mouth of these two noblemen. "I was required to despatch ambassadors to Spain; and I sent them. The edicts and the Inquisition were complained of as too rigorous; I have rendered both more lenient. A general assembly of the states of the realm was proposed; I have submitted this request to the king because I could not grant it from my own authority. What, then, have I unwittingly either omitted or done that should render necessary this assembling in St. Truyen? Is it perhaps fear of the king's anger and of its consequences that disturbs the confederates? The provocation certainly is great, but his mercy is even greater. Where now is the promise of the league to excite no disturbances amongst the people? Where those high-sounding professions that they were ready to die at my feet rather than offend against any of the prerogatives of the crown? The innovators already venture on things which border closely on rebellion, and threaten the state with destruction; and it is to the league that they appeal. If it continues silently to tolerate this it will justly bring on itself the charge of participating in the guilt of their offences; if it is honestly disposed towards the sovereign it cannot remain longer inactive in this licentiousness of the mob. But, in truth, does it not itself outstrip the insane population by its dangerous example, concluding, as it is known to do, alliances with the enemies of the country, and confirming the evil report of its designs by the present illegal meeting?"

Against these reproaches the league formally justified itself in a memorial which it deputed three of its members to deliver to the council of state at Brussels.

"All," it commenced, "that your highness has done in respect to our petition we have felt with the most lively gratitude; and we cannot complain of any new measure, subsequently adopted, inconsistent with your promise; but we cannot help coming to the conclusion that the orders of your highness are by the judicial courts, at least, very little regarded; for we are continually hearing — and our own eyes attest to the truth of the report — that in all quarters our fellow-citizens are in spite of the orders of your highness still mercilessly dragged before the courts of justice and condemned to death for religion. What the league engaged on its part to do it has honestly fulfilled; it has, too, to the utmost of its power endeavored to prevent the public preachings; but it certainly is no wonder if the long delay of an answer from Madrid fills the mind of the people with distrust, and if the disappointed hopes of a general assembly of the states disposes them to put little faith in any further assurances. The league has never allied, nor ever felt any temptation to ally, itself with the enemies of the country. If the arms of France were to appear in the provinces we, the confederates, would be the first to mount and drive them back again. The league, however, desires to be candid with your highness. We thought we read marks of displeasure in your countenance; we see men in exclusive possession of your favor who are notorious for their hatred against us. We daily hear that persons are warned from associating with us, as with those infected with the plague, while we are denounced with the arrival of the king as with the opening of a day of judgment — what is more natural than that such distrust shown to us should at last rouse our own? That the attempt to blacken our league with the reproach of treason, that the warlike preparations of the Duke of Savoy and of other princes, which, according to common report, are directed against ourselves; the negotiations of the king with the French court to obtain a passage through that kingdom for a Spanish army, which is destined, it is said, for the Netherlands — what wonder if these and similar occurrences should have stimulated us to think in time of the means of self-defence, and to strengthen ourselves by an alliance with our friends beyond the frontier? On a general, uncertain, and vague rumor we are accused of a share in this licentiousness of the Protestant mob; but who is safe from general rumor? True it is, certainly, that of our numbers some are Protestants, to whom religious toleration would be a welcome boon; but even they have never forgotten what they owe to their sovereign. It is not fear of the king's anger which instigated us to hold this assembly. The king is good, and we still hope that he is also just. It cannot, therefore, be pardon that we seek from him, and just as little can it be oblivion that we solicit for our actions, which are far from being the least considerable of the services we have at different times rendered his majesty. Again, it is true, that the delegates of the Lutherans and Calvinists are with us in St. Truyen; nay, more, they have delivered to us a petition which, annexed to this memorial, we here present to your highness. In it they offer to go unarmed to their preachings if the league will tender its security to them, and be willing to engage for a general meeting of the states. We have thought it incumbent upon us to communicate both these matters to you, for our guarantee can have no force unless it is at the same time confirmed by your highness and some of your principal counsellors. Among these no one can be so well acquainted with the circumstances of our cause, or be so upright in intention towards us, as the Prince of Orange and Counts Horn and Egmont. We gladly accept these three as meditators if the necessary powers are given to them, and assurance is afforded us that no troops will be enlisted without their knowledge. This guarantee, however, we only require for a given period, before the expiration of which it will rest with the king whether he will cancel or confirm it for the future. If the first should be his will it will then be but fair that time should be allowed us to place our persons and our property in security; for this three weeks will be sufficient. Finally, and in conclusion, we on our part also pledge ourselves to undertake nothing new without the concurrence of those three persons, our mediators."

The league would not have ventured to hold such bold language if it had not reckoned on powerful support and protection; but the regent was as little in a condition to concede their demands as she was incapable of vigorously opposing them. Deserted in Brussels by most of her counsellors of state, who had either departed to their provinces, or under some pretext or other had altogether withdrawn from public affairs; destitute as well of advisers as of money (the latter want had compelled her, in the first instance, to appeal to the liberality of the clergy; when this proved insufficient, to have recourse to a lottery), dependent on orders from Spain, which were ever expected and never received, she was at last reduced to the degrading expedient of entering into a negotiation with the confederates in St. Truyen, that they should wait twenty-four days longer for the king's resolution before they took any further steps. It was certainly surprising that the king still continued to delay a decisive answer to the petition, although it was universally known that he had answered letters of a much later date, and that the regent earnestly importuned him on this head. She had also, on the commencement of the public preaching, immediately despatched the Marquis of Bergen after the Baron of Montigny, who, as an eye-witness of these new occurrences, could confirm her written statements, to move the king to an earlier decision.

1566. In the meanwhile, the Flemish ambassador, Florence of Montigny, had arrived in Madrid, where he was received with a great show of consideration. His instructions were to press for the abolition of the Inquisition and the mitigation of the edicts; the augmentation of the council of state, and the incorporation with it of the two other councils; the calling of a general assembly of the states, and, lastly, to urge the solicitations of the regent for a personal visit from the king. As the latter, however, was only desirous of gaining time, Montigny was put off with fair words until the arrival of his coadjutor, without whom the king was not willing to come to any final determination. In the meantime, Montigny had every day and at any hour that he desired, an audience with the king, who also commanded that on all occasions the despatches of the duchess and the answers to them should be communicated to himself. He was, too, frequently admitted to the council for Belgian affairs, where he never omitted to call the king's attention to the necessity of a general assembly of the states, as being the only means of successfully meeting the troubles which had arisen, and as likely to supersede the necessity of any other measure. He moreover impressed upon him that a general and unreserved indemnity for the past would alone eradicate the distrust, which was the source of all existing complaints, and would always counteract the good effects of every measure, however well advised. He ventured, from a thorough acquaintance with circumstances and accurate knowledge of the character of his countrymen, to pledge himself to the king for their inviolable loyalty, as soon as they should be convinced of the honesty of his intentions by the straightforwardness of his proceedings; while, on the contrary, he assured him that there would be no hopes of it as long as they were not relieved of the fear of being made the victims of the oppression, and sacrificed to the envy of the Spanish nobles. At last Montigny's coadjutor made his appearance, and the objects of their embassy were made the subject of repeated deliberations.

1566. The king was at that time at his palace at Segovia, where also he assembled his state council. The members were: the Duke of Alva; Don Gomez de Figueroa; the Count of Feria; Don Antonio of Toledo, Grand Commander of St. John; Don John Manriquez of Lara, Lord Steward to the Queen; Ruy Gomez, Prince of Eboli and Count of Melito; Louis of Quixada, Master of the Horse to the Prince; Charles Tyssenacque, President of the Council for the Netherlands; Hopper, State Counsellor and Keeper of the Seal; and State Counsellor Corteville. The sitting of the council was protracted for several days; both ambassadors were in attendance, but the king was not himself present. Here, then, the conduct of the Belgian nobles was examined by Spanish eyes; step by step it was traced back to the most distant source; circumstances were brought into relation with others which, in reality, never had any connection; and what had been the offspring of the moment was made out to be a well-matured and far-sighted plan. All the different transactions and attempts of the nobles which had been governed solely by chance, and to which the natural order of events alone assigned their particular shape and succession, were said to be the result of a preconcerted scheme for introducing universal liberty in religion, and for placing all the power of the state in the hands of the nobles. The first step to this end was, it was said, the violent expulsion of the minister Granvella, against whom nothing could be charged, except that he was in possession of an authority which they preferred to exercise themselves. The second step was sending Count Egmont to Spain to urge the abolition of the Inquisition and the mitigation of the penal statutes, and to prevail on the king to consent to an augmentation of the council of state. As, however, this could not be surreptitiously obtained in so quiet a manner, the attempt was made to extort it from the court by a third and more daring step — by a formal conspiracy, the league of the Gueux. The fourth step to the same end was the present embassy, which at length boldly cast aside the mask, and by the insane proposals which they were not ashamed to make to their king, clearly brought to light the object to which all the preceding steps had tended. Could the abolition of the Inquisition, they exclaimed, lead to anything less than a complete freedom of belief? Would not the guiding helm of conscience be lost with it? Did not the proposed "moderation" introduce an absolute impunity for all heresies? What was the project of augmenting the council of state and of suppressing the two other councils but a complete remodelling of the government of the country in favor of the nobles? — a general constitution for all the provinces of the Netherlands? Again, what was this compact of the ecclesiastics in their public preachings but a third conspiracy, entered into with the very same objects which the league of the nobles in the council of state and that of the Gueux had failed to effect?

However, it was confessed that whatever might be the source of the evil it was not on that account the less important and imminent. The immediate personal presence of the king in Brussels was, indubitably, the most efficacious means speedily and thoroughly to remedy it. As, however, it was already so late in the year, and the preparations alone for the journey would occupy the short time which was to elapse before the winter set in; as the stormy season of the year, as well as the danger from French and English ships, which rendered the sea unsafe, did not allow of the king's taking the northern route, which was the shorter of the two; as the rebels themselves meanwhile might become possessed of the island of Walcheren, and oppose the landing of the king; for all these reasons, the journey was not to be thought of before the spring, and in absence of the only complete remedy it was necessary to rest satisfied with a partial expedient. The council, therefore, agreed to propose to the king, in the first place, that he should recall the papal Inquisition from the provinces and rest satisfied with that of the bishops; in the second place, that a new plan for the mitigation of the edicts should be projected, by which the honor of religion and of the king would be better preserved than it had been in the transmitted "moderation;" thirdly, that in order to reassure the minds of the people, and to leave no means untried, the king should impart to the regent full powers to extend free grace and pardon to all those who had not already committed any heinous crime, or who had not as yet been condemned by any judicial process; but from the benefit of this indemnity the preachers and all who harbored them were to be excepted. On the other hand, all leagues, associations, public assemblies, and preachings were to be henceforth prohibited under heavy penalties; if, however, this prohibition should be infringed, the regent was to be at liberty to employ the regular troops and garrisons for the forcible reduction of the refractory, and also, in case of necessity, to enlist new troops, and to name the commanders over them according as should be deemed advisable. Finally, it would have a good effect if his majesty would write to the most eminent towns, prelates, and leaders of the nobility, to some in his own hand, and to all in a gracious tone, in order to stimulate their zeal in his service.

When this resolution of his council of state was submitted to the king his first measure was to command public processions and prayers in all the most considerable places of the kingdom and also of the Netherlands, imploring the Divine guidance in his decision. He appeared in his own person in the council of state in order to approve this resolution and render it effective. He declared the general assembly of the states to be useless and entirely abolished it. He, however, bound himself to retain some German regiments in his pay, and, that they might serve with the more zeal, to pay them their long-standing arrears. He commanded the regent in a private letter to prepare secretly for war; three thousand horse and ten thousand infantry were to be assembled by her in Germany, to which end he furnished her with the necessary letters and transmitted to her a sum of three hundred thousand gold florins. He also accompanied this resolution with several autograph letters to some private individuals and towns, in which he thanked them in the most gracious terms for the zeal which they had already displayed in his service and called upon them to manifest the same for the future. Notwithstanding that he was inexorable on the most important point, and the very one on which the nation most particularly insisted — the convocation of the states, notwithstanding that his limited and ambiguous pardon was as good as none, and depended too much on arbitrary will to calm the public mind; notwithstanding, in fine, that he rejected, as too lenient, the proposed "moderation," but which, on the part of the people, was complained of as too severe; still he had this time made an unwonted step in the favor of the nation; he had sacrificed to it the papal Inquisition and left only the episcopal, to which it was accustomed. The nation had found more equitable judges in the

Spanish council than they could reasonably have hoped for. Whether at another time and under other circumstances this wise concession would have had the desired effect we will not pretend to say. It came too late; when (1566) the royal letters reached Brussels the attack on images had already commenced.

BOOK IV.

THE ICONOCLASTS.

The springs of this extraordinary occurrence are plainly not to be sought for so far back as many historians affect to trace them. It is certainly possible, and very probable, that the French Protestants did industriously exert themselves to raise in the Netherlands a nursery for their religion, and to prevent by all means in their power an amicable adjustment of differences between their brethren in the faith in that quarter and the King of Spain, in order to give that implacable foe of their party enough to do in his own country. It is natural, therefore, to suppose that their agents in the provinces left nothing undone to encourage their oppressed brethren with daring hopes, to nourish their animosity against the ruling church, and by exaggerating the oppression under which they sighed to hurry them imperceptibly into illegal courses. It is possible, too, that there were many among the confederates who thought to help out their own lost cause by increasing the number of their partners in guilt; who thought they could not otherwise maintain the legal character of their league unless the unfortunate results against which they had warned the king really came to pass, and who hoped in the general guilt of all to conceal their own individual criminality. It is, however, incredible that the outbreak of the Iconoclasts was the fruit of a deliberate plan, preconcerted, as it is alleged, at the convent of St. Truyen. It does not seem likely that in a solemn assembly of so many nobles and warriors, of whom the greater part were the adherents of popery, an individual should be found insane enough to propose an act of positive infamy, which did not so much injure any religious party in particular, as rather tread under foot all respect for religion in general, and even all morality too, and which could have been conceived only in the mind of the vilest reprobate. Besides, this outrage was too sudden in its outbreak, too vehement in its execution altogether, too monstrous to have been anything more than the offspring of the moment in which it saw the light; it seemed to flow so naturally from the circumstances which preceded it that it does not require to be traced far back to remount to its origin.

A rude mob, consisting of the very dregs of the populace, made brutal by harsh treatment, by sanguinary decrees which dogged them in every town, scared from place to place and driven almost to despair, were compelled to worship their God, and to hide like a work of darkness the universal, sacred privilege of humanity. Before their eyes proudly rose the temples of the dominant church, in which their haughty brethren indulged in ease their magnificent devotion, while they themselves were driven from the walls, expelled, too, by the weaker number perhaps, and forced, here in the wild woods, under the burning heat of noon, in disgraceful secrecy to worship the same God; cast out from civil society into a state of nature, and reminded in one dread moment of the rights of that state! The greater their superiority of numbers the more unnatural did their lot appear; with wonder they perceive the truth. The free heaven, the arms lying ready, the frenzy in their brains and fury in their hearts combine to aid the suggestions of some preaching fanatic; the occasion calls; no premeditation is necessary where all eyes at once declare consent; the resolution is formed ere yet the word is scarcely uttered; ready for any unlawful act, no one yet clearly knows what, the furious band rushes onwards. The smiling prosperity of the hostile religion insults the poverty of their own; the pomp of the authorized temples casts contempt on their proscribed belief; every cross they set up upon the highway, every image of the saints that they meet, is a trophy erected over their own humiliation, and they all must be removed by their avenging hands. Fanaticism suggests these detestable proceedings, but base passions carry them into execution.

1566. The commencement of the attack on images took place in West Flanders and Artois, in the districts between Lys and the sea. A frantic herd of artisans, boatmen, and peasants, mixed with prostitutes, beggars, vagabonds, and thieves, about three hundred in number, furnished with clubs, axes, hammers, ladders, and cords (a few only were provided with swords or fire arms), cast themselves, with fanatical fury, into the villages and hamlets near St. Omer, and breaking open the gates of such churches and cloisters as they find locked, overthrow everywhere the altars, break to pieces the images of the saints, and trample them under foot. With their excitement increased by its indulgence, and reinforced by newcomers, they press on by the direct road to Ypres, where they can count on the support of a strong body of Calvinists. Unopposed, they break into the cathedral, and mounting on ladders they hammer to pieces the pictures, hew down with axes the pulpits and pews, despoil the altars of their ornaments, and steal the holy vessels. This example was quickly followed in Menin, Comines, Verrich, Lille, and Oudenard; in a few days the same fury spreads through the whole of Flanders. At the very time when the first tidings of this occurrence arrived Antwerp was swarming with a crowd of houseless people, which the feast of the Assumption of the Virgin had brought together in that city. Even the presence of the Prince of Orange was hardly sufficient to restrain the licentious mob, who burned to imitate the doings of their brethren in St. Omer; but an order from the court which summoned him to Brussels, where the regent was just assembling her council of state, in order to lay before them the royal letters, obliged him to abandon Antwerp to the outrages of this band. His departure was the signal for tumult. Apprehensive of the lawless violence of which, on the very first day of the festival, the mob had given indications in derisory allusions, the priests, after carrying about the image of the Virgin for a short time, brought it for safety to the choir, without, as formerly, setting it up in the middle of the church. This incited some mischievous boys from among the people to pay it a visit there, and jokingly inquire why she had so soon absented herself from among them? Others mounting the pulpit, mimicked the preacher, and challenged the papists to a dispute. A Roman Catholic waterman, indignant at this jest, attempted to pull them down, and blows were exchanged in the preacher's seat. Similar scenes occurred on the following evening. The numbers increased, and many came already provided with suspicious implements and secret weapons. At last it came into the head of one of them to cry, "Long live the Gueux!" immediately the whole band took up the cry, and the image of the Virgin was called upon to do the same. The few Roman Catholics who were present, and who had given up the hope of effecting anything against these desperadoes, left the church after locking all the doors except one. So soon as they found themselves alone it was proposed to sing one of the psalms in the new version, which was prohibited by the government. While they were yet singing they all, as at a given signal, rushed furiously upon the image of the Virgin, piercing it with swords and daggers, and striking off its head; thieves and prostitutes tore the great wax-lights from the altar, and lighted them to the work. The beautiful organ of the church, a masterpiece of the art of that period, was broken to pieces, all the paintings were effaced, the statues smashed to atoms. A crucifix, the size of life, which was set up between the two thieves, opposite the high altar, an ancient and highly valued piece of workmanship, was pulled to the ground with cords, and cut to pieces with axes, while the two malefactors at its side were respectfully spared. The holy wafers were strewed on the ground and trodden under foot; in the wine used for the Lord's Supper, which was accidentally found there, the health of the Gueux was drunk, while with the holy oil they rubbed their shoes. The very tombs were opened, and the half-decayed corpses torn up and trampled on. All this was done with as much wonderful regularity as if each had previously had his part assigned to him; every one worked into his neigh-

bor's hands; no one, dangerous as the work was, met with
injury; in the midst of thick darkness, which the tapers
only served to render more sensible, with heavy masses
falling on all sides, and though on the very topmost steps
of the ladders, they scuffled with each other for the honors of demolition — yet no one suffered the least injury.
In spite of the many tapers which lighted them below in
their villanous work not a single individual was recognized. With incredible rapidity was the dark deed accomplished; a number of men, at most a hundred, despoiled in a few hours a temple of seventy altars — after
St. Peter's at Rome, perhaps the largest and most magnificent in Christendom.

The devastation of the cathedral did not content them;
with torches and tapers purloined from it they set out at
midnight to perform a similar work of havoc on the
remaining churches, cloisters, and chapels. The destructive hordes increased with every fresh exploit of infamy,
and thieves were allured by the opportunity. They carried away whatever they found of value—the consecrated
vessels, altar-cloths, money, and vestments; in the cellars
of the cloisters they drank to intoxication; to escape
greater indignities the monks and nuns abandoned everything to them. The confused noises of these riotous acts
had startled the citizens from their first sleep; but night
made the danger appear more alarming than it really was,
and instead of hastening to defend their churches the
citizens fortified themselves in their houses, and in terror
and anxiety awaited the dawn of morning. The rising sun
at length revealed the devastation which had been going
on during the night; but the havoc did not terminate
with the darkness. Some churches and cloisters still
remained uninjured; the same fate soon overtook them
also. The work of destruction lasted three whole days.
Alarmed at last lest the frantic mob, when it could no
longer find anything sacred to destroy, should make a
similar attack on lay property and plunder their warehouses; and encouraged, too, by discovering how small
was the number of the depredators, the wealthier citizens
ventured to show themselves in arms at the doors of their
houses. All the gates of the town were locked but one,

through which the Iconoclasts broke forth to renew the same atrocities in the rural districts. On one occasion only during all this time did the municipal officers venture to exert their authority, so strongly were they held in awe by the superior power of the Calvinists, by whom, as it was believed, this mob of miscreants was hired. The injury inflicted by this work of devastation was incalculable. In the church of the Virgin it was estimated at not less than four hundred thousand gold florins. Many precious works of art were destroyed; many valuable manuscripts; many monuments of importance to history and to diplomacy were thereby lost. The city magistrate ordered the plundered articles to be restored on pain of death; in enforcing this restitution he was effectually assisted by the preachers of the Reformers, who blushed for their followers. Much was in this manner recovered, and the ringleaders of the mob, less animated, perhaps, by the desire of plunder than by fanaticism and revenge, or perhaps being ruled by some unseen head, resolved for the future to guard against these excesses, and to make their attacks in regular bands and in better order.

The town of Ghent, meanwhile, trembled for a like destiny. Immediately on the first news of the outbreak of the Iconoclasts in Antwerp the magistrate of the former town with the most eminent citizens had bound themselves to repel by force the church spoilers; when this oath was proposed to the commonalty also the voices were divided, and many declared openly that they were by no means disposed to hinder so devout a work. In this state of affairs the Roman Catholic clergy found it advisable to deposit in the citadel the most precious movables of their churches, and private families were permitted in like manner to provide for the safety of offerings which had been made by their ancestors. Meanwhile all the services were discontinued, the courts of justice were closed; and, like a town in momentary danger of being stormed by the enemy, men trembled in expectation of what was to come. At last an insane band of rioters ventured to send delegates to the governor with this impudent message: "They were ordered," they said, "by their chiefs to take the images out of the churches, as had been done in the other towns. If they were not opposed it should be done quietly and with as little injury as possible, but otherwise they would storm the churches;" nay, they went so far in their audacity as to ask the aid of the officers of justice therein. At first the magistrate was astounded at this demand; upon reflection, however, and in the hope that the presence of the officers of law would perhaps restrain their excesses, he did not scruple to grant their request.

In Tournay the churches were despoiled of their ornaments within sight of the garrison, who could not be induced to march against the Iconoclasts. As the latter had been told that the gold and silver vessels and other ornaments of the church were buried underground, they turned up the whole floor, and exposed, among others, the body of the Duke Adolph of Gueldres, who fell in battle at the head of the rebellious burghers of Ghent, and had been buried here in Tournay. This Adolph had waged war against his father, and had dragged the vanquished old man some miles barefoot to prison — an indignity which Charles the Bold afterwards retaliated on him. And now, again, after more than half a century fate avenged a crime against nature by another against religion; fanaticism was to desecrate that which was holy in order to expose once more to execration the bones of a parricide. Other Iconoclasts from Valenciennes united themselves with those of Tournay to despoil all the cloisters of the surrounding district, during which a valuable library, the accumulation of centuries, was destroyed by fire. The evil soon penetrated into Brabant, also Malines, Herzogenbusch, Breda, and Bergen-op-Zoom experienced the same fate. The provinces, Namur and Luxemburg, with a part of Artois and of Hainault, had alone the good fortune to escape the contagion of those outrages. In the short period of four or five days four hundred cloisters were plundered in Brabant and Flanders alone.

The northern Netherlands were soon seized with the same mania which had raged so violently through the southern. The Dutch towns, Amsterdam, Leyden, and Gravenhaag, had the alternative of either voluntarily stripping their churches of their ornaments, or of seeing them violently torn from them; the determination of their magistrates saved Delft, Haarlem, Gouda, and Rotterdam from the devastation. The same acts of violence were practised also in the islands of Zealand; the town of Utrecht and many places in Overyssel and Gröningen suffered the same storms. Friesland was protected by the Count of Aremberg, and Gueldres by the Count of Megen from a like fate.

An exaggerated report of these disturbances which came in from the provinces spread the alarm to Brussels, where the regent had just made preparations for an extraordinary session of the council of state. Swarms of Iconoclasts already penetrated into Brabant; and the metropolis, where they were certain of powerful support, was threatened by them with a renewal of the same atrocities then under the very eyes of majesty. The regent, in fear for her personal safety, which, even in the heart of the country, surrounded by provincial governors and Knights of the Fleece, she fancied insecure, was already meditating a flight to Mons, in Hainault, which town the Duke of Arschot held for her as a place of refuge, that she might not be driven to any undignified concession by falling into the power of the Iconoclasts. In vain did the knights pledge life and blood for her safety, and urgently beseech her not to expose them to disgrace by so dishonorable a flight, as though they were wanting in courage or zeal to protect their princess; to no purpose did the town of Brussels itself supplicate her not to abandon them in this extremity, and vainly did the council of state make the most impressive representations that so pusillanimous a step would not fail to encourage still more the insolence of the rebels; she remained immovable in this desperate condition. As messenger after messenger arrived to warn her that the Iconoclasts were advancing against the metropolis, she issued orders to hold everything in readiness for her flight, which was to take place quietly with the first approach of morning. At break of day the aged Viglius presented himself before her, whom, with the view of gratifying the nobles, she had been long accustomed to neglect. He demanded to know the meaning of the preparations he observed, upon which she at last confessed that she intended to make her escape, and assured him that he would himself do well to secure his own safety by accompanying her. "It is now two years," said the old man to her, "that you might have anticipated these results. Because I have spoken more freely than your courtiers you have closed your princely ear to me, which has been open only to pernicious suggestions." The regent allowed that she had been in fault, and had been blinded by an appearance of probity; but that she was now driven by necessity. "Are you resolved," answered Viglius, "resolutely to insist upon obedience to the royal commands?" "I am," answered the duchess. "Then have recourse to the great secret of the art of government, to dissimulation, and pretend to join the princes until, with their assistance, you have repelled this storm. Show them a confidence which you are far from feeling in your heart. Make them take an oath to you that they will make common cause in resisting these disorders. Trust those as your friends who show themselves willing to do it; but be careful to avoid frightening away the others by contemptuous treatment." Viglius kept the regent engaged in conversation until the princes arrived, who he was quite certain would in nowise consent to her flight. When they appeared he quietly withdrew in order to issue commands to the town council to close the gates of the city and prohibit egress to every one connected with the court. This last measure effected more than all the representations had done. The regent, who saw herself a prisoner in her own capital, now yielded to the persuasions of the nobles, who pledged themselves to stand by her to the last drop of blood. She made Count Mansfeld commandant of the town, who hastily increased the garrison and armed her whole court.

The state council was now held, who finally came to a resolution that it was expedient to yield to the emergency; to permit the preachings in those places where they had already commenced; to make known the abolition of the papal Inquisition; to declare the old edicts against the heretics repealed, and before all things to grant the required indemnity to the confederate nobles, without limitation or condition. At the same time the Prince of Orange, Counts Egmont and Horn, with some others, were appointed to confer on this head with the deputies of the league. Solemnly and in the most unequivocal terms the members of the league were declared free from all responsibility by reason of the petition which had been presented, and all royal officers and authorities were enjoined to act in conformity with this assurance, and neither now nor for the future to inflict any injury upon any of the confederates on account of the said petition. In return, the confederates bound themselves to be true and loyal servants of his majesty, to contribute to the utmost of their power to the re-establishment of order and the punishment of the Iconoclasts, to prevail on the people to lay down their arms, and to afford active assistance to the king against internal and foreign enemies. Securities, formally drawn up and subscribed by the plenipotentiaries of both sides, were exchanged between them; the letter of indemnity, in particular, was signed by the duchess with her own hand and attested by her seal. It was only after a severe struggle, and with tears in her eyes, that the regent, as she tremblingly confessed to the king, was at last induced to consent to this painful step. She threw the whole blame upon the nobles, who had kept her a prisoner in Brussels and compelled her to it by force. Above all she complained bitterly of the Prince of Orange.

This business accomplished, all the governors hastened to their provinces; Egmont to Flanders, Orange to Antwerp. In the latter city the Protestants had seized the despoiled and plundered churches, and, as if by the rights of war, had taken possession of them. The prince restored them to their lawful owners, gave orders for their repair, and re-established in them the Roman Catholic form of worship. Three of the Iconoclasts, who had been convicted, paid the penalty of their sacrilege on the gallows; some of the rioters were banished, and many others underwent punishment. Afterwards he assembled four deputies of each dialect, or nations, as they were termed, and agreed with them that, as the approaching winter made preaching in the open air impossible, three places within the town should be granted them, where they might either erect new churches, or convert private houses to that purpose. That they should there perform their service every Sunday and holiday, and always at the same hour, but on no other days. If, however, no holiday happened in the week, Wednesday should be kept by them instead. No religious party should maintain more than two clergymen, and these must be native Netherlanders, or at least have received naturalization from some considerable town of the provinces. All should take an oath to submit in civil matters to the municipal authorities and the Prince of Orange. They should be liable, like the other citizens, to all imposts. No one should attend sermons armed; a sword, however, should be allowed to each. No preacher should assail the ruling religion from the pulpit, nor enter upon controverted points, beyond what the doctrine itself rendered unavoidable, or what might refer to morals. No psalm should be sung by them out of their appointed district. At the election of their preachers, churchwardens, and deacons, as also at all their other consistorial meetings, a person from the government should on each occasion be present to report their proceedings to the prince and the magistrate. As to all other points they should enjoy the same protection as the ruling religion. This arrangement was to hold good until the king, with consent of the states, should determine otherwise; but then it should be free to every one to quit the country with his family and his property. From Antwerp the prince hastened to Holland, Zealand, and Utrecht, in order to make there similar arrangements for the restoration of peace; Antwerp, however, was, during his absence, entrusted to the superintendence of Count Hogstraten, who was a mild man, and although an adherent of the league, had never failed in loyalty to the king. It is evident that in this agreement the prince had far overstepped the powers entrusted to him, and though in the service of the king had acted exactly like a sovereign lord. But he alleged in excuse that it would be far easier to the magistrate to watch these numerous and powerful sects if he himself interfered in their worship, and if this took place under his eyes, than if he were to leave the sectarians to themselves in the open air.

In Gueldres Count Megen showed more severity, and entirely suppressed the Protestant sects and banished all their preachers. In Brussels the regent availed herself of the advantage derived from her personal presence to put a stop to the public preaching, even outside the town. When, in reference to this, Count Nassau reminded her in the name of the confederates of the compact which had been entered into, and demanded if the town of Brussels had inferior rights to the other towns? she answered, if there were public preachings in Brussels before the treaty, it was not her work if they were now discontinued. At the same time, however, she secretly gave the citizens to understand that the first who should venture to attend a public sermon should certainly be hung. Thus she kept the capital at least faithful to her.

It was more difficult to quiet Tournay, which office was committed to Count Horn, in the place of Montigny, to whose government the town properly belonged. Horn commanded the Protestants to vacate the churches immediately, and to content themselves with a house of worship outside the walls. To this their preachers objected that the churches were erected for the use of the people, by which term, they said, not the heads but the majority were meant. If they were expelled from the Roman Catholic churches it was at least fair that they should be furnished with money for erecting churches of their own. To this the magistrate replied even if the Catholic party was the weaker it was indisputably the better. The erection of churches should not be forbidden them; they could not, however, after the injury which the town had already suffered from their brethren, the Iconoclasts, very well expect that it should be further burdened by the erection of their churches. After long quarrelling on both sides, the Protestants contrived to retain possession of some churches, which, for greater security, they occupied with guards. In Valenciennes, too, the Protestants refused submission to the conditions which were offered to them through Philip St. Aldegonde, Baron of Noircarmes, to whom, in the absence of the Marquis of Bergen, the government of that place was entrusted. A reformed preacher, La Grange, a Frenchman by birth, who by his eloquence had gained a complete command over them, urged them to insist on having churches of their own within the town, and to threaten in case of refusal to deliver it up to the Huguenots. A sense of the superior numbers of the Calvinists, and of their understanding with the Huguenots, prevented the governor adopting forcible measures against them.

Count Egmont, also to manifest his zeal for the king's service, did violence to his natural kind-heartedness. Introducing a garrison into the town of Ghent, he caused some of the most refractory rebels to be put to death. The churches were reopened, the Roman Catholic worship renewed, and all foreigners, without exception, ordered to quit the province. To the Calvinists, but to them alone, a site was granted outside the town for the erection of a church. In return they were compelled to pledge themselves to the most rigid obedience to the municipal authorities, and to active co-operation in the proceedings against the Iconoclasts. He pursued similar measures through all Flanders and Artois. One of his noblemen, John Cassembrot, Baron of Beckerzeel, and a leaguer, pursuing the Iconoclasts at the head of some horsemen of the league, surprised a band of them just as they were about to break into a town of Hainault, near Grammont, in Flanders, and took thirty of them prisoners, of whom twenty-two were hung upon the spot, and the rest whipped out of the province.

Services of such importance one would have thought scarcely deserved to be rewarded with the displeasure of the king; what Orange, Egmont, and Horn performed on this occasion evinced at least as much zeal and had as beneficial a result as anything that was accomplished by Noircarmes, Megen, and Aremberg, to whom the king vouchsafed to show his gratitude both by words and deeds. But their zeal, their services came too late. They had spoken too loudly against his edicts, had been too vehement in their opposition to his measures, had insulted him too grossly in the person of his minister Granvella, to leave room for forgiveness. No time, no repentance, no atonement, however great, could efface this one offence from the memory of their sovereign.

Philip lay sick at Segovia when the news of the outbreak of the Iconoclasts and the uncatholic agreement entered into with the Reformers reached him. At the same time the regent renewed her urgent entreaty for his personal visit, of which also all the letters treated, which the President Viglius exchanged with his friend Hopper. Many also of the Belgian nobles addressed special letters to the king, as, for instance, Egmont, Mansfeld, Megen, Aremberg, Noircarmes, and Barlaimont, in which they reported the state of their provinces, and at once explained and justified the arrangements they had made with the disaffected. Just at this period a letter arrived from the German Emperor, in which he recommended Philip to act with clemency towards his Belgian subjects, and offered his mediation in the matter. He had also written direct to the regent herself in Brussels, and added letters to the several leaders of the nobility, which, however, were never delivered. Having conquered the first anger which this hateful occurrence had excited, the king referred the whole matter to his council.

The party of Granvella, which had the preponderance in the council, was diligent in tracing a close connection between the behavior of the Flemish nobles and the excesses of the church desecrators, which showed itself in similarity of the demands of both parties, and especially the time which the latter chose for their outbreak. In the same month, they observed, in which the nobles had sent in their three articles of pacification, the Iconoclasts had commenced their work; on the evening of the very day that Orange quitted Antwerp the churches too were plundered. During the whole tumult not a finger was lifted to take up arms; all the expedients employed were invariably such as turned to the advantage of the sects, while, on the contrary, all others were neglected which tended to the maintenance of the pure faith. Many of the Iconoclasts, it was further said, had confessed that all that they had done was with the knowledge and consent of the princes; though surely nothing was more natural, than for such worthless wretches to seek to screen with great names a crime which they had undertaken solely on their own account. A writing also was produced in which the high nobility were made to promise their services to the "Gueux," to procure the assembly of the states general, the genuineness of which, however, the former strenuously denied. Four different seditious parties were, they said, to be noticed in the Netherlands, which were all more or less connected with one another, and all worked towards a common end. One of these was those bands of reprobates who desecrated the churches; a second consisted of the various sects who had hired the former to perform their infamous acts; the "Gueux," who had raised themselves to be the defenders of the sects were the third; and the leading nobles who were inclined to the "Gueux" by feudal connections, relationship, and friendship, composed the fourth. All, consequently, were alike fatally infected, and all equally guilty. The government had not merely to guard against a few isolated members; it had to contend with the whole body. Since, then, it was ascertained that the people were the seduced party, and the encouragement to rebellion came from higher quarters, it would be wise and expedient to alter the plan hitherto adopted, which now appeared defective in several respects. Inasmuch as all classes had been oppressed without distinction, and as much of severity shown to the lower orders as of contempt to the nobles, both had been compelled to lend support to one another; a party had been given to the latter and leaders to the former. Unequal treatment seemed an infallible expedient to separate them; the mob, always timid and indolent when not goaded by the extremity of distress, would very soon desert its adored protectors and quickly learn to see in their fate well-merited retribution if only it was not driven to share it with them. It was therefore proposed to the king to treat the great multitude for the future with more leniency, and to direct all measures of severity against the leaders of the faction. In order, however, to avoid the appearance of a disgraceful concession, it was considered advisable to accept the mediation of the Emperor, and to impute to it alone and not to the justice of their demands, that the king out of pure generosity had granted to his Belgian subjects as much as they asked.

The question of the king's personal visit to the provinces was now again mooted, and all the difficulties which had formerly been raised on this head appeared to vanish before the present emergency. "Now," said Tyssenacque and Hopper, "the juncture has really arrived at which the king, according to his own declaration formerly made to Count Egmont, will be ready to risk a thousand lives. To restore quiet to Ghent Charles V. had undertaken a troublesome and dangerous journey through an enemy's country. This was done for the sake of a single town; and now the peace, perhaps even the possession, of all the United Provinces was at stake." This was the opinion of the majority; and the journey of the king was looked upon as a matter from which he could not possibly any longer escape.

The question now was, whether he should enter upon it with a numerous body of attendants or with few; and here the Prince of Eboli and Count Figueroa were at issue with the Duke of Alva, as their private interests clashed. If the king journeyed at the head of an army the presence of the Duke of Alva would be indispensable, who, on the other hand, if matters were peaceably adjusted, would be less required, and must make room for his rivals. "An army," said Figueroa, who spoke first, "would alarm the princes through whose territories it must march, and perhaps even be opposed by them; it would, moreover, unnecessarily burden the provinces for whose tranquillization it was intended, and add a new grievance to the many which had already driven the people to such lengths. It would press indiscriminately upon all of the king's subjects, whereas a court of justice, peaceably administering its office, would observe a marked distinction between the innocent and the guilty. The unwonted violence of the former course would tempt the leaders of the faction to take a more alarming view of their behavior, in which wantonness and levity had the chief share, and consequently induce them to proceed with deliberation and union; the thought of having forced the king to such lengths would plunge them into despair, in which they would be ready to undertake anything. If the king placed himself in arms against the rebels he would forfeit the most important advantage which he possessed over them, namely, his authority as sovereign of the country, which would prove the more powerful in proportion as he showed his reliance upon that alone. He would place himself thereby, as it were, on a level with the rebels, who on their side would not be at a loss to raise an army, as the universal hatred of the Spanish forces would operate in their favor with the nation. By this procedure the king would exchange the certain advantage which his position as sovereign of the country conferred upon him for the uncertain result of military operations, which, result as they might, would of necessity destroy a portion of his own subjects. The rumor of his hostile approach would outrun him time enough to allow all who were conscious of a bad cause to place themselves in a posture of defence, and to combine and render availing both their foreign and domestic resources. Here again the general alarm would do them important service; the uncertainty who would be the first object of this warlike approach would drive even the less guilty to the general mass of the rebels, and force those to become enemies to the king who otherwise would never have been so. If, however, he was coming among them without such a formidable accompaniment; if his appearance was less that of a sanguinary judge than of an angry parent, the courage of all good men would rise, and the bad would perish in their own security. They would persuade themselves what had happened was unimportant; that it did not appear to the king of sufficient moment to call for strong measures. They wished if they could to avoid the chance of ruining, by acts of open violence, a cause which might perhaps yet be saved; consequently, by this quiet, peaceable method everything would be gained which by the other would be irretrievably lost; the loyal subject would in no degree be involved in the same punishment with the culpable rebel; on the latter alone would the whole weight of the royal indignation descend. Lastly, the enormous expenses would be avoided which the transport of a Spanish army to those distant regions would occasion.

"But," began the Duke of Alva, " ought the injury of some few citizens to be considered when danger impends over the whole? Because a few of the loyally-disposed may suffer wrong are the rebels therefore not to be chastised? The offence has been universal, why then should not the punishment be the same? What the rebels have incurred by their actions the rest have incurred equally by their supineness. Whose fault is it but theirs that the former have so far succeeded? Why did they not promptly oppose their first attempts? It is said that circumstances were not so desperate as to justify this violent remedy; but who will insure us that they will not be so by the time the king arrives, especially when, according to every fresh despatch of the regent, all is hastening with rapid strides to a ruinous consummation? Is it a hazard we ought to run to leave the king to discover on his entrance into the provinces the necessity of his having brought with him a military force? It is a fact only too well-established that the rebels have secured foreign succors, which stand ready at their command on the first signal; will it then be time to think of preparing for war when the enemy pass the frontiers? Is it a wise risk to rely for aid upon the nearest Belgian troops when their loyalty is so little to be depended upon? And is not the regent perpetually reverting in her despatches to the fact that nothing but the want of a suitable military force has hitherto hindered her from enforcing the edicts, and stopping the progress of the rebels? A well-disciplined and formidable army alone will disappoint all their hopes of maintaining themselves in opposition to their lawful sovereign, and nothing but the certain prospect of destruction will make them lower their demands. Besides, without an adequate force, the king cannot venture his person in hostile countries; he cannot enter into any treaties with his rebellious subjects which would not be derogatory to his honor."

The authority of the speaker gave preponderance to his arguments, and the next question was, when the king should commence his journey and what road he should take. As the voyage by sea was on every account extremely hazardous, he had no other alternative but either to proceed thither through the passes near Trent across Germany, or to penetrate from Savoy over the Apennine Alps. The first route would expose him to the danger of the attack of the German Protestants, who were not likely to view with indifference the objects of his journey, and a passage over the Apennines was at this late season of the year not to be attempted. Moreover, it would be necessary to send for the requisite galleys from Italy, and repair them, which would take several months. Finally, as the assembly of the Cortes of Castile, from which he could not well be absent, was already appointed for December, the journey could not be undertaken before the spring. Meanwhile the regent pressed for explicit instructions how she was to extricate herself from her present embarrassment, without compromising the royal dignity too far; and it was necessary to do something in the interval till the king could undertake to appease the troubles by his personal presence. Two separate letters were therefore despatched to the duchess; one public, which she could lay before the states and the council chambers, and one private, which was intended for herself alone. In the first, the king announced to her his restoration to health, and the fortunate birth of the Infanta Clara Isabella Eugenia, afterwards wife of the Archduke Albert of Austria and Princess of the Netherlands. He declared to her his present firm intention to visit the Netherlands in person, for which he was already making the necessary preparations. The assembling of the states he refused, as he had previously done. No mention was made in this letter of the agreement which she had entered into with the Protestants and with the league, because he did not deem it advisable at present absolutely to reject it, and he was still less disposed to acknowledge its validity. On the other hand, he ordered her to reinforce the army, to draw together new regiments from Germany, and to meet the refractory with force. For the rest, he concluded, he relied upon the loyalty of the leading nobility, among whom he knew many who were sincere in their attachment both to their religion and their king. In the secret letter she was again enjoined to do all in her power to prevent the assembling of the states; but if the general voice should become irresistible, and she was compelled to yield, she was at least to manage so cautiously that the royal dignity should not suffer, and no one learn the king's consent to their assembly.

While these consultations were held in Spain the Protestants in the Netherlands made the most extensive use of the privileges which had been compulsorily granted to them. The erection of churches wherever it was permitted was completed with incredible rapidity; young and old, gentle and simple, assisted in carrying stones; women sacrificed even their ornaments in order to accelerate the work. The two religious parties established in several towns consistories, and a church council of their own, the first move of the kind being made in Antwerp, and placed their form of worship on a well-regulated footing. It was also proposed to raise a common fund by subscription to meet any sudden emergency of the Protestant church in general. In Antwerp a memorial was presented by the Calvinists of that town to the Count of Hogstraten, in which they offered to pay three millions of dollars to secure the free exercise of their religion. Many copies of this writing were circulated in the Netherlands; and in order to stimulate others, many had ostentatiously subscribed their names to large sums. Various interpretations of this extravagant offer were made by the enemies of the Reformers, and all had some appearance of reason. For instance, it was urged that under the pretext of collecting the requisite sum for fulfilling this engagement they hoped, without suspicion, to raise funds for military purposes; for whether they should be called upon to contribute *for or against* they would, it was thought, be more ready to burden themselves with a view of preserving peace than for an oppressive and devasting war. Others saw in this offer nothing more than a temporary stratagem of the Protestants by which they hoped to bind the court and keep it irresolute until they should have gained sufficient strength to confront it. Others again declared it to be a downright bravado in order to alarm the regent, and to raise the courage of their own party by the display of such rich resources. But whatever was the true motive of this proposition, its originators gained little by it; the contributions flowed in scantily and slowly, and the court answered the proposal with silent contempt. The excesses, too, of the Iconoclasts, far from promoting the cause of the league and advancing the Protestants' interests, had done irreparable injury to both. The sight of their ruined churches, which, in the language of Viglius, resembled stables more than houses of God, enraged the Roman Catholics, and above all the clergy. All of that religion, who had hitherto been members of the league, now forsook it, alleging that even if it had not intentionally excited and encouraged the excesses of the Iconoclasts it had beyond question remotely led to them. The intolerance of the Calvinists who, wherever they were the ruling party, cruelly oppressed the Roman Catholics, completely expelled the delusion in which the latter had long indulged, and they withdrew their support from a party from which, if they obtained the upper hand, their own religion had so much cause to fear. Thus the league lost many of its best members; the friends and patrons, too, which it had hitherto found amongst the well-disposed citizens now deserted it, and its character began perceptibly to decline. The severity with which some of its members had acted against the Iconoclasts in order to prove their good disposition towards the regent, and to remove the suspicion of any connection with the malcontents, had also injured them with the people who favored the latter, and thus the league was in danger of ruining itself with both parties at the same time.

The regent had no sooner became acquainted with this change in the public mind than she devised a plan by which she hoped gradually to dissolve the whole league, or at least to enfeeble it through internal dissensions. For this end she availed herself of the private letters which the king had addressed to some of the nobles, and enclosed to her with full liberty to use them at her discretion. These letters, which overflowed with kind expressions were presented to those for whom they were intended, with an attempt at secrecy, which designedly miscarried, so that on each occasion some one or other of those who had received nothing of the sort got a hint of them. In order to spread suspicion the more widely numerous copies of the letters were circulated. This artifice attained its object. Many members of the league began to doubt the honesty of those to whom such brilliant promises were made; through fear of being deserted by their principal members and supporters, they eagerly accepted the conditions which were offered them by the regent, and evinced great anxiety for a speedy reconciliation with the court. The general rumor of the impending visit of the king, which the regent took care to have widely circulated, was also of great service to her in this matter; many who could not augur much good to themselves from the royal presence did not hesitate to accept a pardon, which, perhaps, for what they could tell, was offered them for the last time. Among those who thus received private letters were Egmont and Prince of Orange. Both had complained to the king of the evil reports with which designing persons in Spain had labored to brand their names, and to throw suspicion on their motives and intentions; Egmont, in particular, with the honest simplicity which was peculiar to his character, had asked the monarch only to point out to him what he most desired, to determine the particular action by which his favor could be best obtained and zeal in his service evinced, and it should, he assured him, be done. The king in reply caused the president, Von Tyssenacque, to tell him that he could do nothing better to refute his traducers than to show perfect submission to the royal orders, which were so clearly and precisely drawn up, that no further exposition of them was required, nor any particular instruction. It was the sovereign's part to deliberate, to examine, and to decide; unconditionally to obey was the duty of the subject; the honor of the latter consisted in his obedience. It did not become a member to hold itself wiser than the head. He was assuredly to be blamed for not having done his utmost to curb the unruliness of his sectarians; but it was even yet in his power to make up for past negligence by at least maintaining peace and order until the actual arrival of the king. In thus punishing Count Egmont with reproofs like a disobedient child, the king treated him in accordance with what he knew of his character; with his friend he found it necessary to call in the aid of artifice and deceit. Orange, too, in his letter, had alluded to the suspicions which the king entertained of his loyalty and attachment, but not, like Egmont, in the vain hope of removing them; for this he had long given up; but in order to pass from these complaints to a request for permission to resign his offices. He had already frequently made this request to the regent, but had always received from her a refusal, accompanied with the strongest assurance of her regard. The king also, to whom he now at last addressed a direct application, returned him the same answer, graced with similar strong assurances of his satisfaction and gratitude. In particular he expressed the high satisfaction he entertained of his services, which he had lately rendered the crown in Antwerp, and lamented deeply that the private affairs of the prince (which the latter had made his chief plea for demanding his dismissal) should have fallen into such disorder; but ended with the declaration that it was impossible for him to dispense with his valuable services at a crisis which demanded the increase, rather than diminution, of his good and honest servants. He had thought, he added, that the prince entertained a better opinion of him than to suppose him capable of giving credit to the idle talk of certain persons, who were friends neither to the prince nor to himself. But, at the same time, to give him a proof of his sincerity, he complained to him in confidence of his brother, the Count of Nassau, pretended to ask his advice in the matter, and finally expressed a wish to have the count removed for a period from the Netherlands.

But Philip had here to do with a head which in cunning was superior to his own. The Prince of Orange had for a long time held watch over him and his privy council in Madrid and Segovia, through a host of spies, who reported to him everything of importance that was transacted there. The court of this most secret of all despots had become accessible to his intriguing spirit and his money; in this manner he had gained possession of several autograph letters of the regent, which she had secretly written to Madrid, and had caused copies to be circulated in triumph in Brussels, and in a measure under her own eyes, insomuch that she saw with astonishment in everybody's hands what she thought was preserved with so much care, and entreated the king for the future to destroy her despatches immediately they were read. William's vigilance did not confine itself simply to the court of Spain; he had spies in France, and even at more distant courts. He is also charged with not being over-scrupulous as to the means by which he acquired his intelligence. But the most important disclosure was made by an intercepted letter of the Spanish ambassador in France, Francis Von Alava, to the duchess, in which the former descanted on the fair opportunity which was now afforded to the king, through the guilt of the Netherlandish people, of establishing an arbitrary power in that country. He therefore advised her to deceive the nobles by the very arts which they had hitherto employed against herself, and to secure them through smooth words and an obliging behavior. The king, he concluded, who knew the nobles to be the hidden springs of all the previous troubles, would take good care to lay hands upon them at the first favorable opportunity, as well as the two whom he had already in Spain; and did not mean to let them go again, having sworn to make an example in them which should horrify the whole of Christendom, even if it should cost him his hereditary dominions. This piece of evil news was strongly corroborated by the letters which Bergen and Montigny wrote from Spain, and in which they bitterly complained of the contemptuous behavior of the grandees and the altered deportment of the monarch towards them; and the Prince of Orange was now fully sensible what he had to expect from the fair promises of the king.

The letter of the minister, Alava, together with some others from Spain, which gave a circumstantial account of the approaching warlike visit of the king, and of his evil intentions against the nobles, was laid by the prince before his brother, Count Louis of Nassau, Counts Egmont, Horn, and Hogstraten, at a meeting at Dendermonde in Flanders, whither these five knights had repaired to confer on the measures necessary for their security. Count Louis, who listened only to his feelings of indignation, foolhardily maintained that they ought, without loss of time, to take up arms and seize some strongholds. That they ought at all risks to prevent the king's armed entrance into the provinces. That they should endeavor to prevail on the Swiss, the Protestant princes of Germany, and the Huguenots to arm and obstruct his passage through their territories; and if, notwithstanding, he should force his way through these impediments, that the Flemings should meet him with an army on the frontiers. He would take upon himself to negotiate a defensive alliance in France, in Switzerland, and in Germany, and to raise in the latter empire four thousand horse, together with a proportionate body of infantry. Pretexts would not be wanting for collecting the requisite supplies of money, and the merchants of the reformed sect would, he felt assured, not fail them. But William, more cautious and more wise, declared himself against this proposal, which, in the execution, would be exposed to numberless difficulties, and had as yet nothing to justify it. The Inquisition, he represented, was in fact abolished, the edicts were nearly sunk into oblivion, and a fair degree of religious liberty accorded. Hitherto, therefore, there existed no valid or adequate excuse for adopting this hostile method; he did not doubt, however, that one would be presented to them before long, and in good time for preparation. His own opinion consequently was that they should await this opportunity with patience, and in the meanwhile still keep a watchful eye upon everything, and contrive to give the people a hint of the threatened danger, that they might be ready to act if circumstances should call for their co-operation. If all present had assented to the opinion of the Prince of Orange, there is no doubt but so powerful a league, formidable both by the influence and the high character of its members, would have opposed obstacles to the designs of the king which would have compelled him to abandon them entirely. But the determination of the assembled knights

was much shaken by the declaration with which Count
Egmont surprised them. "Rather," said he, "may all
that is evil befall me than that I should tempt fortune so
rashly. The idle talk of the Spaniard, Alava, does not
move me; how should such a person be able to read the
mind of a sovereign so reserved as Philip, and to decipher
his secrets? The intelligence which Montigny gives us
goes to prove nothing more than that the king has a very
doubtful opinion of our zeal for his service, and believes
he has cause to distrust our loyalty; and for this I for
my part must confess that we have given him only too
much cause. And it is my serious purpose, by redoubling
my zeal, to regain his good opinion, and by my future
behavior to remove, if possible, the distrust which my
actions have hitherto excited. How could I tear myself
from the arms of my numerous and dependent family to
wander as an exile at foreign courts, a burden to every
one who received me, the slave of every one who condescended to assist me, a servant of foreigners, in order to
escape a slight degree of constraint at home? Never
can the monarch act unkindly towards a servant who was
once beloved and dear to him, and who has established a
well-grounded claim to his gratitude. Never shall I be
persuaded that he who has expressed such favorable, such
gracious sentiments towards his Belgian subjects, and
with his own mouth gave me such emphatic, such solemn
assurances, can be now devising, as it is pretended, such
tyrannical schemes against them. If we do but restore
to the country its former repose, chastise the rebels, and
re-establish the Roman Catholic form of worship wherever it has been violently suppressed, then, believe me,
we shall hear no more of Spanish troops. This is the
course to which I now invite you all by my counsel and
my example, and to which also most of our brethren
already incline. I, for my part, fear nothing from the
anger of the king. My conscience acquits me. I trust
my fate and fortunes to his justice and clemency." In
vain did Nassau, Horn, and Orange labor to shake his
resolution, and to open his eyes to the near and inevitable
danger. Egmont was really attached to the king; the
royal favors, and the condescension with which they

were conferred, were still fresh in his remembrance. The attentions with which the monarch had distinguished him above all his friends had not failed of their effect. It was more from false shame than from party spirit that he had defended the cause of his countrymen against him; more from temperament and natural kindness of heart than from tried principles that he had opposed the severe measures of the government. The love of the nation, which worshipped him as its idol, carried him away. Too vain to renounce a title which sounded so agreeable, he had been compelled to do something to deserve it; but a single look at his family, a harsher designation applied to his conduct, a dangerous inference drawn from it, the mere sound of crime, terrified him from his self-delusion, and scared him back in haste and alarm to his duty.

Orange's whole plan was frustrated by Egmont's withdrawal. The latter possessed the hearts of the people and the confidence of the army, without which it was utterly impossible to undertake anything effective. The rest had reckoned with so much certainty upon him that his unexpected defection rendered the whole meeting nugatory. They therefore separated without coming to a determination. All who had met in Dendermonde were expected in the council of state in Brussels; but Egmont alone repaired thither. The regent wished to sift him on the subject of this conference, but she could extract nothing further from him than the production of the letter of Alava, of which he had purposely taken a copy, and which, with the bitterest reproofs, he laid before her. At first she changed color at sight of it, but quickly recovering herself, she boldly declared that it was a forgery. "How can this letter," she said, "really come from Alava, when I miss none? And would he who pretends to have intercepted it have spared the other letters? Nay, how can it be true, when not a single packet has miscarried, nor a single despatch failed to come to hand? How, too, can it be thought likely that the king would have made Alava master of a secret which he has not communicated even to me?"

CIVIL WAR.

1566. Meanwhile the regent hastened to take advantage of the schism amongst the nobles to complete the ruin of the league, which was already tottering under the weight of internal dissensions. Without loss of time she drew from Germany the troops which Duke Eric of Brunswick was holding in readiness, augmented the cavalry, and raised five regiments of Walloons, the command of which she gave to Counts Mansfeld, Megen, Aremberg, and others. To the prince, likewise, she felt it necessary to confide troops, both because she did not wish, by withholding them pointedly, to insult him, and also because the provinces of which he was governor were in urgent need of them; but she took the precaution of joining with him a Colonel Waldenfinger, who should watch all his steps and thwart his measures if they appeared dangerous. To Count Egmont the clergy in Flanders paid a contribution of forty thousand gold florins for the maintenance of fifteen hundred men, whom he distributed among the places where danger was most apprehended. Every governor was ordered to increase his military force, and to provide himself with ammunition. These energetic preparations, which were making in all places, left no doubt as to the measures which the regent would adopt in future. Conscious of her superior force, and certain of this important support, she now ventured to change her tone, and to employ quite another language with the rebels. She began to put the most arbitrary interpretation on the concessions which, through fear and necessity, she had made to the Protestants, and to restrict all the liberties which she had tacitly granted them to the mere permission of their preaching. All other religious exercises and rites, which yet appeared to be involved in the former privilege, were by new edicts expressly forbidden, and all offenders in such matters were to be proceeded against as traitors. The Protestants were permitted to think differently from the ruling church upon the sacrament, but to receive it differently was a crime; baptism, marriage, burial, after

their fashion, were probibited under pain of death. It
was a cruel mockery to allow them their religion, and
forbid the exercise of it; but this mean artifice of the
regent to escape from the obligation of her pledged
word was worthy of the pusillanimity with which she
had submitted to its being extorted from her. She took
advantage of the most trifling innovations and the smallest excesses to interrupt the preachings; and some of the
preachers, under the charge of having performed their
office in places not appointed to them, were brought to
trial, condemned, and executed. On more than one
occasion the regent publicly declared that the confederates had taken unfair advantage of her fears, and that
she did not feel herself bound by an engagement which
had been extorted from her by threats.

Of all the Belgian towns which had participated in the
insurrection of the Iconoclasts none had caused the regent
so much alarm as the town of Valenciennes, in Hainault.
In no other was the party of the Calvinists so powerful,
and the spirit of rebellion for which the province of
Hainault had always made itself conspicuous, seemed to
dwell here as in its native place. The propinquity of
France, to which, as well by language as by manners,
this town appeared to belong, rather than to the Netherlands, had from the first led to its being governed with
great mildness and forbearance, which, however, only
taught it to feel its own importance. At the last outbreak of the church-desecrators it had been on the point
of surrendering to the Huguenots, with whom it maintained the closest understanding. The slightest excitement might renew this danger. On this account Valenciennes was the first town to which the regent proposed,
as soon as should be in her power, to send a strong garrison. Philip of Noircarmes, Baron of St. Aldegonde,
Governor of Hainault in the place of the absent Marquis
of Bergen, had received this charge, and now appeared
at the head of an army before its walls. Deputies came
to meet him on the part of the magistrate from the town,
to petition against the garrison, because the Protestant
citizens, who were the superior number, had declared
against it. Noircarmes acquainted them with the will of

the regent, and gave them the choice between the garrison or a siege. He assured them that not more than four squadrons of horse and six companies of foot should be imposed upon the town; and for this he would give them his son as a hostage. These terms were laid before the magistrate, who, for his part, was much inclined to accept them. But Peregrine Le Grange, the preacher, and the idol of the populace, to whom it was of vital importance to prevent a submission of which he would inevitably become the victim, appeared at the head of his followers, and by his powerful eloquence excited the people to reject the conditions. When their answer was brought to Noircarmes, contrary to all law of nations, he caused the messengers to be placed in irons, and carried them away with him as prisoners; he was, however, by express command of the regent, compelled to set them free again. The regent, instructed by secret orders from Madrid to exercise as much forbearance as possible, caused the town to be repeatedly summoned to receive the garrison; when, however, it obstinately persisted in its refusal, it was declared by public edict to be in rebellion, and Noircarmes was authorized to commence the siege in form. The other provinces were forbidden to assist this rebellious town with advice, money, or arms. All the property contained in it was confiscated. In order to let it see the war before it began in earnest, and to give it time for rational reflection, Noircarmes drew together troops from all Hainault and Cambray (1566), took possession of St. Amant, and placed garrisons in all adjacent places.

The line of conduct adopted towards Valenciennes allowed the other towns which were similarly situated to infer the fate which was intended for them also, and at once put the whole league in motion. An army of the Gueux, between three thousand and four thousand strong, which was hastily collected from the rabble of fugitives, and the remaining bands of the Iconoclasts, appeared in the territories of Tournay and Lille, in order to secure these two towns, and to annoy the enemy at Valenciennes. The commandant of Lille was fortunate enough to maintain that place by routing a detachment of this army, which, in concert with the Protestant inhabitants, had made an attempt to get possession of it. At the same time the army of the Gueux, which was uselessly wasting its time at Lannoy, was surprised by Noircarmes and almost entirely annihilated. The few who with desperate courage forced their way through the enemy, threw themselves into the town of Tournay, which was immediately summoned by the victor to open its gates and admit a garrison. Its prompt obedience obtained for it a milder fate. Noircarmes contented himself with abolishing the Protestant consistory, banishing the preachers, punishing the leaders of the rebels, and again re-establishing the Roman Catholic worship, which he found almost entirely suppressed. After giving it a steadfast Roman Catholic as governor, and leaving in it a sufficient garrison, he again returned with his victorious army to Valenciennes to press the siege.

This town, confident in its strength, actively prepared for defence, firmly resolved to allow things to come to extremes before it surrendered. The inhabitants had not neglected to furnish themselves with ammunition and provisions for a long siege; all who could carry arms (the very artisans not excepted), became soldiers; the houses before the town, and especially the cloisters, were pulled down, that the besiegers might not avail themselves of them to cover their attack. The few adherents of the crown, awed by the multitude, were silent; no Roman Catholic ventured to stir himself. Anarchy and rebellion had taken the place of good order, and the fanaticism of a foolhardy priest gave laws instead of the legal dispensers of justice. The male population was numerous, their courage confirmed by despair, their confidence unbounded that the siege would be raised, while their hatred against the Roman Catholic religion was excited to the highest pitch. Many had no mercy to expect; all abhorred the general thraldom of an imperious garrison. Noircarmes, whose army had become formidable through the reinforcements which streamed to it from all quarters, and was abundantly furnished with all the requisites for a long blockade, once more attempted to prevail on the town by gentle means, but in vain. At last he caused the trenches to be opened and prepared to invest the place.

In the meanwhile the position of the Protestants had grown as much worse as that of the regent had improved. The league of the nobles had gradually melted away to a third of its original number. Some of its most important defenders, Count Egmont, for instance, had gone over to the king; the pecuniary contributions which had been so confidently reckoned upon came in but slowly and scantily; the zeal of the party began perceptibly to cool, and the close of the fine season made it necessary to discontinue the public preachings, which, up to this time, had been continued. These and other reasons combined induced the declining party to moderate its demands, and to try every legal expedient before it proceeded to extremities. In a general synod of the Protestants, which was held for this object in Antwerp, and which was also attended by some of the confederates, it was resolved to send deputies to the regent to remonstrate with her upon this breach of faith, and to remind her of her compact. Brederode undertook this office, but was obliged to submit to a harsh and disgraceful rebuff, and was shut out of Brussels. He had now recourse to a written memorial, in which, in the name of the whole league, he complained that the duchess had, by violating her word, falsified in sight of all the Protestants the security given by the league, in reliance on which all of them had laid down their arms; that by her insincerity she had undone all the good which the confederates had labored to effect; that she had sought to degrade the league in the eyes of the people, had excited discord among its members, and had even caused many of them to be persecuted as criminals. He called upon her to recall her late ordinances, which deprived the Protestants of the free exercise of their religion, but above all to raise the siege of Valenciennes, to disband the troops newly enlisted, and ended by assuring her that on these conditions and these alone the league would be responsible for the general tranquillity.

To this the regent replied in a tone very different from her previous moderation. "Who these confederates are who address me in this memorial is, indeed, a mystery to me. The confederates with whom I had formerly to do, for ought I know to the contrary, have dispersed. All at least cannot participate in this statement of grievances, for I myself know of many, who, satisfied in all their demands, have returned to their duty. But still, whoever he may be, who without authority and right, and without name addresses me, he has at least given a very false interpretation to my word if he asserts that I guaranteed to the Protestants complete religious liberty. No one can be ignorant how reluctantly I was induced to permit the preachings in the places where they had sprung up unauthorized, and this surely cannot be counted for a concession of freedom in religion. Is it likely that I should have entertained the idea of protecting these illegal consistories, of tolerating this state within a state? Could I forget myself so far as to grant the sanction of law to an objectionable sect; to overturn all order in the church and in the state, and abominably to blaspheme my holy religion? Look to him who has given you such permission, but you must not argue with me. You accuse me of having violated the agreement which gave you impunity and security. The past I am willing to look over, but not what may be done in future. No advantage was to be taken of you on account of the petition of last April, and to the best of my knowledge nothing of the kind has as yet been done; but whoever again offends in the same way against the majesty of the king must be ready to bear the consequences of his crime. In fine, how can you presume to remind me of an agreement which you have been the first to break? At whose instigation were the churches plundered, the images of the saints thrown down, and the towns hurried into rebellion? Who formed alliances with foregn powers, set on foot illegal enlistments, and collected unlawful taxes from the subjects of the king? These are the reasons which have impelled me to draw together my troops, and to increase the severity of the edicts. Whoever now asks me to lay down my arms cannot mean well to his country or his king, and if ye value your own lives, look to it that your own actions acquit you, instead of judging mine."

All the hopes which the confederates might have entertained of an amicable adjustment sank with this high-toned declaration. Without being confident of possessing powerful support, the regent would not, they argued, employ such language. An army was in the field, the enemy was before Valenciennes, the members who were the heart of the league had abandoned it, and the regent required unconditional submission. Their cause was now so bad that open resistance could not make it worse. If they gave themselves up defenceless into the hands of their exasperated sovereign their fate was certain; an appeal to arms could at least make it a matter of doubt; they, therefore, chose the latter, and began seriously to take steps for their defence. In order to insure the assistance of the German Protestants, Louis of Nassau attempted to persuade the towns of Amsterdam, Antwerp, Tournay, and Valenciennes to adopt the confession of Augsburg, and in this manner to seal their alliance with a religious union. But the proposition was not successful, because the hatred of the Calvinists to the Lutherans exceeded, if possible, that which they bore to popery. Nassau also began in earnest to negotiate for supplies from France, the Palatinate, and Saxony. The Count of Bergen fortified his castles; Brederode threw himself with a small force into his strong town of Vianne on the Leck, over which he claimed the rights of sovereignty, and which he hastily placed in a state of defense, and there awaited a reinforcement from the league, and the issue of Nassua's negotiations. The flag of war was now unfurled, everywhere the drum was heard to beat; in all parts troops were seen on the march, contributions collected, and soldiers enlisted. The agents of each party often met in the same place, and hardly had the collectors and recruiting officers of the regent quitted a town when it had to endure a similar visit from the agents of the league.

From Valenciennes the regent directed her attention to Herzogenbusch, where the Iconoclasts had lately committed fresh excesses, and the party of the Protestants had gained a great accession of strength. In order to prevail on the citizens peaceably to receive a garrison, she sent thither, as ambassador, the Chancellor Scheiff, from Brabant, with counsellor Merode of Petersheim, whom she appointed governor of the town; they were instructed to secure the place by judicious means, and to exact from the citizens a new oath of allegiance. At the same time the Count of Megen, who was in the neighborhood with a body of troops, was ordered to support the two envoys in effecting their commission, and to afford the means of throwing in a garrison immediately. But Brederode, who obtained information of these movements in Viane, had already sent thither one of his creatures, a certain Anton von Bomberg, a hot Calvinist, but also a brave soldier, in order to raise the courage of his party, and to frustrate the designs of the regent. This Bomberg succeeded in getting possession of the letters which the chancellor brought with him from the duchess, and contrived to substitute in their place counterfeit ones, which, by their harsh and imperious language, were calculated to exasperate the minds of the citizens. At the same time he attempted to throw suspicion on both the ambassadors of the duchess as having evil designs upon the town. In this he succeeded so well with the mob that in their mad fury they even laid hands on the ambassadors and placed them in confinement. He himself, at the head of eight thousand men, who had adopted him as their leader, advanced against the Count of Megen, who was moving in order of battle, and gave him so warm a reception, with some heavy artillery, that he was compelled to retire without accomplishing his object. The regent now sent an officer of justice to demand the release of her ambassadors, and in case of refusal to threaten the place with siege; but Bomberg with his party surrounded the town hall and forced the magistrate to deliver to him the key of the town. The messenger of the regent was ridiculed and dismissed, and an answer sent through him that the treatment of the prisoners would depend upon Brederode's orders. The herald, who was remaining outside before the town, now appeared to declare war against her, which, however, the chancellor prevented.

After his futile attempt on Herzogenbusch the Count of Megen threw himself into Utrecht in order to prevent the execution of a design which Count Brederode had formed against that town. As it had suffered much from the army of the confederates, which was encamped in its immediate neighborhood, near Viane, it received Megen with open arms as its protector, and conformed to all the alterations which he made in the religious worship. Upon this he immediately caused a redoubt to be thrown up on the bank of the Leck, which would command Viane. Brederode, not disposed to await his attack, quitted that rendezvous with the best part of his army and hastened to Amsterdam.

However unprofitably the Prince of Orange appeared to be losing his time in Antwerp during these operations he was, nevertheless, busily employed. At his instigation the league had commenced recruiting, and Brederode had fortified his castles, for which purpose he himself presented him with three cannons which he had had cast at Utrecht. His eye watched all the movements of the court, and he kept the league warned of the towns which were next menaced with attack. But his chief object appeared to be to get possession of the principal places in the districts under his own government, to which end he with all his power secretly assisted Brederode's plans against Utrecht and Amsterdam. The most important place was the Island of Walcheren, where the king was expected to land; and he now planned a scheme for the surprise of this place, the conduct of which was entrusted to one of the confederate nobles, an intimate friend of the Prince of Orange, John of Marnix, Baron of Thoulouse, and brother of Philip of Aldegonde.

1567. Thoulouse maintained a secret understanding with the late mayor of Middleburg, Peter Haak, by which he expected to gain an opportunity of throwing a garrison into Middleburg and Flushing. The recruiting, however, for this undertaking, which was set on foot in Antwerp, could not be carried on so quietly as not to attract the notice of the magistrate. In order, therefore, to lull the suspicions of the latter, and at the same time to promote the success of the scheme, the prince caused the herald by public proclamation to order all foreign soldiers and strangers who were in the service of the state, or employed in other business, forthwith to quit

the town. He might, say his adversaries, by closing the
gates have easily made himself master of all these suspected recruits; but he expelled them from the town in
order to drive them the more quickly to the place of their
destination. They immediately embarked on the Scheldt,
and sailed down to Rammekens; as, however, a market-
vessel of Antwerp, which ran into Flushing a little before
them had given warning of their design they were forbidden to enter the port. They found the same difficulty
at Arnemuiden, near Middleburg, although the Protestants in that place exerted themselves to raise an insurrection in their favor. Thoulouse, therefore, without
having accomplished anything, put about his ships and
sailed back down the Scheldt as far as Osterweel, a
quarter of a mile from Antwerp, where he disembarked
his people and encamped on the shore, with the hope of
getting men from Antwerp, and also in order to revive
by his presence the courage of his party, which had been
cast down by the proceedings of the magistrate. By the
aid of the Calvinistic clergy, who recruited for him, his
little army increased daily, so that at last he began to be
formidable to the Antwerpians, whose whole territory he
laid waste. The magistrate was for attacking him here
with the militia, which, however, the Prince of Orange
successfully opposed by the pretext that it would not be
prudent to strip the town of soldiers.

Meanwhile the regent had hastily brought together a
small army under the command of Philip of Launoy,
which moved from Brussels to Antwerp by forced
marches. At the same time Count Megen managed to
keep the army of the Gueux shut up and employed at
Viane, so that it could neither hear of these movements
nor hasten to the assistance of its confederates. Launoy,
on his arrival attacked by surprise the dispersed crowds,
who, little expecting an enemy, had gone out to plunder,
and destroyed them in one terrible carnage. Thoulouse
threw himself with the small remnant of his troops into a
country house, which had served him as his headquarters,
and for a long time defended himself with the courage of
despair, until Launoy, finding it impossible to dislodge
him, set fire to the house. The few who escaped the

flames fell on the swords of the enemy or were drowned in the Scheldt. Thoulouse himself preferred to perish in the flames rather than to fall into the hands of the enemy. This victory, which swept off more than a thousand of the enemy, was purchased by the conqueror cheaply enough, for he did not lose more than two men. Three hundred of the leaguers who surrendered were cut down without mercy on the spot, as a sally from Antwerp was momentarily dreaded.

Before the battle actually commenced no anticipation of such an event had been entertained at Antwerp. The Prince of Orange, who had got early information of it, had taken the precaution the day before of causing the bridge which unites the town with Osterweel to be destroyed, in order, as he gave out, to prevent the Calvinists within the town going out to join the army of Thoulouse. A more probable motive seems to have been a fear lest the Catholics should attack the army of the Gueux general in the rear, or lest Launoy should prove victorious, and try to force his way into the town. On the same pretext the gates of the city were also shut by his orders, and the inhabitants, who did not comprehend the meaning of all these movements, fluctuated between curiosity and alarm, until the sound of artillery from Osterweel announced to them what there was going on. In clamorous crowds they all ran to the walls and ramparts, from which, as the wind drove the smoke from the contending armies, they commanded a full view of the whole battle. Both armies were so near to the town that they could discern their banners, and clearly distinguish the voices of the victors and the vanquished. More terrible even than the battle itself was the spectacle which this town now presented. Each of the conflicting armies had its friends and its enemies on the wall. All that went on in the plain roused on the ramparts exultation or dismay; on the issue of the conflict the fate of each spectator seemed to depend. Every movement on the field could be read in the faces of the townsmen; defeat and triumph, the terror of the conquered, and the fury of the conqueror. Here a painful but idle wish to support those who are giving way, to rally those who fly;

there an equally futile desire to overtake them, to slay them, to extirpate them. Now the 'Gueux fly, and ten thousand men rejoice; Thoulouse's last place and refuge is in flames, and the hopes of twenty thousand citizens are consumed with him.

But the first bewilderment of alarm soon gave place to a frantic desire of revenge. Shrieking aloud, wringing her hands and with dishevelled hair, the widow of the slain general rushed amidst the crowds to implore their pity and help. Excited by their favorite preacher, Hermann, the Calvinists fly to arms, determined to avenge their brethren, or to perish with them; without reflection, without plan or leader, guided by nothing but their anguish, their delirium, they rush to the Red Gate of the city which leads to the field of battle; but there is no egress, the gate is shut and the foremost of the crowd recoil on those that follow. Thousands and thousands collect together, a dreadful rush is made to the Meer Bridge. We are betrayed! we are prisoners! is the general cry. Destruction to the papists, death to him who has betrayed us! — a sullen murmur, portentous of a revolt, runs through the multitude. They begin to suspect that all that has taken place has been set on foot by the Roman Catholics to destroy the Calvinists. They had slain their defenders, and they would now fall upon the defenceless. With fatal speed this suspicion spreads through the whole of Antwerp. Now they can, they think, understand the past, and they fear something still worse in the background; a frightful distrust gains possession of every mind. Each party dreads the other; every one sees an enemy in his neighbor; the mystery deepens the alarm and horror; a fearful condition for a populous town, in which every accidental concourse instantly becomes tumult, every rumor started amongst them becomes a fact, every small spark a blazing flame, and by the force of numbers and collision all passions are furiously inflamed. All who bore the name of Calvinists were roused by this report. Fifteen thousand of them take possession of the Meer Bridge, and plant heavy artillery upon it, which they had taken by force from the arsenal; the same thing also happens at another bridge;

their number makes them formidable, the town is in their hands; to escape an imaginary danger they bring all Antwerp to the brink of ruin.

Immediately on the commencement of the tumult the Prince of Orange hastened to the Meer Bridge, where, boldly forcing his way through the raging crowd, he commanded peace and entreated to be heard. At the other bridge Count Hogstraten, accompanied by the Burgomaster Strahlen, made the same attempt; but not possessing a sufficient share either of eloquence or of popularity to command attention, he referred the tumultuous crowd to the prince, around whom all Antwerp now furiously thronged. The gate, he endeavored to explain to them, was shut simply to keep off the victor, whoever he might be, from the city, which would otherwise become the prey of an infuriated soldiery. In vain! the frantic people would not listen, and one more daring than the rest presented his musket at him, calling him a traitor. With tumultuous shouts they demanded the key of the Red Gate, which he was ultimately forced to deliver into the hands of the preacher Hermann. But, he added with happy presence of mind, they must take heed what they were doing; in the suburbs six hundred of the enemy's horse were waiting to receive them. This invention, suggested by the emergency, was not so far removed from the truth as its author perhaps imagined; for no sooner had the victorous general perceived the commotion in Antwerp than he caused his whole cavalry to mount in the hope of being able, under favor of the disturbance, to break into the town. I, at least, continued the Prince of Orange, shall secure my own safety in time, and he who follows my example will save himself much future regret. These words opportunely spoken and immediately acted upon had their effect. Those who stood nearest followed him, and were again followed by the next, so that at last the few who had already hastened out of the city when they saw no one coming after them lost the desire of coping alone with the six hundred horse. All accordingly returned to the Meer Bridge, where they posted watches and videttes, and the night was passed tumultuously under arms.

The town of Antwerp was now threatened with fearful bloodshed and pillage. In this pressing emergency Orange assembled an extraordinary senate, to which were summoned all the best-disposed citizens of the four nations. If they wished, said he, to repress the violence of the Calvinists they must oppose them with an army strong enough and prepared to meet them. It was therefore resolved to arm with speed the Roman Catholic inhabitants of the town, whether natives, Italians, or Spaniards, and, if possible, to induce the Lutherans also to join them. The haughtiness of the Calvinists, who, proud of their wealth and confident in their numbers, treated every other religious party with contempt, had long made the Lutherans their enemies, and the mutual exasperation of these two Protestant churches was even more implacable than their common hatred of the dominant church. This jealousy the magistrate had turned to advantage, by making use of one party to curb the other, and had thus contrived to keep the Calvinists in check, who, from their numbers and insolence, were most to be feared. With this view, he had tacitly taken into his protection the Lutherans, as the weaker and more peaceable party, having moreover invited for them, from Germany, spiritual teachers, who, by controversial sermons, might keep up the mutual hatred of the two bodies. He encouraged the Lutherans in the vain idea that the king thought more favorably of their religious creed than that of the Calvinists, and exhorted them to be careful how they damaged their good cause by any understanding with the latter. It was not, therefore, difficult to bring about, for the moment, a union with the Roman Catholics and the Lutherans, as its object was to keep down their detested rivals. At dawn of day an army was opposed to the Calvinists which was far superior in force to their own. At the head of this army, the eloquence of Orange had far greater effect, and found far more attention than on the preceding evening, unbacked by such strong persuasion. The Calvinists, though in possession of arms and artillery, yet, alarmed at the superior numbers arrayed against them, were the first to send envoys, and to treat for an amicable adjustment of differences, which by the tact and good temper of the Prince of Orange, he concluded to the satisfaction of all parties. On the proclamation of this treaty the Spaniards and Italians immdiately laid down their arms. They were followed by the Calvinists, and these again by the Roman Catholics; last of all the Lutherans disarmed.

Two days and two nights Antwerp had continued in this alarming state. During the tumult the Roman Catholics had succeeded in placing barrels of gunpowder under the Meer Bridge, and threatened to blow into the air the whole army of the Calvinists, who had done the same in other places to destroy their adversaries. The destruction of the town hung on the issue of a moment, and nothing but the prince's presence of mind saved it.

Noircarmes, with his army of Walloons, still lay before Valenciennes, which, in firm reliance on being relieved by the Gueux, obstinately refused to listen to all the representations of the regent, and rejected every idea of surrender. An order of the court had expressly forbidden the royalist general to press the siege until he should receive reinforcements from Germany. Whether from forbearance or fear, the king regarded with abhorrence the violent measure of storming the place, as necessarily involving the innocent in the fate of the guilty, and exposing the loyal subject to the same ill-treatment as the rebel. As, however, the confidence of the besieged augmented daily, and emboldened by the inactivity of the besiegers, they annoyed him by frequent sallies, and after burning the cloisters before the town, retired with the plunder — as the time uselessly lost before this town was put to good use by the rebels and their allies, Noircarmes besought the duchess to obtain immediate permission from the king to take it by storm. The answer arrived more quickly than Philip was ever before wont to reply. As yet they must be content, simply to make the necessary preparations, and then to wait awhile to allow terror to have its effect; but if upon this they did not appear ready to capitulate, the storming might take place, but, at the same time, with the greatest possible regard for the lives of the inhabitants. Before the regent allowed Noircarmes to proceed to this extremity she empowered Count Egmont, with the Duke Arschot, to treat once more with the rebels amicably. Both conferred with the deputies of the town, and omitted no argument calculated to dispel their delusion. They acquainted them with the defeat of Thoulouse, their sole support, and with the fact that the Count of Megen had cut off the army of the Gueux from the town, and assured them that if they had held out so long they owed it entirely to the king's forbearance. They offered them full pardon for the past; every one was to be free to prove his innocence before whatever tribunal he should chose; such as did not wish to avail themselves of this privilege were to be allowed fourteen days to quit the town with all their effects. Nothing was required of the townspeople but the admission of the garrison. To give time to deliberate on these terms an armistice of three days was granted. When the deputies returned they found their fellow-citizens less disposed than ever to an accommodation, reports of new levies by the Gueux having, in the meantime, gained currency. Thoulouse, it was pretended, had conquered, and was advancing with a powerful army to relieve the place. Their confidence went so far that they even ventured to break the armistice, and to fire upon the besiegers. At last the burgomaster, with difficulty, succeeded in bringing matters so far towards a peaceful settlement that twelve of the town counsellors were sent into the camp with the following conditions: The edict by which Valenciennes had been charged with treason and declared an enemy to the country was required to be recalled, the confiscation of their goods revoked, and the prisoners on both sides restored to liberty; the garrison was not to enter the town before every one who thought good to do so had placed himself and his property in security; and a pledge to be given that the inhabitants should not be molested in any manner, and that their expenses should be paid by the king.

Noircarmes was so indignant with these conditions that he was almost on the point of ill-treating the deputies. If they had not come, he told them, to give up the place, they might return forthwith, lest he should send them home with their hands tied behind their backs. Upon this the deputies threw the blame on the obstinacy of the Calvinists, and entreated him, with tears in their eyes, to keep them in the camp, as they did not, they said, wish to have anything more to do with their rebellious townsmen, or to be joined in their fate. They even knelt to beseech the intercession of Egmont, but Noircarmes remained deaf to all their entreaties, and the sight of the chains which he ordered to be brought out drove them reluctantly enough back to Valenciennes. Necessity, not severity, imposed this harsh procedure upon the general. The detention of ambassadors had on a former occasion drawn upon him the reprimand of the duchess; the people in the town would not have failed to have ascribed the non-appearance of their present deputies to the same cause as in the former case had detained them. Besides, he was loath to deprive the town of any out of the small residue of well-disposed citizens, or to leave it a prey to a blind, foolhardy mob. Egmont was so mortified at the bad result of his embassy that he the night following rode round to reconnoitre its fortifications, and returned well satisfied to have convinced himself that it was no longer tenable.

Valenciennes stretches down a gentle acclivity into the level plain, being built on a site as strong as it is delightful. On one side enclosed by the Scheldt and another smaller river, and on the other protected by deep ditches, thick walls, and towers, it appears capable of defying every attack. But Noircarmes had discovered a few points where neglect had allowed the fosse to be filled almost up to the level of the natural surface, and of these he determined to avail himself in storming. He drew together all the scattered corps by which he had invested the town, and during a tempestuous night carried the suburb of Berg without the loss of a single man. He then assigned separate points of attack to the Count of Bossu, the young Charles of Mansfeld, and the younger Barlaimont, and under a terrible fire, which drove the enemy from his walls, his troops were moved up with all possible speed. Close before the town, and opposite the gate under the eyes of the besiegers, and with very little loss, a battery was thrown up to an equal height with the fortifications. From this point the town was bombarded with an unceasing fire for four hours. The Nicolaus tower, on which the besieged had planted some artillery, was among the first that fell, and many perished under its ruins. The guns were directed against all the most conspicuous buildings, and a terrible slaughter was made amongst the inhabitants. In a few hours their principal works were destroyed, and in the gate itself so extensive a breach was made that the besieged, despairing of any longer defending themselves, sent in haste two trumpeters to entreat a parley. This was granted, but the storm was continued without intermission. The ambassador entreated Noircarmes to grant them the same terms which only two days before they had rejected. But circumstances had now changed, and the victor would hear no more of conditions. The unceasing fire left the inhabitants no time to repair the ramparts, which filled the fosse with their débris, and opened many a breach for the enemy to enter by. Certain of utter destruction, they surrendered next morning at discretion after a bombardment of six-and-thirty hours without intermission, and three thousand bombs had been thrown into the city. Noircarmes marched into the town with his victorious army under the strictest discipline, and was received by a crowd of women and children, who went to meet him, carrying green boughs, and beseeching his pity. All the citizens were immediately disarmed, the commandant and his son beheaded; thirty-six of the most guilty of the rebels, among whom were La Grange and another Calvinistic preacher, Guido de Bresse, atoned for their obstinacy at the gallows; all the municipal functionaries were deprived of their offices, and the town of all its privileges. The Roman Catholic worship was immediately restored in full dignity, and the Protestant abolished. The Bishop of Arras was obliged to quit his residence in the town, and a strong garrison placed in it to insure its future obedience.

The fate of Valenciennes, towards which all eyes had been turned, was a warning to the other towns which had similarly offended. Noircarmes followed up his victory, and marched immediately against Maestricht, which surrendered without a blow, and received a garrison. From thence he marched to Tornhut to awe by his presence the people of Herzogenbusch and Antwerp. The Gueux in this place, who under the command of Bomberg had carried all things before them, were now so terrified at his approach that they quitted the town in haste. Noircarmes was received without opposition. The ambassadors of the duchess were immediately set at liberty. A strong garrison was thrown into Tornhut. Cambray also opened its gates, and joyfully recalled its archbishop, whom the Calvinists had driven from his see, and who deserved this triumph as he did not stain his entrance with blood. Ghent, Ypres, and Oudenarde submitted and received garrisons. Gueldres was now almost entirely cleared of the rebels and reduced to obedience by the Count of Megen. In Friesland and Gröningen the Count of Aremberg had eventually the same success; but it was not obtained here so rapidly or so easily, since the count wanted consistency and firmness, and these warlike republicans maintained more pertinaciously their privileges, and were greatly supported by the strength of their position. With the exception of Holland all the provinces had yielded before the victorious arms of the duchess. The courage of the disaffected sunk entirely, and nothing was left to them but flight or submission.

RESIGNATION OF WILLIAM OF ORANGE.

Ever since the establishment of the Guesen league, but more perceptibly since the outbreak of the Iconoclasts, the spirit of rebellion and disaffection had spread so rapidly among all classes, parties had become so blended and confused, that the regent had difficulty in distinguishing her own adherents, and at last hardly knew on whom to rely. The lines of demarcation between the loyal and the disaffected had grown gradually fainter, until at last they almost entirely vanished. The frequent alterations, too, which she had been obliged to make in the laws, and which were at most the expedients and suggestions of the moment, had taken from them their precision and binding force, and had given full scope to the arbitrary will of every individual whose office it was to interpret them. And at last, amidst the number and variety of the interpretations, the spirit was lost and the intention of the lawgiver baffled. The close connection which in many cases subsisted between Protestants and Roman Catholics, between Gueux and Royalists, and which not unfrequently gave them a common interest, led the latter to avail themselves of the loophole which the vagueness of the laws left open, and in favor of their Protestant friends and associates evaded by subtle distinctions all severity in the discharge of their duties. In their minds it was enough not to be a declared rebel, not one of the Gueux, or at least not a heretic, to be authorized to mould their duties to their inclinations, and to set the most arbitrary limits to their obedience to the king. Feeling themselves irresponsible, the governors of the provinces, the civil functionaries, both high and low, the municipal officers, and the military commanders had all become extremely remiss in their duty, and presuming upon this impunity showed a pernicious indulgence to the rebels and their adherents which rendered abortive all the regent's measures of coercion. This general indifference and corruption of so many servants of the state had further this injurious result, that it led the turbulent to reckon on far stronger support than in reality they had cause for, and to count on their own side all who were but lukewarm adherents of the court. This way of thinking, erroneous as it was, gave them greater courage and confidence; it had the same effect as if it had been well founded; and the uncertain vassals of the king became in consequence almost as injurious to him as his declared enemies, without at the same time being liable to the same measures of severity. This was especially the case with the Prince of Orange, Counts Egmont, Bergen, Hogstraten, Horn, and several others of the higher nobility. The regent felt the necessity of bringing these doubtful subjects to an explanation, in order either to deprive the rebels of a fancied support or to unmask the enemies of the king. And the latter reason was of the more urgent moment when being obliged to send an army into the field it was of the utmost importance to entrust the command of the troops to none but those of whose fidelity she was fully assured. She caused, therefore, an oath to be drawn up which bound all who took it to advance the Roman Catholic faith, to pursue and punish the Iconoclasts, and to help by every means in their power in extirpating all kinds of heresy. It also pledged them to treat the king's enemies as their own, and to serve without distinction against all whom the regent in the king's name should point out. By this oath she did not hope so much to test their sincerity, and still less to secure them, as rather to gain a pretext for removing the suspected parties if they declined to take it, and for wresting from their hands a power which they abused, or a legitimate ground for punishing them if they took it and broke it. This oath was exacted from all Knights of the Fleece, all civil functionaries and magistrates, all officers of the army — from every one in short who held any appointment in the state. Count Mansfeld was the first who publicly took it in the council of state at Brussels; his example was followed by the Duke of Arschot, Counts Egmont, Megen, and Barlaimont. Hogstraten and Horn endeavored to evade the necessity. The former was offended at a proof of distrust which shortly before the regent had given him. Under the pretext that Malines could not safely be left any longer without its governor, but that the presence of the count was no less necessary in Antwerp, she had taken from him that province and given it to another whose fidelity she could better reckon upon. Hogstraten expressed his thanks that she had been pleased to release him from one of his burdens, adding that she would complete the obligation if she would relieve him from the other also. True to his determination Count Horn was living on one of his estates in the strong town of Weerdt, having retired altogether from public affairs. Having quitted the service of the state, he owed, he thought, nothing more either to the republic or to the king, and declined the oath, which in his case appears at last to have been waived.

The Count of Brederode was left the choice of either taking the prescribed oath or resigning the command of his squadron of cavalry. After many fruitless attempts to evade the alternative, on the plea that he did not hold office in the state, he at last resolved upon the latter course, and thereby escaped all risk of perjuring himself.

Vain were all the attempts to prevail on the Prince of Orange to take the oath, who, from the suspicion which had long attached to him, required more than any other this purification; and from whom the great power which it had been necessary to place in his hands fully justified the regent in exacting it. It was not, however, advisable to proceed against him with the laconic brevity adopted towards Brederode and the like; on the other hand, the voluntary resignation of all his offices, which he tendered, did not meet the object of the regent, who foresaw clearly enough how really dangerous he would become, as soon as he should feel himself independent, and be no longer checked by any external considerations of character or duty in the prosecution of his secret designs. But ever since the consultation in Dendermonde the Prince of Orange had made up his mind to quit the service of the King of Spain on the first favorable opportunity, and till better days to leave the country itself. A very disheartening experience had taught him how uncertain are hopes built on the multitude, and how quickly their zeal is cooled by the necessity of fulfilling its lofty promises. An army was already in the field, and a far stronger one was, he knew, on its road, under the command of the Duke of Alva. The time for remonstrances was past; it was only at the head of an army that an advantageous treaty could now be concluded with the regent, and by preventing the entrance of the Spanish general. But now where was he to raise this army, in want as he was of money, the sinews of warfare, since the Protestants had retracted their boastful promises and deserted him in this pressing emergency?*

* How valiant the wish, and how sorry the deed was, is proved by the following instance amongst others. Some friends of the national liberty, Roman Catholics as well as Protestants, had solemnly engaged in Amsterdam to subscribe to a common fund the hundredth penny of their estates, until a sum of eleven thousand florins should be collected, which was to be devoted

Religious jealousy and hatred, moreover, separated the two Protestant churches, and stood in the way of every salutary combination against the common enemy of their faith. The rejection of the Confession of Augsburg by the Calvinists had exasperated all the Protestant princes of Germany, so that no support was to be looked for from the empire. With Count Egmont the excellent army of Walloons was also lost to the cause, for they followed with blind devotion the fortunes of their general, who had taught them at St. Quentin and Gravelines to be invincible. And again, the outrages which the Iconoclasts had perpetrated on the churches and convents had estranged from the league the numerous, wealthy, and powerful class of the established clergy, who, before this unlucky episode, were already more than half gained over to it; while, by her intrigues, the regent daily contrived to deprive the league itself of some one or other of its most influential members.

All these considerations combined induced the prince to postpone to a more favorable season a project for which the present juncture was little suited, and to leave a country where his longer stay could not effect any advantage for it, but must bring certain destruction on himself. After intelligence gleaned from so many quarters, after so many proofs of distrust, so many warnings from Madrid, he could be no longer doubtful of the sentiments of Philip towards him. If even he had any doubt, his uncertainty would soon have been dispelled by the formidable armament which was preparing in Spain, and which was to have for its leader, not the king, as was falsely given out, but, as he was better informed, the Duke of Alva, his personal enemy, and the very man he had most cause to fear. The prince had seen too deeply into Philip's heart to believe in the sincerity of his reconciliation after having once awakened his fears. He judged his own conduct too justly to reckon, like his

to the common cause and interests. An alms-box, protected by three locks, was prepared for the reception of these contributions. After the expiration of the prescribed period it was opened, and a sum was found amounting to seven hundred florins, which was given to the hostess of the Count of Brederode, in part payment of his unliquidated score. Univ. Hist. of the N., vol. 3.

friend Egmont, on reaping a gratitude from the king to
which he had not sown. He could therefore expect
nothing but hostility from him, and prudence counselled
him to screen himself by a timely flight from its actual
outbreak. He had hitherto obstinately refused to take
the new oath, and all the written exhortations of the
regent had been fruitless. At last she sent to him at
Antwerp her private secretary, Berti, who was to put
the matter emphatically to his conscience, and forcibly
remind him of all the evil consequences which so sudden
a retirement from the royal service would draw upon the
country, as well as the irreparable injury it would do to his
own fair fame. Already, she informed him by her ambassador, his declining the required oath had cast a shade
upon his honor, and imparted to the general voice, which
accused him of an understanding with the rebels, an
appearance of truth which this unconditional resignation
would convert to absolute certainty. It was for the sovereign to discharge his servants, but it did not become
the servant to abandon his sovereign. The envoy of the
regent found the prince in his palace at Antwerp,
already, as it appeared, withdrawn from the public service, and entirely devoted to his private concerns. The
prince told him, in the presence of Hogstraten, that he
had refused to take the required oath because he could
not find that such a proposition had ever before been
made to a governor of a province; because he had already
bound himself, once for all, to the king, and therefore, by
taking this new oath, he would tacitly acknowledge that
he had broken the first. He had also refused because
the old oath enjoined him to protect the rights and privileges of the country, but he could not tell whether this
new one might not impose upon him duties which would
contravene the first; because, too, the clause which
bound him to serve, if required, against all without distinction, did not except even the emperor, his feudal
lord, against whom, however, he, as his vassal, could not
conscientiously make war. He had refused to take this
oath because it might impose upon him the necessity of
surrendering his friends and relations, his children, nay,
even his wife, who was a Lutheran, to butchery. Ac-

cording to it, moreover, he must lend himself to every thing which it should occur to the king's fancy or passion to demand. But the king might thus exact from him things which he shuddered even to think of, and even the severities which were now, and had been all along, exercised upon the Protestants, were the most revolting to his heart. This oath, in short, was repugnant to his feelings as a man, and he could not take it. In conclusion, the name of the Duke of Alva dropped from his lips in a tone of bitterness, and he became immediately silent.

All these objections were answered, point by point, by Berti. Certainly such an oath had never been required from a governor before him, because the provinces had never been similarly circumstanced. It was not exacted because the governors had broken the first, but in order to remind them vividly of their former vows, and to freshen their activity in the present emergency. This oath would not impose upon him anything which offended against the rights and privileges of the country, for the king had sworn to observe these as well as the Prince of Orange. The oath did not, it was true, contain any reference to a war with the emperor, or any other sovereign to whom the prince might be related; and if he really had scruples on this point, a distinct clause could easily be inserted, expressly providing against such a contingency. Care would be taken to spare him any duties which were repugnant to his feelings as a man, and no power on earth would compel him to act against his wife or against his children. Berti was then passing to the last point, which related to the Duke of Alva, but the prince, who did not wish to have this part of his discourse canvassed, interrupted him. "The king was coming to the Netherlands," he said, "and he knew the king. The king would not endure that one of his servants should have wedded a Lutheran, and he had therefore resolved to go with his whole family into voluntary banishment before he was obliged to submit to the same by compulsion. But," he concluded, "wherever he might be, he would always conduct himself as a subject of the king." Thus far-fetched were the motives which the prince adduced to avoid touching upon the single one which really decided him.

Berti had still a hope of obtaining, through Egmont's eloquence, what by his own he despaired of effecting. He therefore proposed a meeting with the latter (1567), which the prince assented to the more willingly as he himself felt a desire to embrace his friend once more before his departure, and if possible to snatch the deluded man from certain destruction. This remarkable meeting, at which the private secretary, Berti, and the young Count Mansfeld, were also present, was the last that the two friends ever held, and took place in Villebroeck, a village on the Rupel, between Brussels and Antwerp. The Calvinists, whose last hope rested on the issue of this conference, found means to acquaint themselves of its import by a spy, who concealed himself in the chimney of the apartment where it was held. All three attempted to shake the determination of the prince, but their united eloquence was unable to move him from his purpose. "It will cost you your estates, Orange, if you persist in this intention," said the Prince of Gaure, as he took him aside to a window. "And you your life, Egmont, if you change not yours," replied the former. "To me it will at least be a consolation in my misfortunes that I desired, in deed as well as in word, to help my country and my friends in the hour of need; but you, my friend, you are dragging friends and country with you to destruction." And saying these words, he once again exhorted him, still more urgently than ever, to return to the cause of his country, which his arm alone was yet able to preserve; if not, at least for his own sake to avoid the tempest which was gathering against him from Spain.

But all the arguments, however lucid, with which a far-discerning prudence supplied him, and however urgently enforced, with all the ardor and animation which the tender anxiety of friendship could alone inspire, did not avail to destroy the fatal confidence which still fettered Egmont's better reason. The warning of Orange seemed to come from a sad and dispirited heart; but for Egmont the world still smiled. To abandon the pomp and affluence in which he had grown up to youth and manhood; to part with all the thousand conveniences of life which alone made it valuable to him, and all this to escape an evil which his buoyant spirit regarded as remote, if not imaginary; no, that was not a sacrifice which could be asked from Egmont. But had he even been less given to indulgence than he was, with what heart could he have consigned a princess, accustomed by uninterrupted prosperity to ease and comfort, a wife who loved him as dearly as she was beloved, the children on whom his soul hung in hope and fondness, to privations at the prospect of which his own courage sank, and which a sublime philosophy alone can enable sensuality to undergo. "You will never persuade me, Orange," said Egmont, "to see things in the gloomy light in which they appear to thy mournful prudence. When I have succeeded in abolishing the public preachings, and chastising the Iconoclasts, in crushing the rebels, and restoring peace and order in the provinces, what can the king lay to my charge? The king is good and just; I have claims upon his gratitude, and I must not forget what I owe to myself." "Well, then," cried Orange, indignantly and with bitter anguish, "trust, if you will, to this royal gratitude; but a mournful presentiment tells me — and may Heaven grant that I am deceived! — that you, Egmont, will be the bridge by which the Spaniards will pass into our country to destroy it." After these words, he drew him to his bosom, ardently clasping him in his arms. Long, as though the sight was to serve for the remainder of his life, did he keep his eyes fixed upon him; the tears fell; they saw each other no more.

The very next day the Prince of Orange wrote his letter of resignation to the regent, in which he assured her of his perpetual esteem, and once again entreated her to put the best interpretation on his present step. He then set off with his three brothers and his whole family for his own town of Breda, where he remained only as long as was requisite to arrange some private affairs. His eldest son, Prince Philip William, was left behind at the University of Louvain, where he thought him sufficiently secure under the protection of the privileges of Brabant and the immunities of the academy; an imprudence which, if it was really not designed, can hardly be reconciled with the just estimate which, in so many other cases, he had taken of the character of his adversary. In Breda the heads of the Calvinists once more consulted him whether there was still hope for them, or whether all was irretrievably lost. "He had before advised them," replied the prince, "and must now do so again, to accede to the Confession of Augsburg; then they might rely upon aid from Germany. If they would still not consent to this, they must raise six hundred thousand florins, or more, if they could." "The first," they answered, "was at variance with their conviction and their conscience; but means might perhaps be found to raise the money if he would only let them know for what purpose he would use it. "No!" cried he, with the utmost displeasure, "if I must tell you that, it is all over with the use of it." With these words he immediately broke off the conference and dismissed the deputies.

The Prince of Orange was reproached with having squandered his fortune, and with favoring the innovations on account of his debts; but he asserted that he still enjoyed sixty thousand florins yearly rental. Before his departure he borrowed twenty thousand florins from the states of Holland on the mortgage of some manors. Men could hadly persuade themselves that he would have succumbed to necessity so entirely, and without an effort at resistance given up all his hopes and schemes. But what he secretly meditated no one knew, no one had read in his heart. Being asked how he intended to conduct himself towards the King of Spain, "Quietly," was his answer, "unless he touches my honor or my estates." He left the Netherlands soon afterwards, and betook himself in retirement to the town of Dillenburg, in Nassau, at which place he was born. He was accompanied to Germany by many hundreds, either as his servants or as volunteers, and was soon followed by Counts Hogstraten, Kuilemberg, and Bergen, who preferred to share a voluntary exile with him rather than recklessly involve themselves in an uncertain destiny. In his departure the nation saw the flight of its guardian angel; many had adored, all had honored him. With him the last stay of the Protestants gave way; they, however, had greater hopes from this man in exile than from all the others together who remained behind. Even the Roman Catholics could not witness his departure without regret. Them also had he shielded from tyranny; he had not unfrequently protected them against the oppression of their own church, and he had rescued many of them from the sanguinary jealousy of their religious opponents. A few fanatics among the Calvinists, who were offended with his proposal of an alliance with their brethren, who avowed the Confession of Augsburg, solemnized with secret thanksgivings the day on which the enemy left them. (1567).

DECAY AND DISPERSION OF THE GEUSEN LEAGUE.

Immediately after taking leave of his friend, the Prince of Gaure hastened back to Brussels, to receive from the regent the reward of his firmness, and there, in the excitement of the court and in the sunshine of his good fortune, to dispel the light cloud which the earnest warnings of the Prince of Orange had cast over his natural gayety. The flight of the latter now left him in possession of the stage. He had now no longer any rival in the republic to dim his glory. With redoubled zeal he wooed the transient favor of the court, above which he ought to have felt himself far exalted. All Brussels must participate in his joy. He gave splendid banquets and public entertainments, at which, the better to eradicate all suspicion from his mind, the regent herself frequently attended. Not content with having taken the required oath, he outstripped the most devout in devotion; outran the most zealous in zeal to extirpate the Protestant faith, and to reduce by force of arms the refractory towns of Flanders. He declared to his old friend, Count Hogstraten, as also to the rest of the Gueux, that he would withdraw from them his friendship forever if they hesitated any longer to return into the bosom of the church, and reconcile themselves with their king. All the confidential letters which had been exchanged between him and them were returned, and by this last step the breach between them was made public and irreparable. Egmont's secession, and the flight of the Prince of Orange, destroyed the last hope of the Protestants and dissolved the whole league of the Gueux. Its members vied with each other in readiness — nay, they could not soon enough abjure the covenant and take the new oath proposed to them by the government. In vain did the Protestant merchants exclaim at this breach of faith on the part of the nobles; their weak voice was no longer listened to, and all the sums were lost with which they had supplied the league.

The most important places were quickly reduced and garrisoned; the rebels had fled, or perished by the hand of the executioner; in the provinces no protector was left. All yielded to the fortune of the regent, and her victorious army was advancing against Antwerp. After a long and obstinate contest this town had been cleared of the worst rebels; Hermann and his adherents took to flight; the internal storms had spent their rage. The minds of the people became gradually composed, and no longer excited at will by every furious fanatic, began to listen to better counsels. The wealthier citizens earnestly longed for peace to revive commerce and trade, which had suffered severely from the long reign of anarchy. The dread of Alva's approach worked wonders; in order to prevent the miseries which a Spanish army would inflict upon the country, the people hastened to throw themselves on the gentler mercies of the regent. Of their own accord they despatched plenipotentiaries to Brussels to negotiate for a treaty and to hear her terms. Agreeably as the regent was surprised by this voluntary step, she did not allow herself to be hurried away by her joy. She declared that she neither could nor would listen to any overtures or representations until the town had received a garrison. Even this was no longer opposed, and Count Mansfeld marched in the day after with sixteen squadrons in battle array. A solemn treaty was now made between the town and duchess, by which the former bound itself to prohibit the Calvinistic form of worship, to banish all preachers of that persuasion, to restore the Roman Catholic religion to its former dignity, to decorate the despoiled churches with their former ornaments, to administer the old edicts as before, to take the new oath which the other towns had sworn to, and, lastly, to deliver into the hands of justice all who been guilty of treason, in bearing arms, or taking part in the desecration of the churches. On the other hand, the regent pledged herself to forget all that had passed, and even to intercede for the offenders with the king. All those who, being dubious of obtaining pardon, preferred banishment, were to be allowed a month to convert their property into money, and place themselves in safety. From this grace none were to be excluded but such as had been guilty of a capital offence, and who were excepted by the previous article. Immediately upon the conclusion of this treaty all Calvinist and Lutheran preachers in Antwerp, and the adjoining territory, were warned by the herald to quit the country within twenty-four hours. All the streets and gates were now thronged with fugitives, who for the honor of their God abandoned what was dearest to them, and sought a more peaceful home for their persecuted faith. Here husbands were taking an eternal farewell of their wives, fathers of their children; there whole families were preparing to depart. All Antwerp resembled a house of mourning; wherever the eye turned some affecting spectacle of painful separation presented itself. A seal was set on the doors of the Protestant churches; the whole worship seemed to be extinct. The 10th of April (1567) was the day appointed for the departure of the preachers. In the town hall, where they appeared for the last time to take leave of the magistrate, they could not command their grief; but broke forth into bitter reproaches. They had been sacrificed, they exclaimed, they had been shamefully betrayed; but a time would come when Antwerp would pay dearly enough for this baseness. Still more bitter were the complaints of the Lutheran clergy, whom the magistrate himself had invited into the country to preach against the Calvinists. Under the delusive representation that the king was not unfavorable to their religion they had been seduced into a combination against the Calvinists, but as soon as the latter had been by their co-operation brought under subjection, and their own services were no longer required, they were left to bewail their folly, which had involved themselves and their enemies in common ruin.

A few days afterwards the regent entered Antwerp in triumph, accompanied by a thousand Walloon horse, the Knights of the Golden Fleece, all the governors and counsellors, a number of municipal officers, and her whole court. Her first visit was to the cathedral, which still bore lamentable traces of the violence of the Iconoclasts, and drew from her many and bitter tears. Immediately afterwards four of the rebels, who had been overtaken in their flight, were brought in and executed in the public market-place. All the children who had been baptized after the Protestant rites were rebaptized by Roman Catholic priests; all the schools of heretics were closed, and their churches levelled to the ground. Nearly all the towns in the Netherlands followed the example of Antwerp and banished the Protestant preachers. By the end of April the Roman Catholic churches were repaired and embellished more splendidly than ever, while all the Protestant places of worship were pulled down, and every vestige of the proscribed belief obliterated in the seventeen provinces. The populace, whose sympathies are generally with the successful party, was now as active in accelerating the ruin of the unfortunate as a short time before it had been furiously zealous in its cause; in Ghent a large and beautiful church which the Calvinists had erected was attacked, and in less than an hour had wholly disappeared. From the beams of the roofless churches gibbets were erected for those who had profaned the sanctuaries of the Roman Catholics. The places of execution were filled with corpses, the prisons with condemned victims, the high roads with fugitives. Innumerable were the victims of this year of murder; in the smallest towns fifty at least, in several of the larger as many as three hundred, were put to death, while no account was kept of the numbers in the open country who fell into the hands of the provost-marshal and were immediately strung up as miscreants, without trial and without mercy.

The regent was still in Antwerp when ambassadors

presented themselves from the Electors of Brandenburg, Saxony, Hesse, Würtemberg, and Baden to intercede for their fugitive brethren in the faith. The expelled preachers of the Augsburg Confession had claimed the rights assured to them by the religious peace of the Germans, in which Brabant, as part of the empire, participated, and had thrown themselves on the protection of those princes. The arrival of the foreign ministers alarmed the regent, and she vainly endeavored to prevent their entrance into Antwerp; under the guise, however, of showing them marks of honor, she continued to keep them closely watched lest they should encourage the malcontents in any attempts against the peace of the town. From the high tone which they most unreasonably adopted towards the regent it might almost be inferred that they were little in earnest in their demand. "It was but reasonable," they said, "that the Confession of Augsburg, as the only one which met the spirit of the gospel, should be the ruling faith in the Netherlands; but to persecute it by such cruel edicts as were in force was positively unnatural and could not be allowed. They therefore required of the regent, in the name of religion, not to treat the people entrusted to her rule with such severity. She replied through the Count of Staremberg, her minister for German affairs, that such an exordium deserved no answer at all. From the sympathy which the German princes had shown for the Belgian fugitives it was clear that they gave less credit to the letters of the king, in explanation of his measures, than to the reports of a few worthless wretches who, in the desecrated churches, had left behind them a worthier memorial of their acts and characters. It would far more become them to leave to the King of Spain the care of his own subjects, and abandon the attempt to foster a spirit of rebellion in foreign countries, from which they would reap neither honor nor profit. The ambassadors left Antwerp in a few days without having effected anything. The Saxon minister, indeed, in a private interview with the regent even assured her that his master had most reluctantly taken this step.

The German ambassadors had not quitted Antwerp when intelligence from Holland completed the triumph of the regent. From fear of Count Megen Count Brederode had deserted his town of Viane, and with the aid of the Protestants inhabitants had succeeded in throwing himself into Amsterdam, where his arrival caused great alarm to the city magistrate, who had previously found difficulty in preventing a revolt, while it revived the courage of the Protestants. Here Brederode's adherents increased daily, and many noblemen flocked to him from Utrecht, Friesland, and Gröningen, whence the victorious arms of Megen and Aremberg had driven them. Under various disguises they found means to steal into the city, where they gathered round Brederode, and served him as a strong body-guard. The regent, apprehensive of a new outbreak, sent one of her private secretaries, Jacob de la Torre, to the council of Amsterdam, and ordered them to get rid of Count Brederode on any terms and at any risk. Neither the magistrate nor de la Torre himself, who visited Brederode in person to acquaint him with the will of the duchess, could prevail upon him to depart. The secretary was even surprised in his own chamber by a party of Brederode's followers, and deprived of all his papers, and would, perhaps, have lost his life also if he had not contrived to make his escape. Brederode remained in Amsterdam a full month after this occurrence, a powerless idol of the Protestants, and an oppressive burden to the Roman Catholics; while his fine army, which he had left in Viane, reinforced by many fugitives from the southern provinces, gave Count Megen enough to do without attempting to harass the Protestants in their flight. At last Brederode resolved to follow the example of Orange, and, yielding to necessity, abandon a desperate cause. He informed the town council that he was willing to leave Amsterdam if they would enable him to do so by furnishing him with the pecuniary means. Glad to get quit of him, they hastened to borrow the money on the security of the town council. Brederode quitted Amsterdam the same night, and was conveyed in a gunboat as far as Vlie, from whence he fortunately escaped to Embden. Fate treated him more mildly than the majority of those he had implicated in his foolhardy enterprise; he died the year after, 1568, at one of his castles in Germany, from the effects of drinking, by which he sought ultimately to drown his grief and disappointments. His widow, Countess of Moers in her own right, was remarried to the Prince Palatine, Frederick III. The Protestant cause lost but little by his demise; the work which he had commenced, as it had not been kept alive by him, so it did not die with him.

The little army, which in his disgraceful flight he had deserted, was bold and valiant, and had a few resolute leaders. It disbanded, indeed, as soon as he, to whom it looked for pay, had fled; but hunger and courage kept its parts together some time longer. One body, under command of Dietrich of Battenburgh, marched to Amsterdam in the hope of carrying that town; but Count Megen hastened with thirteen companies of excellent troops to its relief, and compelled the rebels to give up the attempt. Contenting themselves with plundering the neighboring cloisters, among which the abbey of Egmont in particular was hardly dealt with, they turned off towards Waaterland, where they hoped the numerous swamps would protect them from pursuit. But thither Count Megen followed them, and compelled them in all haste to seek safety in the Zuyderzee. The brothers Van Battenburg, and two Friesan nobles, Beima and Galama, with a hundred and twenty men and the booty they had taken from the monasteries, embarked near the town of Hoorne, intending to cross to Friesland, but through the treachery of the steersman, who ran the vessel on a sand-bank near Harlingen, they fell into the hands of one of Aremberg's captains, who took them all prisoners. The Count of Aremberg immediately pronounced sentence upon all the captives of plebeian rank, but sent his noble prisoners to the regent, who caused seven of them to be beheaded. Seven others of the most noble, including the brothers Van Battenburg and some Frieslanders, all in the bloom of youth, were reserved for the Duke of Alva, to enable him to signalize the commencement of his administration by a deed which was in every way worthy of him. The troops in four other vessels which set sail from Medenblick, and were pursued by Count Megen in small boats, were more successful. A contrary wind had forced them out of their course and driven them ashore on the coast of Gueldres, where they all got safe to land; crossing the Rhine, near Heusen, they fortunately escaped into Cleves, where they tore their flags in pieces and dispersed. In North Holland Count Megen overtook some squadrons who had lingered too long in plundering the cloisters, and completely overpowered them. He afterwards formed a junction with Noircarmes and garrisoned Amsterdam. The Duke Erich of Brunswick also surprised three companies, the last remains of the army of the Gueux, near Viane, where they were endeavoring to take a battery, routed them and captured their leader, Rennesse, who was shortly afterwards beheaded at the castle of Freudenburg, in Utrecht. Subsequently, when Duke Erich entered Viane, he found nothing but deserted streets, the inhabitants having left it with the garrison on the first alarm. He immediately razed the fortifications, and reduced this arsenal of the Gueux to an open town without defences. All the originators of the league were now dispersed; Brederode and Louis of Nassau had fled to Germany, and Counts Hogstraten, Bergen, and Kuilemberg had followed their example. Mansfeld had seceded, the brothers Van Battenburg awaited in prison an ignomonious fate, while Thoulouse alone had found an honorable death on the field of battle. Those of the confederates who had escaped the sword of the enemy and the axe of the executioner had saved nothing but their lives, and thus the title which they had assumed for show became at last a terrible reality.

Such was the inglorious end of the noble league, which in its beginning awakened such fair hopes and promised to become a powerful protection against oppression. Unanimity was its strength, distrust and internal dissension its ruin. It brought to light and developed many rare and beautiful virtues, but it wanted the most indispensable of all, prudence and moderation, without which any undertaking must miscarry, and all the fruits of the most laborious industry perish. If its objects had been as pure as it pretended, or even had they remained as pure as they really were at its first establishment, it might have defied the unfortunate combination of circumstances which prematurely overwhelmed it, and even if unsuccessful it would still have deserved an honorable mention in history. But it is too evident that the confederate nobles, whether directly or indirectly, took a greater share in the frantic excesses of the Iconoclasts than comported with the dignity and blamelessness of their confederation, and many among them openly exchanged their own good cause for the mad enterprise of these worthless vagabonds. The restriction of the Inquisition and a mitigation of the cruel inhumanity of the edicts must be laid to the credit of the league; but this transient relief was dearly purchased, at the cost of so many of the best and bravest citizens, who either lost their lives in the field, or in exile carried their wealth and industry to another quarter of the world; and of the presence of Alva and the Spanish arms. Many, too, of its peaceable citizens, who without its dangerous temptations would never have been seduced from the ranks of peace and order, were beguiled by the hope of success into the most culpable enterprises, and by their failure plunged into ruin and misery. But it cannot be denied that the league atoned in some measure for these wrongs by positive benefits. It brought together and emboldened many whom a selfish pusillanimity kept asunder and inactive; it diffused a salutary public spirit amongst the Belgian people, which the oppression of the government had almost 'entirely extinguished, and gave unanimity and a common voice to the scattered members of the nation, the absence of which alone makes despots bold. The attempt, indeed, failed, and the knots, too carelessly tied, were quickly unloosed; but it was through such failures that the nation was eventually to attain to a firm and lasting union, which should bid defiance to change.

The total destruction of the Geusen army quickly brought the Dutch towns also back to their obedience, and in the provinces there remained not a single place which had not submitted to the regent; but the increasing emigration, both of the natives and the foreign residents, threatened the country with depopulation. In Amsterdam the crowd of fugitives was so great that vessels were wanting to convey them across the North

Sea and the Zuyderzee, and that flourishing emporium beheld with dismay the approaching downfall of its prosperity. Alarmed at this general flight, the regent hastened to write letters to all the towns, to encourage the citizens to remain, and by fair promises to revive a hope of better and milder measures. In the king's name she promised to all who would freely swear to obey the state and the church complete indemnity, and by public proclamation invited the fugitives to trust to the royal clemency and return to their homes. She engaged also to relieve the nation from the dreaded presence of a Spanish army, even if it were already on the frontiers; nay, she went so far as to drop hints that, if necessary, means might be found to prevent it by force from entering the provinces, as she was fully determined not to relinquish to another the glory of a peace which it had cost her so much labor to effect. Few, however, returned in reliance upon her word, and these few had cause to repent it in the sequel; many thousands had already quitted the country, and several thousands more quickly followed them. Germany and England were filled with Flemish emigrants, who, wherever they settled, retained their usages and manners, and even their costume, unwilling to come to the painful conclusion that they should never again see their native land, and to give up all hopes of return. Few carried with them any remains of their former affluence; the greater portion had to beg their way, and bestowed on their adopted country nothing but industrious skill and honest citizens.

And now the regent hastened to report to the king tidings such as, during her whole administration, she had never before been able to gratify him with. She announced to him that she had succeeded in restoring quiet throughout the provinces, and that she thought herself strong enough to maintain it. The sects were extirpated, and the Roman Catholic worship re-established in all its former splendor; the rebels had either already met with, or were awaiting in prison, the punishment they deserved; the towns were secured by adequate garrisons. There was therefore no necessity for sending Spanish troops into the Netherlands, and nothing to justify their entrance. Their arrival would tend to destroy the existing repose, which it had cost so much to establish, would check the much-desired revival of commerce and trade, and, while it would involve the country in new expenses, would at the same time deprive them of the only means of supporting them. The mere rumor of the approach of a Spanish army had stripped the country of many thousands of its most valuable citizens; its actual appearance would reduce it to a desert. As there was no longer any enemy to subdue, or rebellion to suppress, the people would see no motive for the march of this army but punishment and revenge, and under this supposition its arrival would neither be welcomed nor honored. No longer excused by necessity, this violent expedient would assume the odious aspect of oppression, would exasperate the national mind afresh, drive the Protestants to desperation, and arm their brethren in other countries in their defence. The regent, she said, had in the king's name promised the nation it should be relieved from this foreign army, and to this stipulation she was principally indebted for the present peace; she could not therefore guarantee its long continuance if her pledge was not faithfully fulfilled. The Netherlands would receive him as their sovereign, the king, with every mark of attachment and veneration, but he must come as a father to bless, not as a despot to chastise them. Let him come to enjoy the peace which she had bestowed on the country, but not to destroy it afresh.

ALVA'S ARMAMENT AND EXPEDITION TO THE NETHERLANDS.

But it was otherwise determined in the council at Madrid. The minister, Granvella, who, even while absent himself, ruled the Spanish cabinet by his adherents; the Cardinal Grand Inquisitor, Spinosa, and the Duke of Alva, swayed respectively by hatred, a spirit of persecution, or private interest, had outvoted the milder councils of the Prince Ruy Gomes of Eboli, the Count of Feria, and the king's confessor, Fresneda. The insurrection, it was urged by the former, was indeed quelled for the present, but only because the rebels were awed by the rumor of the king's armed approach; it was to fear of punishment alone, and not to sorrow for their crime, that the present calm was to be ascribed, and it would soon again be broken if that feeling were allowed to subside. In fact, the offences of the people fairly afforded the king the opportunity he had so long desired of carrying out his despotic views with an appearance of justice. The peaceable settlement for which the regent took credit to herself was very far from according with his wishes, which sought rather for a legitimate pretext to deprive the provinces of their privileges, which were so obnoxious to his despotic temper.

With an impenetrable dissimulation Philip had hitherto fostered the general delusion that he was about to visit the provinces in person, while all along nothing could have been more remote from his real intentions. Travelling at any time ill suited the methodical regularity of his life, which moved with the precision of clockwork; and his narrow and sluggish intellect was oppressed by the variety and multitude of objects with which new scenes crowded it. The difficulties and dangers which would attend a journey to the Netherlands must, therefore, have been peculiarly alarming to his natural timidity and love of ease. Why should he, who, in all that he did, was accustomed to consider himself alone, and to make men accommodate themselves to his principles, not his principles to men, undertake so perilous an expedition, when he could see neither the advantage nor necessity of it. Moreover, as it had ever been to him an utter impossibility to separate, even for a moment, his person from his royal dignity, which no prince ever guarded so tenaciously and pedantically as himself, so the magnificence and ceremony which in his mind were inseparably connected with such a journey, and the expenses which, on this account, it would necessarily occasion, were of themselves sufficient motives to account for his indisposition to it, without its being at all requisite to call in the aid of the influence of his favorite, Ruy Gomes, who is said to have desired to separate his rival, the Duke of Alva, from the king. Little, however, as he seriously intended this journey, he still deemed it advisable to keep up the expectation of it, as well with a view of sustaining the courage of the loyal as of preventing a dangerous combination of the disaffected, and stopping the further progress of the rebels.

In order to carry on the deception as long as possible, Philip made extensive preparations for his departure, and neglected nothing which could be required for such an event. He ordered ships to be fitted out, appointed the officers and others to attend him. To allay the suspicion such warlike preparations might excite in all foreign courts, they were informed through his ambassadors of his real design. He applied to the King of France for a passage for himself and attendants through that kingdom, and consulted the Duke of Savoy as to the preferable route. He caused a list to be drawn up of all the towns and fortified places that lay in his march, and directed all the intermediate distances to be accurately laid down. Orders were issued for taking a map and survey of the whole extent of country between Savoy and Burgundy, the duke being requested to furnish the requisite surveyors and scientific officers. To such lengths was the deception carried that the regent was commanded to hold eight vessels at least in readiness off Zealand, and to despatch them to meet the king the instant she heard of his having sailed from Spain; and these ships she actually got ready, and caused prayers to be offered up in all the churches for the king's safety during the voyage, though in secret many persons did not scruple to remark that in his chamber at Madrid his majesty would not have much cause to dread the storms at sea. Philip played his part with such masterly skill that the Belgian ambassadors at Madrid, Lords Bergen and Montigny, who at first had disbelieved in the sincerity of his pretended journey, began at last to be alarmed, and infected their friends in Brussels with similar apprehensions. An attack of tertian ague, which about this time the king suffered, or perhaps feigned, in Segovia, afforded a plausible pretence for postponing his journey, while meantime the preparations for it were carried on with the utmost activity. At last, when the urgent and repeated solicitations of his sister compelled him to make a definite explanation of his plans, he gave orders that the Duke of Alva should set out forthwith with an army, both to clear the way before him of rebels, and to enhance the splendor of his own royal arrival. He did not yet venture to throw off the mask and announce the duke as his substitute. He had but too much reason to fear that the submission which his Flemish nobles would cheerfully yield to their sovereign would be refused to one of his servants, whose cruel character was well known, and who, moreover, was detested as a foreigner and the enemy of their constitution. And, in fact, the universal belief that the king was soon to follow, which long survived Alva's entrance into the country, restrained the outbreak of disturbances which otherwise would assuredly have been caused by the cruelties which marked the very opening of the duke's government.

The clergy of Spain, and especially the Inquisition, contributed richly towards the expenses of this expedition as to a holy war. Throughout Spain the enlisting was carried on with the utmost zeal. The viceroys and governors of Sardinia, Sicily, Naples, and Milan received orders to select the best of their Italian and Spanish troops in the garrisons and despatch them to the general rendezvous in the Genoese territory, where the Duke of Alva would exchange them for the Spanish recruits which he should bring with him. At the same time the regent was commanded to hold in readiness a few more regiments of German infantry in Luxembourg, under the command of the Counts Eberstein, Schaumburg, and Lodrona, and also some squadrons of light cavalry in the Duchy of Burgundy to reinforce the Spanish general immediately on his entrance into the provinces. The Count of Barlaimont was commissioned to furnish the necessary provision for the armament, and a sum of two hundred thousand gold florins was remitted to the regent to enable her to meet these expenses and to maintain her own troops.

The French court, however, under pretence of the danger to be apprehended from the Huguenots, had refused to allow the Spanish army to pass through France. Philip applied to the Dukes of Savoy and Lorraine, who were too dependent upon him to refuse his request. The former merely stipulated that he should be allowed to maintain two thousand infantry and a squadron of horse at the king's expense in order to protect his country from the injuries to which it might otherwise be exposed from the passage of the Spanish army. At the same time he undertook to provide the necessary supplies for its maintenance during the transit.

The rumor of this arrangement roused the Huguenots, the Genevese, the Swiss, and the Grisons. The Prince of Condé and the Admiral Coligny entreated Charles IX. not to neglect so favorable a moment of inflicting a deadly blow on the hereditary foe of France. With the aid of the Swiss, the Genevese, and his own Protestant subjects, it would, they alleged, be an easy matter to destroy the flower of the Spanish troops in the narrow passes of the Alpine mountains; and they promised to support him in this undertaking with an army of fifty thousand Huguenots. This advice, however, whose dangerous object was not easily to be mistaken, was plausibly declined by Charles IX., who assured them that he was both able and anxious to provide for the security of his kingdom. He hastily despatched troops to cover the French frontiers; and the republics of Geneva, Bern, Zurich, and the Grisons followed his example, all ready to offer a determined opposition to the dreaded enemy of their religion and their liberty.

On the 5th of May, 1567, the Duke of Alva set sail from Carthagena with thirty galleys, which had been furnished by Andrew Doria and the Duke Cosmo of Florence, and within eight days landed at Genoa, where the four regiments were waiting to join him. But a tertian ague, with which he was seized shortly after his arrival, compelled him to remain for some days inactive in Lombardy — a delay of which the neighboring powers availed themselves to prepare for defence. As soon as the duke recovered he held at Asti, in Montferrat, a review of all his troops, who were more formidable by their valor than by their numbers, since cavalry and infantry together did not amount to much above ten thousand men. In his long and perilous march he did not wish to encumber himself with useless supernumeraries, which would only impede his progress and increase the difficulty of supporting his army. These ten thousand veterans were to form the nucleus of a greater army, which, according as circumstances and occasion might require, he could easily assemble in the Netherlands themselves.

This army, however, was as select as it was small. It consisted of the remains of those victorious legions at whose head Charles V. had made Europe tremble; sanguinary, indomitable bands, in whose battalions the firmness of the old Macedonian phalanx lived again; rapid in their evolutions from long practice, hardy and enduring, proud of their leader's success, and confident from past victories, formidable by their licentiousness, but still more so by their discipline; let loose with all the passions of a warmer climate upon a rich and peaceful country, and inexorable towards an enemy whom the church had cursed. Their fanatical and sanguinary spirit, their thirst for glory and innate courage was aided by a rude sensuality, the instrument by which the Spanish general firmly and surely ruled his otherwise intractable troops. With a prudent indulgence he allowed riot and voluptuousness to reign throughout the camp. Under his tacit connivance Italian courtezans followed the standards; even in the march across the Apennines, where the high price of the necessaries of life compelled him to reduce his force to the smallest possible number, he preferred to have a few regiments less rather than to leave behind these instruments of voluptuousness.*

But industriously as Alva strove to relax the morals of his soldiers, he enforced the more rigidly a strict military discipline, which was interrupted only by a victory or rendered less severe by a battle. For all this he had, he said, the authority of the Athenian General Iphicrates, who awarded the prize of valor to the pleasure-loving and rapacious soldier. The more irksome the restraint

* The bacchanalian procession of this army contrasted strangely enough with the gloomy seriousness and pretended sanctity of his aim. The number of these women was so great that to restrain the disorders and quarrelling among themselves they hit upon the expedient of establishing a discipline of their own. They ranged themselves under particular flags, marched in ranks and sections, and in admirable military order, after each battalion, and classed themselves with strict etiquette according to their rank and pay.

by which the passions of the soldiers were kept in check, the greater must have been the vehemence with which they broke forth at the sole outlet which was left open to them.

The duke divided his infantry, which was about nine thousand strong, and chiefly Spaniards, into four brigades, and gave the command of them to four Spanish officers. Alphonso of Ulloa led the Neapolitan brigade of nine companies, amounting to three thousand two hundred and thirty men; Sancho of Lodogno commanded the Milan brigade, three thousand two hundred men in ten companies; the Sicilian brigade, with the same number of companies, and consisting of sixteen hundred men, was under Julian Romero, an experienced warrior, who had already fought on Belgian ground;* while Gonsalo of Braccamonte headed that of Sardinia, which was raised by three companies of recruits to the full complement of the former. To every company, moreover, were added fifteen Spanish musqueteers. The horse, in all twelve hundred strong, consisted of three Italian, two Albanian, and seven Spanish squadrons, light and heavy cavalry, and the chief command was held by Ferdinand and Frederick of Toledo, the two sons of Alva. Chiappin Vitelli, Marquis of Cetona, was field-marshal; a celebrated general whose services had been made over to the King of Spain by Cosmo of Florence; and Gabriel Serbellon was general of artillery. The Duke of Savoy lent Alva an experienced engineer, Francis Pacotto, of Urbino, who was to be employed in the erection of new fortifications. His standard was likewise followed by a number of volunteers, and the flower of the Spanish nobility, of whom the greater part had fought under Charles V. in Germany, Italy, and before Tunis. Among these were Christopher Mondragone, one of the ten Spanish heroes who, near Mühlberg, swam across the Elbe with their swords between their teeth, and, under a shower of bullets from the enemy, brought over from the opposite shore the boats which the emperor required for the construction of a bridge. Sancho of Avila, who

* The same officer who commanded one of the Spanish regiments about which so much complaint had formerly been made in the States-General.

had been trained to war under Alva himself, Camillo of Monte, Francis Ferdugo, Karl Davila, Nicolaus Basta, and Count Martinego, all fired with a noble ardor, either to commence their military career under so eminent a leader, or by another glorious campaign under his command to crown the fame they had already won. After the review the army marched in three divisions across Mount Cenis, by the very route which sixteen centuries before Hannibal is said to have taken. The duke himself led the van; Ferdinand of Toledo, with whom was associated Lodogno as colonel, the centre; and the Marquis of Cetona the rear. The Commissary General, Francis of Ibarra, was sent before with General Serbellon to open the road for the main body, and get ready the supplies at the several quarters for the night. The places which the van left in the morning were entered in the evening by the centre, which in its turn made room on the following day for the rear. Thus the army crossed the Alps of Savoy by regular stages, and with the fourteenth day completed that dangerous passage. A French army of observation accompanied it side by side along the frontiers of Dauphiné, and the course of the Rhone, and the allied army of the Genevese followed it on the right, and was passed by it at a distance of seven miles. Both these armies of observation carefully abstained from any act of hostility, and were merely intended to cover their own frontiers. As the Spanish legions ascended and descended the steep mountain crags, or while they crossed the rapid Iser, or file by file wound through the narrow passes of the rocks, a handful of men would have been sufficient to put an entire stop to their march, and to drive them back into the mountains, where they would have been irretrievably lost, since at each place of encampment supplies were provided for no more than a single day, and for a third part only of the whole force. But a supernatural awe and dread of the Spanish name appeared to have blinded the eyes of the enemy so that they did not perceive their advantage, or at least did not venture to profit by it. In order to give them as little opportunity as possible of remembering it, the Spanish general hastened through this dangerous pass.

Convinced, too, that if his troops gave the slightest umbrage he was lost, the strictest discipline was maintained during the march; not a single peasant's hut, not a single field was injured;* and never, perhaps, in the memory of man was so numerous an army led so far in such excellent order. Destined as this army was for vengeance and murder, a malignant and baleful star seemed to conduct it safe through all dangers; and it would be difficult to decide whether the prudence of its general or the blindness of its enemies is most to be wondered at.

In Franche Comté, four squadrons of Burgundian cavalry, newly-raised, joined the main army, which, at Luxembourg, was also reinforced by three regiments of German infantry under the command of Counts Eberstein, Schaumburg, and Lodrona. From Thionville, where he halted a few days, Alva sent his salutations to the regent by Francis of Ibarra, who was, at the same time, directed to consult her on the quartering of the troops. On her part, Noircarmes and Barlaimont were despatched to the Spanish camp to congratulate the duke on his arrival, and to show him the customary marks of honor. At the same time they were directed to ask him to produce the powers entrusted to him by the king, of which, however, he only showed a part. The envoys of the regent were followed by swarms of the Flemish nobility, who thought they could not hasten soon enough to conciliate the favor of the new viceroy, or by a timely submission avert the vengeance which was preparing. Among them was Count Egmont. As he came forward the duke pointed him out to the bystanders. "Here comes an arch-heretic," he exclaimed, loud enough to be heard by Egmont himself, who, surprised at these words, stopped and changed color. But when the duke, in order to repair his imprudence, went up to him with a serene countenance, and greeted him

---

* Once only on entering Lorraine three horsemen ventured to drive away a few sheep from a flock, of which circumstance the duke was no sooner informed than he sent back to the owner what had been taken from him and sentenced the offenders to be hung. This sentence was, at the intercession of the Lorraine general, who had come to the frontiers to pay his respects to the duke, executed on only one of the three, upon whom the lot fell at the drum-head.

with a friendly embrace, the Fleming was ashamed of his fears, and made light of this warning, by putting some frivolous interpretation upon it. Egmont sealed this new friendship with a present of two valuable chargers, which Alva accepted with a grave condescension.

Upon the assurance of the regent that the provinces were in the enjoyment of perfect peace, and that no opposition was to be apprehended from any quarter, the duke discharged some German regiments, which had hitherto drawn their pay from the Netherlands. Three thousand six hundred men, under the command of Lodrona, were quartered in Antwerp, from which town the Walloon garrison, in which full reliance could not be placed, was withdrawn; garrisons proportionably stronger were thrown into Ghent and other important places; Alva himself marched with the Milan brigade towards Brussels, whither he was accompanied by a splendid cortège of the noblest in the land.

Here, as in all the other towns of the Netherlands, fear and terror had preceded him, and all who were conscious of any offences, and even those who were sensible of none, alike awaited his approach with a dread similar to that with which criminals see the coming of their day of trial. All who could tear themselves from the ties of family, property, and country had already fled, or now at last took to flight. The advance of the Spanish army had already, according to the report of the regent, diminished the population of the provinces by the loss of one hundred thousand citizens, and this general flight still continued. But the arrival of the Spanish general could not be more hateful to the people of the Netherlands than it was distressing and dispiriting to the regent. At last, after so many years of anxiety, she had begun to taste the sweets of repose, and that absolute authority, which had been the long-cherished object of eight years of a troubled and difficult administration. This late fruit of so much anxious industry, of so many cares and nightly vigils, was now to be wrested from her by a stranger, who was to be placed at once in possession of all the advantages which she had been forced to extract from adverse circumstances, by a long and tedious course of intrigue and patient endurance. Another was lightly to bear away the prize of promptitude, and to triumph by more rapid success over her superior but less glittering merits. Since the departure of the minister, Granvella, she had tasted to the full the pleasures of independence. The flattering homage of the nobility, which allowed her more fully to enjoy the shadow of power, the more they deprived her of its substance, had, by degrees, fostered her vanity to such an extent, that she at last estranged by her coldness even the most upright of all her servants, the state counsellor Viglius, who always addressed her in the language of truth. All at once a censor of her actions was placed at her side, a partner of her power was associated with her, if indeed it was not rather a master who was forced upon her, whose proud, stubborn, and imperious spirit, which no courtesy could soften, threatened the deadliest wounds to her self-love and vanity. To prevent his arrival she had, in her representations to the king, vainly exhausted every political argument. To no purpose had she urged that the utter ruin of the commerce of the Netherlands would be the inevitable consequence of this introduction of the Spanish troops; in vain had she assured the king that peace was universally restored, and reminded him of her own services in procuring it, which deserved, she thought, a better guerdon than to see all the fruits of her labors snatched from her and given to a foreigner, and more than all, to behold all the good which she had effected destroyed by a new and different line of conduct. Even when the duke had already crossed Mount Cenis she made one more attempt, entreating him at least to diminish his army; but that also failed, for the duke insisted upon acting up to the powers entrusted to him. In poignant grief she now awaited his approach, and with the tears she shed for her country were mingled those of offended self-love.

On the 22d of August, 1567, the Duke of Alva appeared before the gates of Brussels. His army immediately took up their quarters in the suburbs, and he himself made it his first duty to pay his respects to the sister of his king. She gave him a private audience on

the plea of suffering from sickness. Either the mortification she had undergone had in reality a serious effect upon her health, or, what is not improbable, she had recourse to this expedient to pain his haughty spirit, and in some degree to lessen his triumph. He delivered to her letters from the king, and laid before her a copy of his own appointment, by which the supreme command of the whole military force of the Netherlands was committed to him, and from which, therefore, it would appear, that the administration of civil affairs remained, as heretofore, in the hands of the regent. But as soon as he was alone with her he produced a new commission, which was totally different from the former. According to this, the power was delegated to him of making war at his discretion, of erecting fortifications, of appointing and dismissing at pleasure the governors of provinces, the commandants of towns, and other officers of the king; of instituting inquiries into the past troubles, of punishing those who originated them, and of rewarding the loyal. Powers of this extent, which placed him almost on a level with a sovereign prince, and far surpassed those of the regent herself, caused her the greatest consternation, and it was with difficulty that she could conceal her emotion. She asked the duke whether he had not even a third commission, or some special orders in reserve which went still further, and were drawn up still more precisely, to which he replied distinctly enough in the affirmative, but at the same time gave her to understand that this commission might be too full to suit the present occasion, and would be better brought into play hereafter with due regard to time and circumstances. A few days after his arrival he caused a copy of the first instructions to be laid before the several councils and the states, and had them printed to insure their rapid circulation. As the regent resided in the palace, he took up his quarters temporarily in Kuilemberg house, the same in which the association of the Gueux had received its name, and before which, through a wonderful vicissitude, Spanish tyranny now planted its flag.

A dead silence reigned in Brussels, broken only at times by the unwonted clang of arms. The duke had entered the town but a few hours when his attendants, like bloodhounds that have been slipped, dispersed themselves in all directions. Everywhere foreign faces were to be seen; the streets were empty, all the houses carefully closed, all amusements suspended, all public places deserted. The whole metropolis resembled a place visited by the plague. Acquaintances hurried on without stopping for their usual greeting; all hastened on the moment a Spaniard showed himself in the streets. Every sound startled them, as if it were the knock of the officials of justice at their doors; the nobility, in trembling anxiety, kept to their houses; they shunned appearing in public lest their presence should remind the new viceroy of some past offence. The two nations now seemed to have exchanged characters. The Spaniard had become the talkative man and the Brabanter taciturn; distrust and fear had scared away the spirit of cheerfulness and mirth; a constrained gravity fettered even the play of the features. Every moment the impending blow was looked for with dread.

This general straining of expectation warned the duke to hasten the accomplishment of his plans before they should be anticipated by the timely flight of his victims. His first object was to secure the suspected nobles, in order, at once and forever, to deprive the faction of its leaders, and the nation, whose freedom was to be crushed, of all its supporters. By a pretended affability he had succeeded in lulling their first alarm, and in restoring Count Egmont in particular to his former perfect confidence, for which purpose he artfully employed his sons, Ferdinand and Frederick of Toledo, whose companionableness and youth assimilated more easily with the Flemish character. By this skilful advice he succeeded also in enticing Count Horn to Brussels, who had hitherto thought it advisable to watch the first measures of the duke from a distance, but now suffered himself to be seduced by the good fortune of his friend. Some of the nobility, and Count Egmont at the head of them, even resumed their former gay style of living. But they themselves did not do so with their whole hearts, and they had not many imitators. Kuilemberg house was incessantly besieged by a numerous crowd, who thronged around the person of the new viceroy, and exhibited an affected gayety on their countenances, while their hearts were wrung with distress and fear. Egmont in particular assumed the appearance of a light heart, entertaining the duke's sons, and being fêted by them in return. Meanwhile, the duke was fearful lest so fair an opportunity for the accomplishment of his plans might not last long, and lest some act of imprudence might destroy the feeling of security which had tempted both his victims voluntarily to put themselves into his power; he only waited for a third; Hogstraten also was to be taken in the same net. Under a plausible pretext of business he therefore summoned him to the metropolis. At the same time that he purposed to secure the three counts in Brussels, Colonel Lodrona was to arrest the burgomaster, Strahlen, in Antwerp, an intimate friend of the Prince of Orange, and suspected of having favored the Calvinists; another officer was to seize the private secretary of Count Egmont, whose name was John Cassembrot von Beckerzeel, as also some secretaries of Count Horn, and was to possess themselves of their papers.

When the day arrived which had been fixed upon for the execution of this plan, the duke summoned all the counsellors and knights before him to confer with them upon matters of state. On this occasion the Duke of Arschot, the Counts Mansfeld, Barlaimont, and Aremberg attended on the part of the Netherlands, and on the part of the Spaniards besides the duke's sons, Vitelli, Serbellon, and Ibarra. The young Count Mansfeld, who likewise appeared at the meeting, received a sign from his father to withdraw with all speed, and by a hasty flight avoid the fate which was impending over him as a former member of the Geusen league. The duke purposely prolonged the consultation to give time before he acted for the arrival of the couriers from Antwerp, who were to bring him the tidings of the arrest of the other parties. To avoid exciting any suspicion, the engineer, Pacotto, was required to attend the meeting to lay before it the plans for some fortifications. At last intelligence was brought him that Lodrona had successfully executed his commission. Upon this the duke dexterously broke off the debate and dismissed the council. And now, as Count Egmont was about to repair to the apartment of Don Ferdinand, to finish a game that he had commenced with him, the captain of the duke's body guard, Sancho D'Avila, stopped him, and demanded his sword in the king's name. At the same time he was surrounded by a number of Spanish soldiers, who, as had been preconcerted, suddenly advanced from their concealment. So unexpected a blow deprived Egmont for some moments of all powers of utterance and recollection; after a while, however, he collected himself, and taking his sword from his side with dignified composure, said, as he delivered it into the hands of the Spaniard, "This sword has before this on more than one occasion successfully defended the king's cause." Another Spanish officer arrested Count Horn as he was returning to his house without the least suspicion of danger. Horn's first inquiry was after Egmont. On being told that the same fate had just happened to his friend he surrendered himself without resistance. "I have suffered myself to be guided by him," he exclaimed, "it is fair that I should share his destiny." The two counts were placed in confinement in separate apartments. While this was going on in the interior of Kuilemberg house the whole garrison were drawn out under arms in front of it. No one knew what had taken place inside, a mysterious terror diffused itself throughout Brussels until rumor spread the news of this fatal event. Each felt as if he himself were the sufferer; with many indignation at Egmont's blind infatuation preponderated over sympathy for his fate; all rejoiced that Orange had escaped. The first question of the Cardinal Granvella, too, when these tidings reached him in Rome, is said to have been, whether they had taken the Silent One also. On being answered in the negative he shook his head: "then as they have let him escape they have got nothing." Fate ordained better for the Count of Hogstraten. Compelled by ill-health to travel slowly, he was met by the report of this event while he was yet on his way. He hastily turned back, and fortunately escaped destruction. Immediately after Egmont's seizure a writing was

extorted from him, addressed to the commandant of
the citadel of Ghent, ordering that officer to deliver the
fortress to the Spanish Colonel Alphonso d'Ulloa. Upon
this the two counts were then (after they had been for
some weeks confined in Brussels) conveyed under a guard
of three thousand Spaniards to Ghent, where they remained imprisoned till late in the following year. In the
meantime all their papers had been seized. Many of the
first nobility who, by the pretended kindness of the Duke
of Alva, had allowed themselves to be cajoled into
remaining experienced the same fate. Capital punishment was also, without further delay, inflicted on all who
before the duke's arrival had been taken with arms in
their hands. Upon the news of Egmont's arrest a second
body of about twenty thousand inhabitants took up the
wanderer's staff, besides the one hundred thousand who,
prudently declining to await the arrival of the Spanish
general, had already placed themselves in safety.* After
so noble a life had been assailed no one counted himself
safe any longer; but many found cause to repent that
they had so long deferred this salutary step; for every
day flight was rendered more difficult, for the duke
ordered all the ports to be closed, and punished the
attempt at emigration with death. The beggars were
now esteemed fortunate, who had abandoned country
and property in order to preserve at least their liberty
and their lives.

ALVA'S FIRST MEASURES, AND DEPARTURE OF THE DUCHESS OF PARMA.

Alva's first step, after securing the most suspected of
the nobles, was to restore the Inquisition to its former
authority, to put the decrees of Trent again in force,
abolish the "*moderation,*" and promulgate anew the
edicts against heretics in all their original severity. The

---

* A great part of these fugitives helped to strengthen the army of the
Huguenots, who had taken occasion, from the passage of the Spanish army
through Lorraine, to assemble their forces, and now pressed Charles IX.
hard. On these grounds the French court thought it had a right to demand
aid from the regent of the Netherlands. It asserted that the Huguenots had
looked upon the march of the Spanish army as the result of a preconcerted
plan which had been formed against them by the two courts at Bayonne, and

court of Inquisition in Spain had pronounced the whole nation of the Netherlands guilty of treason in the highest degree, Catholics and heterodox, loyalists and rebels, without distinction; the latter as having offended by overt acts, the former as having incurred equal guilt by their supineness. From this sweeping condemnation a very few were excepted, whose names, however, were purposely reserved, while the general sentence was publicly confirmed by the king. Philip declared himself absolved from all his promises, and released from all engagements which the regent in his name had entered into with the people of the Netherlands, and all the justice which they had in future to expect from him must depend on his own good-will and pleasure. All who had aided in the expulsion of the minister, Granvella, who had taken part in the petition of the confederate nobles, or had but even spoken in favor of it; all who had presented a petition against the decrees of Trent, against the edicts relating to religion, or against the installation of the bishops; all who had permitted the public preachings, or had only feebly resisted them; all who had worn the insignia of the Gueux, had sung Geusen songs, or who in any way whatsoever had manifested their joy at the establishment of the league; all who had sheltered or concealed the reforming preachers, attended Calvinistic funerals, or had even merely known of their secret meetings, and not given information of them; all who had appealed to the national privileges; all, in fine, who had expressed an opinion that they ought to obey God rather than man; all these indiscriminately were declared liable to the penalties which the law imposed upon any violation of the royal prerogative, and upon high treason; and these penalties were, according to the instruction which Alva had received, to be executed on the guilty persons without forbearance or favor; without regard to rank, sex, or age, as an example to posterity, and for a

that this had roused them from their slumber. That consequently it behooved the Spanish court to assist in extricating the French king from difficulties into which the latter had been brought simply by the march of the Spanish troops. Alva actually sent the Count of Aremberg with a considerable force to join the army of the Queen Mother in France, and even offered to command these subsidiaries in person, which, however, was declined. Strada, 206. Thuan, 541.

terror to all future times. According to this declaration there was no longer an innocent person to be found in the whole Netherlands, and the new viceroy had it in his power to make a fearful choice of victims. Property and life were alike at his command, and whoever should have the good fortune to preserve one or both must receive them as the gift of his generosity and humanity. By this stroke of policy, as refined as it was detestable, the nation was disarmed, and unanimity rendered impossible. As it absolutely depended on the duke's arbitrary will upon whom the sentence should be carried in force which had been passed without exception upon all, each individual kept himself quiet, in order to escape, if possible, the notice of the viceroy, and to avoid drawing the fatal choice upon himself. Every one, on the other hand, in whose favor he was pleased to make an exception stood in a degree indebted to him, and was personally under an obligation which must be measured by the value he set upon his life and property. As, however, this penalty could only be executed on the smaller portion of the nation, the duke naturally secured the greater by the strongest ties of fear and gratitude, and for one whom he sought out as a victim he gained ten others whom he passed over. As long as he continued true to this policy he remained in quiet possession of his rule, even amid the streams of blood which he caused to flow, and did not forfeit this advantage till the want of money compelled him to impose a burden upon the nation which oppressed all indiscriminately.

In order to be equal to this bloody occupation, the details of which were fast accumulating, and to be certain of not losing a single victim through the want of instruments; and, on the other hand, to render his proceedings independent of the states, with whose privileges they were so much at variance, and who, indeed, were far too humane for him, he instituted an extraordinary court of justice. This court consisted of twelve criminal judges, who, according to their instructions, to the very letter of which they must adhere, were to try and pronounce sentence upon those implicated in the past disturbances. The mere institution of such a board was a violation of the liberties of the country, which expressly stipulated that no citizen should be tried out of his own province; but the duke filled up the measure of his injustice when, contrary to the most sacred privileges of the nation, he proceeded to give seats and votes in that court to Spaniards, the open and avowed enemies of Belgian liberty. He himself was the president of this court, and after him a certain licentiate, Vargas, a Spaniard by birth, of whose iniquitous character the historians of both parties are unanimous; cast out like a plague-spot from his own country, where he had violated one of his wards, he was a shameless, hardened villain, in whose mind avarice, lust, and the thirst for blood struggled for ascendancy. The principal members were Count Aremberg, Philip of Noircarmes, and Charles of Barlaimont, who, however, never sat in it; Hadrian Nicolai, chancellor of Gueldres; Jacob Mertens and Peter Asset, presidents of Artois and Flanders; Jacob Hesselts and John de la Porte, counsellors of Ghent; Louis del Roi, doctor of theology, and by birth a Spaniard; John du Bois, king's advocate; and De la Torre, secretary of the court. In compliance with the representations of Viglius the privy council was spared any part in this tribunal; nor was any one introduced into it from the great council at Malines. The votes of the members were only recommendatory, not conclusive, the final sentence being reserved by the duke to himself. No particular time was fixed for the sitting of the court; the members, however, assembled at noon, as often as the duke thought good. But after the expiration of the third month Alva began to be less frequent in his attendance, and at last resigned his place entirely to his favorite, Vargas, who filled it with such odious fitness that in a short time all the members, with the exception merely of the Spanish doctor, Del Rio, and the secretary, De la Torre,* weary of the atrocities of which they were compelled to be both eye-witnesses and accomplices, remained away from the assembly. It is revolting to the feelings to think how the

---

* The sentences passed upon the most eminent persons (for example, the sentence of death passed upon Strahlen, the burgomaster of Antwerp), were signed only by Vargas, Del Rio, and De la Torre.

lives of the noblest and best were thus placed at the mercy of Spanish vagabonds, and how even the sanctuaries of the nation, its deeds and charters, were unscrupulously ransacked, the seals broken, and the most secret contracts between the sovereign and the state profaned and exposed.*

From the council of twelve (which, from the object of its institution, was called the council for disturbances, but on account of its proceedings is more generally known under the appellation of the council of blood, a name which the nation in their exasperation bestowed upon it), no appeal was allowed. Its proceedings could not be revised. Its verdicts were irrevocable and independent of all other authority. No other tribunal in the country could take cognizance of cases which related to the late insurrection, so that in all the other courts justice was nearly at a standstill. The great council at Malines was as good as abolished; the authority of the council of state entirely ceased, insomuch that its sittings were discontinued. On some rare occasions the duke conferred with a few members of the late assembly, but even when this did occur the conference was held in his cabinet, and was no more than a private consultation, without any of the proper forms being observed. No privilege, no charter of immunity, however carefully protected, had any weight with the council for disturbances.† It compelled all deeds and contracts to be laid before it, and often forced upon them the most strained interpetations and alterations. If the duke caused a sentence to be drawn out which there was reason to fear might be opposed by the states of Brabant, it was legalized with-

---

* For an example of the unfeeling levity with which the most important matters, even decisions in cases of life and death, were treated in this sanguinary council, it may serve to relate what is told of the Counsellor Hesselts. He was generally asleep during the meeting, and when his turn came to vote on a sentence of death he used to cry out, still half asleep: "Ad patibulum! Ad patibulum!" so glibly did his tongue utter this word. It is further to be remarked of this Hesselts, that his wife, a daughter of the President Viglius, had expressly stipulated in the marriage-contract that he should resign the dismal office of attorney for the king, which made him detested by the whole nation. Vigl. ad Hopp. lxvii., L.

† Vargas, in a few words of barbarous Latin, demolished at once the boasted liberties of the Netherlands. "Non curamus vestros privilegios," he replied to one who wished to plead the immunities of the University of Louvain.

out the Brabant seal. The most sacred rights of individuals were assailed, and a tyranny without example forced its arbitrary will even into the circle of domestic life. As the Protestants and rebels had hitherto contrived to strengthen their party so much by marriages with the first families in the country, the duke issued an edict forbidding all Netherlanders, whatever might be their rank or office, under pain of death and confiscation of property, to conclude a marriage without previously obtaining his permission.

All whom the council for disturbances thought proper to summon before it were compelled to appear, clergy as well as laity; the most venerable heads of the senate, as well as the reprobate rabble of the Iconoclasts. Whoever did not present himself, as indeed scarcely anybody did, was declared an outlaw, and his property was confiscated; but those who were rash or foolish enough to appear, or who were so unfortunate as to be seized, were lost without redemption. Twenty, forty, often fifty were summoned at the same time and from the same town, and the richest were always the first on whom the thunderbolt descended. The meaner citizens, who possessed nothing that could render their country and their homes dear to them, were taken unawares and arrested without any previous citation. Many eminent merchants, who had at their disposal fortunes of from sixty thousand to one hundred thousand florins, were seen with their hands tied behind their backs, dragged like common vagabonds at the horse's tail to execution, and in Valenciennes fifty-five persons were decapitated at one time. All the prisons — and the duke immediately on commencing his administration had built a great number of them — were crammed full with the accused; hanging, beheading, quartering, burning were the prevailing and ordinary occupations of the day; the punishment of the galleys and banishment were more rarely heard of, for there was scarcely any offence which was reckoned too trival to be punished with death. Immense sums were thus brought into the treasury, which, however, served rather to stimulate the new viceroy's and his colleagues' thirst for gold than to quench it. It seemed to be his insane purpose to make beggars of the whole people, and to throw all their riches into the hands of the king and his servants. The yearly income derived from these confiscations was computed to equal the revenues of the first kingdoms of Europe; it is said to have been estimated, in a report furnished to the king, at the incredible amount of twenty million of dollars. But these proceedings were the more inhuman, as they often bore hardest precisely upon the very persons who were the most peaceful subjects, and most orthodox Roman Catholics, whom they could not want to injure. Whenever an estate was confiscated all the creditors who had claims upon it were defrauded. The hospitals, too, and public institutions, which such properties had contributed to support, were now ruined, and the poor, who had formerly drawn a pittance from this source, were compelled to see their only spring of comfort dried up. Whoever ventured to urge their well-grounded claims on the forfeited property before the council of twelve (for no other tribunal dared to interfere with these inquiries), consumed their substance in tedious and expensive proceedings, and were reduced to beggary before they saw the end of them. The histories of civilized states furnish but one instance of a similar perversion of justice, of such violation of the rights of property, and of such waste of human life; but Cinna, Sylla, and Marius entered vanquished Rome as incensed victors, and practised without disguise what the viceroy of the Netherlands performed under the venerable veil of the laws.

Up to the end of the year 1567 the king's arrival had been confidently expected, and the well-disposed of the people had placed all their last hopes on this event. The vessels, which Philip had caused to be equipped expressly for the purpose of meeting him, still lay in the harbor of Flushing, ready to sail at the first signal; and the town of Brussels had consented to receive a Spanish garrison, simply because the king, it was pretended, was to reside within its walls. But this hope gradually vanished, as he put off the journey from one season to the next, and the new viceroy very soon began to exhibit powers which announced him less as a precursor of royalty than as an absolute minister, whose presence made that of the

monarch entirely superfluous. To complete the distress
of the provinces their last good angel was now to leave
them in the person of the regent.

From the moment when the production of the duke's
extensive powers left no doubt remaining as to the practical termination of her own rule, Margaret had formed
the resolution of relinquishing the name also of regent.
To see a successor in the actual possession of a dignity
which a nine years' enjoyment had made indispensable to
her; to see the authority, the glory, the splendor, the
adoration, and all the marks of respect, which are the
usual concomitants of supreme power, pass over to
another; and to feel that she had lost that which she
could never forget she had once held, was more than a
woman's mind could endure; moreover, the Duke of Alva
was of all men the least calculated to make her feel her
privation the less painful by a forbearing use of his newly-acquired dignity. The tranquillity of the country, too,
which was put in jeopardy by this divided rule, seemed
to impose upon the duchess the necessity of abdicating.
Many governors of provinces refused, without an express
order from the court, to receive commands from the duke
and to recognize him as co-regent.

The rapid change of their point of attraction could not
be met by the courtiers so composedly and imperturbably but that the duchess observed the alteration, and
bitterly felt it. Even the few who, like State Counsellor
Viglius, still firmly adhered to her, did so less from attachment to her person than from vexation at being
displaced by novices and foreigners, and from being too
proud to serve a fresh apprenticeship under a new viceroy.
But far the greater number, with all their endeavors to
keep an exact mean, could not help making a difference
between the homage they paid to the rising sun and that
which they bestowed on the setting luminary. The royal
palace in Brussels became more and more deserted, while
the throng at Kuilemberg house daily increased. But
what wounded the sensitiveness of the duchess most
acutely was the arrest of Horn and Egmont, which was
planned and executed by the duke without her knowledge
or consent, just as if there had been no such person as

herself in existence. Alva did, indeed, after the act was done, endeavor to appease her by declaring that the design had been purposely kept secret from her in order to spare her name from being mixed up in so odious a transaction; but no such considerations of delicacy could close the wound which had been inflicted on her pride. In order at once to escape all risk of similar insults, of which the present was probably only a forerunner, she despatched her private secretary, Macchiavell, to the court of her brother, there to solicit earnestly for permission to resign the regency. The request was granted without difficulty by the king, who accompanied his consent with every mark of his highest esteem. He would put aside (so the king expressed himself) his own advantage and that of the provinces in order to oblige his sister. He sent a present of thirty thousand dollars, and allotted to her a yearly pension of twenty thousand.* At the same time a diploma was forwarded to the Duke of Alva, constituting him, in her stead, viceroy of all the Netherlands, with unlimited powers.

Gladly would Margaret have learned that she was permitted to resign the regency before a solemn assembly of the states, a wish which she had not very obscurely hinted to the king. But she was not gratified. She was particularly fond of solemnity, and the example of the Emperor, her father, who had exhibited the extraordinary spectacle of his abdication of the crown in this very city, seemed to have great attractions for her. As she was compelled to part with supreme power, she could scarcely be blamed for wishing to do so with as much splendor as possible. Moreover, she had not failed to observe how much the general hatred of the duke had effected in her own favor, and she looked, therefore, the more wistfully forward to a scene, which promised to be at once so flattering to her

* Which, however, does not appear to have been very punctually paid, if a pamphlet may be trusted which was printed during her lifetime. (It bears the title: Discours sur la Blessure de Monseigneur Prince d'Orange, 1582, without notice of the place where it was printed, and is to be found in the Elector's library at Dresden.) She languished, it is there stated, at Namur in poverty, and so ill-supported by her son (the then governor of the Netherlands), that her own secretary, Aldrobandin, called her sojourn there an exile. But the writer goes on to ask what better treatment could she expect from a son who, when still very young, being on a visit to her at Brussels, snapped his fingers at her behind her back.

and so affecting. She would have been glad to mingle her own tears with those which she hoped to see shed by the Netherlanders for their good regent. Thus the bitterness of her descent from the throne would have been alleviated by the expression of general sympathy. Little as she had done to merit the general esteem during the nine years of her administration, while fortune smiled upon her, and the approbation of her sovereign was the limit to all her wishes, yet now the sympathy of the nation had acquired a value in her eyes as the only thing which could in some degree compensate to her for the disappointment of all her other hopes. Fain would she have persuaded herself that she had become a voluntary sacrifice to her goodness of heart and her too humane feelings towards the Netherlanders. As, however, the king was very far from being disposed to incur any danger by calling a general assembly of the states, in order to gratify a mere caprice of his sister, she was obliged to content herself with a farewell letter to them. In this document she went over her whole administration, recounted, not without ostentation, the difficulties with which she had had to struggle, the evils which, by her dexterity, she had prevented, and wound up at last by saying that she left a finished work, and had to transfer to her successor nothing but the punishment of offenders. The king, too, was repeatly compelled to hear the same statement, and she left nothing undone to arrogate to herself the glory of any future advantages which it might be the good fortune of the duke to realize. Her own merits, as something which did not admit of a doubt, but was at the same time a burden oppressive to her modesty, she laid at the feet of the king.

Dispassionate posterity may, nevertheless, hesitate to subscribe unreservedly to this favorable opinion. Even though the united voice of her contemporaries, and the testimony of the Netherlands themselves vouch for it, a third party will not be denied the right to examine her claims with stricter scrutiny. The popular mind, easily affected, is but too ready to count the absence of a vice as an additional virtue, and, under the pressure of existing evil, to give excess of praise for past benefits.

The Netherlander seems to have concentrated all his hatred upon the Spanish name. To lay the blame of the national evils on the regent would tend to remove from the king and his minister the curses which he would rather shower upon them alone and undividedly; and the Duke of Alva's government of the Netherlands was, perhaps, not the proper point of view from which to test the merits of his predecessor. It was undoubtedly no light task to meet the king's expectations without infringing the rights of the people and the duties of humanity; but in struggling to effect these two contradictory objects Margaret had accomplished neither. She had deeply injured the nation, while comparatively she had done little service to the king. It is true that she at last crushed the Protestant faction, but the accidental outbreak of the Iconoclasts assisted her in this more than all her dexterity. She certainly succeeded by her intrigues in dissolving the league of the nobles, but not until the first blow had been struck at its roots by internal dissensions. The object, to secure which she had for many years vainly exhaused her whole policy, was effected at last by a single enlistment of troops, for which, however, the orders were issued from Madrid. She delivered to the duke, no doubt, a tranquillized country; but it cannot be denied that the dread of his approach had the chief share in tranquillizing it. By her reports she led the council in Spain astray; because she never informed it of the disease, but only of the occasional symptoms; never of the universal feeling and voice of the nation, but only of the misconduct of factions. Her faulty administration, moreover, drew the people into the crime, because she exasperated without sufficiently awing them. She it was that brought the murderous Alva into the country by leading the king to believe that the disturbances in the provinces were to be ascribed, not so much to the severity of the royal ordinances, as to the unworthiness of those who were charged with their execution. Margaret possessed natural capacity and intellect; and an acquired political tact enabled her to meet any ordinary case; but she wanted that creative genius which, for new and extraordinary emergencies, invents new maxims, or wisely oversteps old ones. In a country where honesty was the best policy, she adopted the unfortunate plan of practising her insidious Italian policy, and thereby sowed the seeds of a fatal distrust in the minds of the people. The indulgence which has been so liberally imputed to her as a merit was, in truth, extorted from her weakness and timidity by the courageous opposition of the nation; she had never departed from the strict letter of the royal commands by her own spontaneous resolution; never did the gentle feelings of innate humanity lead her to misinterpret the cruel purport of her instructions. Even the few concessions to which necessity compelled her were granted with an uncertain and shrinking hand, as if fearing to give too much; and she lost the fruit of her benefactions because she mutilated them by a sordid closeness. What in all the other relations of her life she was too little, she was on the throne too much — a woman! She had it in her power, after Granvella's expulsion, to become the benefactress of the Belgian nation, but she did not. Her supreme good was the approbation of her king, her greatest misfortune his displeasure; with all the eminent qualities of her mind she remained an ordinary character because her heart was destitute of native nobility. She used a melancholy power with much moderation, and stained her government with no deed of arbitrary cruelty; nay, if it had depended on her, she would have always acted humanely. Years afterwards, when her idol, Philip II., had long forgotten her, the Netherlanders still honored her memory; but she was far from deserving the glory which her successor's inhumanity reflected upon her.

She left Brussels about the end of December, 1567. The duke escorted her as far as the frontiers of Brabant, and there left her under the protection of Count Mansfeld in order to hasten back to the metropolis and show himself to the Netherlanders as sole regent.

TRIAL AND EXECUTION OF COUNTS EGMONT AND HORN.

THE two counts were a few weeks after their arrest conveyed to Ghent under an escort of three thousand Spaniards, where they were confined in the citadel for more than eight months. Their trial commenced in due form before the council of twelve, and the solicitor-general, John Du Bois, conducted the proceedings. The indictment against Egmont consisted of ninety counts, and that against Horn of sixty. It would occupy too much space to introduce them here. Every action, however innocent, every omission of duty, was interpreted on the principle which had been laid down in the opening of the indictment, "that the two counts, in conjunction with the Prince of Orange, had planned the overthrow of the royal authority in the Netherlands, and the usurpation of the government of the country;" the expulsion of Granvella; the embassy of Egmont to Madrid; the confederacy of the Gueux; the concessions which they made to the Protestants in the provinces under their government — all were made to have a connection with, and reference to, this deliberate design. Thus importance was attached to the most insignificant occurrences, and one action made to darken and discolor another. By taking care to treat each of the charges as in itself a treasonable offence it was the more easy to justify a sentence of high treason by the whole.

The accusations were sent to each of the prisoners, who were required to reply to them within five days. After doing so they were allowed to employ solicitors and advocates, who were permitted free access to them; but as they were accused of treason their friends were prohibited from visiting them. Count Egmont employed for his solicitor Von Landas, and made choice of a few eminent advocates from Brussels.

The first step was to demur against the tribunal which was to try them, since by the privilege of their order they, as Knights of the Golden Fleece, were amenable only to the king himself, the grand master. But this demurrer was overruled, and they were required to produce their witnesses, in default of which they were to be proceeded against *in contumaciam*. Egmont had satisfactorily answered to eighty-two counts, while Count Horn had refuted the charges against him, article by article. The accusation and the defence are still extant; on that defence every impartial tribunal would have acquitted them both. The Procurator Fiscal pressed for the production of their evidence, and the Duke of Alva issued his repeated commands to use despatch. They delayed, however, from week to week, while they renewed their protests against the illegality of the court. At last the duke assigned them nine days to produce their proofs; on the lapse of that period they were to be declared guilty, and as having forfeited all right of defence.

During the progress of the trial the relations and friends of the two counts were not idle. Egmont's wife, by birth a duchess of Bavaria, addressed petitions to the princes of the German empire, to the Emperor, and to the King of Spain. The Countess Horn, mother of the imprisoned count, who was connected by the ties of friendship or of blood with the principal royal families of Germany, did the same. All alike protested loudly against this illegal proceeding, and appealed to the liberty of the German empire, on which Horn, as a count of the empire, had special claims; the liberty of the Netherlands and the privileges of the Order of the Golden Fleece were likewise insisted upon. The Countess Egmont succeeded in obtaining the intercession of almost every German court in behalf of her husband. The King of Spain and his viceroy were besieged by applications in behalf of the accused, which were referred from one to the other, and made light of by both. Countess Horn collected certificates from all the Knights of the Golden Fleece in Spain, Germany, and Italy to prove the privileges of the order. Alva rejected them with a declaration that they had no force in such a case as the present. "The crimes of which the counts are accused relate to the affairs of the Belgian provinces, and he, the duke, was appointed by the king sole judge of all matters connected with those countries."

Four months had been allowed to the solicitor-general to draw up the indictment, and five were granted to the two counts to prepare for their defence. But instead of losing their time and trouble in adducing their evidence, which, perhaps, would have profited them but little, they preferred wasting it in protests against the judges, which availed them still less. By the former course they would probably have delayed the final sentence, and in the time thus gained the powerful intercession of their friends might perhaps have not been ineffectual. By obstinately persisting in denying the competency of the tribunal which was to try them, they furnished the duke with an excuse for cutting short the proceedings. After the last assigned period had expired, on the 1st of June, 1658, the council of twelve declared them guilty, and on the 4th of that month sentence of death was pronounced against them.

The execution of twenty-five noble Netherlanders, who were beheaded in three successive days in the market-place at Brussels, was the terrible prelude to the fate of the two counts. John Casembrot von Beckerzeel, secretary to Count Egmont, was one of the unfortunates, who was thus rewarded for his fidelity to his master, which he steadfastly maintained even upon the rack, and for his zeal in the service of the king, which he had manifested against the Iconoclasts. The others had either been taken prisoners, with arms in their hands, in the insurrection of the "Gueux," or apprehended and condemned as traitors on account of having taken a part in the petition of the nobles.

The duke had reason to hasten the execution of the sentence. Count Louis of Nassau had given battle to the Count of Aremberg, near the monastery of Heiligerlee, in Gröningen, and had the good fortune to defeat him. Immediately after his victory he had advanced against Gröningen, and laid siege to it. The success of his arms had raised the courage of his faction; and the Prince of Orange, his brother, was close at hand with an army to support him. These circumstances made the duke's presence necessary in those distant provinces; but he could not venture to leave Brussels before the fate of two such important prisoners was decided. The whole nation loved them, which was not a little increased by their unhappy fate. Even the strict papists disapproved of the execution of these eminent nobles. The slightest advantage which the arms of the rebels might gain over the duke, or even the report of a defeat, would cause a revolution in Brussels, which would immediately set the two counts at liberty. Moreover, the petitions and intercessions which came to the viceroy, as well as to the King of Spain, from the German princes, increased daily; nay, the Emperor, Maximilian II., himself caused the countess to be assured " that she had nothing to fear for the life of her spouse." These powerful applications might at last turn the king's heart in favor of the prisoners. The king might, perhaps, in reliance on his viceroy's usual dispatch, put on the appearance of yielding to the representations of so many sovereigns, and rescind the sentence of death under the conviction that his mercy would come too late. These considerations moved the duke not to delay the execution of the sentence as soon as it was pronounced.

On the day after the sentence was passed the two counts were brought, under an escort of three thousand Spaniards, from Ghent to Brussels, and placed in confinement in the *Brodhause*, in the great market-place. The next morning the council of twelve were assembled; the duke, contrary to his custom, attended in person, and both the sentences, in sealed envelopes, were opened and publicly read by Secretary Pranz. The two counts were declared guilty of treason, as having favored and promoted the abominable conspiracy of the Prince of Orange, protected the confederated nobles, and been convicted of various misdemeanors against their king and the church in their governments and other appointments. Both were sentenced to be publicly beheaded, and their heads were to be fixed upon pikes and not taken down without the duke's express command. All their possessions, fiefs, and rights escheated to the royal treasury. The sentence was signed only by the duke and the secretary, Pranz, without asking or caring for the consent of the other members of the council.

During the night between the 4th and 5th of June the sentences were brought to the prisoners, after they had already gone to rest. The duke gave them to the Bishop of Ypres, Martin Rithov, whom he had expressly summoned to Brussels to prepare the prisoners for death. When the bishop received this commission he threw himself at the feet of the duke, and supplicated him with tears in his eyes for mercy, at least for respite for the prisoners; but he was answered in a rough and angry voice that he had been sent for from Ypres, not to oppose the sentence, but by his spiritual consolation to reconcile the unhappy noblemen to it.

Egmont was the first to whom the bishop communicated the sentence of death. "That is indeed a severe sentence," exclaimed the count, turning pale, and with a faltering voice. "I did not think that I had offended his majesty so deeply as to deserve such treatment. If, however, it must be so I submit to my fate with resignation. May this death atone for my offence, and save my wife and children from suffering. This at least I think I may claim for my past services. As for death, I will meet it with composure, since it so pleases God and my king." He then pressed the bishop to tell him seriously and candidly if there was no hope of pardon. Being answered in the negative, he confessed and received the sacrament from the priest, repeating after him the mass with great devoutness. He asked what prayer was the best and most effective to recommend him to God in his last hour. On being told that no prayer could be more effectual than the one which Christ himself had taught, he prepared immediately to repeat the Lord's prayer. The thoughts of his family interrupted him; he called for pen and ink, and wrote two letters, one to his wife, the other to the king. The latter was as follows:

"Sire,—This morning I have heard the sentence which your majesty has been pleased to pass upon me. Far as I have ever been from attempting anything against the person or service of your majesty, or against the true, old, and Catholic religion, I yet submit myself with patience to the fate which it has pleased God to ordain I should suffer. If, during the past disturbances, I have omitted, advised, or done anything that seems at variance with my duty, it was most assuredly performed with the best intentions, or was forced upon me by the pressure of circumstances. I therefore pray your majesty to forgive me, and, in consideration of my past services, show mercy to my unhappy wife, my poor children, and servants. In a firm hope of this, I commend myself to the infinite mercy of God.

"Your majesty's most faithful vassal and servant,
"LAMORAL COUNT EGMONT.

"BRUSSELS, June 5, 1568, near my last moments."

This letter he placed in the hands of the bishop, with the strongest injunctions for its safe delivery; and for greater security he sent a duplicate in his own handwriting to State Counsellor Viglius, the most upright man in the senate, by whom, there is no doubt, it was actually delivered to the king. The family of the count were subsequently reinstated in all his property, fiefs, and rights, which, by virtue of the sentence, had escheated to the royal treasury.

Meanwhile a scaffold had been erected in the market-place, before the town hall, on which two poles were fixed with iron spikes, and the whole covered with black cloth. Two-and-twenty companies of the Spanish garrison surrounded the scaffold, a precaution which was by no means superfluous. Between ten and eleven o'clock the Spanish guard appeared in the apartment of the count; they were provided with cords to tie his hands according to custom. He begged that this might be spared him, and declared that he was willing and ready to die. He himself cut off the collar from his doublet to facilitate the executioner's duty. He wore a robe of red damask, and over that a black Spanish cloak trimmed with gold lace. In this dress he appeared on the scaffold, and was attended by Don Julian Romero, maitre-de-camp; Salinas, a Spanish captain; and the Bishop of Ypres. The grand provost of the court, with a red wand in his hand, sat on horseback at the foot of the scaffold; the executioner was concealed beneath.

Egmont had at first shown a desire to address the people from the scaffold. He desisted, however, on the bishop's representing to him that either he would not be heard, or that if he were, he might — such at present was the dangerous disposition of the people — excite them to acts of violence, which would only plunge his friends into destruction. For a few moments he paced the scaffold with noble dignity, and lamented that it had not been permitted him to die a more honorable death for his king and his country. Up to the last he seemed unable to persuade himself that the king was in earnest, and that his severity would be carried any further than the mere terror of execution. When the decisive period approached, and he was to receive the extreme unction, he looked wistfully round, and when there still appeared no prospect of a reprieve, he turned to Julian Romero, and asked him once more if there was no hope of pardon for him. Julian Romero shrugged his shoulders, looked on the ground, and was silent.

He then closely clenched his teeth, threw off his mantle and robe, knelt upon the cushion, and prepared himself for the last prayer. The bishop presented him the crucifix to kiss, and administered to him extreme unction, upon which the count made him a sign to leave him. He drew a silk cap over his eyes, and awaited the stroke. Over the corpse and the streaming blood a black cloth was immediately thrown.

All Brussels thronged around the scaffold, and the fatal blow seemed to fall on every heart. Loud sobs alone broke the appalling silence. The duke himself, who watched the execution from a window of the townhouse, wiped his eyes as his victim died.

Shortly afterwards Count Horn advanced on the scaffold. Of a more violent temperament than his friend, and stimulated by stronger reasons for hatred against the king, he had received the sentence with less composure, although in his case, perhaps, it was less unjust. He burst forth in bitter reproaches against the king, and the bishop with difficulty prevailed upon him to make a better use of his last moments than to abuse them in imprecations on his enemies. At last, however, he became more collected, and made his confession to the bishop, which at first he was disposed to refuse.

He mounted the scaffold with the same attendants as his friend. In passing he saluted many of his acquaintances; his hands were, like Egmont's, free, and he was dressed in a black doublet and cloak, with a Milan cap of the same color upon his head. When he had ascended, he cast his eyes upon the corpse, which lay under the cloth, and asked one of the bystanders if it was the body of his friend. On being answered in the affirmative, he said some words in Spanish, threw his cloak from him, and knelt upon the cushion. All shrieked aloud as he received the fatal blow.

The heads of both were fixed upon the poles which were set up on the scaffold, where they remained until past three in the afternoon, when they were taken down, and, with the two bodies, placed in leaden coffins and deposited in a vault.

In spite of the number of spies and executioners who surrounded the scaffold, the citizens of Brussels would not be prevented from dipping their handkerchiefs in the streaming blood, and carrying home with them these precious memorials.

SIEGE OF ANTWERP BY THE PRINCE OF PARMA, IN THE YEARS 1584 AND 1585.

IT is an interesting spectacle to observe the struggle of man's inventive genius in conflict with powerful opposing elements, and to see the difficulties which are insurmountable to ordinary capacities overcome by prudence, resolution, and a determined will. Less attractive, but only the more instructive, perhaps, is the contrary spectacle, where the absence of those qualities renders all efforts of genius vain, throws away all the favors of fortune, and where inability to improve such advantages renders hopeless a success which otherwise seemed sure and inevitable. Examples of both kinds are afforded by the celebrated siege of Antwerp by the Spaniards towards the close of the sixteenth century, by which that flourishing city was forever deprived of its commercial prosperity, but which, on the other hand, conferred immortal fame on the general who undertook and accomplished it.

Twelve years had the war continued which the northern provinces of Belgium had commenced at first in vindication simply of their religious freedom, and the privileges of their states, from the encroachments of the Spanish viceroy, but maintained latterly in the hope of establishing their independence of the Spanish crown. Never completely victors, but never entirely vanquished, they wearied out the Spanish valor by tedious operations on an unfavorable soil, and exhausted the wealth of the sovereign of both the Indies while they themselves were called beggars, and in a degree actually were so. The league of Ghent, which had united the whole Netherlands, Roman Catholic and Protestant, in a common and (could such a confederation have lasted) invincible body, was indeed dissolved; but in place of this uncertain and unnatural combination the northern provinces had, in the year 1579, formed among themselves the closer union of Utrecht, which promised to be more lasting, inasmuch as it was linked and held together by common political and religious interests. What the new republic had lost in extent through this separation from the Roman Catholic provinces it was fully compensated for by the closeness of alliance, the unity of enterprise, and energy of execution; and perhaps it was fortunate in thus timely losing what no exertion probably would ever have enabled it to retain.

The greater part of the Walloon provinces had, in the year 1584, partly by voluntary submission and partly by force of arms, been again reduced under the Spanish yoke. The northern districts alone had been able at all successfully to oppose it. A considerable portion of Brabant and Flanders still obstinately held out against the arms of the Duke Alexander of Parma, who at that time administered the civil government of the provinces, and the supreme command of the army, with equal energy and prudence, and by a series of splendid victories had revived the military reputation of Spain. The peculiar formation of the country, which by its numerous rivers and canals facilitated the connection of the towns with one another and with the sea, baffled all attempts effectually to subdue it, and the possession of one place could only be maintained by the occupation of another. So long as this communication was kept up Holland and Zealand could with little difficulty assist their allies, and supply them abundantly by water as well as by land with all necessaries, so that valor was of no use, and the strength of the king's troops was fruitlessly wasted on tedious sieges.

Of all the towns in Brabant Antwerp was the most important, as well from its wealth, its population, and its military force, as by its position on the mouth of the Scheldt. This great and populous town, which at this date contained more than eighty thousand inhabitants, was one of the most active members of the national league, and had in the course of the war distinguished itself above all the towns of Belgium by an untamable spirit of liberty. As it fostered within its bosom all the three Christian churches, and owed much of its prosperity to this unrestricted religious liberty, it had the more cause to dread the Spanish rule, which threatened to abolish this toleration, and by the terror of the Inquisition to drive all the Protestant merchants from its markets. Moreover it had had but too terrible experience of the brutality of the Spanish garrisons, and it was quite evident that if it once more suffered this insupportable yoke to be imposed upon it it would never again during the whole course of the war be able to throw it off.

But powerful as were the motives which stimulated Antwerp to resistance, equally strong were the reasons which determined the Spanish general to make himself master of the place at any cost. On the possession of this town depended in a great measure that of the whole province of Brabant, which by this channel chiefly derived its supplies of corn from Zealand, while the capture of this place would secure to the victor the command of the Scheldt. It would also deprive the league of Brabant, which held its meetings in the town, of its principal support; the whole faction of its dangerous influence, of its example, its counsels, and its money, while the treasures of its inhabitants would open plentiful supplies for the military exigencies of the king. Its fall would sooner or later necessarily draw after it that of all Brabant, and the preponderance of power in that quarter would decide the whole dispute in favor of the king. Determined by these grave considerations, the Duke of Parma drew his forces together in July, 1584, and advanced from his position at Dornick to the neighborhood of Antwerp, with the intention of investing it.

But both the natural position and fortifications of the town appeared to defy attacks. Surrounded on the side of Brabant with insurmountable works and moats, and towards Flanders covered by the broad and rapid stream of the Scheldt, it could not be carried by storm; and to blockade a town of such extent seemed to require a land force three times larger than that which the duke had, and moreover a fleet, of which he was utterly destitute. Not only did the river yield the town all necessary supplies from Ghent, it also opened an easy communication with the bordering province of Zealand. For, as the tide of the North Sea extends far up the Scheldt, and ebbs and flows regularly, Antwerp enjoys the peculiar advantage that the same tide flows past it at different times in two opposite directions. Besides, the adjacent towns of Brussels, Malines, Ghent, Dendermonde, and others, were all at this time in the hands of the league, and could aid the place from the land side also. To blockade, therefore, the town by land, and to cut off its communication with Flanders and Brabant, required two different armies, one on each bank of the river. A sufficient fleet was likewise needed to guard the passage of the Scheldt, and to prevent all attempts at relief, which would most certainly be made from Zealand. But by the war which he had still to carry on in other quarters, and by the numerous garrisons which he was obliged to leave in the towns and fortified places, the army of the duke was reduced to ten thousand infantry and seventeen hundred horse, a force very inadequate for an undertaking of such magnitude. Moreover, these troops were deficient in the most necessary supplies, and the long arrears of pay had excited them to subdued murmurs, which hourly threatened to break out into open mutiny. If, notwithstanding these difficulties, he should still attempt the seige, there would be much occasion to fear from the strongholds of the enemy, which were left in the rear, and from which it would be easy, by vigorous sallies, to annoy an army distributed over so many places, and to expose it to want by cutting off its supplies.

All these considerations were brought forward by the council of war, before which the Duke of Parma now laid his scheme. However great the confidence which they placed in themselves, and in the proved abilities of such a leader, nevertheless the most experienced generals did not disguise their despair of a fortunate result. Two only were exceptions, Capizucchi and Mondragone, whose ardent courage placed them above all apprehensions; the rest concurred in dissuading the duke from attempting so hazardous an enterprise, by which they ran the risk of forfeiting the fruit of all their former victories and tarnishing the glory they had already earned.

But objections, which he had already made to himself and refuted, could not shake the Duke of Parma in his purpose. Not in ignorance of its inseparable dangers, not from thoughtless overvaluing his forces had he taken this bold resolve. But that instinctive genius which leads great men by paths which inferior minds either never enter upon or never finish, raised him above the influence of the doubts which a cold and narrow prudence would oppose to his views; and, without being able to convince his generals, he felt the correctness of his calculations in a conviction indistinct, indeed, but not on that account less indubitable. A succession of fortunate results had raised his confidence, and the sight of his army, unequalled in Europe for discipline, experience, and valor, and commanded by a chosen body of the most distinguished officers, did not permit him to entertain fear for a moment. To those who objected to the small number of his troops, he answered, that however long the pike, it is only the point that kills; and that in military enterprise, the moving power was of more importance than the mass to be moved. He was aware, indeed, of the discontent of his troops, but he knew also their obedience; and he thought, moreover, that the best means to stifle their murmurs was by keeping them employed in some important undertaking, by stimulating their desire of glory by the splendor of the enterprise, and their rapacity by hopes of the rich booty which the capture of so wealthy a town would hold out.

In the plan which he now formed for the conduct of the siege he endeavored to meet all these difficulties. Famine was the only instrument by which he could hope to subdue the town; but effectually to use this formidable weapon, it would be expedient to cut off all its land and water communications. With this view, the first object was to stop, or at least to impede, the arrival of supplies from Zealand. It was, therefore, requisite not only to carry all the outworks, which the people of Antwerp had built on both shores of the Scheldt for the protection of their shipping; but also, wherever feasible, to throw up new batteries which should command the whole course of the river; and to prevent the place from drawing supplies from the land side, while efforts were being made to intercept their transmission by sea, all the adjacent towns of Brabant and Flanders were comprehended in the plan of the siege, and the fall of Antwerp was based on the destruction of all those places. A bold and, considering the duke's scanty force, an almost extravagant project, which was, however, justified by the genius of its author, and crowned by fortune with a brilliant result.

As, however, time was required to accomplish a plan of this magnitude, the Prince of Parma was content, for the present, with the erection of numerous forts on the canals and rivers which connected Antwerp with Dendermonde, Ghent, Malines, Brussels, and other places. Spanish garrisons were quartered in the vicinity, and almost at the very gates of those towns, which laid waste the open country, and by their incursions kept the surrounding territory in alarm. Thus, round Ghent alone were encamped about three thousand men, and proportionate numbers round the other towns. In this way, and by means of the secret understanding which he maintained with the Roman Catholic inhabitants of those towns, the duke hoped, without weakening his own forces, gradually to exhaust their strength, and by the harassing operations of a petty but incessant warfare, even without any formal siege, to reduce them at last to capitulate.

In the meantime the main force was directed against Antwerp, which he now closely invested. He fixed his headquarters at Bevern in Flanders, a few miles from Antwerp, where he found a fortified camp. The protection of the Flemish bank of the Scheldt was entrusted to the Margrave of Rysburg, general of cavalry; the Brabant bank to the Count Peter Ernest Von Mansfeld, who was joined by another Spanish leader, Mondragone. Both the latter succeeded in crossing the Scheldt upon pontoons, notwithstanding the Flemish admiral's ship was sent to oppose them, and, passing Antwerp, took up their position at Stabroek in Bergen. Detached corps dispersed themselves along the whole Brabant side, partly to secure the dykes and the roads.

Some miles below Antwerp the Scheldt was guarded by two strong forts, of which one was situated at Liefkenshoek ōn the island Doel, in Flanders, the other at Lillo, exactly opposite the coast of Brabant. The last had been erected by Mondragone himself, by order of the Duke of Alva, when the latter was still master of Antwerp, and for this very reason the Duke of Parma now entrusted to him the attack upon it. On the possession of these two forts the success of the siege seemed wholly to depend, since all the vessels sailing from Zealand to Antwerp must pass under their guns. Both forts had a short time before been strengthened by the besieged, and the former was scarcely finished when the Margrave of Rysburg attacked it. The celerity with which he went to work surprised the enemy before they were sufficiently prepared for defence, and a brisk assault quickly placed Liefkenshoek in the hands of the Spaniards. The confederates sustained this loss on the same fatal day that the Prince of Orange fell at Delft by the hands of an assassin. The other batteries, erected on the island of Doel, were partly abandoned by their defenders, partly taken by surprise, so that in a short time the whole Flemish side was cleared of the enemy. But the fort at Lillo, on the Brabant shore, offered a more vigorous resistance, since the people of Antwerp had had time to strengthen its fortifications and to provide it with a strong garrison. Furious sallies of the besieged, led by Odets von Teligny, supported by the cannon of the fort, destroyed all the works of the Spaniards, and an inundation, which was effected by opening the sluices, finally drove them away from the place after a three weeks' siege, and with the loss of nearly two thousand killed. They now retired into their fortified camp at Stabroek, and contented themselves with taking possession of the dams which run across the lowlands of Bergen, and oppose a breastwork to the encroachments of the East Scheldt.

The failure of his attempt upon the fort of Lillo compelled the Prince of Parma to change his measures. As he could not succeed in stopping the passage of the Scheldt by his original plan, on which the success of the siege entirely depended, he determined to effect his purpose by throwing a bridge across the whole breadth of the river. The thought was bold, and there were many who held it to be rash. Both the breadth of the stream, which at this part exceeds twelve hundred paces, as well as its violence, which is still further augmented by the tides of the neighboring sea, appeared to render every attempt of this kind impracticable. Moreover, he had to contend with a deficiency of timber, vessels, and workmen, as well as with the dangerous position between the fleets of Antwerp and of Zealand, to which it would necessarily be an easy task, in combination with a boisterous element, to interrupt so tedious a work. But the Prince of Parma knew his power, and his settled resolution would yield to nothing short of absolute impossibility. After he had caused the breadth as well as the depth of the river to be measured, and had consulted with two of his most skilful engineers, Barocci and Plato, it was settled that the bridge should be constructed between Calloo in Flanders and Ordam in Brabant. This spot was selected because the river is here narrowest, and bends a little to the right, and so detains vessels a while by compelling them to tack. To cover the bridge strong bastions were erected at both ends, of which the one on the Flanders side was named Fort St. Maria, the other, on the Brabant side, Fort St. Philip, in honor of the king.

While active preparations were making in the Spanish camp for the execution of this scheme, and the whole attention of the enemy was directed to it, the duke made an unexpected attack upon Dendermonde, a strong town between Ghent and Antwerp, at the confluence of the Dender and the Scheldt. As long as this important place was in the hands of the enemy the towns of Ghent and Antwerp could mutually support each other, and by the facility of their communication frustrate all the efforts of the besiegers. Its capture would leave the prince free to act against both towns, and might decide the fate of his undertaking. The rapidity of his attack left the besieged no time to open their sluices and lay the country under water. A hot cannonade was opened upon the chief bastion of the town before the Brussels gate, but was answered by the fire of the besieged, which made great havoc amongst the Spaniards. It increased, however, rather than discouraged their ardor, and the insults of the garrison, who mutilated the statue of a saint before their eyes, and after treating it with the most contumelious indignity, hurled it down from the rampart, raised their fury to the highest pitch. Clamorously they demanded to be led against the bastion before their fire had made a sufficient breach in it, and the prince, to avail himself of the first ardor of their impetuosity, gave the signal for the assault. After a sanguinary contest of two hours the rampart was mounted, and those who were not sacrificed to the first fury of the Spaniards threw themselves into the town. The latter was indeed now more exposed, a fire being directed upon it from the works which had been carried; but its strong walls and the broad moat which surrounded it gave reason to expect a protracted resistance. The inventive resources of the Prince of Parma soon overcame this obstacle also. While the bombardment was carried on night and day, the troops were incessantly employed in diverting the course of the Dender, which supplied the fosse with water, and the besieged were seized with despair as they saw the water of the trenches, the last defence of the town, gradually disappear. They hastened to capitulate, and in August, 1584, received a Spanish garrison. Thus, in the space of eleven days, the Prince of Parma accomplished an undertaking which, in the opinion of competent judges, would require as many weeks.

The town of Ghent, now cut off from Antwerp and the sea, and hard pressed by the troops of the king, which were encamped in its vicinity, and without hope of immediate succor, began to despair, as famine, with all its dreadful train, advanced upon them with rapid steps. The inhabitants therefore despatched deputies to the Spanish camp at Bevern, to tender its submission to the king upon the same terms as the prince had a short time previously offered. The deputies were informed that the time for treaties was past, and that an unconditional submission alone could appease the just anger of the monarch whom they had offended by their rebellion. Nay, they were even given to understand that it would be only through his great mercy if the same humiliation were not exacted from them as their rebellious ancestors were forced to undergo under Charles V., namely, to implore pardon half-naked, and with a cord round their necks. The deputies returned to Ghent in despair, but three days afterwards a new deputation was sent to the Spanish camp, which at last, by the intercession of one of the prince's friends, who was a prisoner in Ghent, obtained peace upon moderate terms. The town was to pay a fine of two hundred thousand florins, recall the banished papists, and expel the Protestant inhabitants, who, however, were to be allowed two years for the settlement of their affairs. All the inhabitants except six, who were reserved for capital punishment (but afterwards pardoned), were included in a general amnesty, and the garrison, which amounted to two thousand men, was allowed to evacuate the place with the honors of war. This treaty was concluded in September of the same year, at the headquarters at Bevern, and immediately three thousand Spaniards marched into the town as a garrison.

It was more by the terror of his name and the dread of famine than by the force of arms that the Prince of Parma had succeeded in reducing this city to submission, the largest and strongest in the Netherlands, which was little inferior to Paris within the barriers of its inner town, consisted of thirty-seven thousand houses, and was built on twenty islands, connected by ninety-eight stone bridges. The important privileges which in the course of several centuries this city had contrived to extort from its rulers fostered in its inhabitants a spirit of independence, which not unfrequently degenerated into riot and license, and naturally brought it in collision with the Austrian-Spanish government. And it was exactly this bold spirit of liberty which procured for the Reformation the rapid and extensive success it met with in this town, and the combined incentives of civil and religious freedom produced all those scenes of violence by which, during the rebellion, it had unfortunately distinguished itself. Besides the fine levied, the prince found within the walls a large store of artillery, carriages, ships, and building materials of all kinds, with numerous workmen and sailors, who materially aided him in his plans against Antwerp.

Before Ghent surrendered to the king Vilvorden and Herentals had fallen into the hands of the Spaniards, and the capture of the block-houses near the village of Willebrock had cut off Antwerp from Brussels and Malines. The loss of these places within so short a period deprived Antwerp of all hope of succor from Brabant and Flanders, and limited all their expectations to the assistance which might be looked for from Zealand. But to deprive them also of this the Prince of Parma was now making the most energetic preparations.

The citizens of Antwerp had beheld the first operations of the enemy against their town with the proud security with which the sight of their invincible river inspired them. This confidence was also in a degree justified by the opinion of the Prince of Orange, who, upon the first intelligence of the design, had said that the Spanish army would inevitably perish before the walls of Antwerp. That nothing, however, might be neglected, he sent, a short time before his assassination, for the burgomaster of Antwerp, Philip Marnix of St. Aldegonde, his intimate friend, to Delft, where he consulted with him as to the means of maintaining defensive operations. It was agreed between them that it would be advisable to demolish forthwith the great dam between Sanvliet and Lillo called the Blaaugarendyk, so as to allow the waters of the East Scheldt to inundate, if necessary, the lowlands of Bergen, and thus, in the event of the Scheldt being closed, to open a passage for the Zealand vessels to the town across the inundated country. Aldegonde had, after his return, actually persuaded the magistrate and the majority of the citizens to agree to this proposal, when it was resisted by the guild of butchers, who claimed that they would be ruined by such a measure; for the plain which it was wished to lay under water was a vast tract of pasture land, upon which about twelve thousand oxen were annually put to graze. The objection of the butchers was successful, and they managed to prevent the execution of this salutary scheme until the enemy had got possession of the dams as well as the pasture land.

At the suggestion of the burgomaster St. Aldegonde,

who, himself a member of the states of Brabant, was possessed of great authority in that council, the fortifications on both sides the Scheldt had, a short time before the arrival of the Spaniards, been placed in repair, and many new redoubts erected round the town. The dams had been cut through at Saftingen, and the water of the West Scheldt let out over nearly the whole country of Waes. In the adjacent Marquisate of Bergen troops had been enlisted by the Count of Hohenlohe, and a Scotch regiment, under the command of Colonel Morgan, was already in the pay of the republic, while fresh reinforcements were daily expected from England and France. Above all, the states of Holland and Zealand were called upon to hasten their supplies. But after the enemy had taken strong positions on both sides of the river, and the fire of their batteries made the navigation dangerous, when place after place in Brabant fell into their hands, and their cavalry had cut off all communication on the land side, the inhabitants of Antwerp began at last to entertain serious apprehensions for the future. The town then contained eighty-five thousand souls, and according to calculation three hundred thousand quarters of corn were annually required for their support. At the beginning of the siege neither the supply nor the money was wanting for the laying in of such a store; for in spite of the enemy's fire the Zealand victualing ships, taking advantage of the rising tide, contrived to make their way to the town. All that was requisite was to prevent any of the richer citizens from buying up these supplies, and, in case of scarcity, raising the price. To secure his object, one Gianibelli from Mantua, who had rendered important services in the course of the siege, proposed a property tax of one penny in every hundred, and the appointment of a board of respectable persons to purchase corn with this money, and distribute it weekly. And until the returns of this tax should be available the richer classes should advance the required sum, holding the corn purchased, as a deposit, in their own magazines; and were also to share in the profit. But this plan was unwelcome to the wealthier citizens, who had resolved to profit by the general distress. They recommended that every individual should be required to provide himself with a sufficient supply for two years; a proposition which, however it might suit their own circumstances, was very unreasonable in regard to the poorer inhabitants, who, even before the siege, could scarcely find means to supply themselves for so many months. They obtained indeed their object, which was to reduce the poor to the necessity of either quitting the place or becoming entirely their dependents. But when they afterwards reflected that in the time of need the rights of property would not be respected, they found it advisable not to be over-hasty in making their own purchases.

The magistrate, in order to avert an evil that would have pressed upon individuals only, had recourse to an expedient which endangered the safety of all. Some enterprising persons in Zealand had freighted a large fleet with provisions, which succeeded in passing the guns of the enemy, and discharged its cargo at Antwerp. The hope of a large profit had tempted the merchants to enter upon this hazardous speculation; in this, however, they were disappointed, as the magistrate of Antwerp had, just before their arrival, issued an edict regulating the price of all the necessaries of life. At the same time to prevent individuals from buying up the whole cargo and storing it in their magazines with a view of disposing of it afterwards at a dearer rate, he ordered that the whole should be publicly sold in any quantities from the vessels. The speculators, cheated of their hopes of profit by these precautions, set sail again, and left Antwerp with the greater part of their cargo, which would have sufficed for the support of the town for several months.

This neglect of the most essential and natural means of preservation can only be explained by the supposition that the inhabitants considered it absolutely impossible ever to close the Scheldt completely, and consequently had not the least apprehension that things would come to extremity. When the intelligence arrived in Antwerp that the prince intended to throw a bridge over the Scheldt the idea was universally ridiculed as chimerical. An arrogant comparison was drawn between the republic and the stream, and it was said that the one would bear the Spanish yoke as little as the other. "A river which is twenty-four hundred feet broad, and, with its own waters alone, above sixty feet deep, but which with the tide rose twelve feet more — would such a stream," it was asked, "submit to be spanned by a miserable piece of paling? Where were beams to be found high enough to reach to the bottom and project above the surface? and how was a work of this kind to stand in winter, when whole islands and mountains of ice, which stone walls could hardly resist, would be driven by the flood against its weak timbers, and splinter them to pieces like glass? Or, perhaps, the prince purposed to construct a bridge of boats; if so, where would he procure the latter, and how bring them into his intrenchments? They must necessarily be brought past Antwerp, where a fleet was ready to capture or sink them."

But while they were trying to prove the absurdity of the Prince of Parma's undertaking he had already completed it. As soon as the forts St. Maria and St. Philip were erected, and protected the workmen and the work by their fire, a pier was built out into the stream from both banks, for which purpose the masts of the largest vessels were employed; by a skilful arrangement of the timbers they contrived to give the whole such solidity that, as the result proved, it was able to resist the violent pressure of the ice. These timbers, which rested firmly and securely on the bottom of the river, and projected a considerable height above it, being covered with planks, afforded a commodious roadway. It was wide enough to allow eight men to cross abreast, and a balustrade that ran along it on both sides, protected them from the fire of small-arms from the enemy's vessels. This "stacade," as it was called, ran from the two opposite shores as far as the increasing depth and force of the stream allowed. It reduced the breadth of the river to about eleven hundred feet; as, however, the middle and proper current would not admit of such a barrier, there remained, therefore, between the two stacades a space of more than six hundred paces through which a whole fleet of transports could sail with ease. This intervening space the prince designed to close by a bridge of boats, for which purpose the craft must be procured from Dunkirk. But, besides that they could not be obtained in any number at that place, it would be difficult to bring them past Antwerp without great loss. He was, therefore, obliged to content himself for the time with having narrowed the stream one-half, and rendered the passage of the enemy's vessels so much the more difficult. Where the stacades terminated in the middle of the stream they spread out into parallelograms, which were mounted with heavy guns, and served as a kind of battery on the water. From these a heavy fire was opened on every vessel that attempted to pass through this narrow channel. Whole fleets, however, and single vessels still attempted and succeeded in passing this dangerous strait.

Meanwhile Ghent surrendered, and this unexpected success at once rescued the prince from his dilemma. He found in this town everything necessary to complete his bridge of boats; and the only difficulty now was its safe transport, which was furnished by the enemy themselves. By cutting the dams at Saftingen a great part of the country of Waes, as far as the village of Borcht, had been laid under water, so that it was not difficult to cross it with flat-bottomed boats. The prince, therefore, ordered his vessels to run out from Ghent, and after passing Dendermonde and Rupelmonde to pass through the left dyke of the Scheldt, leaving Antwerp to the right, and sail over the inundated fields in the direction of Borcht. To protect this passage a fort was erected at the latter village, which would keep the enemy in check. All succeeded to his wishes, though not without a sharp action with the enemy's flotilla, which was sent out to intercept this convoy. After breaking through a few more dams on their route, they reached the Spanish quarters at Calloo, and successfully entered the Scheldt again. The exultation of the army was greater when they discovered the extent of the danger the vessels had so narrowly escaped. Scarcely had they got quit of the enemy's vessels when a strong reinforcement from Antwerp got under weigh, commanded by the valiant defender of Lillo, Odets von Teligny. When this officer saw that the affair was over, and that the enemy had escaped, he took possession of the dam through which their fleet had passed, and threw up a fort on the spot in order to stop the passage of any vessels from Ghent which might attempt to follow them.

By this step the prince was again thrown into embarrassment. He was far from having as yet a sufficient number of vessels, either for the construction of the bridge or for its defence, and the passage by which the former convoy had arrived was now closed by the fort erected by Teligny. While he was reconnoitring the country to discover a new way for his fleets an idea occurred to him which not only put an end to his present dilemma, but greatly accelerated the success of his whole plan. Not far from the village of Stecken, in Waes, which is within some five thousand paces of the commencement of the inundation, flows a small stream called the Moer, which falls into the Scheldt near Ghent. From this river he caused a canal to be dug to the spot where the inundations began, and as the water of these was not everywhere deep enough for the transit of his boats, the canal between Bevern and Verrebroek was continued to Calloo, where it was met by the Scheldt. At this work five hundred pioneers labored without intermission, and in order to cheer the toil of the soldiers the prince himself took part in it. In this way did he imitate the example of the two celebrated Romans, Drusus and Corbulo, who by similar works had united the Rhine with the Zuyder Zee, and the Maes with the Rhine?

This canal, which the army in honor of its projector called the canal of Parma, was fourteen thousand paces in length, and was of proportionable depth and breadth, so as to be navigable for ships of a considerable burden. It afforded to the vessels from Ghent not only a more secure, but also a much shorter course to the Spanish quarters, because it was no longer necessary to follow the many windings of the Scheldt, but entering the Moer at once near Ghent, and from thence passing close to Stecken, they could proceed through the canal and across the inundated country as far as Calloo. As the produce of all Flanders was brought to the town of Ghent, this canal placed the Spanish camp in communication with the whole province. Abundance poured into the camp from all quarters, so that during the whole course of the siege the Spaniards suffered no scarcity of any kind. But the greatest benefit which the prince derived from this work was an adequate supply of flat-bottomed vessels to complete his bridge.

These preparations were overtaken by the arrival of winter, which, as the Scheldt was filled with drift-ice, occasioned a considerable delay in the building of the bridge. The prince had contemplated with anxiety the approach of this season, lest it should prove highly destructive to the work he had undertaken, and afford the enemy a favorable opportunity for making a serious attack upon it. But the skill of his engineers saved him from the one danger, and the strange inaction of the enemy freed him from the other. It frequently happened, indeed, that at flood-time large pieces of ice were entangled in the timbers, and shook them violently, but they stood the assault of the furious element, which only served to prove their stability.

In Antwerp, meanwhile, important moments had been wasted in futile deliberations; and in a struggle of factions the general welfare was neglected. The government of the town was divided among too many heads, and much too great a share in it was held by the riotous mob to allow room for calmness of deliberation or firmness of action. Besides the municipal magistracy itself, in which the burgomaster had only a single voice, there were in the city a number of guilds, to whom were consigned the charge of the internal and external defence, the provisioning of the town, its fortifications, the marine, commerce, etc.; some of whom must be consulted in every business of importance. By means of this crowd of speakers, who intruded at pleasure into the council, and managed to carry by clamor and the number of their adherents what they could not effect by their arguments, the people obtained a dangerous influence in the public debates, and the natural struggle of such discordant interests retarded the execution of every salutary measure. A government so vacillating and impotent could not command the respect of unruly sailors and a lawless soldiery. The orders of the state consequently were but imperfectly obeyed, and the decisive moment was more than once lost by the negligence, not to say the open mutiny, both of the land and sea forces.

The little harmony in the selection of the means by which the enemy was to be opposed would not, however, have proved so injurious had there but existed unanimity as to the end. But on this very point the wealthy citizens and poorer classes were divided; so the former, having everything to apprehend from allowing matters to be carried to extremity, were strongly inclined to treat with the Prince of Parma. This disposition they did not even attempt to conceal after the fort of Liefkenshoek had fallen into the enemy's hands, and serious fears were entertained for the navigation of the Scheldt. Some of them, indeed, withdrew entirely from the danger, and left to its fate the town, whose prosperity they had been ready enough to share, but in whose adversity they were unwilling to bear a part. From sixty to seventy of those who remained memorialized the council, advising that terms should be made with the king. No sooner, however, had the populace got intelligence of it than their indignation broke out in a violent uproar, which was with difficulty appeased by the imprisonment and fining of the petitioners. Tranquillity could only be fully restored by publication of an edict, which imposed the penalty of death on all who either publicly or privately should countenance proposals for peace.

The Prince of Parma did not fail to take advantage of these disturbances; for nothing that transpired within the city escaped his notice, being well served by the agents with whom he maintained a secret understanding with Antwerp, as well as the other towns of Brabant and Flanders. Although he had already made considerable progress in his measures for distressing the town, still he had many steps to take before he could actually make himself master of it; and one unlucky moment might destroy the work of many months. Without, therefore, neglecting any of his warlike preparations, he determined to make one more serious attempt to get possession by fair means. With this object he despatched a letter in November to the great council of Antwerp, in which he skilfully made use of every topic likely to induce the citizens to come to terms, or at least to increase their existing dissensions. He treated them in this letter in the light of persons who had been led astray, and threw the whole blame of their revolt and refractory conduct hitherto upon the intriguing spirit of the Prince of Orange, from whose artifices the retributive justice of heaven had so lately liberated them. "It was," he said, "now in their power to awake from their long infatuation and return to their allegiance to a monarch who was ready and anxious to be reconciled to his subjects. For this end he gladly offered himself as mediator, as he had never ceased to love a country in which he had been born, and where he had spent the happiest days of his youth. He therefore exhorted them to send plenipotentiaries with whom he could arrange the conditions of peace, and gave them hopes of obtaining reasonable terms if they made a timely submission, but also threatened them with the severest treatment if they pushed matters to extremity."

This letter, in which we are glad to recognize a language very different from that which the Duke of Alva held ten years before on a similar occasion, was answered by the townspeople in a respectful and dignified tone. While they did full justice to the personal character of the prince, and acknowledged his favorable intentions towards them with gratitude, they lamented the hardness of the times, which placed it out of his power to treat them in accordance with his character and disposition. They declared that they would gladly place their fate in his hands if he were absolute master of his actions, instead of being obliged to obey the will of another, whose proceedings his own candor would not allow him to approve of. The unalterable resolution of the King of Spain, as well as the vow which he had made to the pope, were only too well known for them to have any hopes in that quarter. They at the same time defended with a noble warmth the memory of the Prince of Orange, their benefactor and preserver, while they enumerated the true cases which had produced this unhappy war, and had caused the provinces to revolt from the Spanish crown. At the same time they did not disguise from him that they had hopes of finding a new and a milder master in the King of France, and that, if only for this reason, they could not enter into any treaty with the Spanish king without incurring the charge of the most culpable fickleness and ingratitude.

The united provinces, in fact, dispirited by a succession of reverses, had at last come to the determination of placing themselves under the protection and sovereignty of France, and of preserving their existence and their ancient privileges by the sacrifice of their independence. With this view an embassy had some time before been despatched to Paris, and it was the prospect of this powerful assistance which principally supported the courage of the people of Antwerp. Henry III., King of France, was personally disposed to accept this offer; but the troubles which the intrigues of the Spaniards contrived to excite within his own kingdom compelled him against his will to abandon it. The provinces now turned for assistance to Queen Elizabeth of England, who sent them some supplies, which, however, came too late to save Antwerp. While the people of this city were awaiting the issue of these negotiations, and expecting aid from foreign powers, they neglected, unfortunately, the most natural and immediate means of defence; the whole winter was lost, and while the enemy turned it to greater advantage the more complete was their indecision and inactivity.

The burgomaster of Antwerp, St. Aldegonde, had, indeed, repeatedly urged the fleet of Zealand to attack the enemy's works, which should be supported on the other side from Antwerp. The long and frequently stormy nights would favor this attempt, and if at the same time a sally were made by the garrison at Lillo, it seemed scarcely possible for the enemy to resist this triple assault. But unfortunately misunderstandings had arisen between the commander of the fleet, William von Blois von Treslong, and the admiralty of Zealand, which caused the equipment of the fleet to be most unaccountably delayed. In order to quicken their movements Teligny at last resolved to go himself to Middleburg,

were the states of Zealand were assembled; but as the
enemy were in possession of all the roads the attempt cost
him his freedom and the republic its most valiant
defender. However, there was no want of enterprising
vessels, which, under the favor of the night and the flood-
tide, passing through the still open bridge in spite of the
enemy's fire, threw provisions into the town and returned
with the ebb. But as many of these vessels fell into the
hands of the enemy the council gave orders that they
should never risk the passage unless they amounted to a
certain number; and the result, unfortunately, was that
none attempted it because the required number could not
be collected at one time. Several attacks were also made
from Antwerp on the ships of the Spaniards, which were
not entirely unsuccessful; some of the latter were captured, others sunk, and all that was required was to execute similar attempts on a grand scale. But however
zealously St. Aldegonde urged this, still not a captain
was to be found who would command a vessel for that
purpose.

Amid these delays the winter expired, and scarcely had
the ice begun to disappear when the construction of the
bridge of boats was actively resumed by the besiegers.
Between the two piers a space of more than six hundred
paces still remained to be filled up, which was effected in
the following manner: Thirty-two flat-bottomed vessels,
each sixty-six feet long and twenty broad, were fastened
together with strong cables and iron chains, but at a distance from each other of about twenty feet to allow a
free passage to the stream. Each boat, moreover, was
moored with two cables, both up and down the stream,
but which, as the water rose with the tide, or sunk with
the ebb, could be slackened or tightened. Upon the
boats great masts were laid which reached from one to
another, and, being covered with planks, formed a regular
road, which, like that along the piers, was protected with
a balustrade. This bridge of boats, of which the two piers
formed a continuation, had, including the latter, a length
of twenty-four thousand paces. This formidable work
was so ingeniously constructed, and so richly furnished
with the instruments of destruction, that it seemed almost

capable, like a living creature, of defending itself at the word of command, scattering death among all who approached. Besides the two forts of St. Maria and St. Philip, which terminated the bridge on either shore, and the two wooden bastions on the bridge itself, which were filled with soldiers and mounted with guns on all sides, each of the two-and-thirty vessels was manned with thirty soldiers and four sailors, and showed the cannon's mouth to the enemy, whether he came up from Zealand or down from Antwerp. There were in all ninety-seven cannon, which were distributed beneath and above the bridge, and more than fifteen hundred men who were posted, partly in the forts, partly in the vessels, and, in case of necessity, could maintain a terrible fire of small-arms upon the enemy.

But with all this the prince did not consider his work sufficiently secure. It was to be expected that the enemy would leave nothing unattempted to burst by the force of his machines the middle and weakest part. To guard against this, he erected in a line with the bridge of boats, but at some distance from it, another distinct defence, intended to break the force of any attack that might be directed against the bridge itself. This work consisted of thirty-three vessels of considerable magnitude, which were moored in a row athwart the stream and fastened in threes by masts, so that they formed eleven different groups. Each of these, like a file of pikemen, presented fourteen long wooden poles with iron heads to the approaching enemy. These vessels were loaded merely with ballast, and were anchored each by a double but slack cable, so as to be able to give to the rise and fall of the tide. As they were in constant motion they got from the soldiers the name of "swimmers." The whole bridge of boats and also a part of the piers were covered by these swimmers, which were stationed above as well as below the bridge. To all these defensive preparations was added a fleet of forty men-of-war, which were stationed on both coasts and served as a protection to the whole.

This astonishing work was finished in March, 1585, the seventh month of the siege, and the day on which it was completed was kept as a jubilee by the troops. The great event was announced to the besieged by a grand *feu de joie*, and the army, as if to enjoy ocular demonstration of its triumph, extended itself along the whole platform to gaze upon the proud stream, peacefully and obediently flowing under the yoke which had been imposed upon it. All the toil they had undergone was forgotten in the delightful spectacle, and every man who had had a hand in it, however insignificant he might be, assumed to himself a portion of the honor which the successful execution of so gigantic an enterprise conferred on its illustrious projector. On the other hand, nothing could equal the consternation which seized the citizens of Antwerp when intelligence was brought them that the Scheldt was now actually closed, and all access from Zealand cut off. To increase their dismay they learned the fall of Brussels also, which had at last been compelled by famine to capitulate. An attempt made by the Count of Hohenlohe about the same time on Herzogenbusch, with a view to recapture the town, or at least form a diversion, was equally unsuccessful; and thus the unfortunate city lost all hope of assistance, both by sea and land.

These evil tidings were brought them by some fugitives who had succeeded in passing the Spanish videttes, and had made their way into the town; and a spy, whom the burgomaster had sent out to reconnoitre the enemy's works, increased the general alarm by his report. He had been seized and carried before the Prince of Parma, who commanded him to be conducted over all the works, and all the defences of the bridge to be pointed out to him. After this had been done he was again brought before the general, who dismissed him with these words: "Go," said he, "and report what you have seen to those who sent you. And tell them, too, that it is my firm resolve to bury myself under the ruins of this bridge or by means of it to pass into your town."

But the certainty of danger now at last awakened the zeal of the confederates, and it was no fault of theirs if the former half of the prince's vow was not fulfilled. The latter had long viewed with apprehension the preparations which were making in Zealand for the relief of the town. He saw clearly that it was from this quarter that he had to fear the most dangerous blow, and that with all his works he could not make head against the combined fleets of Zealand and Antwerp if they were to fall upon him at the same time and at the proper moment. For a while the delays of the admiral of Zealand, which he had labored by all the means in his power to prolong, had been his security, but now the urgent necessity accelerated the expedition, and without waiting for the admiral the states at Middleburg despatched the Count Justin of Nassau, with as many ships as they could muster, to the assistance of the besieged. This fleet took up a position before Liefkenshoek, which was in possession of the Spaniards, and, supported by a few vessels from the opposite fort of Lillo, cannonaded it with such success that the walls were in a short time demolished, and the place carried by storm. The Walloons who formed the garrison did not display the firmness which might have been expected from soldiers of the Duke of Parma; they shamefully surrendered the fort to the enemy, who in a short time were in possession of the whole island of Doel, with all the redoubts situated upon it. The loss of these places, which were, however, soon retaken, incensed the Duke of Parma so much that he tried the officers by court-martial, and caused the most culpable among them to be beheaded. Meanwhile this important conquest opened to the Zealanders a free passage as far as the bridge, and after concerting with the people of Antwerp the time was fixed for a combined attack on this work. It was arranged that, while the bridge of boats was blown up by machines already prepared in Antwerp, the Zealand fleet, with a sufficient supply of provisions, should be in the vicinity, ready to sail to the town through the opening.

While the Duke of Parma was engaged in constructing his bridge an engineer within the walls was already preparing the materials for its destruction. Frederick Gianibelli was the name of the man whom fate had destined to be the Archimedes of Antwerp, and to exhaust in its defence the same ingenuity with the same want of success. He was born in Mantua, and had formerly visited Madrid for the purpose, it was said, of offering his services to King Philip in the Belgian war. But wearied with waiting the offended engineer left the court with the intention of making the King of Spain sensibly feel the value of talents which he had so little known how to appreciate. He next sought the service of Queen Elizabeth of England, the declared enemy of Spain, who, after witnessing a few specimens of his skill, sent him to Antwerp. He took up his residence in that town, and in the present extremity devoted to its defence his knowledge, his energy, and his zeal.

As soon as this artist perceived that the project of erecting the bridge was seriously intended, and that the work was fast approaching to completion, he applied to the magistracy for three large vessels, from a hundred and fifty to five hundred tons, in which he proposed to place mines. He also demanded sixty boats, which, fastened together with cables and chains, furnished with projecting grappling-irons, and put in motion with the ebbing of the tide, were intended to second the operation of the mine-ships by being directed in a wedgelike form against the bridge. But he had to deal with men who were quite incapable of comprehending an idea out of the common way, and even where the salvation of their country was at stake could not forget the calculating habits of trade.

His scheme was rejected as too expensive, and with difficulty he at last obtained the grant of two smaller vessels, from seventy to eighty tons, with a number of flat-bottomed boats. With these two vessels, one of which he called the "Fortune" and the other the "Hope," he proceeded in the following manner: In the hold of each he built a hollow chamber of freestone, five feet broad, three and a half high, and forty long. This magazine he filled with sixty hundredweight of the finest priming powder of his own compounding, and covered it with as heavy a weight of large slabs and millstones as the vessels could carry. Over these he further added a roof of similar stones, which ran up to a point and projected six feet above the ship's side. The deck itself was crammed with iron chains and hooks, knives, nails, and other destructive missiles; the remaining space, which was not occupied by the magazine, was likewise filled up with planks. Several small apertures were left in the chamber for the matches which were to set fire to the mine. For greater certainty he had also contrived a piece of mechanism which, after the lapse of a given time, would strike out sparks, and even if the matches failed would set the ship on fire. To delude the enemy into a belief that these machines were only intended to set the bridge on fire, a composition of brimstone and pitch was placed in the top, which could burn a whole hour. And still further to divert the enemy's attention from the proper seat of danger, he also prepared thirty-two flat-bottomed boats, upon which there were only fireworks burning, and whose sole object was to deceive the enemy. These fire-ships were to be sent down upon the bridge in four separate squadrons, at intervals of half an hour, and keep the enemy incessantly engaged for two whole hours, so that, tired of firing and wearied by vain expectation, they might at last relax their vigilance before the real fire-ships came. In addition to all this he also despatched a few vessels in which powder was concealed in order to blow up the floating work before the bridge, and to clear a passage for the two principal ships. At the same time he hoped by this preliminary attack to engage the enemy's attention, to draw them out, and expose them to the full deadly effect of the volcano.

The night between the 4th and 5th of April was fixed for the execution of this great undertaking. An obscure rumor of it had already diffused itself through the Spanish camp, and particularly from the circumstance of many divers from Antwerp having been detected endeavoring to cut the cables of the vessels. They were prepared, therefore, for a serious attack; they only mistook the real nature of it, and counted on having to fight rather with man than the elements. In this expectation the duke caused the guards along the whole bank to be doubled, and drew up the chief part of his troops in the vicinity of the bridge, where he was present in person; thus meeting the danger while endeavoring to avoid it.

No sooner was it dark than three burning vessels were seen to float down from the city towards the bridge, then three more, and directly after the same number. They beat to arms throughout the Spanish camp, and the whole length of the bridge was crowded with soldiers. Meantime the number of the fire-ships increased, and they came in regular order down the stream, sometimes two and sometimes three abreast, being at first steered by sailors on board them. The admiral of the Antwerp fleet, Jacob Jacobson (whether designedly or through carelessness is not known), had committed the error of sending off the four squadrons of fire-ships too quickly one after another, and caused the two large mine-ships also to follow them too soon, and thus disturbed the intended order of attack.

The array of vessels kept approaching, and the darkness of night still further heightened the extraordinary spectacle. As far as the eye could follow the course of the stream all was fire; the fire-ships burning as brilliantly as if they were themselves in the flames; the surface of the water glittered with light; the dykes and the batteries along the shore, the flags, arms, and accoutrements of the soldiers who lined the rivers as well as the bridges were clearly distinguishable in the glare. With a mingled sensation of awe and pleasure the soldiers watched the unusual sight, which rather resembled a *fête* than a hostile preparation, but from the very strangeness of the contrast filled the mind with a mysterious awe. When the burning fleet had come within two thousand paces of the bridge those who had the charge of it lighted the matches, impelled the two mine-vessels into the middle of the stream, and leaving the others to the guidance of the current of the waves, they hastily made their escape in boats which had been kept in readiness.

Their course, however, was irregular, and destitute of steersmen they arrived singly and separately at the floating works, where they continued hanging or were dashed off sidewise on the shore. The foremost powder-ships, which were intended to set fire to the floating works, were cast, by the force of a squall which arose at that instant, on the Flemish coast. One of the two, the " Fortune," grounded in its passage before it reached the bridge, and killed by its explosion some Spanish soldiers who were at work in a neighboring battery. The other and larger fire-ship, called the "Hope," narrowly escaped a similar fate. The current drove her against the floating defences towards the Flemish bank, where it remained hanging, and had it taken fire at that moment the greatest part of its effect would have been lost. Deceived by the flames which this machine, like the other vessels, emitted, the Spaniards took it for a common fire-ship, intended to burn the bridge of boats. And as they had seen them extinguished one after the other without further effect all fears were dispelled, and the Spaniards began to ridicule the preparations of the enemy, which had been ushered in with so much display and now had so absurd an end. Some of the boldest threw themselves into the stream in order to get a close view of the fire-ship and extinguish it, when by its weight it suddenly broke through, burst the floating work which had detained it, and drove with terrible force on the bridge of boats. All was now in commotion on the bridge, and the prince called to the sailors to keep the vessel off with poles, and to extinguish the flames before they caught the timbers.

At this critical moment he was standing at the farthest end of the left pier, where it formed a bastion in the water and joined the bridge of boats. By his side stood the Margrave of Rysburg, general of cavalry and governor of the province of Artois, who had formerly served the states, but from a protector of the republic had become its worst enemy; the Baron of Billy, governor of Friesland and commander of the German regiments; the Generals Cajetan and Guasto, with several of the principal officers; all forgetful of their own danger and entirely occupied with averting the general calamity. At this moment a Spanish ensign approached the Prince of Parma and conjured him to remove from a place where his life was in manifest and imminent peril. No attention being paid to his entreaty he repeated it still more urgently, and at last fell at his feet and implored him in this one instance to take advice from his servant. While he said this he had laid hold of the duke's coat as though

he wished forcibly to draw him away from the spot, and
the latter, surprised rather at the man's boldness than
persuaded by his arguments, retired at last to the shore,
attended by Cajetan and Guasto. He had scarcely time
to reach the fort St. Maria at the end of the bridge when
an explosion took place behind him, just as if the earth
had burst or the vault of heaven given way. The duke
and his whole army fell to the ground as dead, and
several minutes elapsed before they recovered their consciousness.

But then what a sight presented itself! The waters of
the Scheldt had been divided to its lowest depth, and
driven with a surge which rose like a wall above the dam
that confined it, so that all the fortifications on the banks
were several feet under water. The earth shook for three
miles round. Nearly the whole left pier, on which the
fire-ship had been driven, with a part of the bridge of
boats, had been burst and shattered to atoms, with all
that was upon it; spars, cannon, and men blown into the
air. Even the enormous blocks of stone which had
covered the mine had, by the force of the explosion, been
hurled into the neighboring fields, so that many of them
were afterwards dug out of the ground at a distance of a
thousand paces from the bridge. Six vessels were buried,
several had gone to pieces. But still more terrible was
the carnage which the murderous machine had dealt
amongst the soldiers. Five hundred, according to other
reports even eight hundred, were sacrificed to its fury,
without reckoning those who escaped with mutilated or
injured bodies. The most opposite kinds of death were
combined in this frightful moment. Some were consumed by the flames of the explosion, others scalded to
death by the boiling water of the river, others stifled
by the poisonous vapor of the brimstone; some were
drowned in the stream, some buried under the hail of
falling masses of rock, many cut to pieces by the knives
and hooks, or shattered by the balls which were poured
from the bowels of the machine. Some were found lifeless without any visible injury, having in all probability
been killed by the mere concussion of the air. The spectacle which presented itself directly after the firing of the

mine was fearful. Men were seen wedged between the palisades of the bridge, or struggling to release themselves from beneath ponderous masses of rock, or hanging in the rigging of the ships; and from all places and quarters the most heartrending cries for help arose, but as each was absorbed in his own safety these could only be answered by helpless wailings.

Many had escaped in the most wonderful manner. An officer named Tucci was carried by the whirlwind like a feather high into the air, where he was for a moment suspended, and then dropped into the river, where he saved himself by swimming. Another was taken up by the force of the blast from the Flanders shore and deposited on that of Brabant, incurring merely a slight contusion on the shoulder; he felt, as he afterwards said, during this rapid aerial transit, just as if he had been fired out of a cannon. The Prince of Parma himself had never been so near death as at that moment, when half a minute saved his life. He had scarcely set foot in the fort of St. Maria when he was lifted off his feet as if by a hurricane, and a beam which struck him on the head and shoulders stretched him senseless on the earth. For a long time he was believed to be actually killed, many remembering to have seen him on the bridge only a few minutes before the fatal explosion. He was found at last between his attendants, Cajetan and Guasto, raising himself up with his hand on his sword; and the intelligence stirred the spirits of the whole army. But vain would be the attempt to depict his feelings when he surveyed the devastation which a single moment had caused in the work of so many months. The bridge of boats, upon which all his hopes rested, was rent asunder; a great part of his army was destroyed; another portion maimed and rendered ineffective for many days; many of his best officers were killed; and, as if the present calamity were not sufficient, he had now to learn the painful intelligence that the Margrave of Rysburg, whom of all his officers he prized the highest, was missing. And yet the worst was still to come, for every moment the fleets of the enemy were to be expected from Antwerp and Lillo, to which this fearful position of the army would disable him from offering any effectual resistance. The bridge was entirely destroyed, and nothing could prevent the fleet from Zealand passing through in full sail; while the confusion of the troops in this first moment was so great and general that it would have been impossible to give or obey orders, as many corps had lost their commanding officers, and many commanders their corps; and even the places where they had been stationed were no longer to be recognized amid the general ruin. Add to this that all the batteries on shore were under water, that several cannon were sunk, that the matches were wet, and the ammunition damaged. What a moment for the enemy if they had known how to avail themselves of it!

It will scarcely be believed, however, that this success, which surpassed all expectation, was lost to Antwerp, simply because nothing was known of it. St. Aldegonde, indeed, as soon as the explosion of the mine was heard in the town, had sent out several galleys in the direction of the bridge, with orders to send up fire-balls and rockets the moment they had passed it, and then to sail with the intelligence straight on to Lillo, in order to bring up, without delay, the Zealand fleet, which had orders to co-operate. At the same time the admiral of Antwerp was ordered, as soon as the signal was given, to sail out with his vessels and attack the enemy in their first consternation. But although a considerable reward was promised to the boatmen sent to reconnoitre they did not venture near the enemy, but returned without effecting their purpose, and reported that the bridge of boats was uninjured, and the fire-ship had had no effect. Even on the following day also no better measures were taken to learn the true state of the bridge; and as the fleet at Lillo, in spite of the favorable wind, was seen to remain inactive, the belief that the fire-ships had accomplished nothing was confirmed. It did not seem to occur to any one that this very inactivity of the confederates, which misled the people of Antwerp, might also keep back the Zealanders at Lillo, as in fact it did. So signal an instance of neglect could only have occurred in a government, which, without dignity of independence, was guided by the tumultuous multitude it ought to have governed. The more supine, however, they were themselves in opposing the enemy, the more violently did their rage boil against Gianibelli, whom the frantic mob would have torn in pieces if they could have caught him. For two days the engineer was in the most imminent danger, until at last, on the third morning, a courier from Lillo, who had swam under the bridge, brought authentic intelligence of its having been destroyed, but at the same time announced that it had been repaired.

This rapid restoration of the bridge was really a miraculous effort of the Prince of Parma. Scarcely had he recovered from the shock, which seemed to have overthrown all his plans, when he contrived, with wonderful presence of mind, to prevent all its evil consequences. The absence of the enemy's fleet at this decisive moment revived his hopes. The ruinous state of the bridge appeared to be a secret to them, and though it was impossible to repair in a few hours the work of so many months, yet a great point would be gained if it could be done even in appearance. All his men were immediately set to work to remove the ruins, to raise the timbers which had been thrown down, to replace those which were demolished, and to fill up the chasms with ships. The duke himself did not refuse to share in the toil, and his example was followed by all his officers. Stimulated by this popular behavior, the common soldiers exerted themselves to the utmost; the work was carried on during the whole night under the constant sounding of drums and trumpets, which were distributed along the bridge to drown the noise of the work-people. With dawn of day few traces remained of the night's havoc; and although the bridge was restored only in appearance, it nevertheless deceived the spy, and consequently no attack was made upon it. In the meantime the prince contrived to make the repairs solid, nay, even to introduce some essential alterations in the structure. In order to guard against similar accidents for the future, a part of the bridge of boats was made movable, so that in case of necessity it could be taken away and a passage opened to the fire-ships. His loss of men was supplied from the garrisons of the adjoining places, and by a German regiment which arrived very opportunely from Gueldres. He filled up the vacancies of the officers who were killed, and in doing this he did not forget the Spanish ensign who had saved his life.

The people of Antwerp, after learning the success of their mine-ship, now did homage to the inventor with as much extravagance as they had a short time before mistrusted him, and they encouraged his genius to new attempts. Gianibelli now actually obtained the number of flat-bottomed vessels which he had at first demanded in vain, and these he equipped in such a manner that they struck with irresistible force on the bridge, and a second time also burst and separated it. But this time, the wind was contrary to the Zealand fleet, so that they could not put out, and thus the prince obtained once more the necessary respite to repair the damage. The Archimedes of Antwerp was not deterred by any of these disappointments. Anew he fitted out two large vessels which were armed with iron hooks and similar instruments in order to tear asunder the bridge. But when the moment came for these vessels to get under weigh no one was found ready to embark in them. The engineer was therefore obliged to think of a plan for giving to these machines such a self-impulse that, without being guided by a steersman, they would keep the middle of the stream, and not, like the former ones, be driven on the bank by the wind. One of his workmen, a German, here hit upon a strange invention, if Strada's description of it is to be credited. He affixed a sail under the vessel, which was to be acted upon by the water, just as an ordinary sail is by the wind, and could thus impel the ship with the whole force of the current. The result proved the correctness of his calculation; for this vessel, with the position of its sails reversed, not only kept the centre of the stream, but also ran against the bridge with such impetuosity that the enemy had not time to open it and was actually burst asunder. But all these results were of no service to the town, because the attempts were made at random and were supported by no adequate force. A new fire-ship, equipped like the former, which had succeeded so well, and which Gianibelli had filled with four thousand pounds of the finest powder was not even used; for a new mode of attempting their deliverance had now occurred to the people of Antwerp.

Terrified by so many futile attempts from endeavoring to clear a passage for vessels on the river by force, they at last came to the determination of doing without the stream entirely. They remembered the example of the town of Leyden, which, when besieged by the Spaniards ten years before, had saved itself by opportunely inundating the surrounding country, and it was resolved to imitate this example. Between Lillo and Stabroek, in the district of Bergen, a wide and somewhat sloping plain extends as far as Antwerp, being protected by numerous embankments and counter-embankments against the irruptions of the East Scheldt. Nothing more was requisite than to break these dams, when the whole plain would become a sea, navigable by flat-bottomed vessels almost to the very walls of Antwerp. If this attempt should succeed, the Duke of Parma might keep the Scheldt guarded with his bridge of boats as long as he pleased; a new river would be formed, which, in case of necessity, would be equally serviceable for the time. This was the very plan which the Prince of Orange had at the commencement of the siege recommended, and in which he had been strenuously, but unsuccessfully, seconded by St. Aldegonde, because some of the citizens could not be persuaded to sacrifice their own fields. In the present emergency they reverted to this last resource, but circumstances in the meantime had greatly changed.

The plain in question is intersected by a broad and high dam, which takes its name from the adjacent Castle of Cowenstein, and extends for three miles from the village of Stabroek, in Bergen, as far as the Scheldt, with the great dam of which it unites near Ordam. Beyond this dam no vessels can proceed, however high the tide, and the sea would be vainly turned into the fields as long as such an embankment remained in the way, which would prevent the Zealand vessels from descending into the plain before Antwerp. The fate of the town would therefore depend upon the demolition of this Cowenstein dam; but, foreseeing this, the Prince of Parma had, immediately on commencing the blockade, taken possession of it, and spared no pains to render it tenable to the last. At the village of Stabroek, Count Mansfeld was encamped with the greatest part of his army, and by means of this very Cowenstein dam kept open the communication with the bridge, the headquarters, and the Spanish magazines at Calloo. Thus the army formed an uninterrupted line from Stabroek in Brabant, as far as Bevern in Flanders, intersected indeed, but not broken by the Scheldt, and which could not be cut off without a sanguinary conflict. On the dam itself within proper distances five different batteries had been erected, the command of which was given to the most valiant officers in the army. Nay, as the Prince of Parma could not doubt that now the whole fury of the war would be turned to this point, he entrusted the defence of the bridge to Count Mansfeld, and resolved to defend this important post himself. The war, therefore, now assumed a different aspect, and the theatre of it was entirely changed.

Both above and below Lillo, the Netherlanders had in several places cut through the dam, which follows the Brabant shore of the Scheldt; and where a short time before had been green fields, a new element now presented itself, studded with masts and boats. A Zealand fleet, commanded by Count Hohenlohe, navigated the inundated fields, and made repeated movements against the Cowenstein dam, without, however, attempting a serious attack on it, while another fleet showed itself in the Scheldt, threatening the two coasts alternately with a landing, and occasionally the bridge of boats with an attack. For several days this manœuvre was practised on the enemy, who, uncertain of the quarter whence an attack was to be expected, would, it was hoped, be exhausted by continual watching, and by degrees lulled into security by so many false alarms. Antwerp had promised Count Hohenlohe to support the attack on the dam by a flotilla from the town; three beacons on the principal tower were to be the signal that this was on the way. When, therefore, on a dark night the expected columns of fire really ascended above Antwerp, Count Hohenlohe immediately caused five hundred of his troops to scale the dam between two of the enemy's redoubts, who surprised part of the Spanish garrison asleep, and cut down the others who attempted to defend themselves. In a short time they had gained a firm footing upon the dam, and were just on the point of disembarking the remainder of their force, two thousand in number, when the Spaniards in the adjoining redoubts marched out and, favored by the narrowness of the ground, made a desperate attack on the crowded Zealanders. The guns from the neighboring batteries opened upon the approaching fleet, and thus rendered the landing of the remaining troops impossible; and as there were no signs of co-operation on the part of the city, the Zealanders were overpowered after a short conflict and again driven down from the dam. The victorious Spaniards pursued them through the water as far as their boats, sunk many of the latter, and compelled the rest to retreat with heavy loss. Count Hohenlohe threw the blame of this defeat upon the inhabitants of Antwerp, who had deceived him by a false signal, and it certainly must be attributed to the bad arrangement of both parties that the attempt failed of better success.

But at last the allies determined to make a systematic assault on the enemy with their combined force, and to put an end to the siege by a grand attack as well on the dam as on the bridge. The 16th of May, 1585, was fixed upon for the execution of this design, and both armies used their utmost endeavors to make this day decisive. The force of the Hollanders and Zealanders, united to that of Antwerp, exceeded two hundred ships, to man which they had stripped their towns and citadels, and with this force they purposed to attack the Cowenstein dam on both sides. The bridge over the Scheldt was to be assailed with new machines of Gianibelli's invention, and the Duke of Parma thereby hindered from assisting the defence of the dam.

Alexander, apprised of the danger which threatened him, spared nothing on his side to meet it with energy. Immediately after getting possession of the dam he had caused redoubts to be erected at five different places, and had given the command of them to the most experienced officers of the army. The first of these, which was called the Cross battery, was erected on the spot where the Cowenstein dam enters the great embankment of the Scheldt, and makes with the latter the form of a cross; the Spaniard, Mondragone, was appointed to the command of this battery. A thousand paces farther on, near the castle of Cowenstein, was posted the battery of St. James, which was entrusted to the command of Camillo di Monte. At an equal distance from this lay the battery of St. George, and at a thousand paces from the latter, the Pile battery, under the command of Gamboa, so called from the pile-work on which it rested; at the farthest end of the dam, near Stabroek, was the fifth redoubt, where Count Mansfeld, with Capizucchi, an Italian, commanded. All these forts the prince now strengthened with artillery and men; on both sides of the dam, and along its whole extent, he caused piles to be driven, as well to render the main embankment firmer, as to impede the labor of the pioneers, who were to dig through it.

Early on the morning of the 16th of May the enemy's forces were in motion. With the dusk of dawn there came floating down from Lillo, over the inundated country, four burning vessels, which so alarmed the guards upon the dams, who recollected the former terrible explosion, that they hastily retreated to the next battery. This was exactly what the enemy desired. In these vessels, which had merely the appearance of fire-ships, soldiers were concealed, who now suddenly jumped ashore, and succeeded in mounting the dam at the undefended spot, between the St. George and Pile batteries. Immediately afterward the whole Zealand fleet showed itself, consisting of numerous ships-of-war, transports, and a crowd of smaller craft, which were laden with great sacks of earth, wool, fascines, gabions, and the like, for throwing up breastworks wherever necessary. The ships-of-war were furnished with powerful artillery, and numerously and bravely manned, and a whole army of pioneers accompanied it in order to dig through the dam as soon as it should be in their possession.

The Zealanders had scarcely begun on their side to ascend the dam when the fleet of Antwerp advanced from Osterweel and attacked it on the other. A high breastwork was hastily thrown up between the two nearest hostile batteries, so as at once to divide the two garrisons and to cover the pioneers. The latter, several hundreds in number, now fell to work with their spades on both sides of the dam, and dug with such energy that hopes were entertained of soon seeing the two seas united. But meanwhile the Spaniards also had gained time to hasten to the spot from the two nearest redoubts, and make a spirited assault, while the guns from the battery of St. George played incessantly on the enemy's fleet. A furious battle now raged in the quarter where they were cutting through the dike and throwing up the breastworks. The Zealanders had drawn a strong line of troops round the pioneers to keep the enemy from interrupting their work, and in this confusion of battle, in the midst of a storm of bullets from the enemy, often up to the breast in water, among the dead and dying, the pioneers pursued their work, under the incessant exhortations of the merchants, who impatiently waited to see the dam opened and their vessels in safety. The importance of the result, which it might be said depended entirely upon their spades, appeared to animate even the common laborers with heroic courage. Solely intent upon their task, they neither saw nor heard the work of death which was going on around them, and as fast as the foremost ranks fell those behind them pressed into their places. Their operations were greatly impeded by the piles which had been driven in, but still more by the attacks of the Spaniards, who burst with desperate courage through the thickest of the enemy, stabbed the pioneers in the pits where they were digging, and filled up again with dead bodies the cavities which the living had made. At last, however, when most of their officers were killed or wounded, and the number of the enemy constantly increasing, while fresh laborers were supplying the place of those who had been slain, the courage of these valiant troops began to give way, and they thought it advisable to retreat to their batteries. Now, therefore, the confederates saw themselves masters of the whole extent of the dam, from Fort St. George as far as

the Pile battery. As, however, it seemed too long to
wait for the thorough demolition of the dam, they hastily
unloaded a Zealand transport, and brought the cargo
over the dam to a vessel of Antwerp, with which Count
Hohenlohe sailed in triumph to that city. The sight of
the provisions at once filled the inhabitants with joy, and
as if the victory was already won, they gave themselves
up to the wildest exultation. The bells were rung, the
cannon discharged, and the inhabitants, transported by
their unexpected success, hurried to the Osterweel gate,
to await the store-ships which were supposed to be at
hand.

In fact, fortune had never smiled so favorably on the
besieged as at that moment. The enemy, exhausted and
dispirited, had thrown themselves into their batteries,
and, far from being able to struggle with the victors for
the post they had conquered, they found themselves
rather besieged in the places where they had taken refuge. Some companies of Scots, led by their brave
colonel, Balfour, attacked the battery of St. George,
which, however, was relieved, but not without severe
loss, by Camillo di Monte, who hastened thither from
St. James' battery. The Pile battery was in a much
worse condition, it being hotly cannonaded by the ships,
and threatened every moment to crumble to pieces. Gamboa, who commanded it, lay wounded, and it was unfortunately deficient in artillery to keep the enemy at a
distance. The breastwork, too, which the Zealanders
had thrown up between this battery and that of St.
George cut off all hope of assistance from the Scheldt.
If, therefore, the Belgians had only taken advantage of
this weakness and inactivity of the enemy to proceed
with zeal and perseverance in cutting through the dam,
there is no doubt that a passage might have been made,
and thus put an end to the whole siege. But here also
the same want of consistent energy showed itself which
had marked the conduct of the people of Antwerp during the whole course of the siege. The zeal with which
the work had been commenced cooled in proportion to
the success which attended it. It was soon found too
tedious to dig through the dyke; it seemed far easier to

transfer the cargoes from the large store-ships into smaller ones, and carry these to the town with the flood tide. St. Aldegonde and Hohenlohe, instead of remaining to animate the industry of the workmen by their personal presence, left the scene of action at the decisive moment, in order, by sailing to the town with a corn vessel, to win encomiums on their wisdom and valor.

While both parties were fighting on the dam with the most obstinate fury the bridge over the Scheldt had been attacked from Antwerp with new machines, in order to give employment to the prince in that quarter. But the sound of the firing soon apprised him of what was going on at the dyke, and as soon as he saw the bridge clear he hastened to support the defence of the dyke. Followed by two hundred Spanish pikemen, he flew to the place of attack, and arrived just in time to prevent the complete defeat of his troops. He hastily posted some guns which he had brought with him in the two nearest redoubts, and maintained from thence a heavy fire upon the enemy's ships. He placed himself at the head of his men, and, with his sword in one hand and shield in the other, led them against the enemy. The news of his arrival, which quickly spread from one end of the dyke to the other, revived the drooping spirits of his troops, and the conflict recommenced with renewed violence, made still more murderous by the nature of the ground where it was fought. Upon the narrow ridge of the dam, which in many places was not more than nine paces broad, about five thousand combatants were fighting; so confined was the spot upon which the strength of both armies was assembled, and which was to decide the whole issue of the siege. With the Antwerpers the last bulwark of their city was at stake; with the Spaniards it was to determine the whole success of their undertaking. Both parties fought with a courage which despair alone could inspire. From both the extremities of the dam the tide of war rolled itself towards the centre, where the Zealanders and Antwerpers had the advantage, and where they had collected their whole strength. The Italians and Spaniards, inflamed by a noble emulation, pressed on from Stabroek; and from the Scheldt the

Walloons and Spaniards advanced, with their general at their head. While the former endeavored to relieve the Pile battery, which was hotly pressed by the enemy, both by sea and land, the latter threw themselves on the breastwork, between the St. George and the Pile batteries, with a fury which carried everything before it. Here the flower of the Belgian troops fought behind a well-fortified rampart, and the guns of the two fleets covered this important post. The prince was already pressing forward to attack this formidable defence with his small army when he received intelligence that the Italians and Spaniards, under Capizucchi and Aquila, had forced their way, sword in hand, into the Pile battery, had got possession of it, and were now likewise advancing from the other side against the enemy's breastwork. Before this intrenchment, therefore, the whole force of both armies was now collected, and both sides used their utmost efforts to carry and to defend this position. The Netherlanders on board the fleet, loath to remain idle spectators of the conflict, sprang ashore from their vessels. Alexander attacked the breastwork on one side, Count Mansfeld on the other; five assaults were made, and five times they were repulsed. The Netherlanders in this decisive moment surpassed themselves; never in the whole course of the war had they fought with such determination. But it was the Scotch and English in particular who baffled the attempts of the enemy by their valiant resistance. As no one would advance to the attack in the quarter where the Scotch fought, the duke himself led on the troops, with a javelin in his hand, and up to his breast in water. At last, after a protracted struggle, the forces of Count Mansfeld succeeded with their halberds and pikes in making a breach in the breastwork, and by raising themselves on one another's shoulders scaled the parapet. Barthelemy Toralva, a Spanish captain, was the first who showed himself on the top; and almost at the same instant the Italian, Capizucchi, appeared upon the edge of it; and thus the contest of valor was decided with equal glory for both nations. It is worth while to notice here the manner in which the Prince of Parma, who was made arbiter of this emulous strife, encouraged this delicate sense of honor among his warriors. He embraced the Italian, Capizucchi, in presence of the troops, and acknowledged aloud that it was principally to the courage of this officer that he owed the capture of the breastwork. He caused the Spanish captain, Toralva, who was dangerously wounded, to be conveyed to his own quarters at Stabroek, laid on his own bed, and covered with the cloak which he himself had worn the day before the battle.

After the capture of the breastwork the victory no longer remained doubtful. The Dutch and Zealand troops, who had disembarked to come to close action with the enemy, at once lost their courage when they looked about them and saw the vessels, which were their last refuge, putting off from the shore.

For the tide had begun to ebb, and the commanders of the fleet, from fear of being stranded with their heavy transports, and, in case of an unfortunate issue to the engagement, becoming the prey of the enemy, retired from the dam, and made for deep water. No sooner did Alexander perceive this than he pointed out to his troops the flying vessels, and encouraged them to finish the action with an enemy who already despaired of their safety. The Dutch auxiliaries were the first that gave way, and their example was soon followed by the Zealanders. Hastily leaping from the dam they endeavored to reach the vessels by wading or swimming; but from their disorderly flight they impeded one another, and fell in heaps under the swords of the pursuers. Many perished even in the boats, as each strove to get on board before the other, and several vessels sank under the weight of the numbers who rushed into them. The Antwerpers, who fought for their liberty, their hearths, their faith, were the last who retreated, but this very circumstance augmented their disaster. Many of their vessels were outstripped by the ebb-tide, and grounded within reach of the enemy's cannon, and were consequently destroyed with all on board. Crowds of fugitives endeavored by swimming to gain the other transports, which had got into deep water; but such was the rage and boldness of the Spaniards that they swam after them with their swords between their teeth, and dragged many even from the ships. The victory of the king's troops was complete· but bloody; for of the Spaniards about eight hundred, of the Netherlanders some thousands (without reckoning those who were drowned), were left on the field, and on both sides many of the principal nobility perished. More than thirty vessels, with a large supply of provisions for Antwerp, fell into the hands of the victors, with one hundred and fifty cannon and other military stores. The dam, the possession of which had been so dearly maintained, was pierced in thirteen different places, and the bodies of those who had cut through it were now used to stop up the openings.

The following day a transport of immense size and singular construction fell into the hands of the royalists. It formed a floating castle, and had been destined for the attack on the Cowenstein dam. The people of Antwerp had built it at an immense expense at the very time when the engineer Gianibelli's useful proposals had been rejected on account of the cost they entailed, and this ridiculous monster was called by the proud title of "End of the War," which appellation was afterwards changed for the more appropriate sobriquet of "Money lost!" When this vessel was launched it turned out, as every sensible person had foretold, that on account of its unwieldly size it was utterly impossible to steer it, and it could hardly be floated by the highest tide. With great difficulty it was worked as far as Ordam, where, deserted by the tide, it went aground, and fell a prey to the enemy.

The attack upon the Cowenstein dam was the last attempt which was made to relieve Antwerp. From this time the courage of the besieged sank, and the magistracy of the town vainly labored to inspirit with distant hopes the lower orders, on whom the present distress weighed heaviest. Hitherto the price of bread had been kept down to a tolerable rate, although the quality of it continued to deteriorate; by degrees, however, provisions became so scarce that a famine was evidently near at hand. Still hopes were entertained of being able to hold out, at least until the corn between the town and the farthest batteries, which was already in full ear, could be reaped; but before that could be done the enemy had carried the last outwork, and had appropriated the whole harvest to their use. At last the neighboring and confederate town of Malines fell into the enemy's hands, and with its fall vanished the only remaining hope of getting supplies from Brabant. As there was, therefore, no longer any means of increasing the stock of provisions nothing was left but to diminish the consumers. All useless persons, all strangers, nay even the women and children were to be sent away out of the town, but this proposal was too revolting to humanity to be carried into execution. Another plan, that of expelling the Catholic inhabitants, exasperated them so much that it had almost ended in open mutiny. And thus St. Aldegonde at last saw himself compelled to yield to the riotous clamors of the populace, and on the 17th of August, 1585, to make overtures to the Duke of Parma for the surrender of the town.

www.ingramcontent.com/pod-product-compliance
Lightning Source LLC
Chambersburg PA
CBHW031246230426
43670CB00005B/64